ITH GIANT
OMIC BOOKS,
E FICTION,
NG, ROBOTS,
N. NO ONE
E WANTED.
OURSELVES.
I0819437

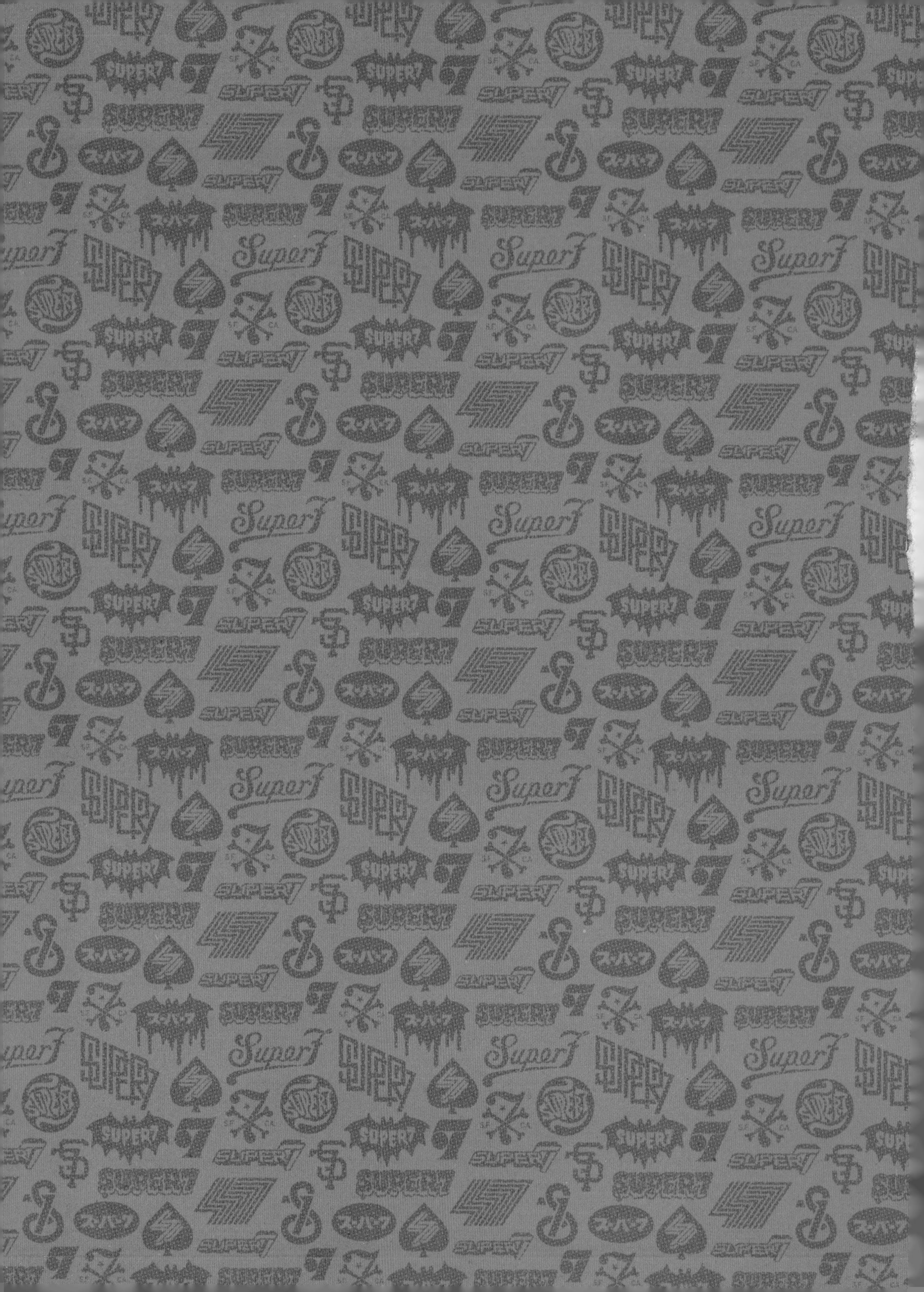
SUPER7
Super7

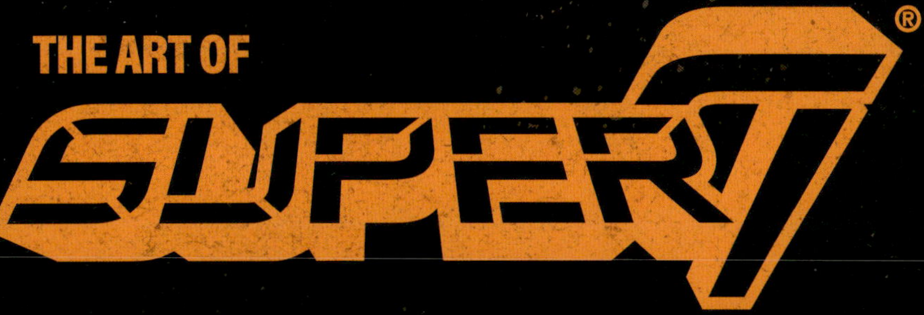
THE ART OF
SUPER7®

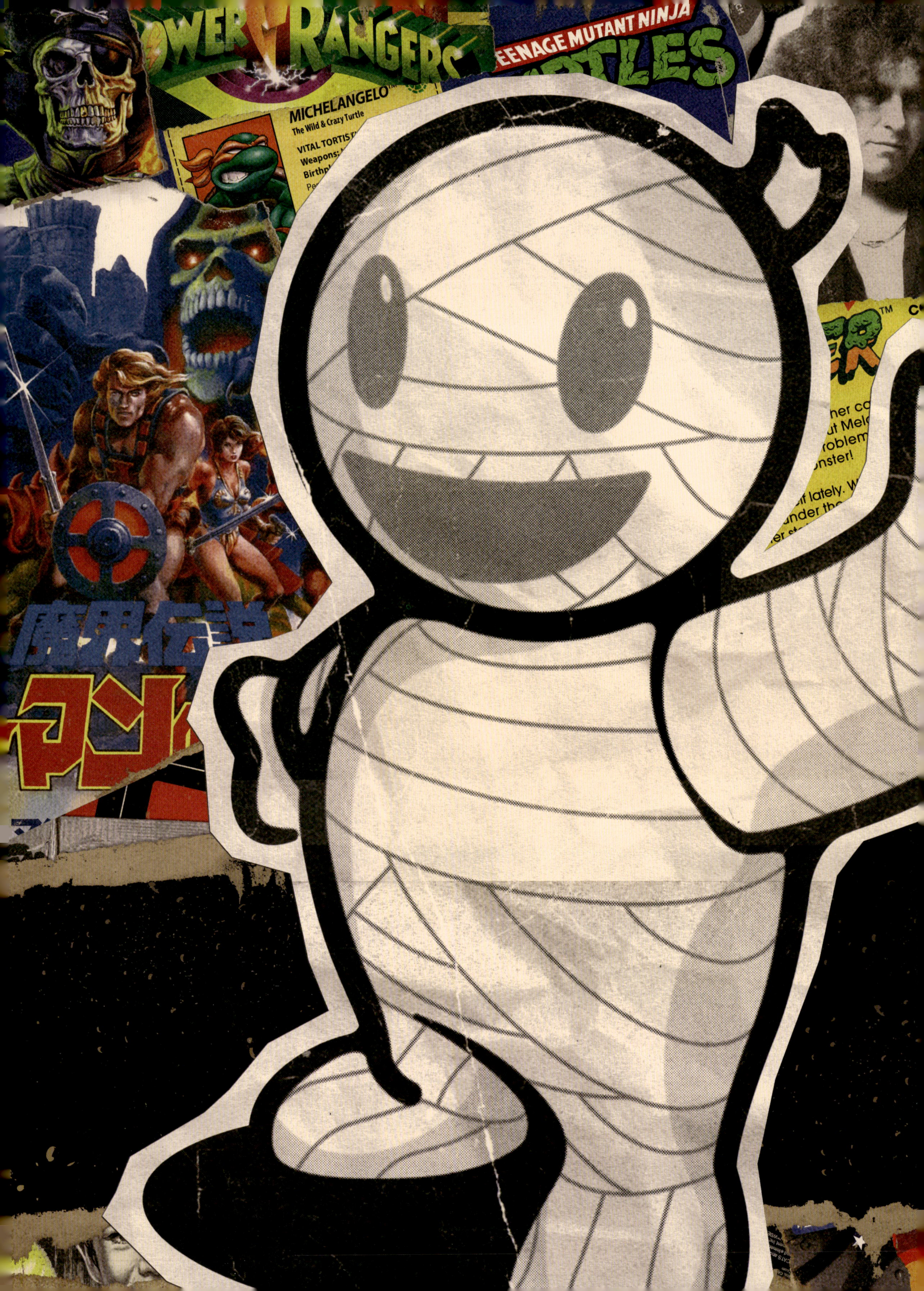

OWER RANGERS
EENAGE MUTANT NINJA
MICHELANGELO™
The Wild & Crazy Turtle
魔界伝説

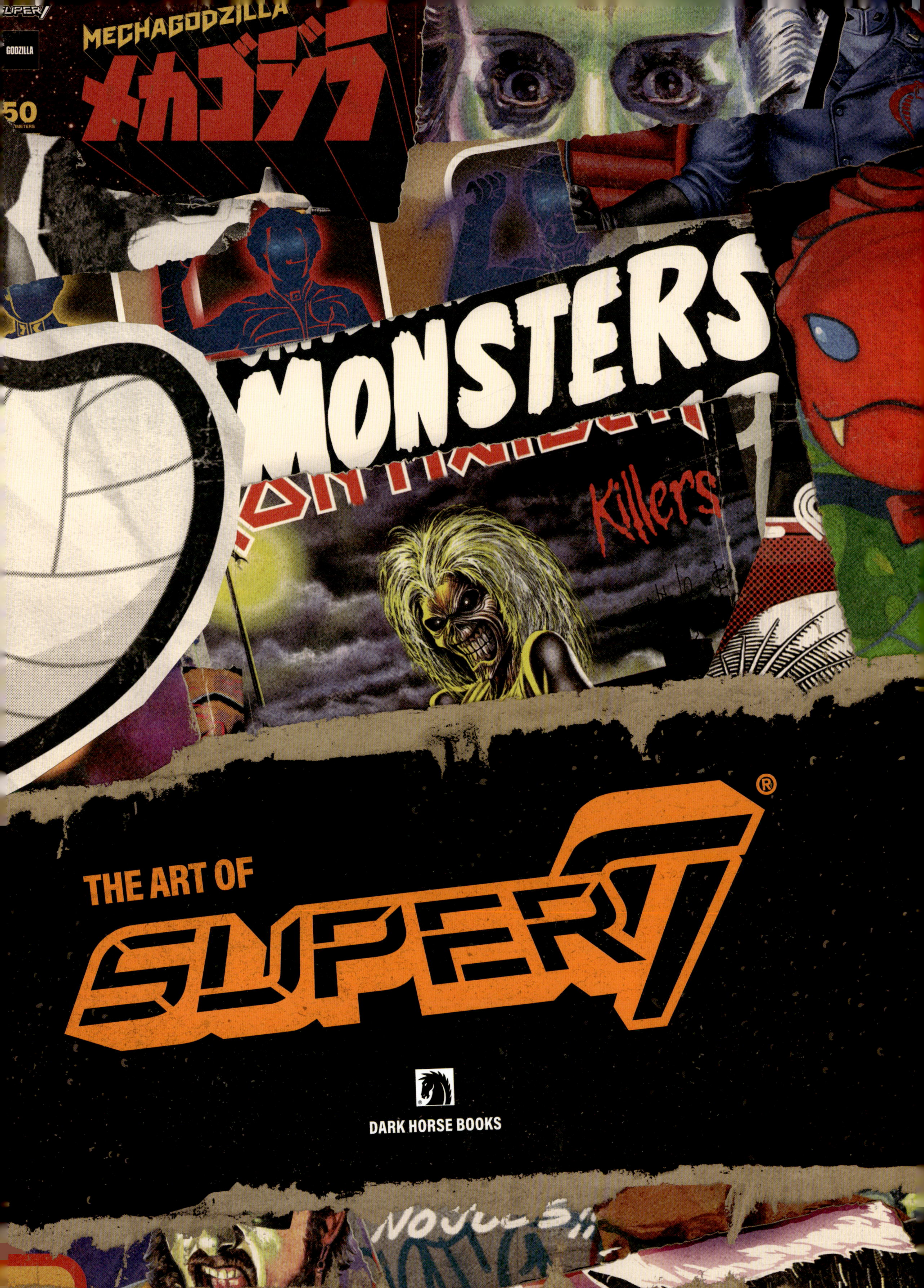
MECHAGODZILLA
メカゴジラ
GODZILLA
MONSTERS
Killers
THE ART OF
SUPER7
DARK HORSE BOOKS

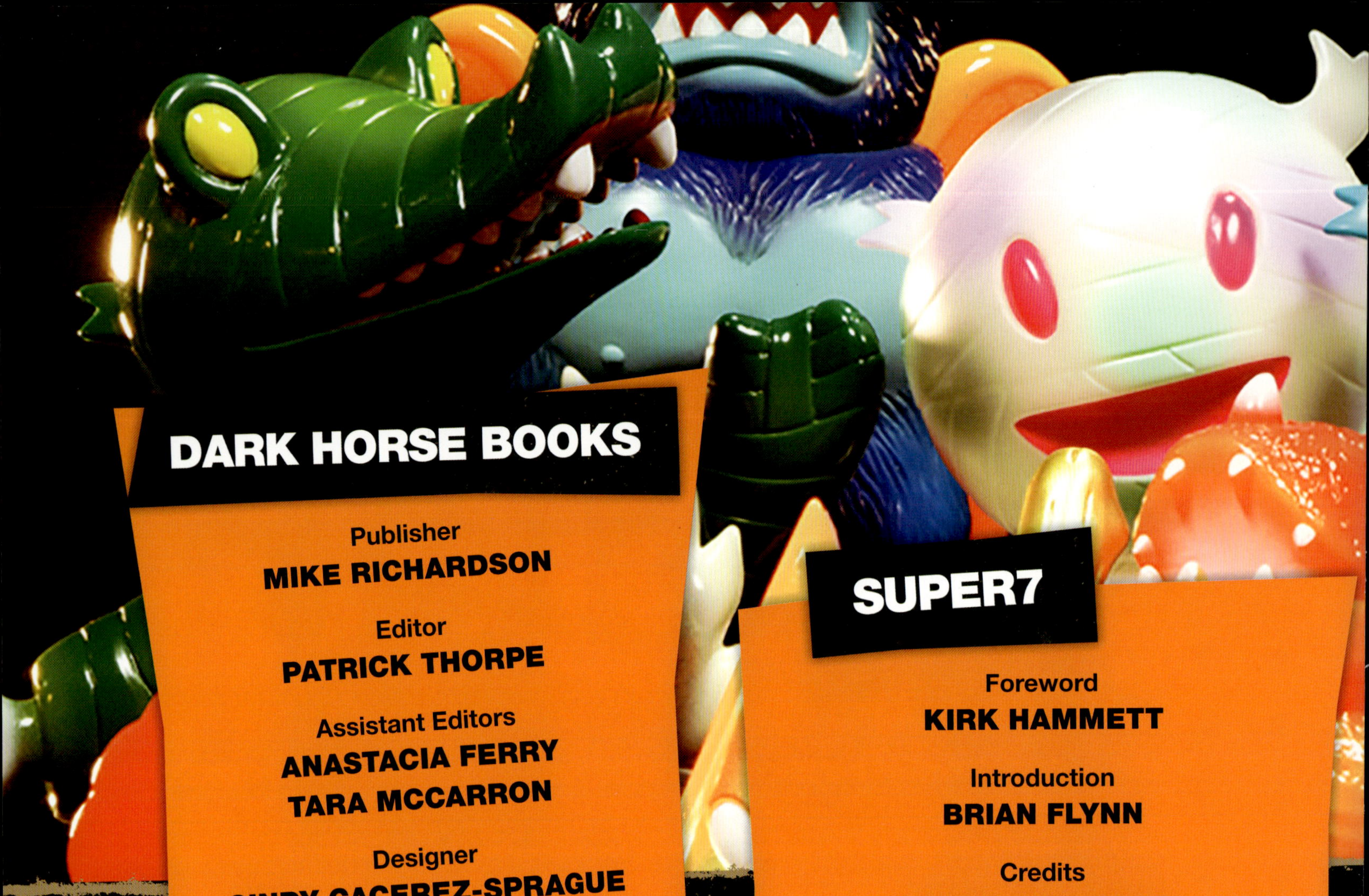

DARK HORSE BOOKS

Publisher
MIKE RICHARDSON

Editor
PATRICK THORPE

Assistant Editors
ANASTACIA FERRY
TARA MCCARRON

Designer
CINDY CACEREZ-SPRAGUE

Digital Art Technician
JOEY WEAVER

Prepress Technician
RIKKI MIDNIGHT

SUPER7

Foreword
KIRK HAMMETT

Introduction
BRIAN FLYNN

Credits
DORA DRIMALAS
AARON EILAND
JOSH HERBOLSHEIMER
NICOLE HASSELFELD
CHELSEA KIMBALL
LINDA OLBOURNE

Paul Schwake Chief Operations Officer • **Tom Weddle** Chief Financial Officer • **Dale LaFountain** Chief Information Officer • **Tim Wiesch** Vice President of Licensing • **Vanessa Todd-Holmes** Vice President of Production and Scheduling • **Mark Bernardi** Vice President of Book Trade and Digital Sales • **Randy Lahrman** Vice President of Product Development and Sales • **Cara O'Neil** Vice President of Marketing • **Dave Marshall** Editor in Chief • **Melissa Teeman** Controller

THE ART OF SUPER7
The Art of Super7 Copyright © 2025 Super7 OpCo LLC. Dark Horse Books® and the Dark Horse logo are registered trademarks of Dark Horse Comics LLC, registered in various categories and countries. All rights reserved. Dark Horse is part of Embracer Group. No portion of this publication may be reproduced or transmitted, in any form or by any means, without the express written permission of Dark Horse Comics LLC. Names, characters, places, and incidents featured in this publication either are the product of the author's imagination or are used fictitiously. Any resemblance to actual persons (living or dead), events, institutions, or locales, without satiric intent, is coincidental.

Published by Dark Horse Books
A division of Dark Horse Comics LLC
10956 SE Main Street, Milwaukie, OR 97222

DarkHorse.com • Super7.com
Facebook.com/DarkHorseComics
X.com/DarkHorseComics

First edition: July 2025

Ebook ISBN 978-1-50673-964-9
Hardcover ISBN 978-1-50673-963-2
10 9 8 7 6 5 4 3 2 1
Printed in China

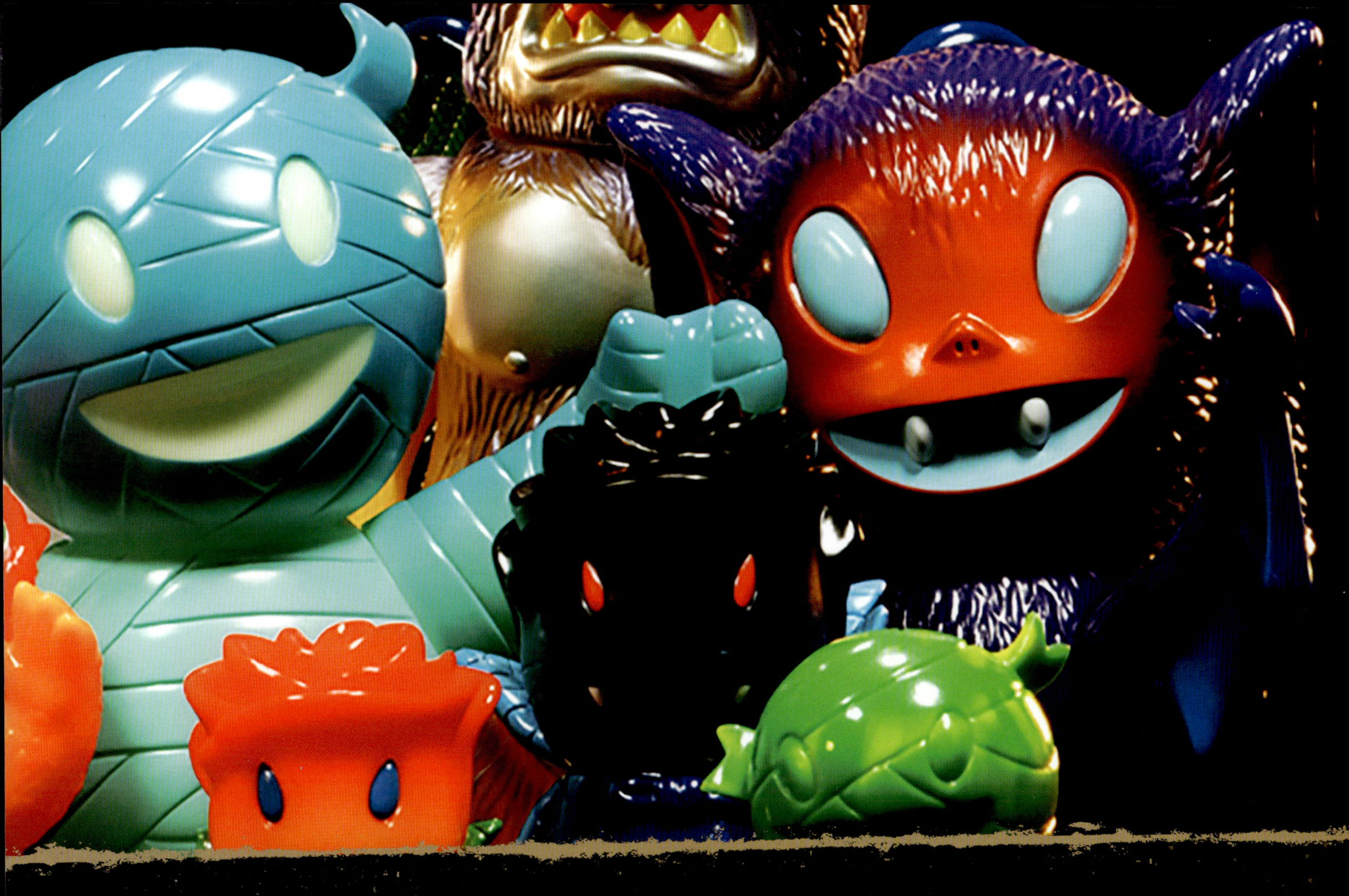

TABLE OF CONTENTS

FEATURING ART BY:

Astor Alexander, Joseph Allard, Leo Alvarez, Attack Peter, BeastWreck, Michael Barnard, Tim Baron, Dennis Brown, Jon Carr, Jason Chalker, Mark Cruz, Dane Danner, Carlos Datolli, Orlando Diez, Jason Edmiston, Diego Estolano, Michael Gambriel, Mike Heath, Jay Hilgenfeld, Līga Kļaviņa, Chris Lee, Mike Lemos, Ben Newman, Josh Newton, Clark Orr, OSH RED, Jose Lorenzo Pacheco, Doug P'gosh, Pitchgrim, Ed Repka, Christian Rimando, Joseph Schmalke, Zack Shereck, Joe Simko, L'Amour Supreme, Matt Ryan Tobin, Turbopork, Johnny Wu, Sarah Young, Alexis Ziritt, Aaron Eiland, Josh Herbolsheimer, Brian Flynn, and more.

SPECIAL THANKS

Kirk Hammett, Chris Casgar, Peter Maulik, Jonathan Weiner, Michael Kesselman, Sandy Boone, Sander Zagzebski, Ryan Powers, Bryan Christner, Tim and Beth Kerr, DJ Amen, iDSTROY, Pixel Dan, Robo and Veebs, Rod and Damien, Augie and Anibal Pires, Val Staples, Egmond O'Donohue, Tim Freyer, Jim, Eric, CB (The Four Horsemen), Gregory Howard, Sean and Patrick Johnson (Swazzle), Civ and Gorilla Biscuits, Hiddy (Secret Base), Kiyoka and Naoya (Gargamel), Chanmen (Gargamel), Leo Alvarez, Ashley Anderson, Luisa Arana, Nikki Arthur, Katie Bell, Jennifer Bizeur, Dennis Brown, Max Bryan, Ashley Bryant, Joseph Buck, Ryan Buckalew, Matthew Buercklin, Kris Butiong, Teresa Callahan, Nathan Carnett, Jon Carr, Jen Cassidy, Thomas Chouinard, Stephanie Comfort, Jose Delgado, Adriana Diaz-Romero, James Dinsdale, Diego Estolano, Alexis Feingold, Oliver Fernandez, Reginald Fields, Mason Fiske, Colin Flynn, Mariel Fredericksen, Brandon Gash, Chloe Gaule Goodrich, Camille Geeter, Joe George, Michael Gulen, Sam Hasirbaf, Arian Hinojosa, Shawn Houser, Andras Jozsi, Nomi Kane, Daryl Kato, Matthew Keown, Shawn Knapp, Alison Labra, Derek Laplante, Brian Lew, Kowanda Liddell, Collin Lindo, Ruben Macias, Luke Martinez, Michael McCorkle, Michael Mehiel, Greta Myers, Tara Newmyer, Jonathan Odom, Jackeline Orrego, Sarah Parzygnat, Karla Perez, Emily Pidgeon, Julia Phuong, Ashly Powell, Christopher Rasmussen, Christian Rimando, Gilbert Rivera, Preston Rodriguez, Eamon Ronayne, Brian Rouspil, Jose Sanchez, Daniel Sant, Chuck Schweiger, Timothy Shoaf, Ariel Shostak, Rosario Silva, Matthew Stewart, Chantel Thrower, Rudy Torreliza, Martin Van Dyke, Brian Walker, Allie Whalen, David White, Kyle Wlodyga, Johnny Wu, Sarah Young, Ashley Zenner. A special thanks to all of our licensing partners who help us make such cool things for fans to enjoy and all of our friends and family and especially Ava, Kate, and Vivian.

FOREWORD BY KIRK HAMMETT

SUPER7. I MEAN, WHAT CAN I SAY? I WAS FORTUNATE ENOUGH TO WORK WITH THEM FOR MY FEAR FESTEVIL IN 2014 AND WE CREATED THESE COOL NOSFERATU SUPER SOAPEEZ. I LOVE THE RETRO FEEL AND THE NOSTALGIA THAT COMES IN WITH THE LOOK AND FEEL OF THESE FIGURES. PLUS, WE'RE BOTH FROM SAN FRANCISCO, WHICH IS GREAT, AND WE BOTH LOVE HORROR, TOYS, AND MUSIC! AND IT'S THESE THREE THINGS THAT SUPER7 MANAGES TO COMBINE IN FANTASTIC AND WELL-DESIGNED PACKAGES. I WAS AWARE OF THEM EARLY ON, BUT WHEN SUPER7 HIT WITH THE REACTION SERIES OF UNIVERSAL MONSTERS IN 2014 I WAS HOOKED. THE COLORS AND DETAIL WERE SPOT ON, AND THE SIZE MEANT I COULD GET THEM ALL. AND I DID!

THEN WHEN THEY STARTED ON THE MUSIC SIDE, THAT WAS PRETTY COOL, TOO. I LOVE HOW IT'S OBVIOUS THEY WORK WITH WHO THEY WANT, REGARDLESS OF GENRE OR STYLE, AND THEY DO IT ALL WITH THE SAME PASSION. THE TOHO REACTION WAVE IS MADE WITH THE SAME LOVE AND EXCITEMENT AS THE PAUL BALOFF FIGURE. AND I LIKE TO MAKE THEM FIGHT. PAUL USUALLY WINS.

SO, YEAH. IT'S JUST REALLY COOL TO SEE SUPER7 GROW AND EXPAND AND KEEP THAT SAME PASSION AND INDIVIDUALITY SHINING THROUGH EACH PROJECT.

—KIRK HAMMETT

INTRODUCTION

OVER TWENTY YEARS AGO, IN 2001, SUPER7 STARTED OUT AS AN IDEA, A CLUBHOUSE MASQUERADING AS A MAGAZINE. A PLACE TO TALK ABOUT TOYS WITH FRIENDS OF OURS. IT WASN'T MEANT TO BE MORE THAN THAT, OR MAYBE WE COULDN'T SEE THAT IT COULD BE MORE THAN THAT. TO BE HONEST, WE WERE MORE THAN HAPPY TO JUST TALK ABOUT TOYS.

ALONG THE WAY, SUPER7 SLOWLY BECAME MORE THAN JUST A MAGAZINE ABOUT TOYS. WE BECAME A STORE, A WEBSITE, A FORUM, AN IMPORTER, AND A MANUFACTURER, EACH OPPORTUNITY BUILDING ON THE LAST. WITH THAT, WE MADE THE TOYS WE ALWAYS WANTED TO HAVE, AND JUST AS IMPORTANTLY, PACKAGED THEM THE WAY WE WANTED, MAKING THE EXPERIENCE OF THE PRODUCT JUST AS IMPORTANT AS THE PRODUCT ITSELF. THIS BOOK IS A TESTAMENT, A SURVEY IF YOU WILL, OF THAT EXPERIENCE. FROM PAINTINGS TO PACKAGING, PRINTS TO PLASTIC, T-SHIRTS TO SNEAKERS, THE ART AND DESIGN OF SUPER7 HAS ALWAYS BEEN INTEGRAL TO OUR SUCCESS.

THANK YOU TO EVERYONE WHO HAS SUPPORTED THIS CRAZY DREAM OF OURS FOR THE LAST TWENTY YEARS. WE ARE HAPPY TO HAVE YOU HERE TO HANG OUT WITH US. HERE IS TO MANY MORE YEARS TO COME!

—BRIAN FLYNN

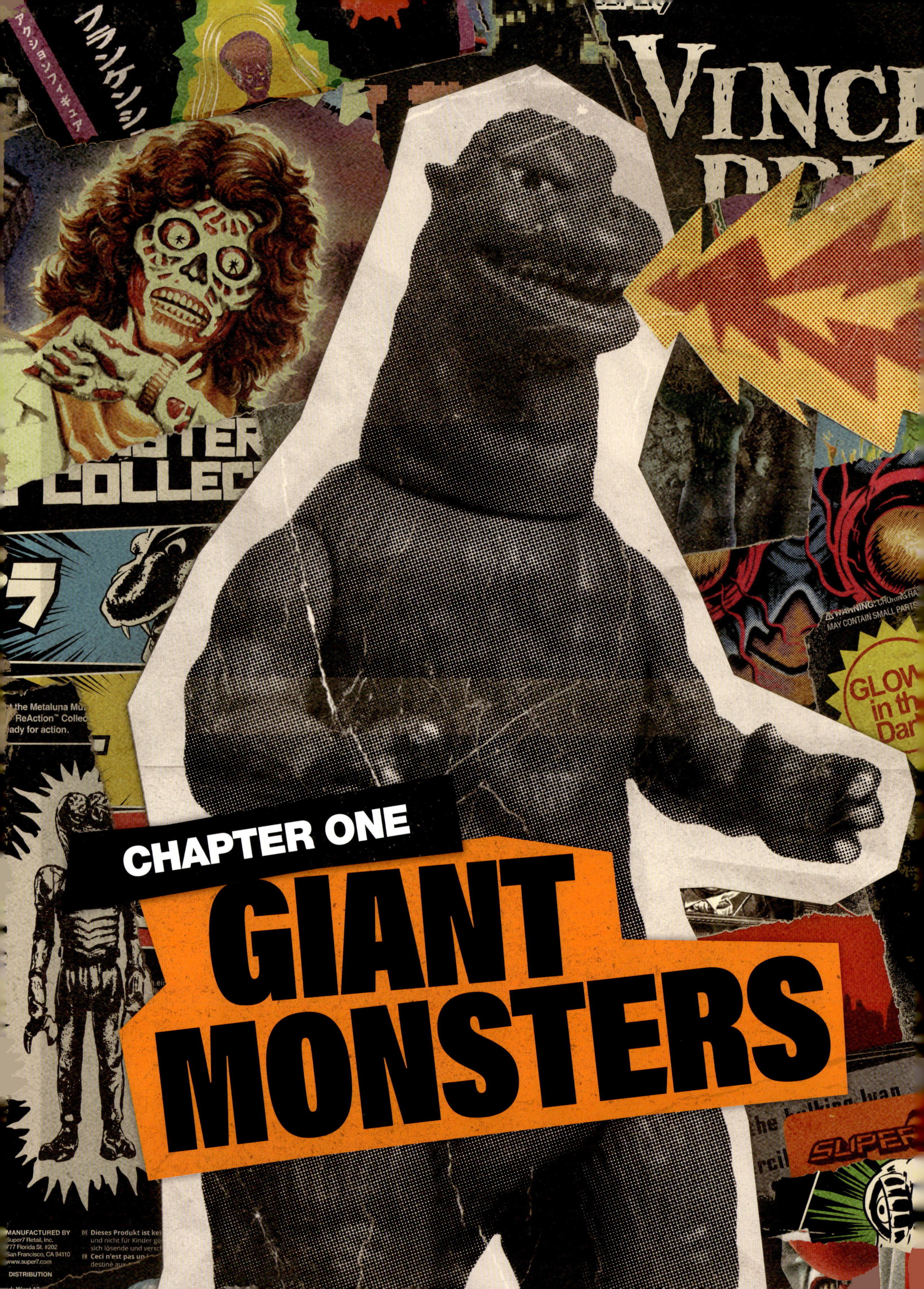

CHAPTER ONE
GIANT MONSTERS

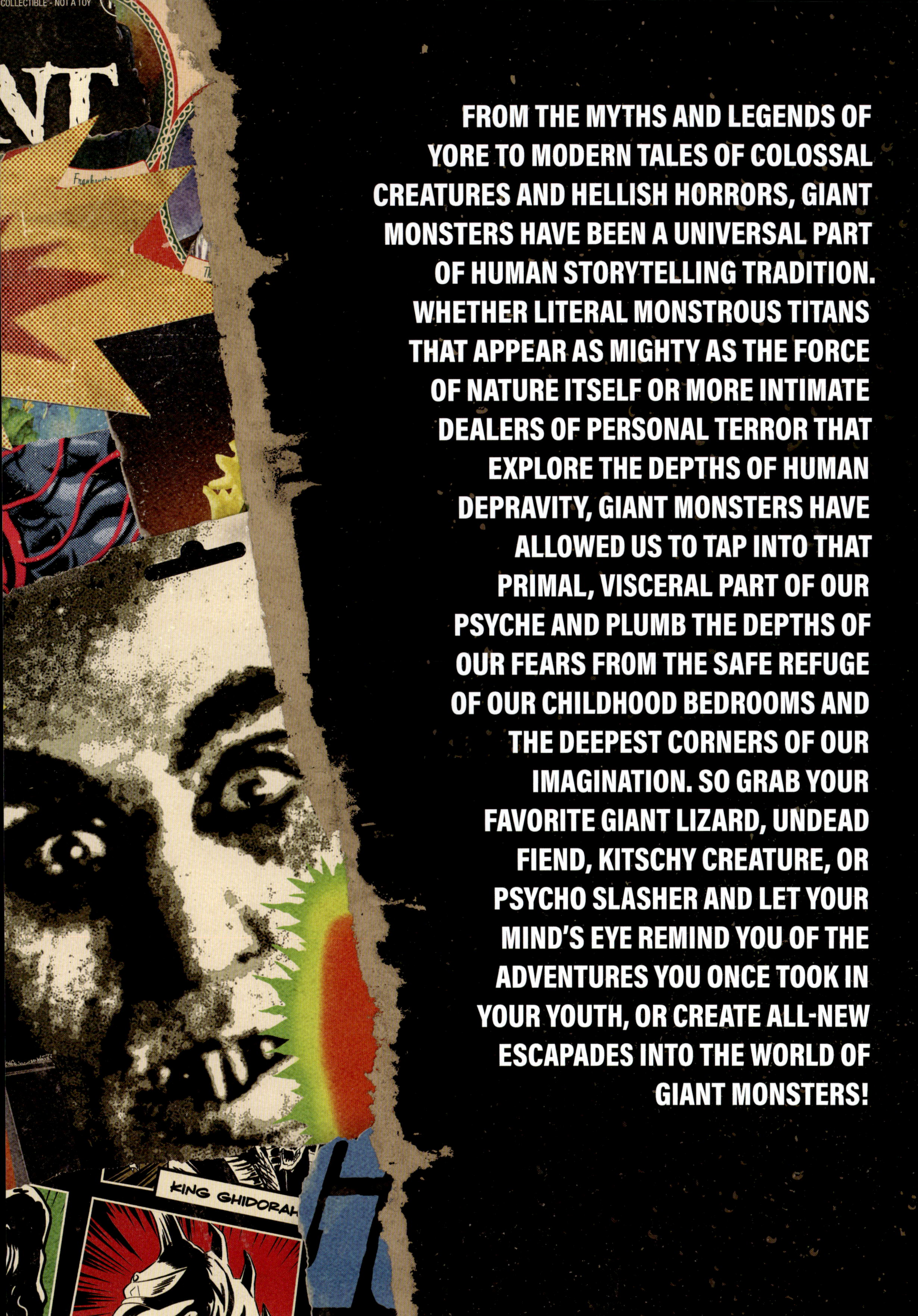

FROM THE MYTHS AND LEGENDS OF YORE TO MODERN TALES OF COLOSSAL CREATURES AND HELLISH HORRORS, GIANT MONSTERS HAVE BEEN A UNIVERSAL PART OF HUMAN STORYTELLING TRADITION. WHETHER LITERAL MONSTROUS TITANS THAT APPEAR AS MIGHTY AS THE FORCE OF NATURE ITSELF OR MORE INTIMATE DEALERS OF PERSONAL TERROR THAT EXPLORE THE DEPTHS OF HUMAN DEPRAVITY, GIANT MONSTERS HAVE ALLOWED US TO TAP INTO THAT PRIMAL, VISCERAL PART OF OUR PSYCHE AND PLUMB THE DEPTHS OF OUR FEARS FROM THE SAFE REFUGE OF OUR CHILDHOOD BEDROOMS AND THE DEEPEST CORNERS OF OUR IMAGINATION. SO GRAB YOUR FAVORITE GIANT LIZARD, UNDEAD FIEND, KITSCHY CREATURE, OR PSYCHO SLASHER AND LET YOUR MIND'S EYE REMIND YOU OF THE ADVENTURES YOU ONCE TOOK IN YOUR YOUTH, OR CREATE ALL-NEW ESCAPADES INTO THE WORLD OF GIANT MONSTERS!

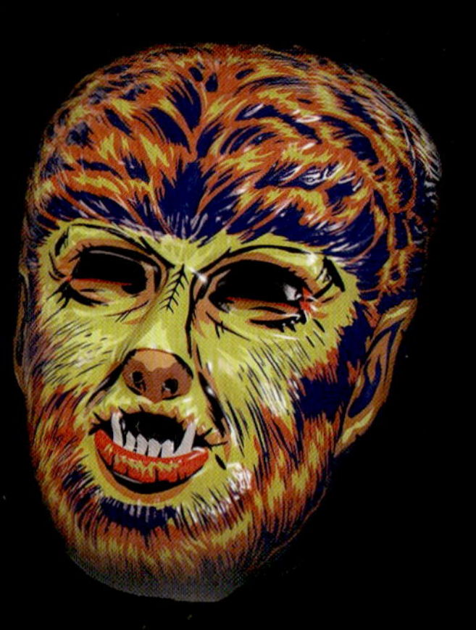

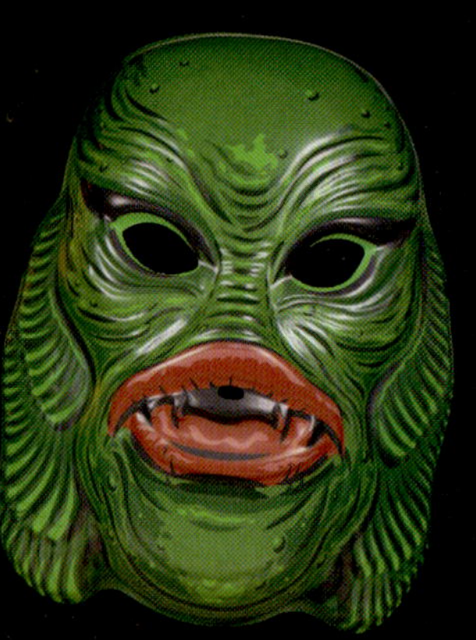

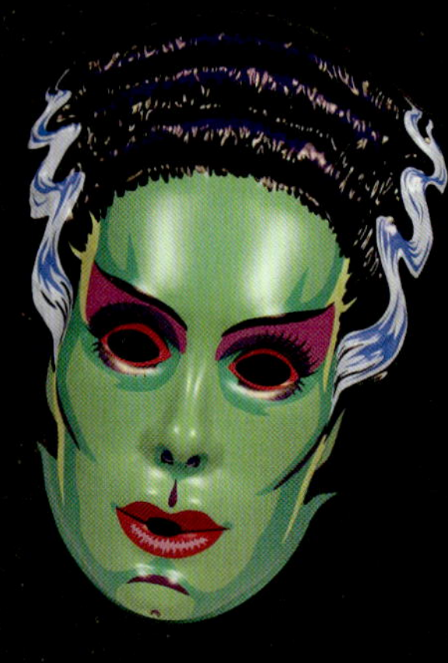

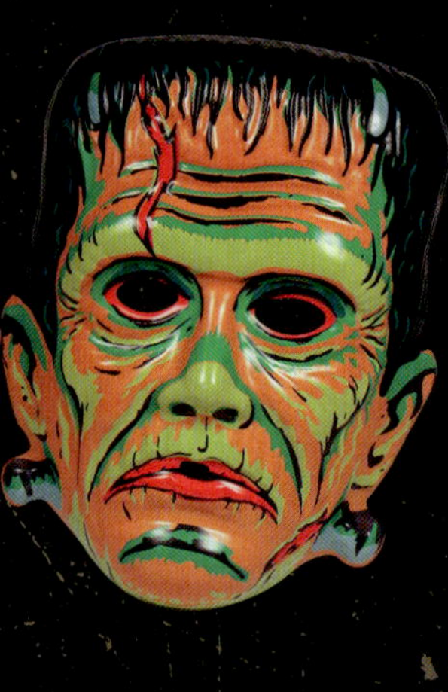

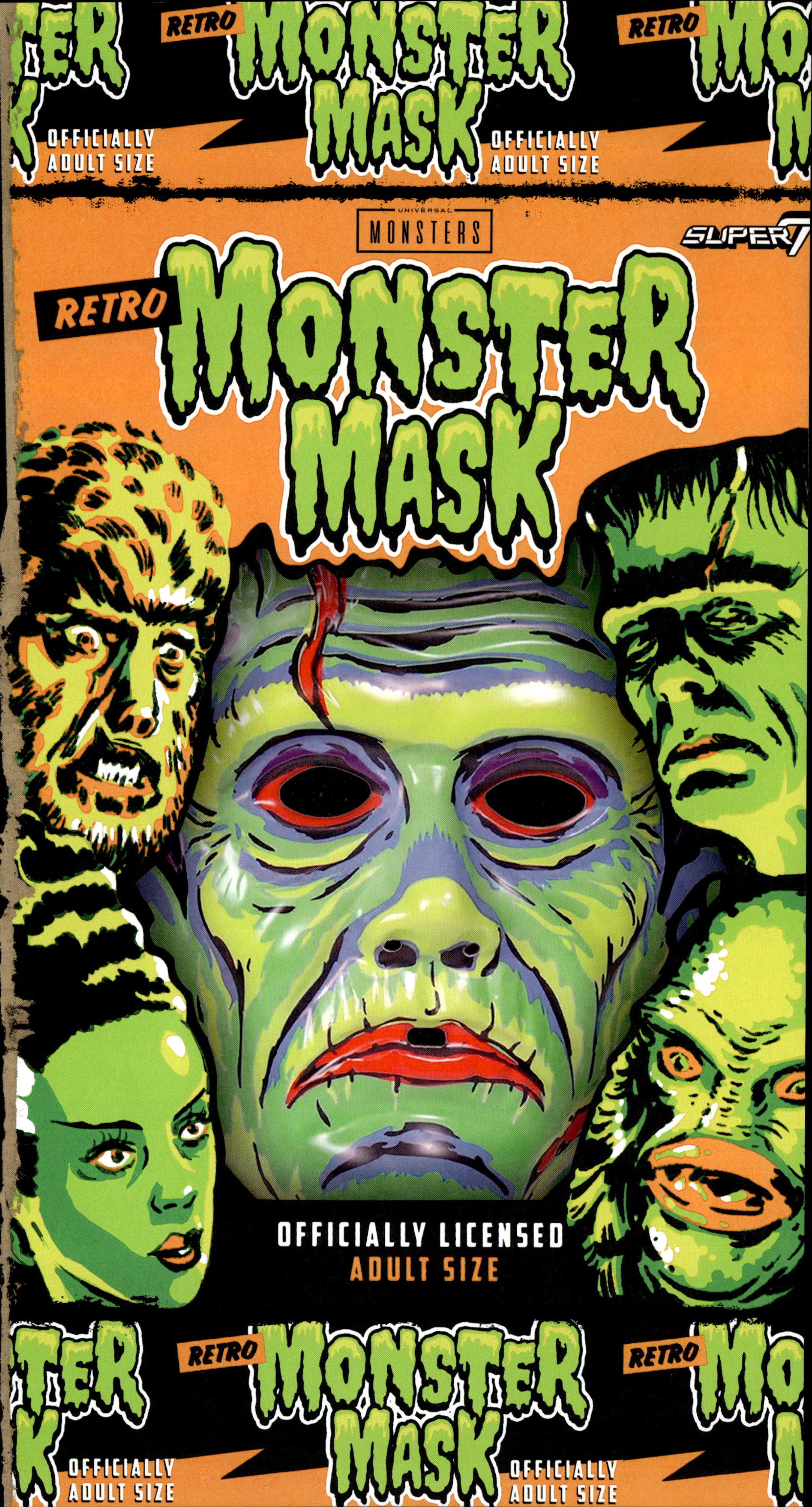

THIS PAGE: Universal Monsters™ Wolf Man, Creature from the Black Lagoon, Bride of Frankenstein, and Frankenstein Halloween masks

UNIVERSAL MONSTERS © Universal City Studios, LLC. All Rights Reserved.

UNIVERSAL MONSTERS

VISIBLE CREATURE

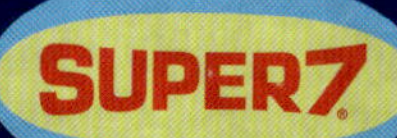

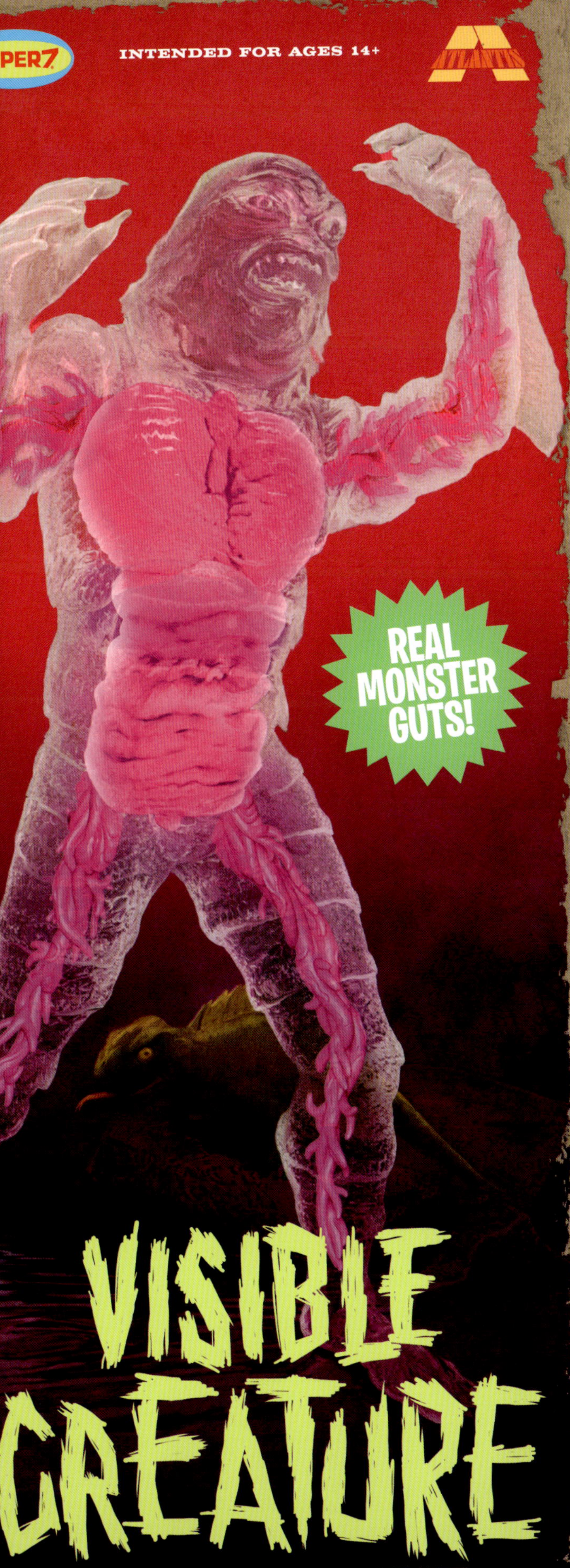

INSTRUCTIONS FOR ASSEMBLY

SUPER7

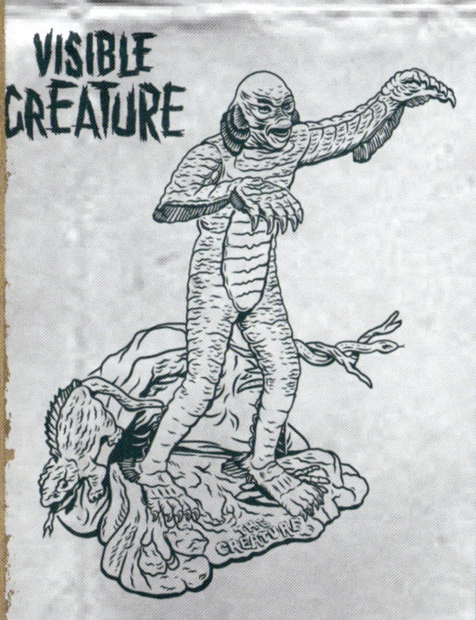

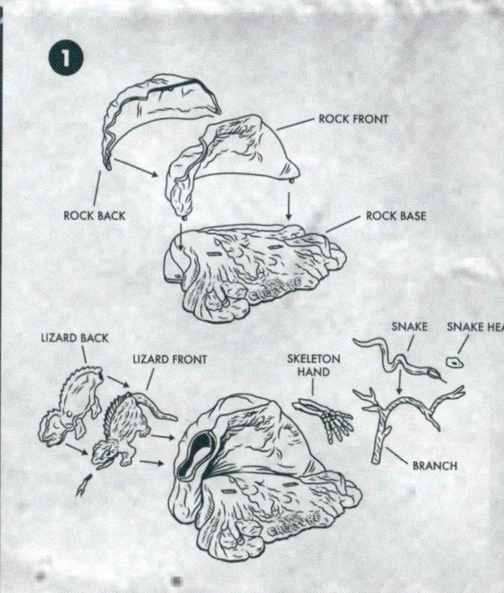

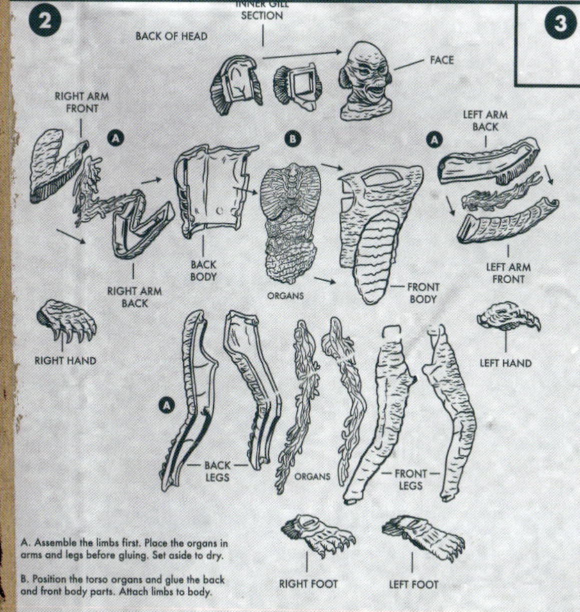

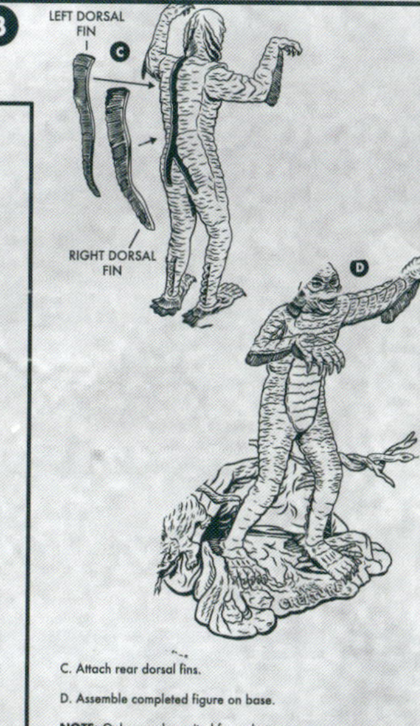

Creature from the Black Lagoon

One of the most iconic science fiction movies of all-time, Creature from the Black Lagoon is a groundbreaking classic, showcasing Hollywood magic at its best. When scientists exploring the Amazon River stumble upon a "missing link" connecting humans and fish, they plan to capture it for later study. However, the Creature has plans of his own, inspired by the lead scientist's (Richard Carlson) beautiful fiancée (Julie Adams).

Now you can see the Creature in a new and exciting see-thru body and be amazed at his visible guts!

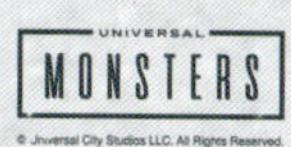

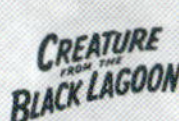

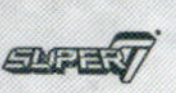

THIS PAGE: Creature from the Black Lagoon model kit

UNIVERSAL MONSTERS © Universal City Studios, LLC. All Rights Reserved.

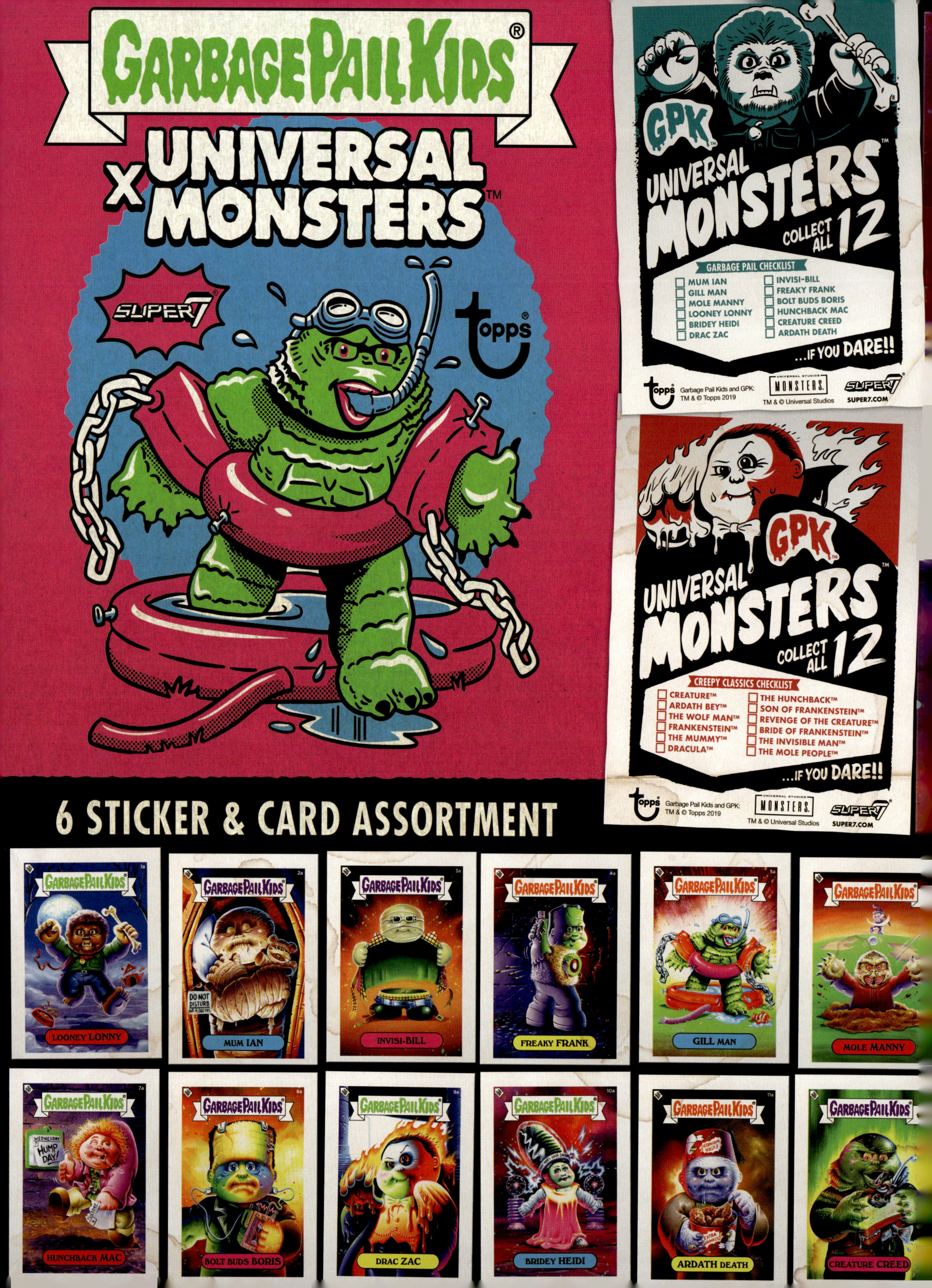

GARBAGE PAIL KIDS®

X UNIVERSAL MONSTERS™

SUPER7®

topps®

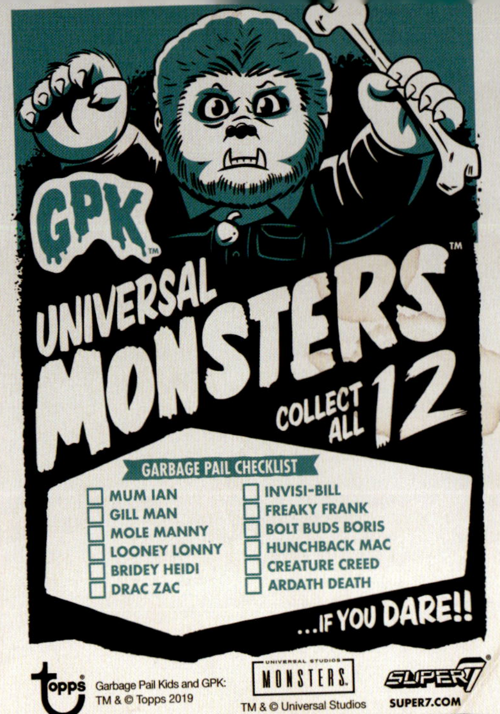

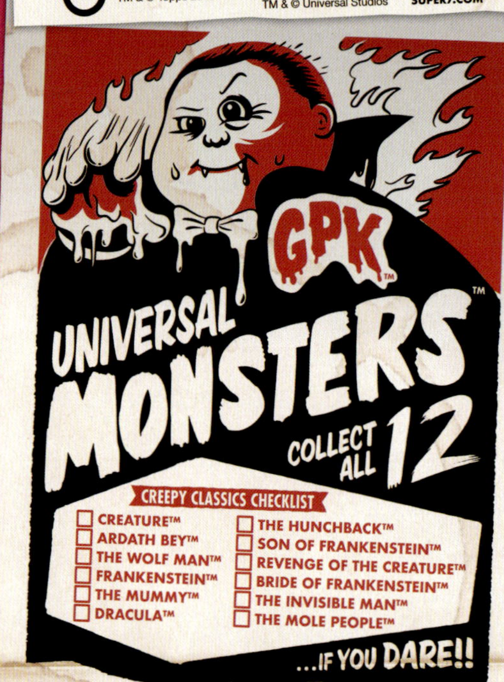

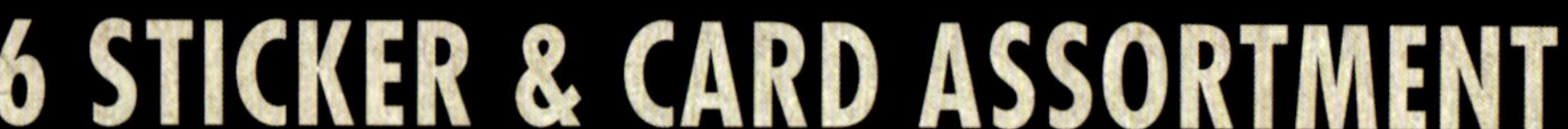

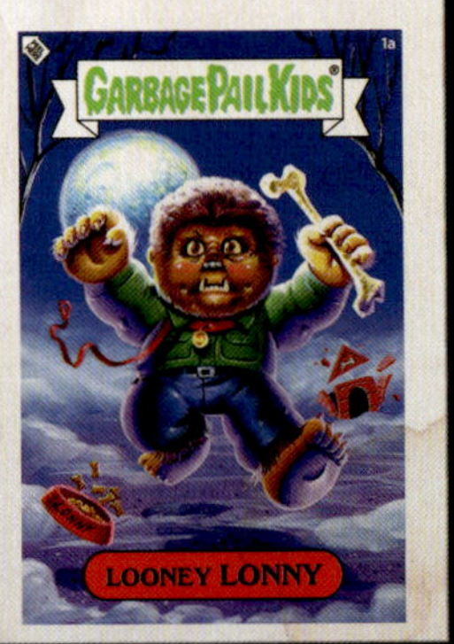

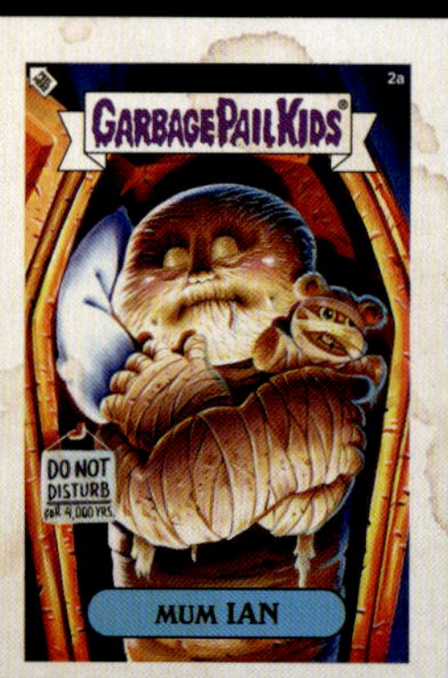

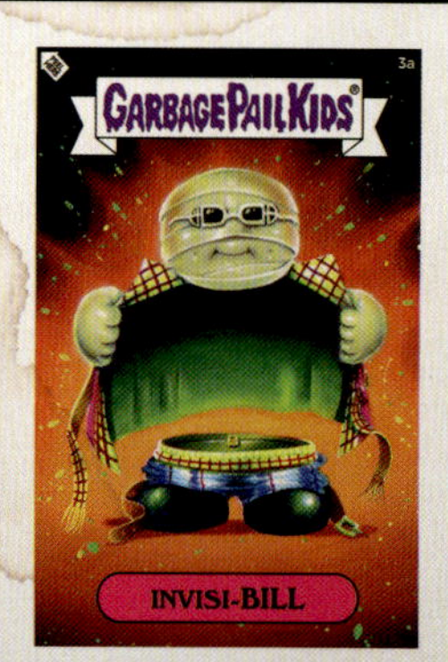

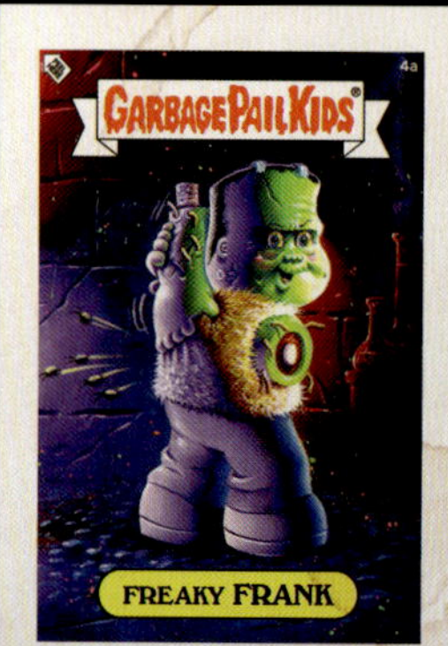

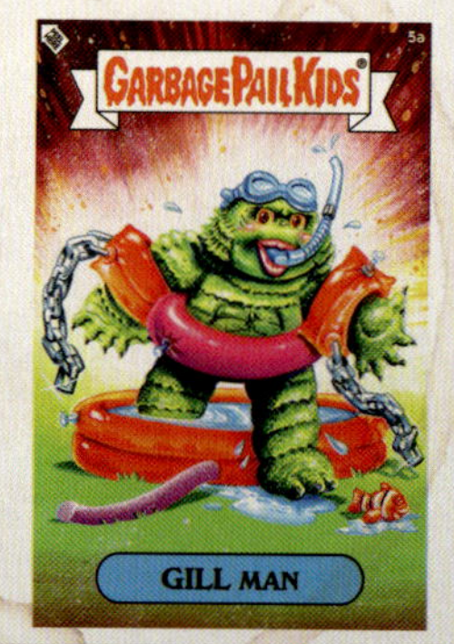

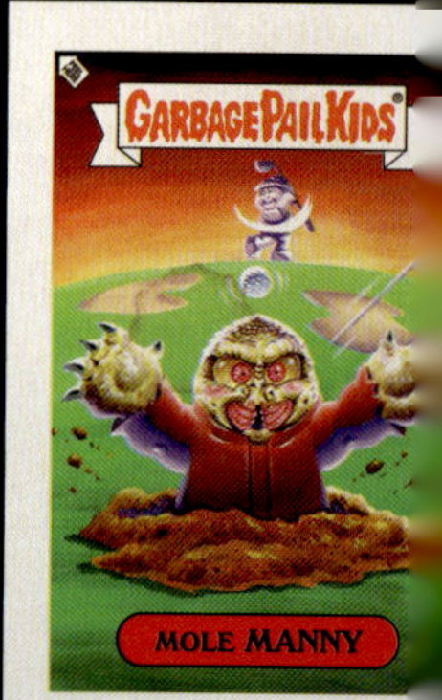

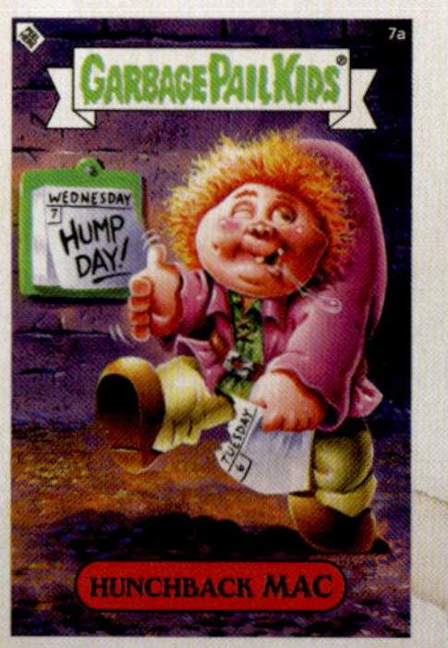

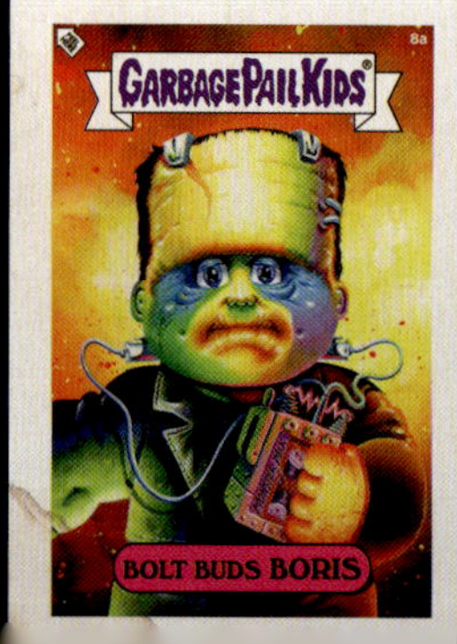

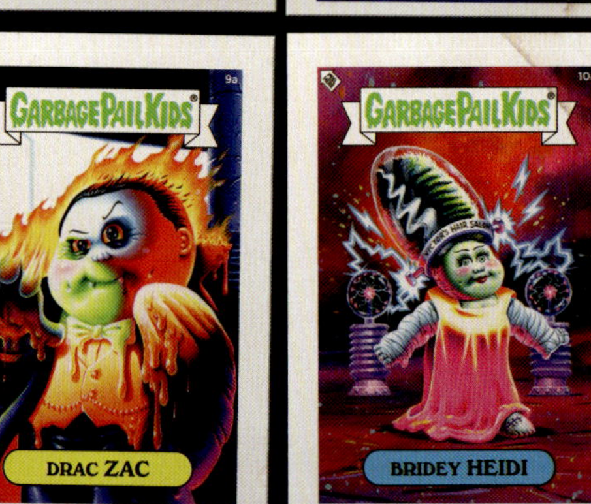

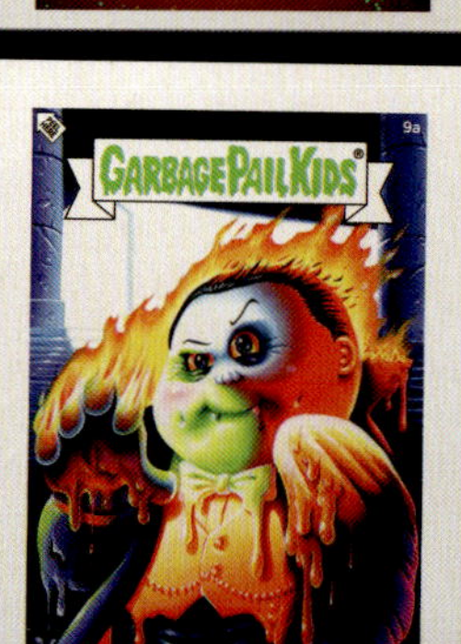

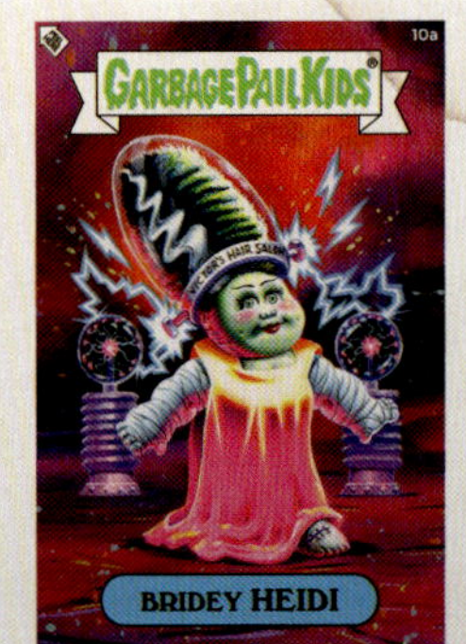

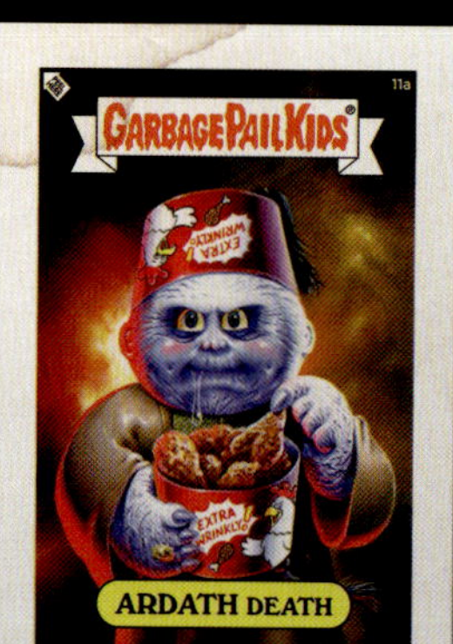

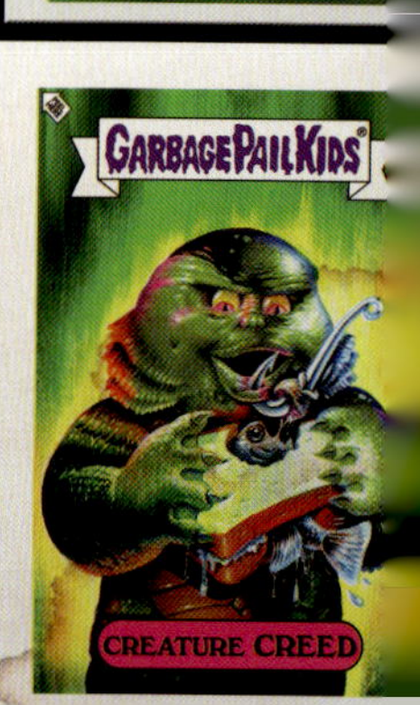

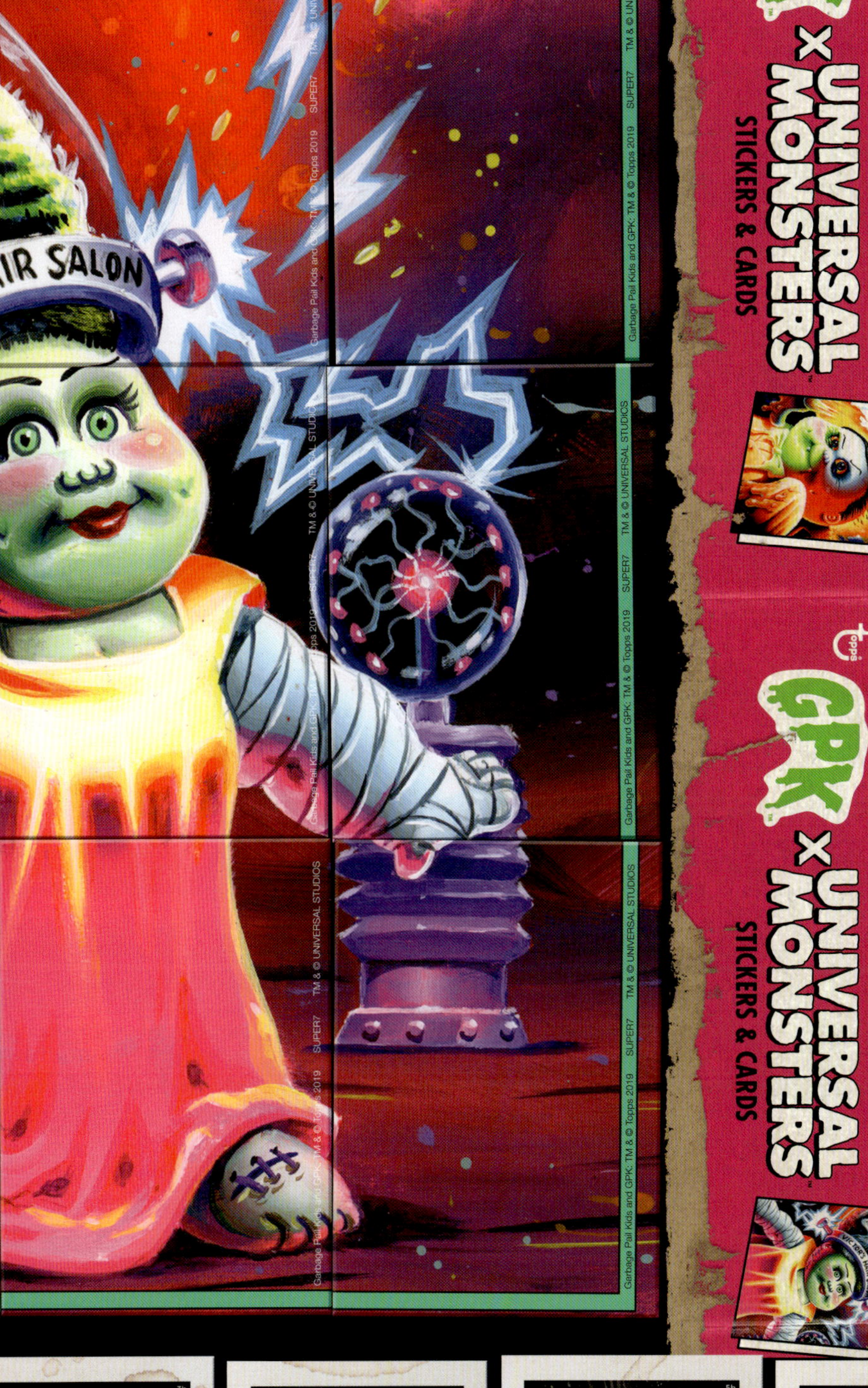

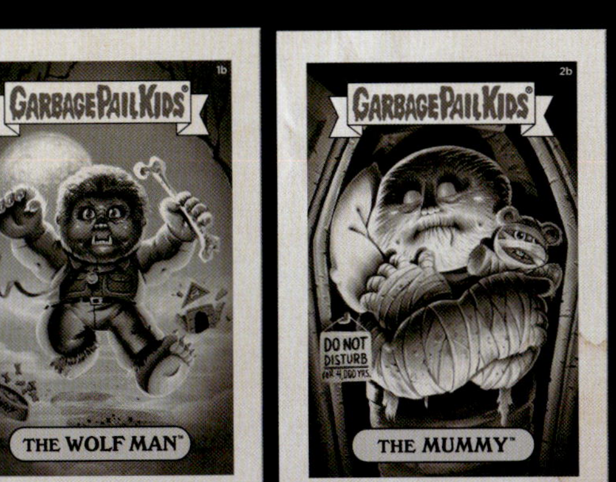

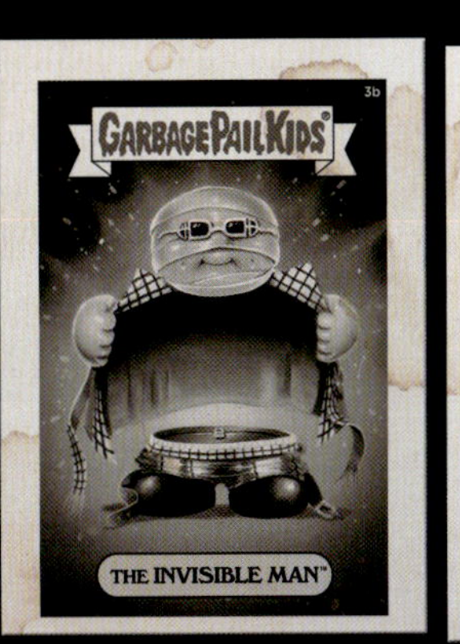

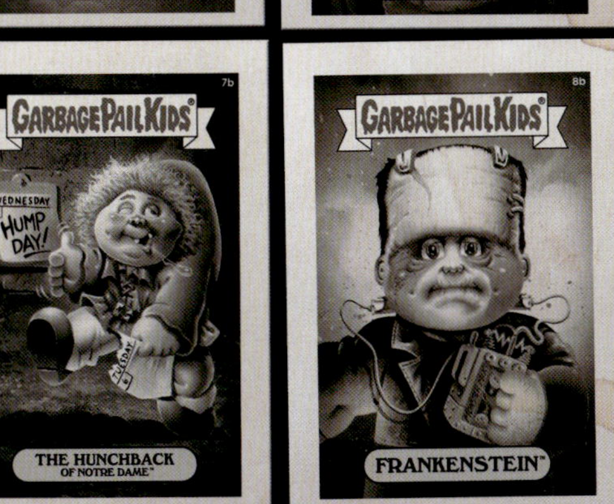

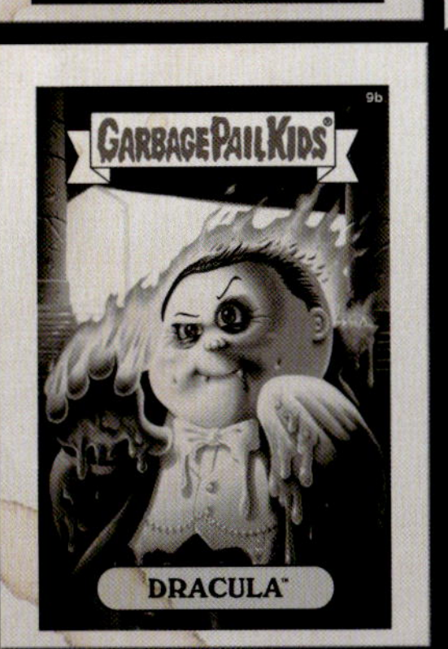

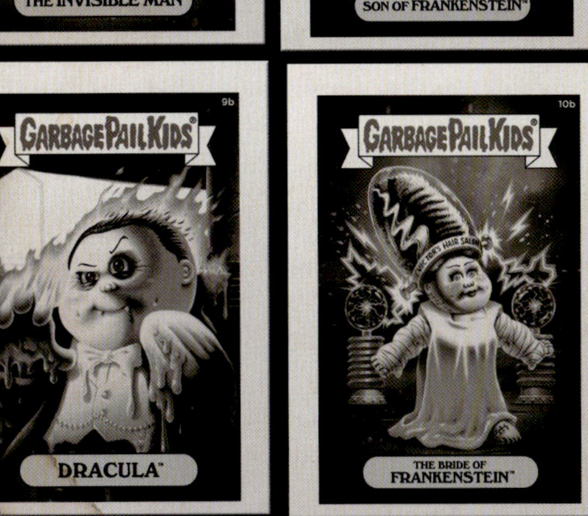

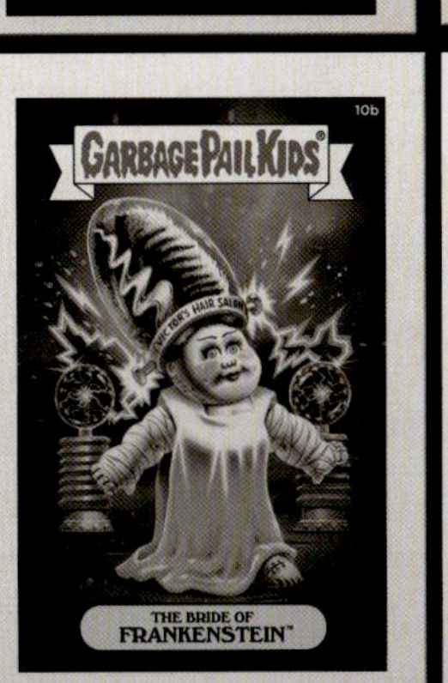

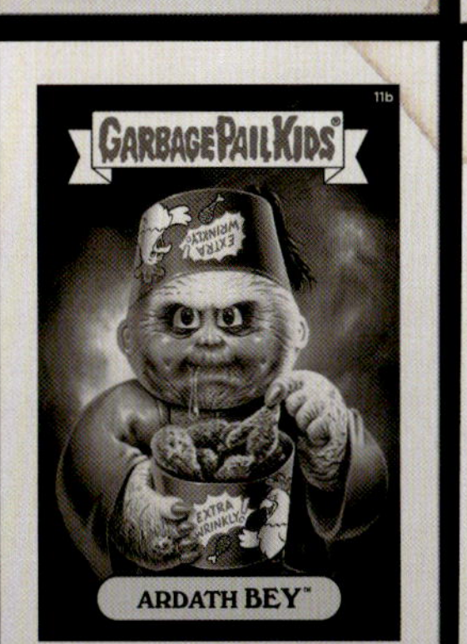

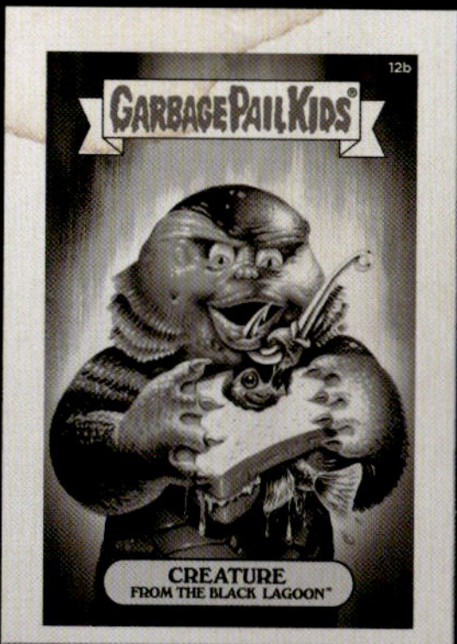

THIS SPREAD: Garbage Pail Kids® x Universal Monsters™ wax pack trading card art

UNIVERSAL MONSTERS © Universal City Studios, LLC. All Rights Reserved.
© 2025 TOPPS. All rights reserved.

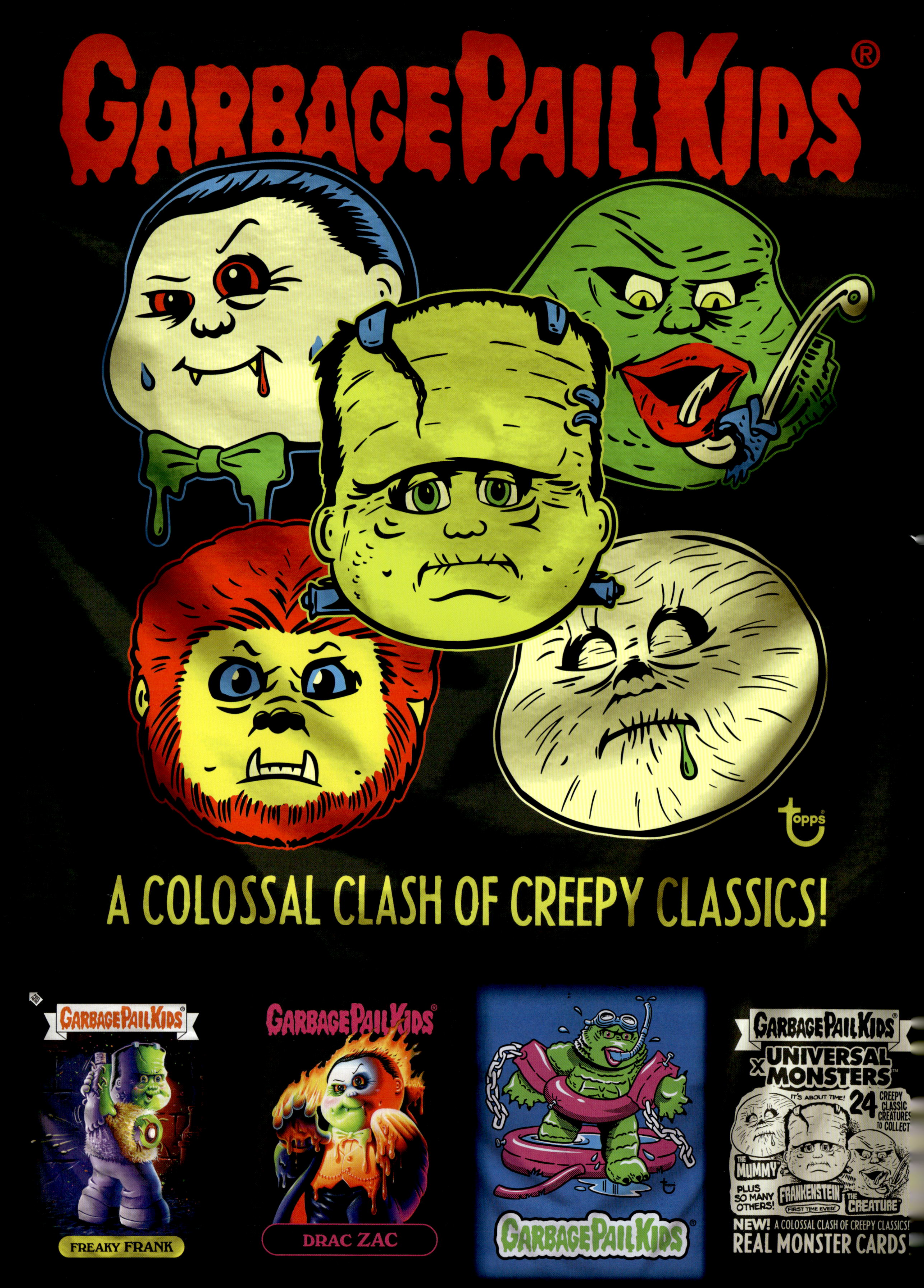

GARBAGE PAIL KIDS®

topps

A COLOSSAL CLASH OF CREEPY CLASSICS!

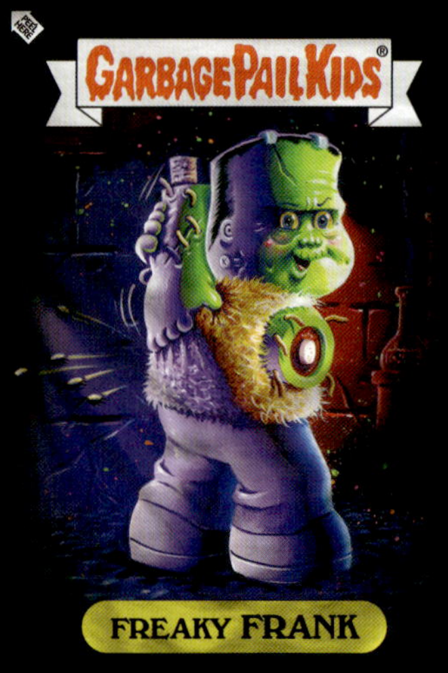

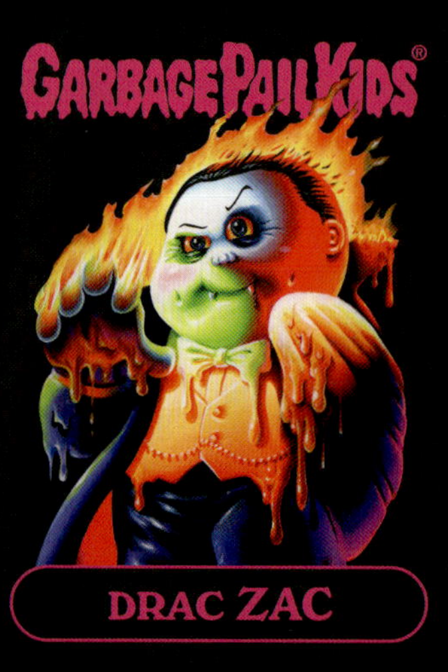

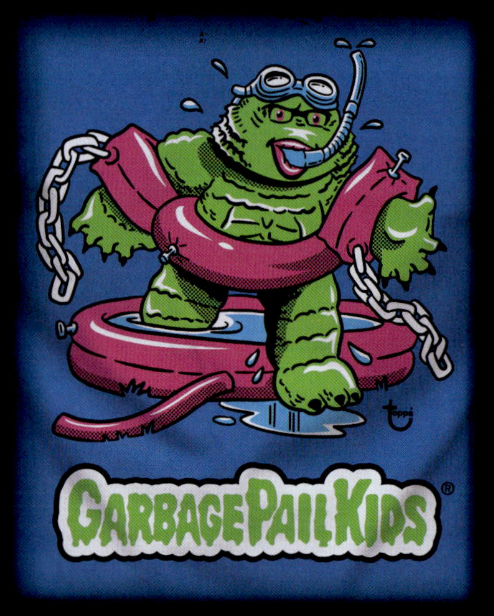

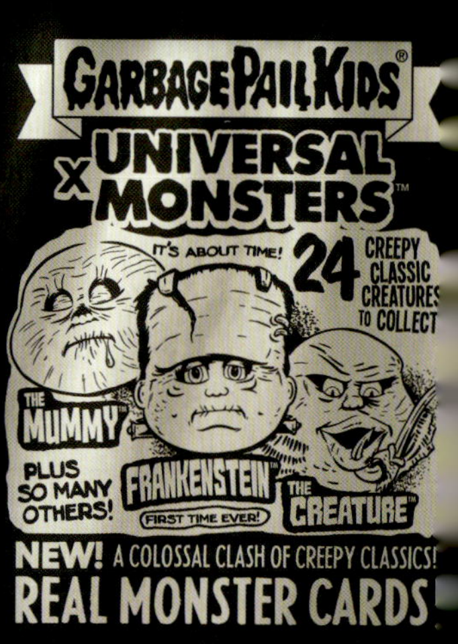

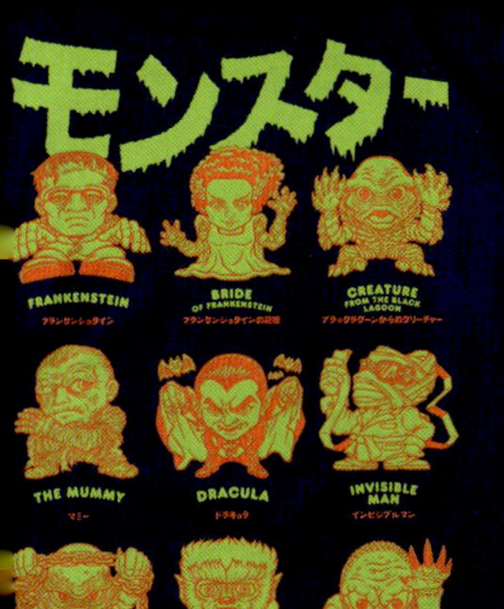

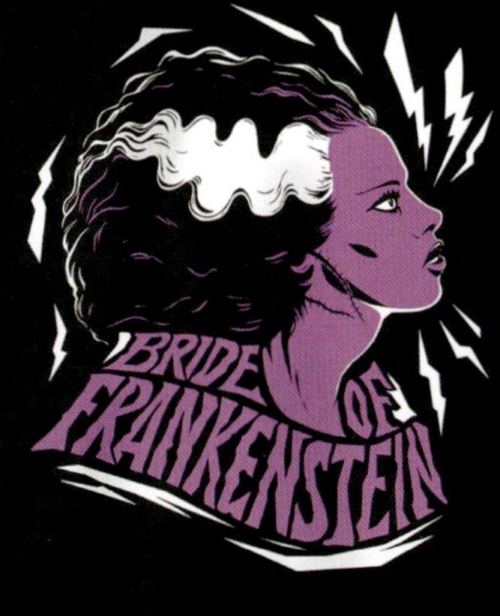

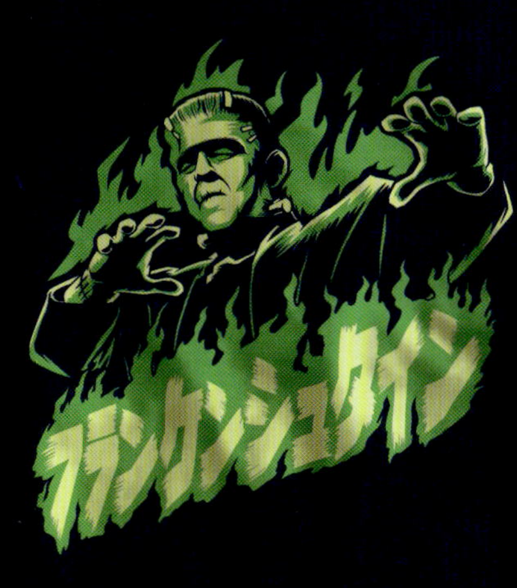

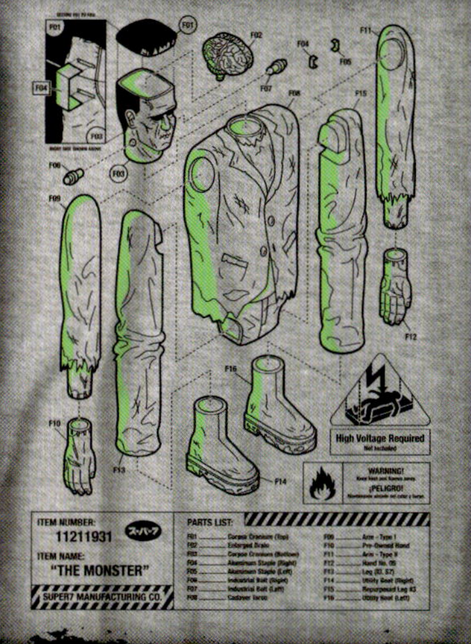

LEFT: Garbage Pail Kids® x Universal Monsters™ apparel

© 2025 TOPPS. All rights reserved.

THIS PAGE: Universal Monsters™ apparel

UNIVERSAL MONSTERS © Universal City Studios, LLC. All Rights Reserved.

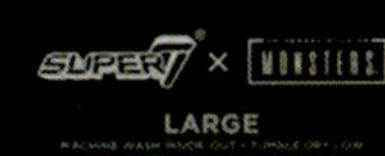

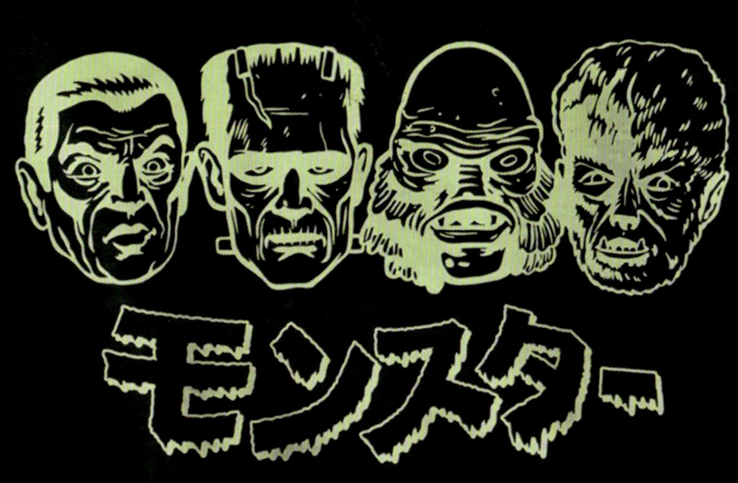

COLLECT THEM ALL! COLLECT THEM ALL! COLLECT THEM ALL!

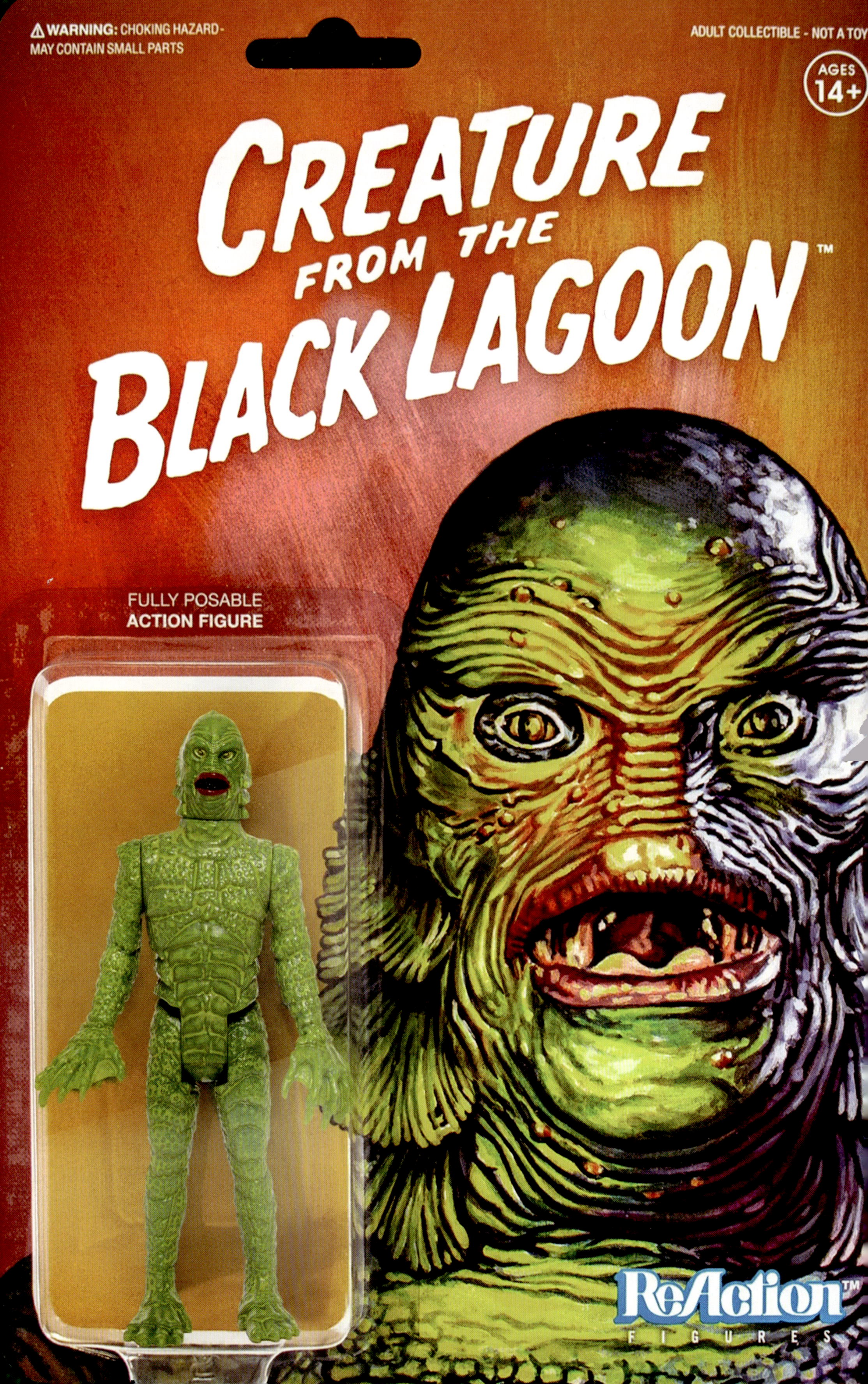

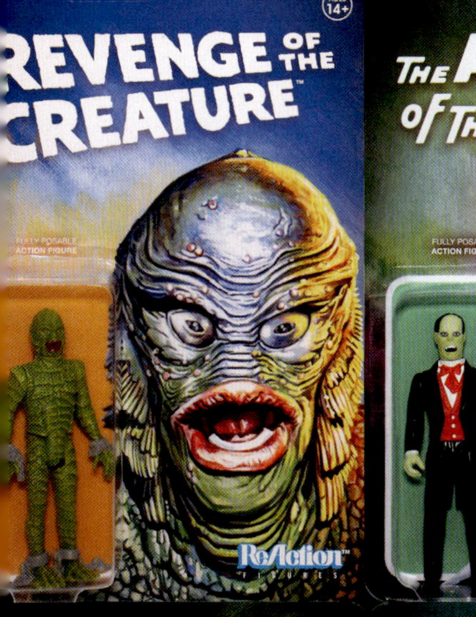

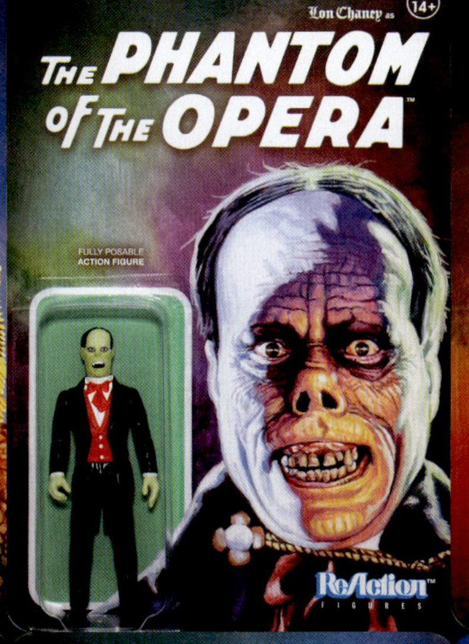

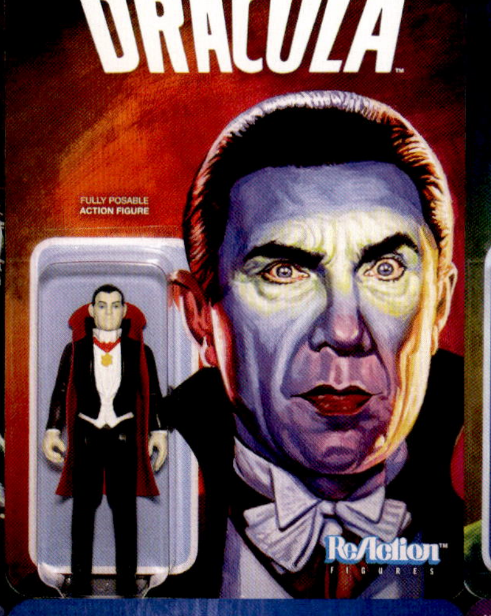

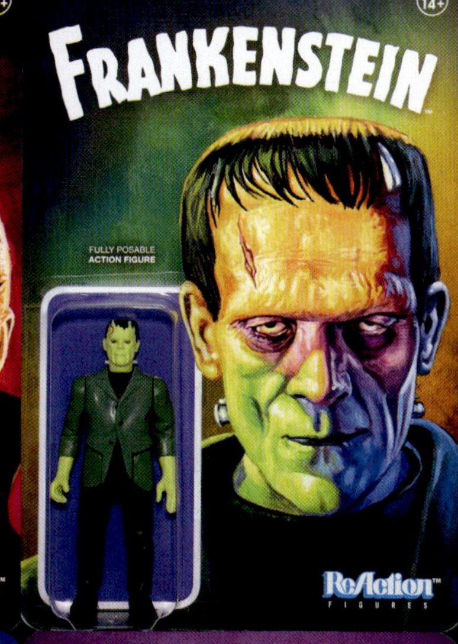

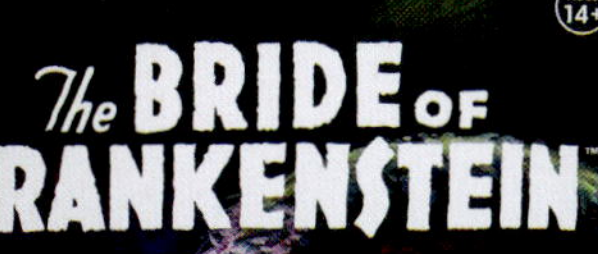

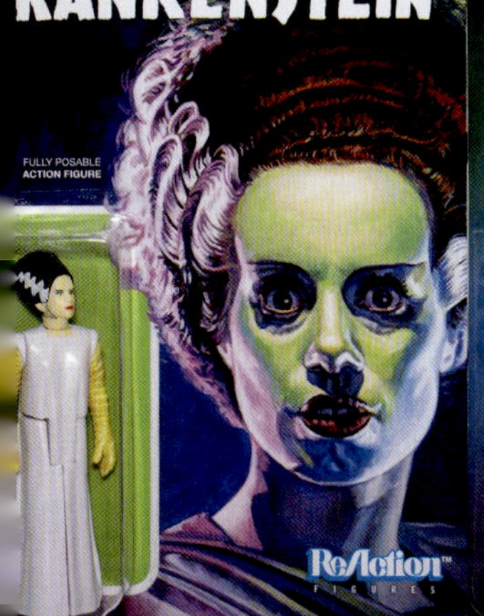

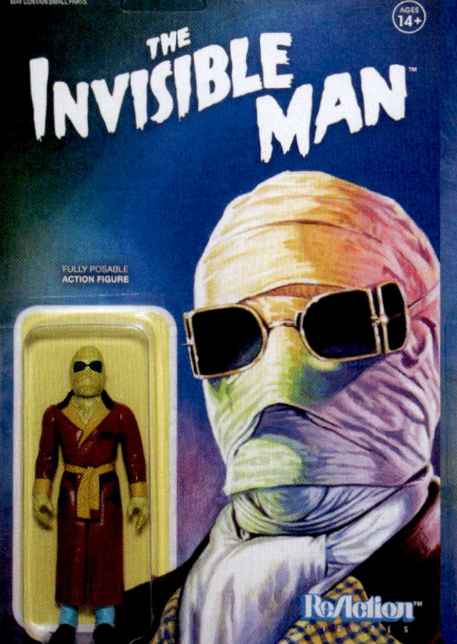

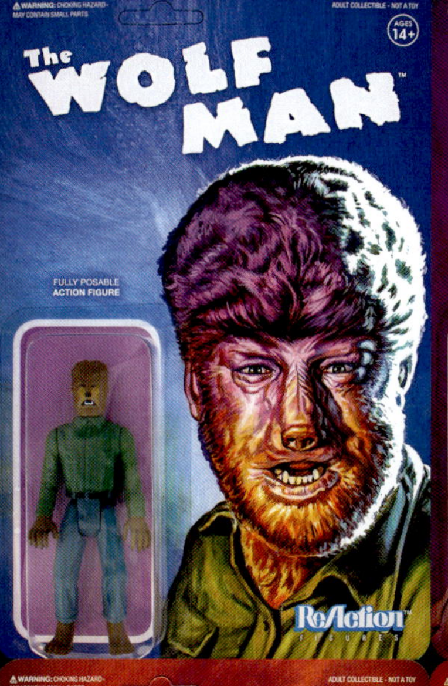

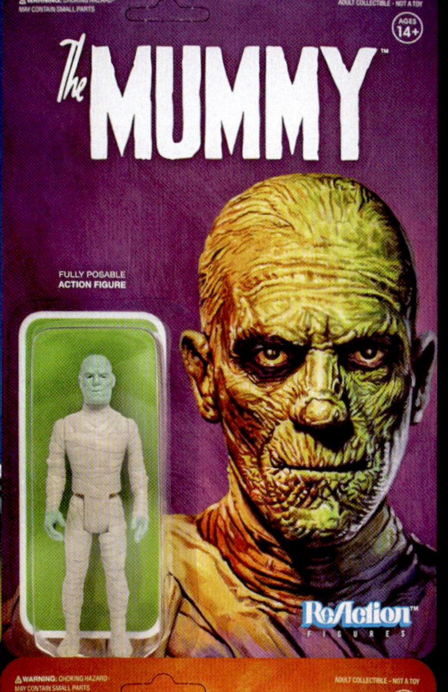

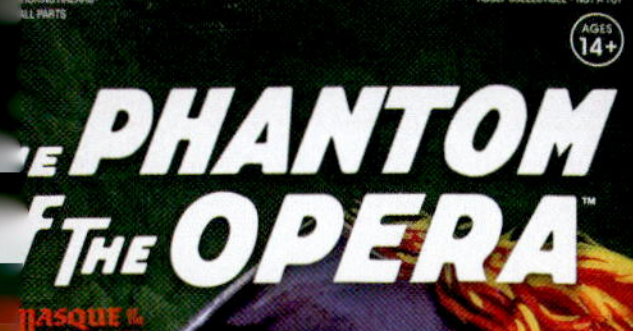

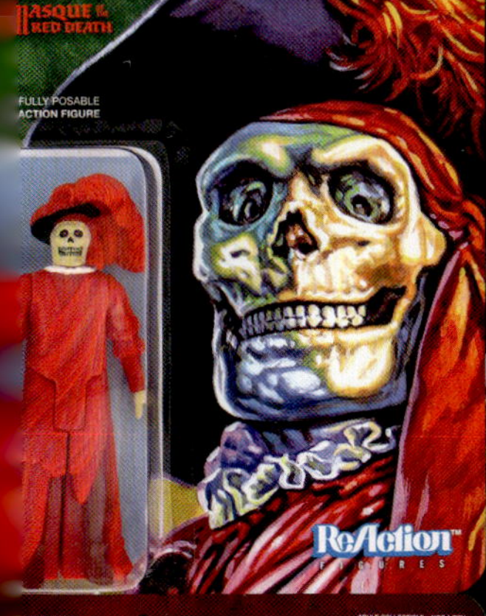

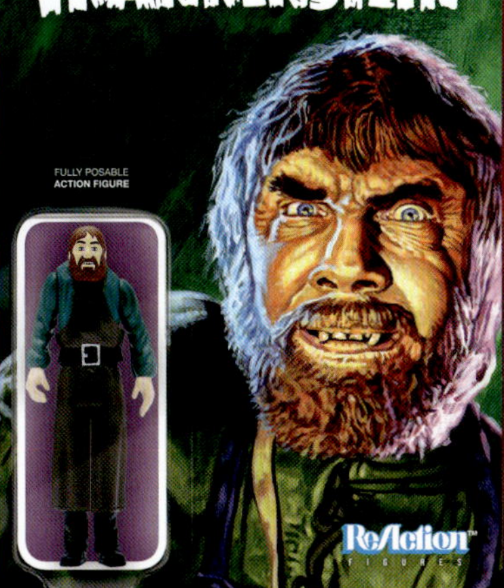

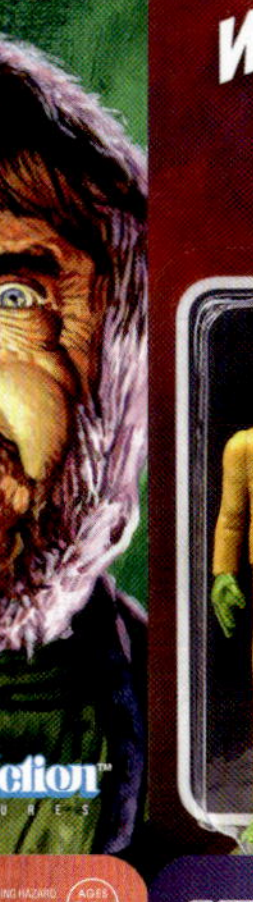
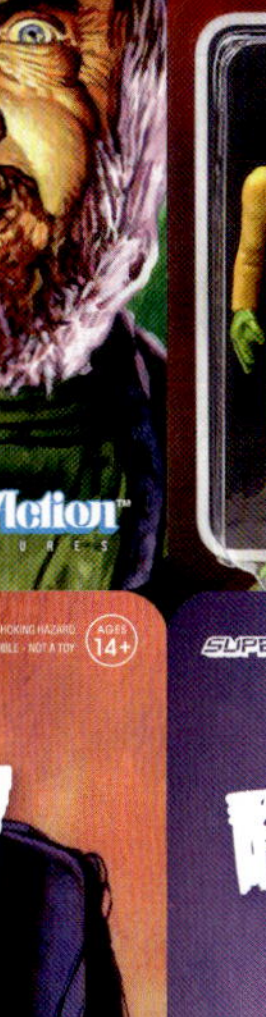

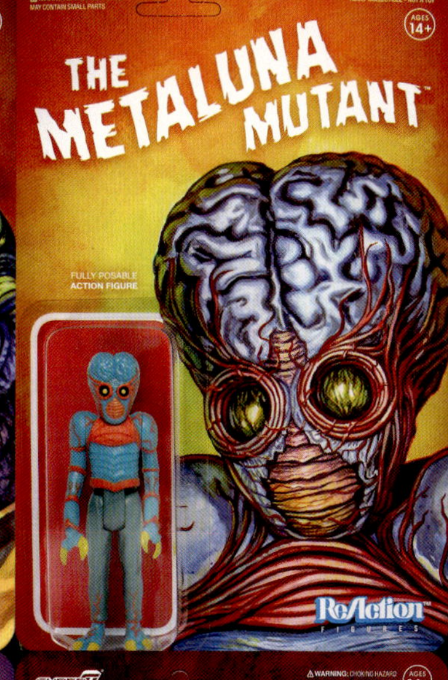

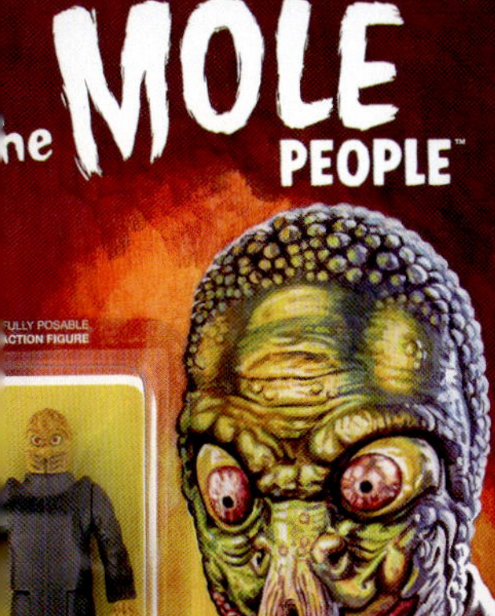

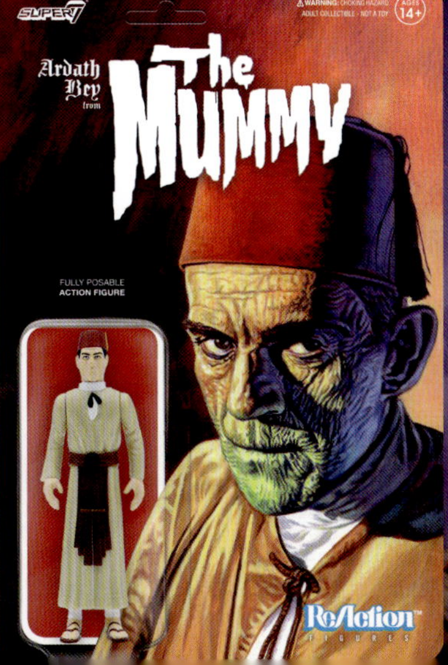

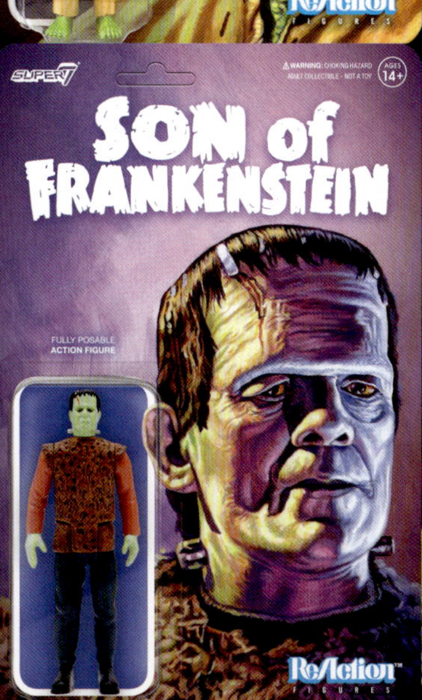

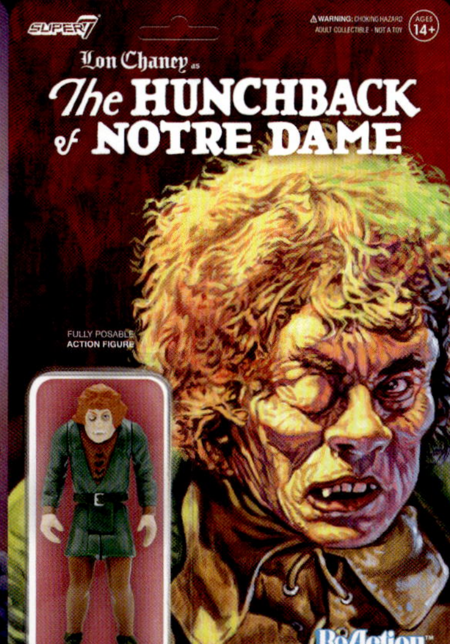

THIS SPREAD: Universal Monsters™ ReAction Figures™ card art

UNIVERSAL MONSTERS © Universal City Studios, LLC. All Rights Reserved.
Bela Lugosi™ and Bela Lugosi as Dracula™ © 2025 Lugosi Enterprises
Lon Chaney™ and Lon Chaney, Jr.™ © 2025 Chaney Entertainment, Inc. All Rights Reserved.

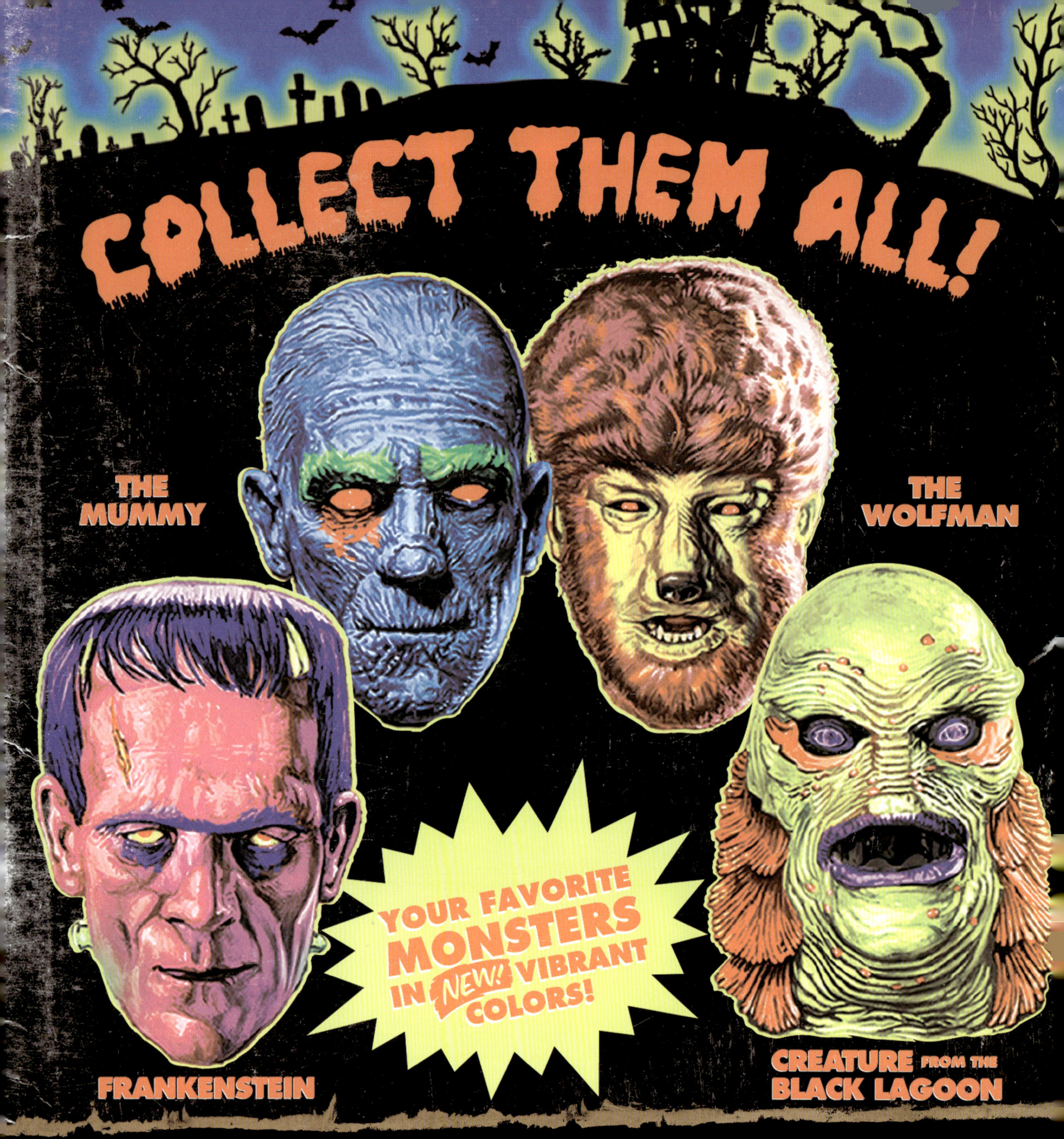

COLLECT THEM ALL!

THE MUMMY

THE WOLFMAN

YOUR FAVORITE MONSTERS IN NEW! VIBRANT COLORS!

FRANKENSTEIN

CREATURE FROM THE BLACK LAGOON

THIS PAGE: Universal Monsters™ "Costume Colors" ReAction Figures™

RIGHT: Creature from the Black Lagoon box art

UNIVERSAL MONSTERS
© Universal City Studios, LLC.
All Rights Reserved.

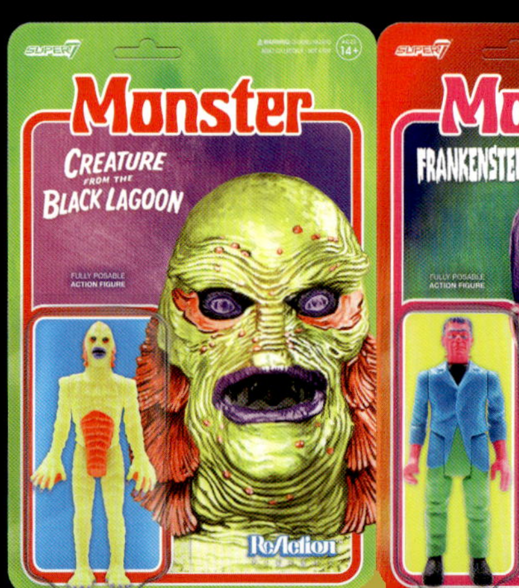

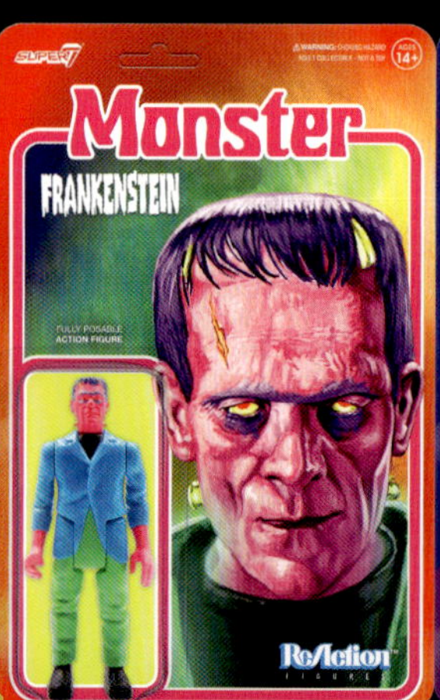

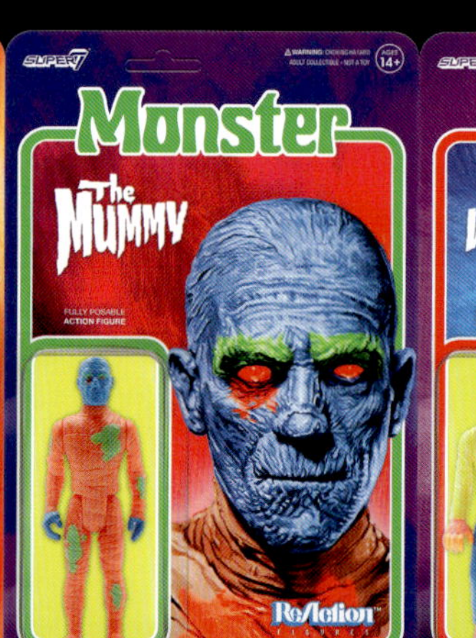

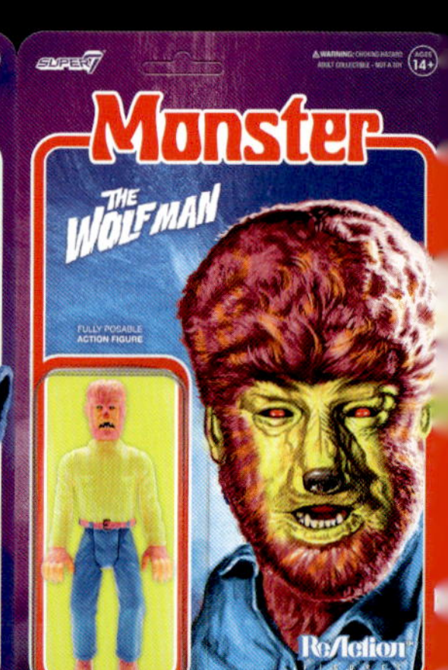

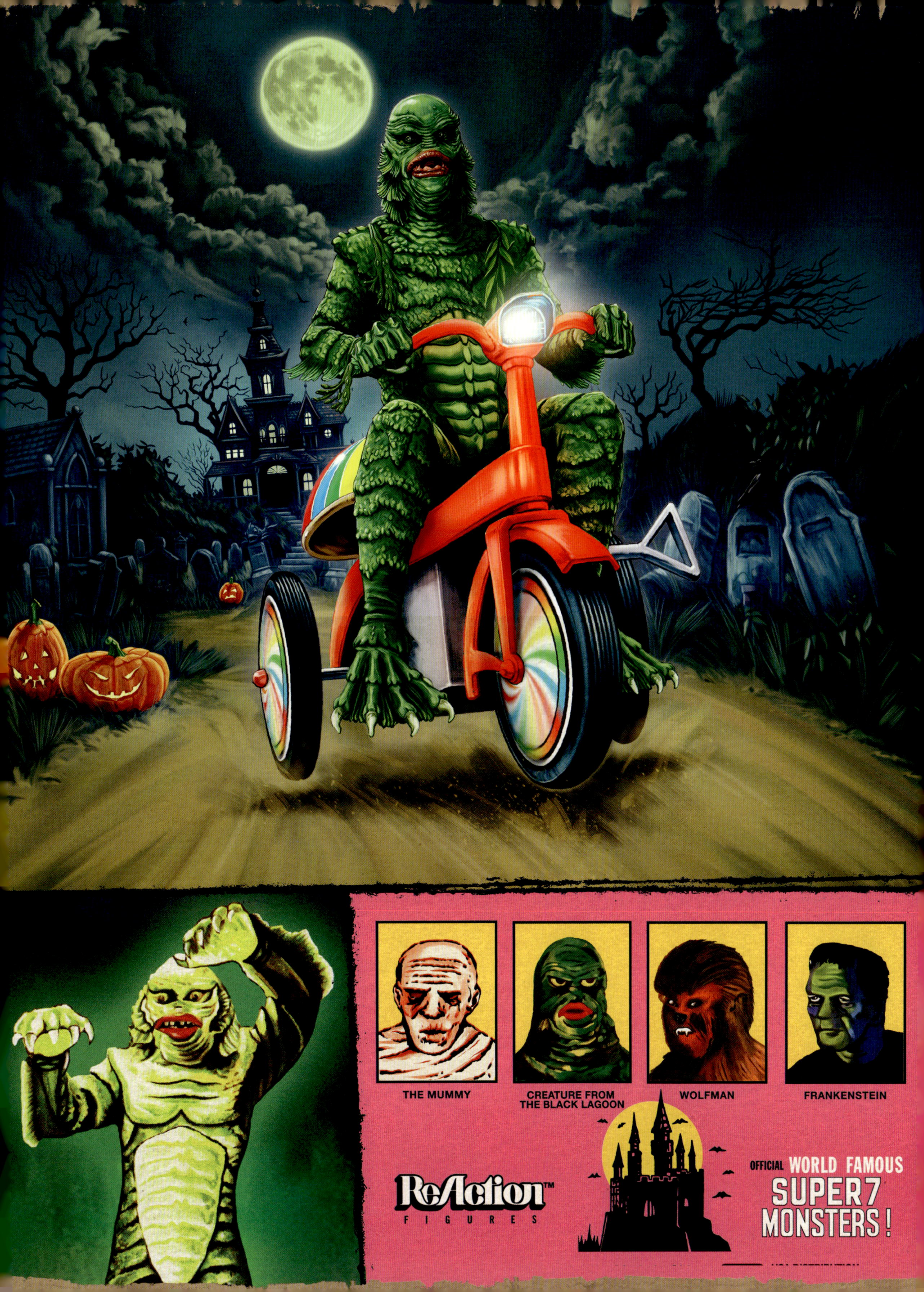

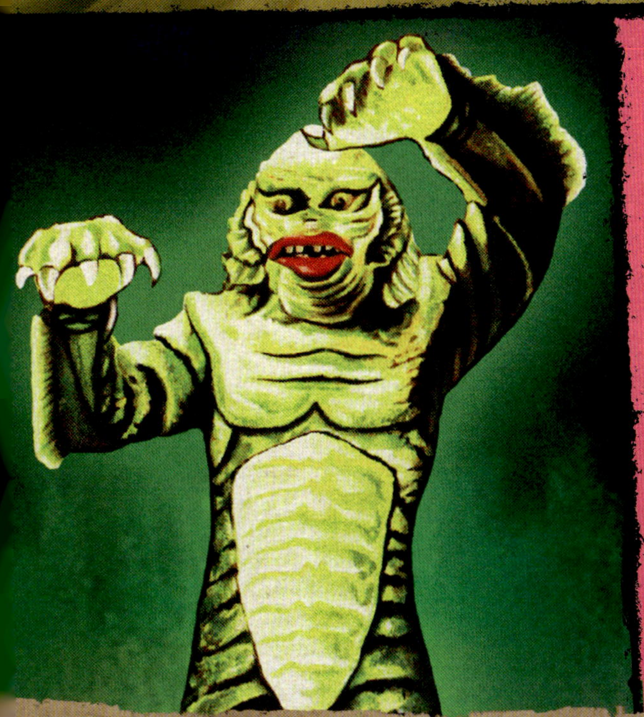

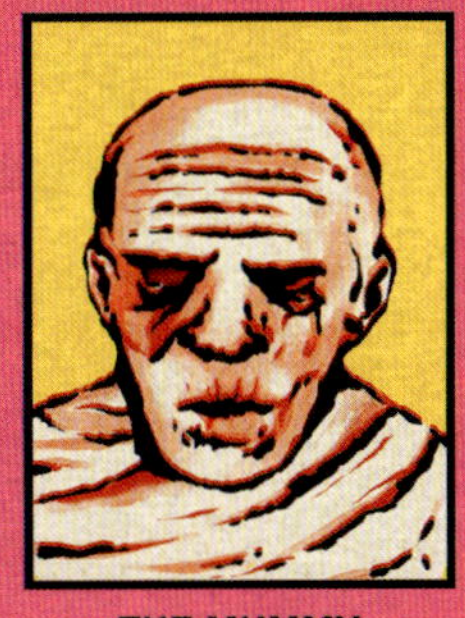
THE MUMMY

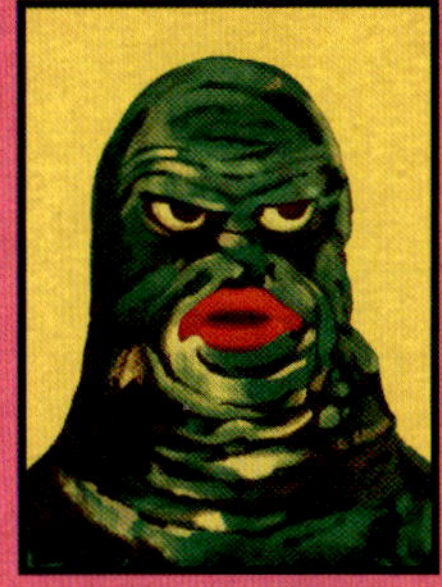
CREATURE FROM THE BLACK LAGOON

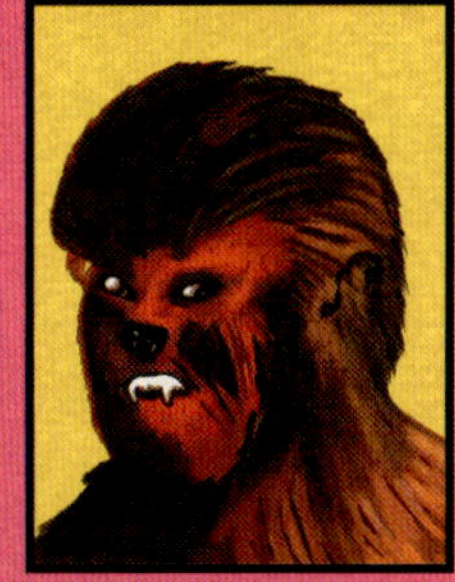
WOLFMAN

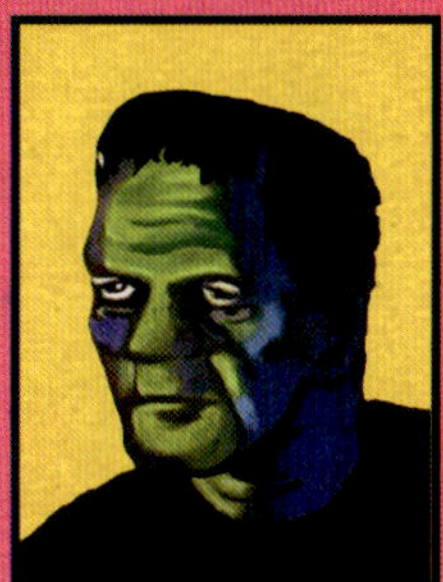
FRANKENSTEIN

ReAction™ FIGURES

OFFICIAL WORLD FAMOUS SUPER7 MONSTERS!

THEY'RE BOLD...

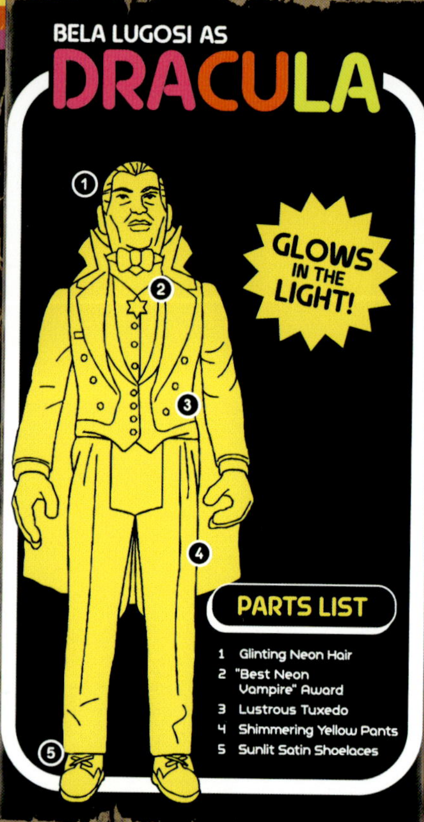

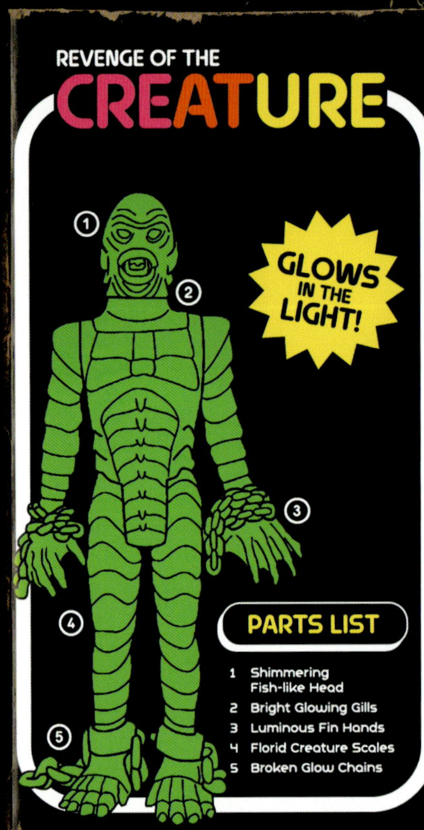

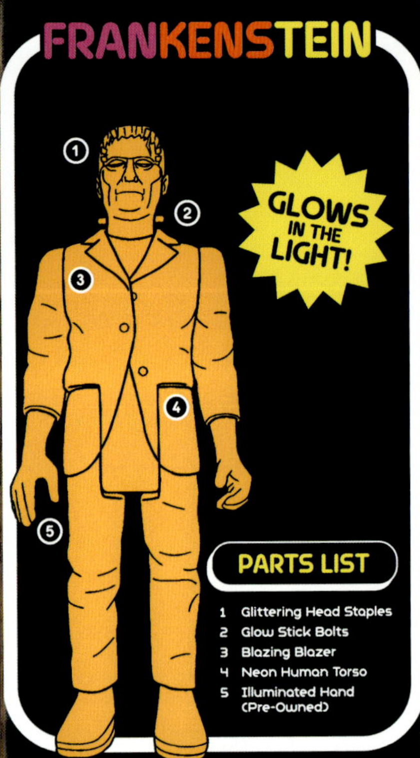

THEY'RE BRIGHT...

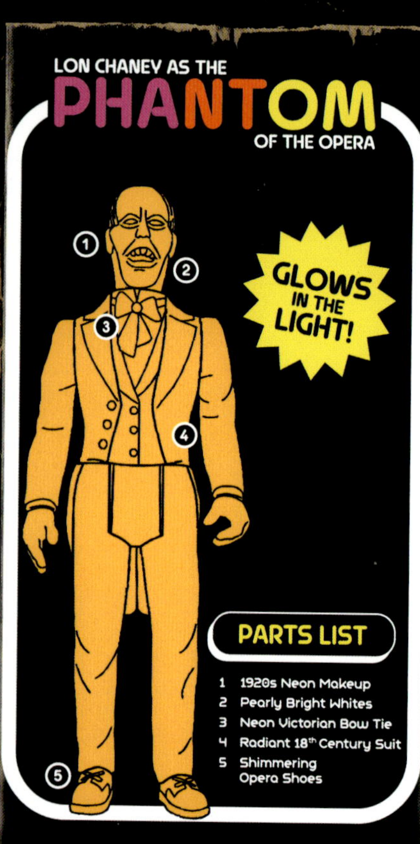

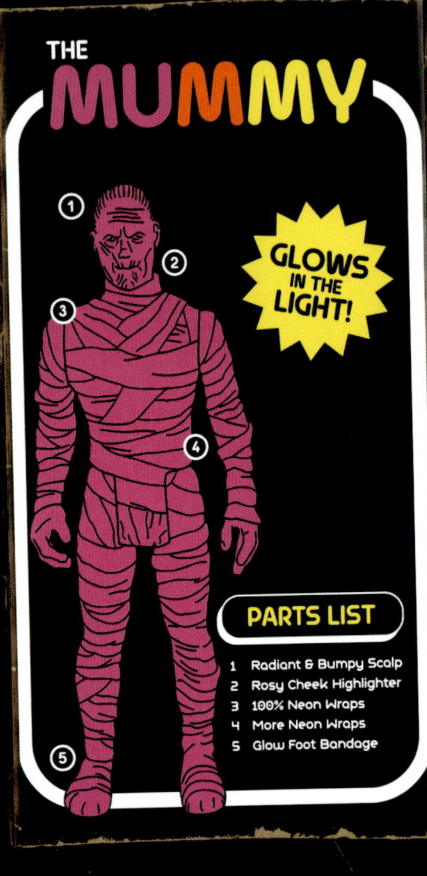

THE
WOLF MAN
GLOWS IN THE LIGHT!
PARTS LIST
1 Fluorescent Facial Hair
2 Howlingly Bright Apparel
3 Brightest Wolf Belt
4 Full Moon Manicure
5 Pedicure "Glow up"

THEY GLOW IN THE LIGHT!

THIS PAGE: Universal Monsters™ "Luminators" box art

RIGHT: Universal Monsters™ Glow "Costume Colors" box art

UNIVERSAL MONSTERS © Universal City Studios, LLC. All Rights Reserved.

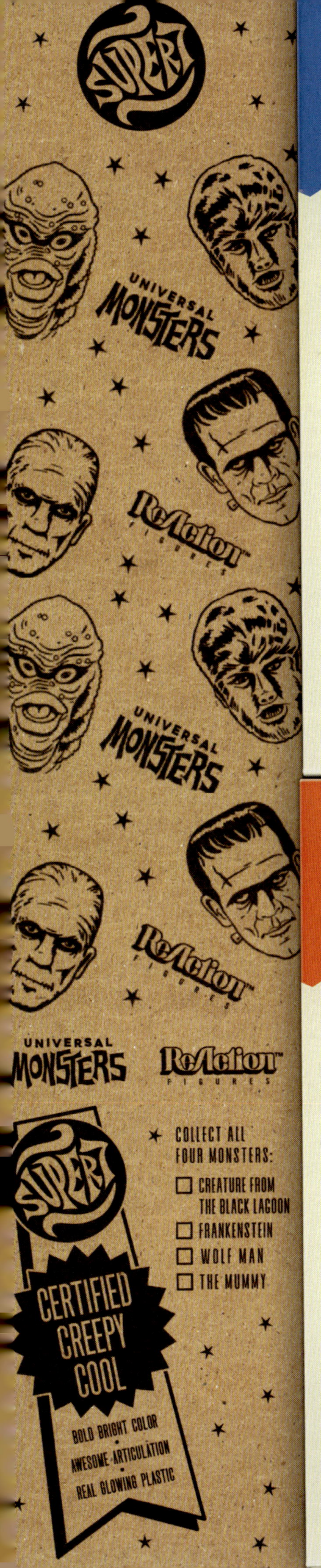
SUPER7
UNIVERSAL MONSTERS
ReAction FIGURES
UNIVERSAL MONSTERS
ReAction FIGURES
UNIVERSAL MONSTERS
ReAction FIGURES
SUPER7
COLLECT ALL FOUR MONSTERS:
CREATURE FROM THE BLACK LAGOON
FRANKENSTEIN
WOLF MAN
THE MUMMY
CERTIFIED CREEPY COOL
BOLD BRIGHT COLOR
AWESOME ARTICULATION
REAL GLOWING PLASTIC

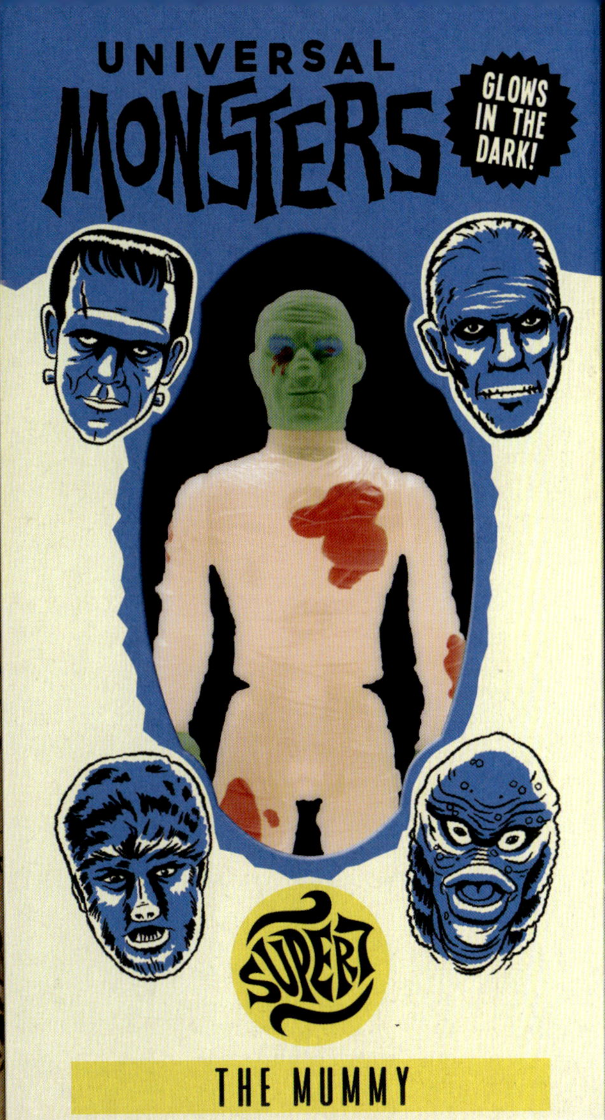
UNIVERSAL MONSTERS
GLOWS IN THE DARK!
SUPER7
THE MUMMY

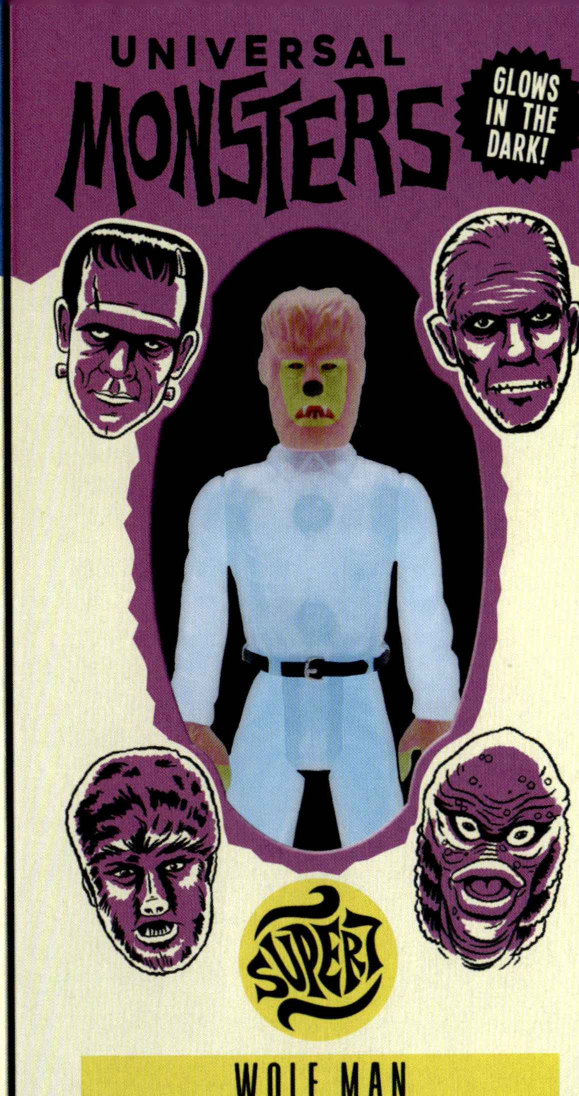
UNIVERSAL MONSTERS
GLOWS IN THE DARK!
SUPER7
WOLF MAN

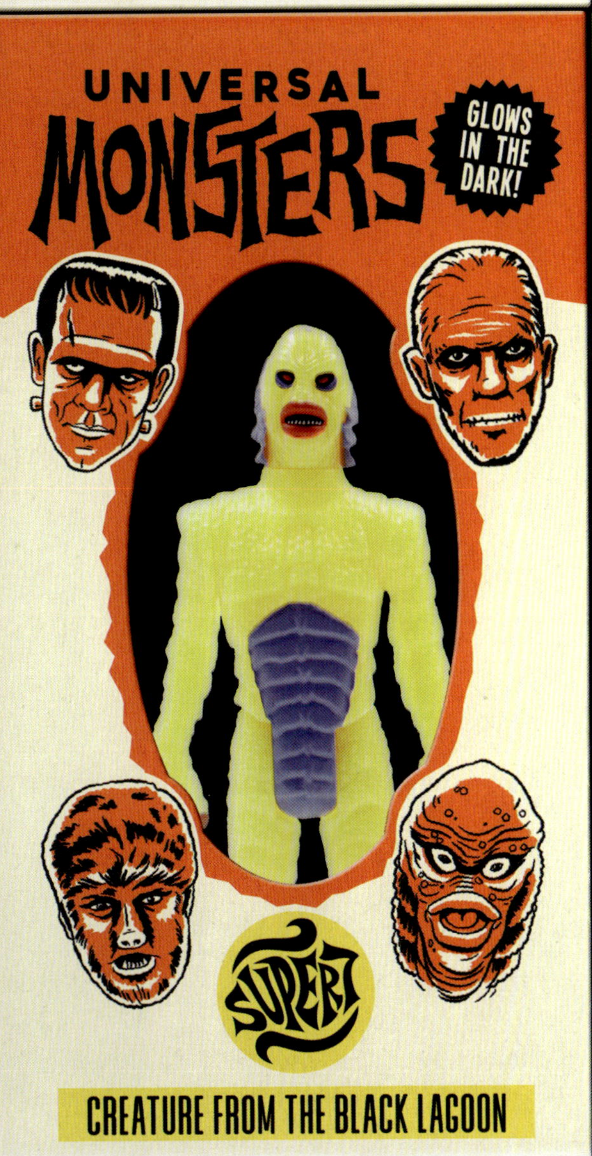
UNIVERSAL MONSTERS
GLOWS IN THE DARK!
SUPER7
CREATURE FROM THE BLACK LAGOON

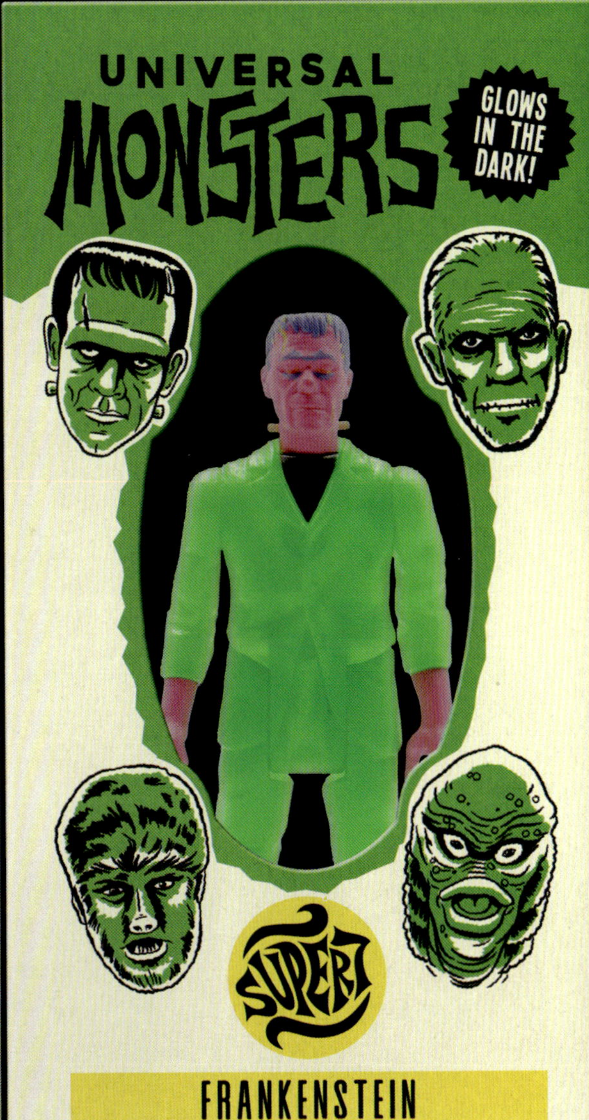
UNIVERSAL MONSTERS
GLOWS IN THE DARK!
SUPER7
FRANKENSTEIN

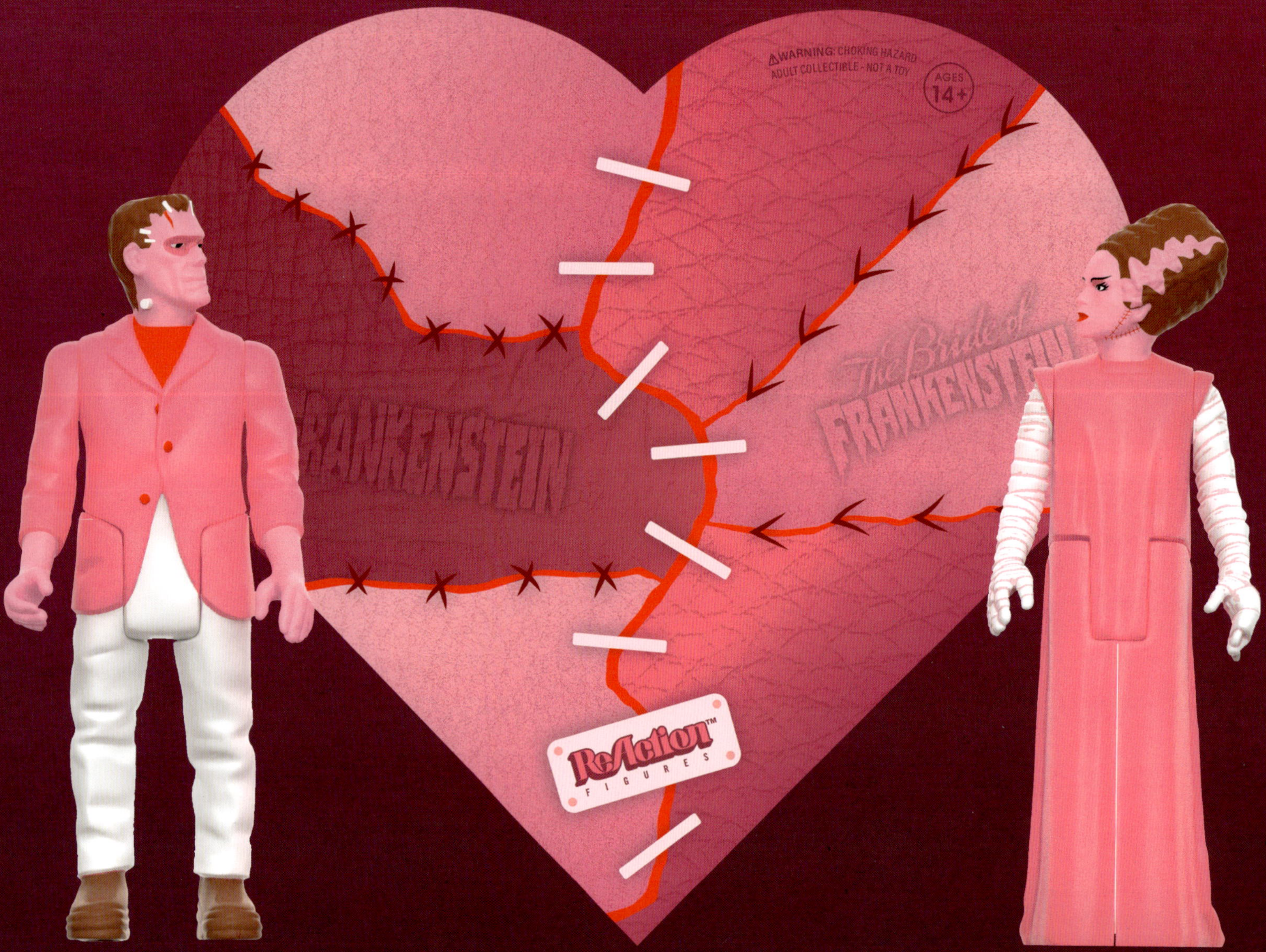

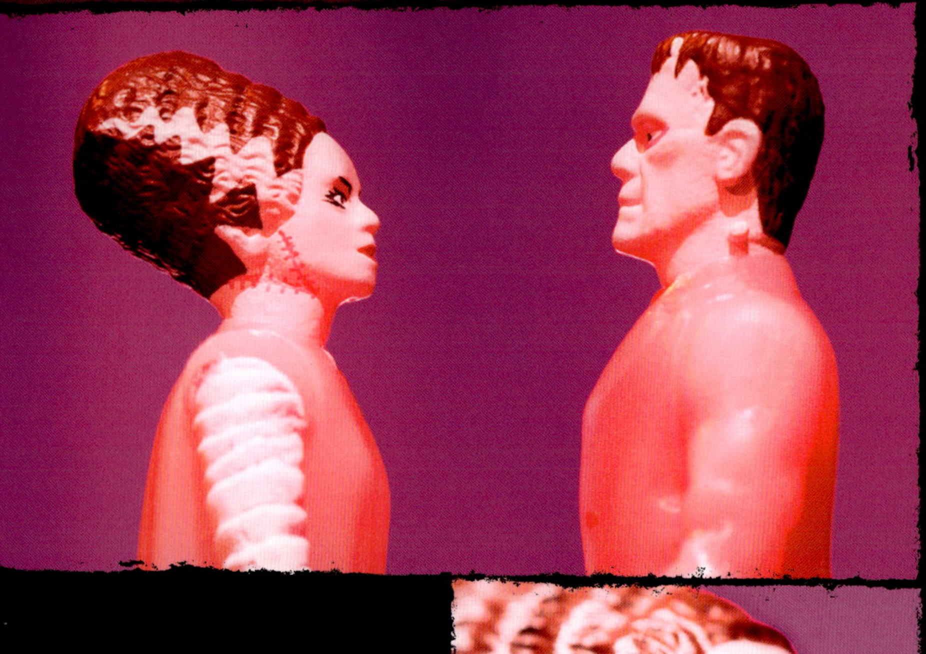

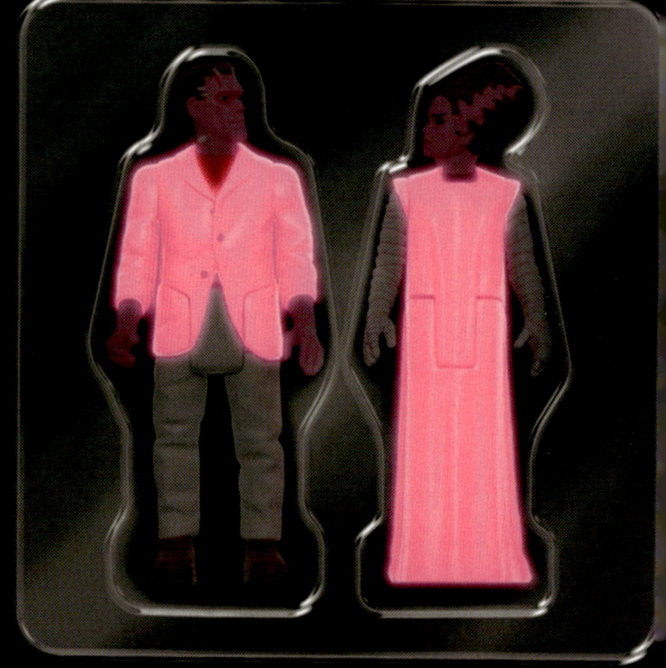

THIS PAGE: Frankenstein and Bride Valentine's 2-pack art

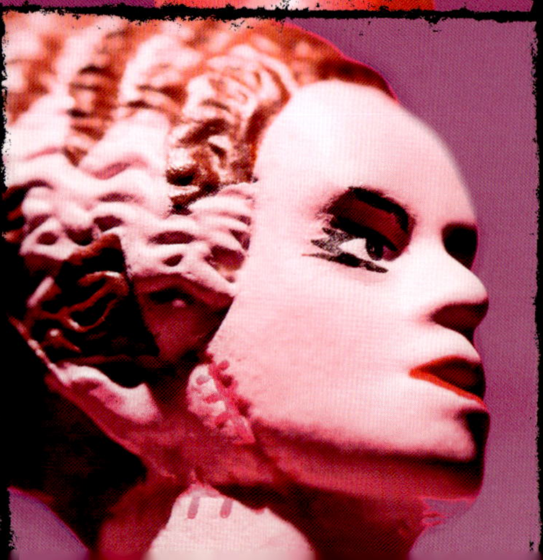

UNIVERSAL MONSTERS
© Universal City Studios, LLC.
All Rights Reserved.

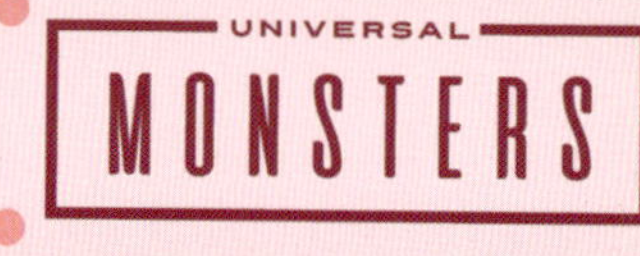

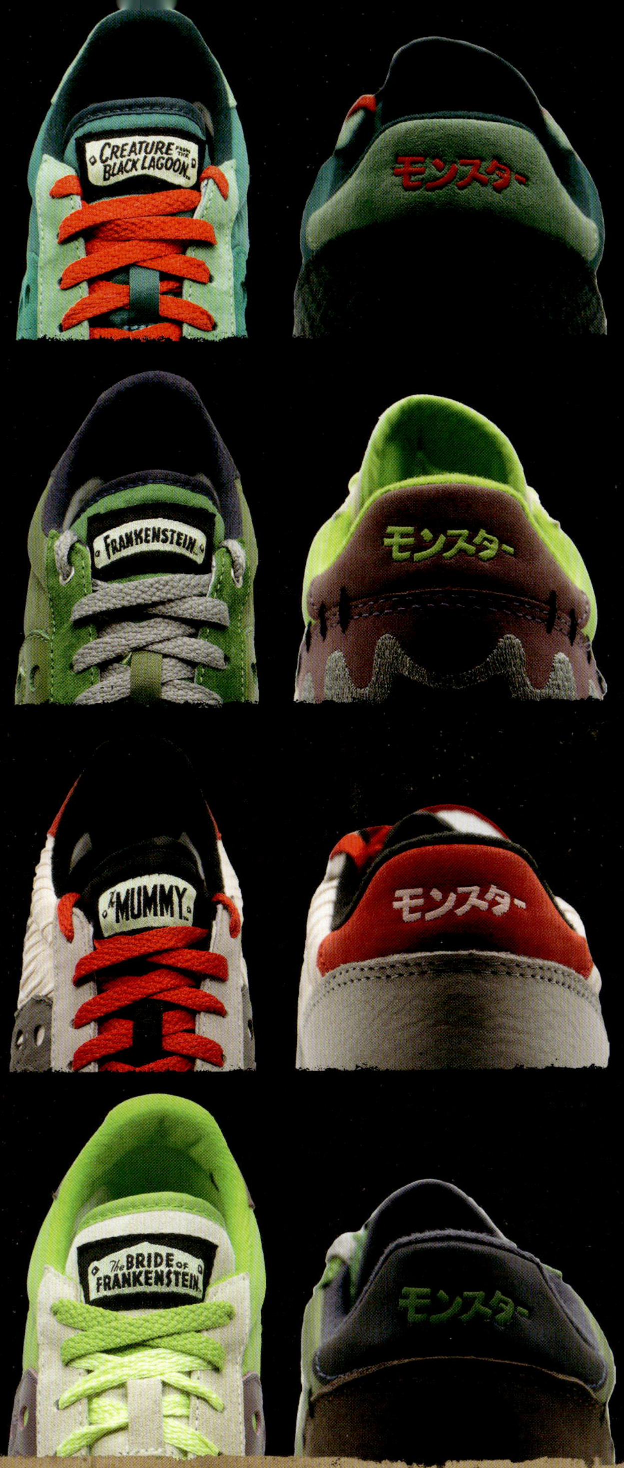

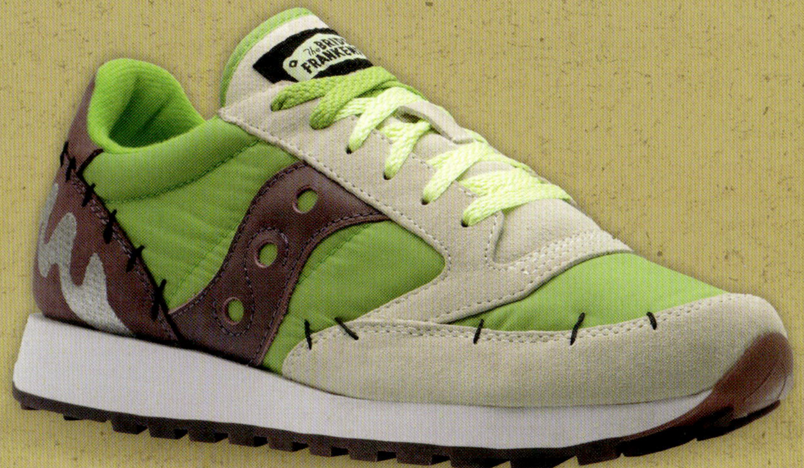

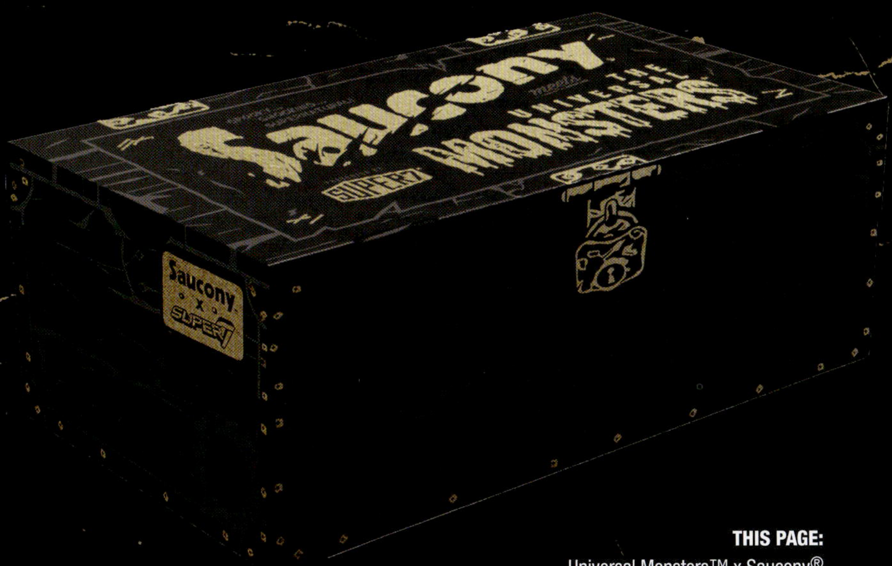

THIS PAGE:
Universal Monsters™ x Saucony®
shoes and Universal Monsters™ Super Soapies

UNIVERSAL MONSTERS © Universal City Studios, LLC. All Rights Reserved.
© 2025 Saucony. All Rights Reserved.

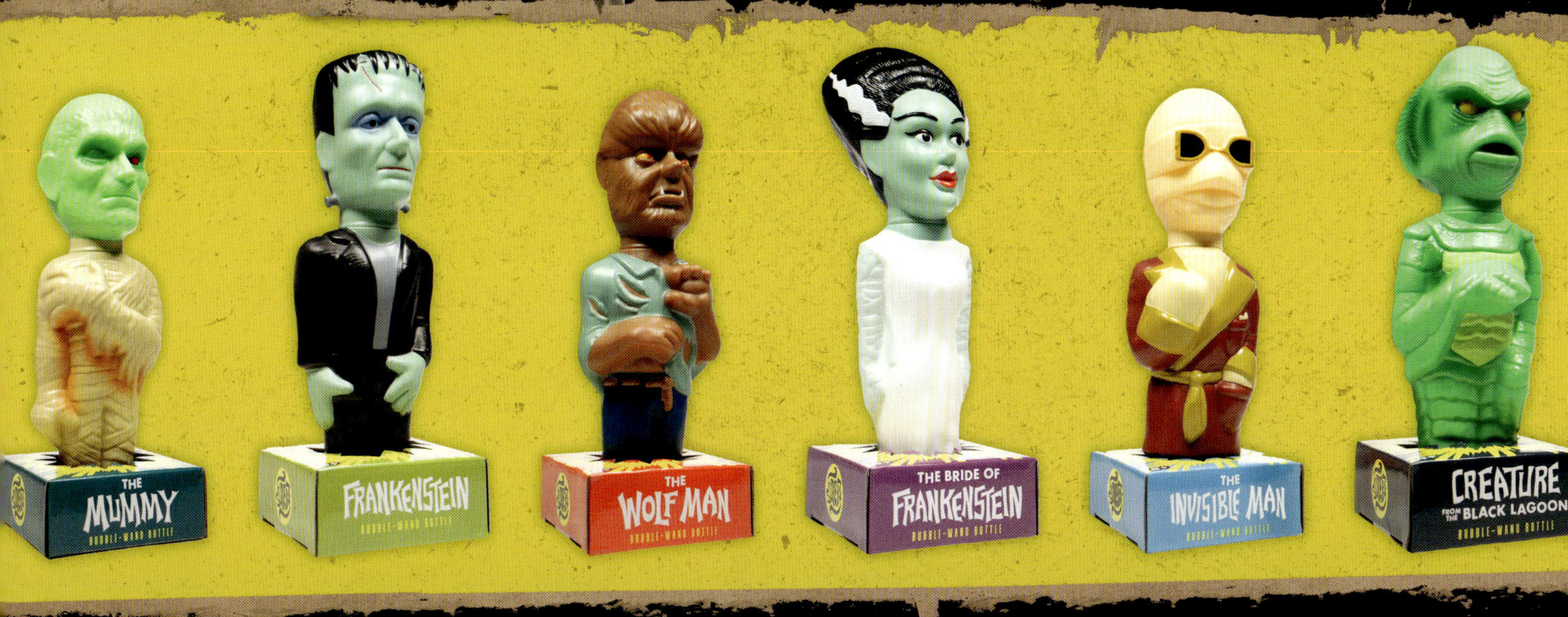

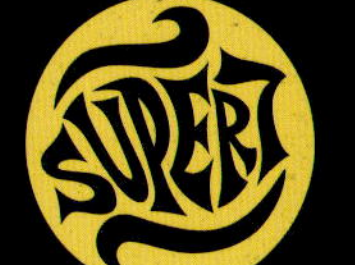
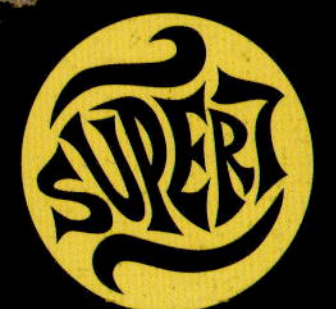
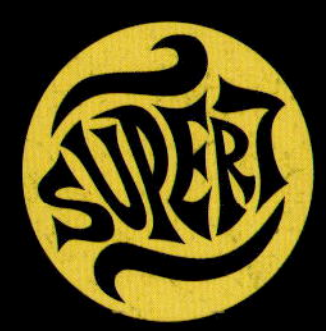
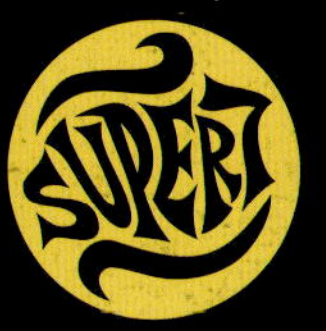
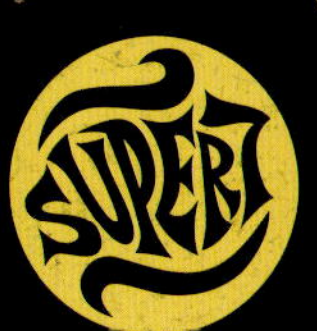
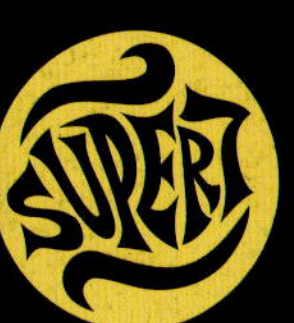
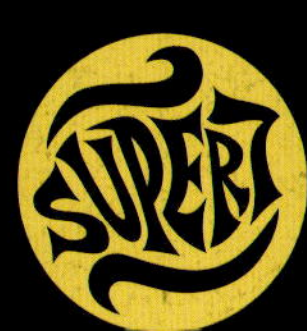
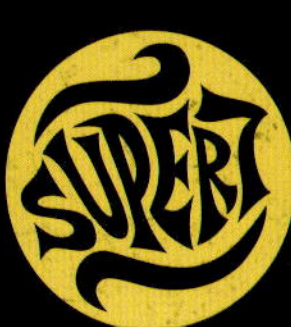

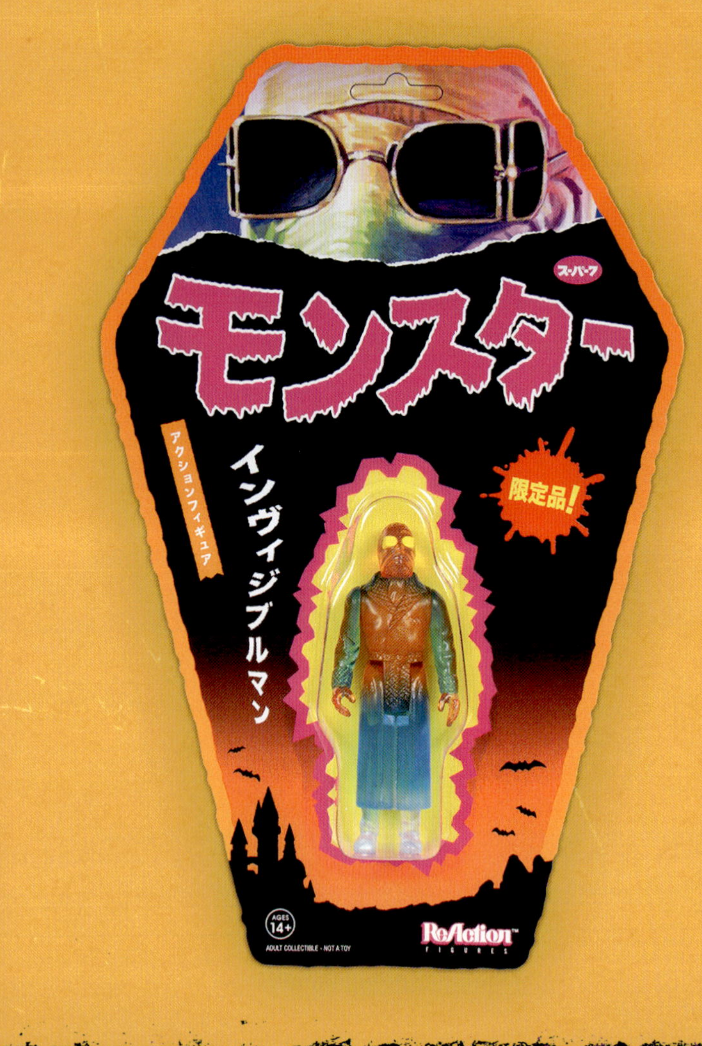
モンスター
スーパー7
アクションフィギュア
インヴィジブルマン
限定品!
AGES 14+
ReAction
FIGURES

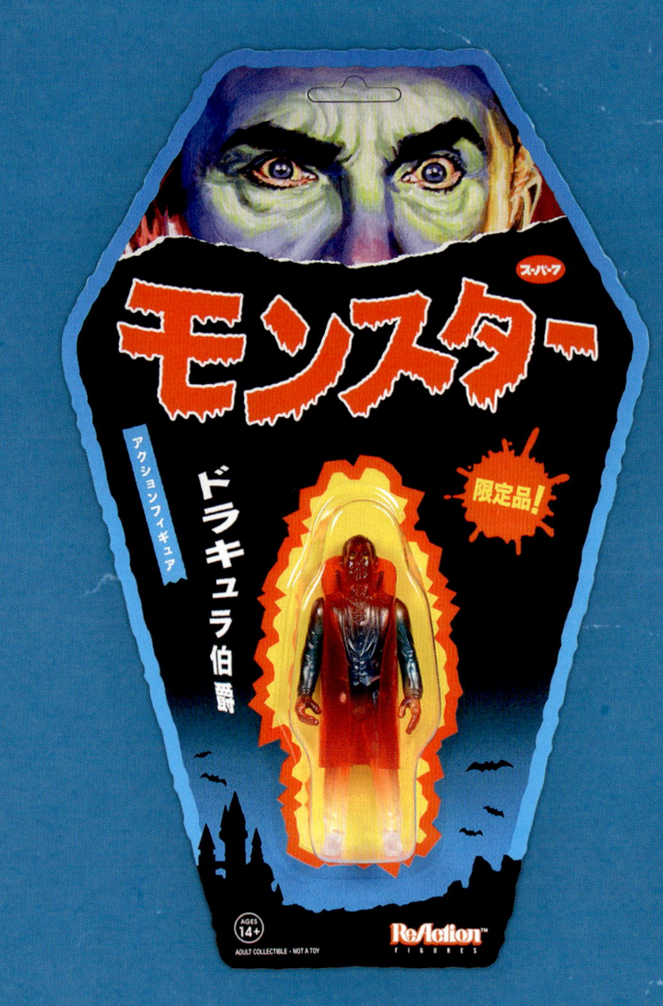
モンスター
スーパー7
アクションフィギュア
ドラキュラ伯爵
限定品!
AGES 14+
ReAction
FIGURES

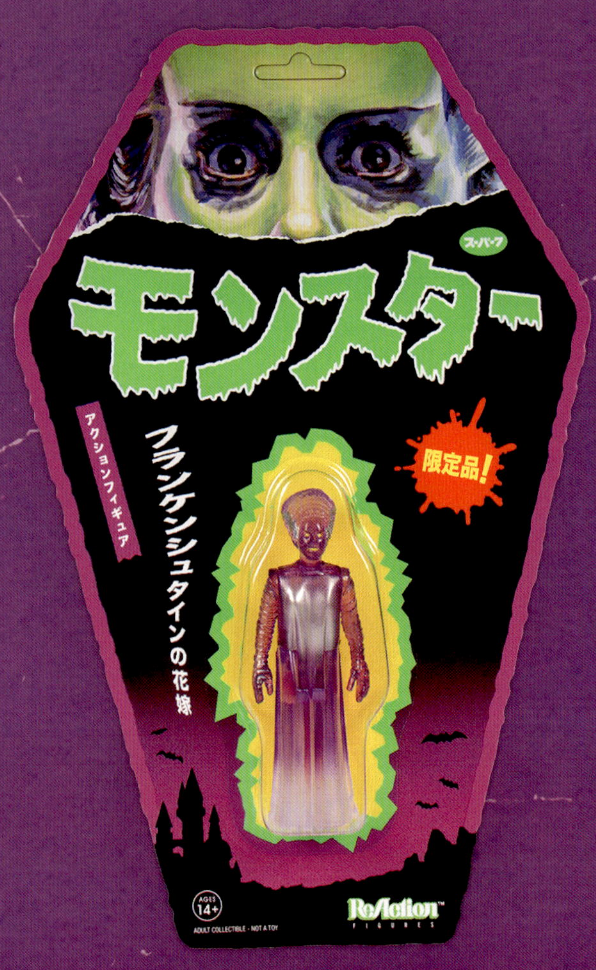
モンスター
スーパー7
アクションフィギュア
フランケンシュタインの花嫁
限定品!
AGES 14+
ReAction
FIGURES

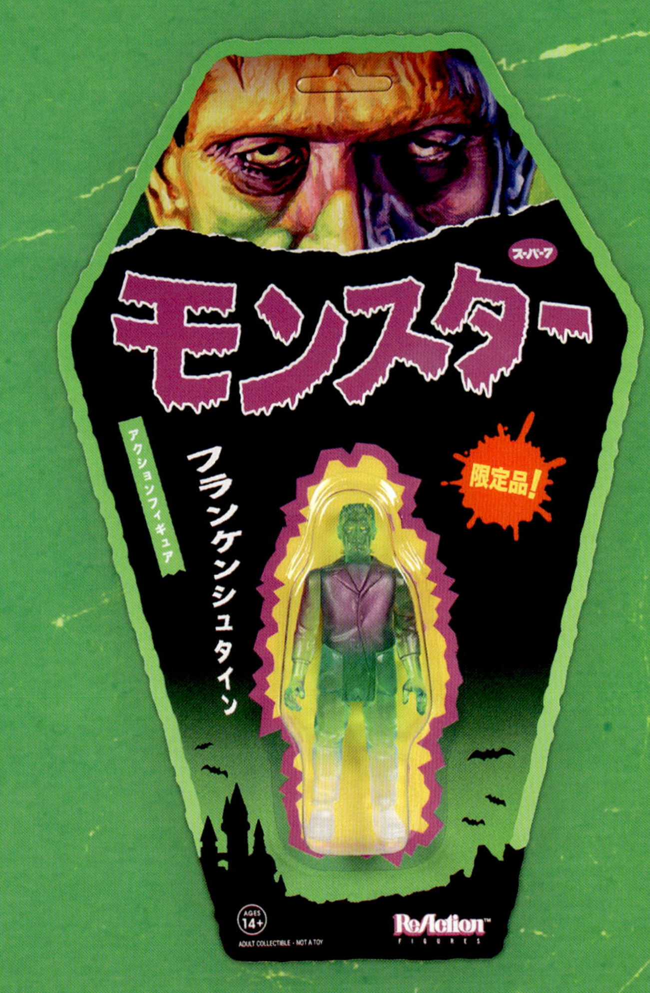
モンスター
スーパー7
アクションフィギュア
フランケンシュタイン
限定品!
AGES 14+
ReAction
FIGURES

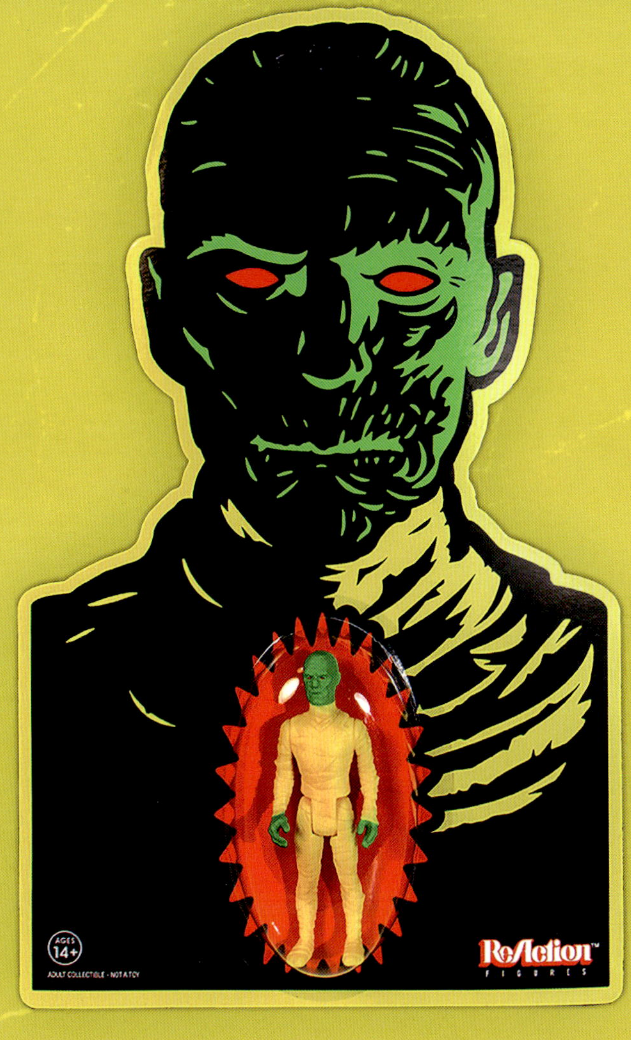

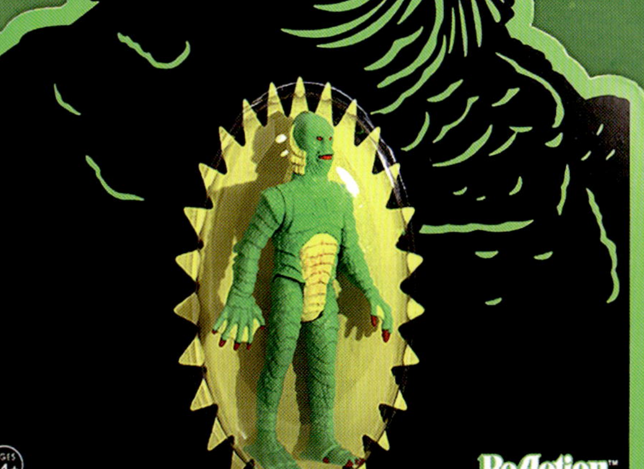

THIS SPREAD: A selection of special release Universal Monsters™ ReAction Figures™ cards

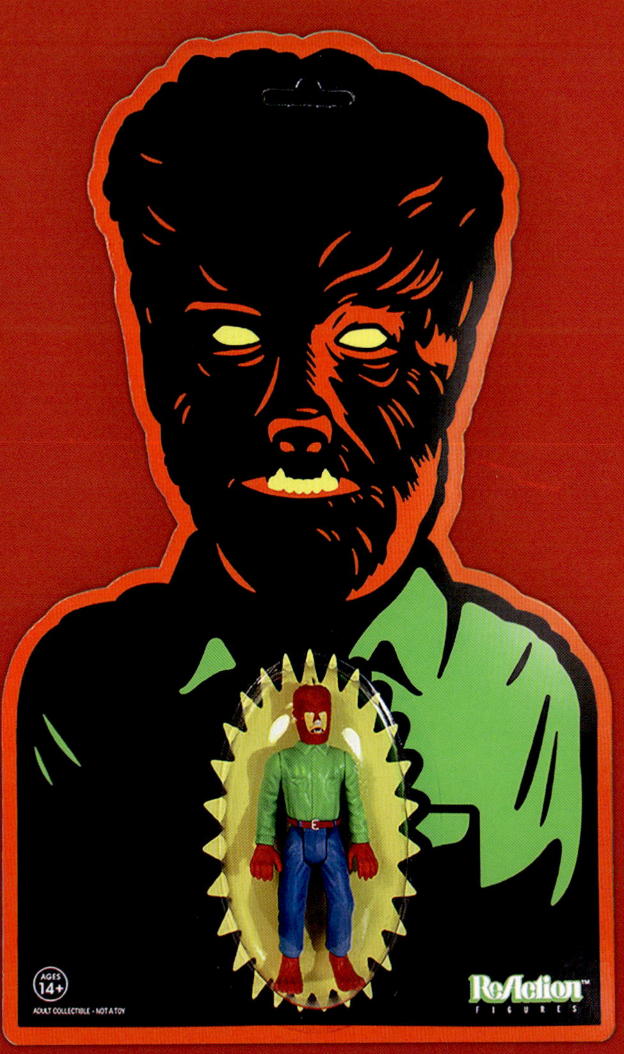

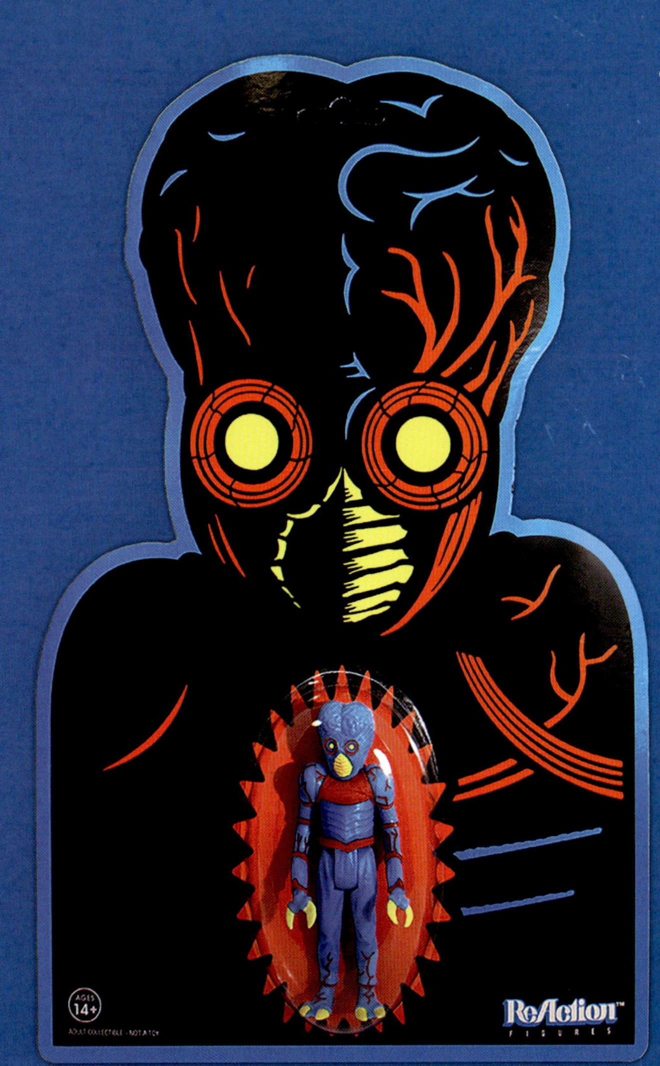

UNIVERSAL MONSTERS © Universal City Studios, LLC. All Rights Reserved.

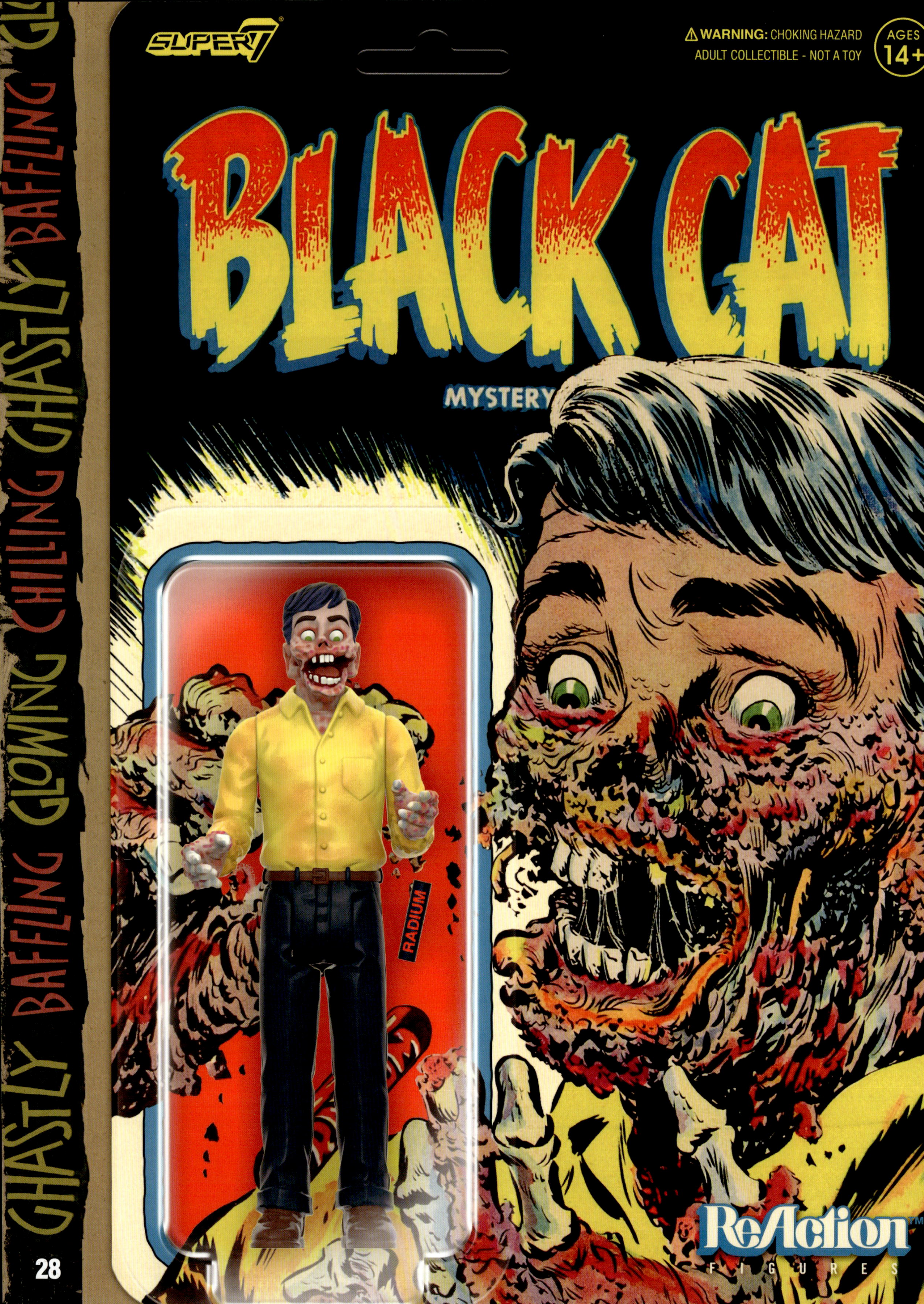
SUPER7
⚠ WARNING: CHOKING HAZARD
ADULT COLLECTIBLE - NOT A TOY
AGES 14+
BLACK CAT
MYSTERY
RADIUM
ReAction™
FIGURES
GHASTLY BAFFLING GLOWING CHILLING GHASTLY BAFFLING GL

HORROR ACTION FIGURES FROM THE PRE-CODE ERA

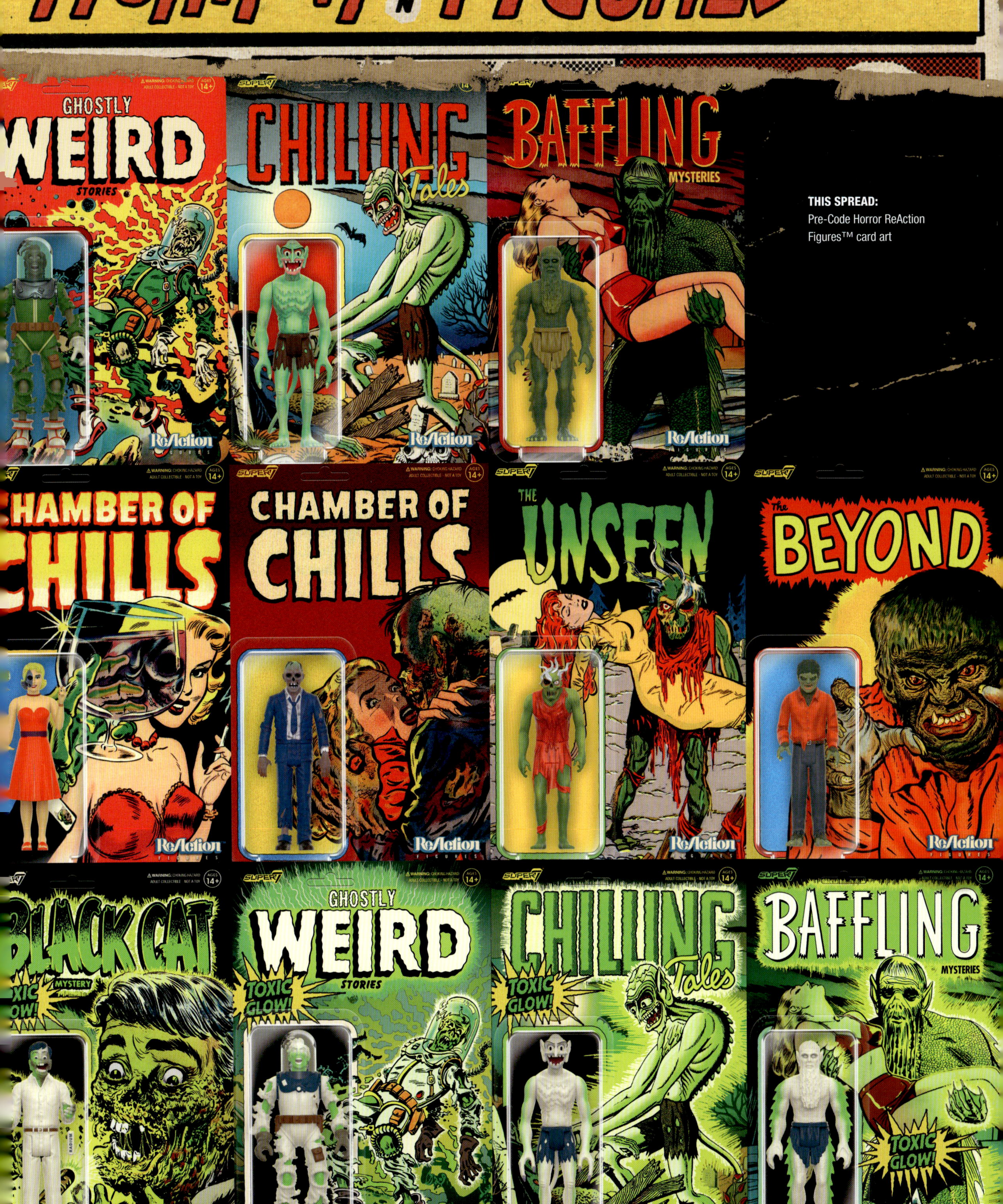

THIS SPREAD: Pre-Code Horror ReAction Figures™ card art

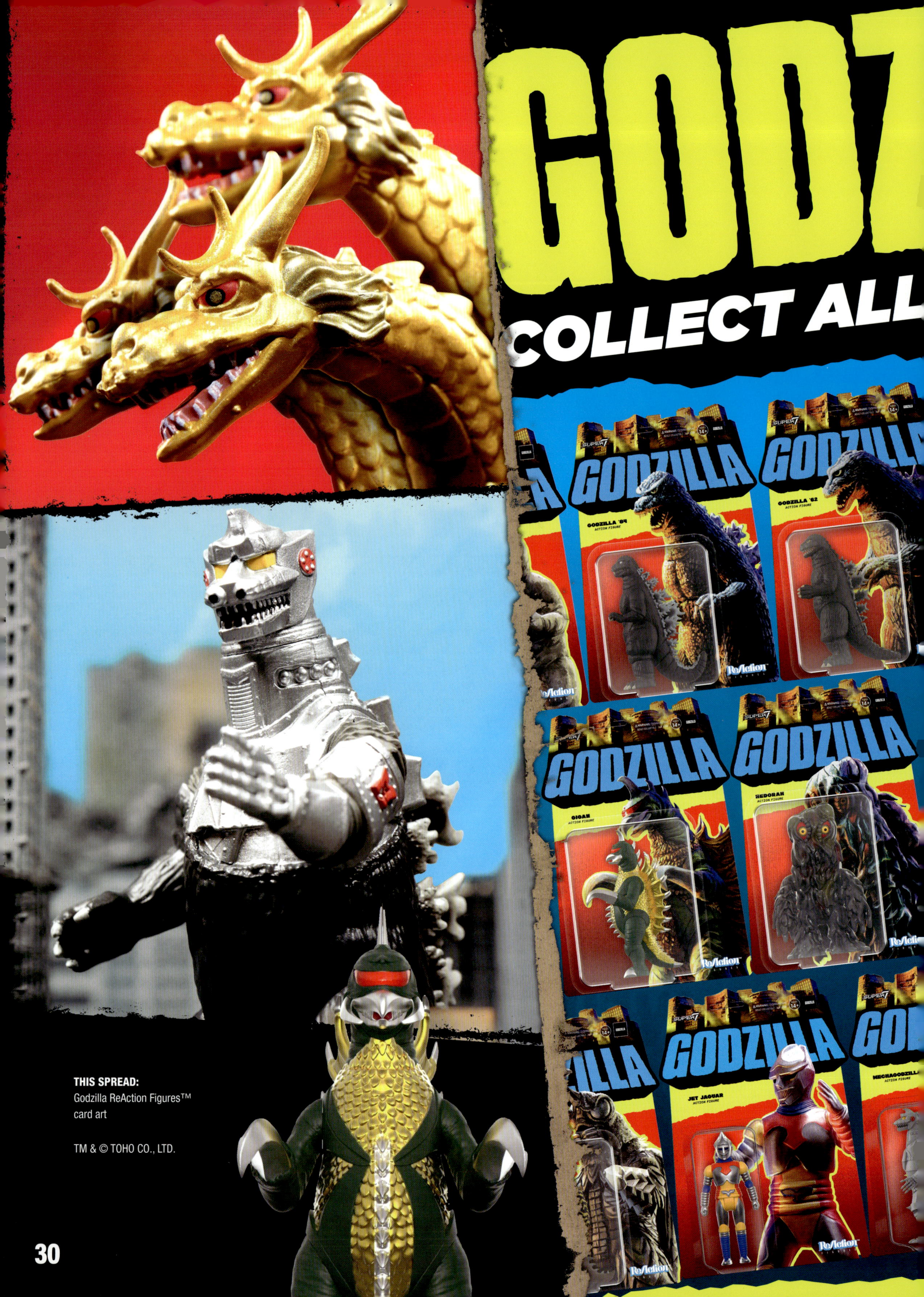

THIS SPREAD:
Godzilla ReAction Figures™ card art

TM & © TOHO CO., LTD.

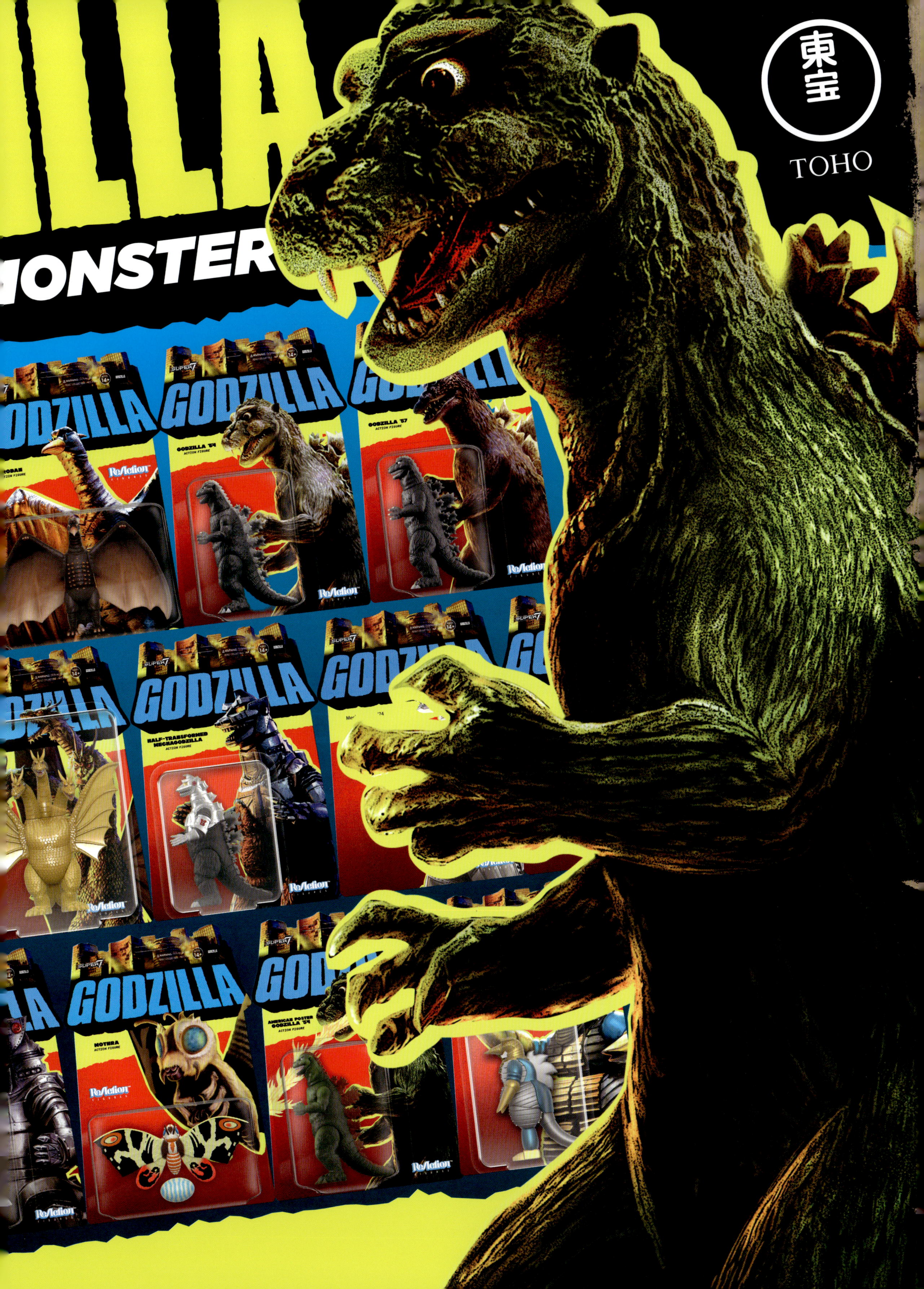
ILLA
ONSTER
東宝
TOHO
GODZILLA
GODZILLA '54
ACTION FIGURE
GODZILLA '57
ACTION FIGURE
HALF-TRANSFORMED
MECHAGODZILLA
ACTION FIGURE
MOTHRA
ACTION FIGURE
AMERICAN POSTER
GODZILLA '54
ACTION FIGURE
ReAction

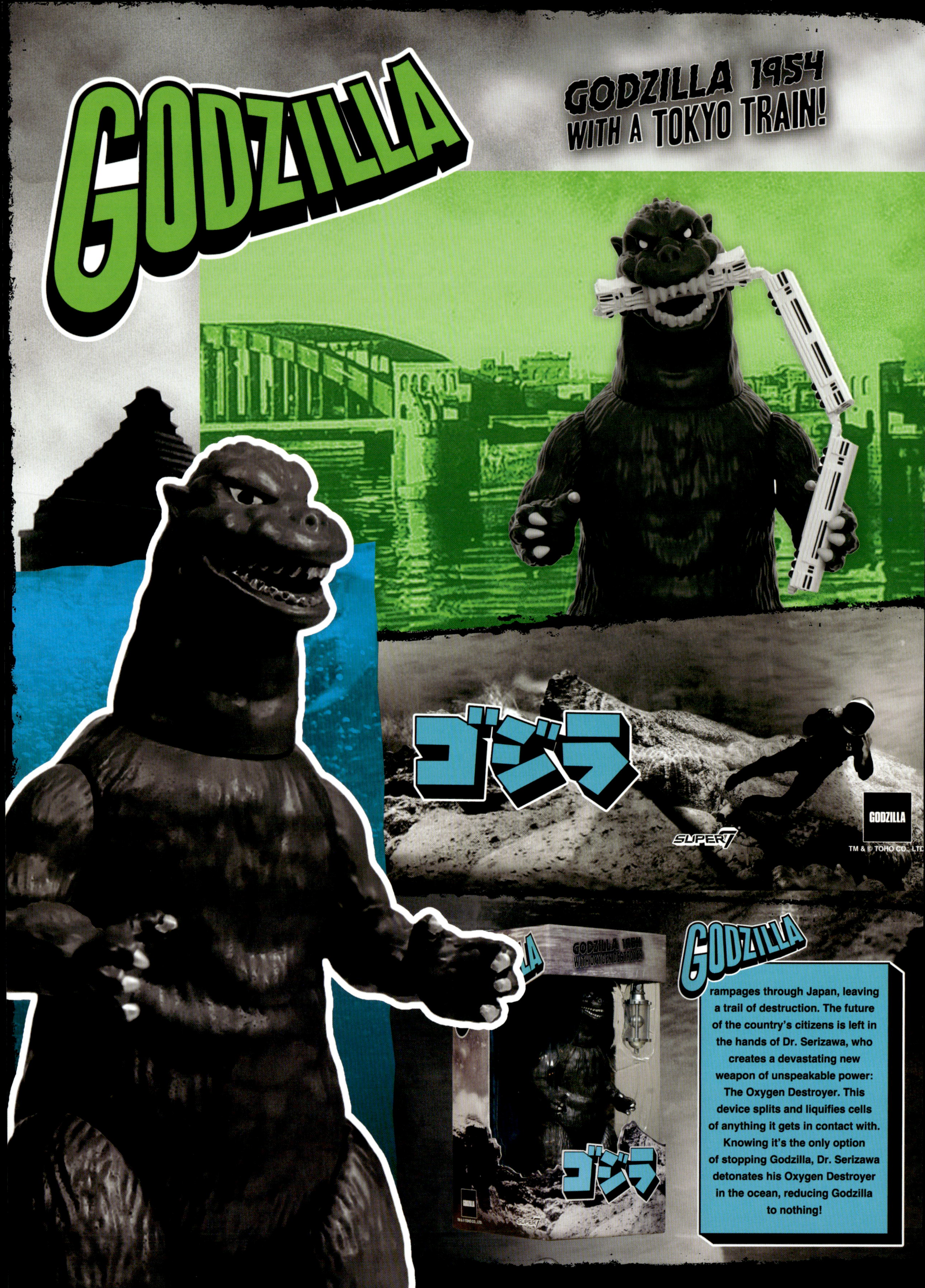
GODZILLA
GODZILLA 1954
WITH A TOKYO TRAIN!
ゴジラ
SUPER7
GODZILLA
TM & © TOHO CO., LTD.
GODZILLA
rampages through Japan, leaving a trail of destruction. The future of the country's citizens is left in the hands of Dr. Serizawa, who creates a devastating new weapon of unspeakable power: The Oxygen Destroyer. This device splits and liquifies cells of anything it gets in contact with. Knowing it's the only option of stopping Godzilla, Dr. Serizawa detonates his Oxygen Destroyer in the ocean, reducing Godzilla to nothing!

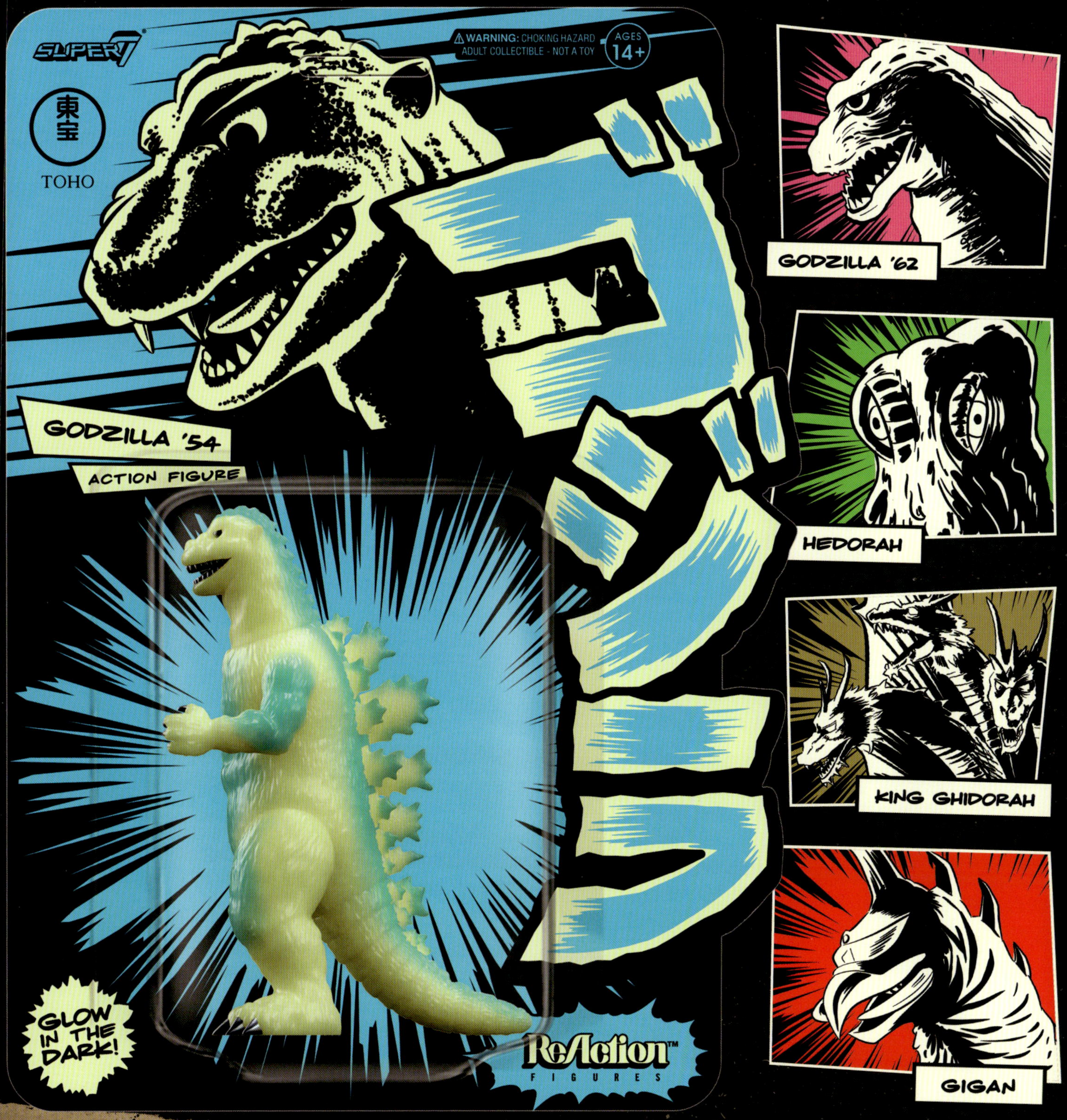

SUPER7

WARNING: CHOKING HAZARD
ADULT COLLECTIBLE - NOT A TOY

AGES 14+

東宝
TOHO

ゴジラ

GODZILLA '54
ACTION FIGURE

GODZILLA '62

HEDORAH

KING GHIDORAH

GIGAN

GLOW IN THE DARK!

ReAction™
FIGURES

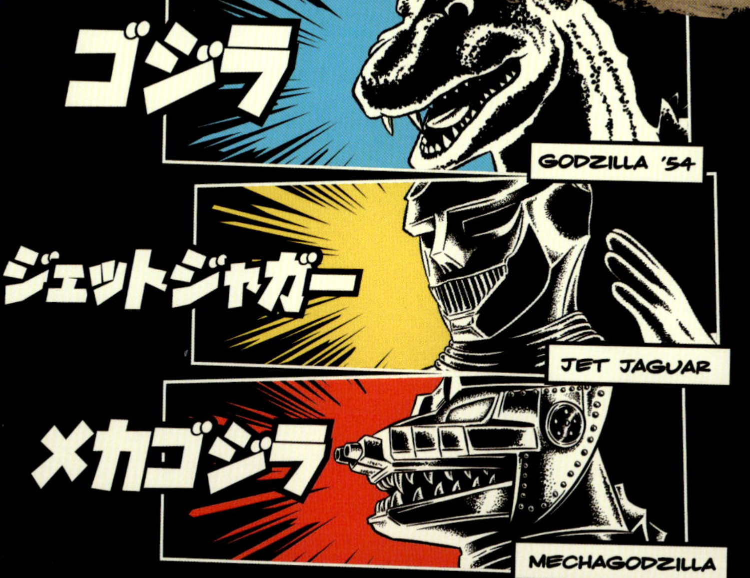

MONSTERS TO COLLECT!!

LEFT: Godzilla '54 ReAction Figures™ Train Biter box art

THIS PAGE: Godzilla Glow ReAction Figures™ card art

TM & © TOHO CO., LTD.

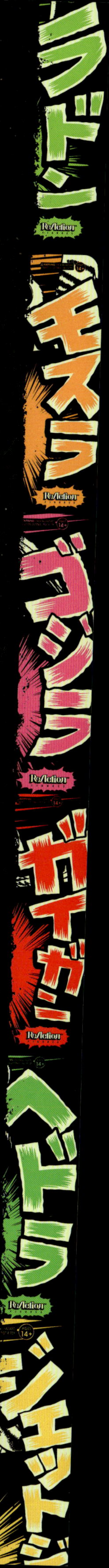

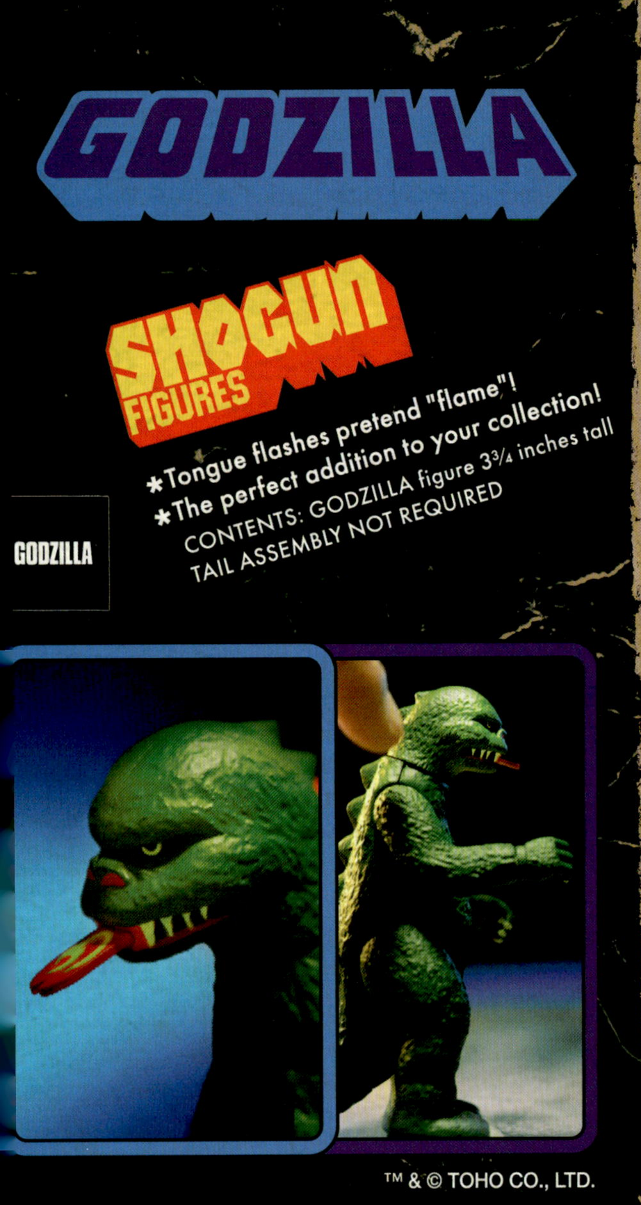

GODZILLA

SHOGUN FIGURES

*Tongue flashes pretend "flame"!
*The perfect addition to your collection!
CONTENTS: GODZILLA figure 3¾ inches tall
TAIL ASSEMBLY NOT REQUIRED

GODZILLA

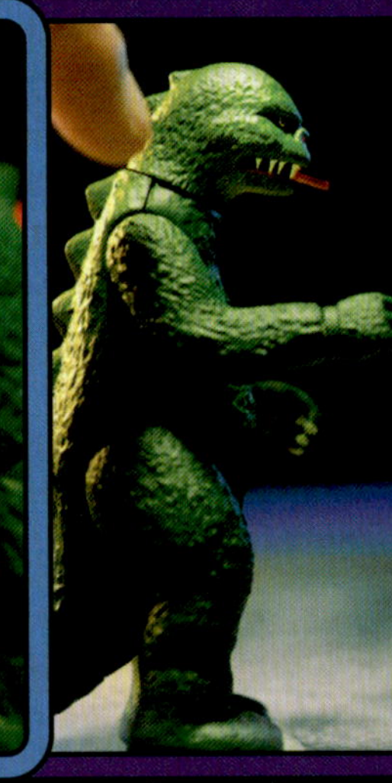

™ & © TOHO CO., LTD.

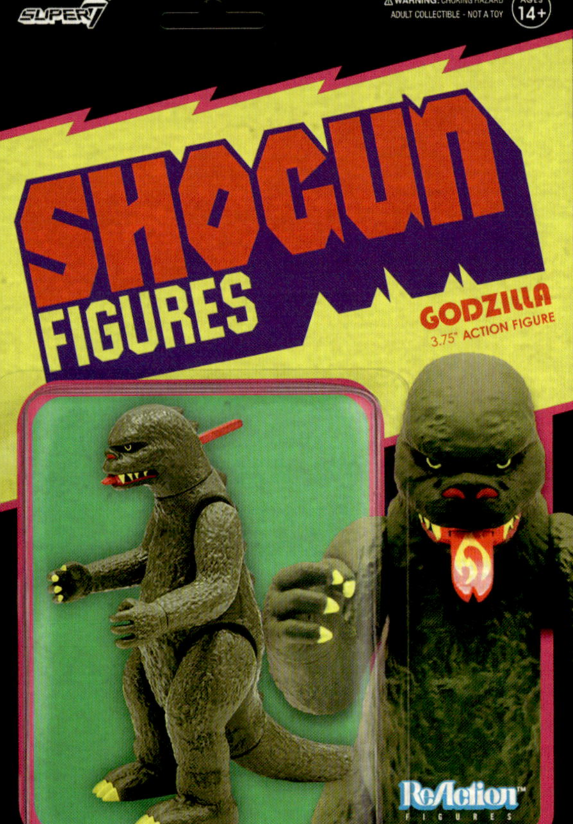

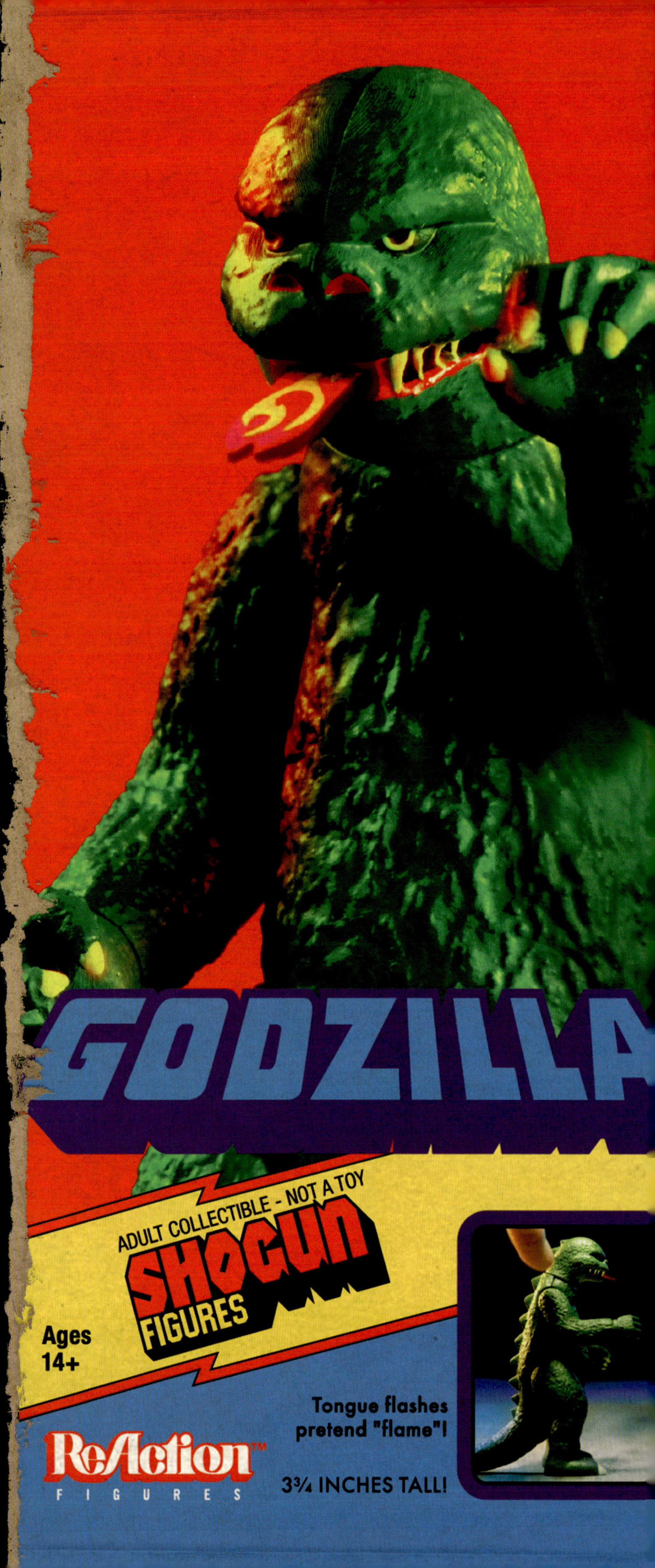

GODZILLA

ADULT COLLECTIBLE - NOT A TOY

SHOGUN FIGURES

Ages 14+

ReAction™
FIGURES

Tongue flashes pretend "flame"!

3¾ INCHES TALL!

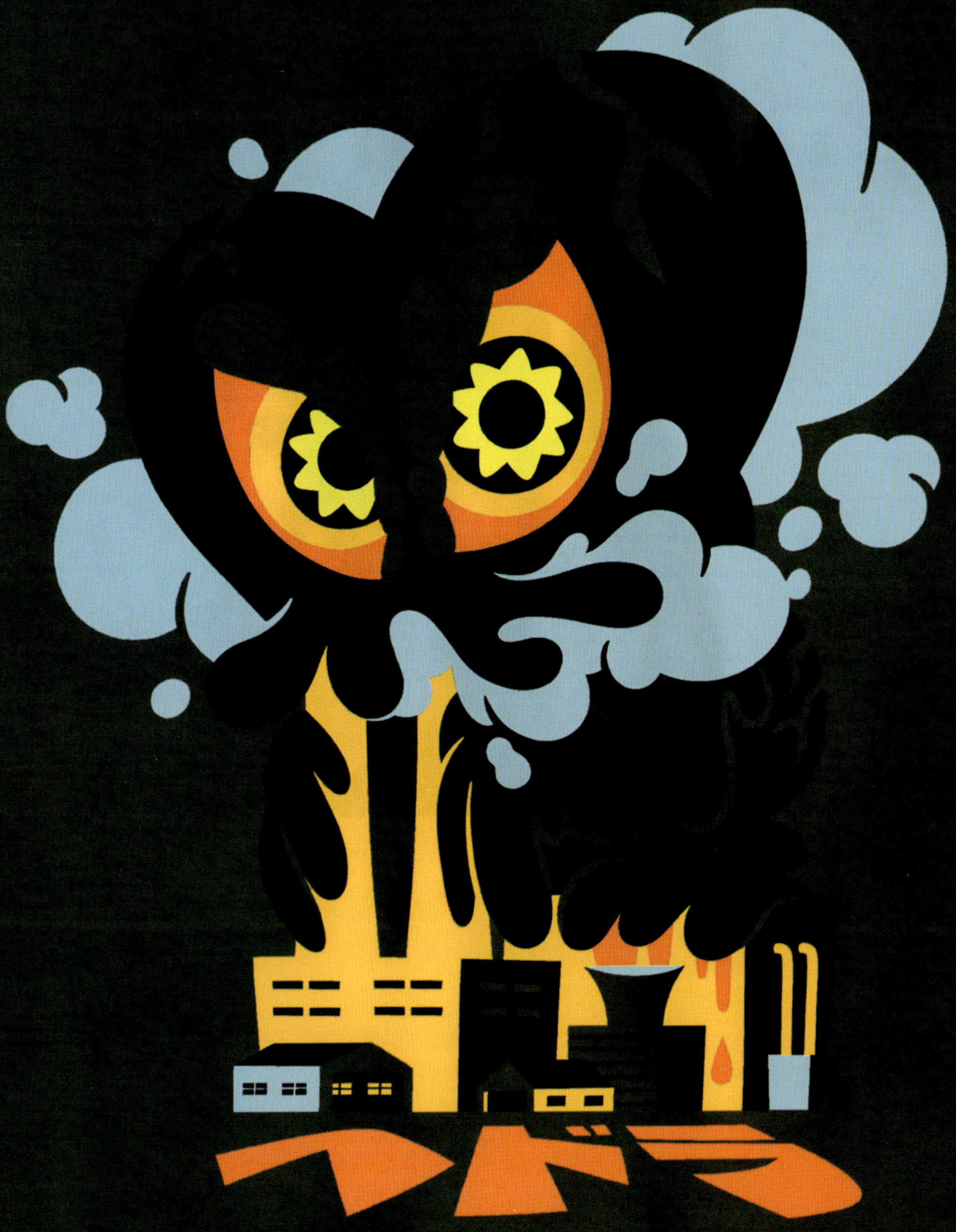

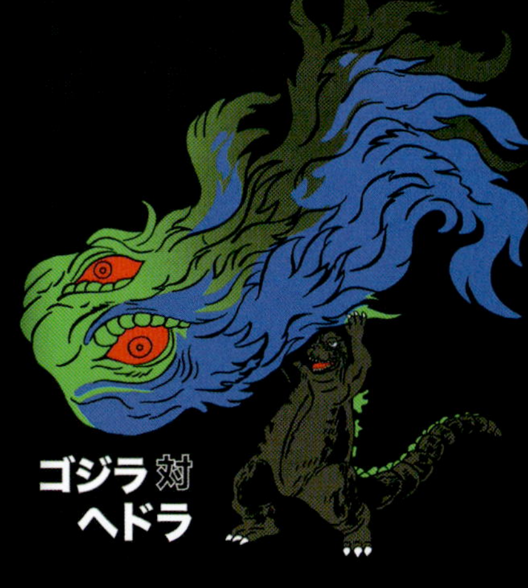

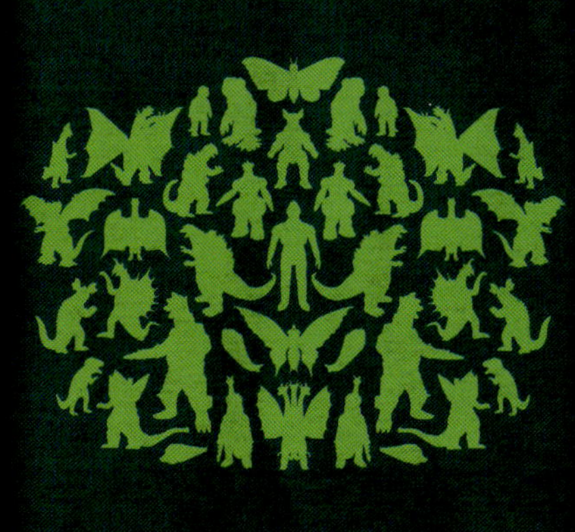

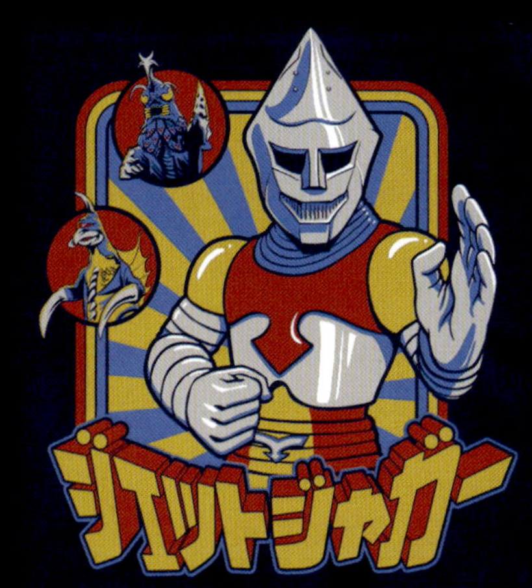

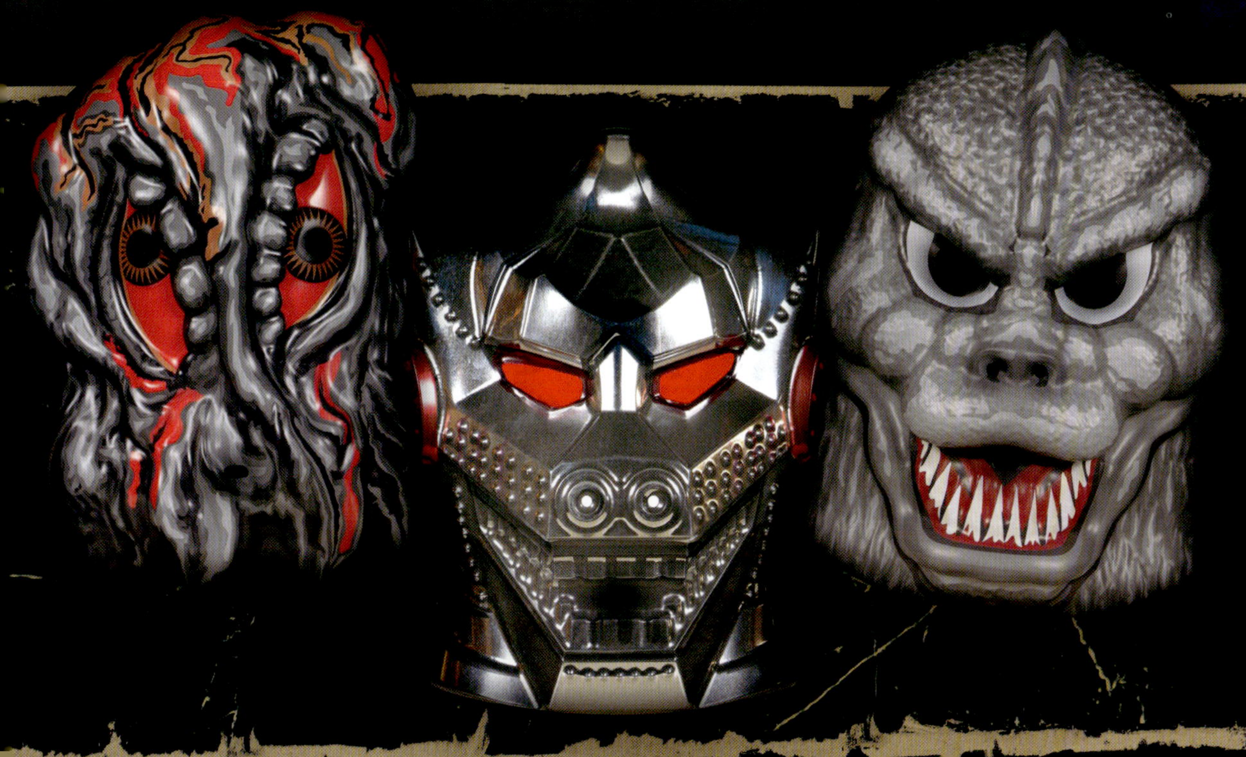

LEFT: Godzilla Shogun Figures box art

THIS PAGE: Godzilla retro masks and apparel

TM & © TOHO CO., LTD.

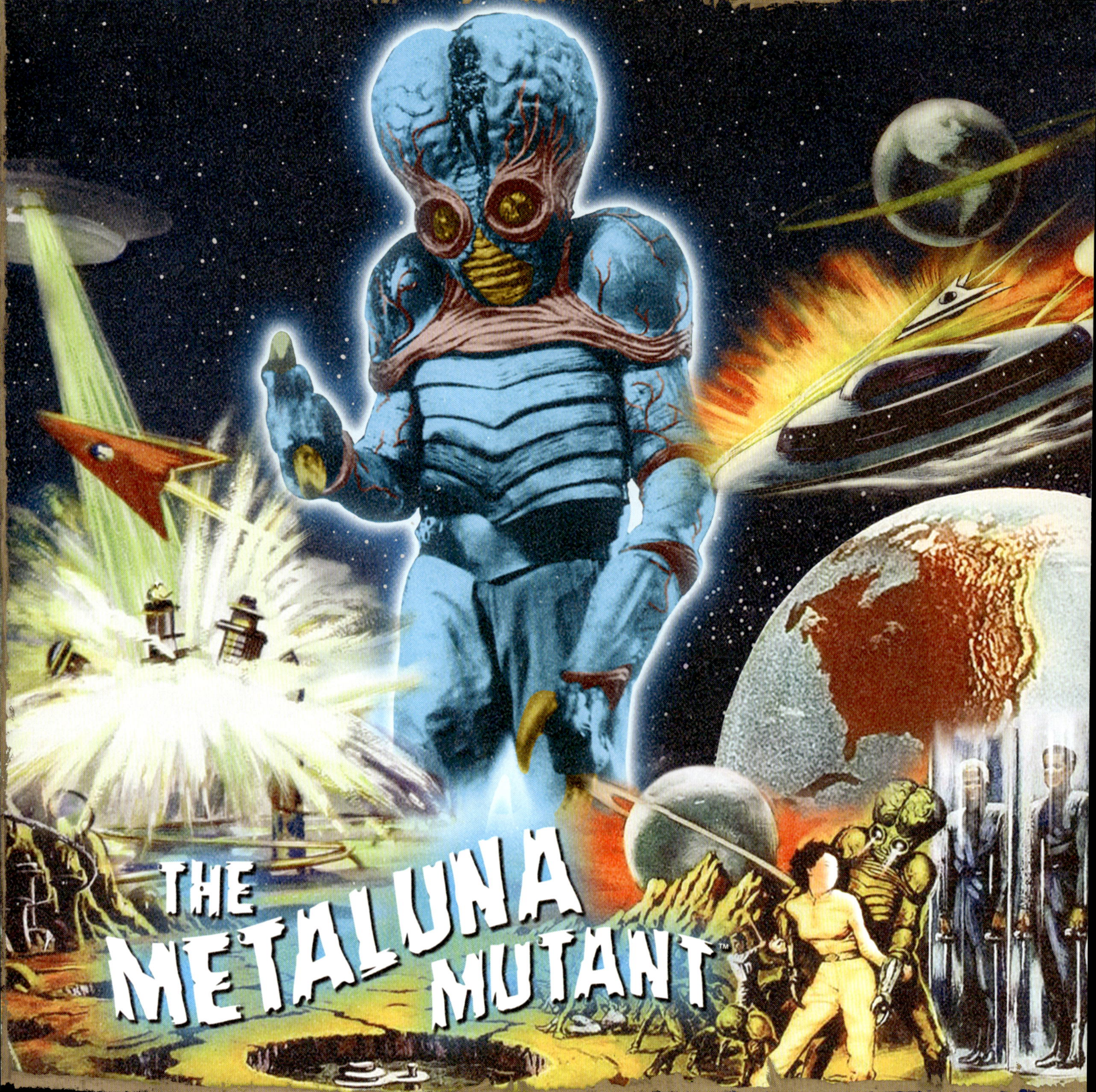

THE METALUNA MUTANT™

THIS PAGE: The Metaluna Mutant ULTIMATES!™ box art and figure

TOP RIGHT: Alfred Hitchcock ReAction Figures™ card art

BOTTOM RIGHT: The Munsters® ReAction Figures™ card art

© 2025 Alfred Hitchcock Estate

THE MUNSTERS © Universal City Studios, LLC. All Rights Reserved.

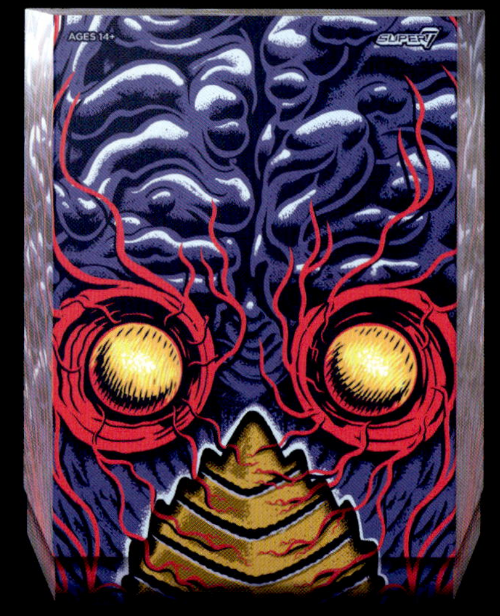

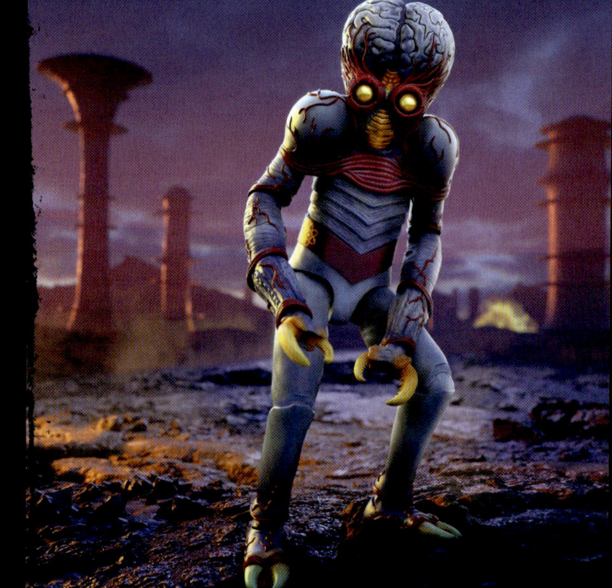

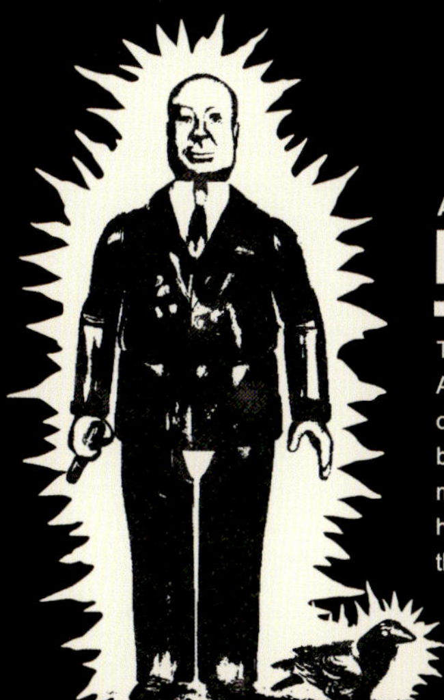

Alfred
Hitchcock

The great master of terror, Alfred Hitchcock shines light on all of your deepest, darkest fears and brings along a bird for good measure. You can't run, you can't hide, you can only scream in the darkness!

COLLECT THEM ALL!

FULLY POSABLE
3.75" ACTION FIGURES

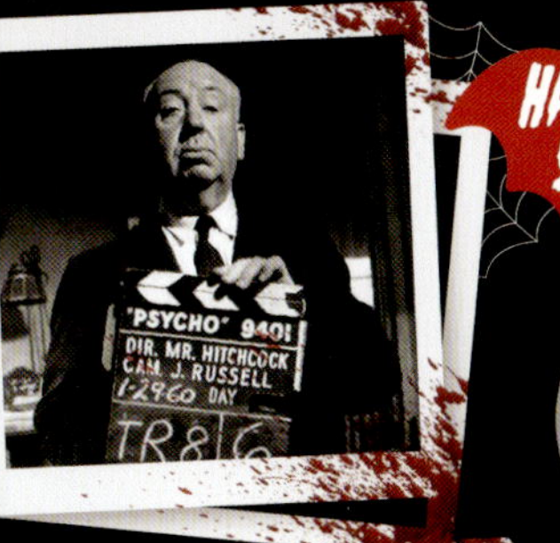

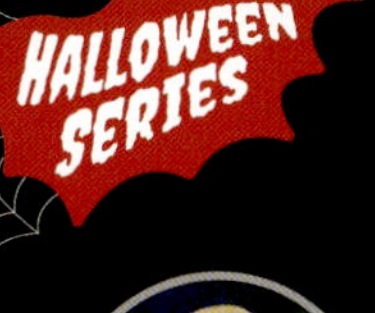

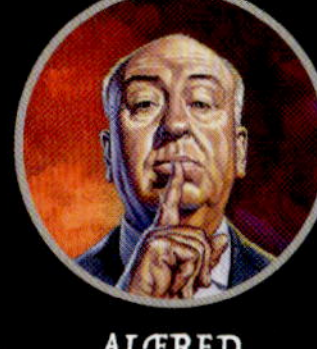

ALFRED
HITCHCOCK

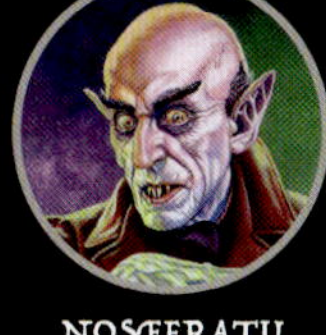

NOSFERATU

ALFRED
HITCHCOCK

"The Master of Suspense" is one of the most revered, and recognizable, directors in film history. Through his classic films *Psycho*, *The Birds*, *Rear Window*, and *Vertigo*, along with his classic television show *Alfred Hitchcock Presents*, Hitchcock has gripped the imaginations and minds of generations with his film making artistry.

ALSO AVAILABLE
MISFITS

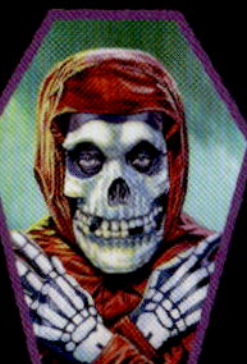

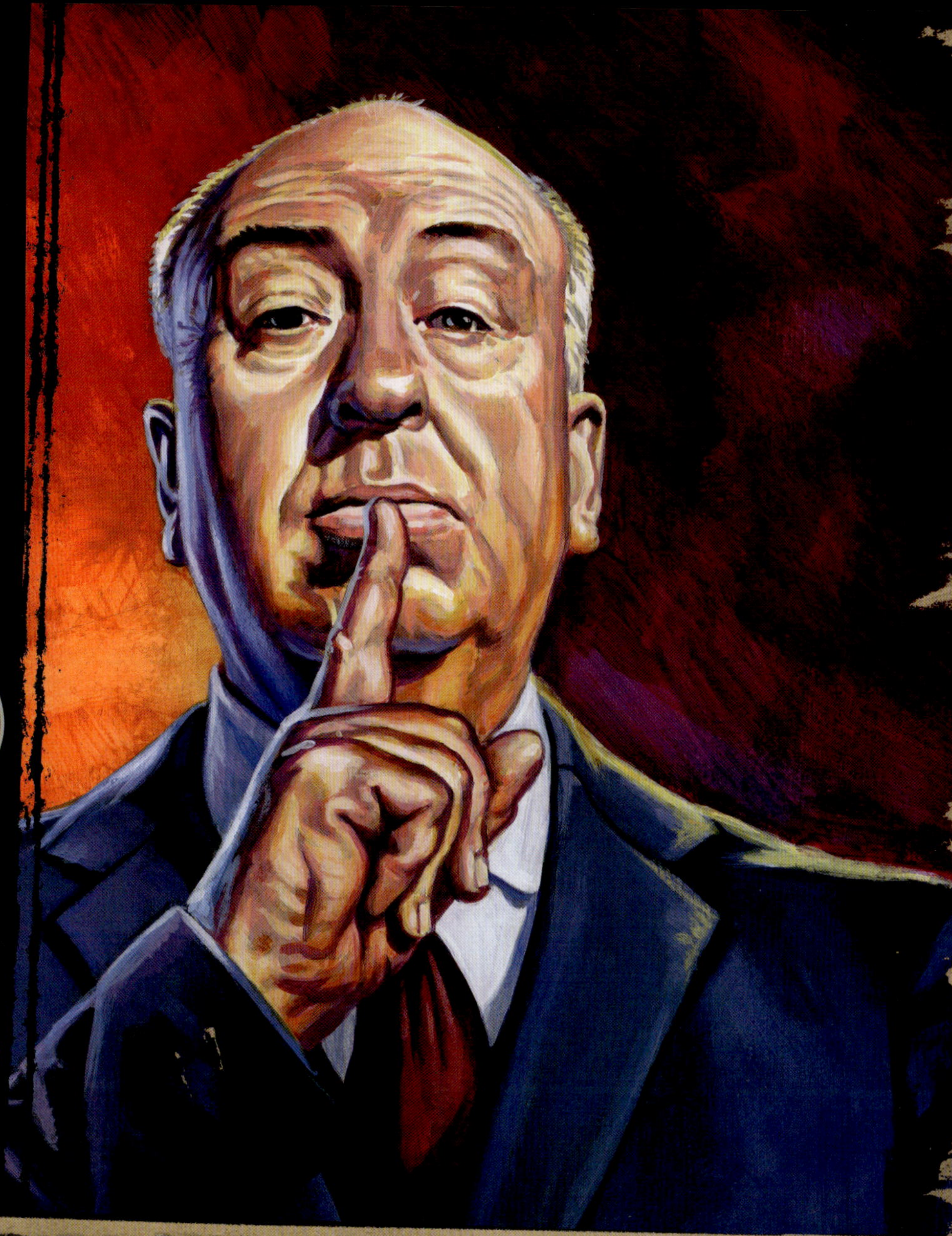

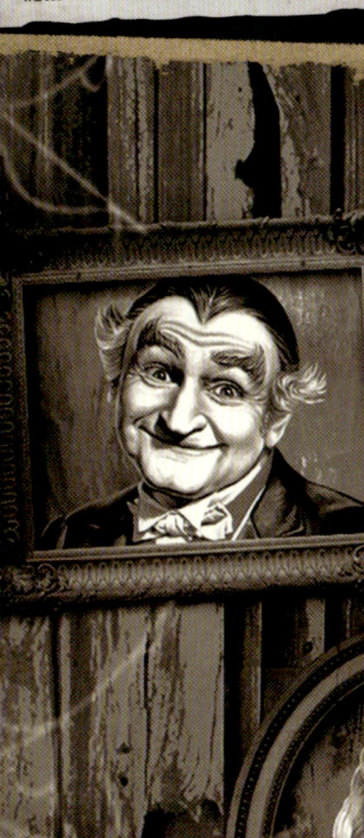

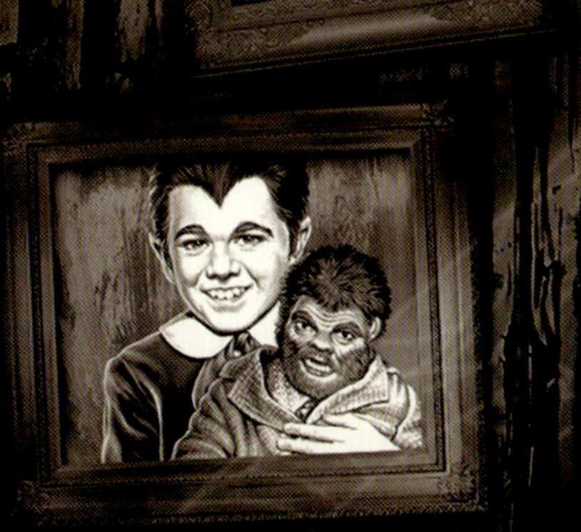

COLLECT
THEM ALL

ADULT COLLECTIBLE - NOT A TOY

AGES
14+

GLOWS
in the
Dark!

SUPER7

The Munsters
Herman

An authentic, posable action figure from the Super7 ReAction™ Collection.

Recommended for ages 14 years and older.

No. 1964 Asst. No. 666

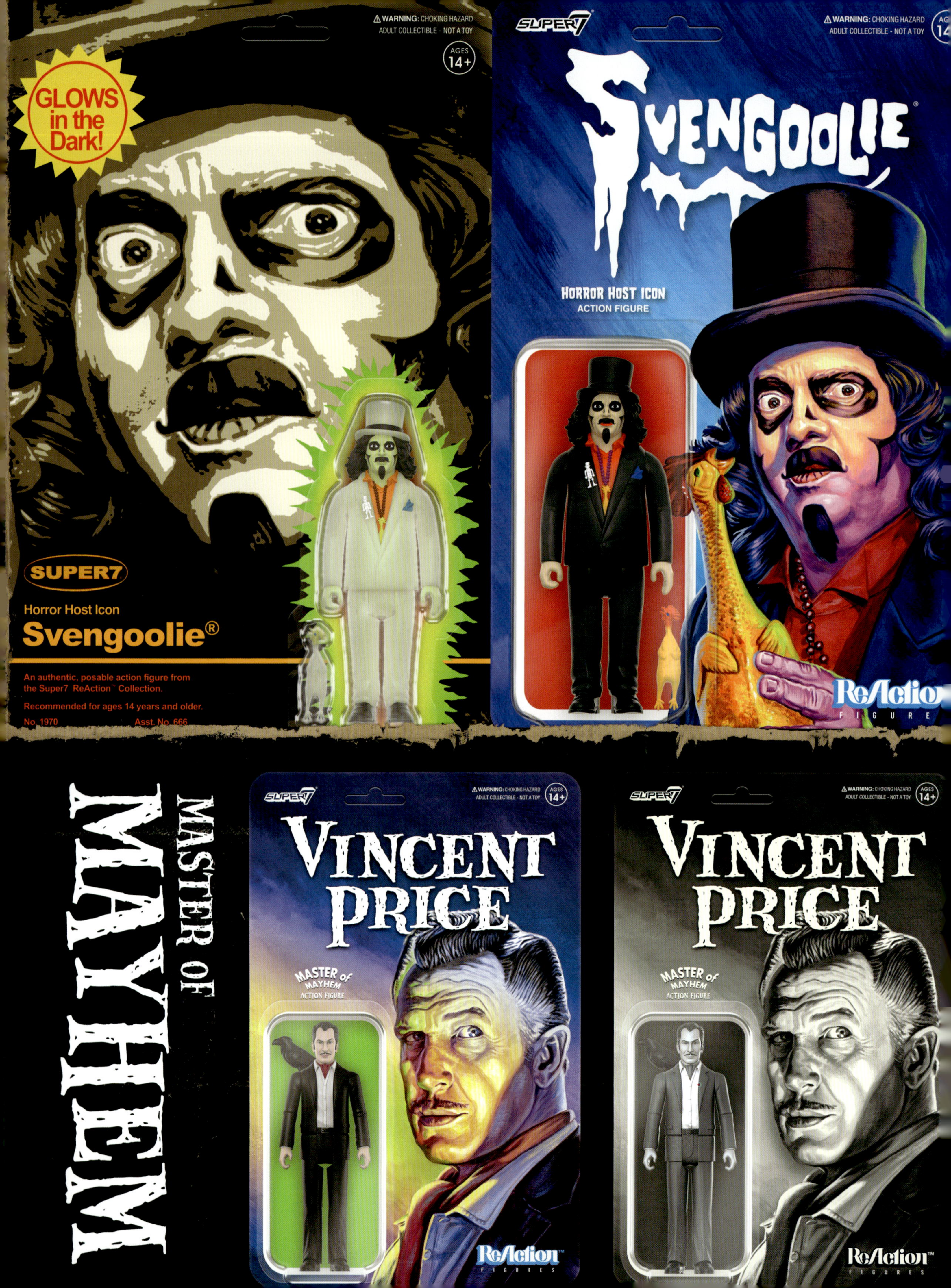

⚠ WARNING: CHOKING HAZARD
ADULT COLLECTIBLE - NOT A TOY

AGES 14+

GLOWS in the Dark!

SUPER7

Horror Host Icon

Svengoolie®

An authentic, posable action figure from the Super7 ReAction™ Collection.

Recommended for ages 14 years and older.

No. 1970 Asst. No. 666

SUPER7

⚠ WARNING: CHOKING HAZARD
ADULT COLLECTIBLE - NOT A TOY

SVENGOOLIE®

HORROR HOST ICON
ACTION FIGURE

MASTER OF
MAYHEM

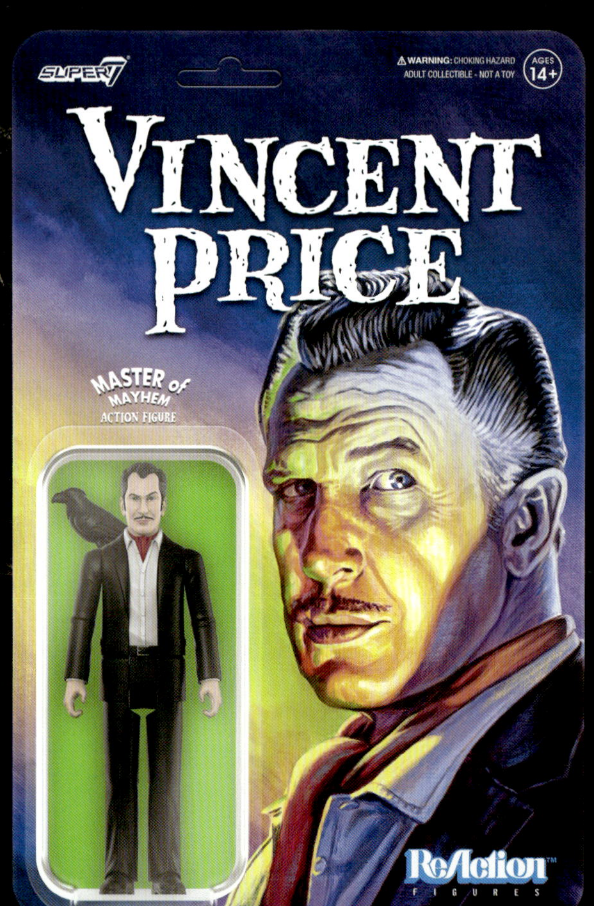

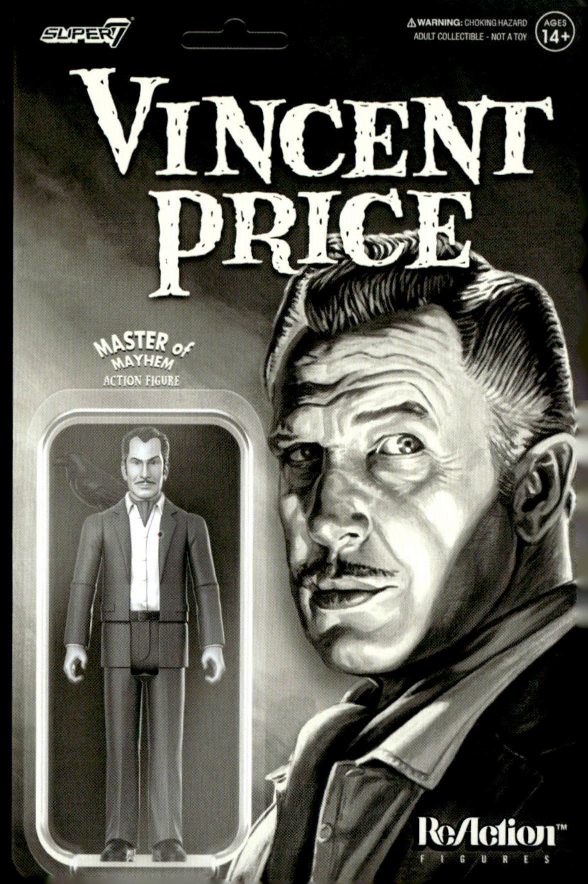

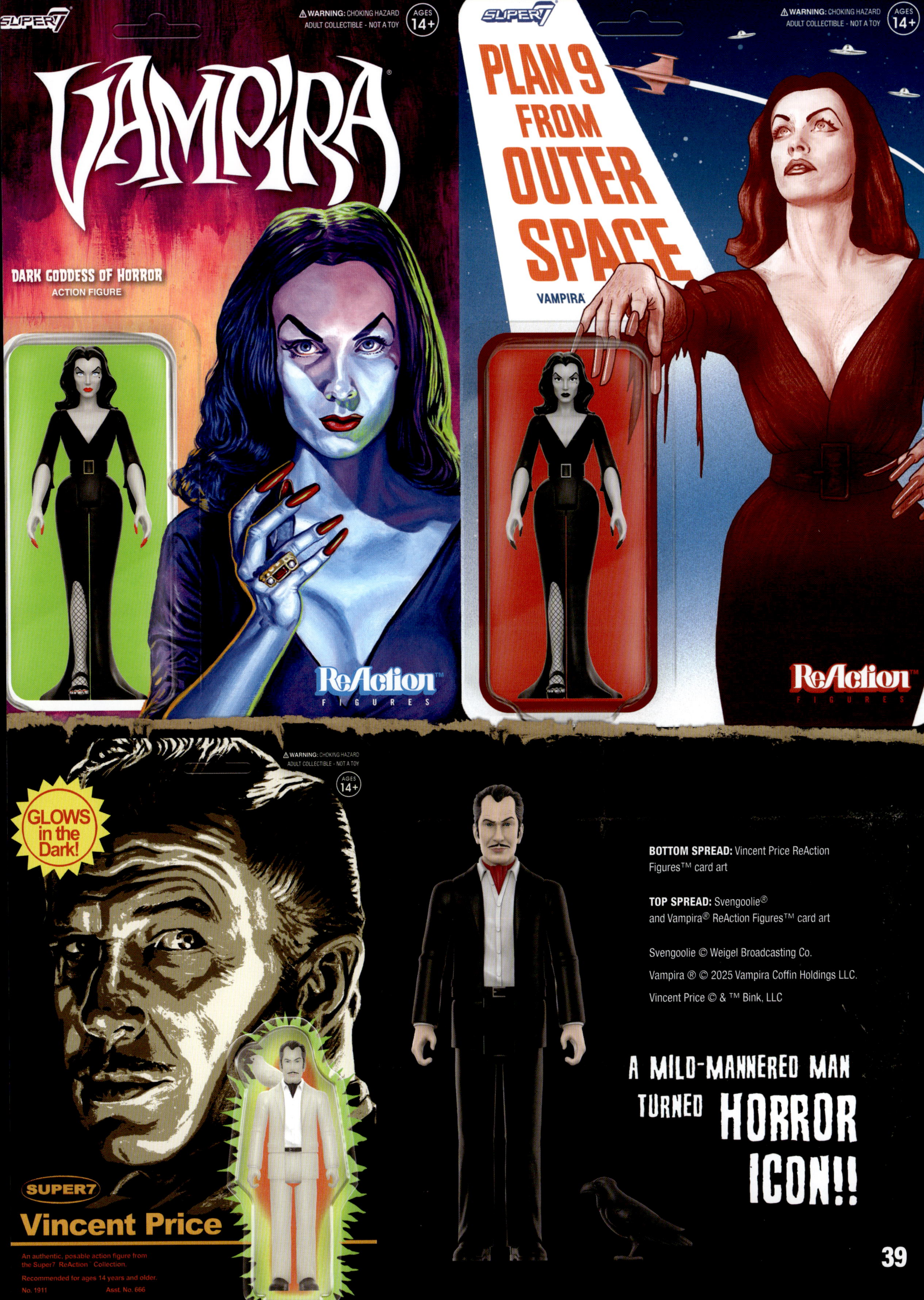

BOTTOM SPREAD: Vincent Price ReAction Figures™ card art

TOP SPREAD: Svengoolie® and Vampira® ReAction Figures™ card art

Svengoolie © Weigel Broadcasting Co.

Vampira ® © 2025 Vampira Coffin Holdings LLC.

Vincent Price © & ™ Bink, LLC

A MILD-MANNERED MAN TURNED HORROR ICON!!

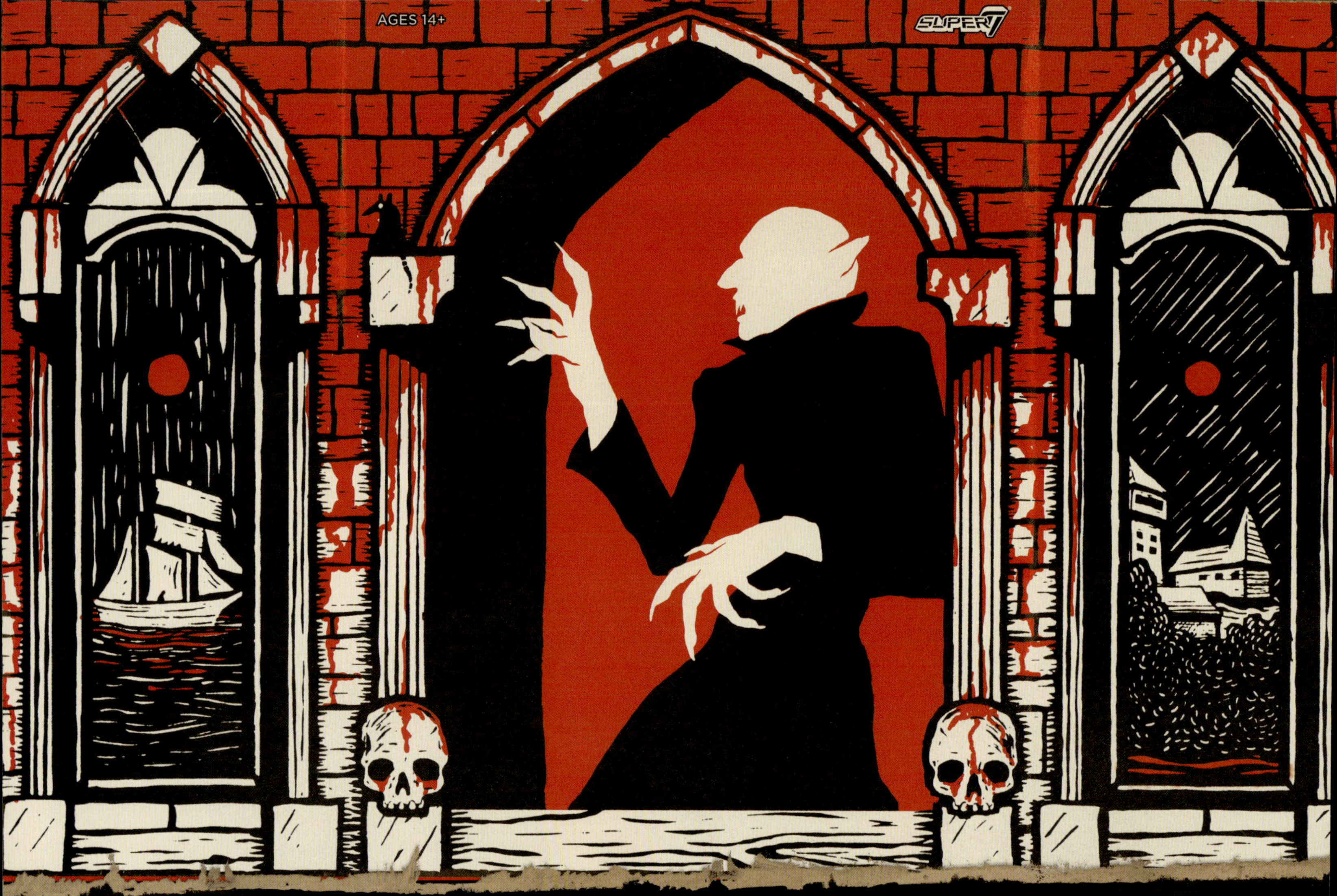

AGES 14+

SUPER7

NOSFERATU

THIS PAGE: Selected Nosferatu apparel and packaging art

RIGHT: The Exorcist, IT The Movie, and The Lost Boys ReAction Figures™ card art

© & ™ WBEI. (s25)

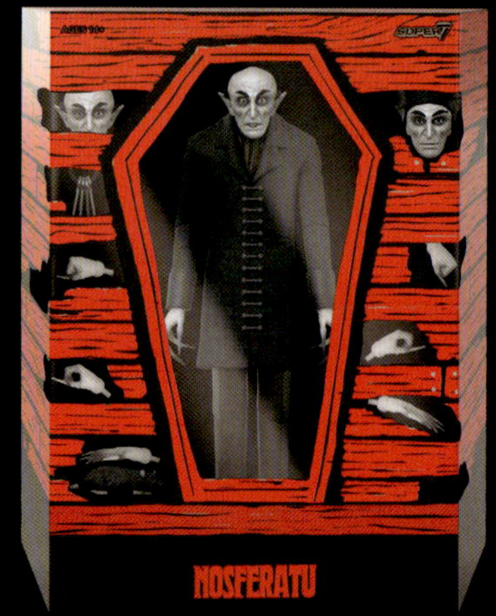

Of Vampires, Terrible Ghosts, Magic, and The Seven Deadly Sins

Out of Belial's seed appeared the vampire, Nosferatu, who lives and feeds on human blood. He lives in terrifying caves, tombs, and coffins. These are filled with goddamned soil from the fields of the Black Death.

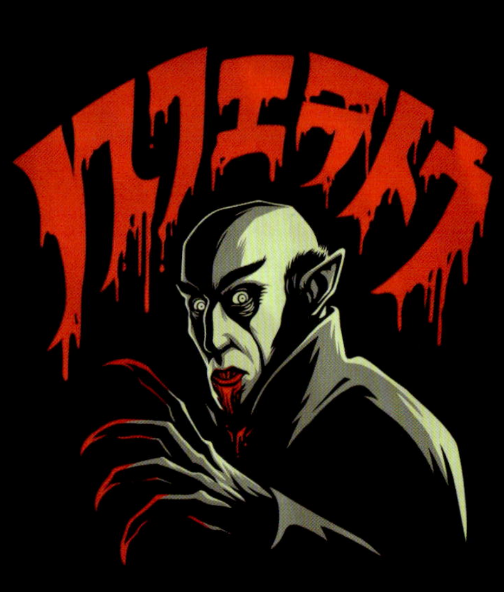

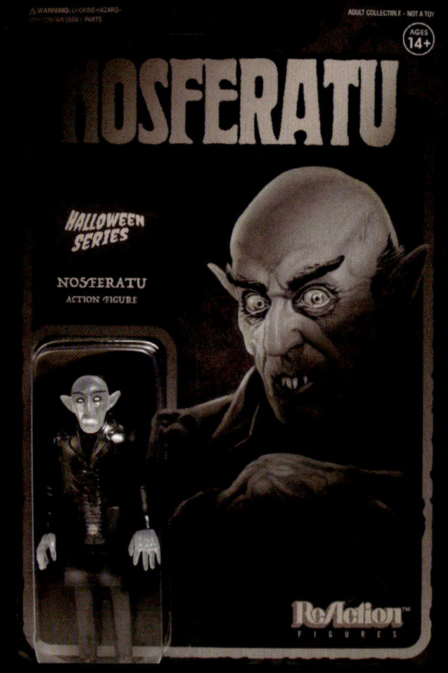

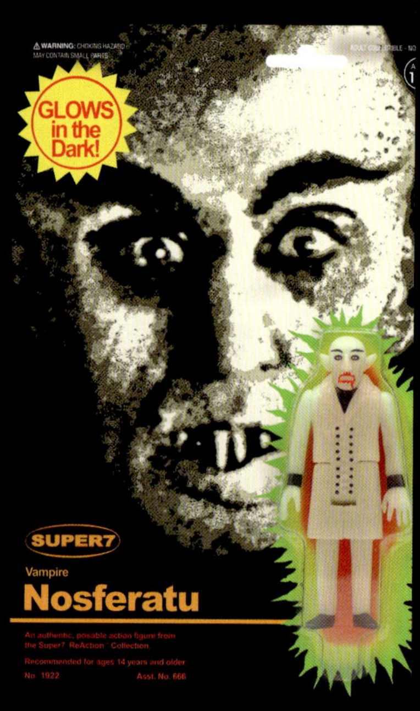

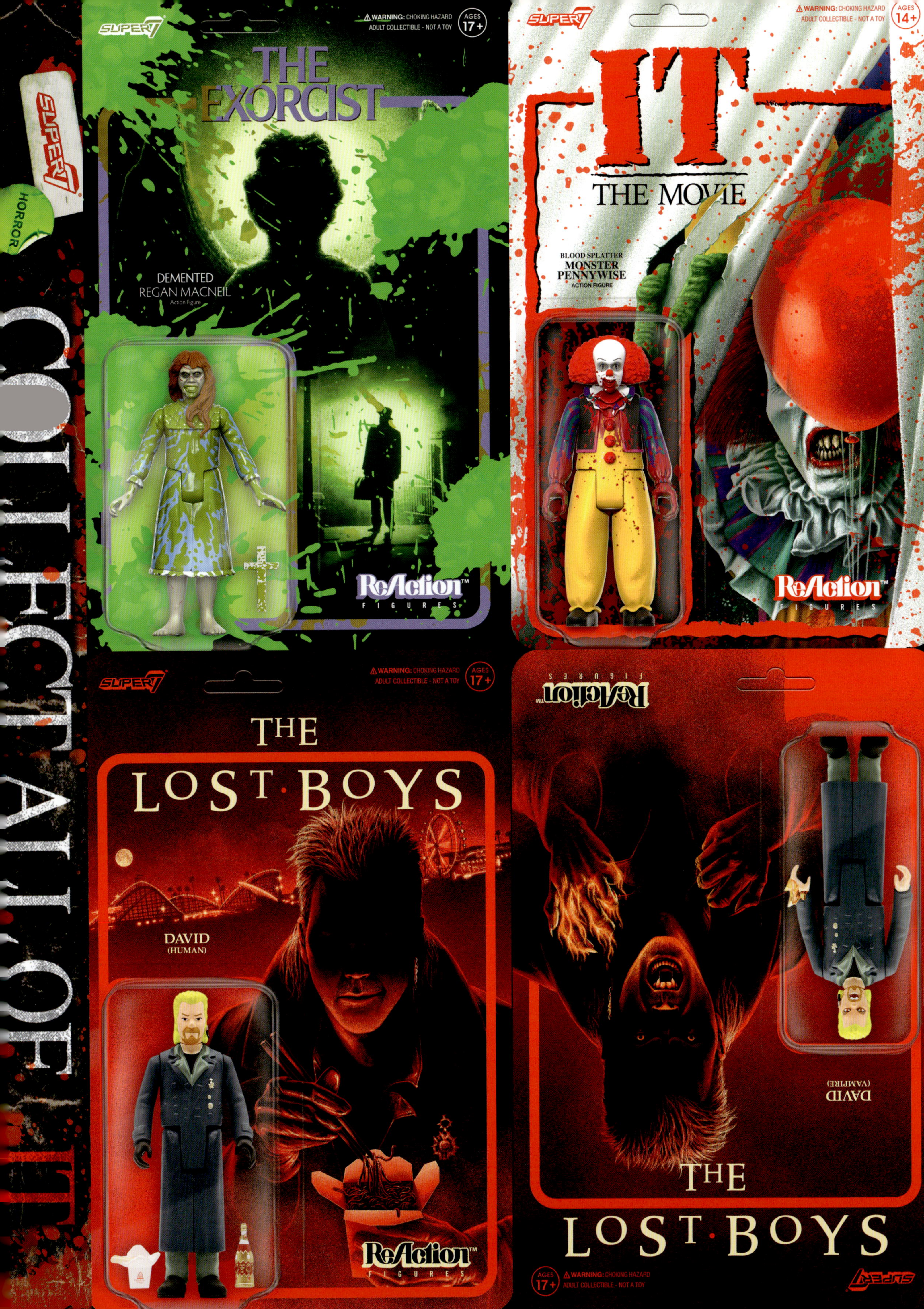
SUPER7
HORROR
SUPER7
WARNING: CHOKING HAZARD
ADULT COLLECTIBLE · NOT A TOY
AGES 17+
THE EXORCIST
DEMENTED
REGAN MACNEIL
Action Figure
ReAction
FIGURES
SUPER7
WARNING: CHOKING HAZARD
ADULT COLLECTIBLE · NOT A TOY
AGES 14+
IT
THE MOVIE
BLOOD SPLATTER
MONSTER
PENNYWISE
ACTION FIGURE
ReAction
FIGURES
SUPER7
WARNING: CHOKING HAZARD
ADULT COLLECTIBLE · NOT A TOY
AGES 17+
THE
LOST BOYS
DAVID
(HUMAN)
ReAction
FIGURES
ReAction
FIGURES
DAVID
(VAMPIRE)
THE
LOST BOYS
AGES 17+
WARNING: CHOKING HAZARD
ADULT COLLECTIBLE · NOT A TOY
SUPER7

COLLECT

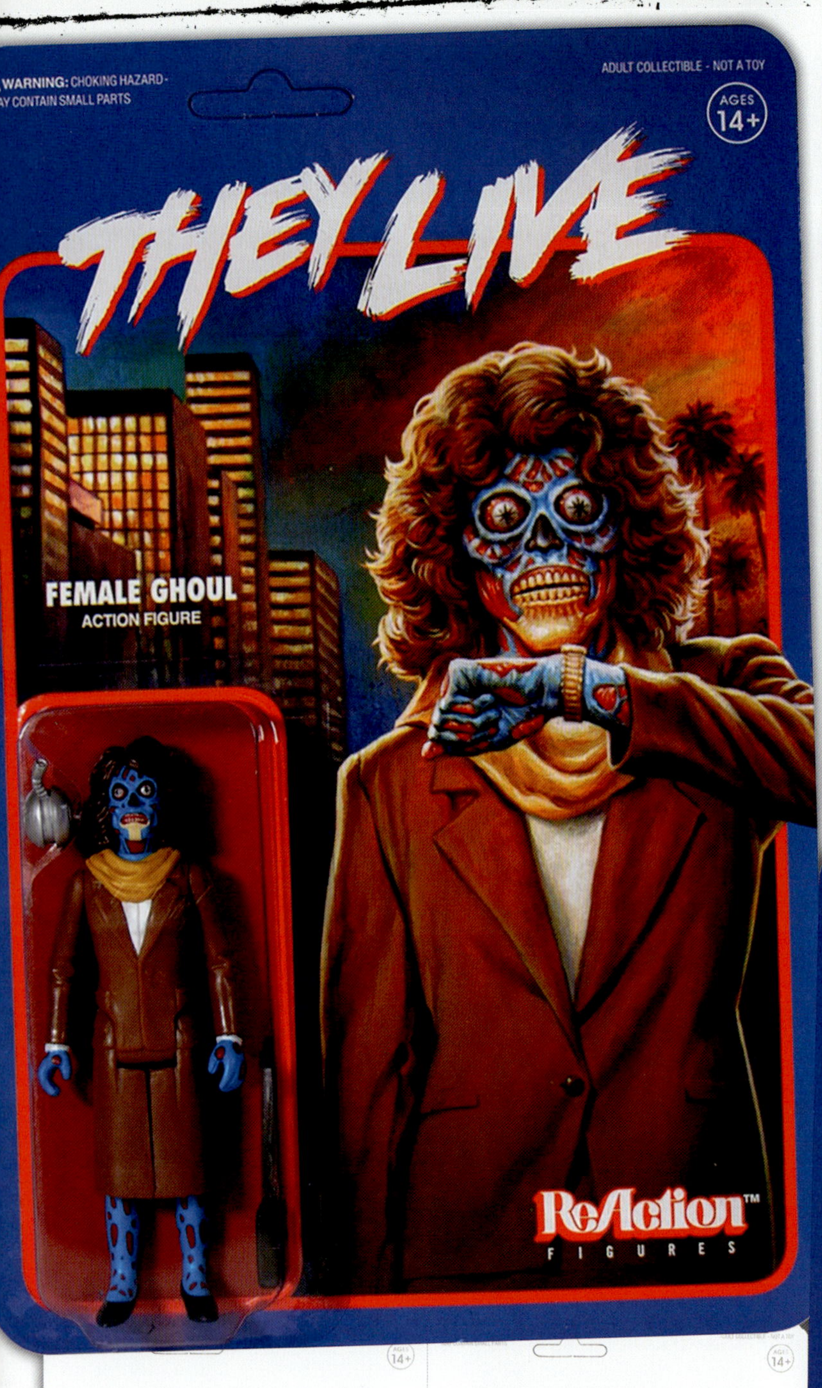

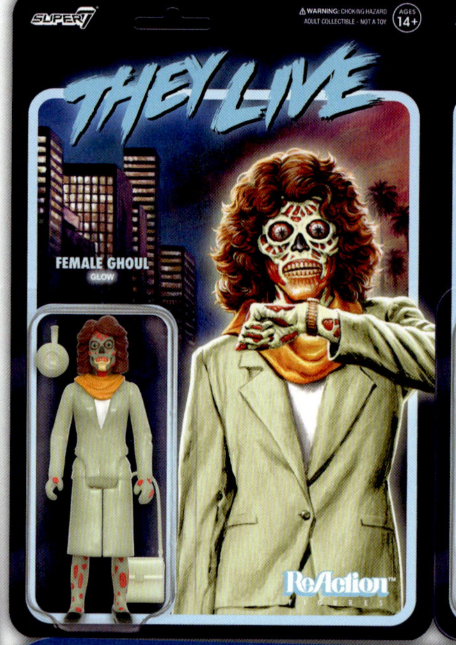

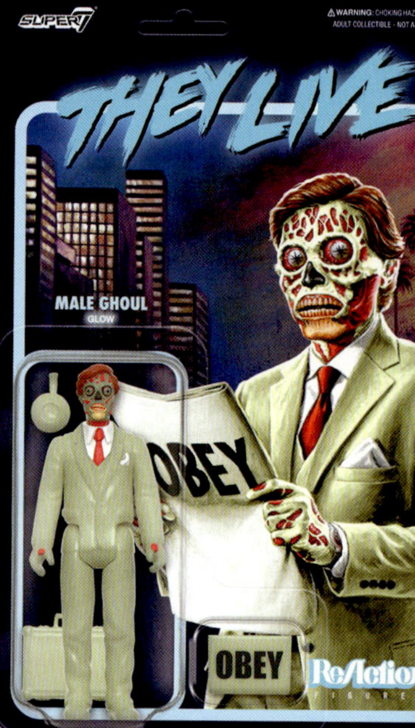

SUBMIT

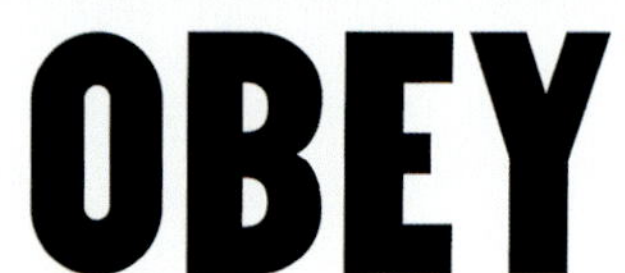

OBEY

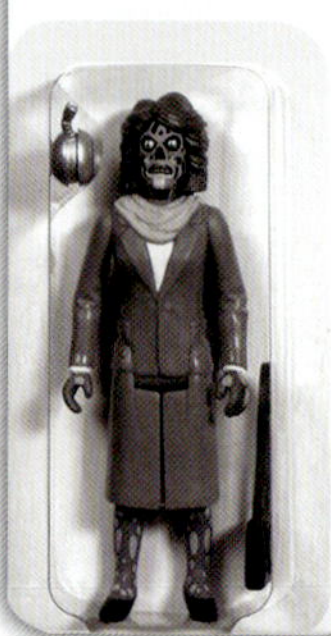

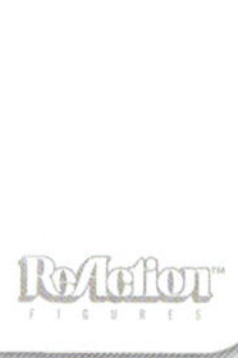

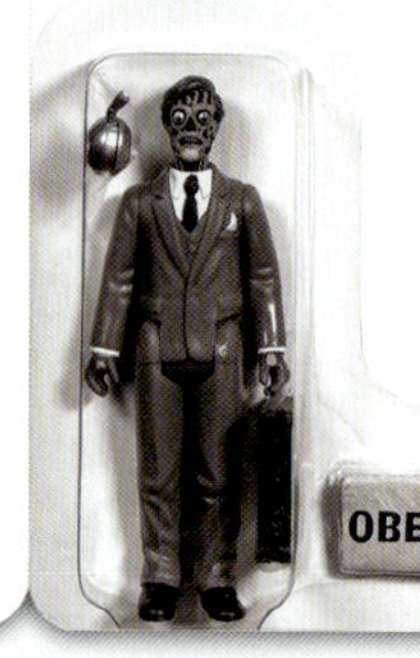

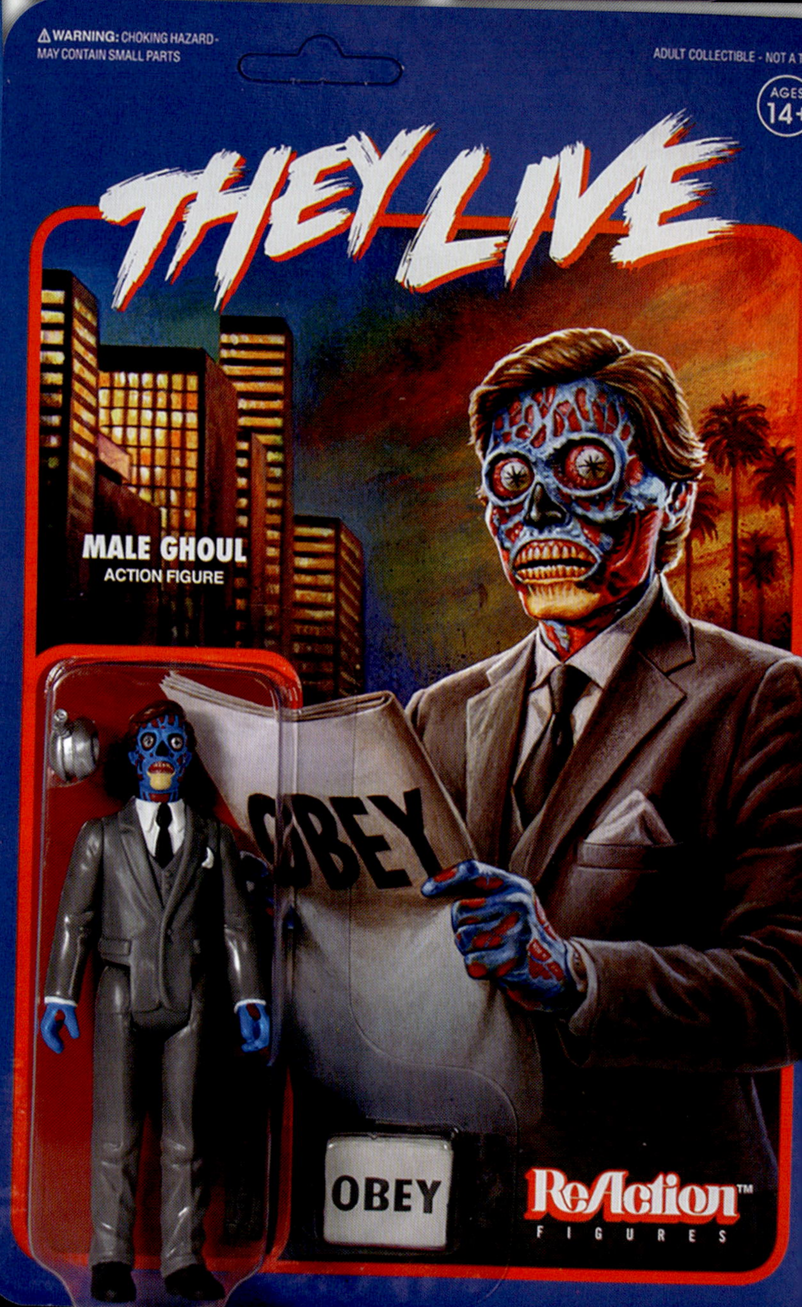

THIS SPREAD: They Live ReAction Figures™ card art

COLLECT THEM ALL COLLECT THEM ALL COLLECT THEM ALL THEM ALL THEM ALL THEM ALL

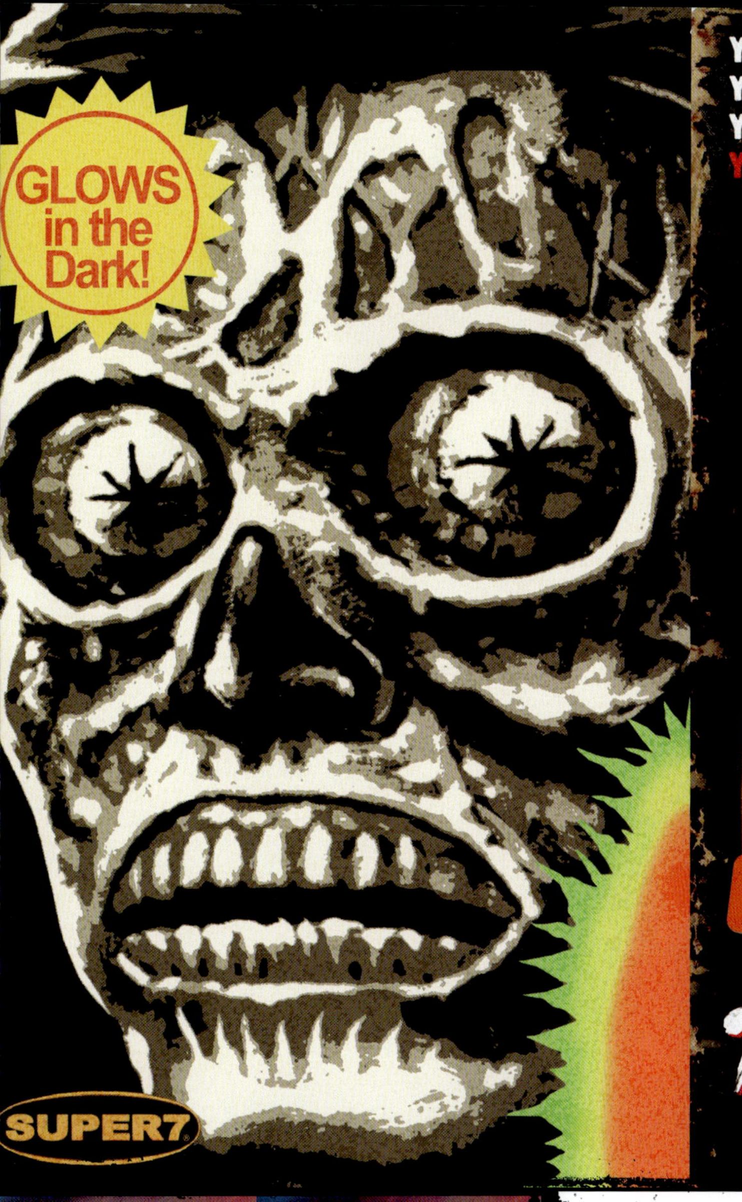

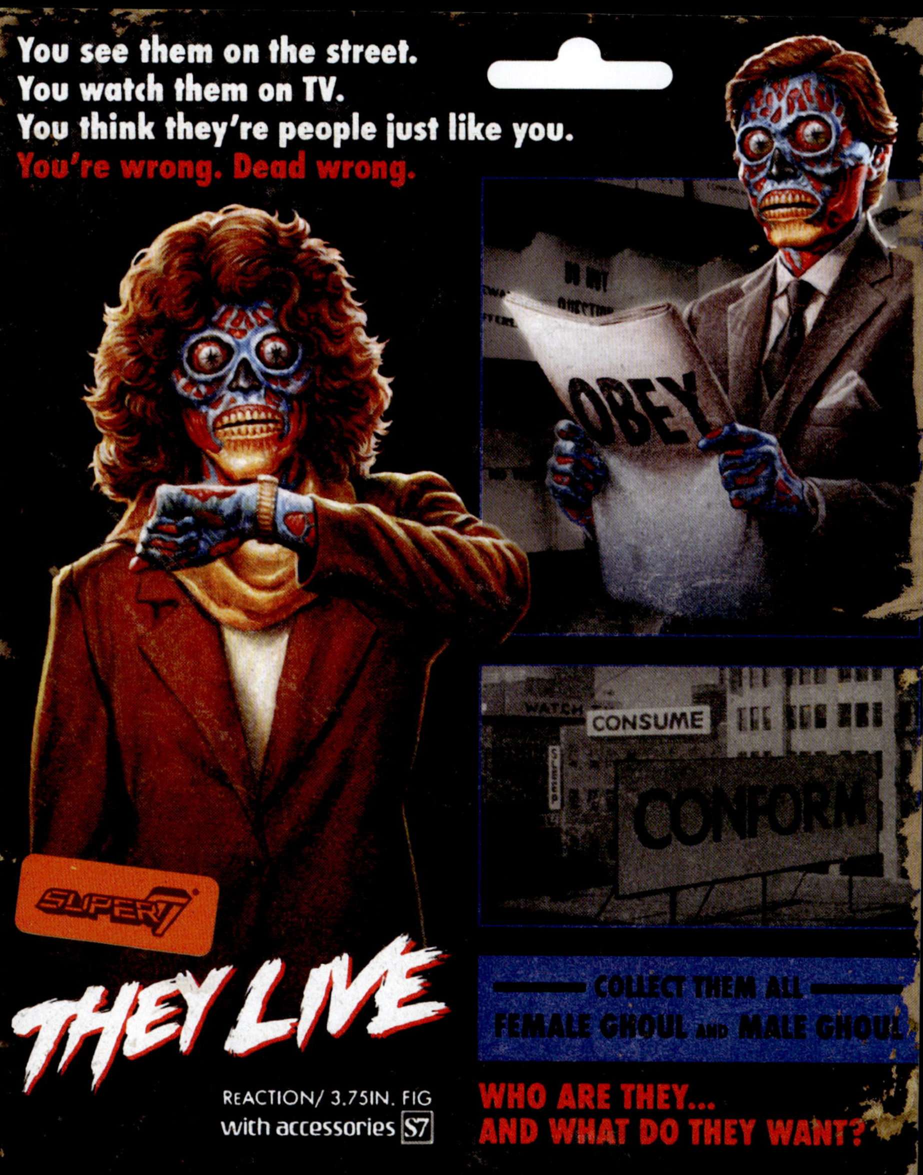

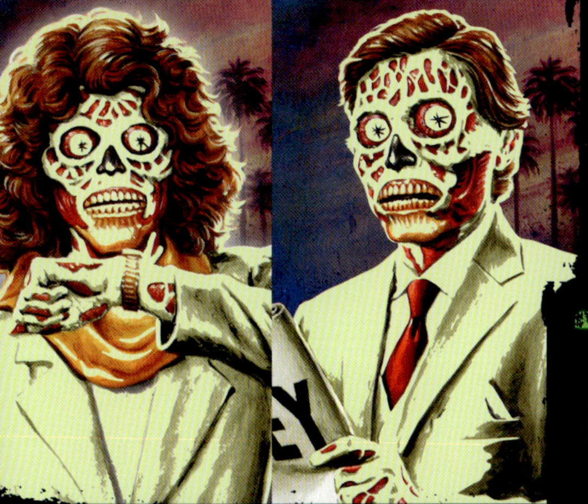

SUBMIT OBEY

CONSUME WATCH TV

They Live

Ghoul

The Ghoul is here, ready to exploit Earth as a third world planet! If you see him in his true form, you'll know this glowing menance wants you to SUBMIT, CONSUME, and OBEY!

THEY LIVE © Universal City Studios, LLC. All Rights Reserved.

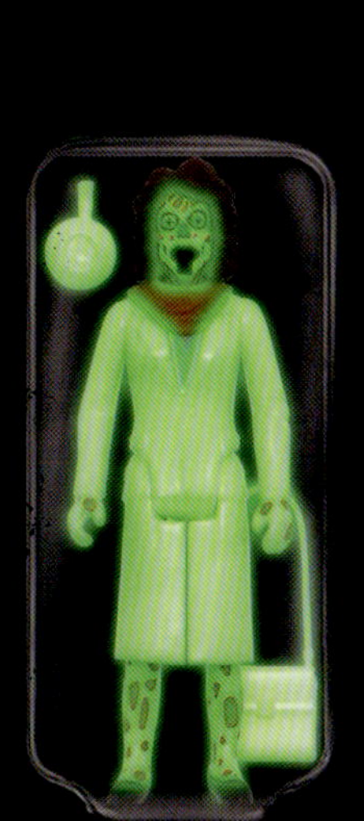

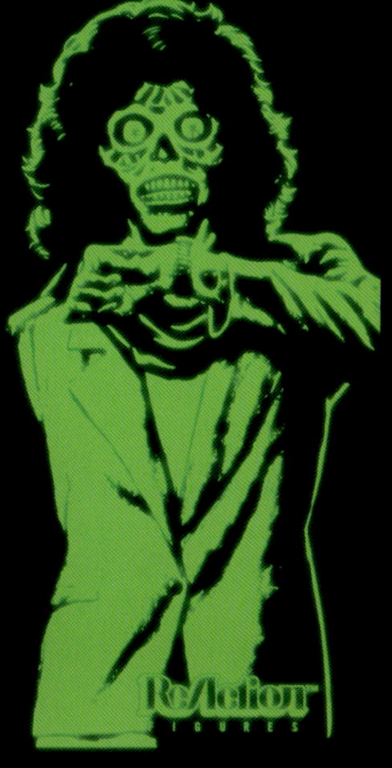

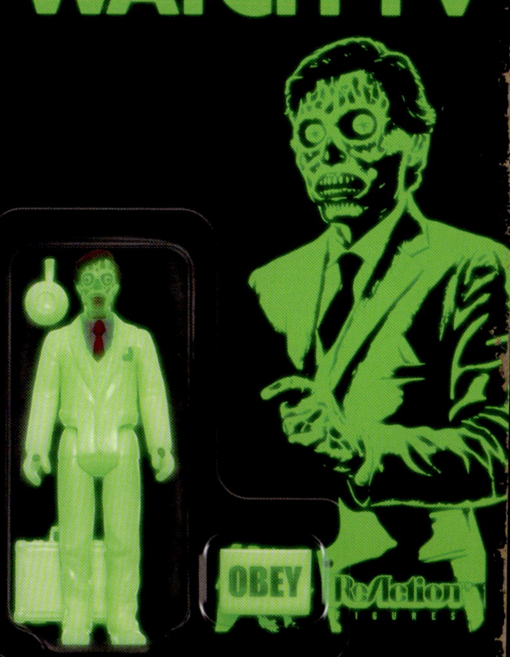

PUNK SAVED OUR LIVES. MAYBE YOU'VE HEARD THAT SENTIMENT BEFORE, BUT IT IS TRUE. PUNK ISN'T JUST A SOUND OR STYLE OF MUSIC, BUT RATHER A STATE OF MIND. A WAY OF BEING, A WAY TO NAVIGATE THE WILD WORLD SWIRLING AROUND US. PUNK PUTS EVERYONE ON THE SAME LEVEL, AND EVERYONE IS INVITED—NO GODS, NO MASTERS. A COMMUNITY BUILT ON INCLUSIVITY AND CELEBRATING THE DIFFERENCES WITHIN IT, AND AT THE SAME TIME WILLING TO CHALLENGE THE RULES THAT KEEP US BOXED IN, WHETHER REAL, UNWRITTEN, OR IMAGINED. PUNK IS ABOUT NOT ONLY WHO YOU ARE, BUT HOW YOU TREAT EACH OTHER AND THE WORLD AROUND YOU. PUNK IS NOT ASKING FOR PERMISSION TO BE WHO YOU WANT TO BE. ONE DAY YOU CAN DECIDE TO START MAKING TOYS, BECAUSE WHY NOT? IT IS NOT LIKE WE HAD ANY TRAINING, ONLY PASSION. SOMETIMES THAT IS ENOUGH. A LIBRARIAN CAN BE PUNK. A DOG WALKER CAN BE PUNK. TOY COLLECTING CAN BE PUNK. YOU CAN BE PUNK. AND WE CAN ALL CHANGE THE WORLD.

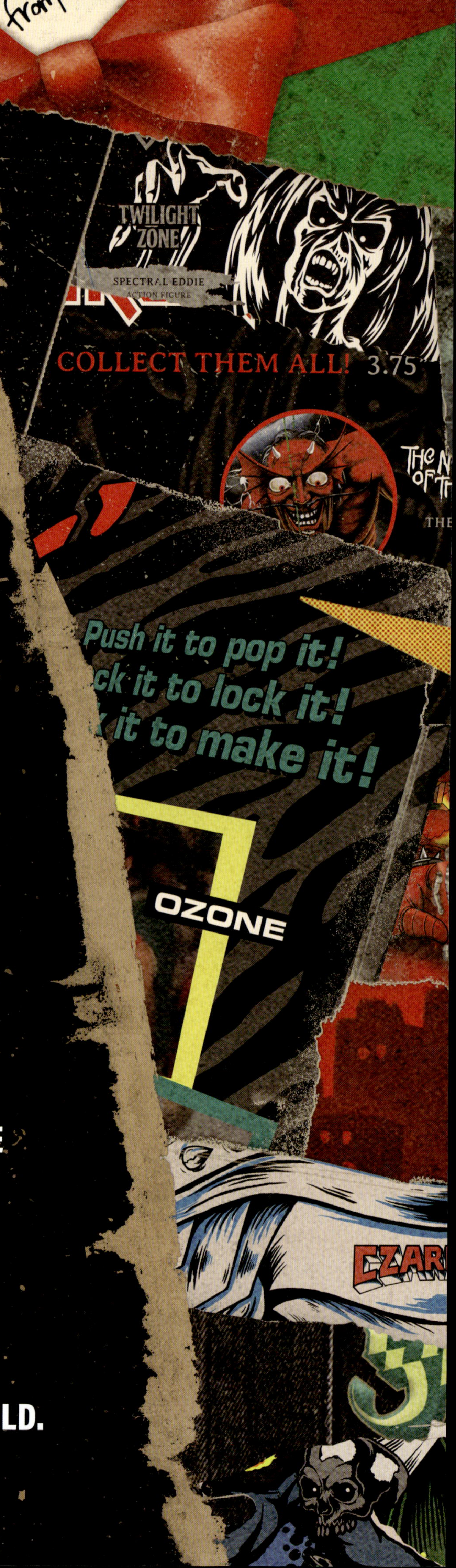

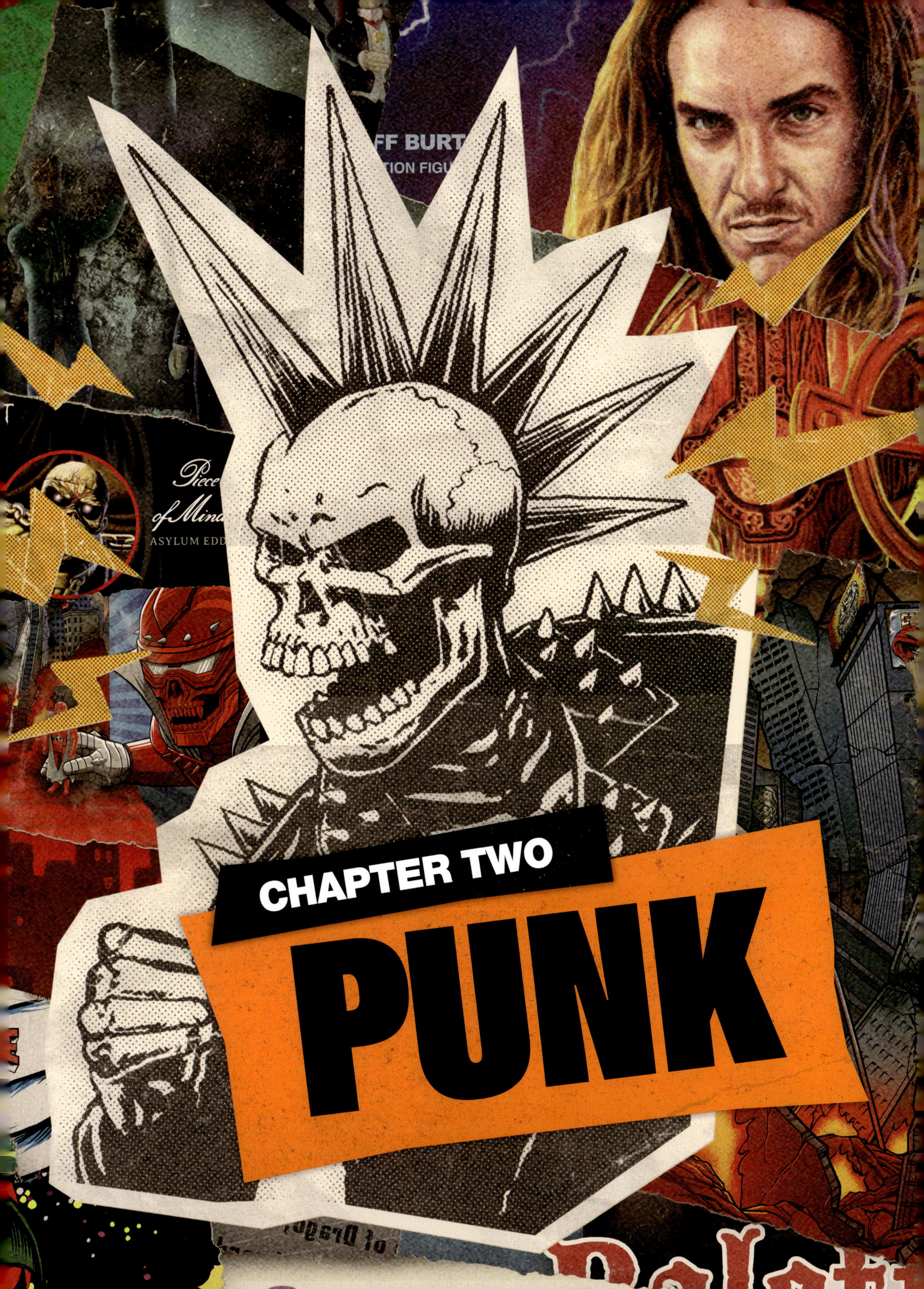
CHAPTER TWO
PUNK

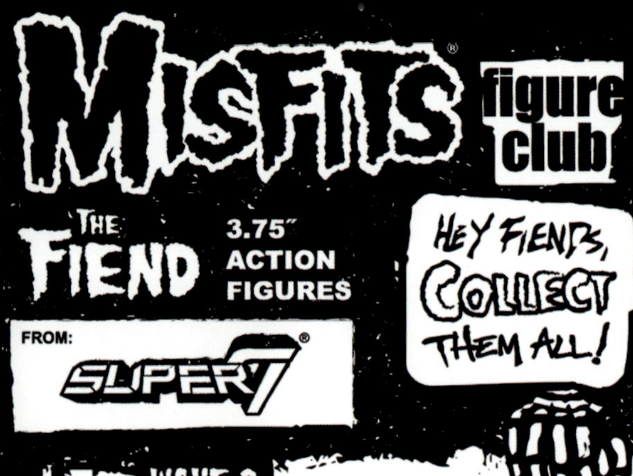

WAVE 2

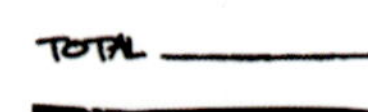

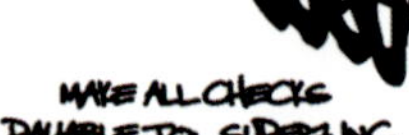

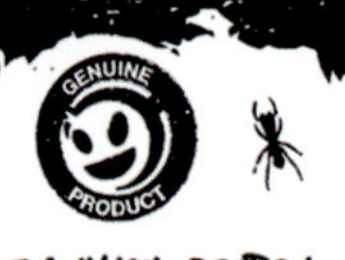

ENJOY YOU CREEPS!

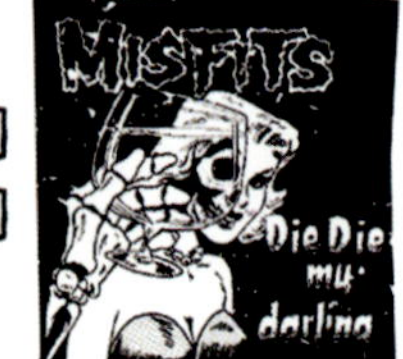

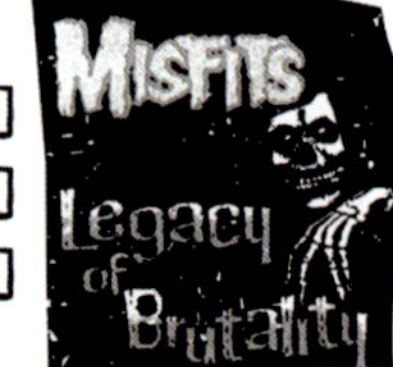

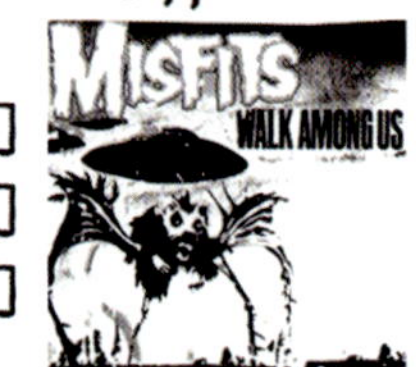

DIE, DIE MY DARLING

LEGACY OF BRUTALITY

WALK AMONG US

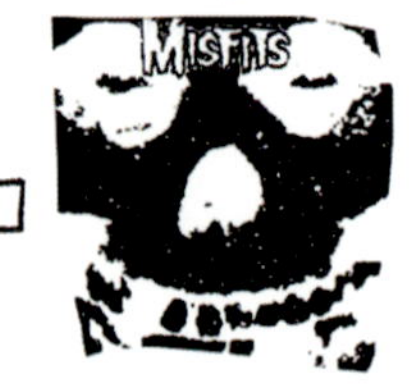

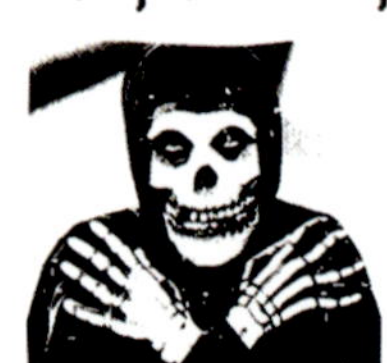

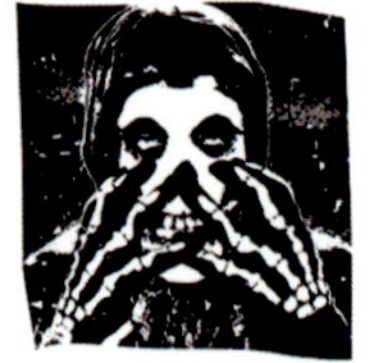

COLLECTION 1

COLLECTION 2

STATIC AGE

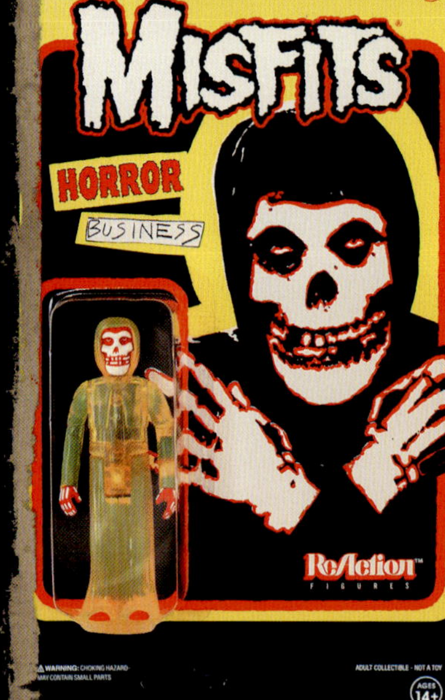

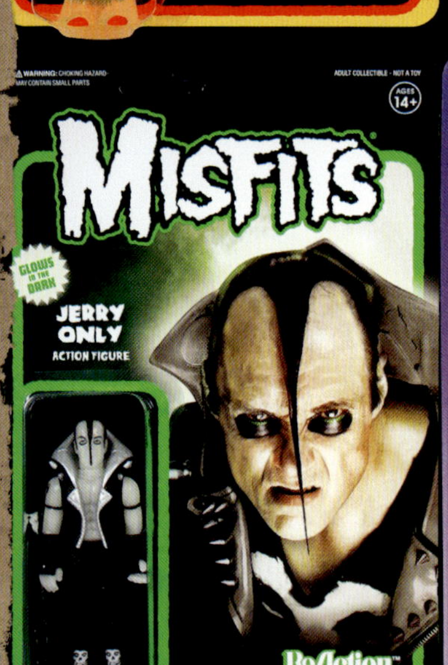

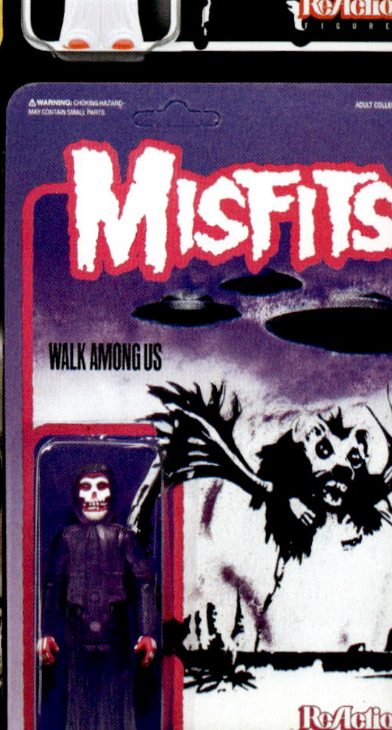

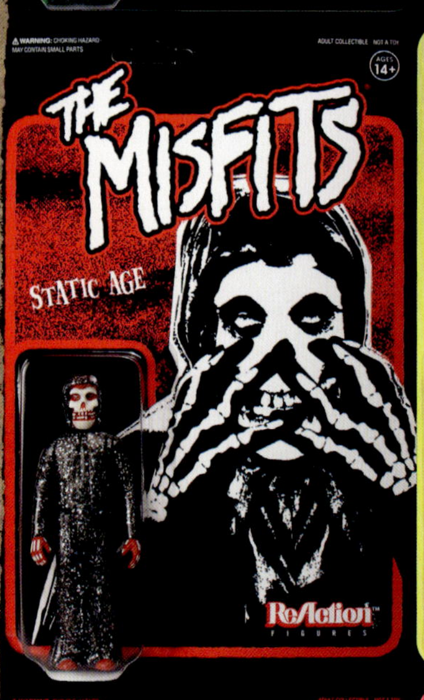

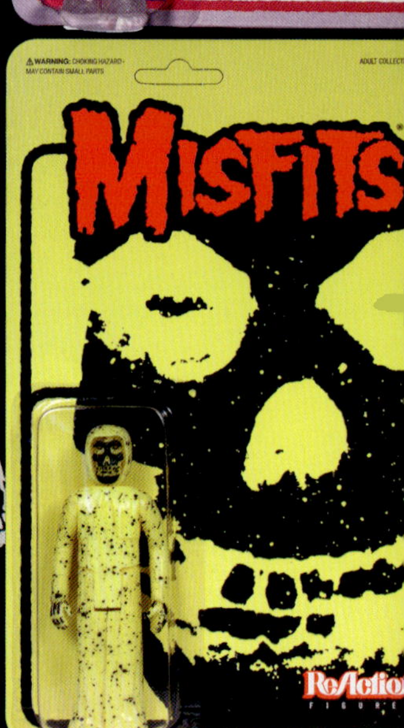

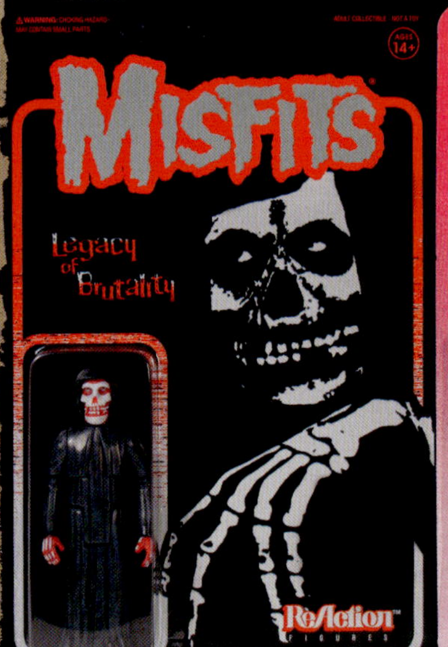

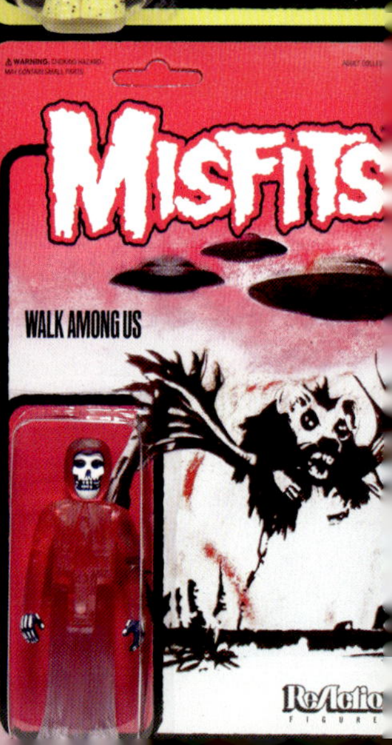

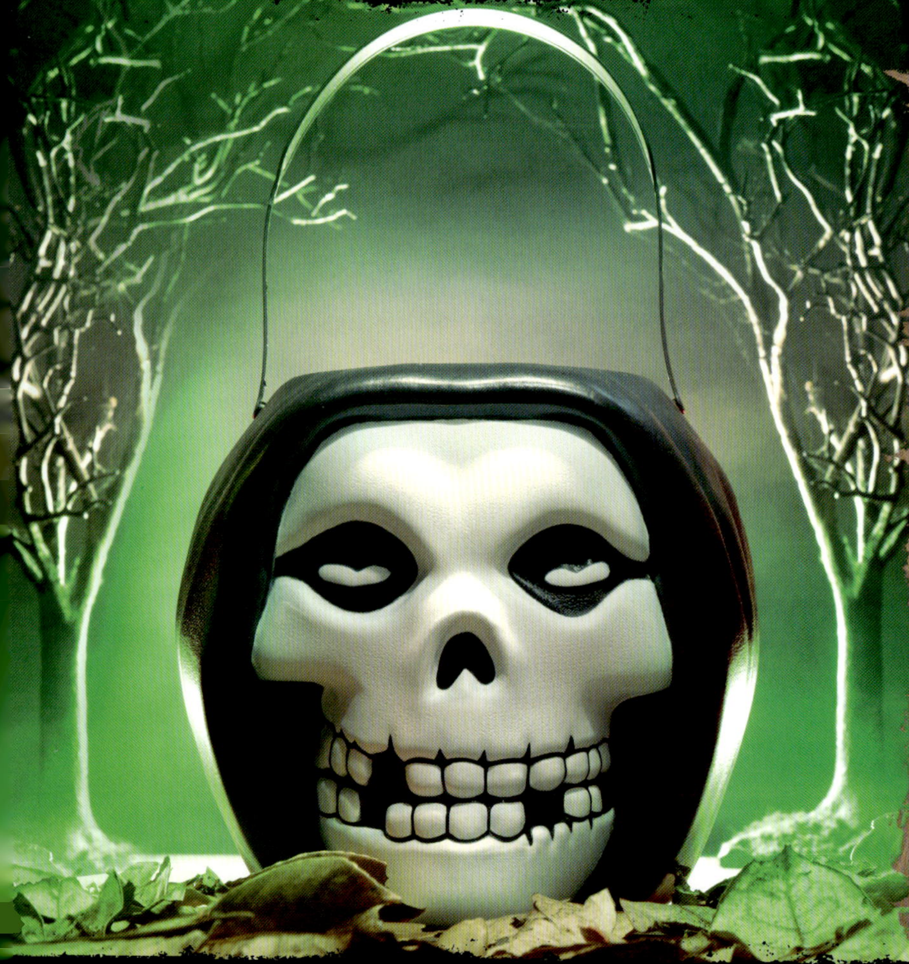

THIS SPREAD: Misfits® ReAction Figures™ art and SuperBucket™

All Misfits trademarks, artwork and intellectual property appear courtesy of TM & © Cyclopian Music, used with permission. All Rights Reserved.

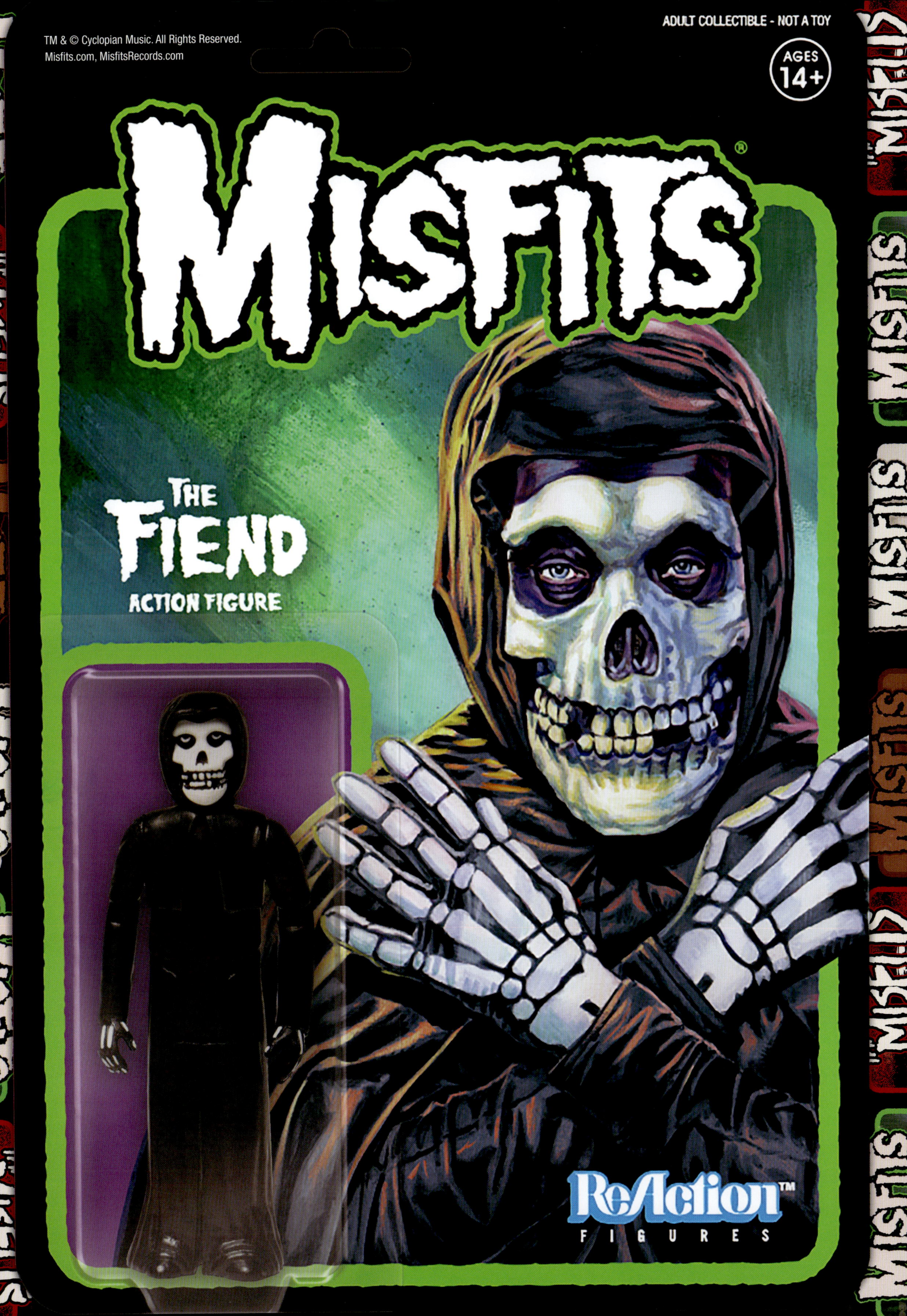

TM & © Cyclopian Music. All Rights Reserved.
Misfits.com, MisfitsRecords.com
ADULT COLLECTIBLE - NOT A TOY
AGES 14+
MISFITS®
THE FIEND
ACTION FIGURE
ReAction™
FIGURES

COLLECT THEM ALL
AGES 14+
RANCID
SKELETIM
ACTION FIGURE
HOOLIGANS
RANCID
SKELETIM
ACTION FIGURE
ReAction
RANCID
SKELETIM (WOLF HEAD)
ACTION FIGURE
ReAction
SKELETIM
ACTION FIGURE

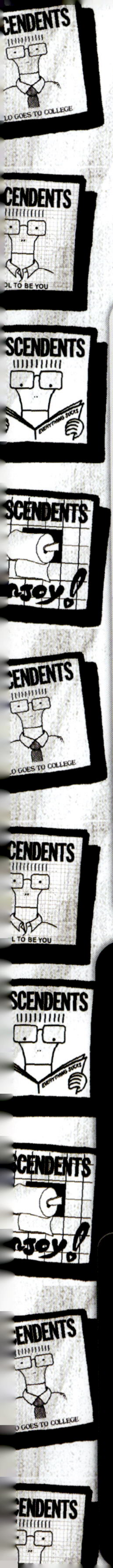

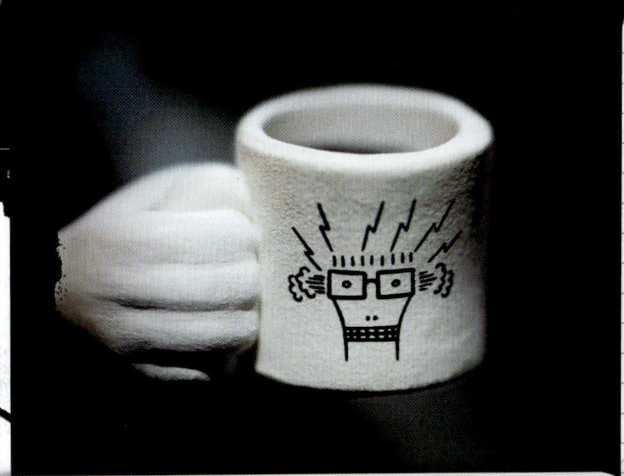

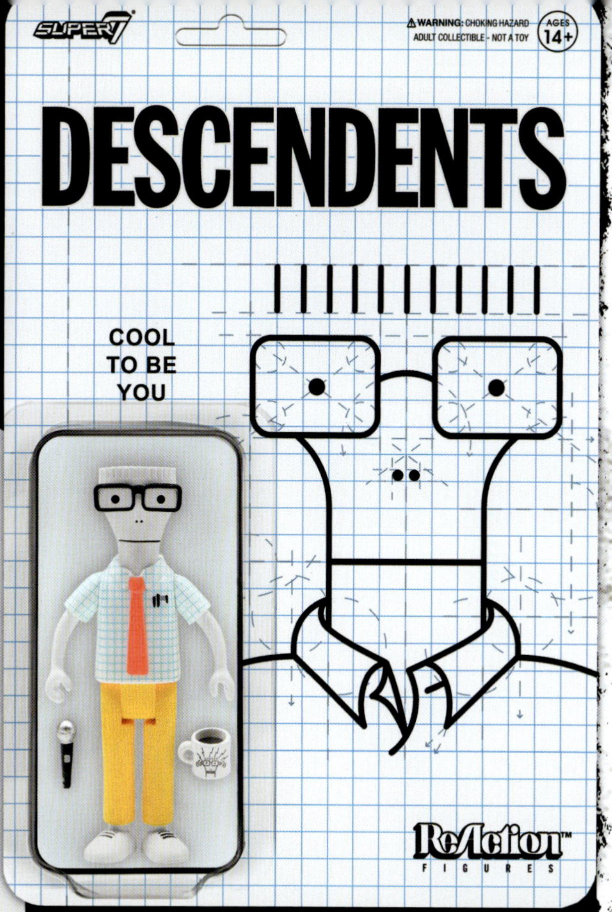

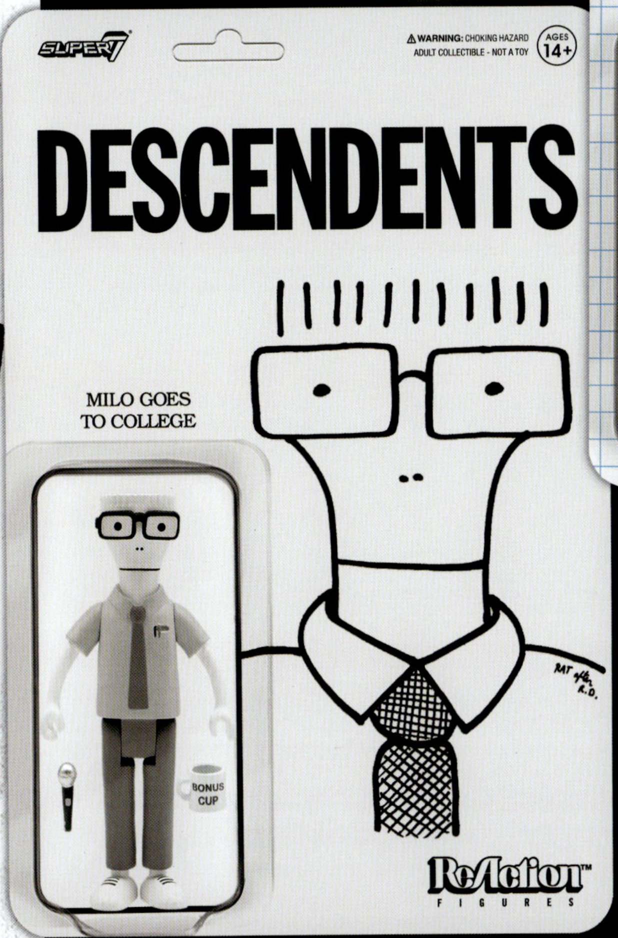

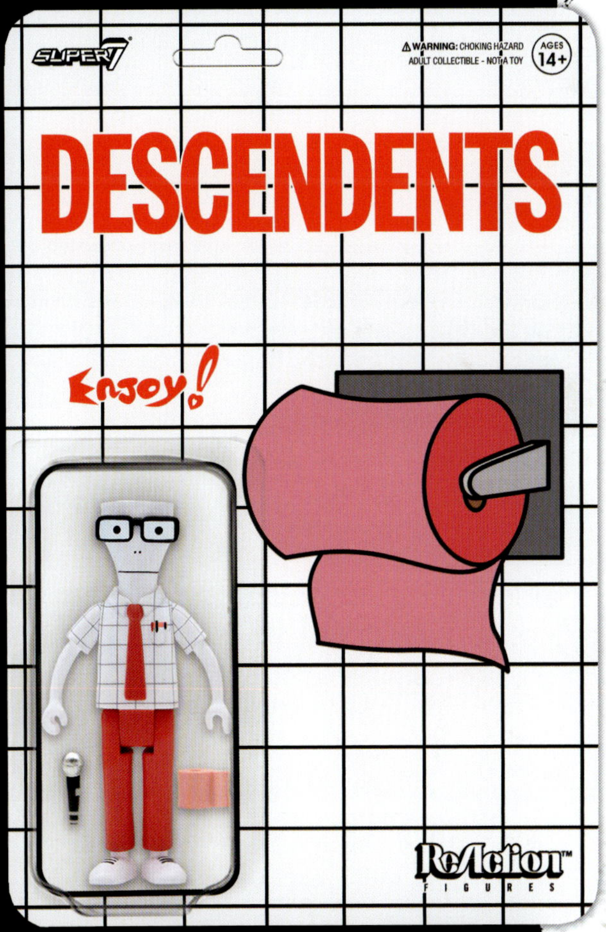

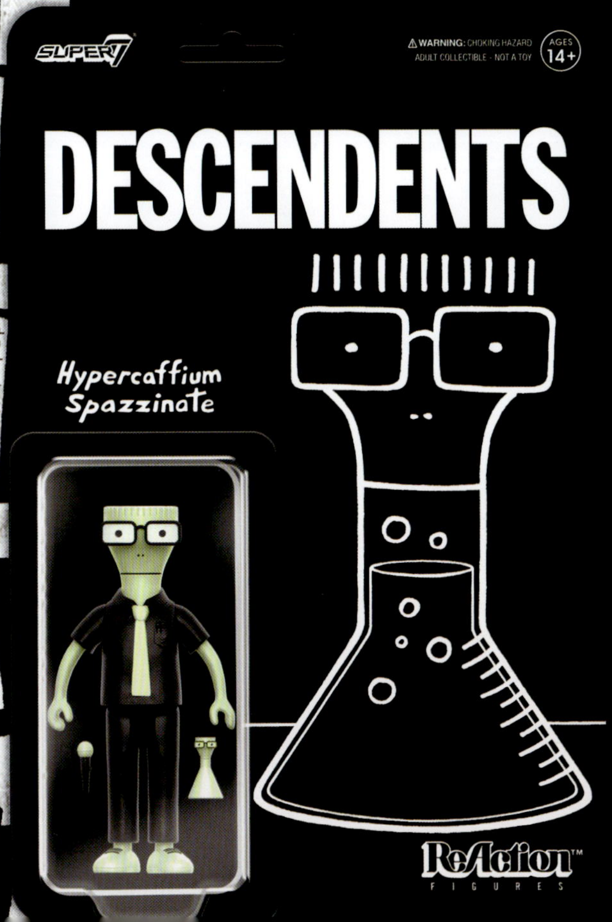

COLLECT THEM ALL!

LEFT: Rancid ReAction Figures™ card art

© Rancid

THIS PAGE: Descendents ReAction Figures™ card art

© 2025 Descendents / All Group

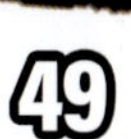

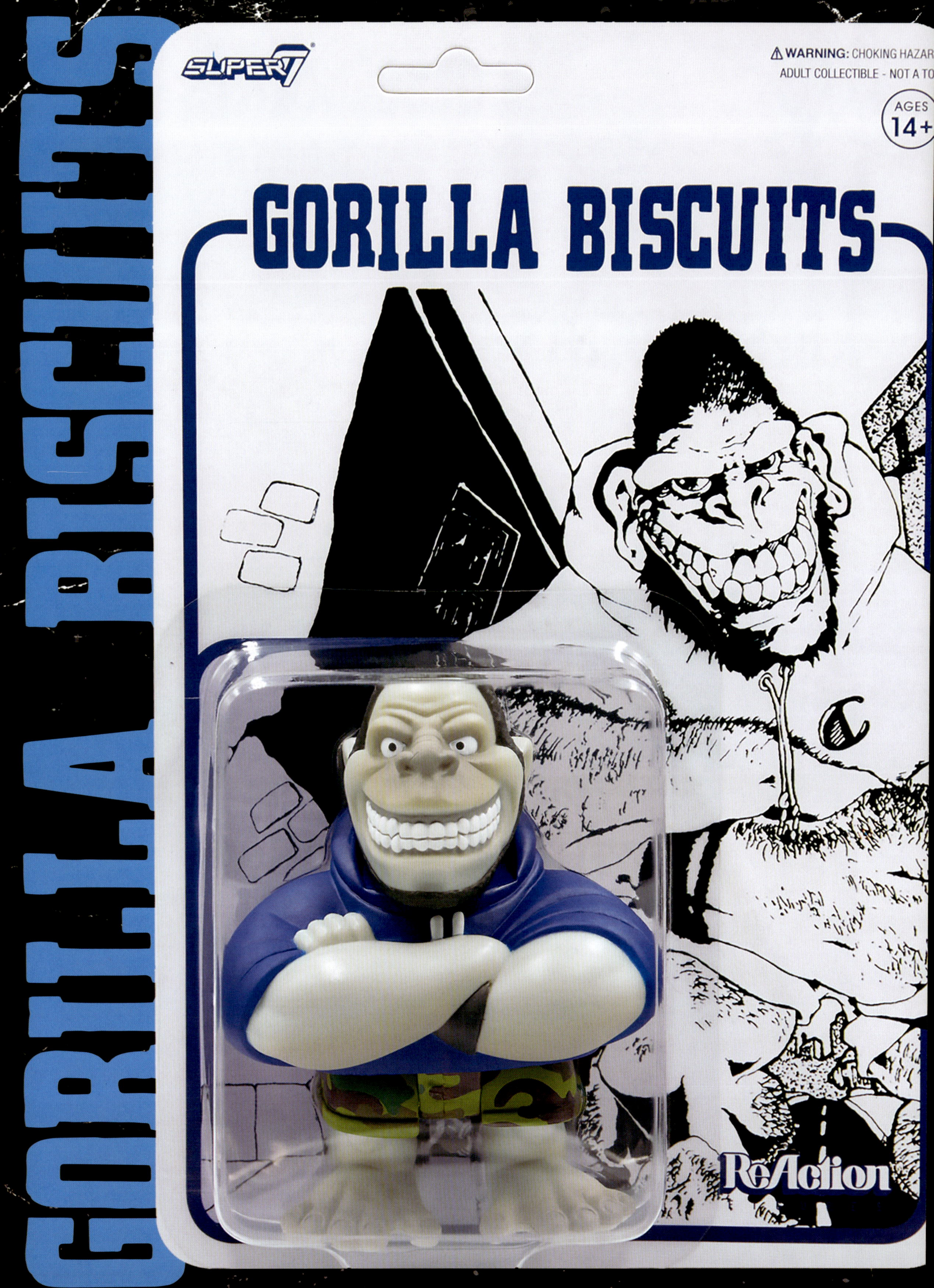

GORILLA BISCUITS

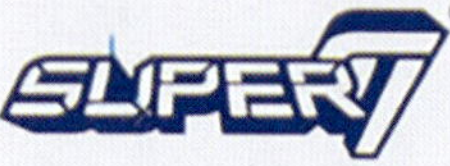

⚠ WARNING: CHOKING HAZAR
ADULT COLLECTIBLE - NOT A TO

AGES 14+

GORILLA BISCUITS

ReAction

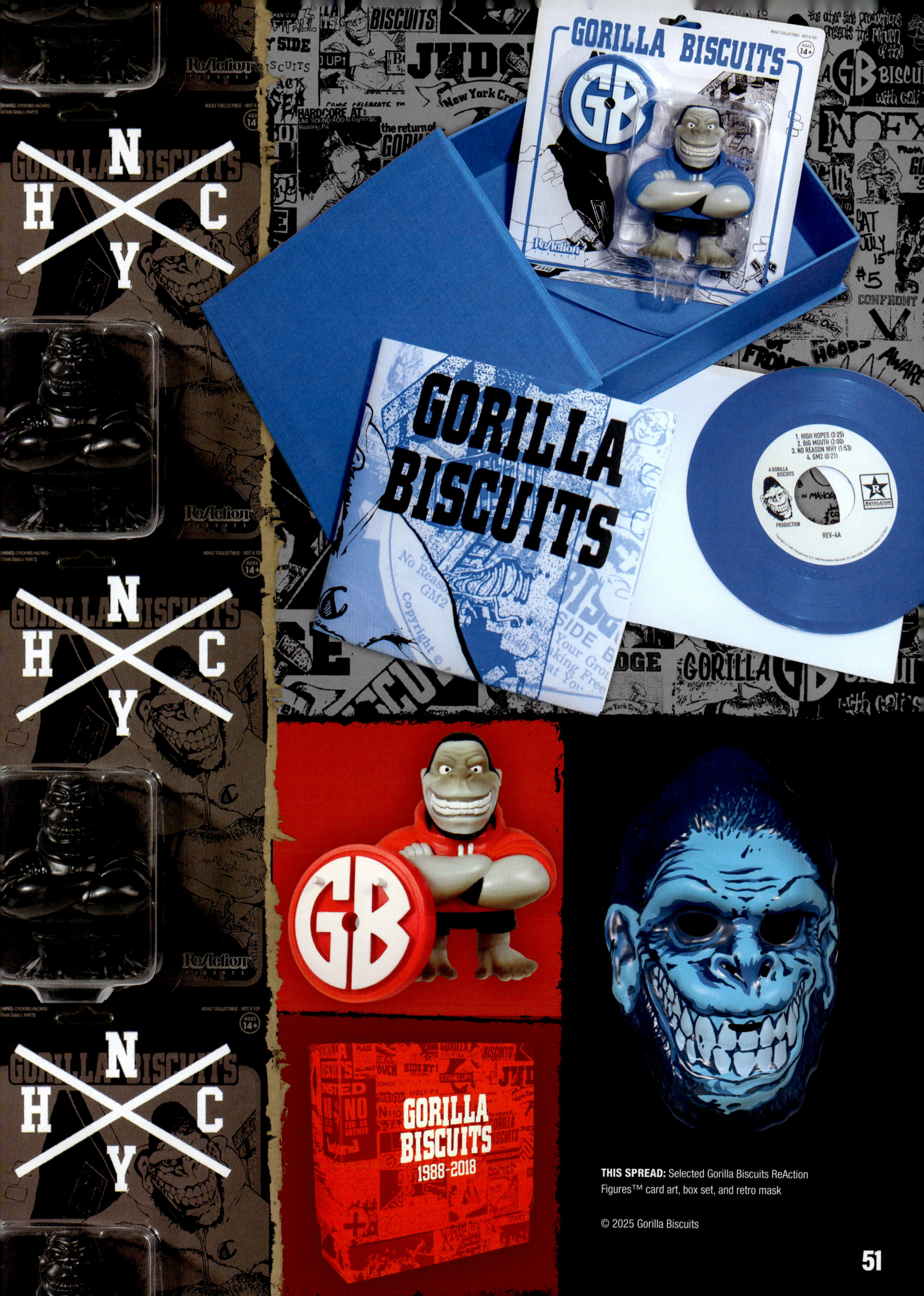

THIS SPREAD: Selected Gorilla Biscuits ReAction Figures™ card art, box set, and retro mask

© 2025 Gorilla Biscuits

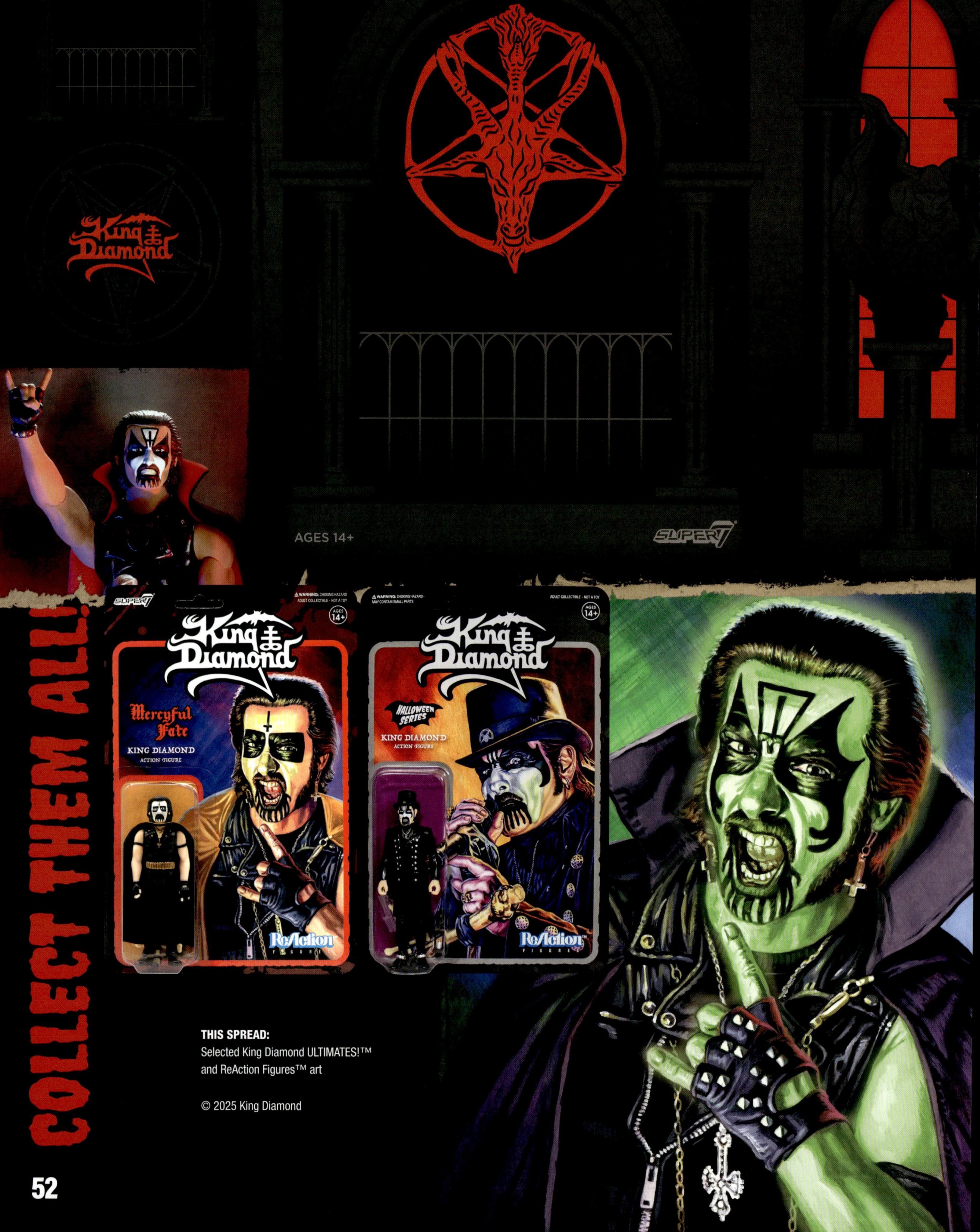

THIS SPREAD:
Selected King Diamond ULTIMATES!™ and ReAction Figures™ art

© 2025 King Diamond

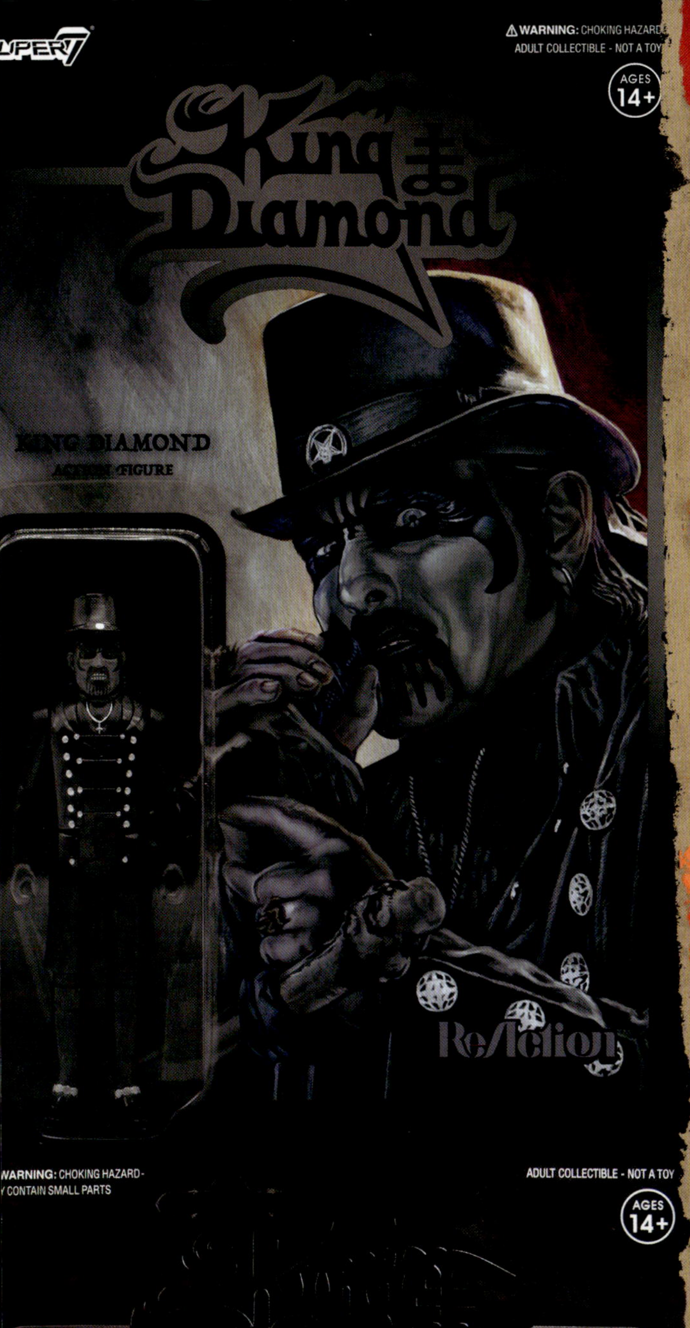

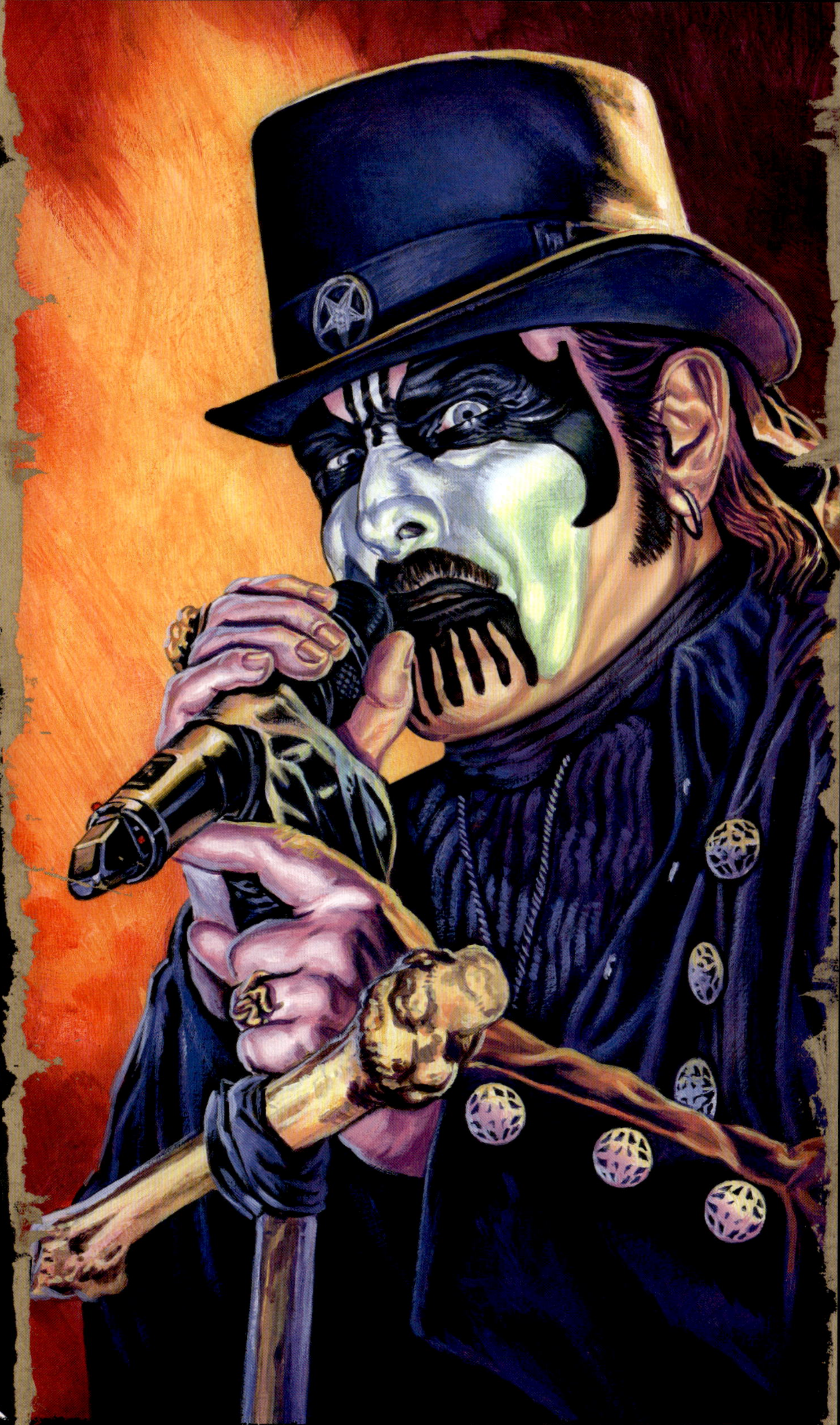

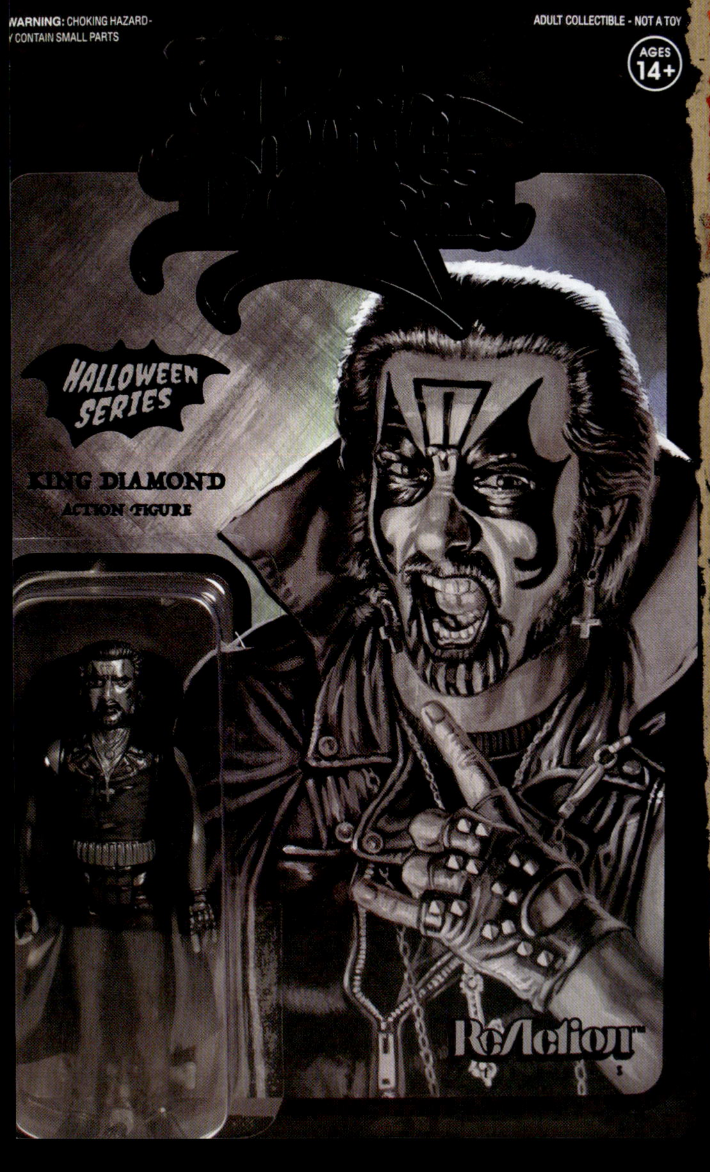

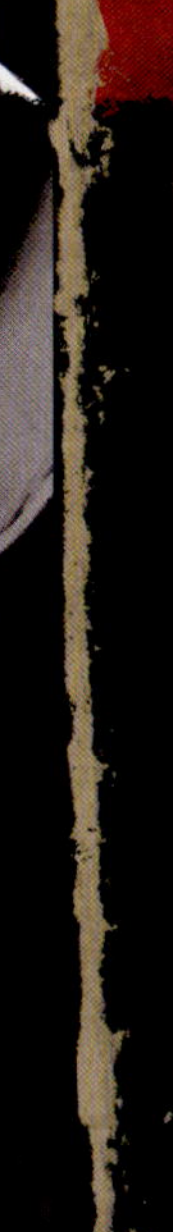

KING DIAMOND

King Diamond is a Danish heavy metal musician and song writer. He is known for his extensive and powerful vocal range, particularly his use of falsetto. Diamond is the lead vocalist for both Mercyful Fate and the eponymous King Diamond.

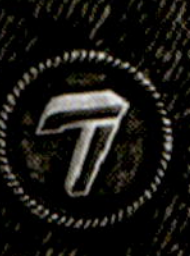

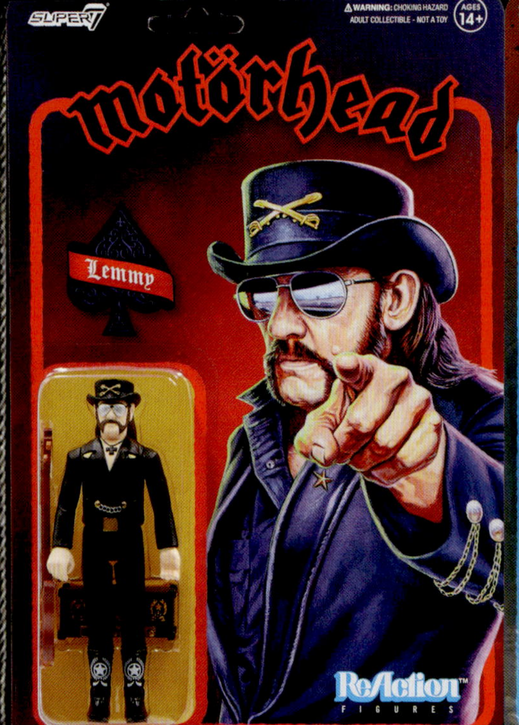

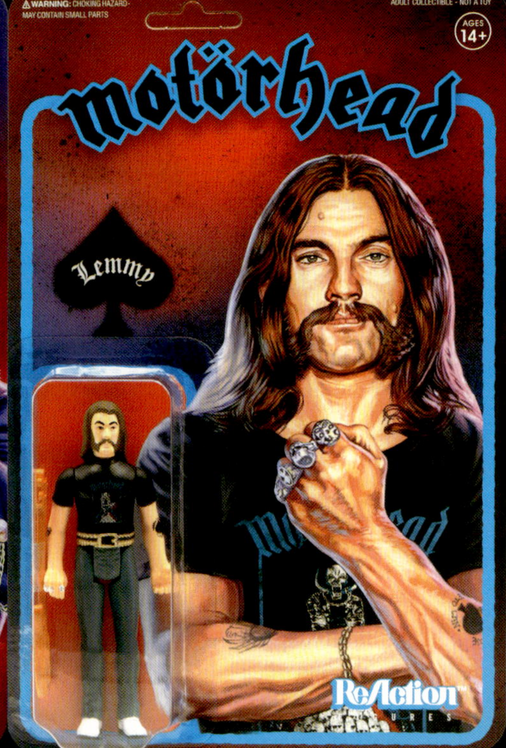

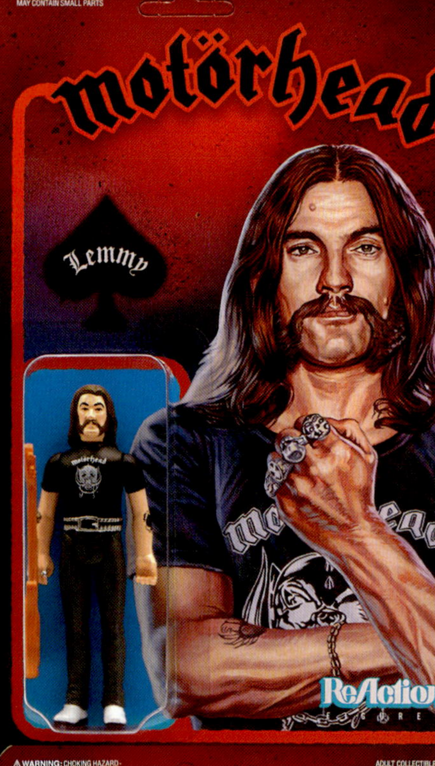

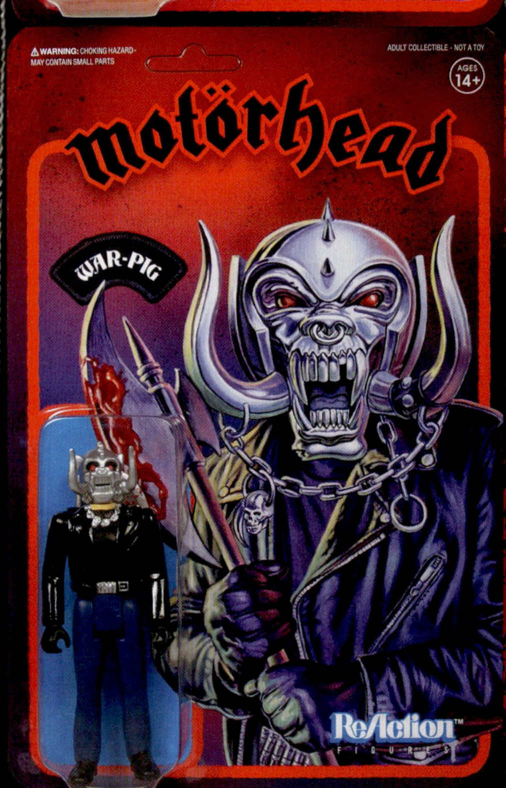

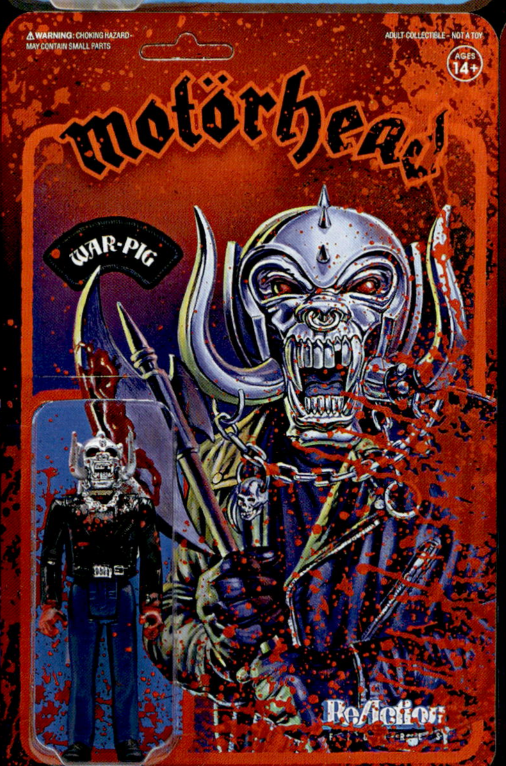

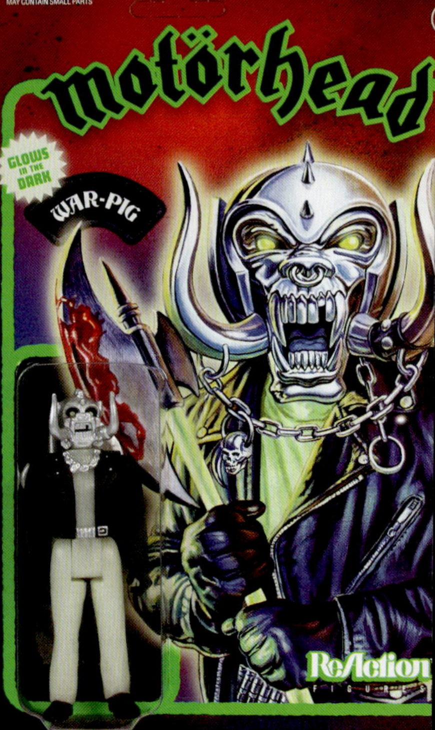

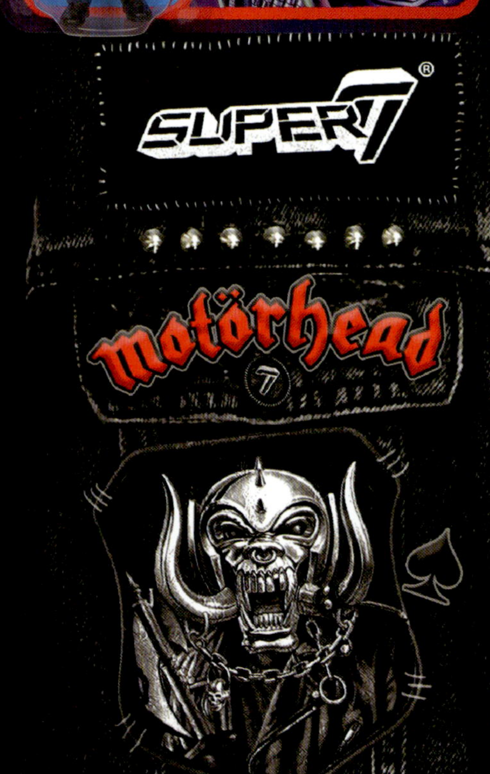

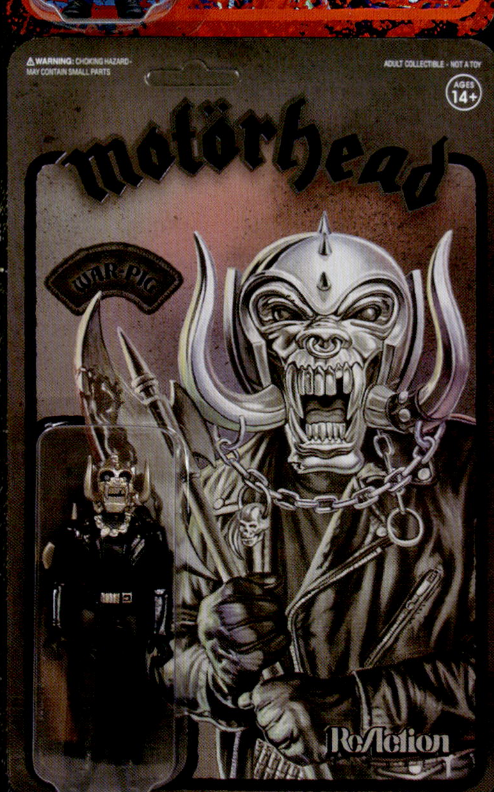

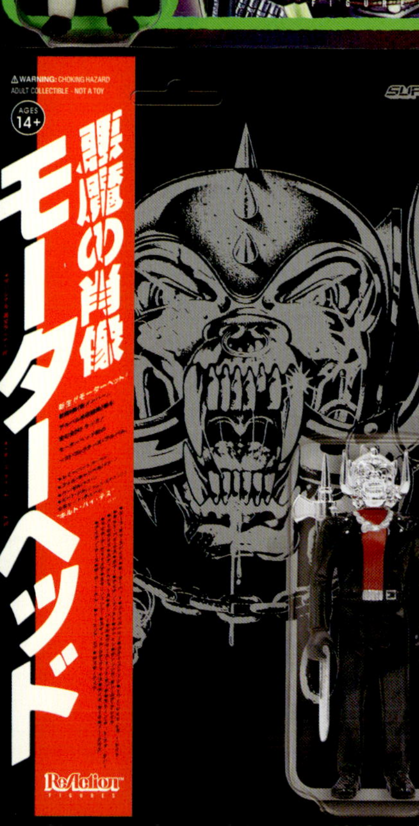

THIS SPREAD: Motörhead ReAction Figures™ and ULTIMATES!™ packaging art

© 2025 Motörhead

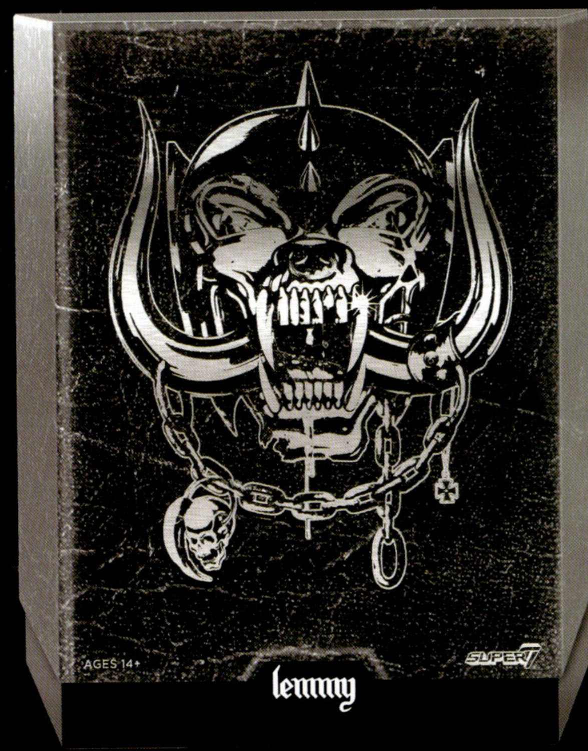

Everything Louder Than Everything Else

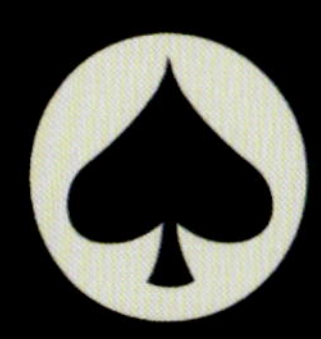

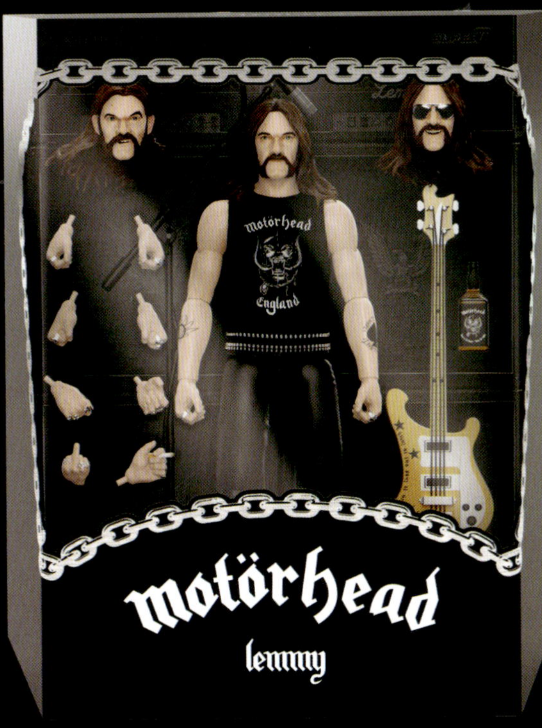

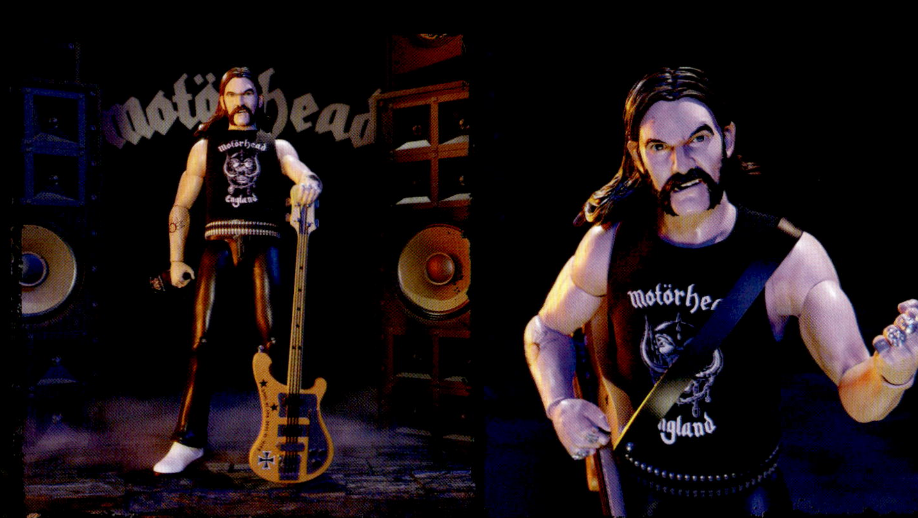

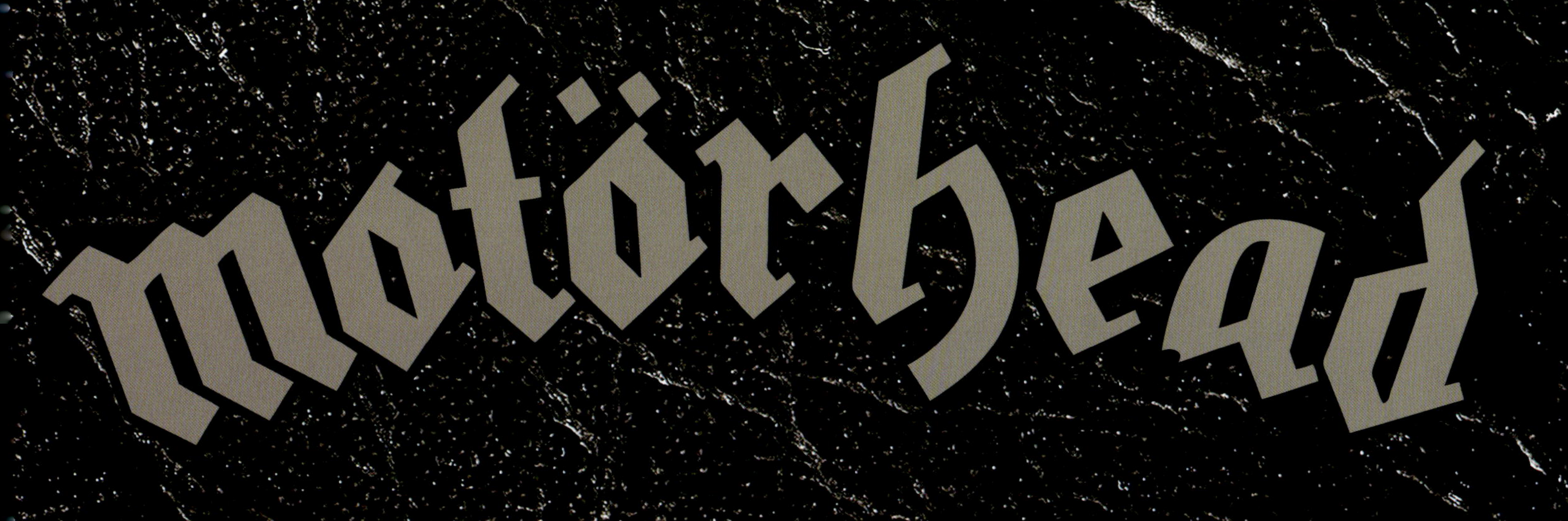

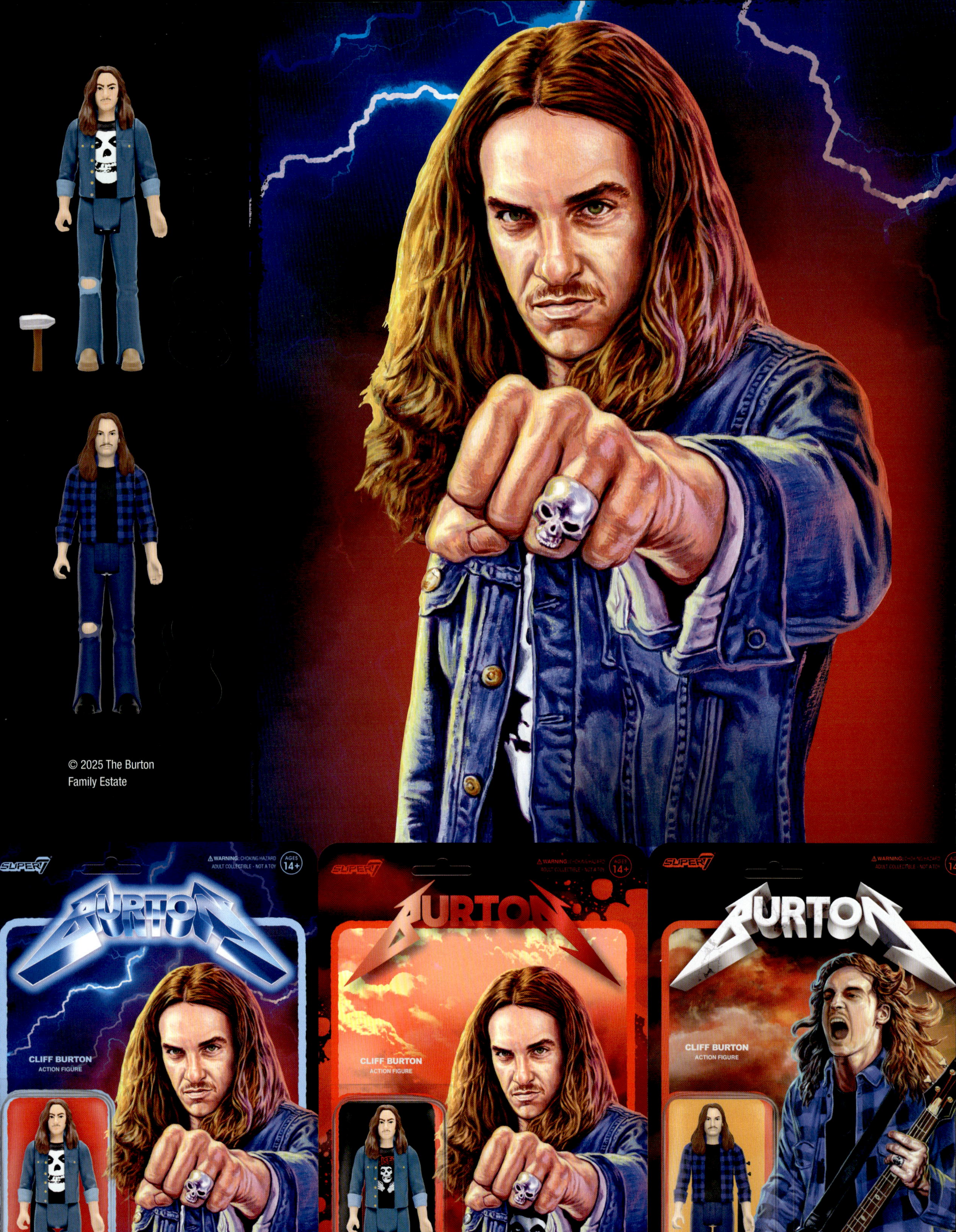

© 2025 The Burton Family Estate

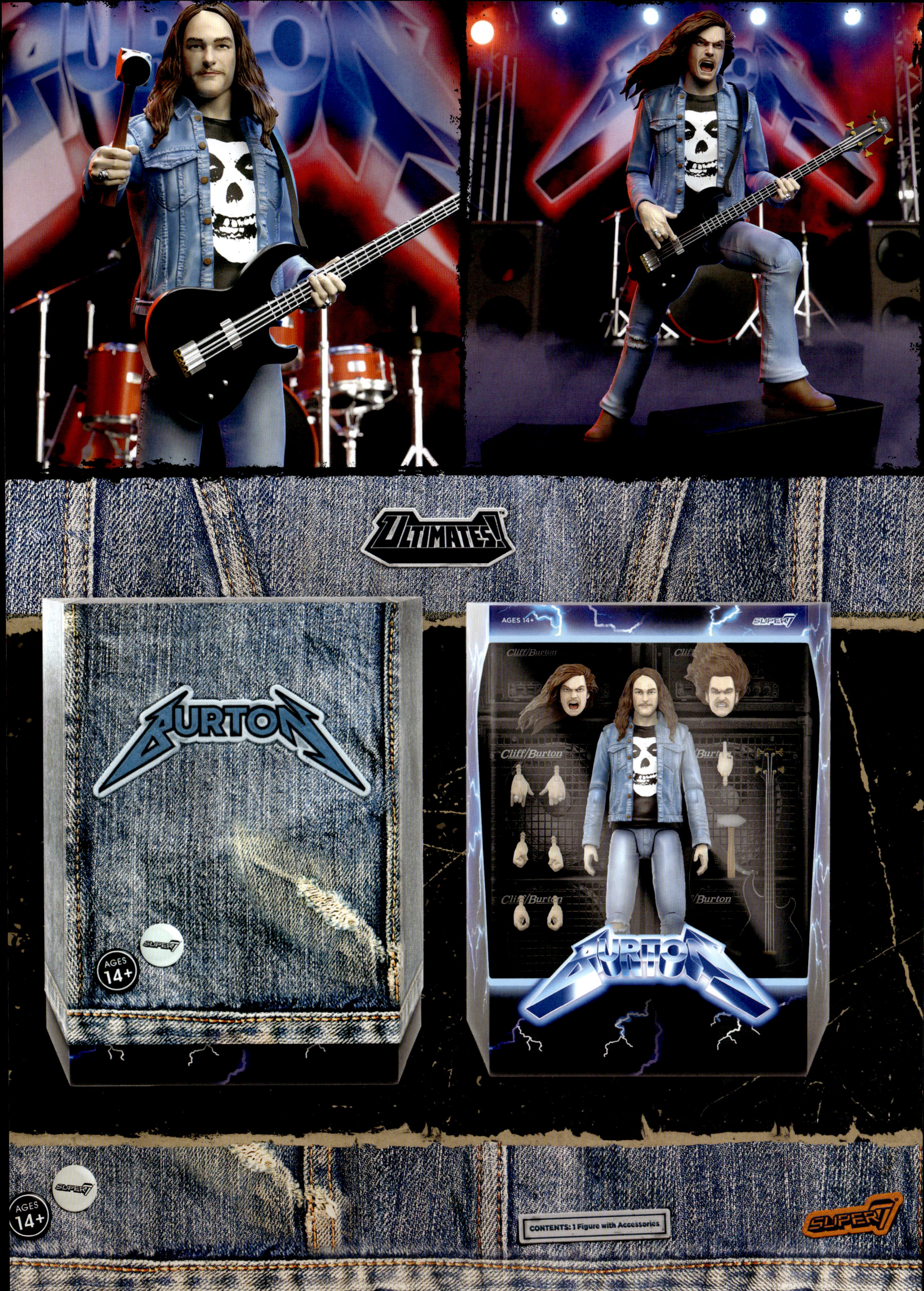
ULTIMATES!
BURTON
AGES 14+
SUPER7
Cliff/Burton
CONTENTS: 1 Figure with Accessories

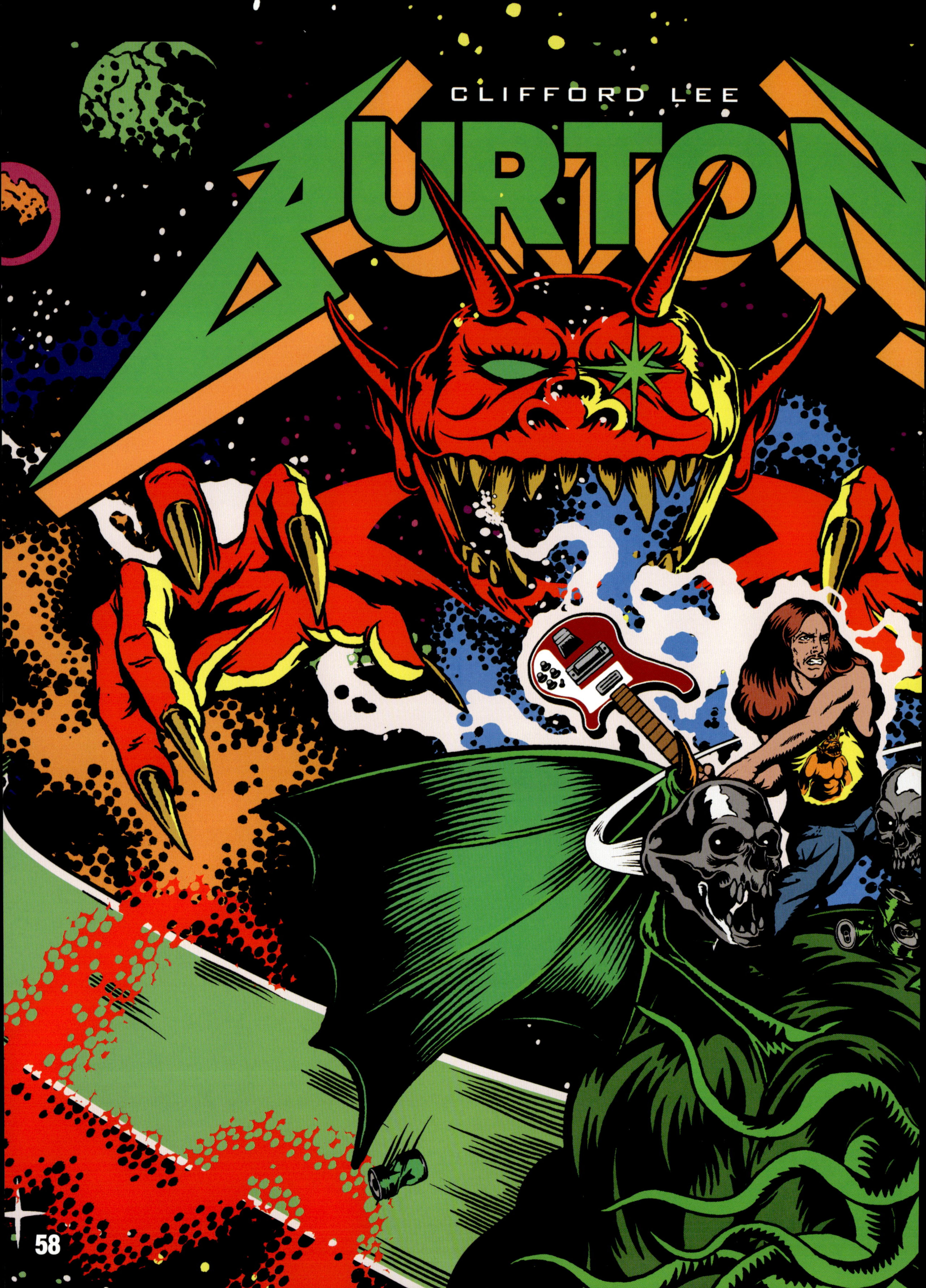
CLIFFORD LEE
BURTON

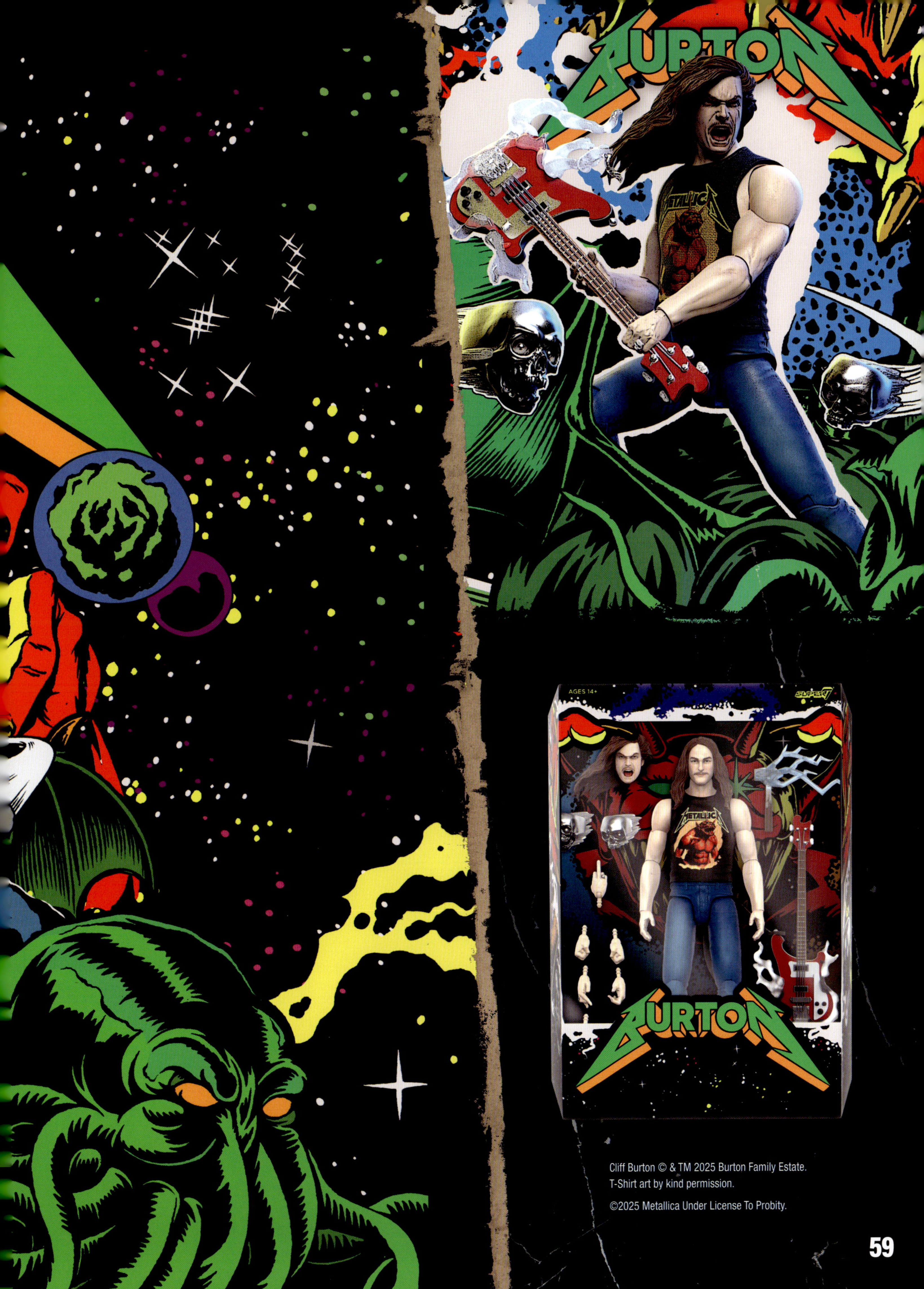

Cliff Burton © & TM 2025 Burton Family Estate.
T-Shirt art by kind permission.

©2025 Metallica Under License To Probity.

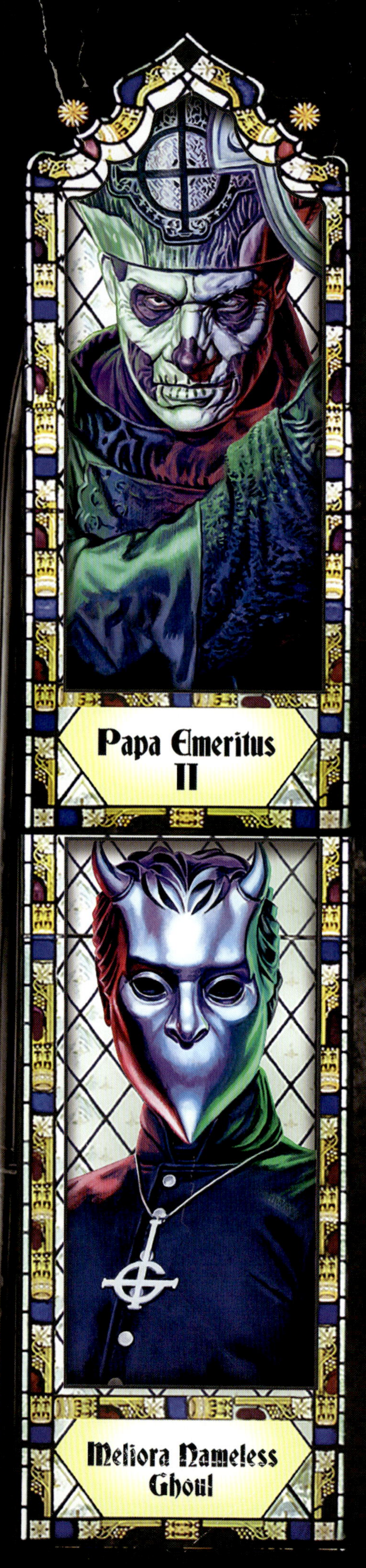
Papa Emeritus
II
Meliora Nameless
Ghoul
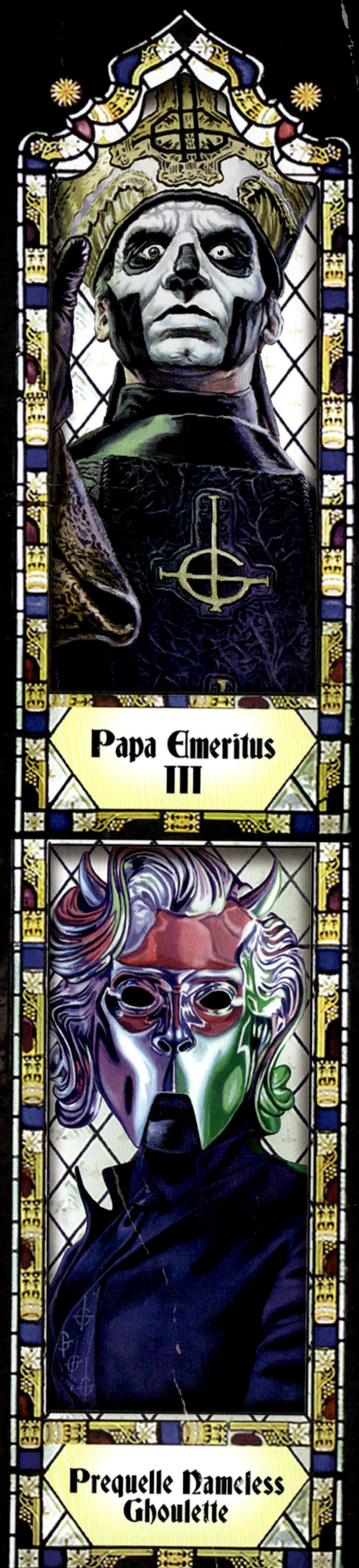
Papa Emeritus
III
Prequelle Nameless
Ghoulette
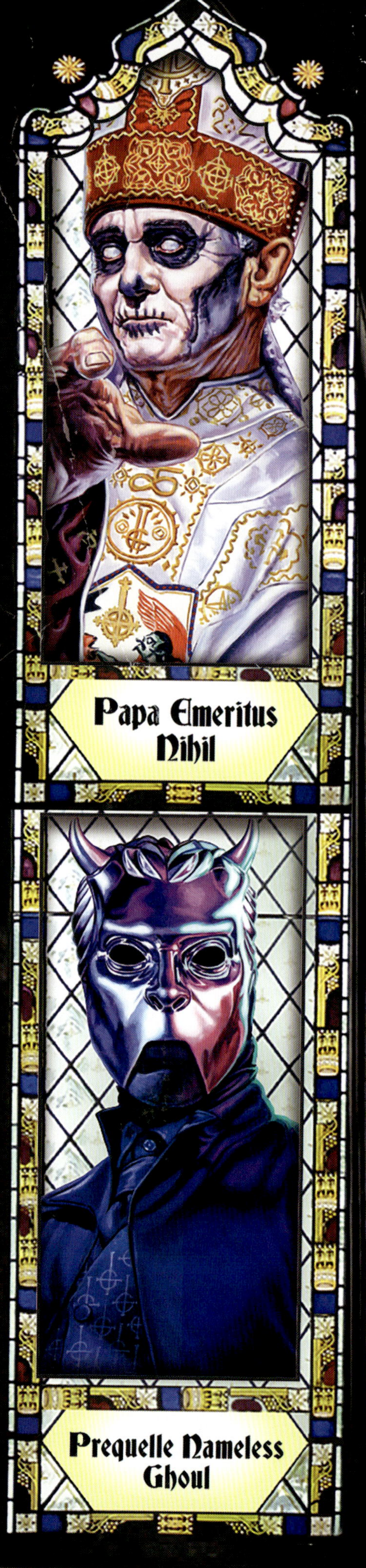
Papa Emeritus
Nihil
Prequelle Nameless
Ghoul

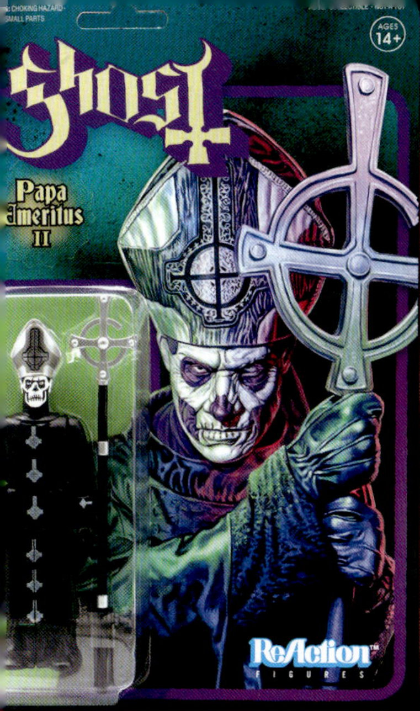

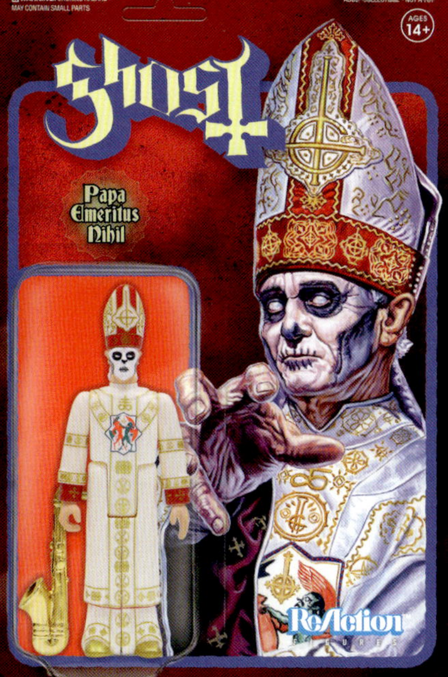

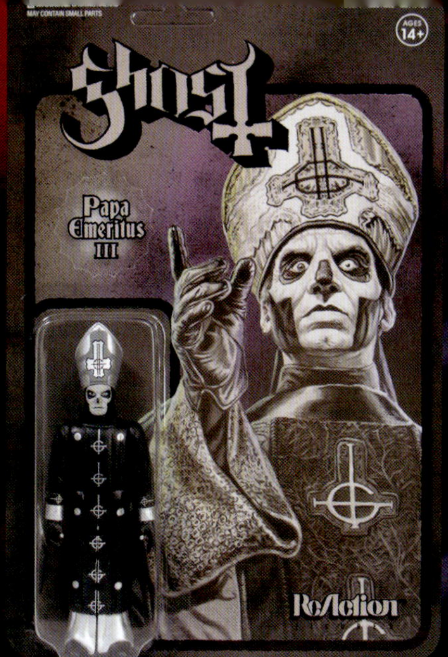

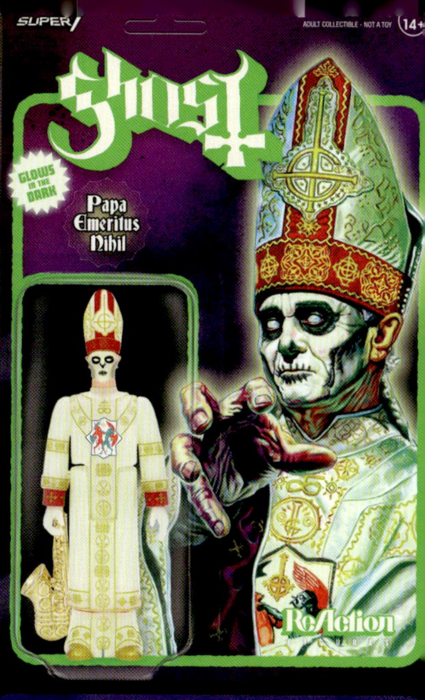

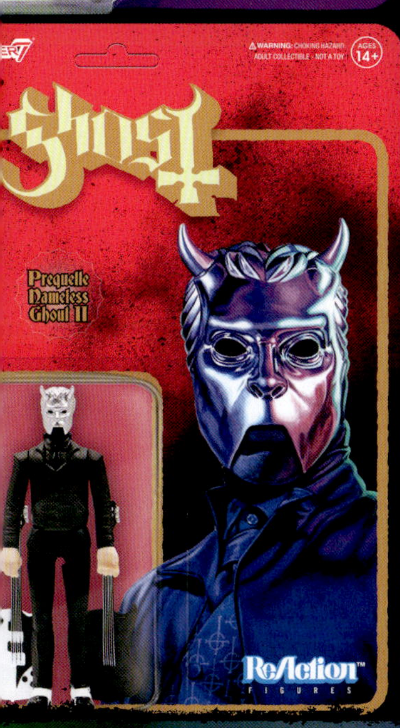

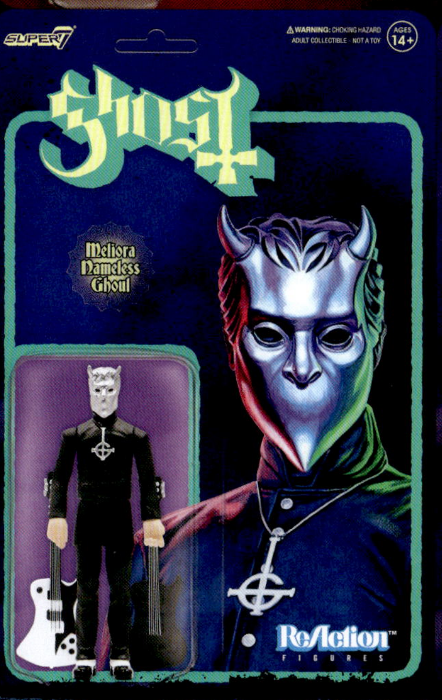

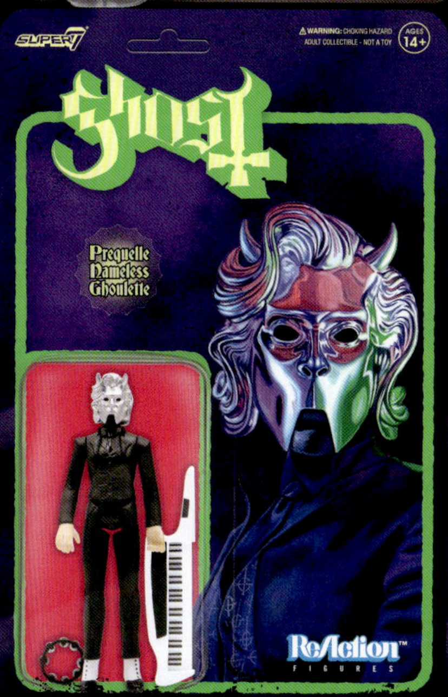

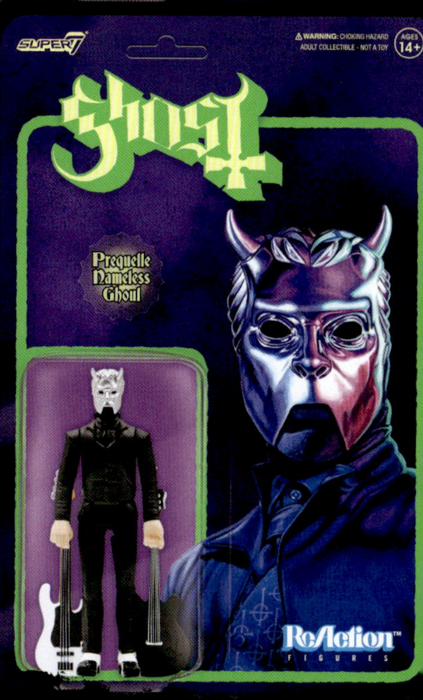

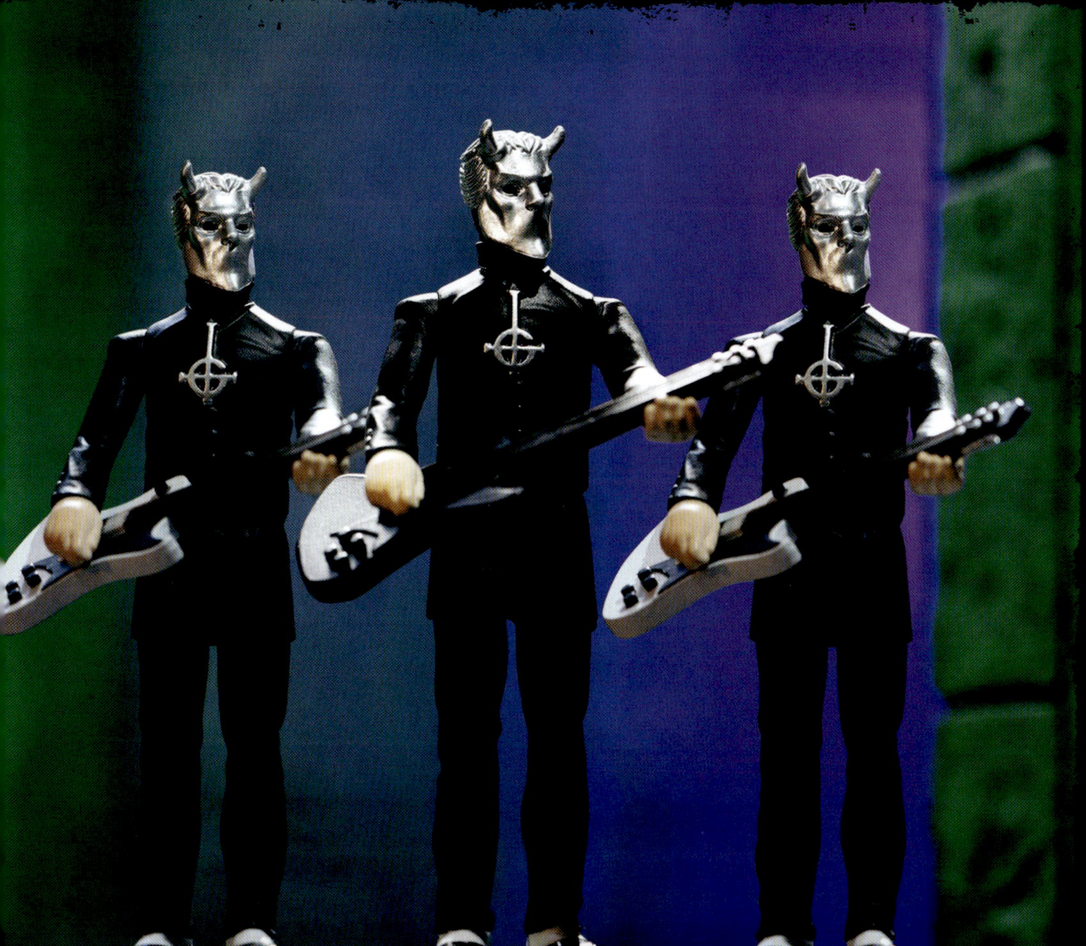
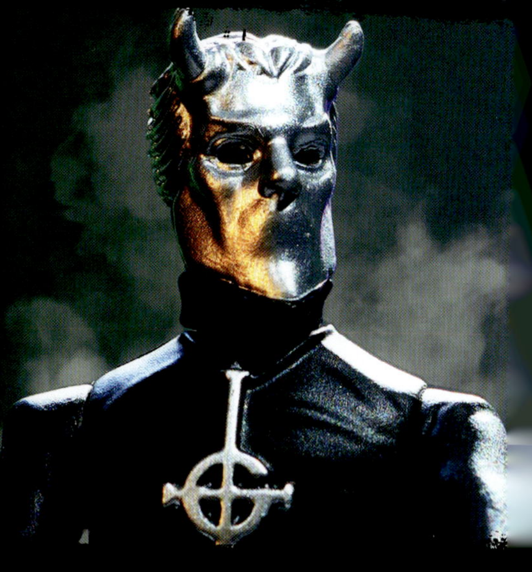

THIS SPREAD: Selected Ghost ReAction Figures™ card art

© 2025 ® TM svensk drama pop AB

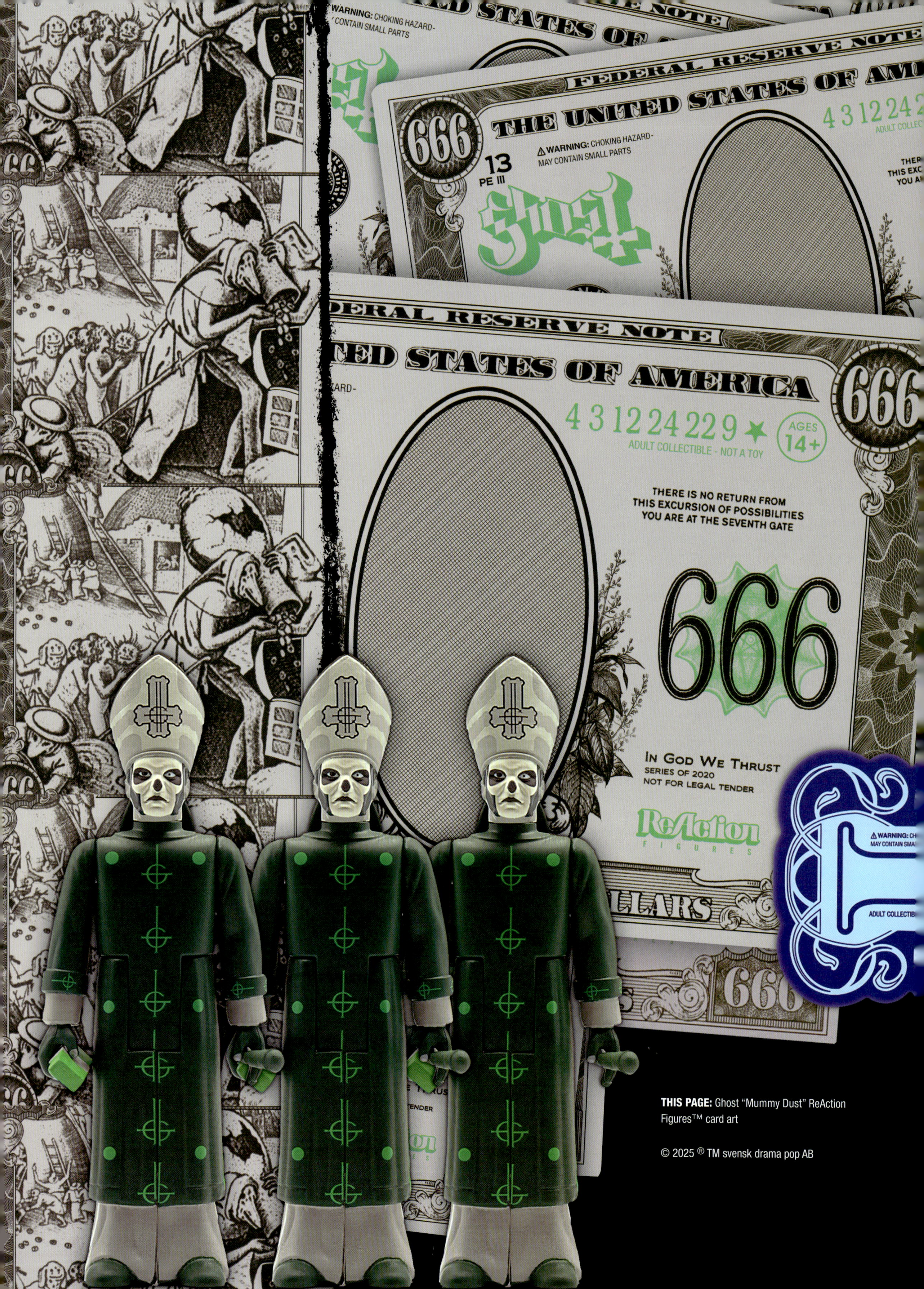

THIS PAGE: Ghost "Mummy Dust" ReAction Figures™ card art

© 2025 ® TM svensk drama pop AB

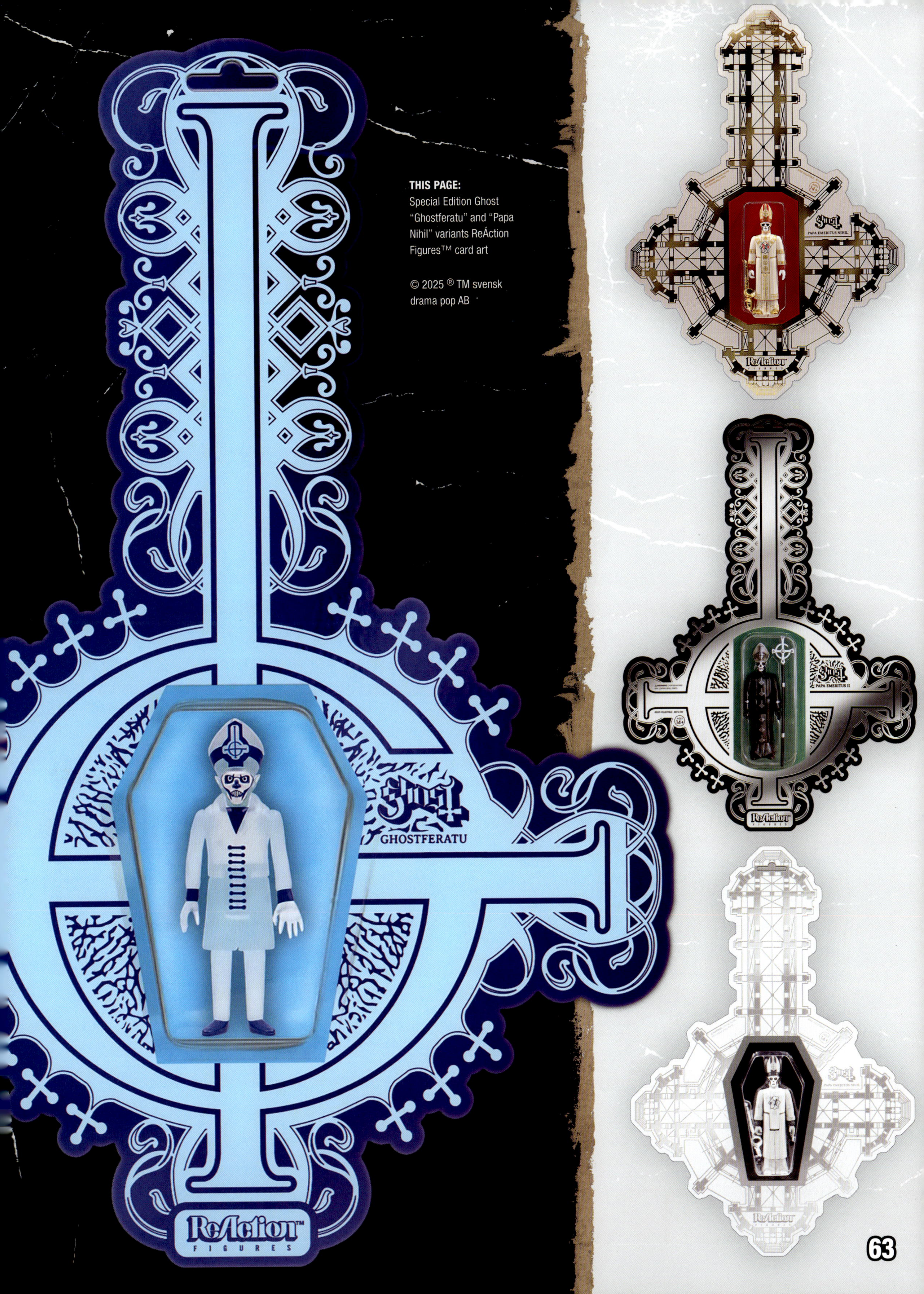

THIS PAGE:
Special Edition Ghost "Ghostferatu" and "Papa Nihil" variants ReÁction Figures™ card art

© 2025 ® TM svensk drama pop AB

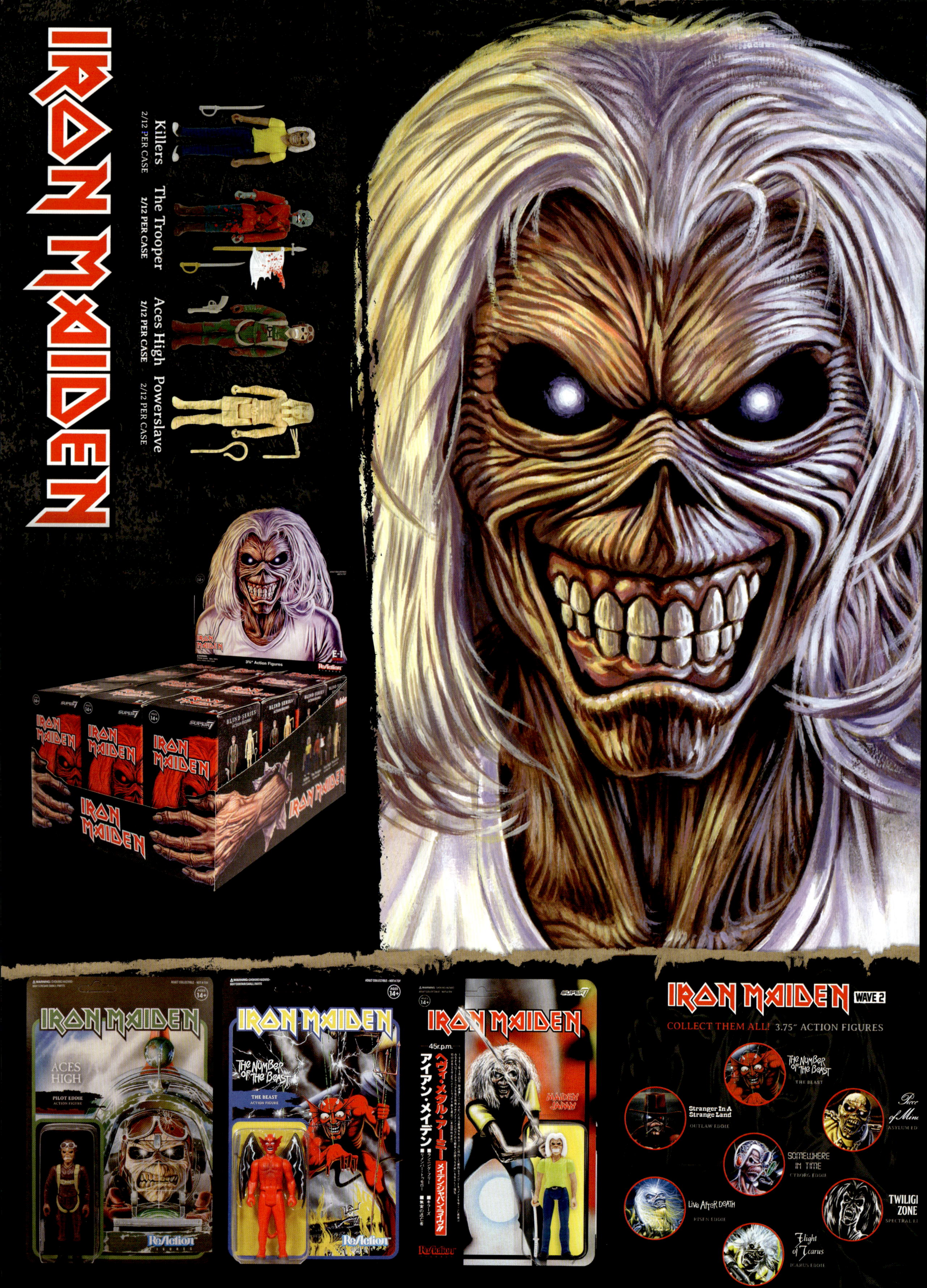

IRON MAIDEN

Killers
2/12 PER CASE

The Tropper
2/12 PER CASE

Aces High
2/12 PER CASE

Powerslave
2/12 PER CASE

3¾" Action Figures

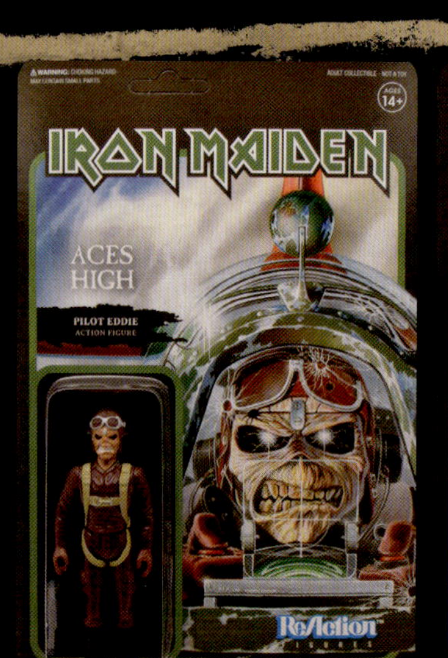

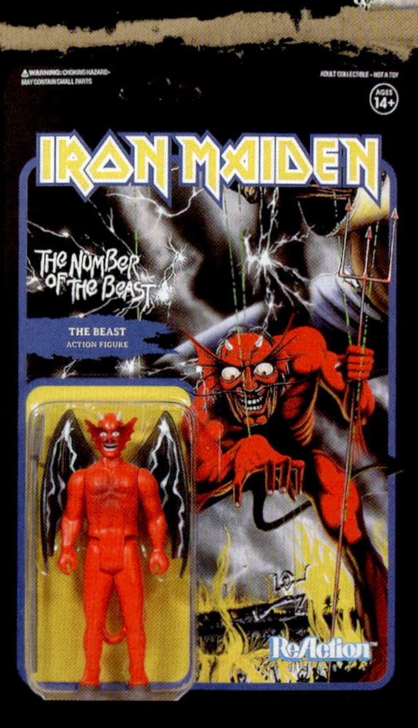

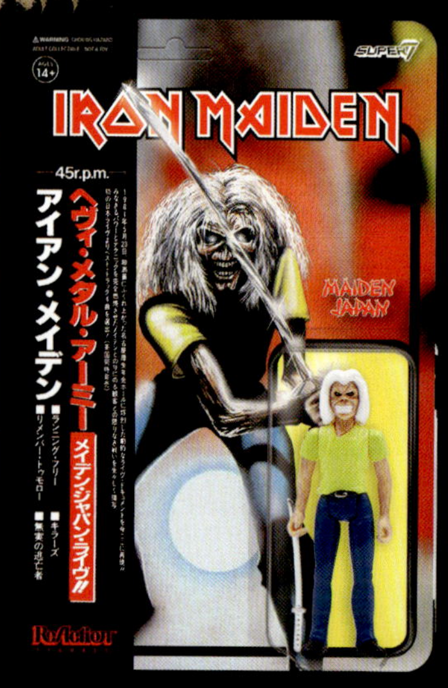

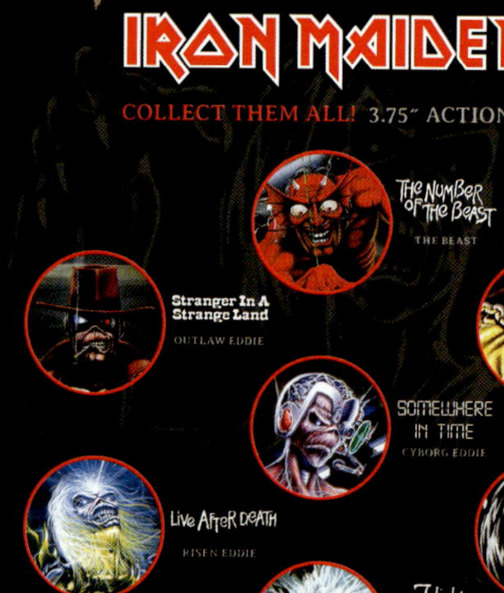

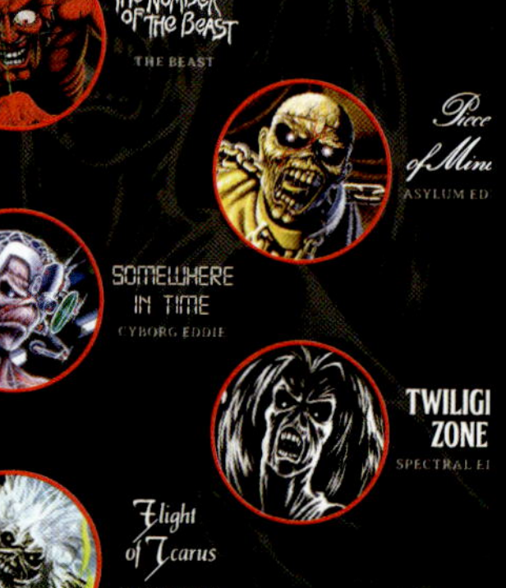

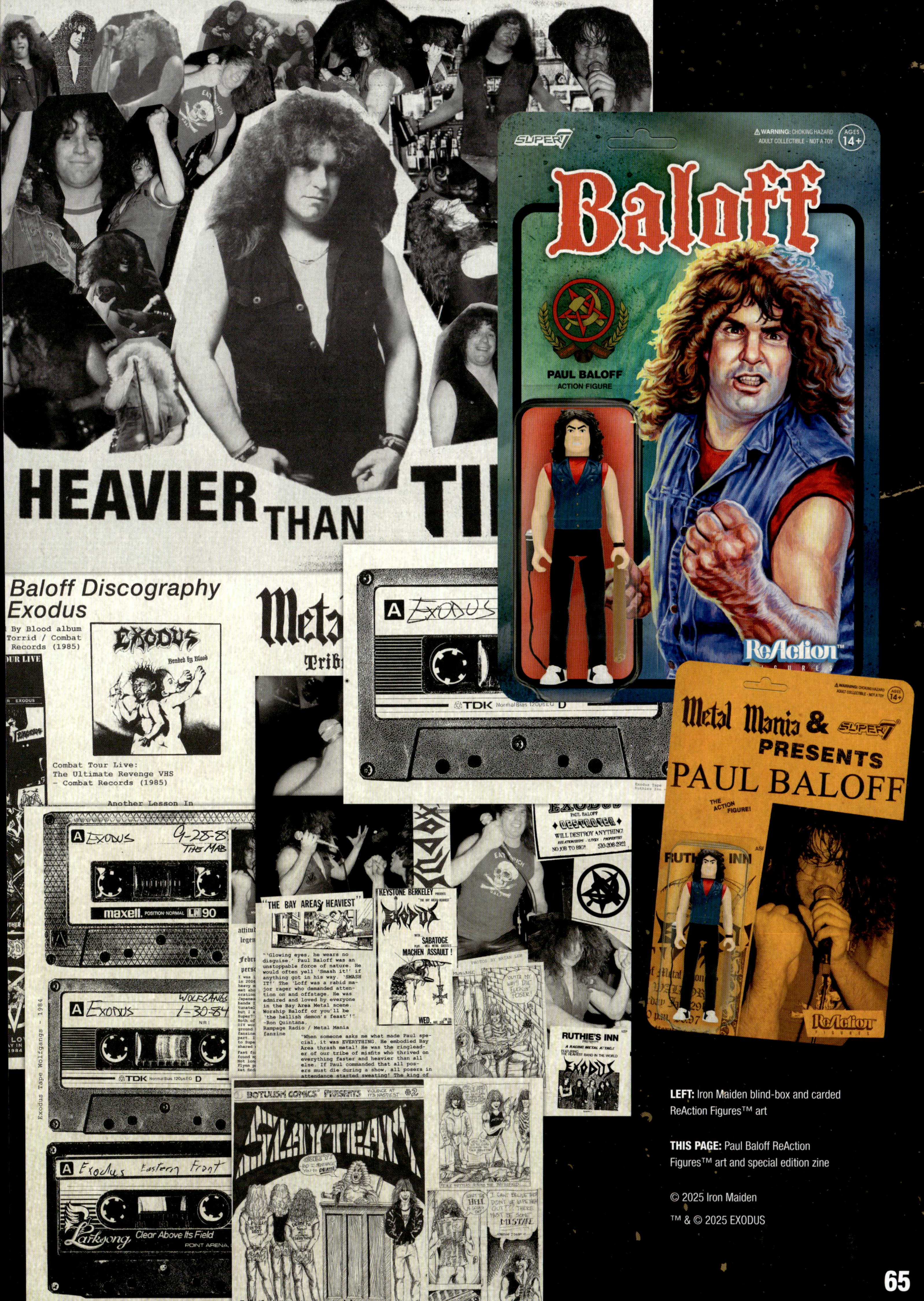

LEFT: Iron Maiden blind-box and carded ReAction Figures™ art

THIS PAGE: Paul Baloff ReAction Figures™ art and special edition zine

© 2025 Iron Maiden

™ & © 2025 EXODUS

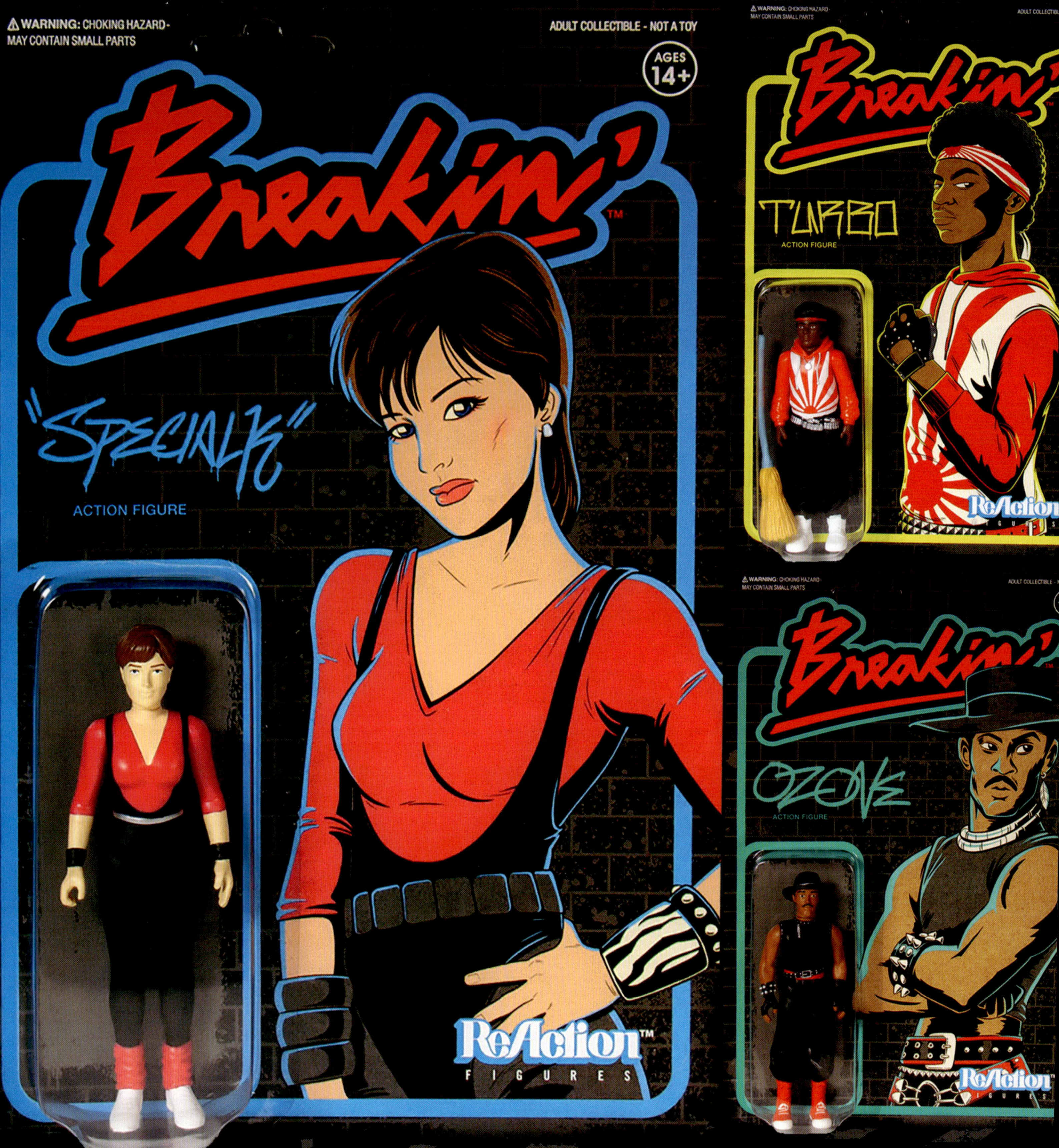

Push it to pop it!
Rock it to lock it!
Break it to make it!

THIS SPREAD: Selected Breakin'™ ReAction Figures™ card art and 3-pack box

™ & © 2025 MGM

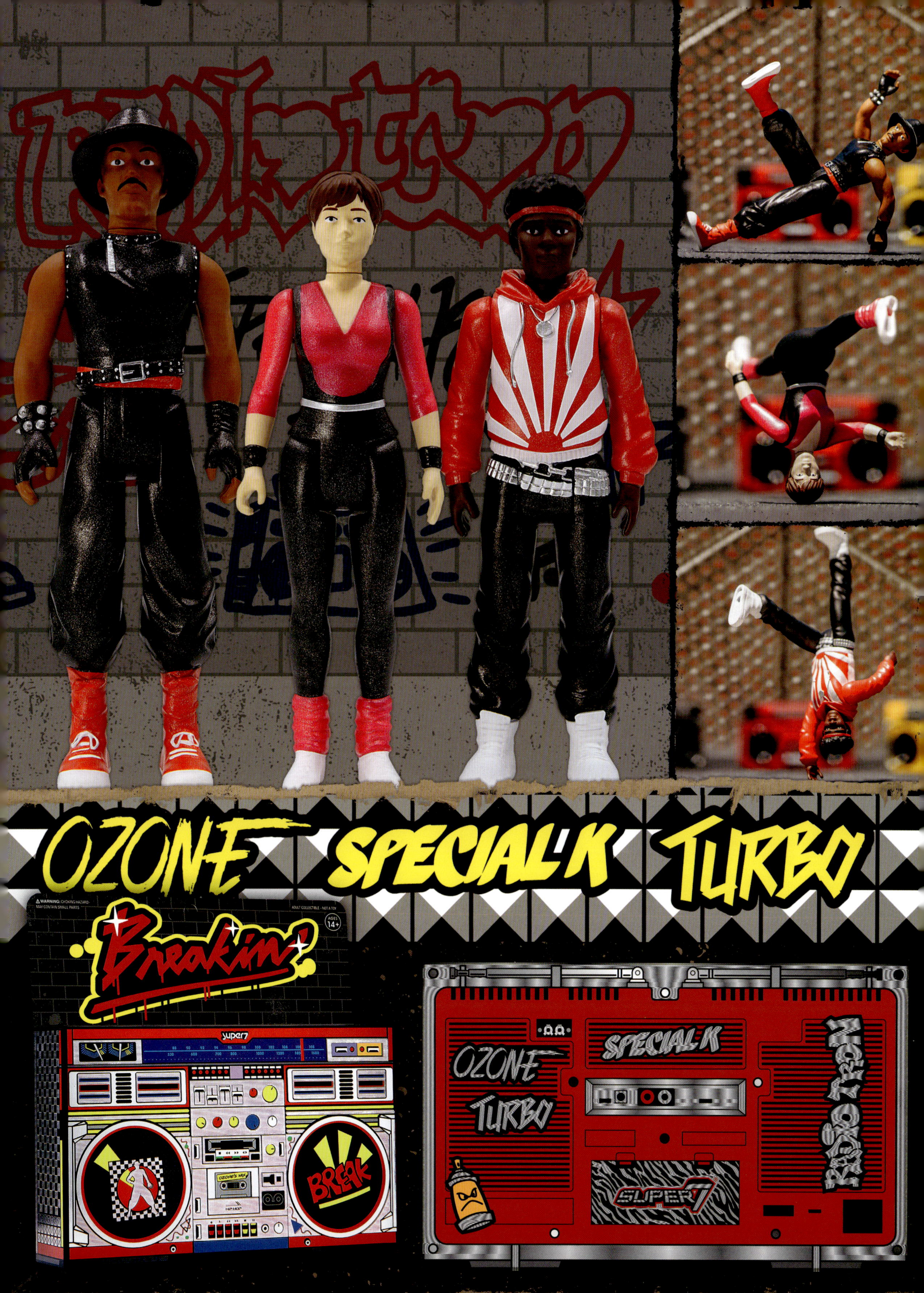
OZONE
SPECIAL K
TURBO
Breakin'
SPECIAL K
OZONE
TURBO
SUPER7

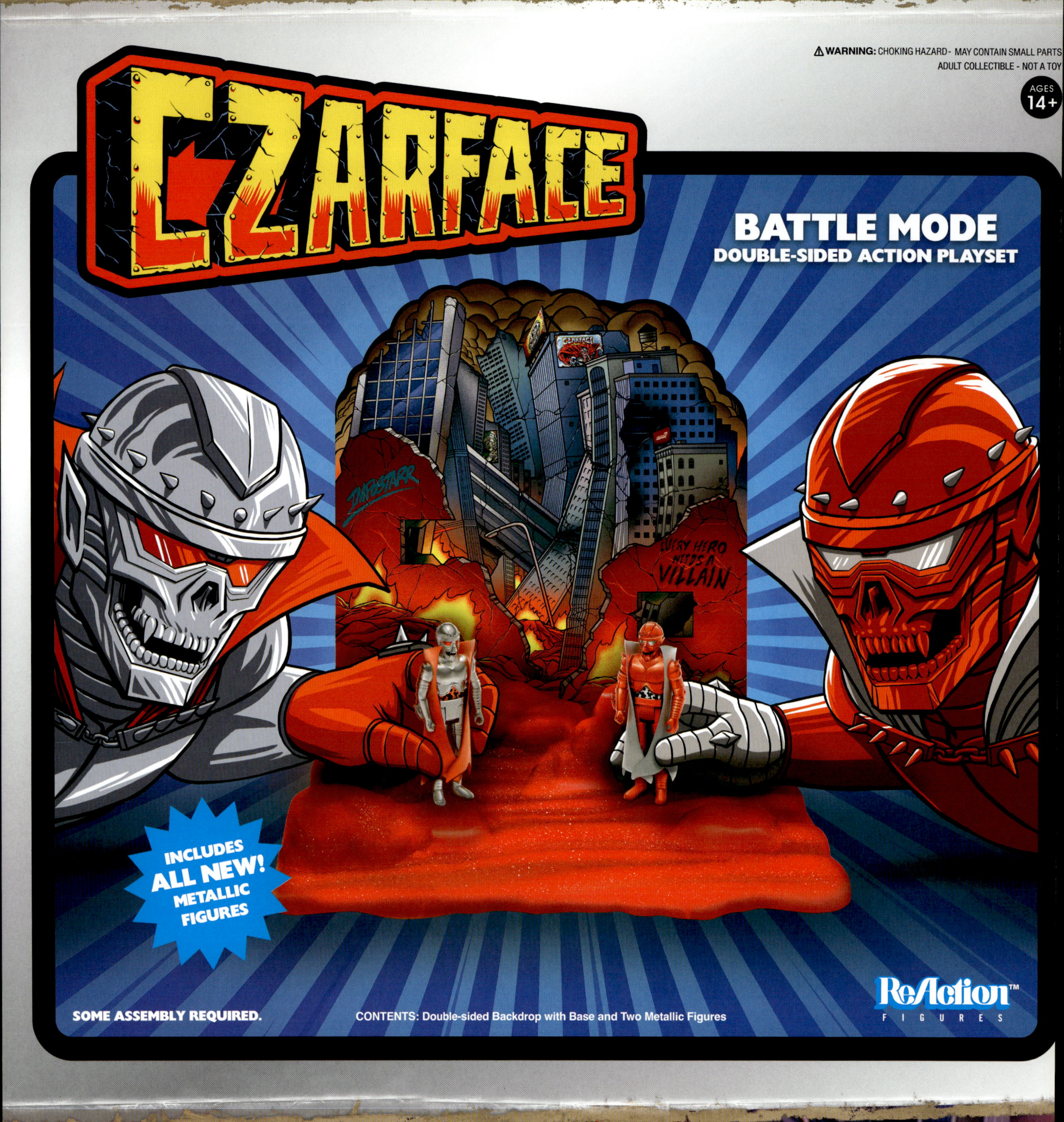

⚠ WARNING: CHOKING HAZARD - MAY CONTAIN SMALL PARTS
ADULT COLLECTIBLE - NOT A TOY
AGES 14+

CZARFACE

BATTLE MODE
DOUBLE-SIDED ACTION PLAYSET

EVERY HERO NEEDS A VILLAIN

INCLUDES ALL NEW! METALLIC FIGURES

SOME ASSEMBLY REQUIRED.

CONTENTS: Double-sided Backdrop with Base and Two Metallic Figures

ReAction™ FIGURES

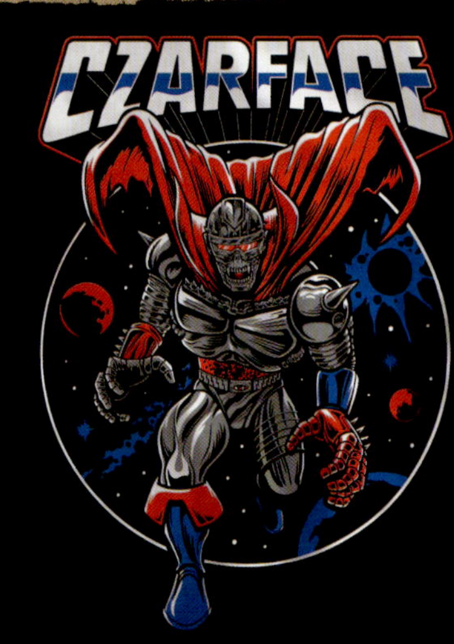

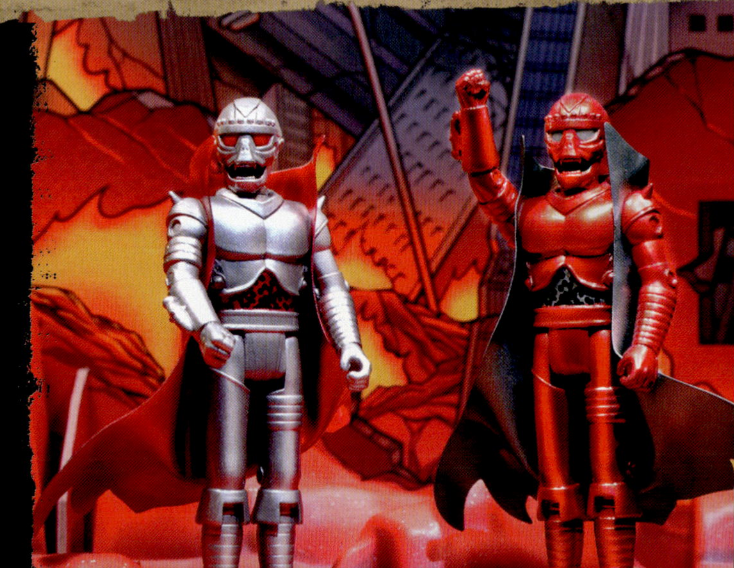

THIS PAGE: Czarface ReAction Figures™ playset and apparel

RIGHT: Selected Czarface™ ReAction Figures™ card art

™ & © CZARFACE

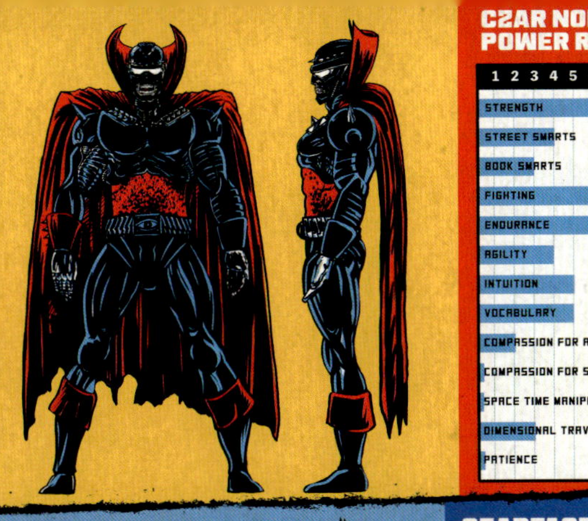

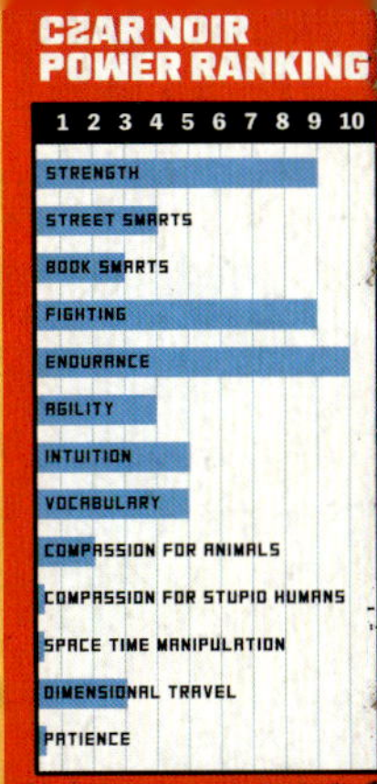

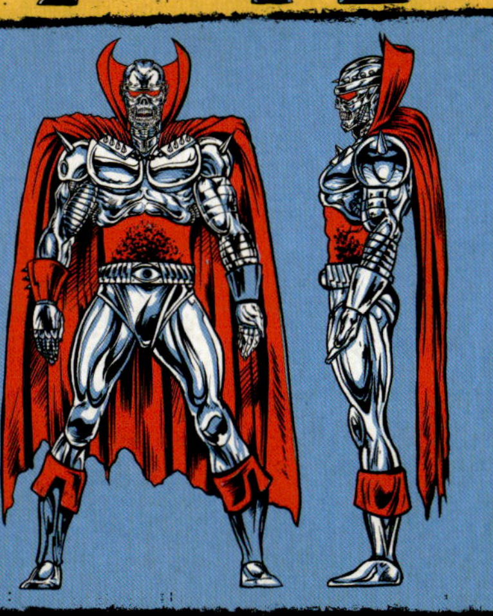

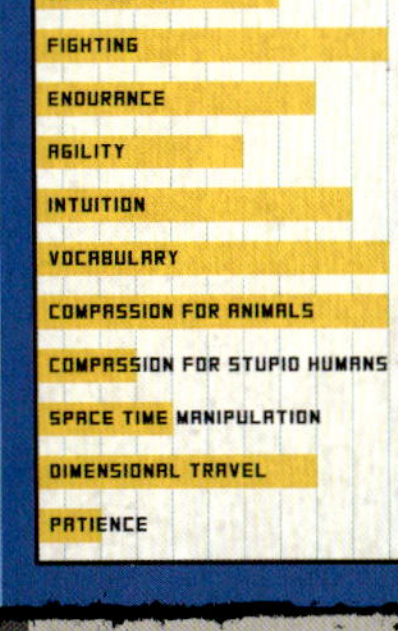

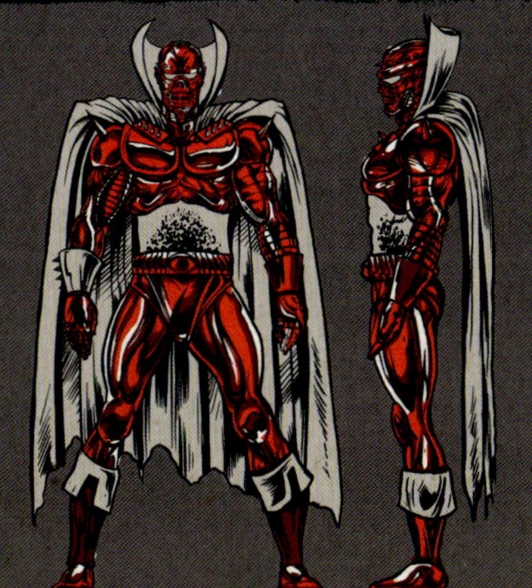

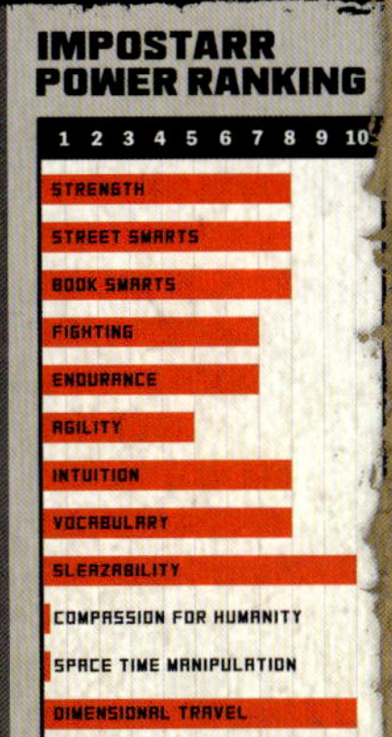

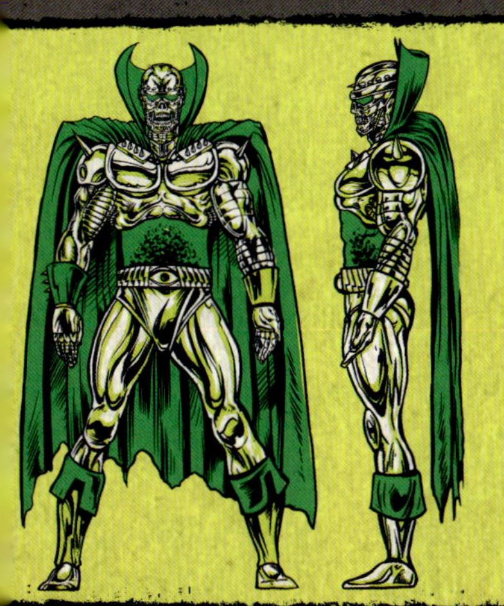

CZARFACE
POWER RANKING
1 2 3 4 5 6 7 8 9 10
STRENGTH
STREET SMARTS
BOOK SMARTS
FIGHTING
ENDURANCE
AGILITY
INTUITION
VOCABULARY
COMPASSION FOR ANIMALS
COMPASSION FOR STUPID HUMANS
SPACE TIME MANIPULATION
DIMENSIONAL TRAVEL
PATIENCE

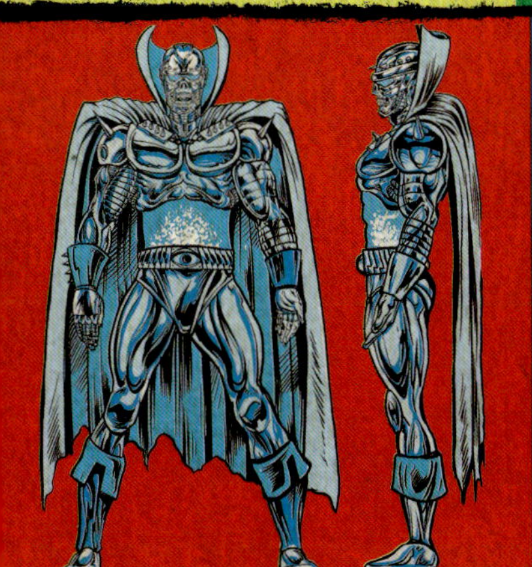

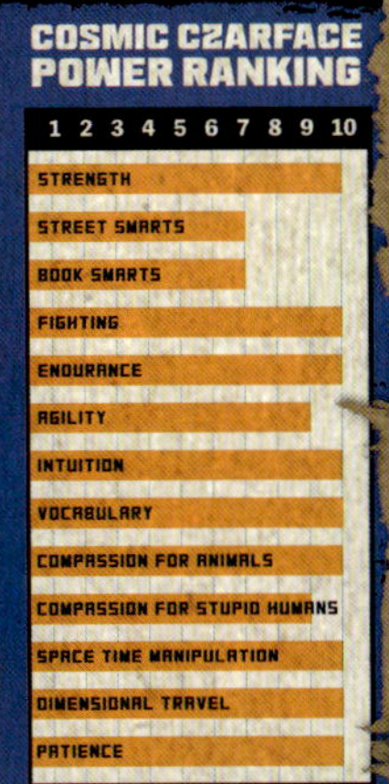

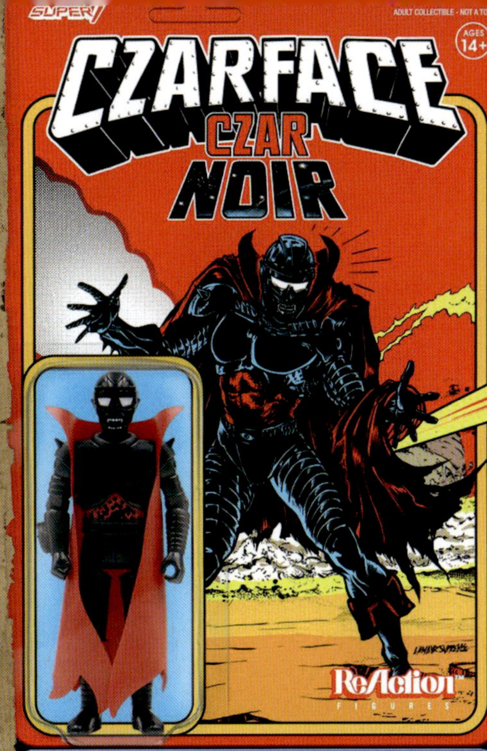

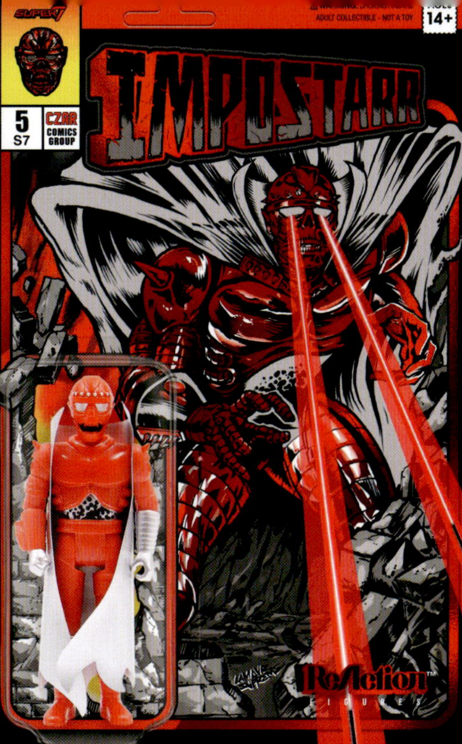

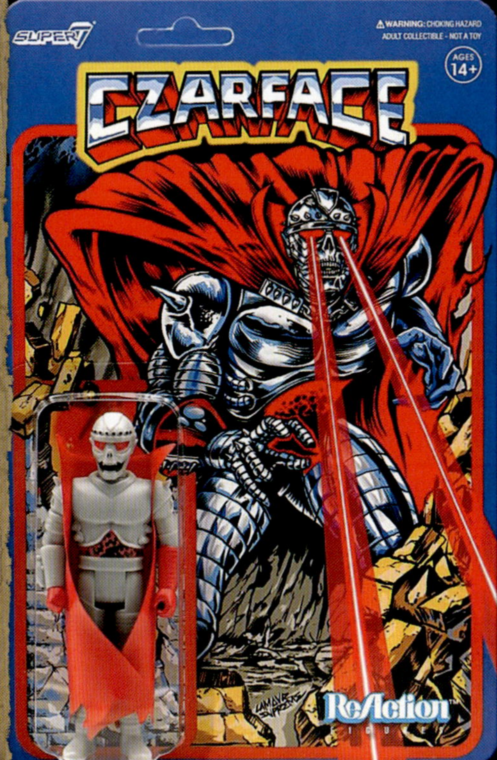

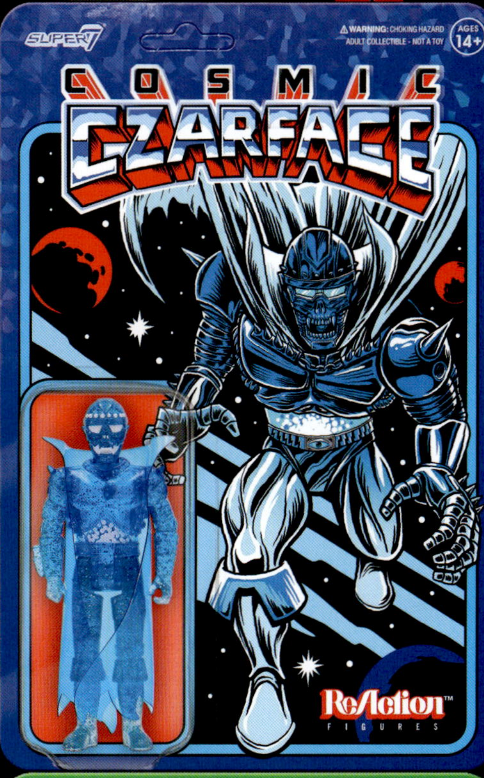

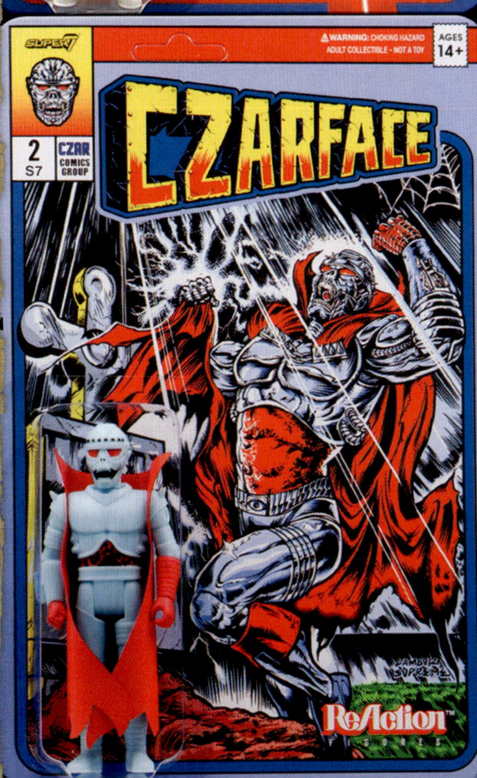

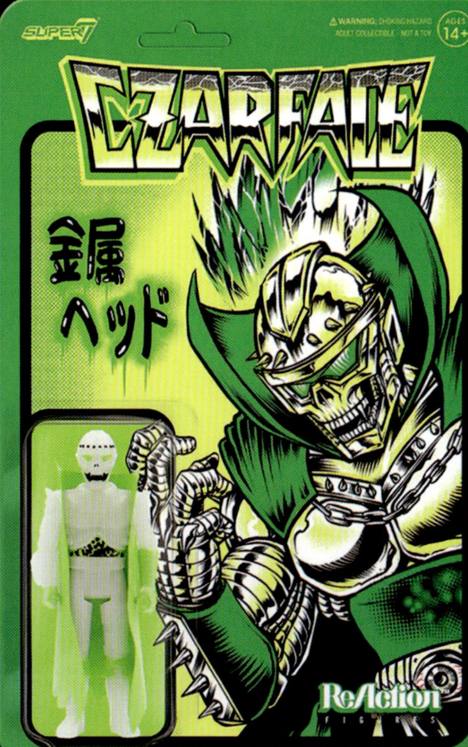

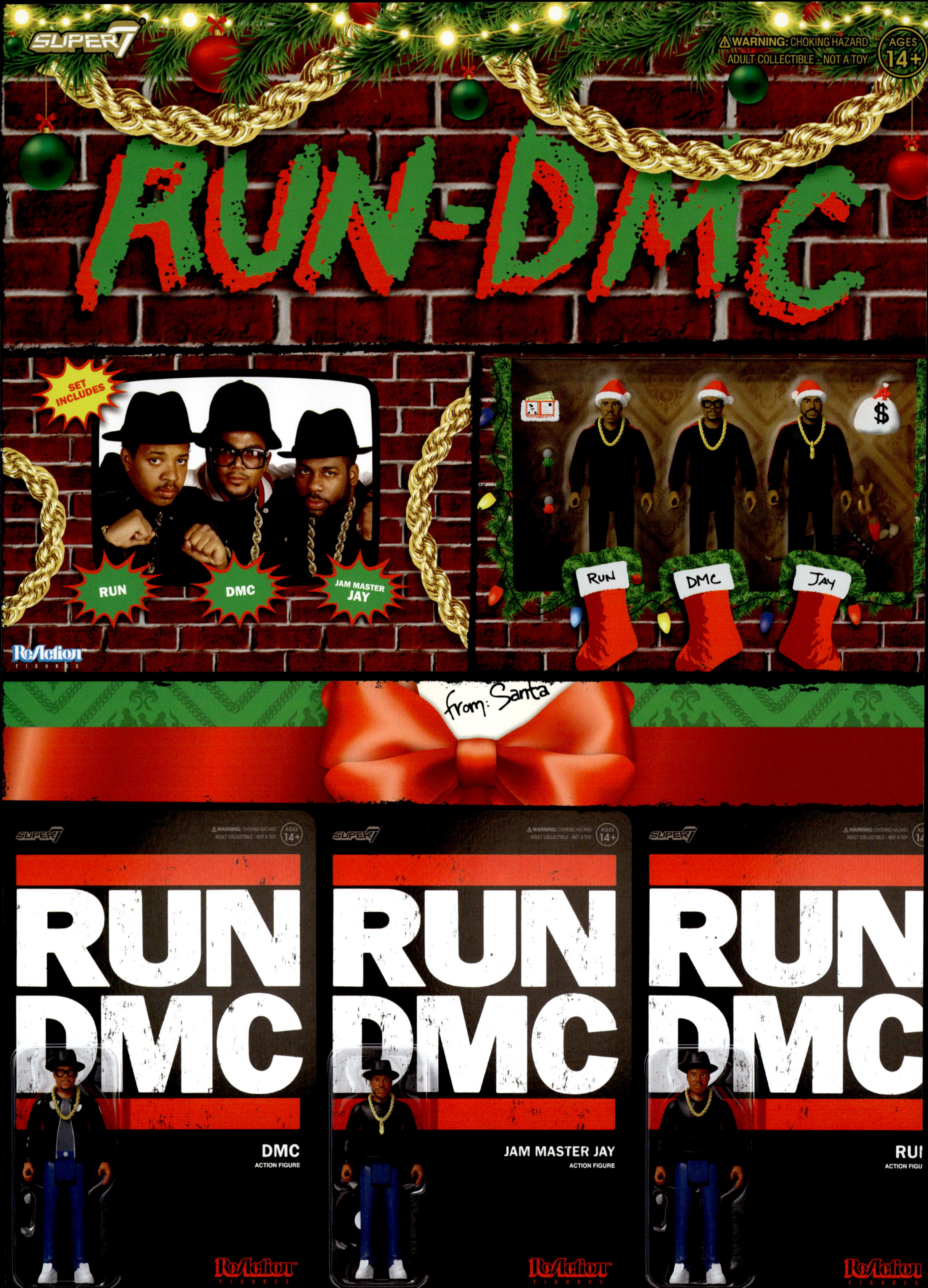

SUPER7

⚠ WARNING: CHOKING HAZARD
ADULT COLLECTIBLE - NOT A TOY
AGES 14+

RUN-DMC

SET INCLUDES

RUN

DMC

JAM MASTER JAY

ReAction FIGURES

RUN

DMC

JAY

from: Santa

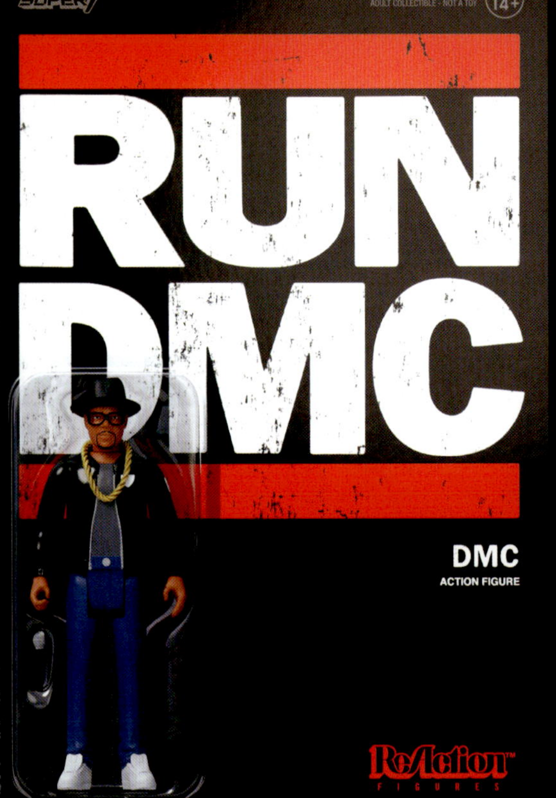

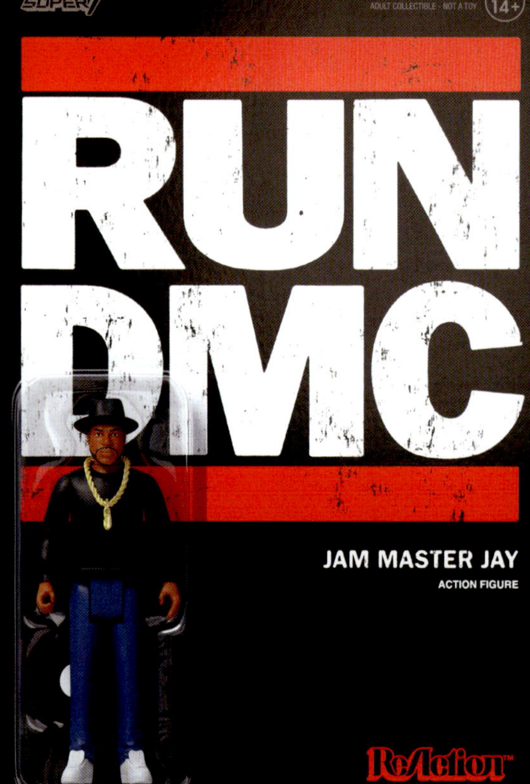

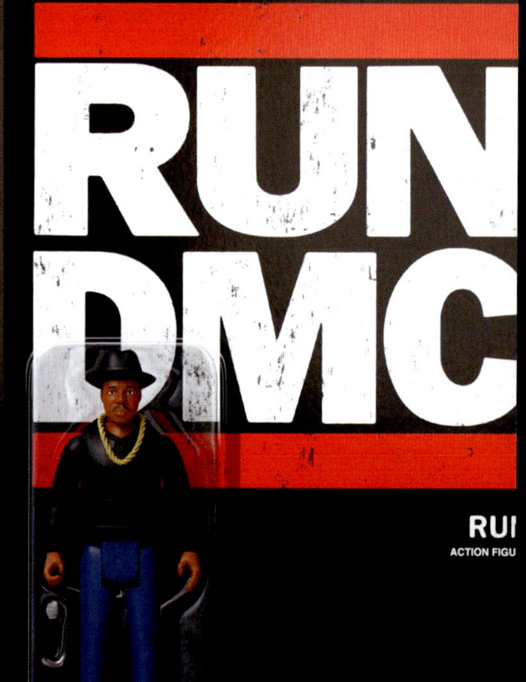

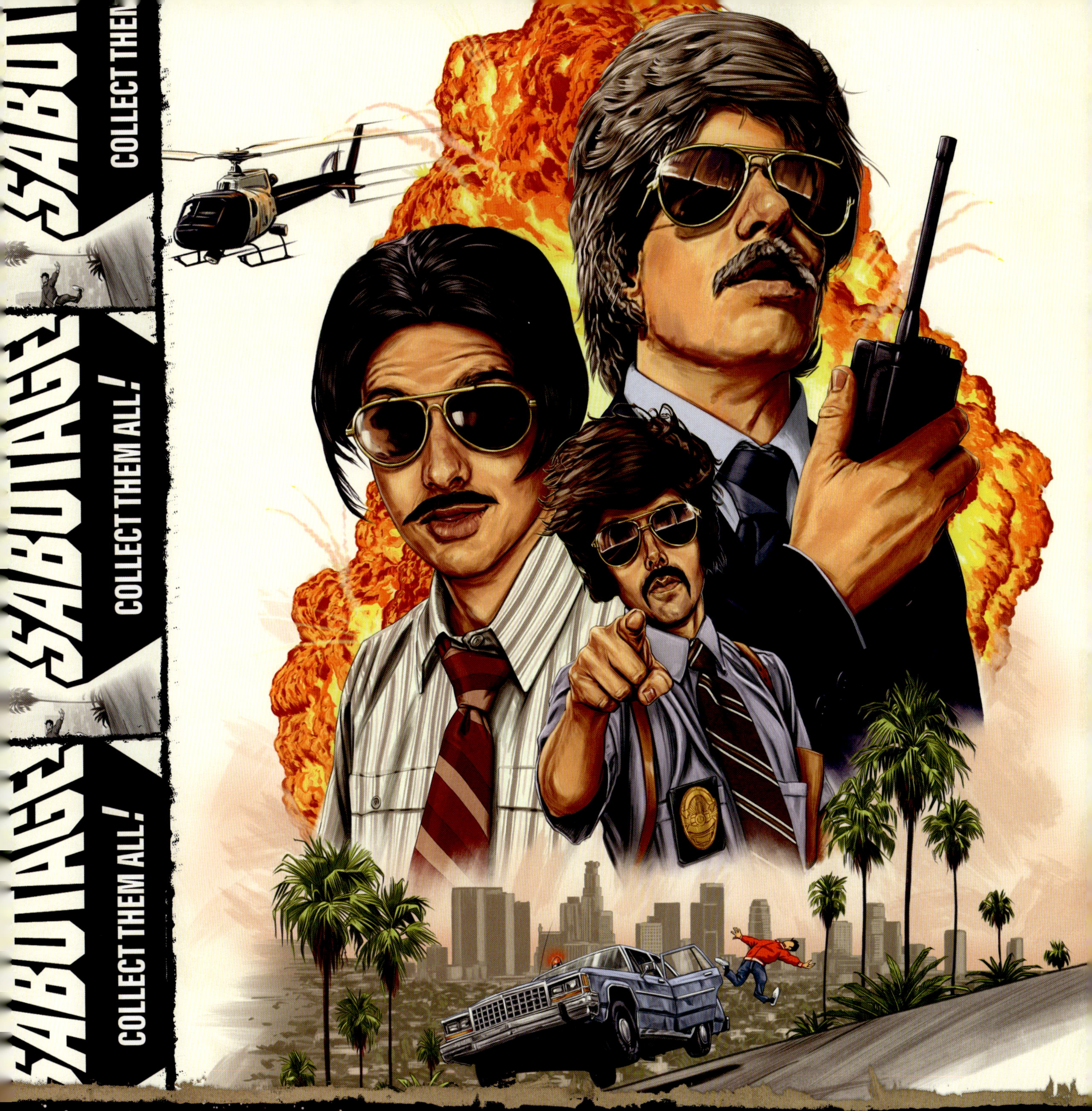

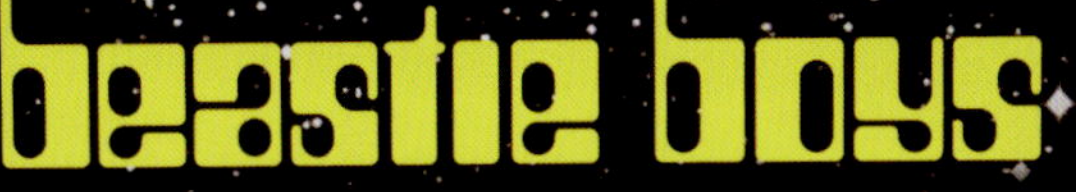

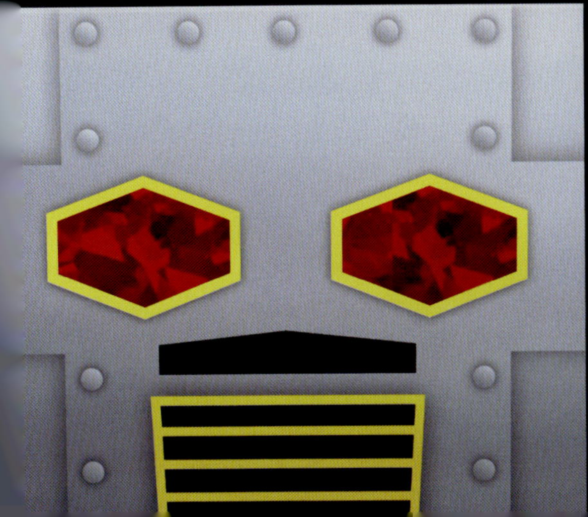

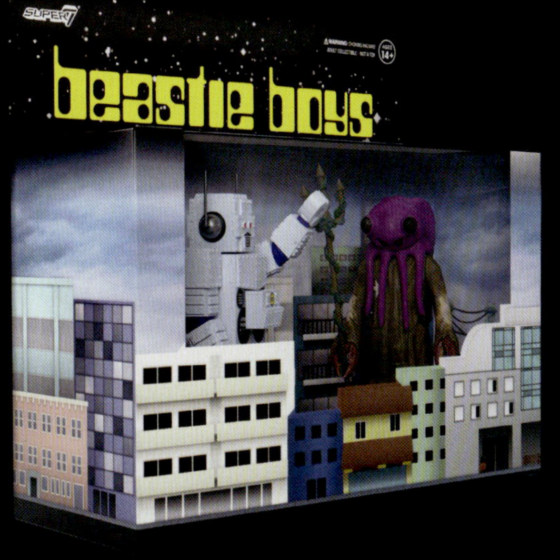

LEFT: Run DMC ReAction Figures™ card art and Holiday 3-pack box

THIS PAGE: Beastie Boys ReAction Figures™ card art and Intergalactic 2-pack box

© 2025 Run DMC

© 2025 Beastie Boys

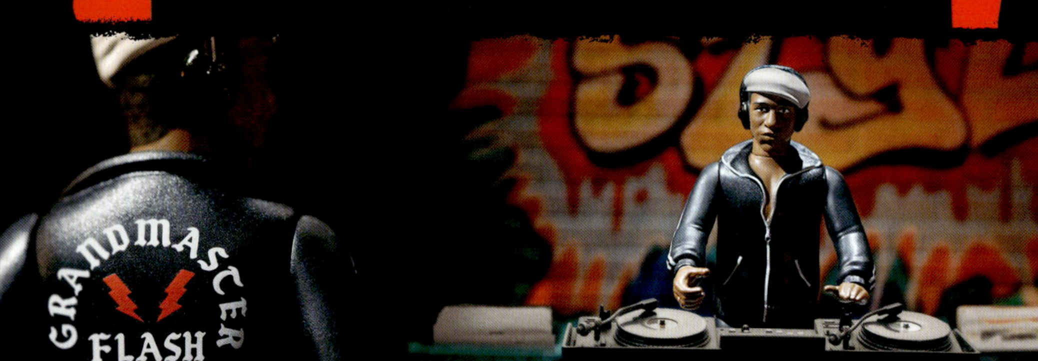

GM

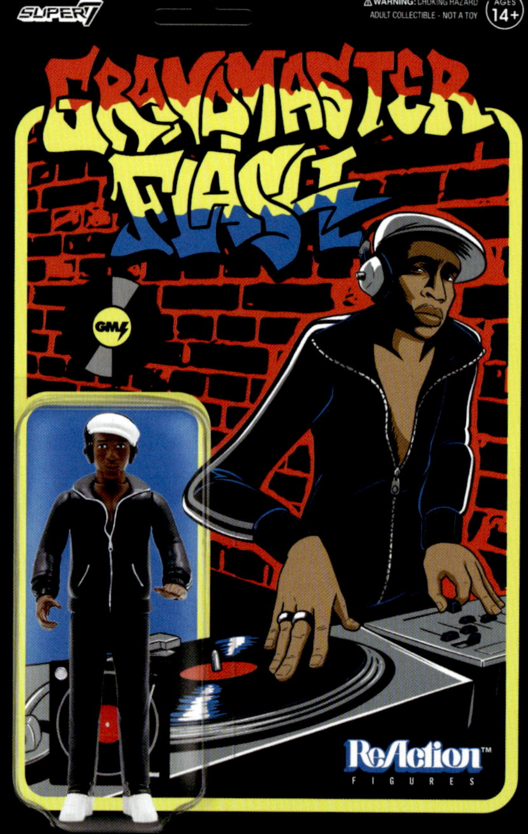

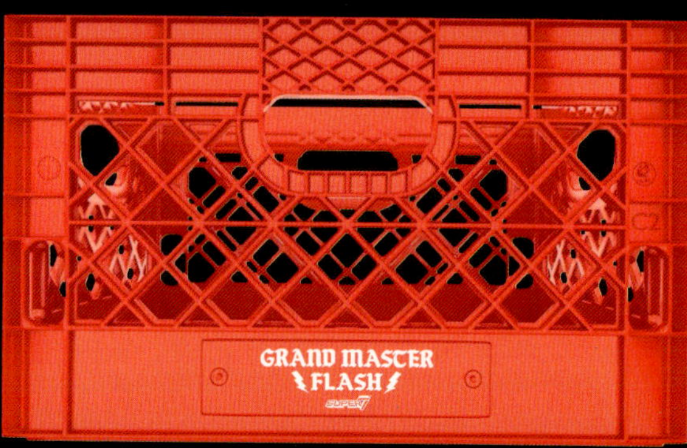

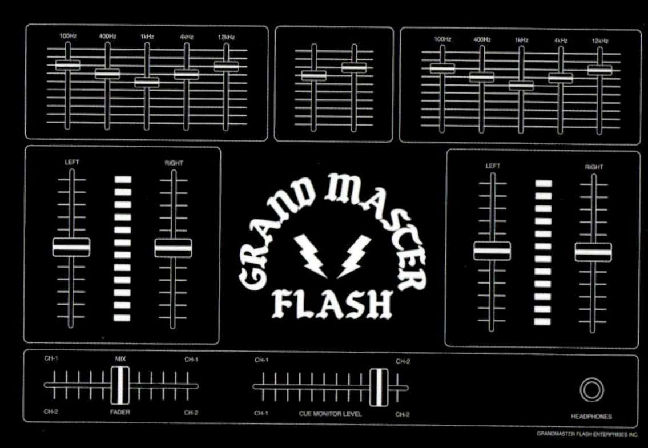

THIS PAGE: Grandmaster Flash ReAction Figures™ card art and box set

RIGHT: Selected Ol' Dirty Bastard ReAction Figures™ card art

© 2025 Grandmaster Flash Enterprises, Inc. All Rights Reserved.

Ol' Dirty Bastard ™ © 2025 Ol' Dirty Bastard. All Rights Reserved.

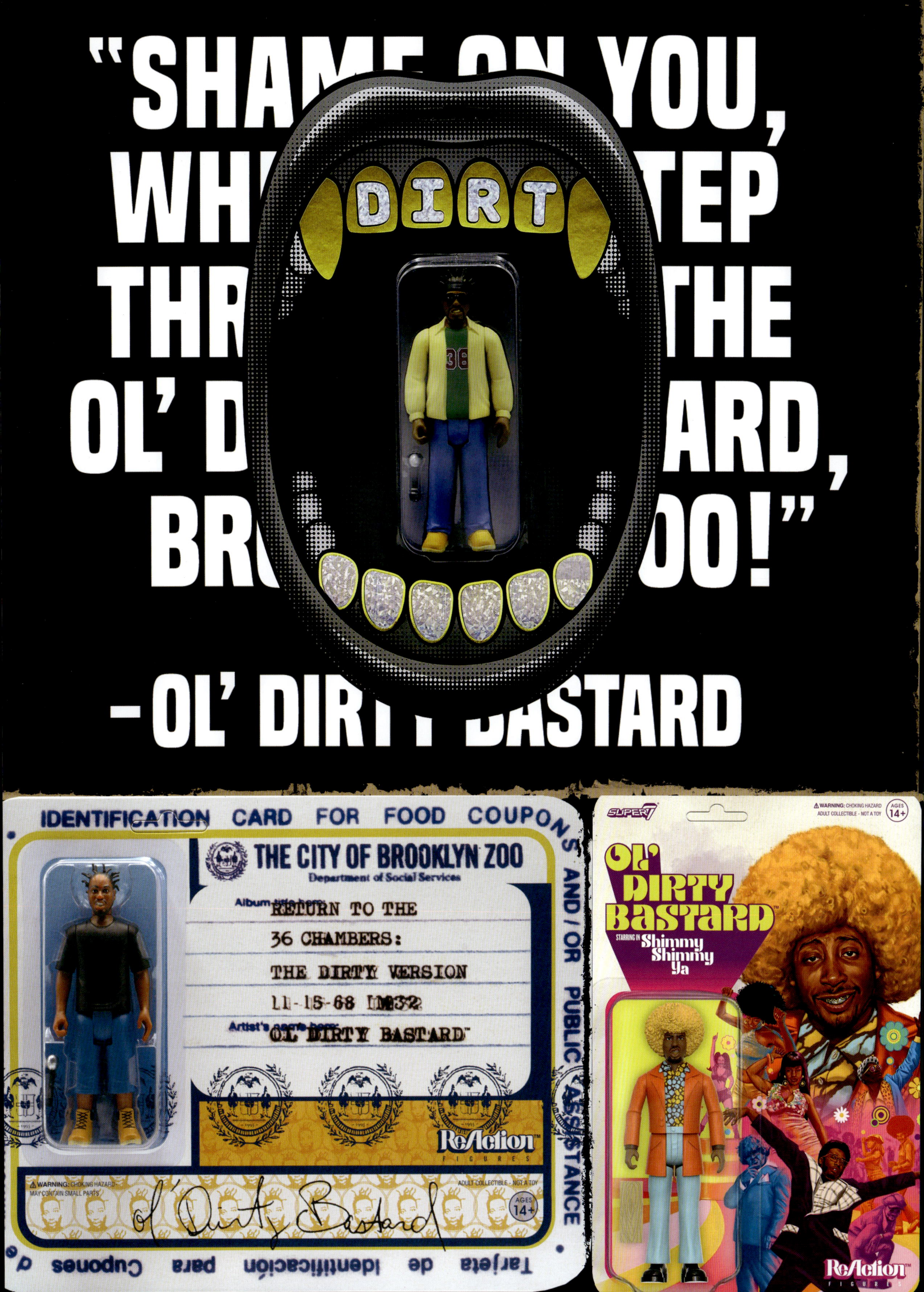

"SHAM... ON YOU,
WH... TEP
THR... THE
OL' D... ARD,
BR... OO!"

-OL' DIRT... BASTARD

DIRT

IDENTIFICATION CARD FOR FOOD COUPONS AND/OR PUBLIC ASSISTANCE

THE CITY OF BROOKLYN ZOO
Department of Social Services

Album title here: RETURN TO THE
36 CHAMBERS:
THE DIRTY VERSION
11-15-68

Artist's name here: OL' DIRTY BASTARD

ReAction FIGURES

WARNING: CHOKING HAZARD
MAY CONTAIN SMALL PARTS

ADULT COLLECTIBLE - NOT A TOY
AGES 14+

Ol' Dirty Bastard

Tarjeta de Identificación para Cupones de

SUPER7
WARNING: CHOKING HAZARD
ADULT COLLECTIBLE - NOT A TOY
AGES 14+

OL' DIRTY BASTARD
STARRING IN Shimmy Shimmy Ya

ReAction FIGURES

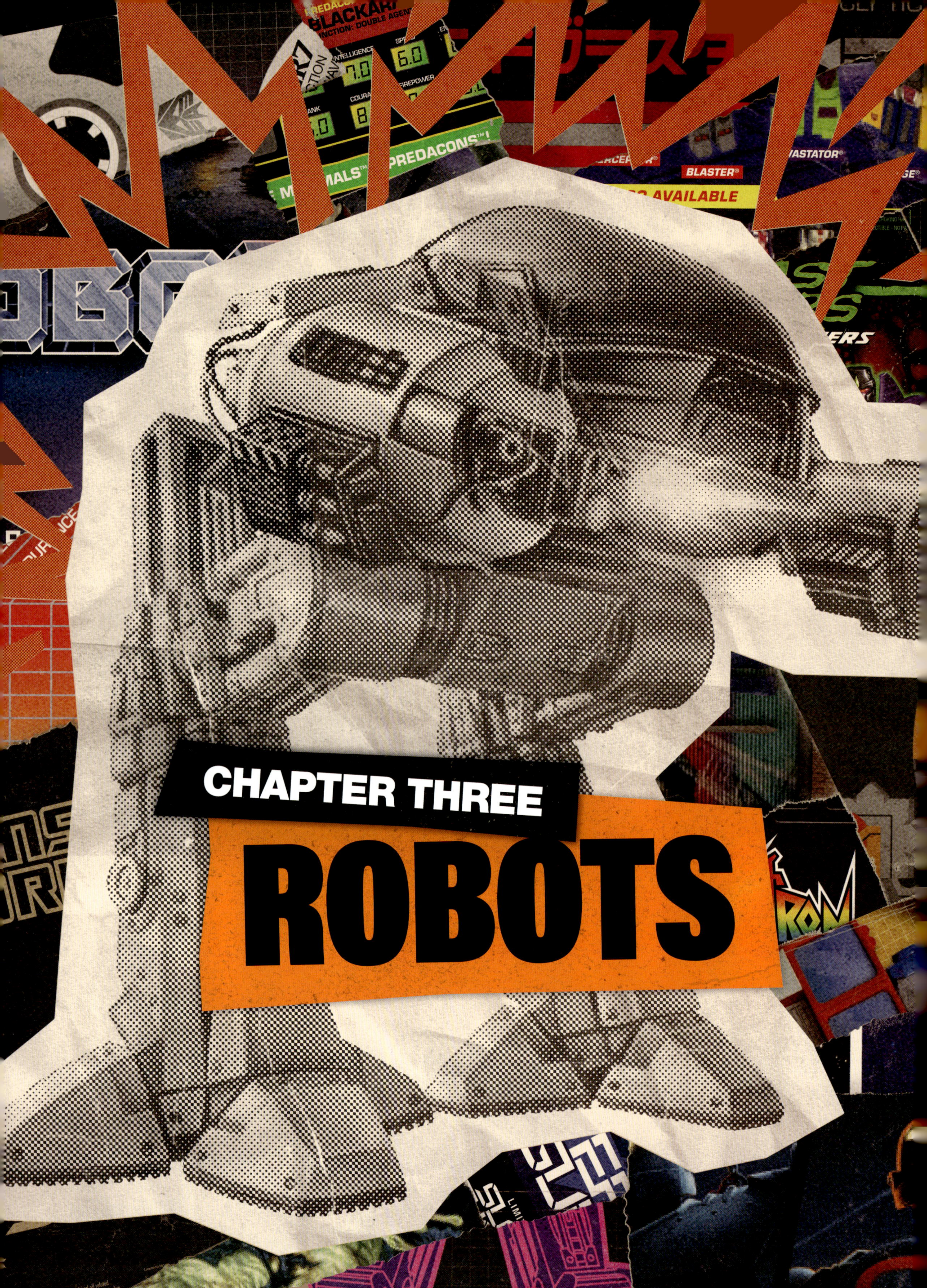

CHAPTER THREE
ROBOTS

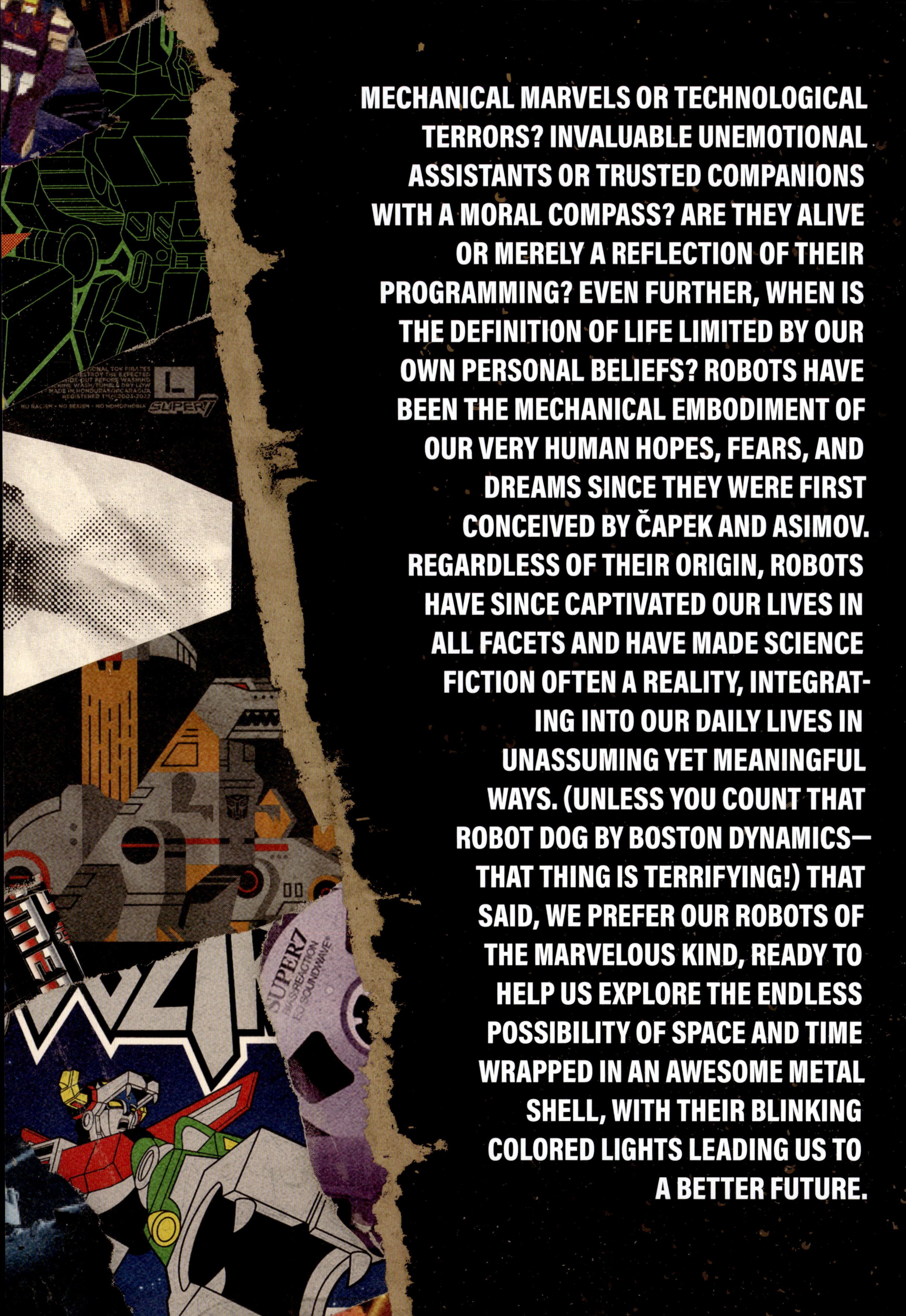

MECHANICAL MARVELS OR TECHNOLOGICAL TERRORS? INVALUABLE UNEMOTIONAL ASSISTANTS OR TRUSTED COMPANIONS WITH A MORAL COMPASS? ARE THEY ALIVE OR MERELY A REFLECTION OF THEIR PROGRAMMING? EVEN FURTHER, WHEN IS THE DEFINITION OF LIFE LIMITED BY OUR OWN PERSONAL BELIEFS? ROBOTS HAVE BEEN THE MECHANICAL EMBODIMENT OF OUR VERY HUMAN HOPES, FEARS, AND DREAMS SINCE THEY WERE FIRST CONCEIVED BY ČAPEK AND ASIMOV. REGARDLESS OF THEIR ORIGIN, ROBOTS HAVE SINCE CAPTIVATED OUR LIVES IN ALL FACETS AND HAVE MADE SCIENCE FICTION OFTEN A REALITY, INTEGRATING INTO OUR DAILY LIVES IN UNASSUMING YET MEANINGFUL WAYS. (UNLESS YOU COUNT THAT ROBOT DOG BY BOSTON DYNAMICS—THAT THING IS TERRIFYING!) THAT SAID, WE PREFER OUR ROBOTS OF THE MARVELOUS KIND, READY TO HELP US EXPLORE THE ENDLESS POSSIBILITY OF SPACE AND TIME WRAPPED IN AN AWESOME METAL SHELL, WITH THEIR BLINKING COLORED LIGHTS LEADING US TO A BETTER FUTURE.

THIS SPREAD: Transformers™ ReAction Figures™ card art

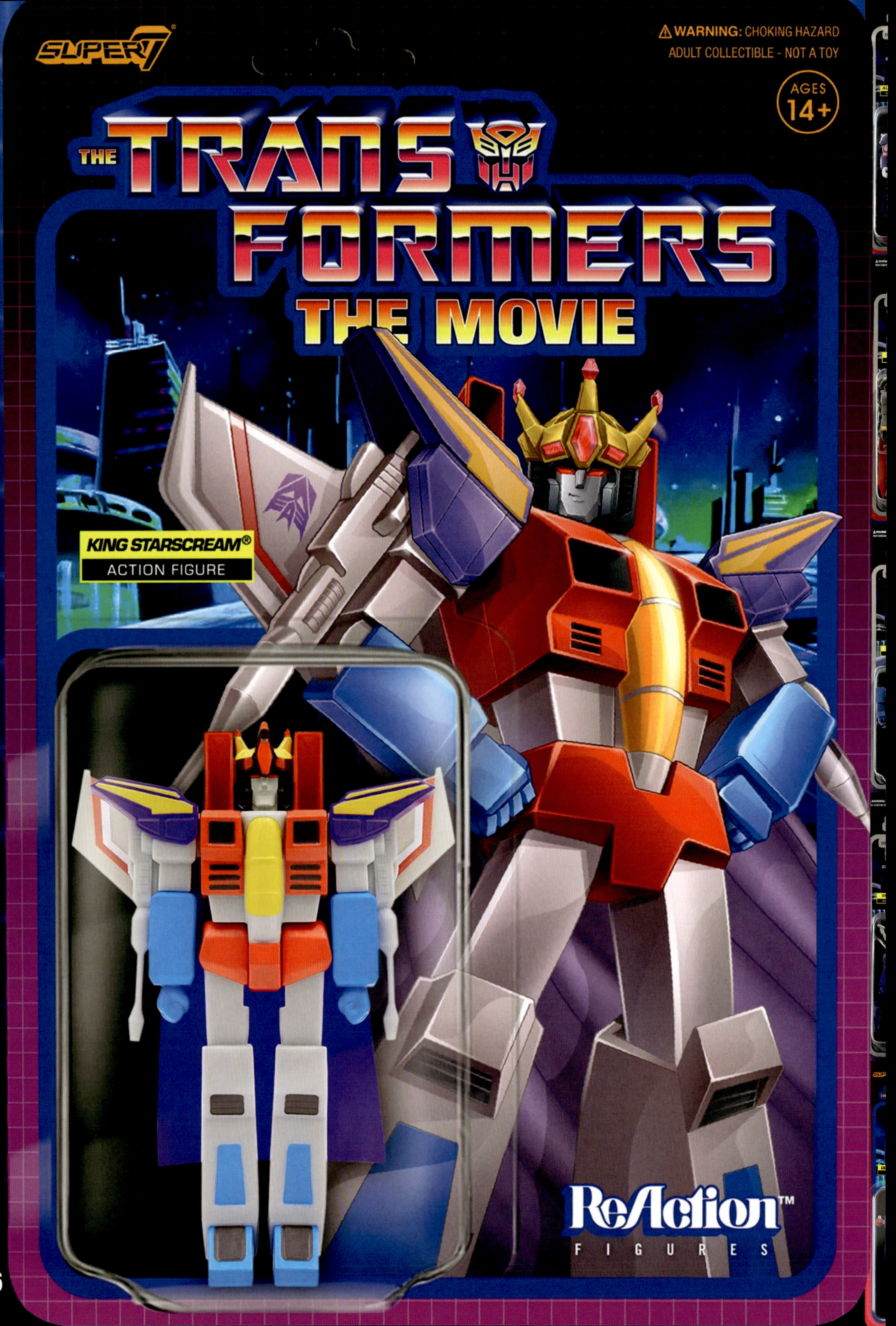

SUPER7

⚠ WARNING: CHOKING HAZARD
ADULT COLLECTIBLE - NOT A TOY

AGES 14+

THE TRANSFORMERS
THE MOVIE

KING STARSCREAM®
ACTION FIGURE

ReAction™
FIGURES

© 2025 HASBRO

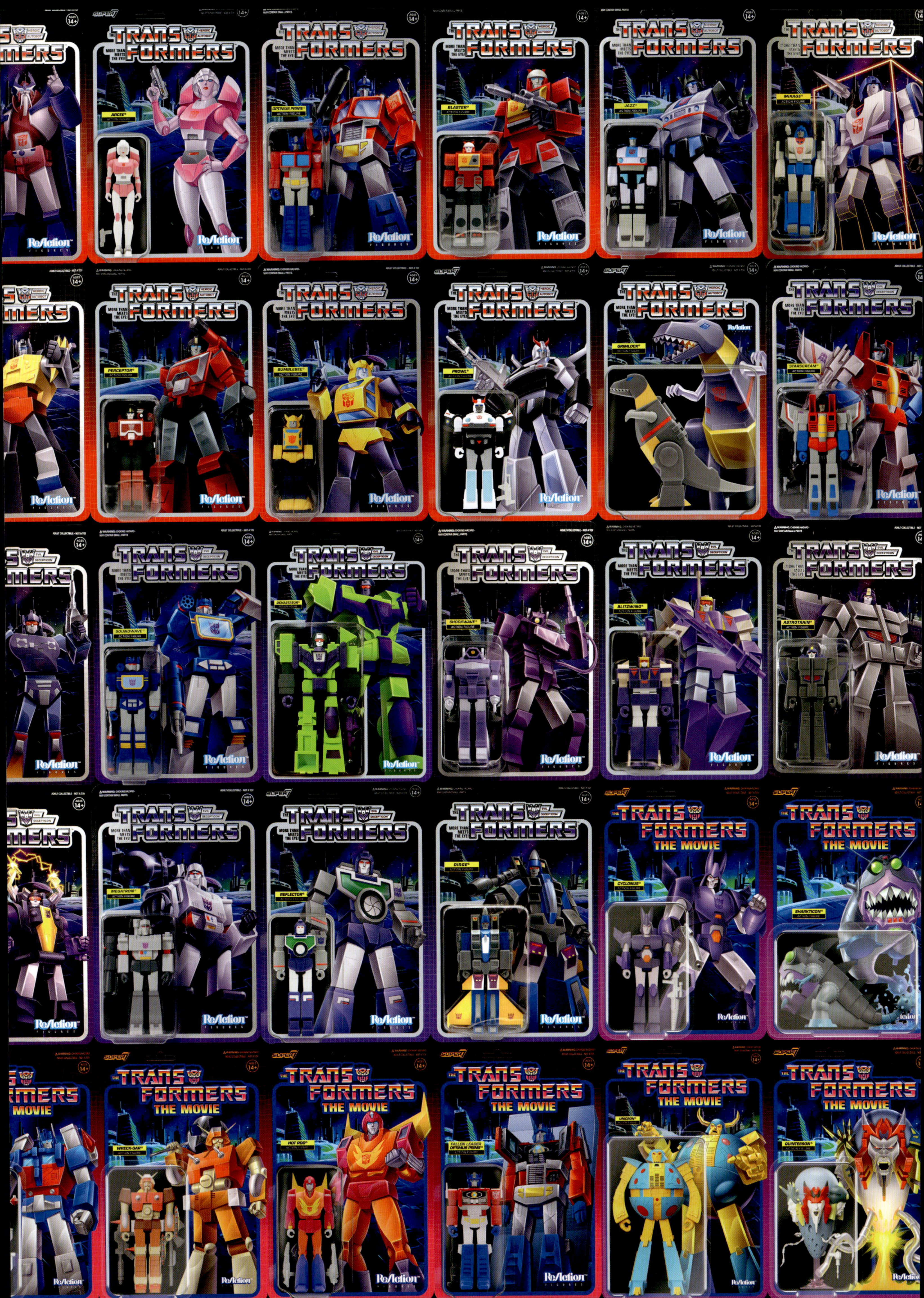

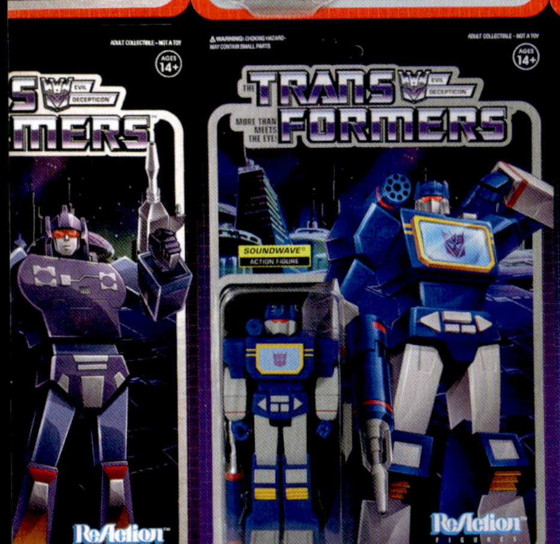
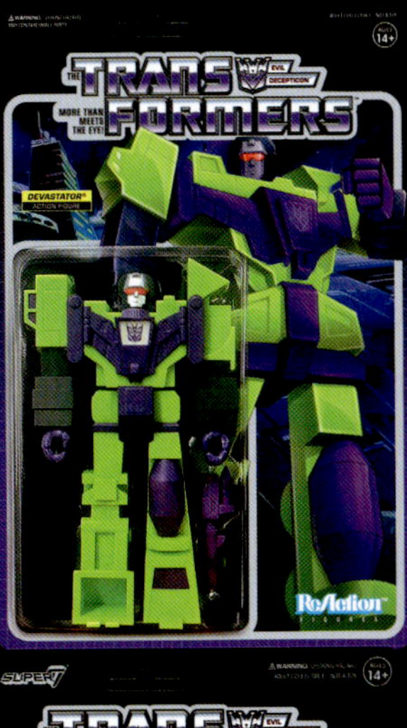
TRANS
FORMERS
SOUNDWAVE
ReAction
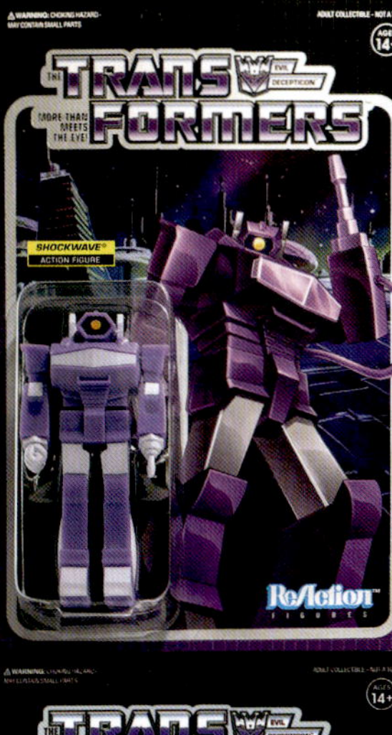
TRANS
FORMERS
DEVASTATOR
ReAction
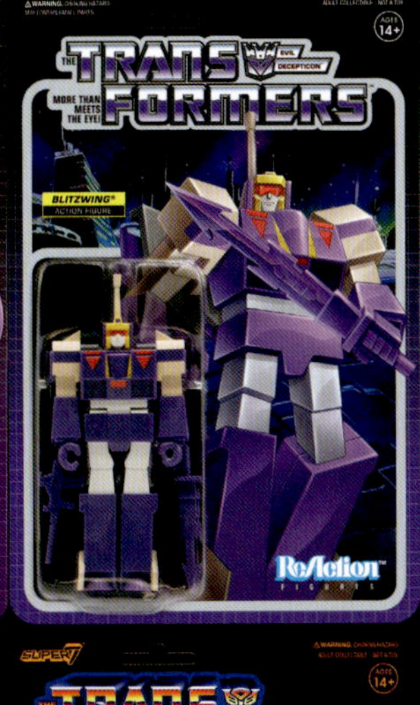
TRANS
FORMERS
SHOCKWAVE
ReAction
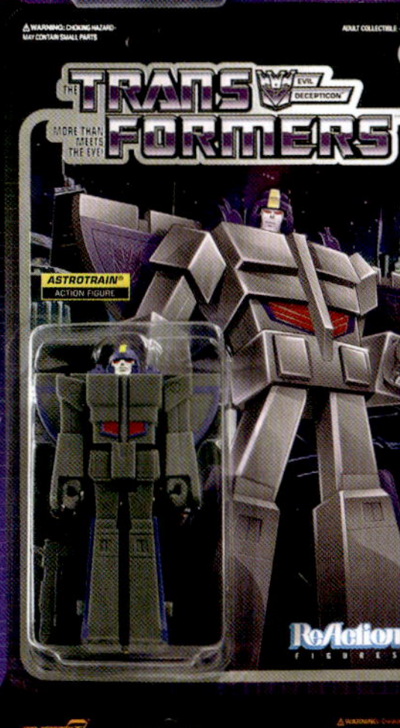
TRANS
FORMERS
BLITZWING
ReAction
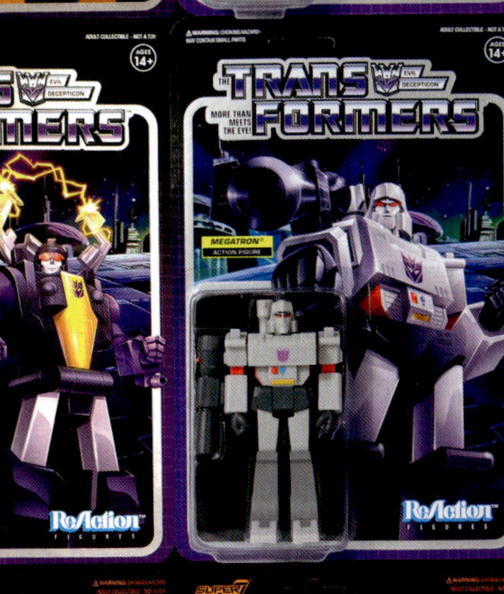
TRANS
FORMERS
MEGATRON
ReAction
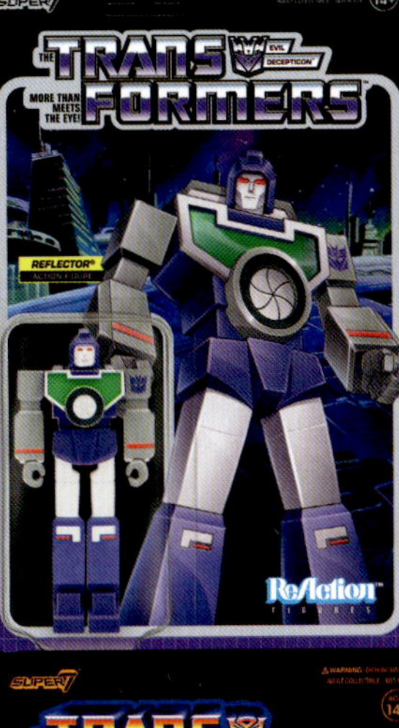
TRANS
FORMERS
REFLECTOR
ReAction
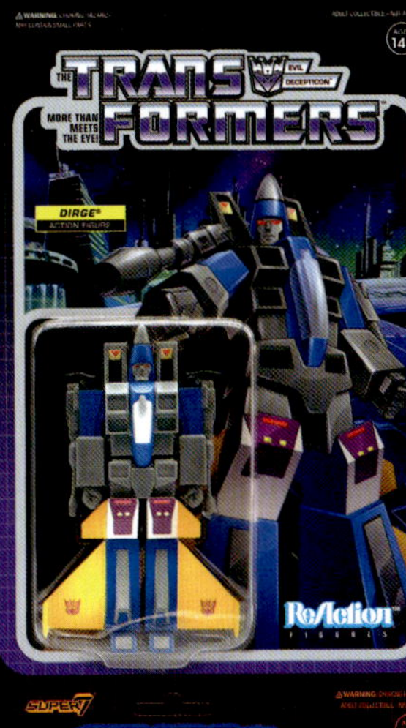
TRANS
FORMERS
DIRGE
ReAction
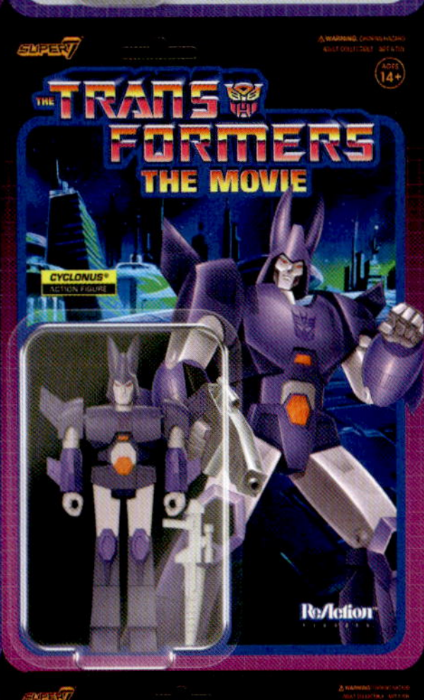
TRANS
FORMERS
THE MOVIE
CYCLONUS
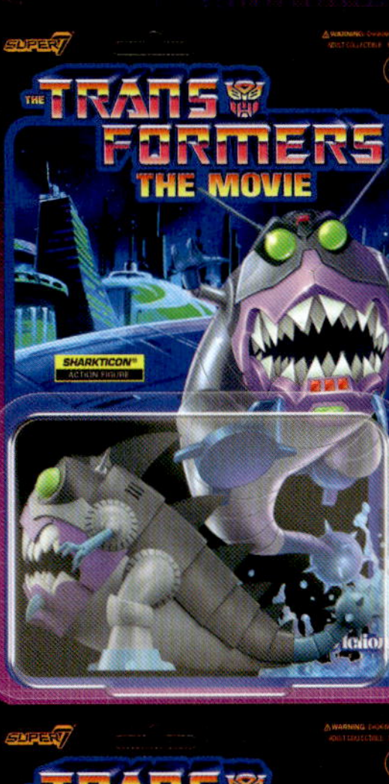
TRANS
FORMERS
THE MOVIE
SHARKTICON
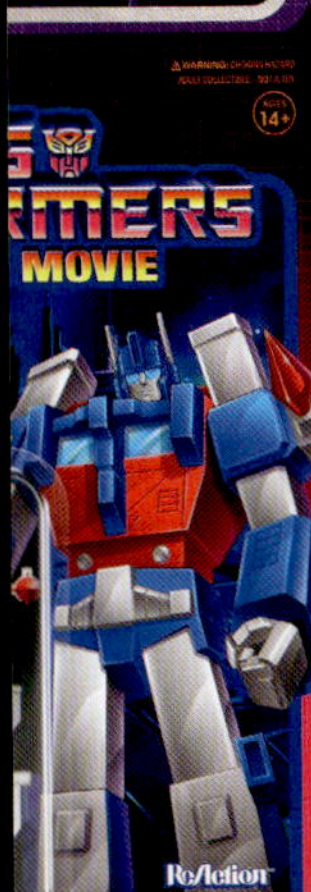
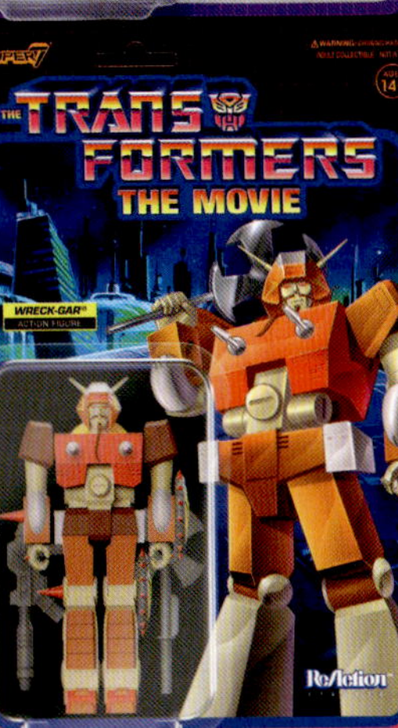
TRANS
FORMERS
THE MOVIE
WRECK-GAR
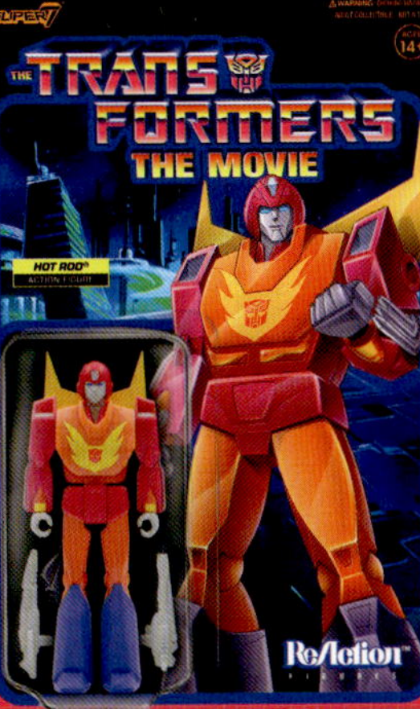
TRANS
FORMERS
THE MOVIE
HOT ROD
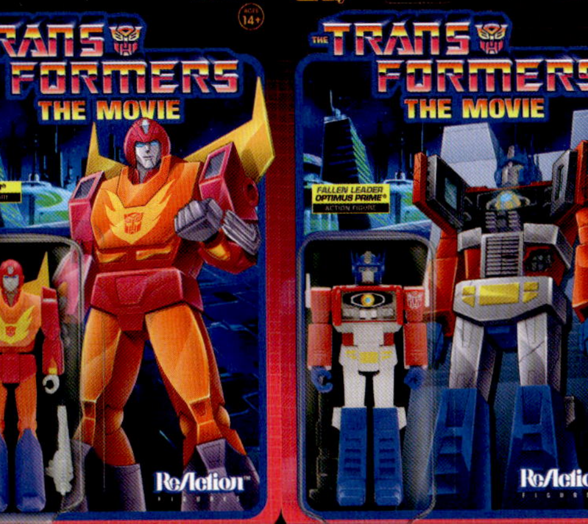
TRANS
FORMERS
THE MOVIE
ReAction
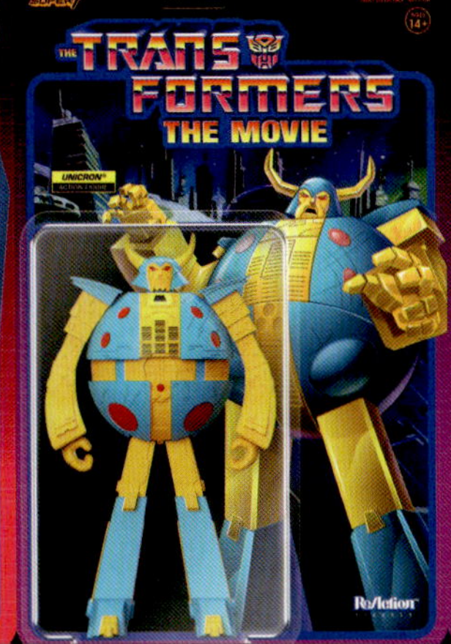
TRANS
FORMERS
THE MOVIE
UNICRON
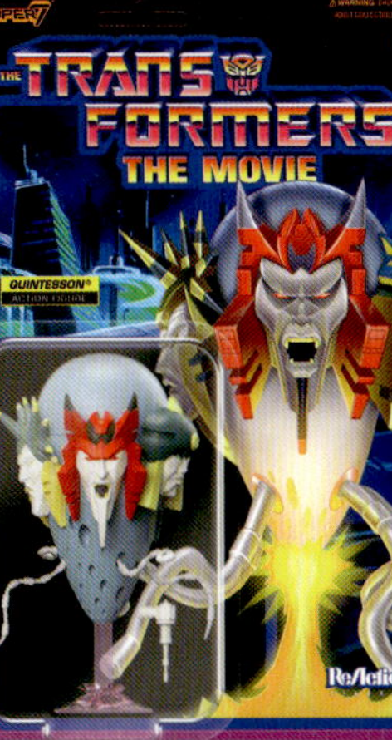
TRANS
FORMERS
THE MOVIE
QUINTESSON

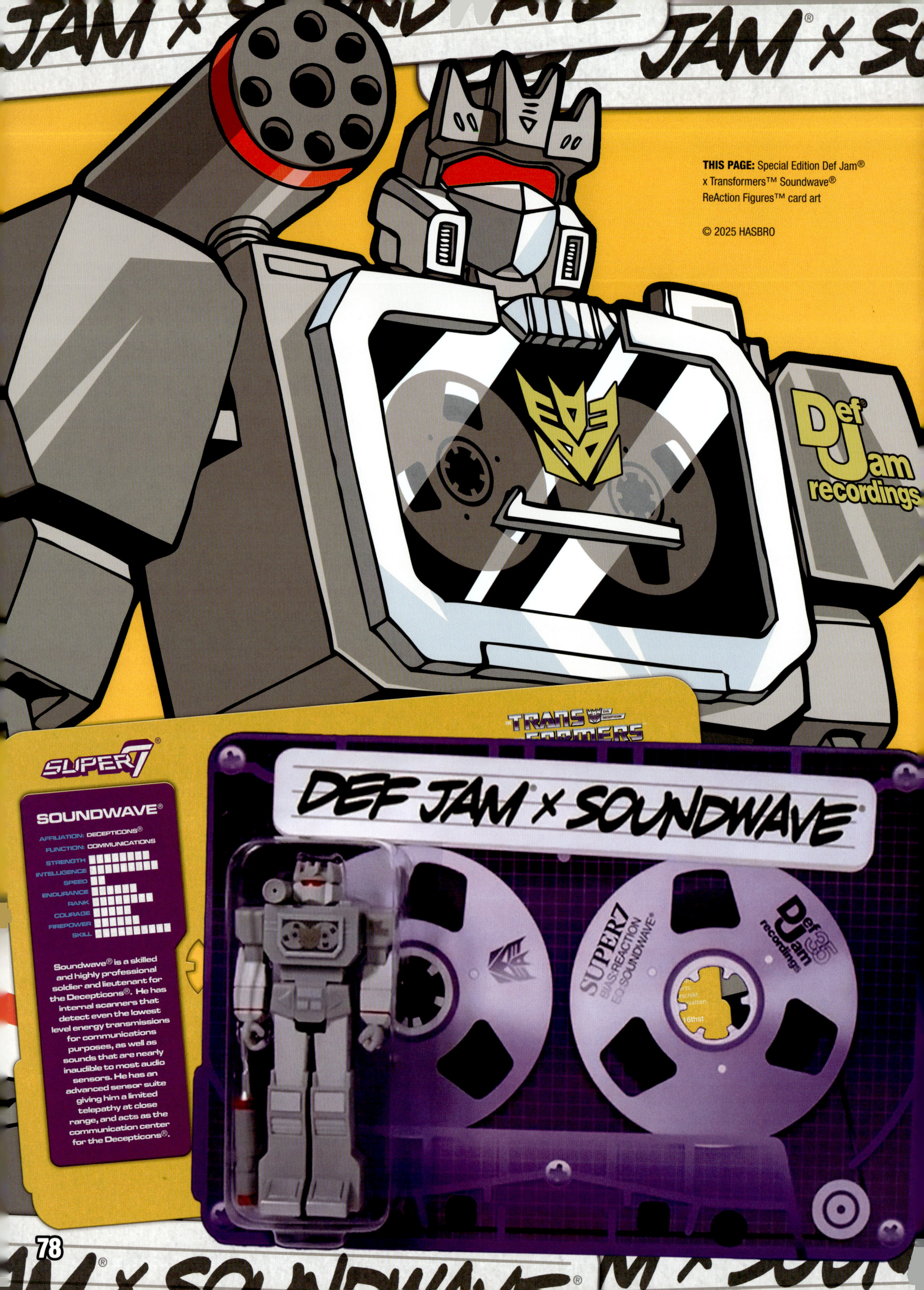

THIS PAGE: Special Edition Def Jam® x Transformers™ Soundwave® ReAction Figures™ card art

© 2025 HASBRO

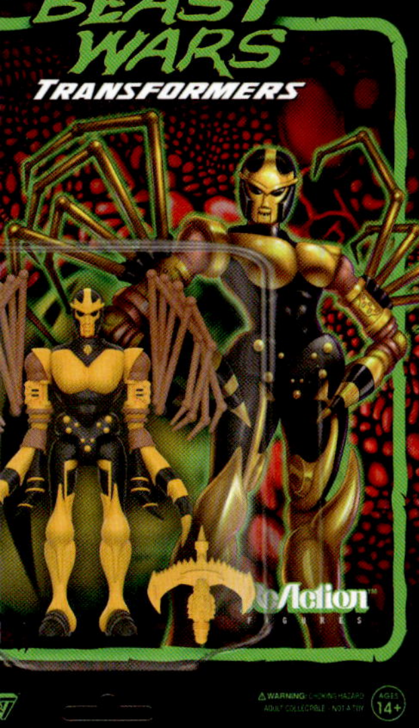

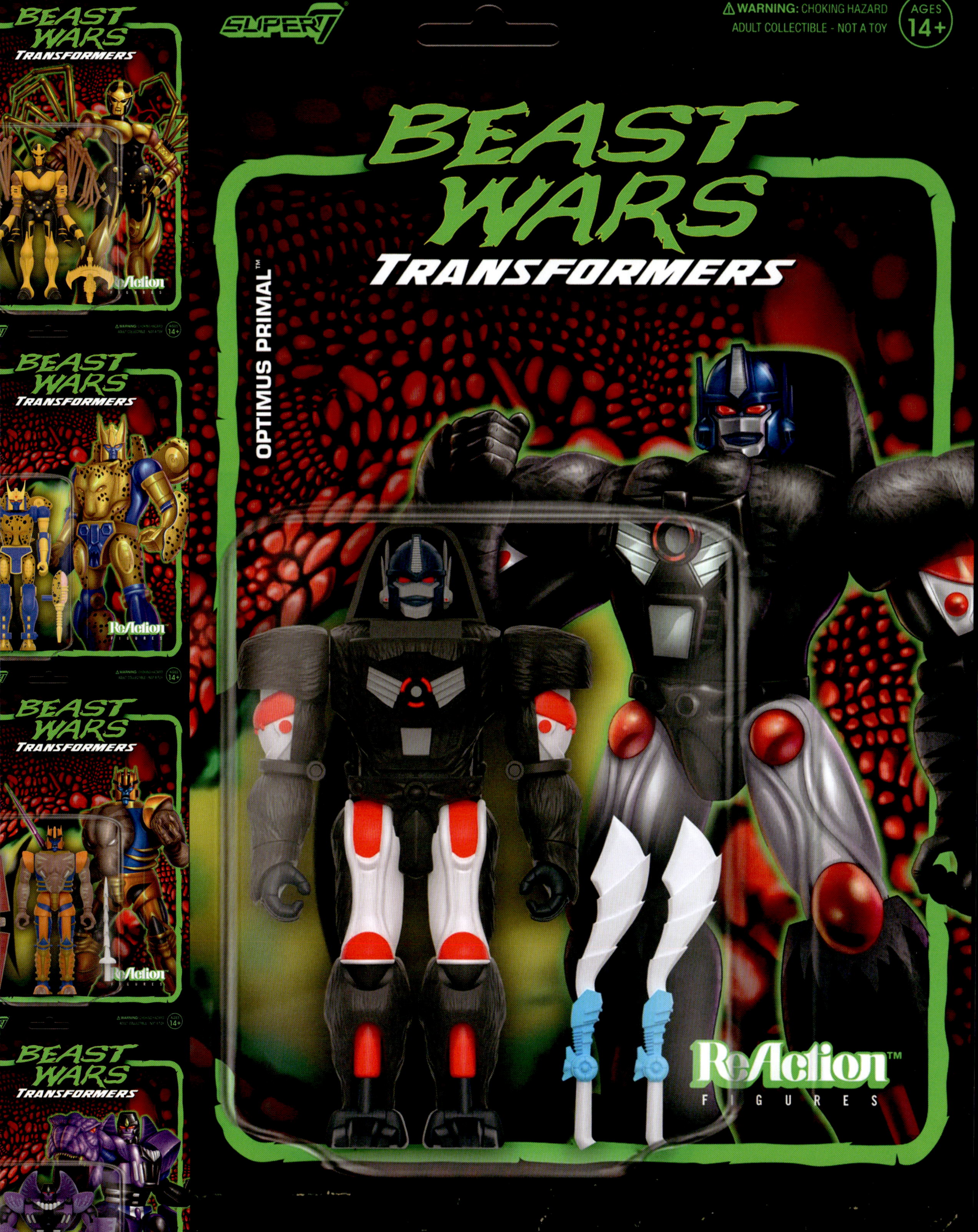

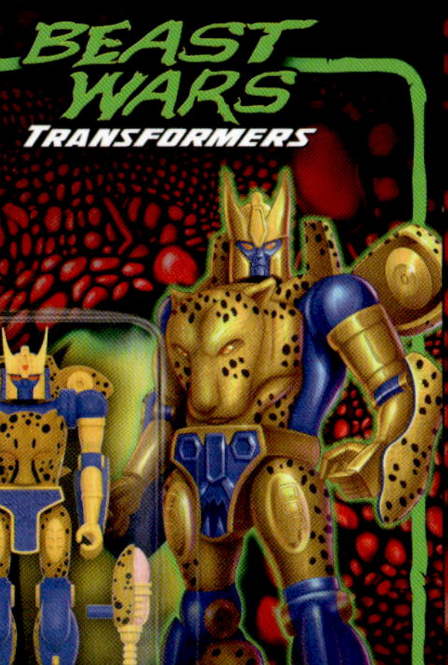

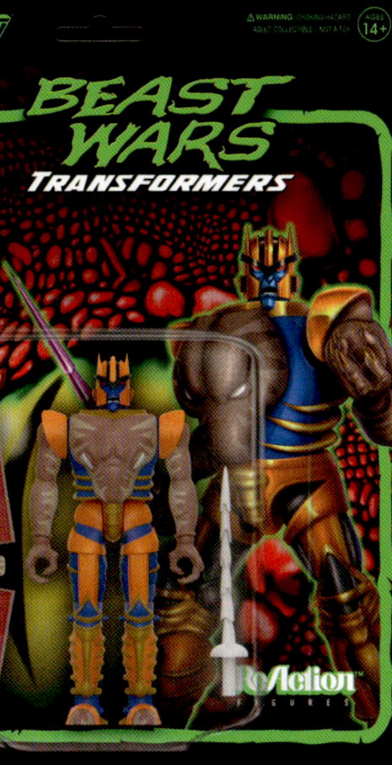

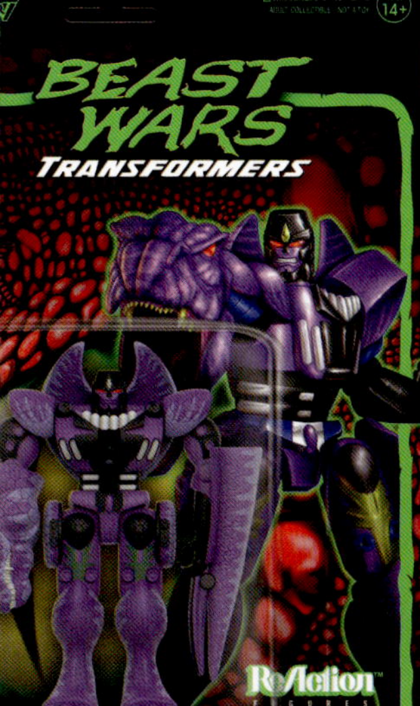

THIS PAGE: Transformers™ Beast Wars ReAction Figures™ card art

© 2025 HASBRO

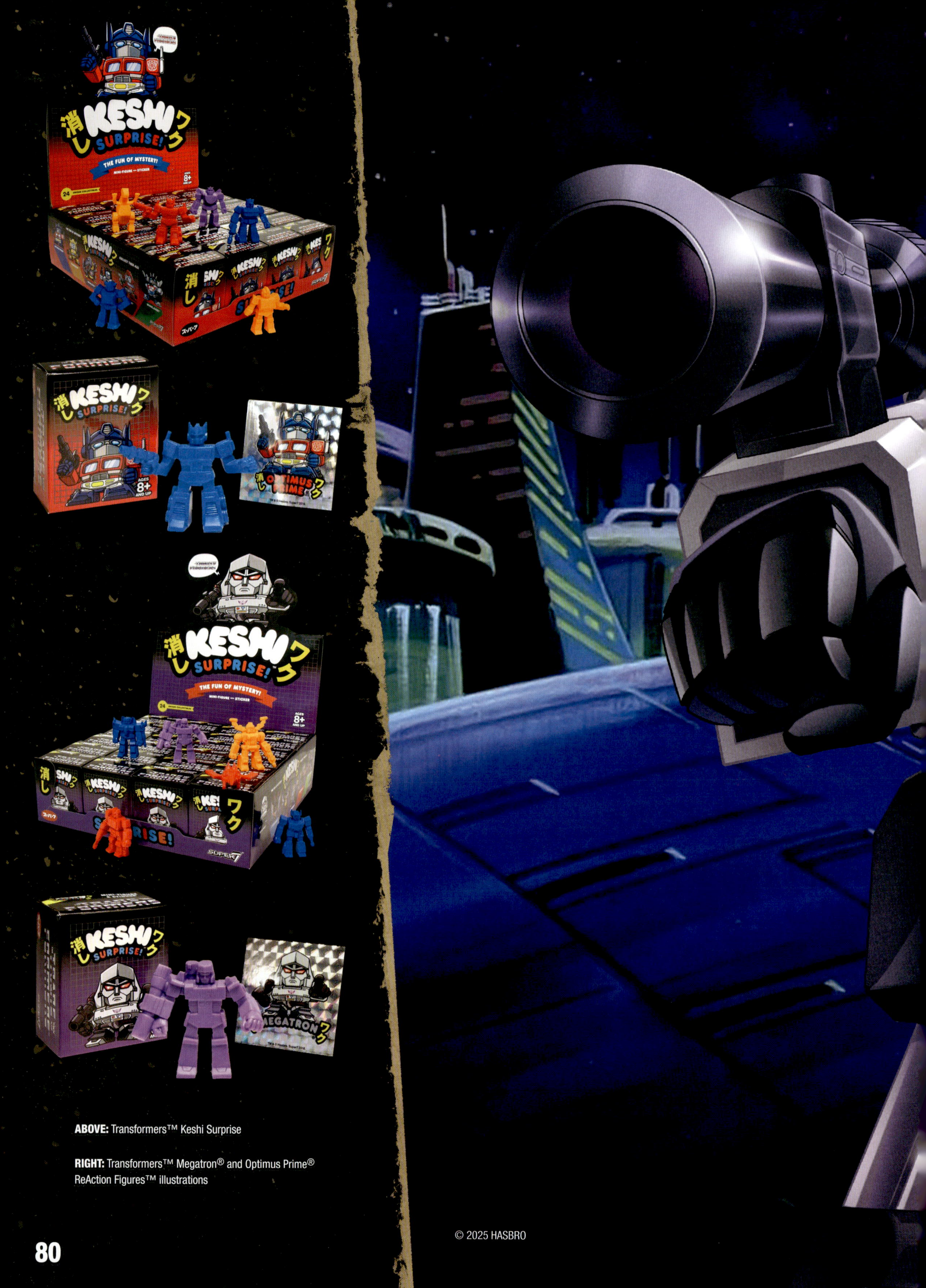

ABOVE: Transformers™ Keshi Surprise

RIGHT: Transformers™ Megatron® and Optimus Prime® ReAction Figures™ illustrations

© 2025 HASBRO

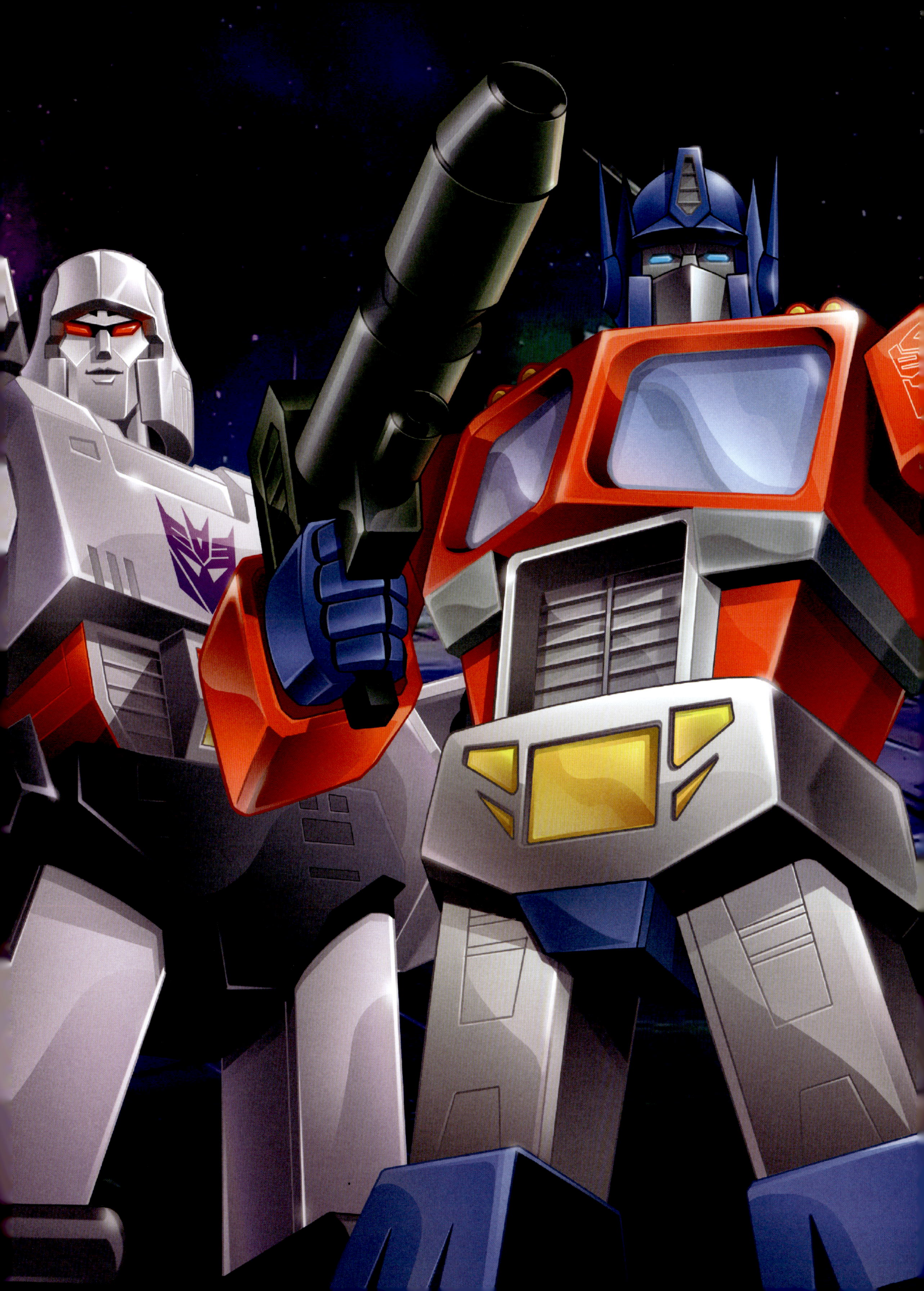

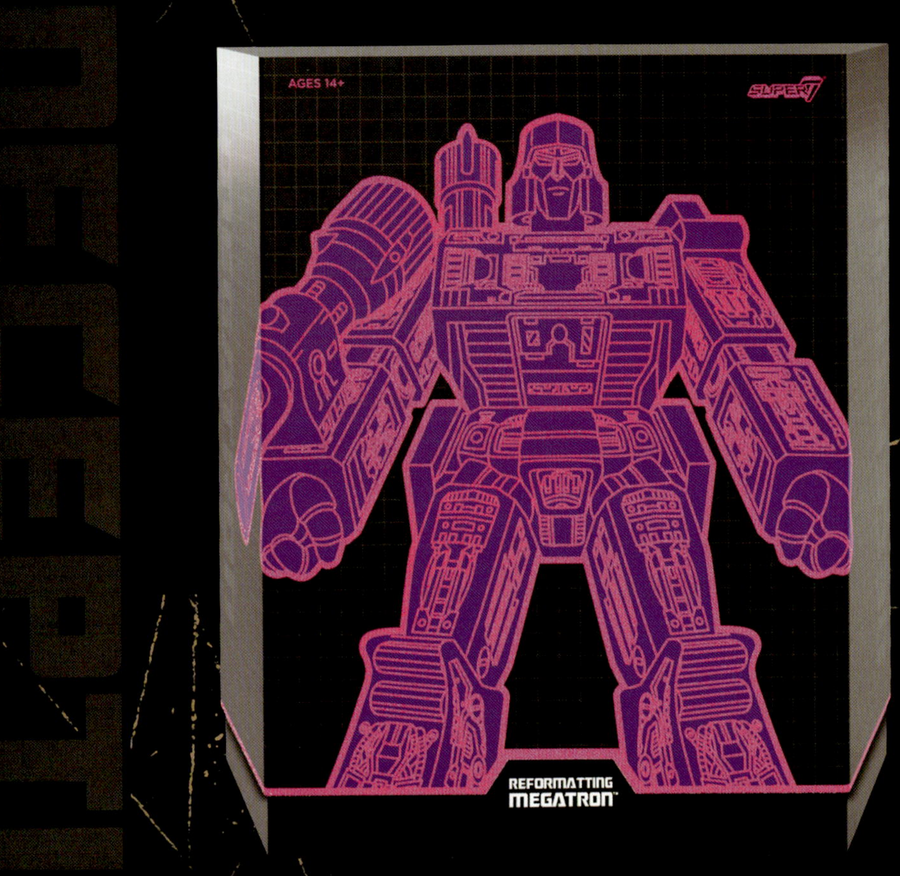

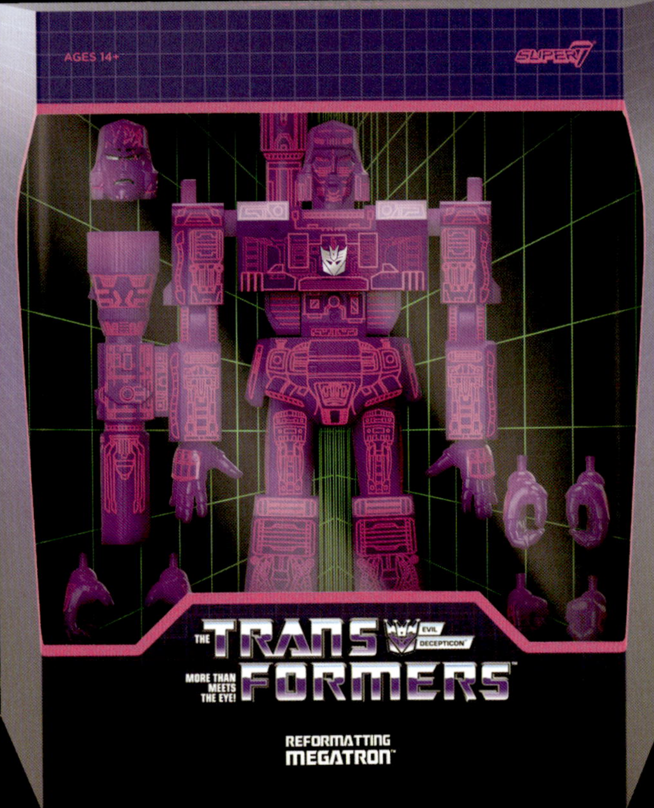

THIS PAGE: Selected Transformers ULTIMATES!™ box art

© 2025 HASBRO

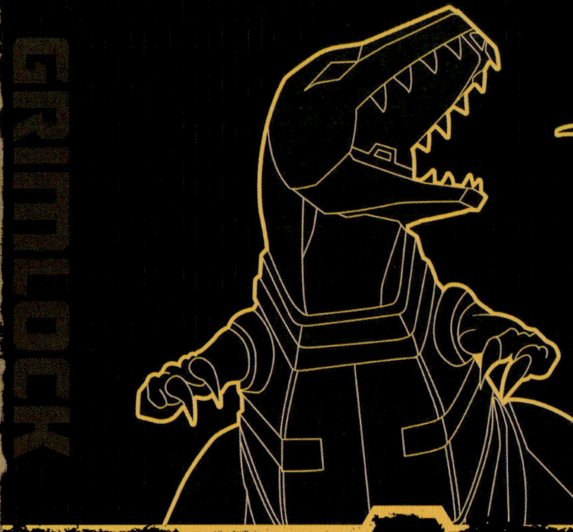

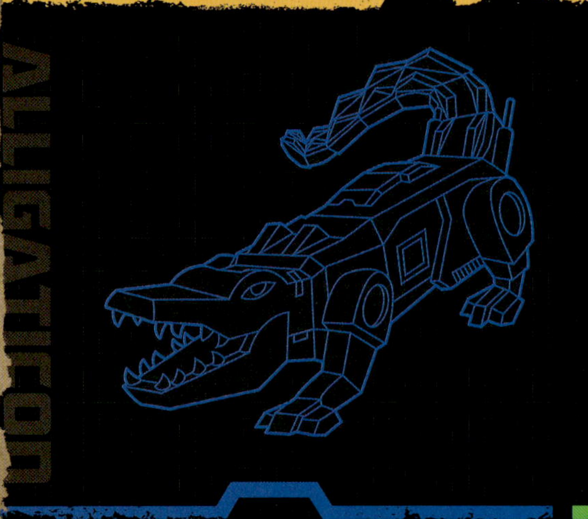

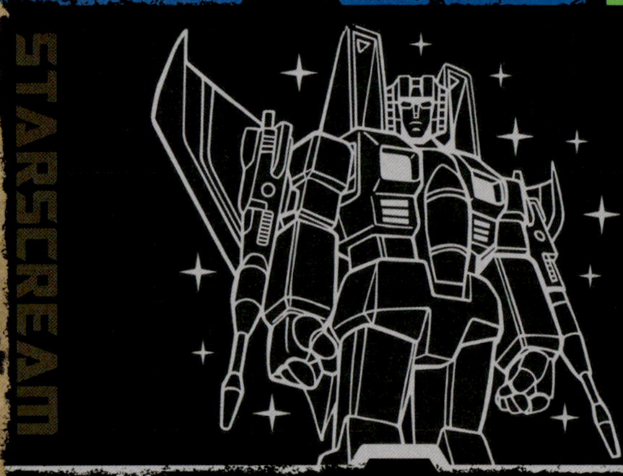

DECEPTICON

GRIMLOCK

ALLIGATICON

STARSCREAM

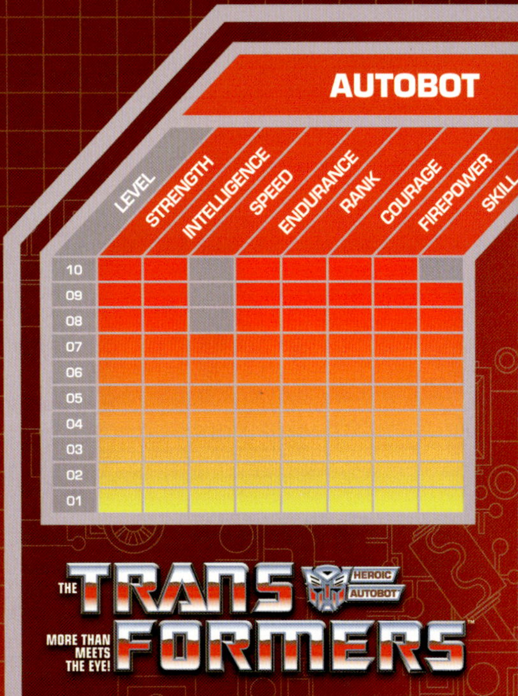

AUTOBOT

LEVEL STRENGTH INTELLIGENCE SPEED ENDURANCE RANK COURAGE FIREPOWER SKILL

10 09 08 07 06 05 04 03 02 01

THE TRANSFORMERS HEROIC AUTOBOT MORE THAN MEETS THE EYE!

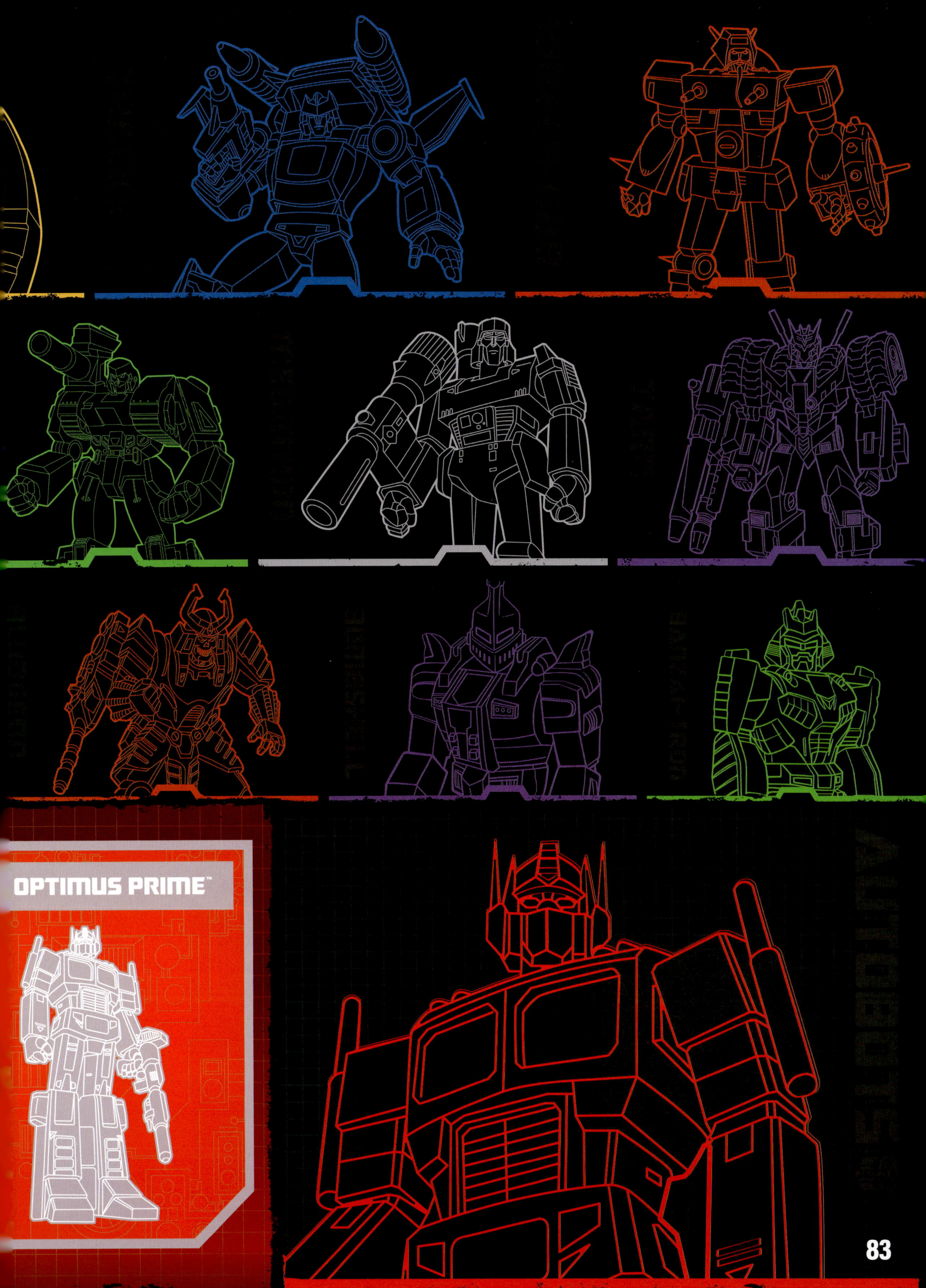
OPTIMUS PRIME™

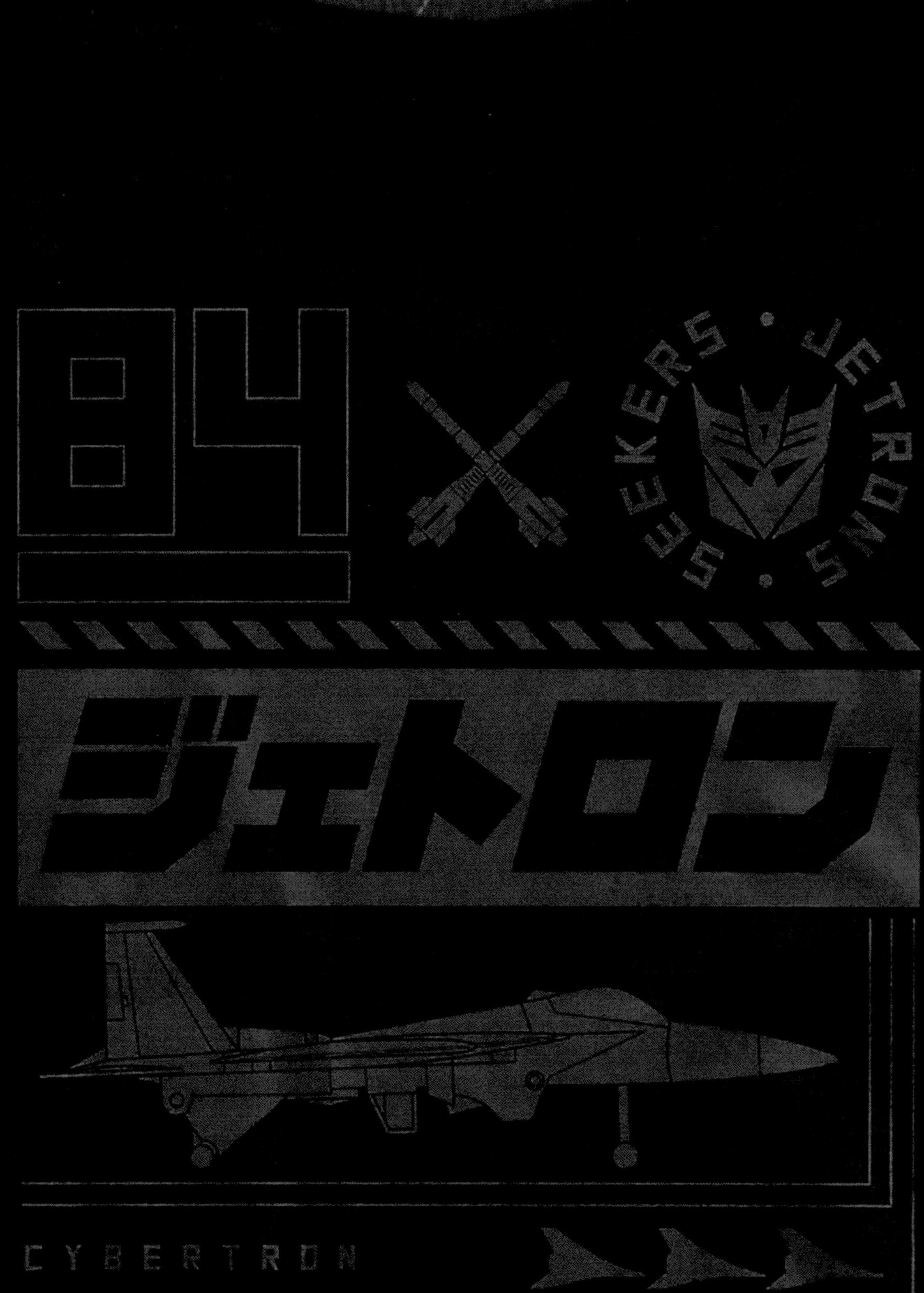
84
SEEKERS • JETRONS •
ジェトロン
CYBERTRON
スタースクリーム
サンダークラッカー

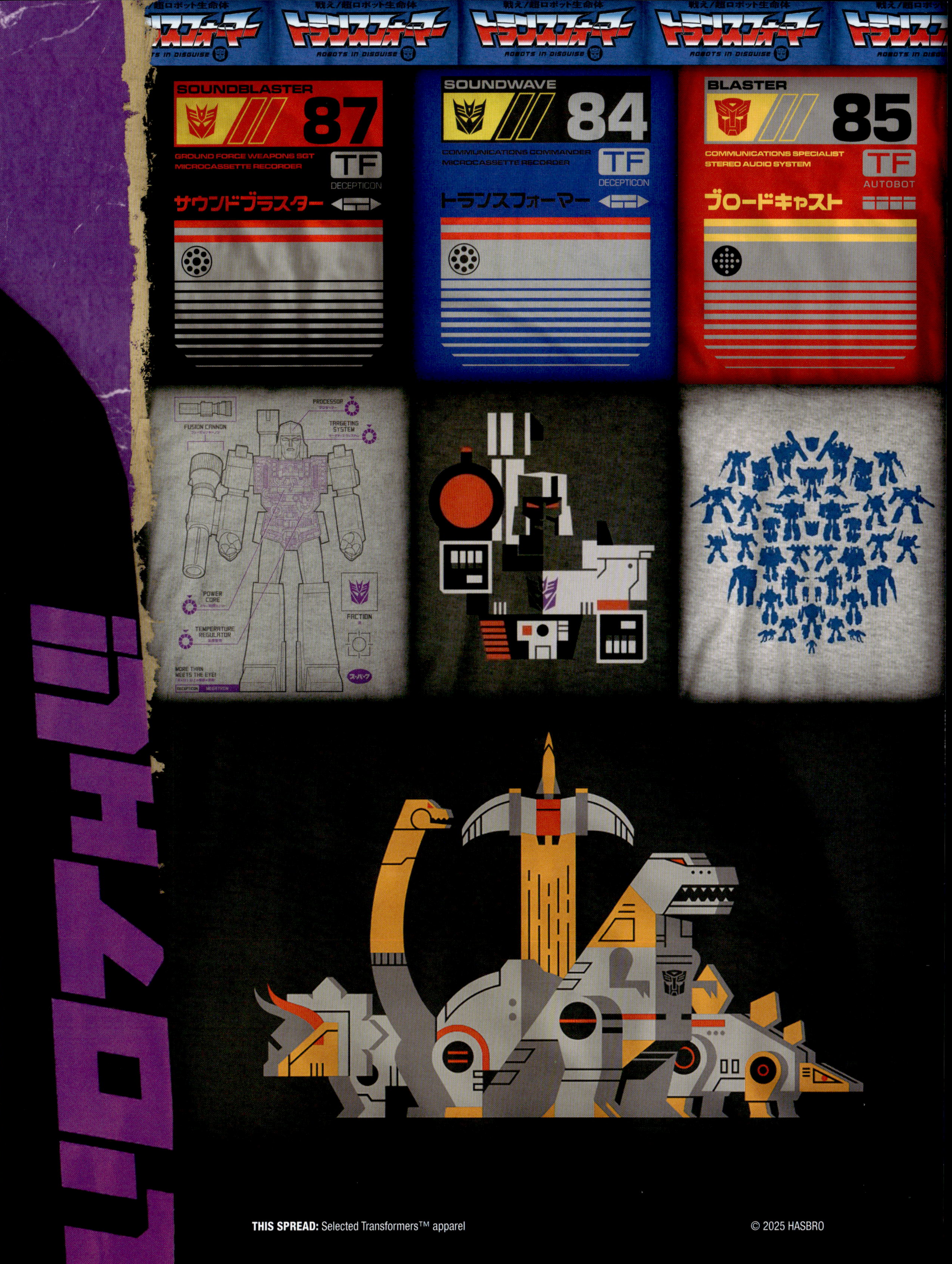

THIS SPREAD: Selected Transformers™ apparel

© 2025 HASBRO

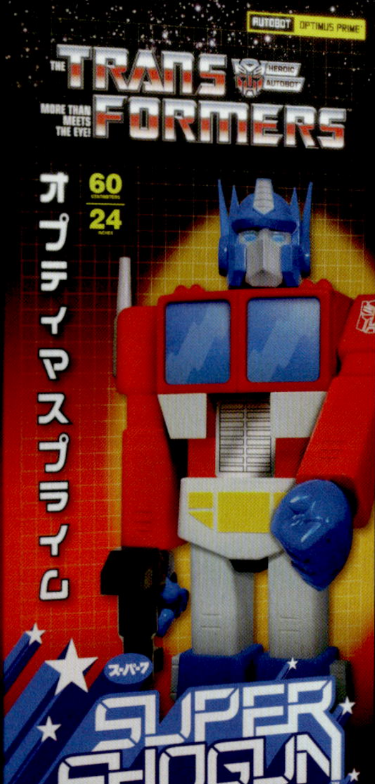

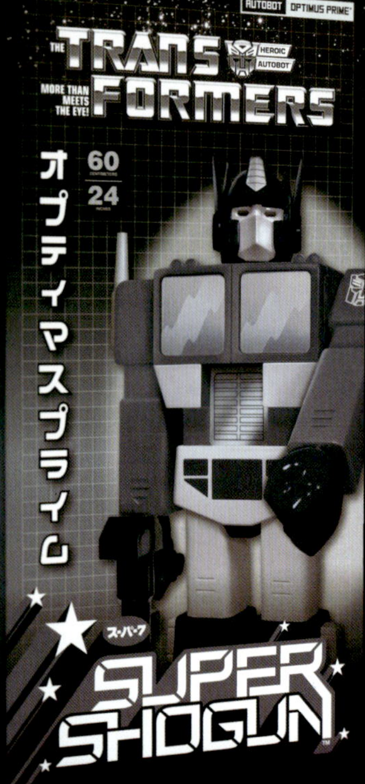

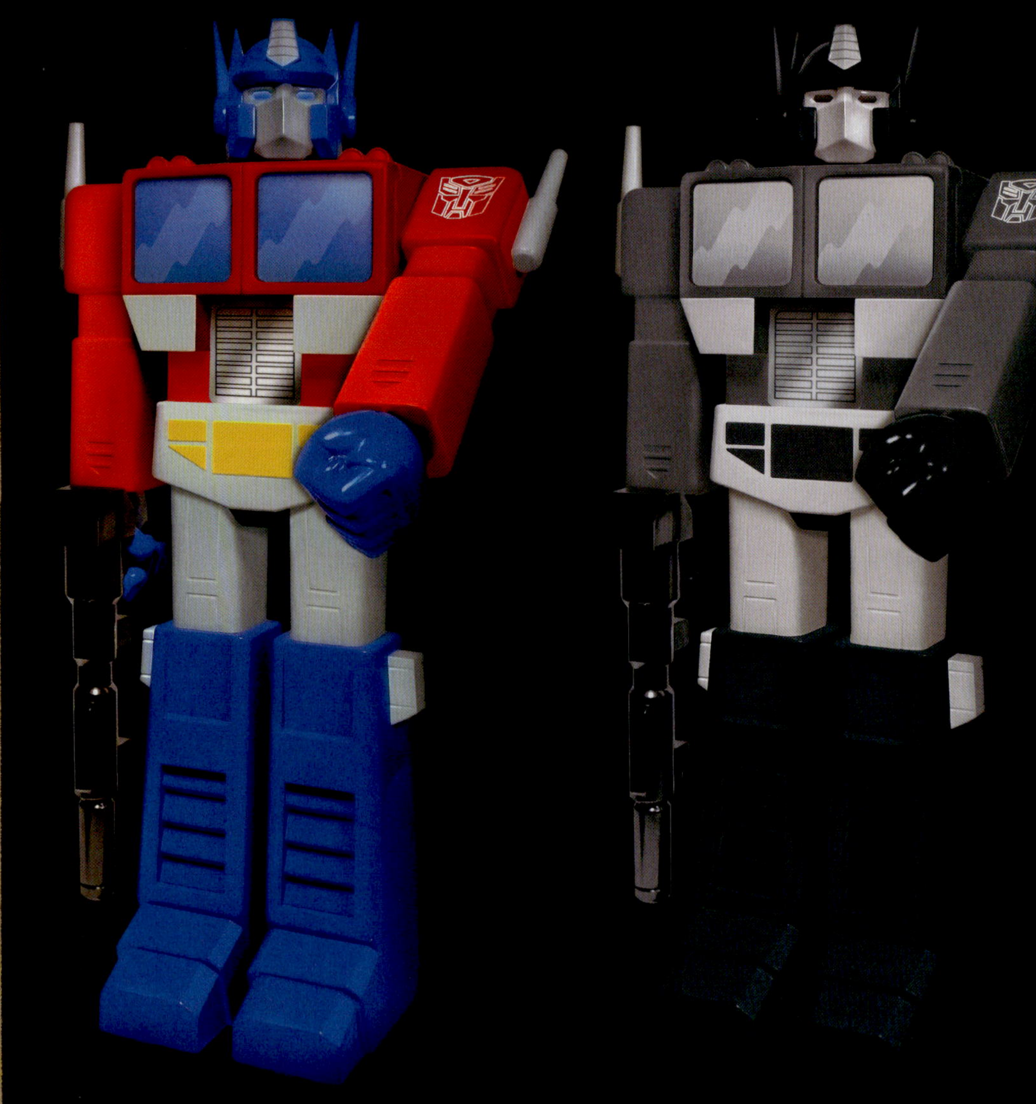

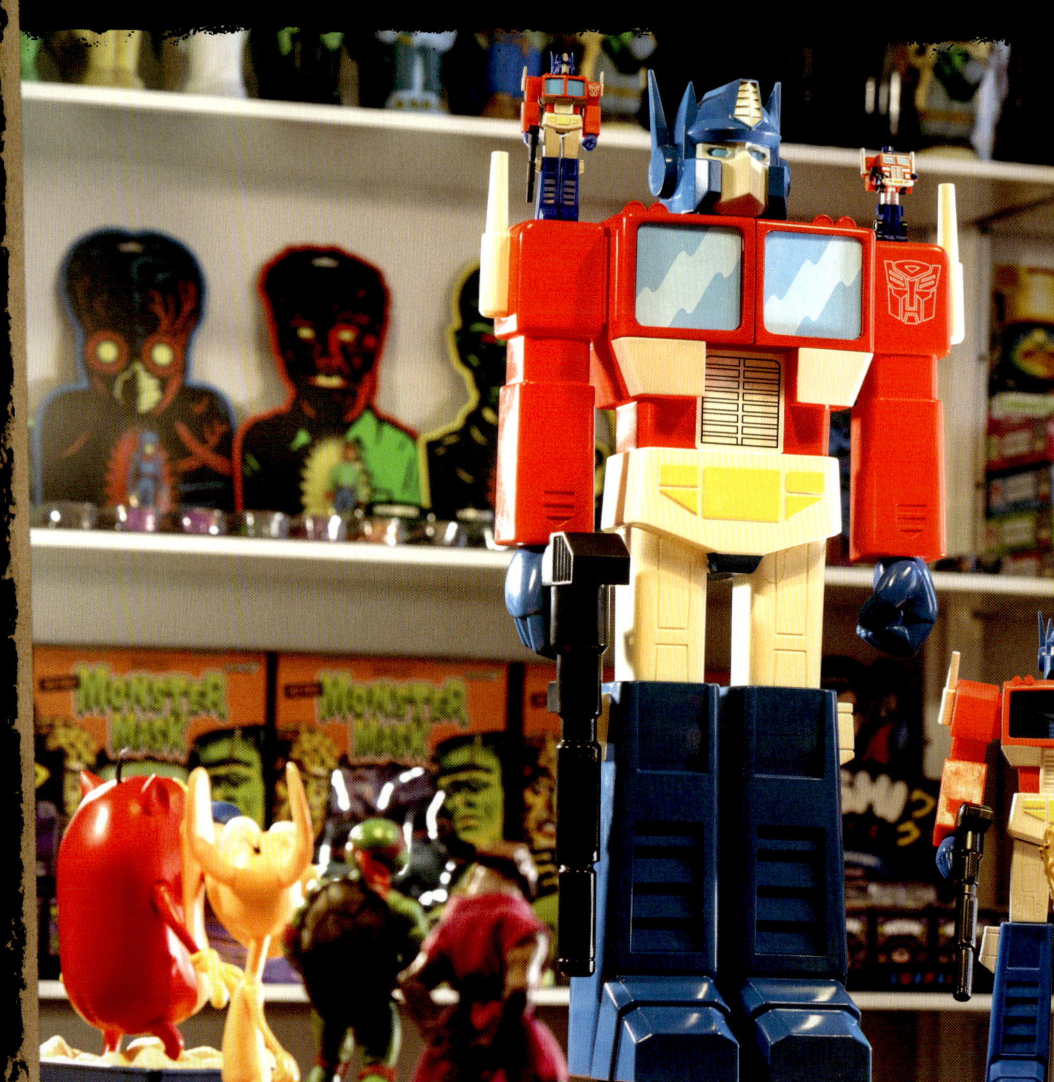

THIS SPREAD: Transformers™ Super Shogun™ box art and figures

© 2025 HASBRO

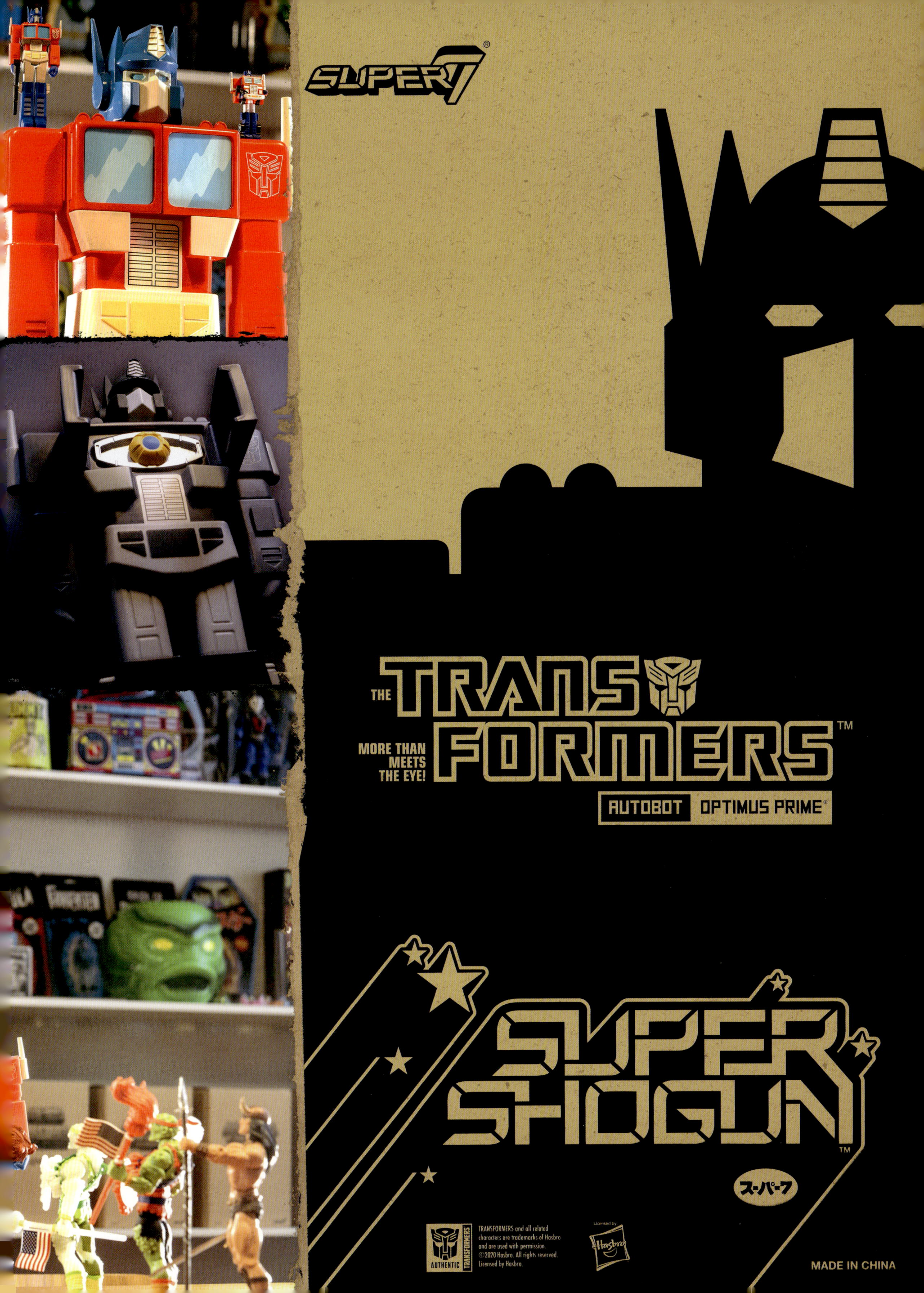

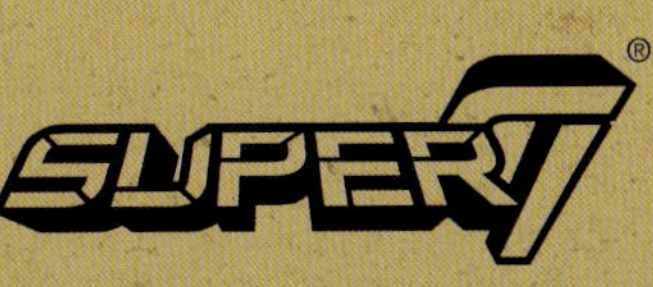

THE TRANSFORMERS™
MORE THAN MEETS THE EYE!
AUTOBOT OPTIMUS PRIME

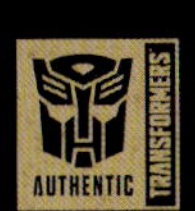

TRANSFORMERS and all related characters are trademarks of Hasbro and are used with permission. ©2020 Hasbro. All rights reserved. Licensed by Hasbro.

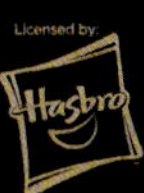

MADE IN CHINA

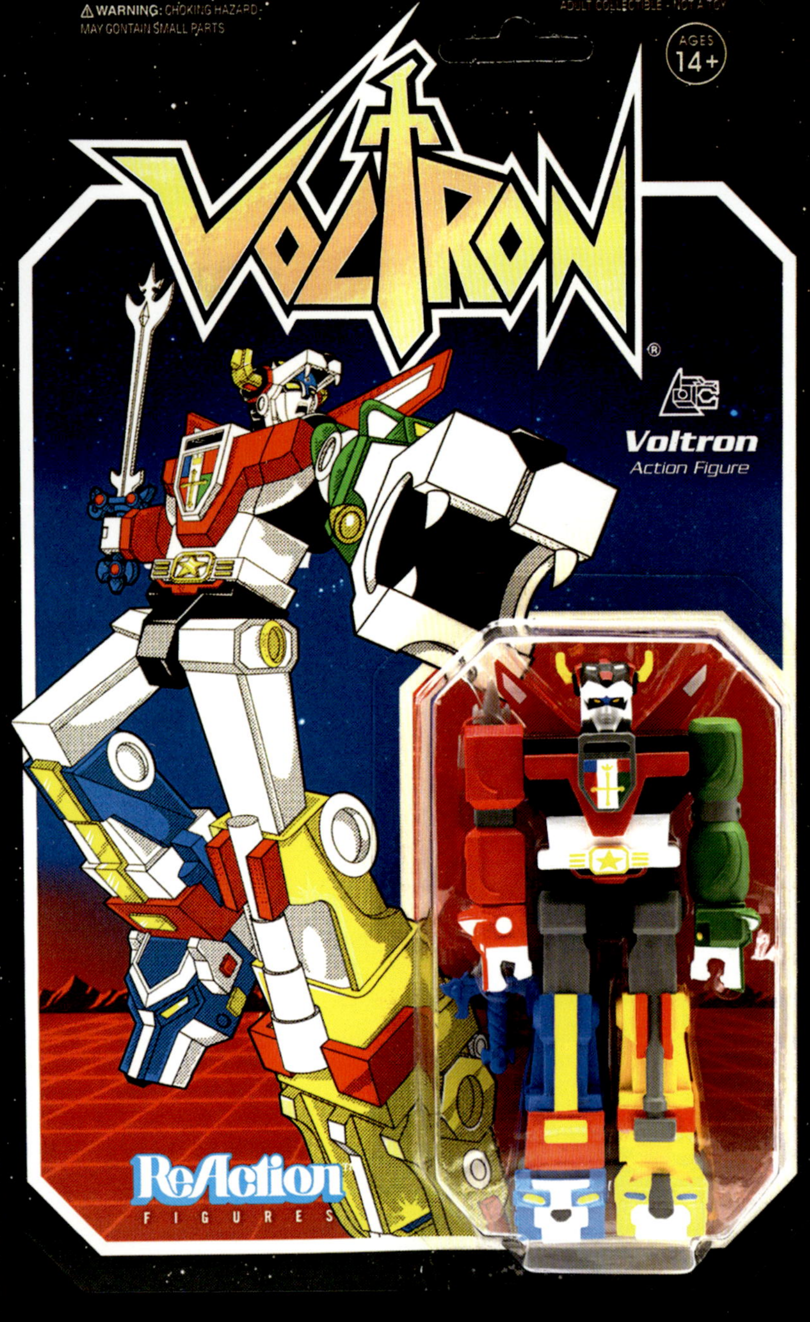
WARNING: CHOKING HAZARD
MAY CONTAIN SMALL PARTS
AGES 14+
VOLTRON
Voltron
Action Figure
ReAction
FIGURES

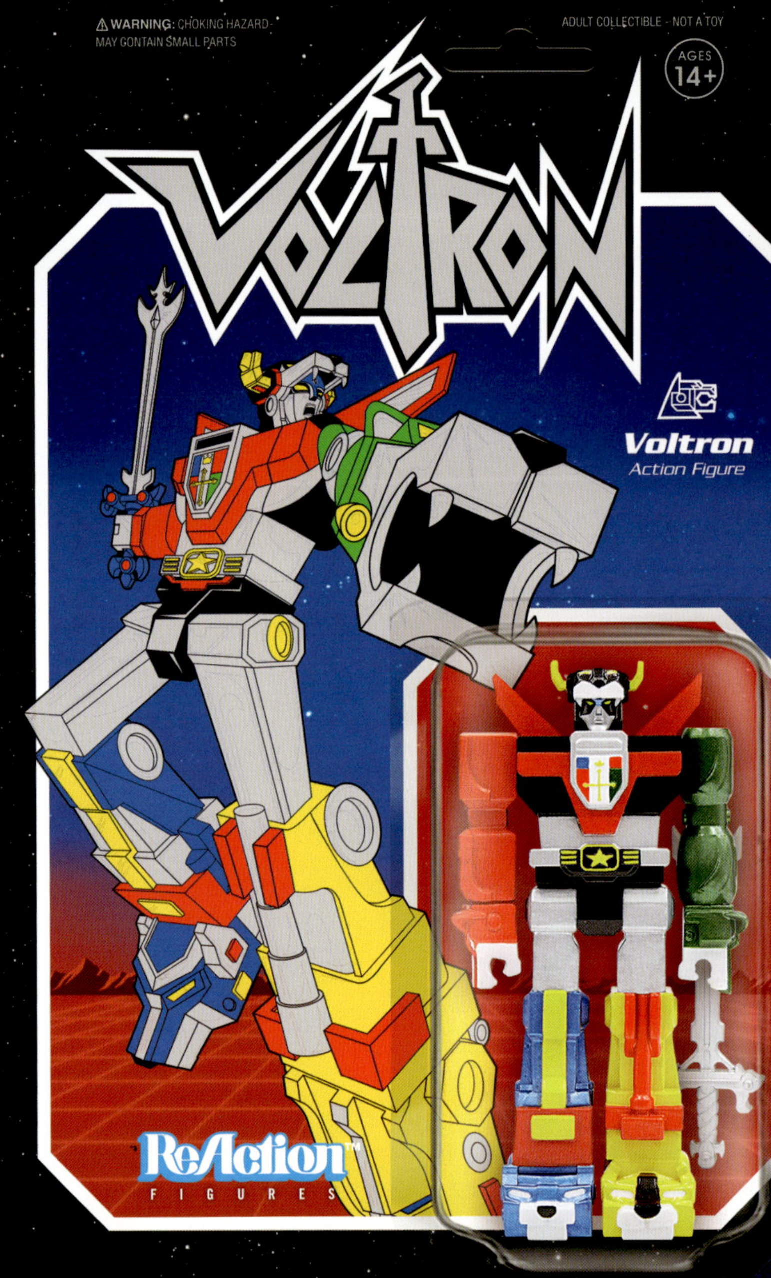
WARNING: CHOKING HAZARD
MAY CONTAIN SMALL PARTS
ADULT COLLECTIBLE - NOT A TOY
AGES 14+
VOLTRON
Voltron
Action Figure
ReAction
FIGURES

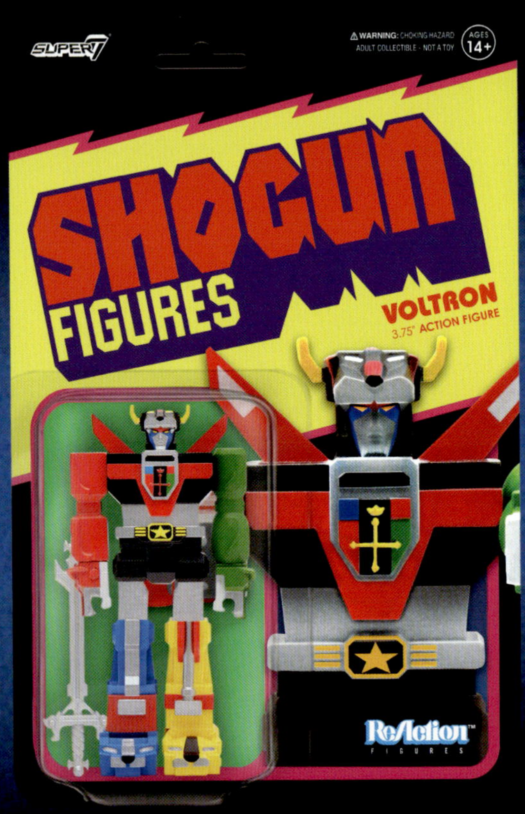
SUPER7
WARNING: CHOKING HAZARD
ADULT COLLECTIBLE - NOT A TOY
AGES 14+
SHOGUN
FIGURES
VOLTRON
3.75" ACTION FIGURE
ReAction
FIGURES

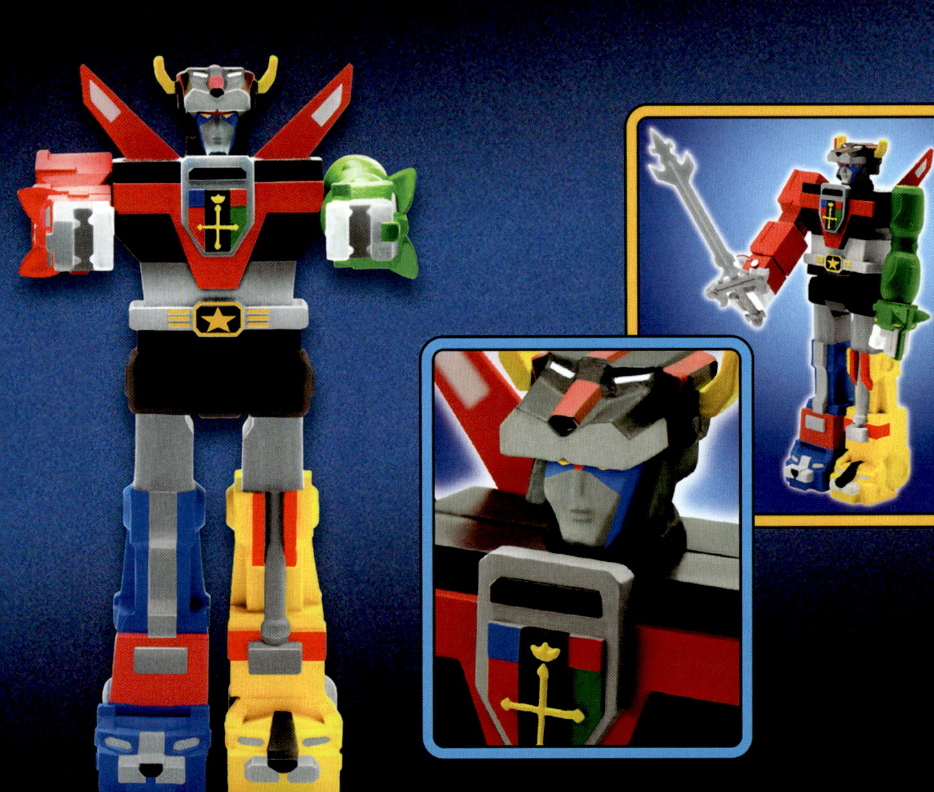

Voltron ™ & © WEP, LLC.
All rights reserved.

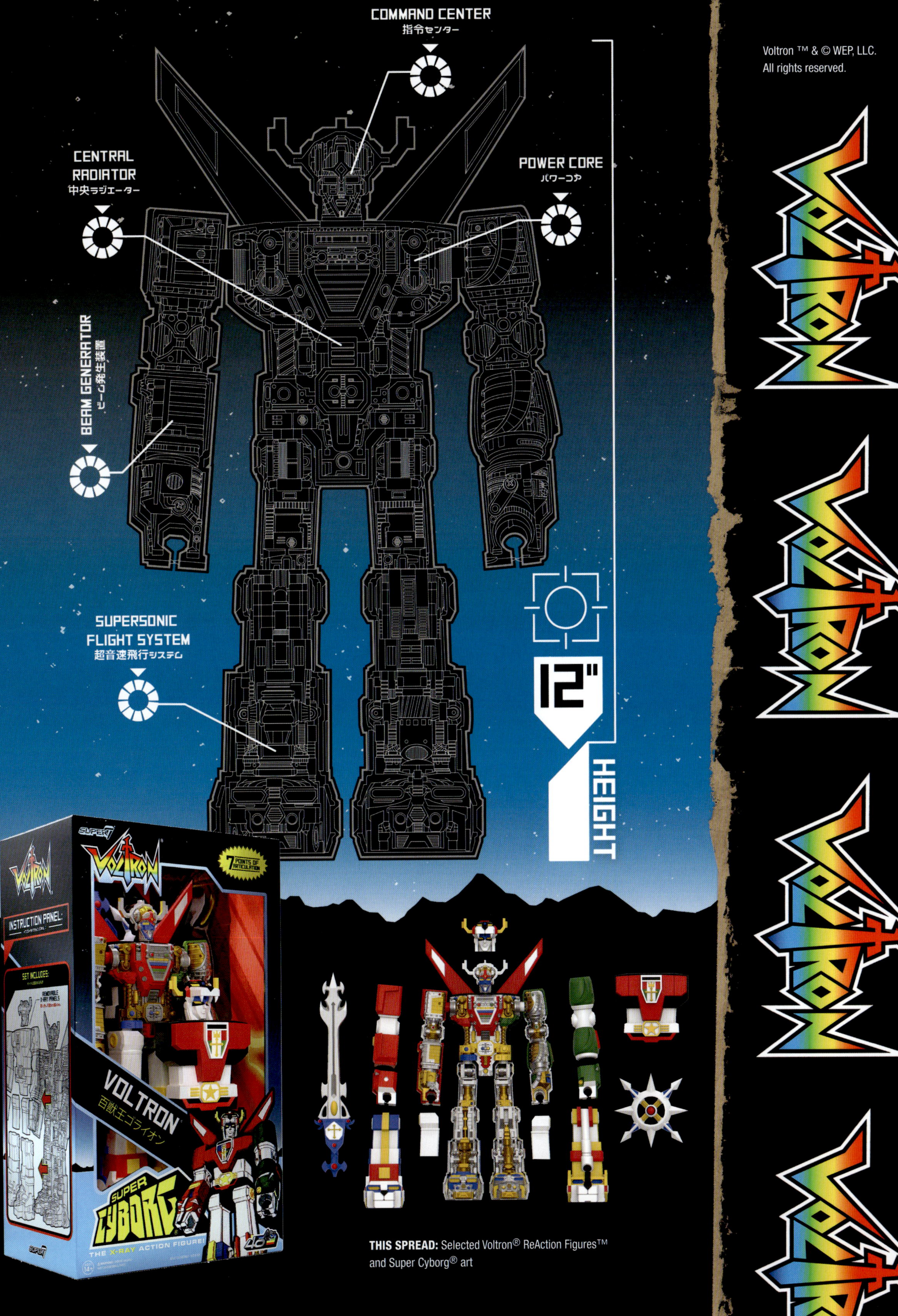

THIS SPREAD: Selected Voltron® ReAction Figures™ and Super Cyborg® art

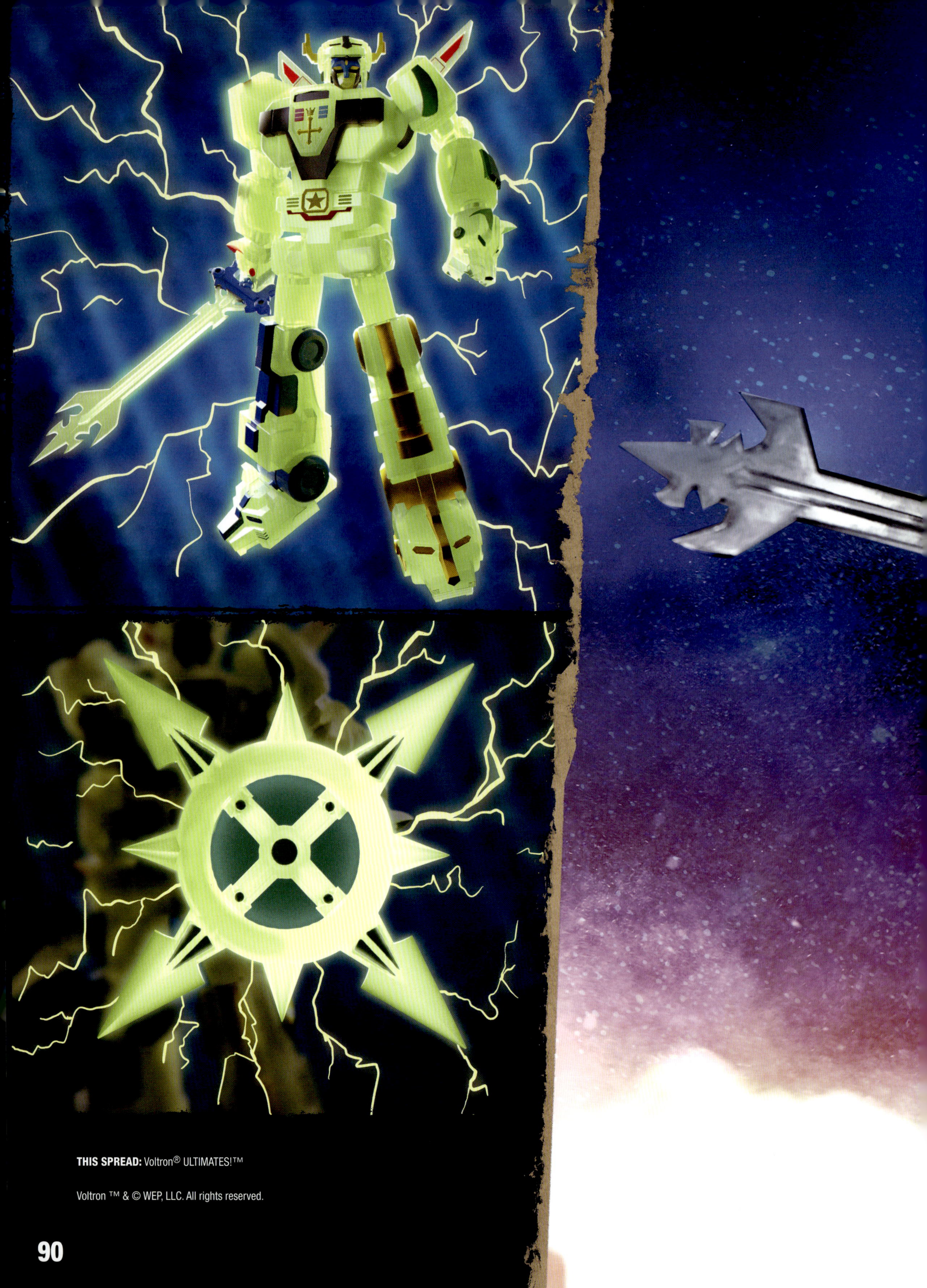

THIS SPREAD: Voltron® ULTIMATES!™

Voltron ™ & © WEP, LLC. All rights reserved.

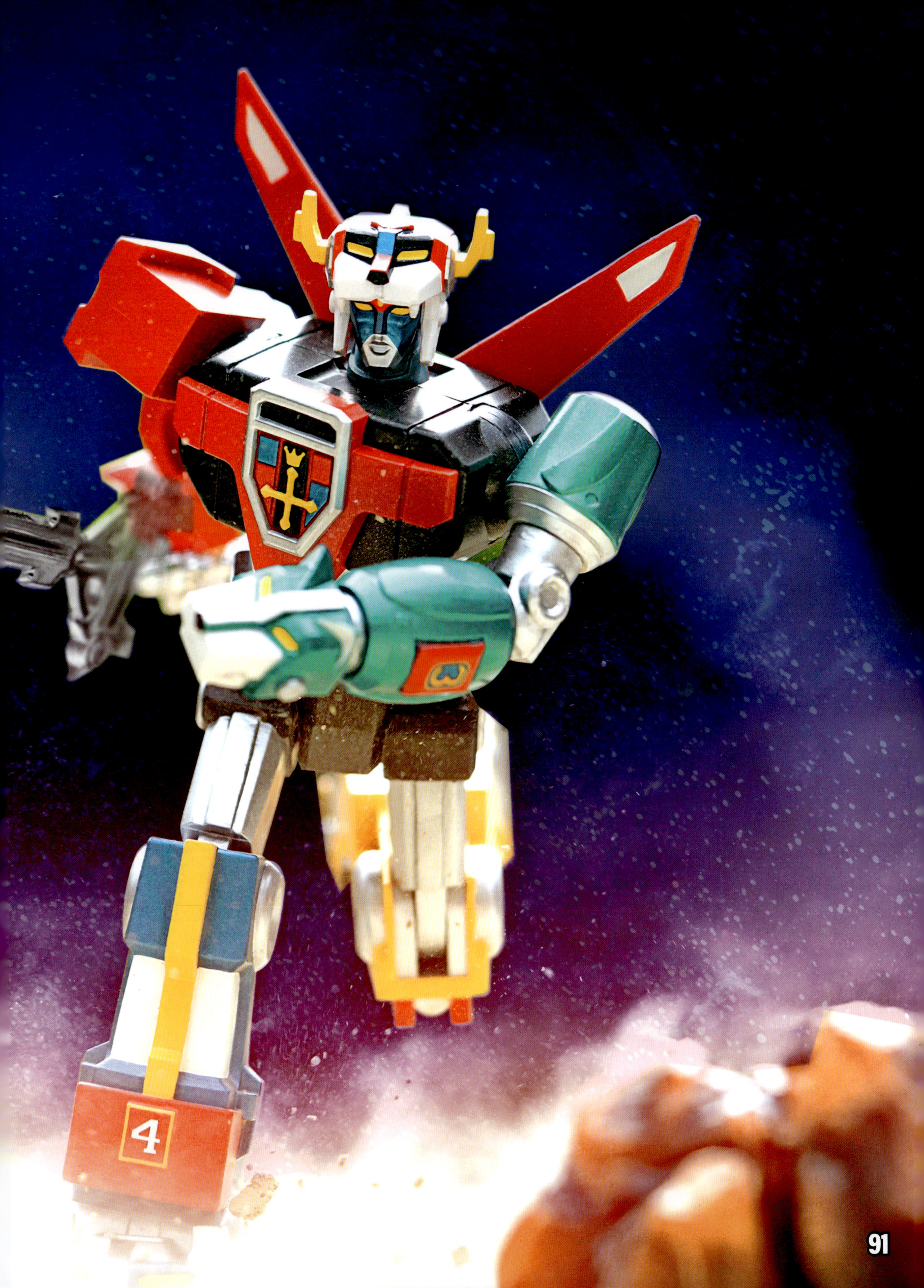

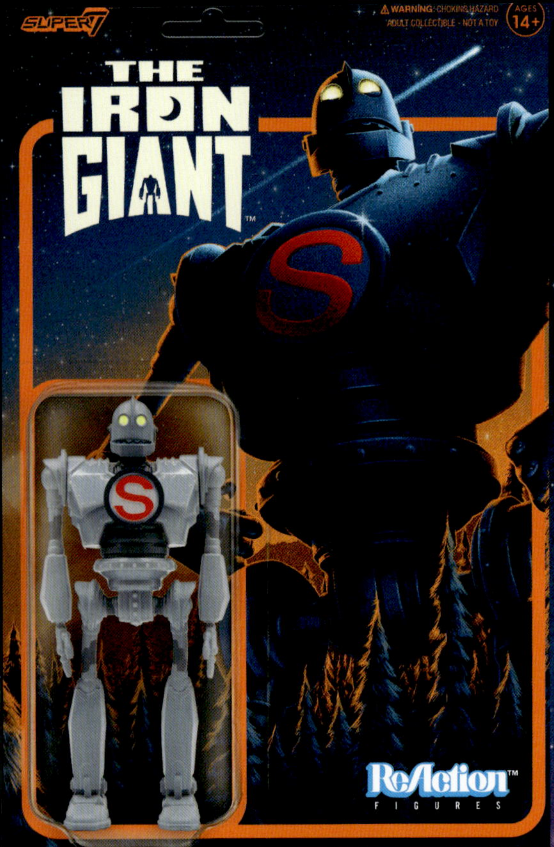

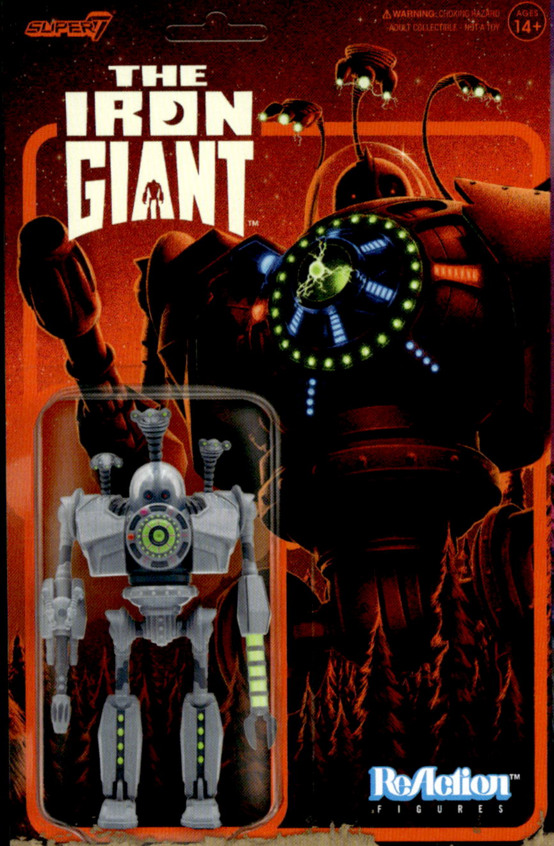

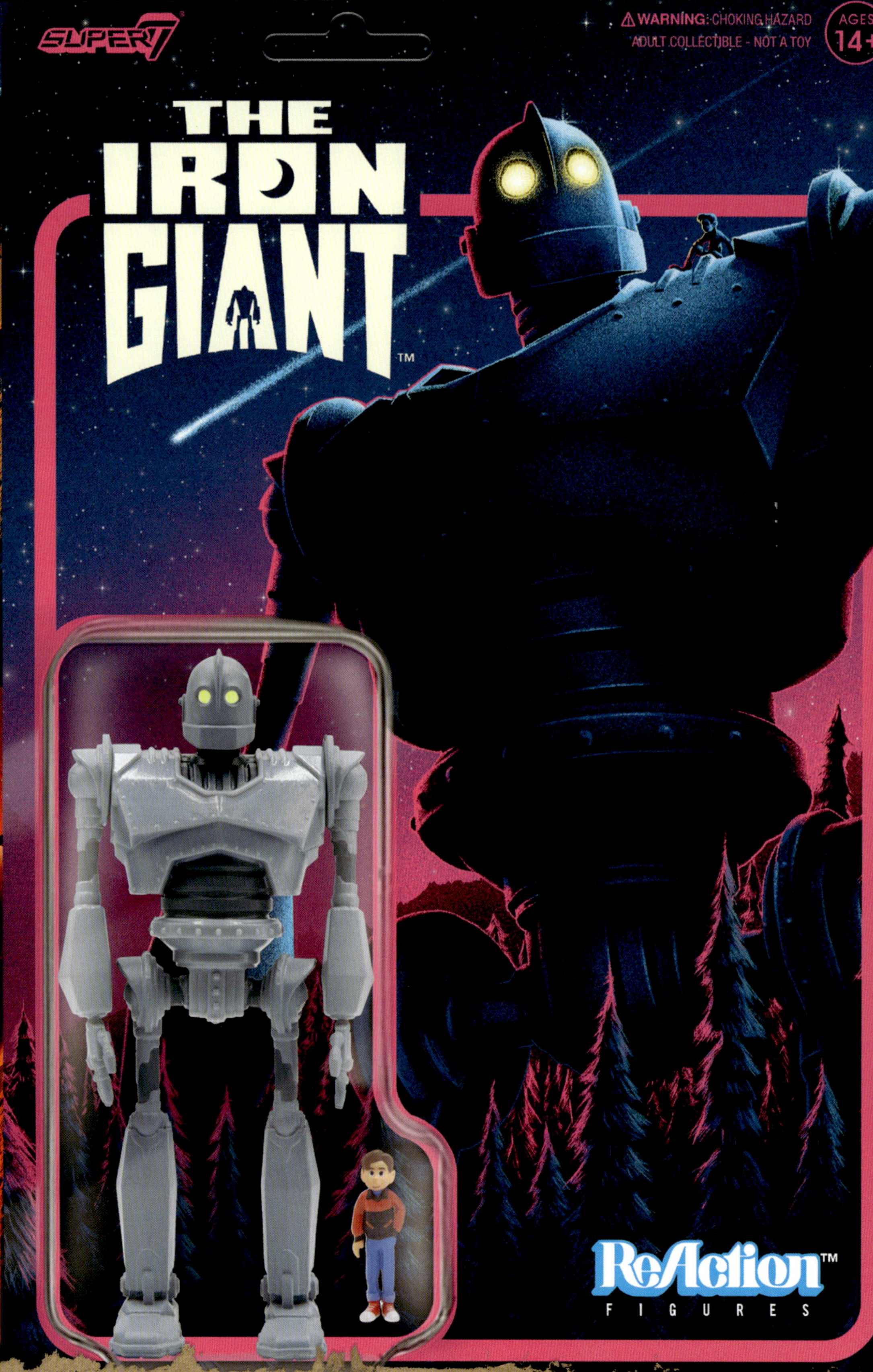

THIS PAGE: The Iron Giant™ ReAction Figures™ card art

RIGHT: RoboCop™ ReAction Figures™ card art

© & ™ WBEI. (s25)

ROBOCOP ™ & © 1987 – 2025 Metro-Goldwyn-Mayer Studios Inc. All Rights Reserved.

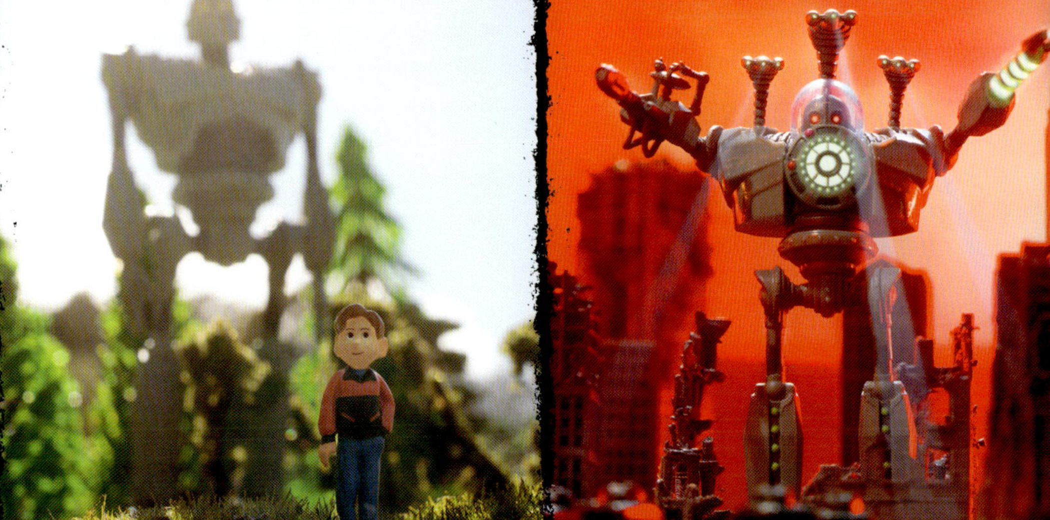

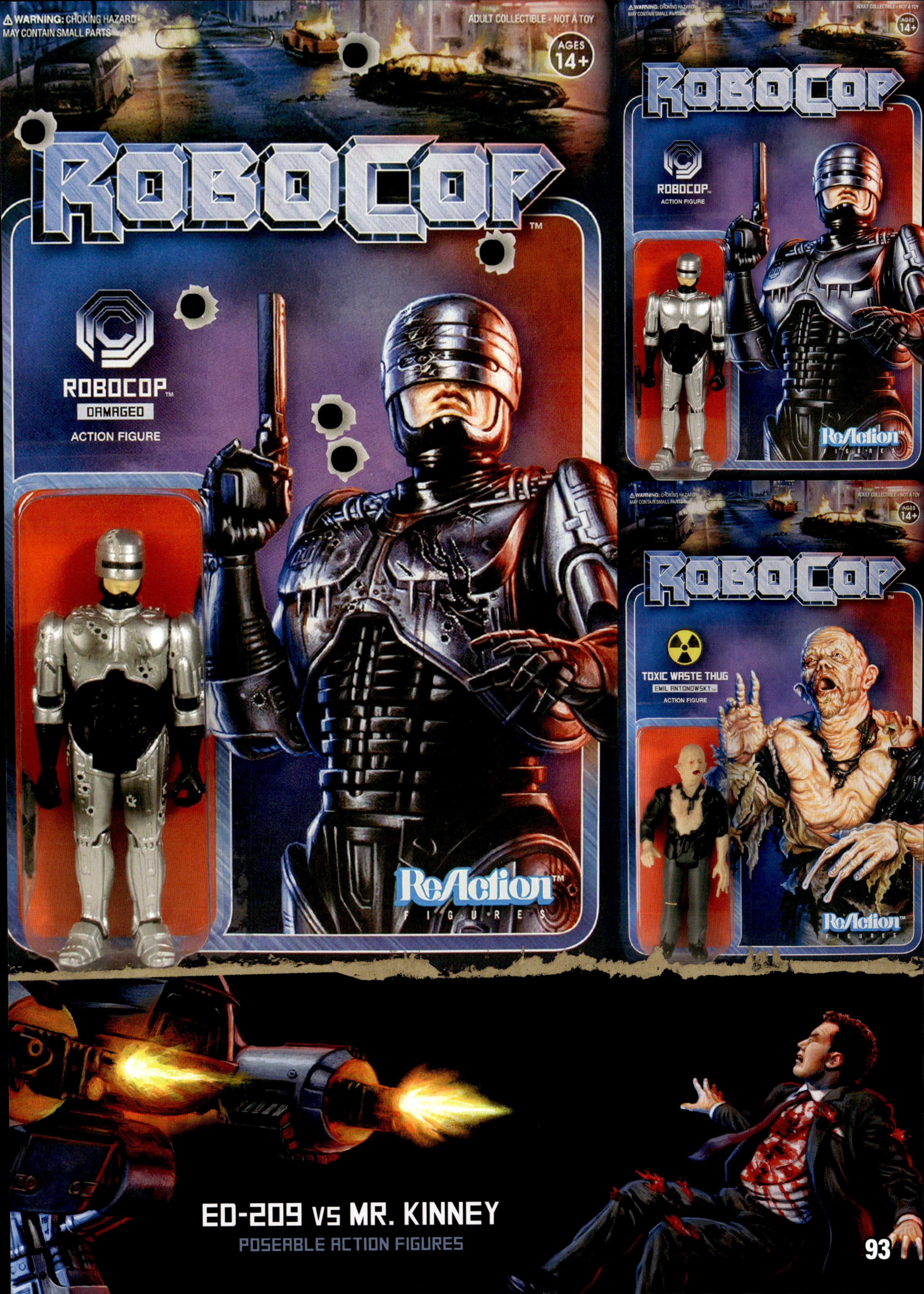

⚠ WARNING: CHOKING HAZARD
MAY CONTAIN SMALL PARTS
ADULT COLLECTIBLE - NOT A TOY
AGES 14+
ROBOCOP™
ROBOCOP™
DAMAGED
ACTION FIGURE
ReAction™
FIGURES
ROBOCOP™
ROBOCOP
ACTION FIGURE
ReAction™
ROBOCOP™
TOXIC WASTE THUG
EMIL ANTONOWSKY
ACTION FIGURE
ReAction™
ED-209 VS MR. KINNEY
POSEABLE ACTION FIGURES

FROM FAR-FLUNG GALAXIES TO HIDDEN WORLDS WITHIN OUR OWN, SCIENCE FICTION HAS ENTHRALLED AND CAPTIVATED US FOR GENERATIONS, ALLOWING US TO IMAGINE THE FUTURE AND THE PAST WITH INFINITELY RADIATING STORYLINES THAT CAN SERVE AS INSPIRATION (OR CAUTION) FOR OUR ACTUAL DAY-TO-DAY LIVES. WE CAN WITNESS CRIME-FIGHTING TEENS (BE THEY MORPHED HUMAN OR MUTANT REPTILIAN) AND INTREPID EXPLORERS FACE OFF WITH NEFARIOUS BIOLOGICAL OR TECHNOLOGICAL TERRORS IN A STORYTELLING CANVAS AS LOCAL AS BACKYARD BATTLES AND UNDERGROUND ADVENTURES OR AS GRAND AS OPERAS OF TIME TRAVEL, SPACE EXPLORATION, AND ENTIRE NEW REALITIES. FROM THAT FIRST IMPRESSIONABLE EXPOSURE, OUR YOUNG, FERTILE MINDS GRASPED THAT WITH SCIENCE FICTION, THE SKY ISN'T THE LIMIT—IT IS ACTUALLY JUST THE BEGINNING.

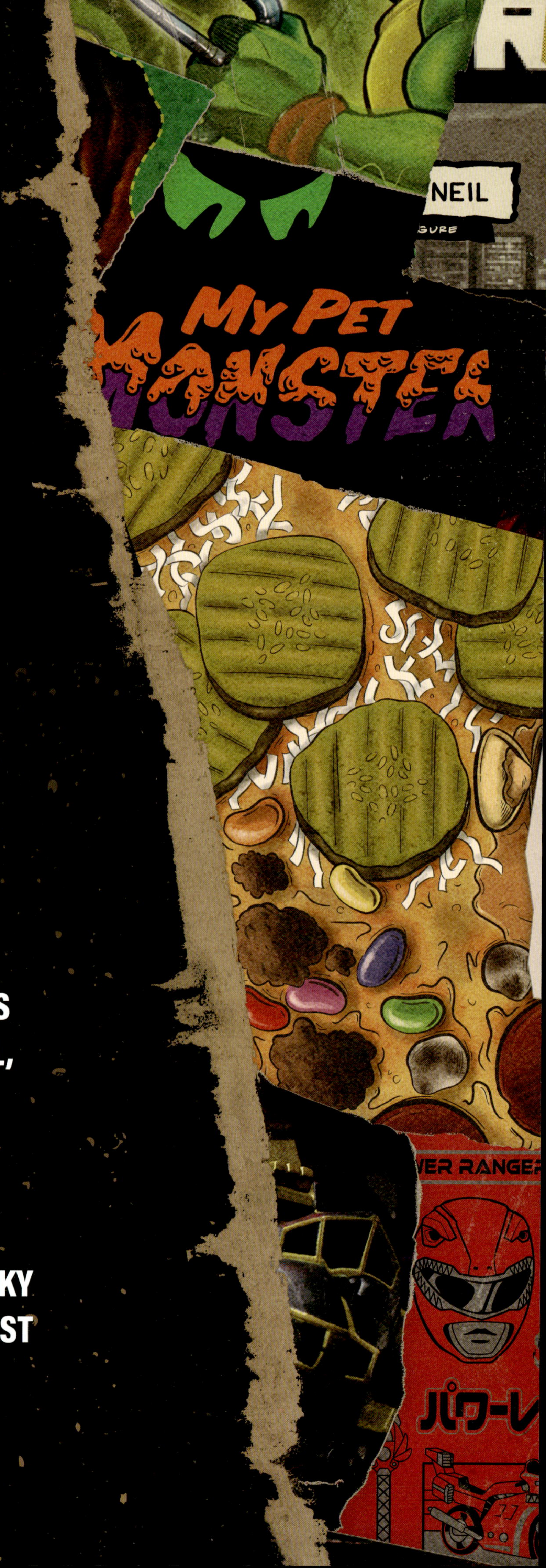

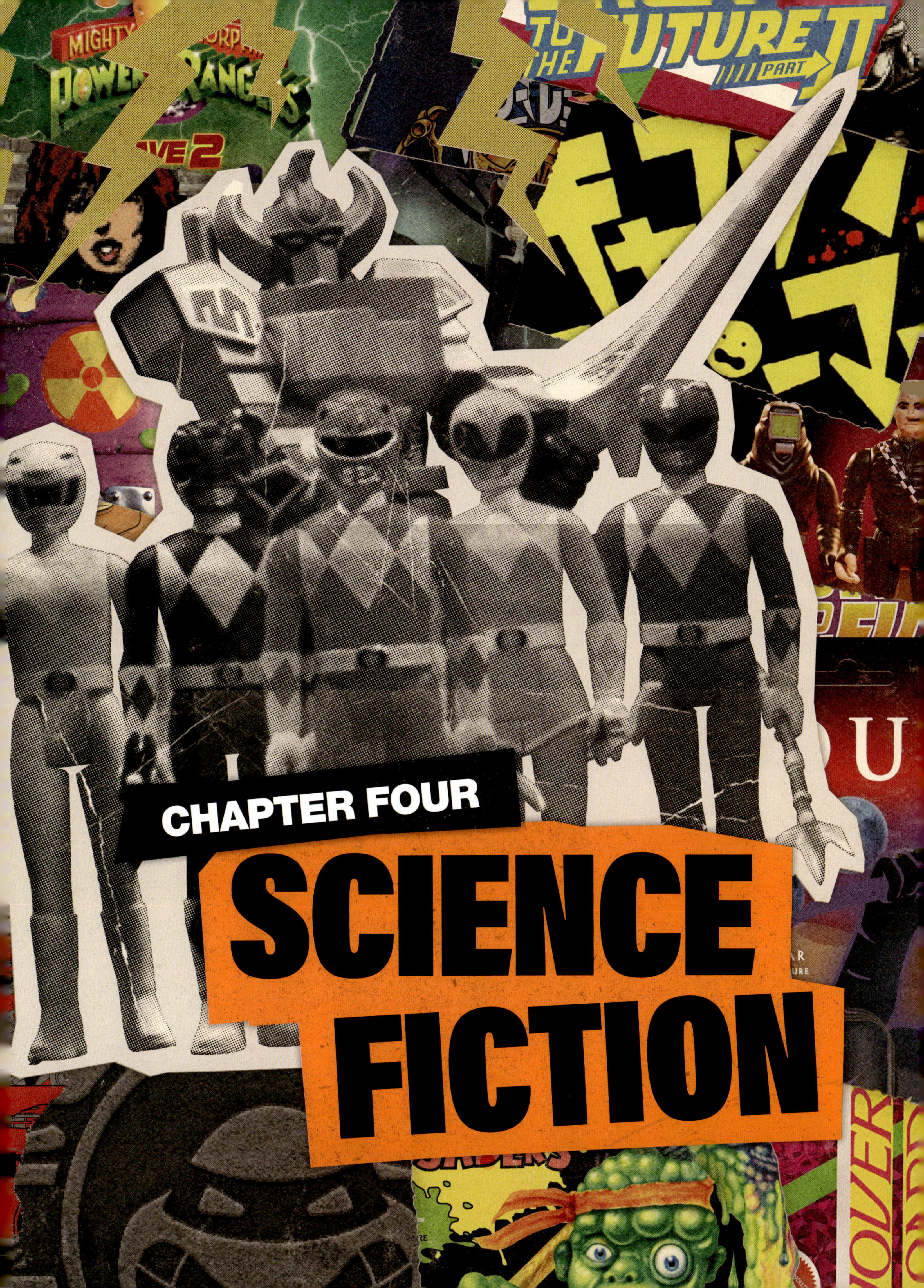

CHAPTER FOUR

SCIENCE FICTION

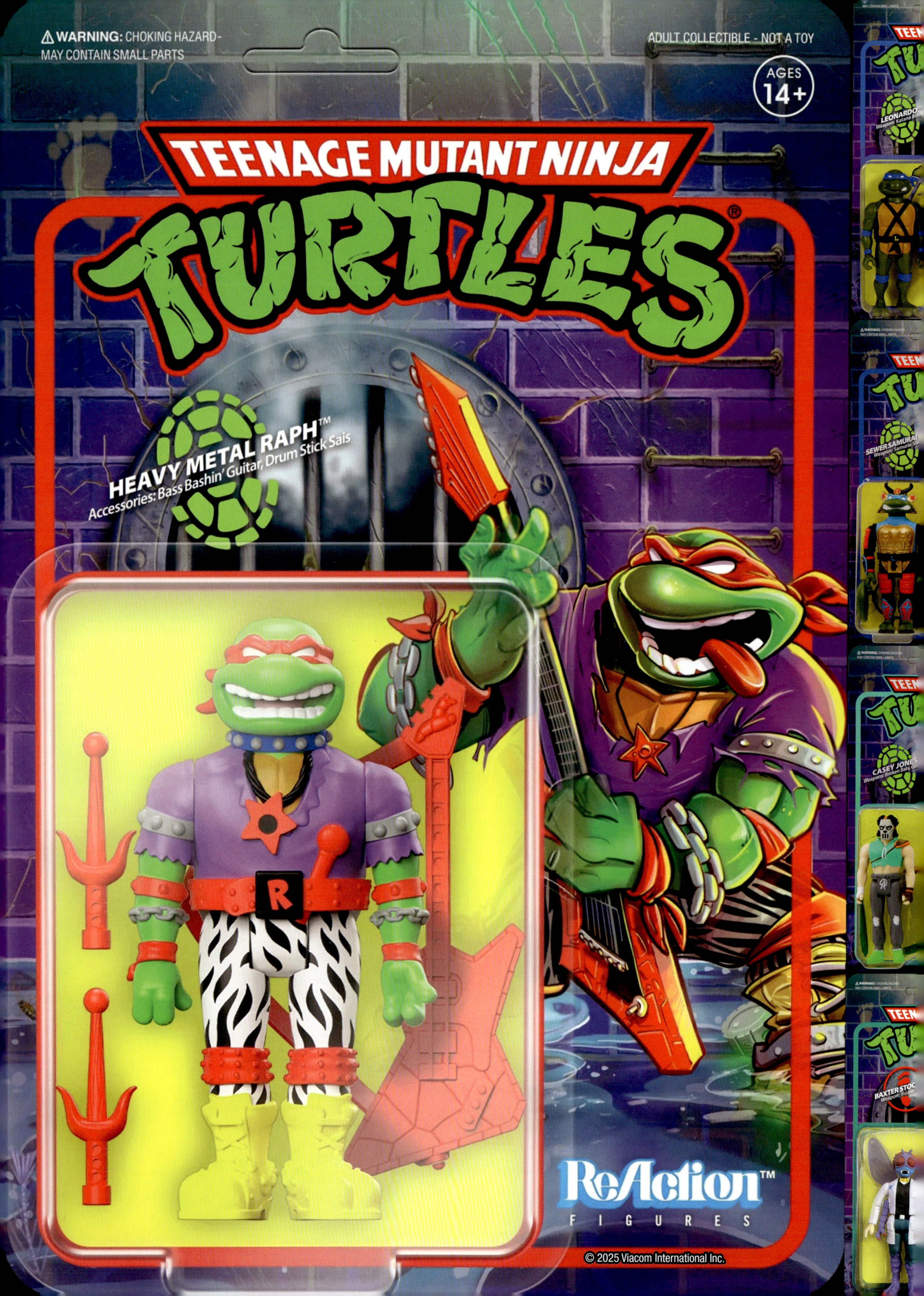

⚠ WARNING: CHOKING HAZARD - MAY CONTAIN SMALL PARTS

ADULT COLLECTIBLE - NOT A TOY

AGES 14+

TEENAGE MUTANT NINJA TURTLES®

HEAVY METAL RAPH™

Accessories: Bass Bashin' Guitar, Drum Stick Sais

ReAction™ FIGURES

© 2025 Viacom International Inc.

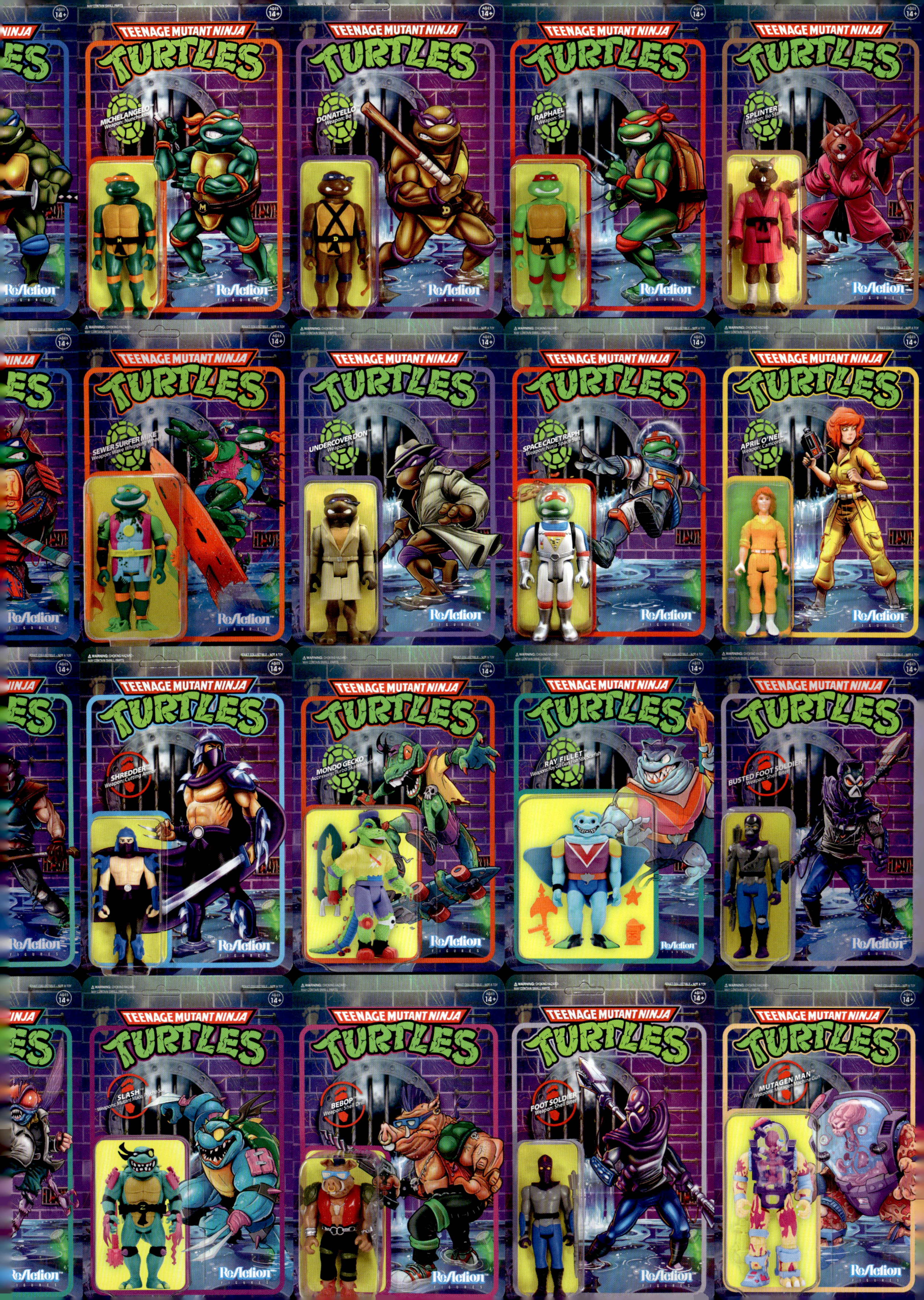
TEENAGE MUTANT NINJA
TURTLES
MICHELANGELO
TEENAGE MUTANT NINJA
TURTLES
DONATELLO
TEENAGE MUTANT NINJA
TURTLES
RAPHAEL
TEENAGE MUTANT NINJA
TURTLES
SPLINTER
TEENAGE MUTANT NINJA
TURTLES
SEWER SURFER MIKE
TEENAGE MUTANT NINJA
TURTLES
UNDERCOVER DON
TEENAGE MUTANT NINJA
TURTLES
SPACE CADET RAPH
TEENAGE MUTANT NINJA
TURTLES
APRIL O'NEIL
TEENAGE MUTANT NINJA
TURTLES
SHREDDER
TEENAGE MUTANT NINJA
TURTLES
MONDO GECKO
TEENAGE MUTANT NINJA
TURTLES
RAY FILLET
TEENAGE MUTANT NINJA
TURTLES
BUSTED FOOT SOLDIER
TEENAGE MUTANT NINJA
TURTLES
SLASH
TEENAGE MUTANT NINJA
TURTLES
BEBOP
TEENAGE MUTANT NINJA
TURTLES
FOOT SOLDIER
TEENAGE MUTANT NINJA
TURTLES
MUTAGEN MAN

EASTMAN AND LAIRD'S TEENAGE MUTANT NINJA TURTLES

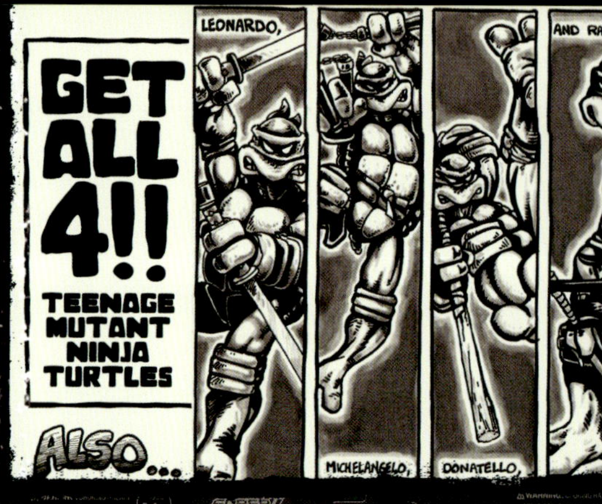

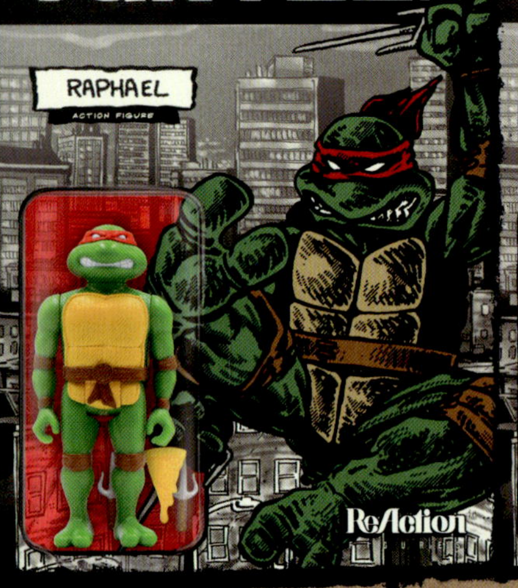

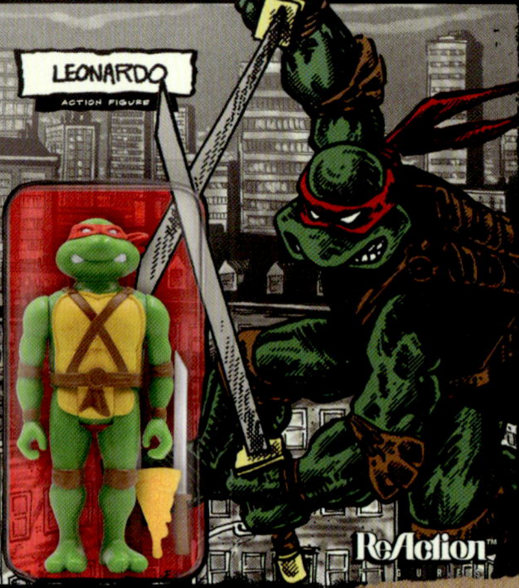

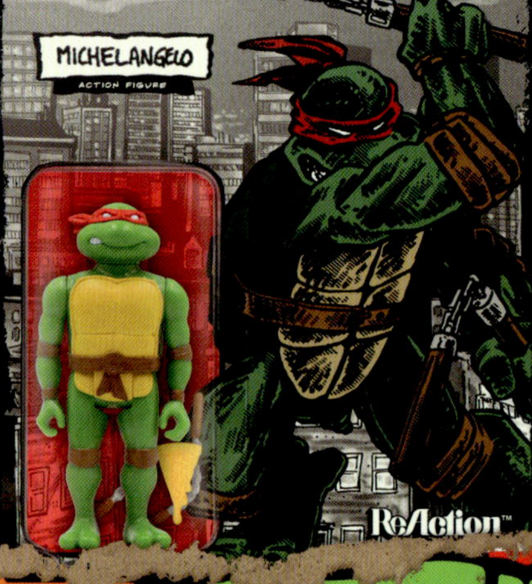

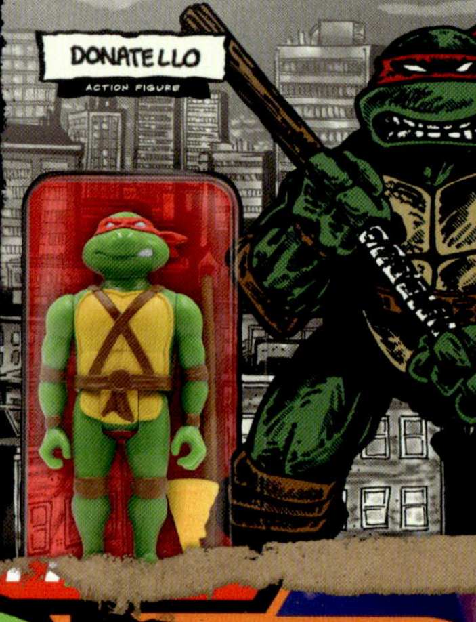

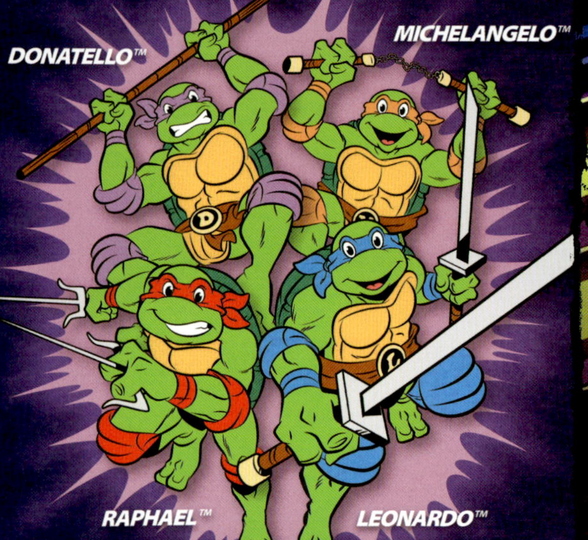

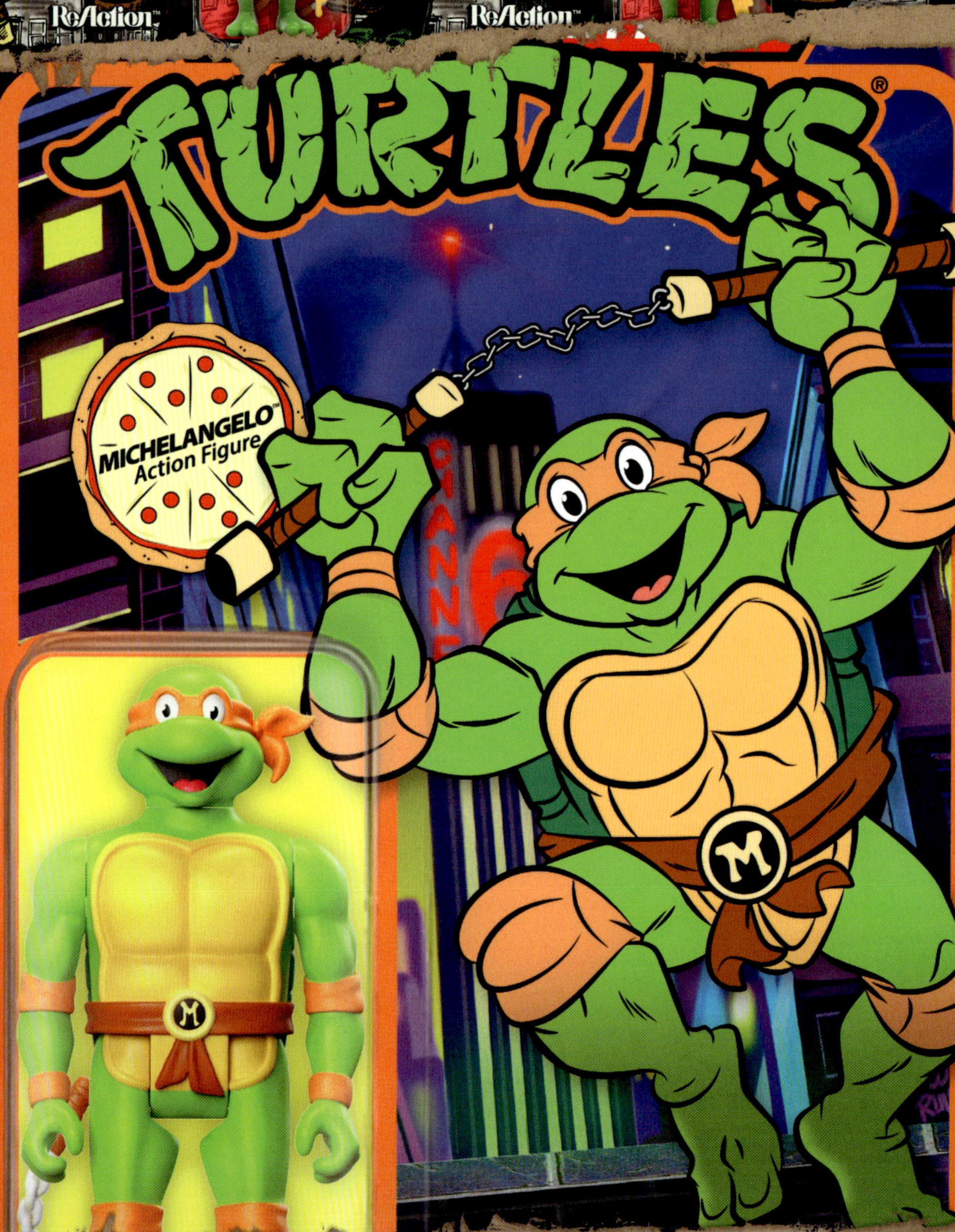

PREVIOUS: Teenage Mutant Ninja Turtles® ReAction Figures™ card art

THIS SPREAD: Selected Teenage Mutant Ninja Turtles® ReAction Figures™ card art

© 2025 Viacom International Inc.

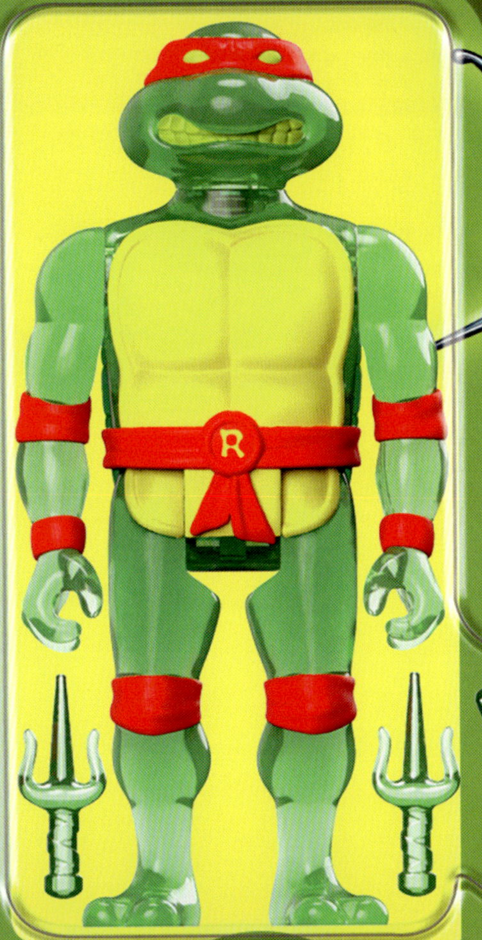

⚠ WARNING: CHOKING HAZARD - MAY CONTAIN SMALL PARTS
ADULT COLLECTIBLE - NOT A TOY
AGES 14+
TEENAGE MUTANT NINJA
TURTLES®
RAPHAEL™
Mutagen Ooze
ReAction™
FIGURES

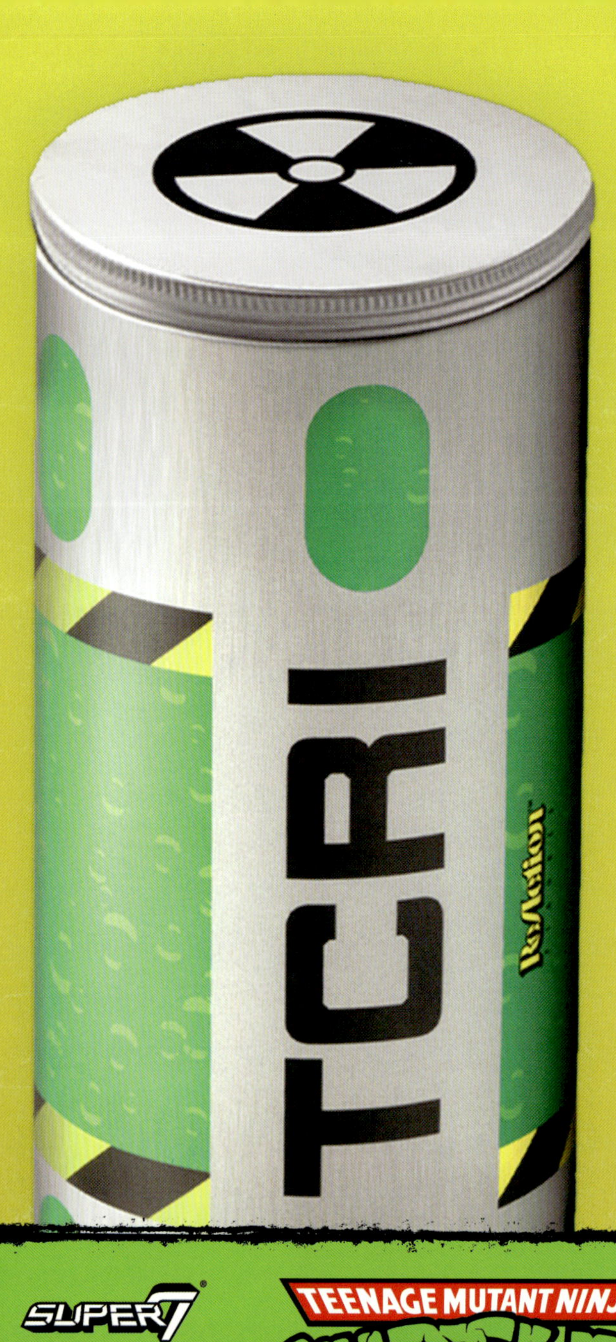
TCRI
ReAction
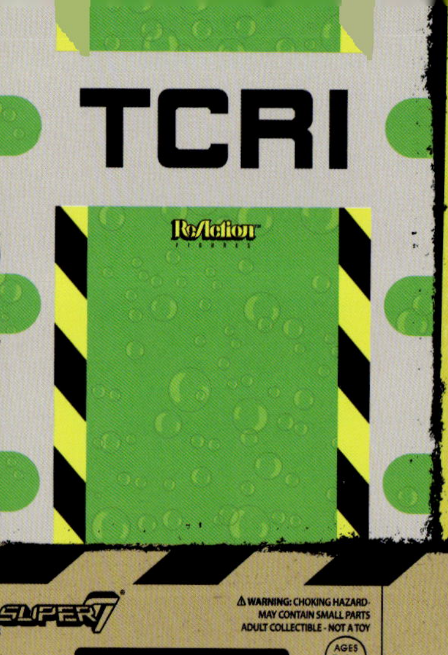
TCRI
ReAction
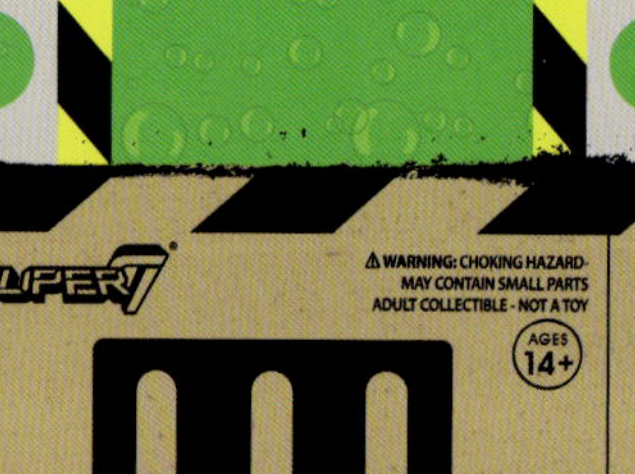
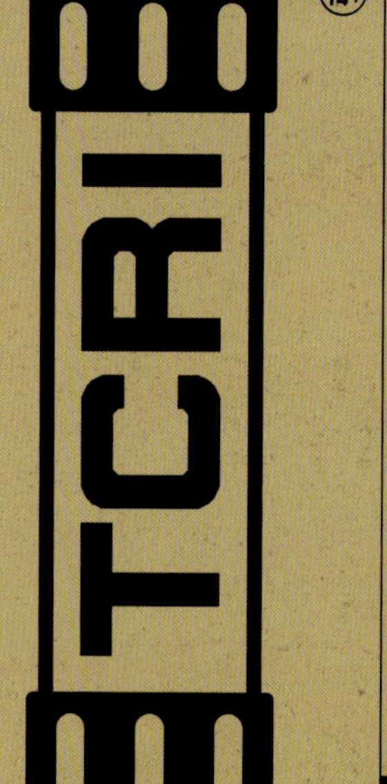
SUPER7
WARNING: CHOKING HAZARD MAY CONTAIN SMALL PARTS ADULT COLLECTIBLE - NOT A TOY
AGES 14+
TCRI
4 GLOW IN THE DARK REACTION FIGURES
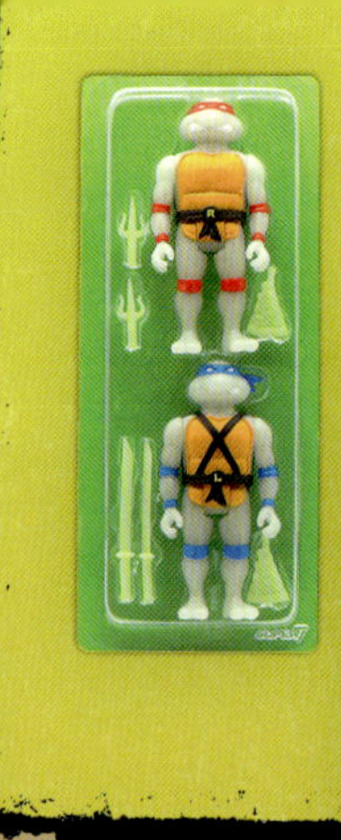
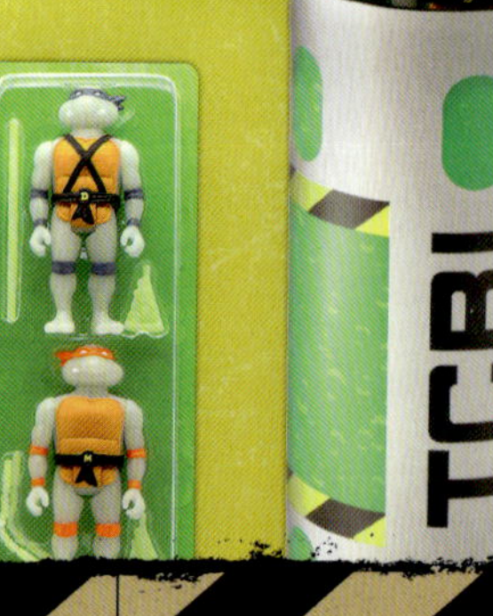
TCRI
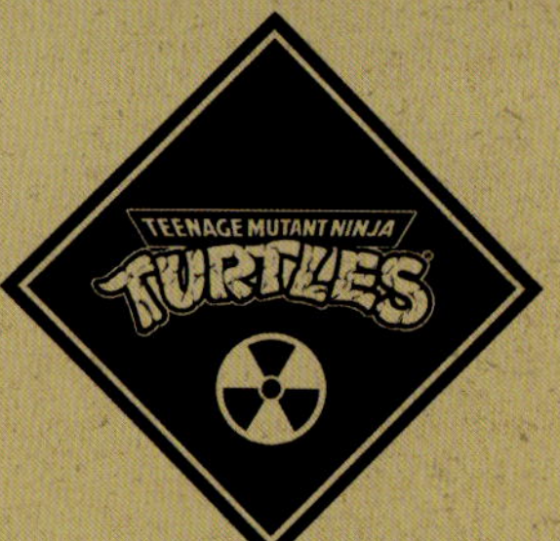
nickelodeon
TEENAGE MUTANT NINJA TURTLES
MUTAGEN OOZE
DANGER TOXIC
CANISTER: 1
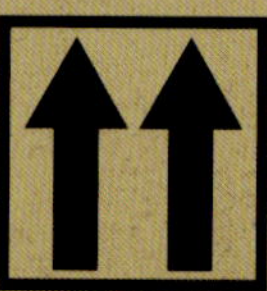
ReAction
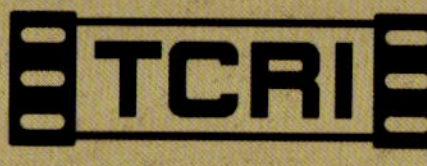
TCRI
CANISTER CONTENTS:
OOZE-POWERED
TEENAGE MUTANT
NINJA TURTLES
TYPE: REACTION
95.25 MM./3.75 IN.
QTY: 4
ACCS: WEAPONS/PIZZA
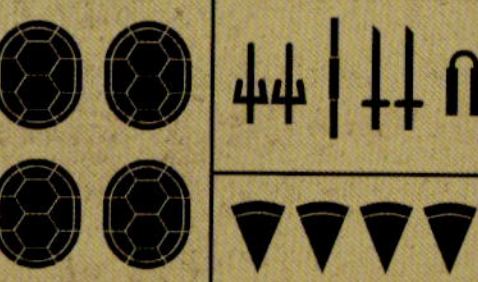
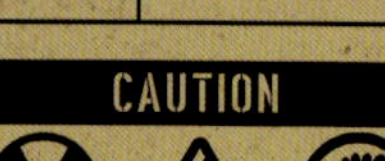
CAUTION
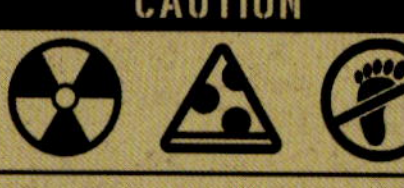
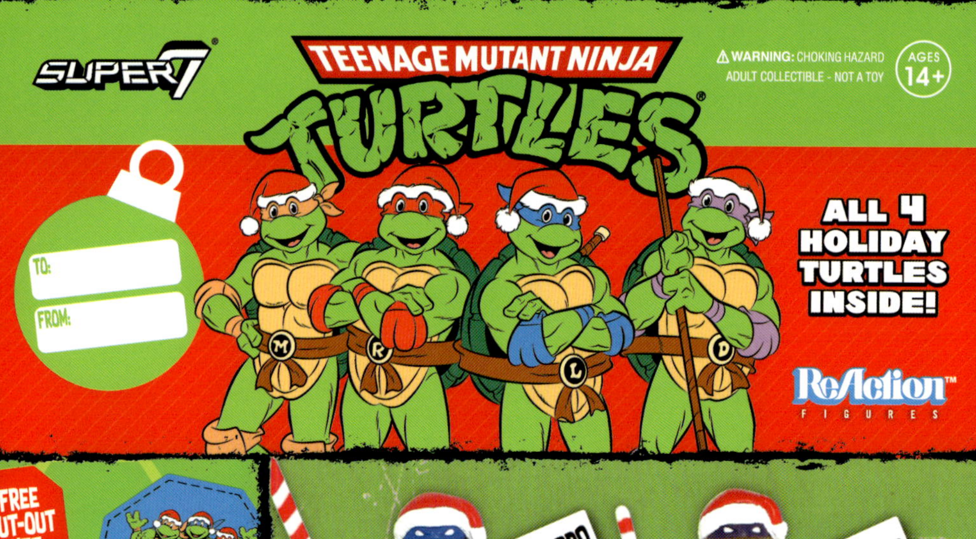
SUPER7
TEENAGE MUTANT NINJA
TURTLES
WARNING: CHOKING HAZARD
ADULT COLLECTIBLE - NOT A TOY
AGES 14+
TO:
FROM:
ALL 4
HOLIDAY
TURTLES
INSIDE!
ReAction FIGURES
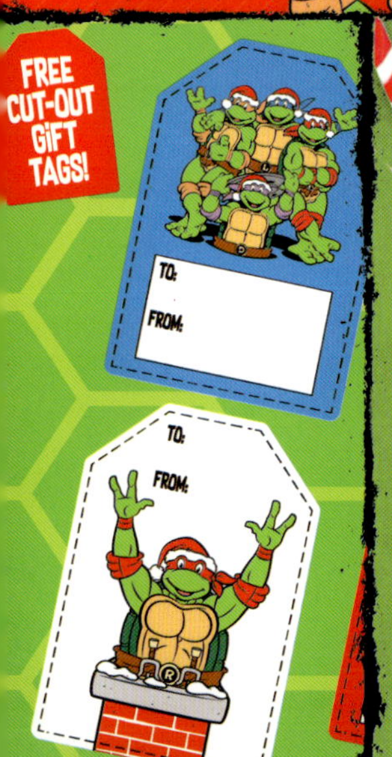
FREE
CUT-OUT
GIFT
TAGS!
TO:
FROM:
TO:
FROM:
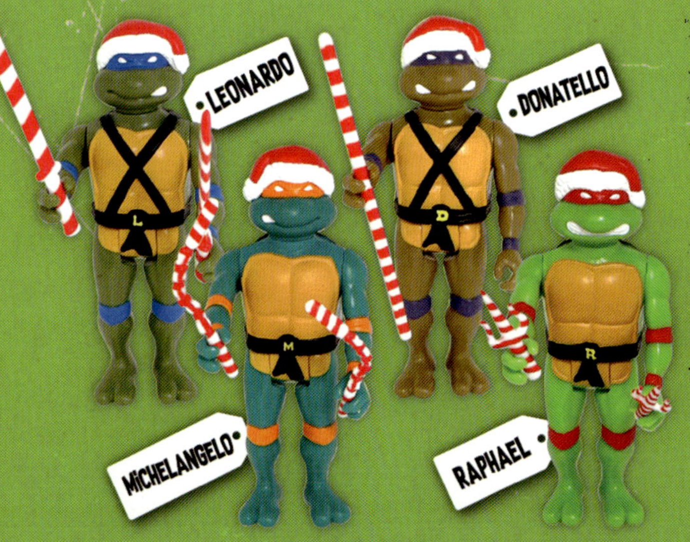
LEONARDO
DONATELLO
MICHELANGELO
RAPHAEL
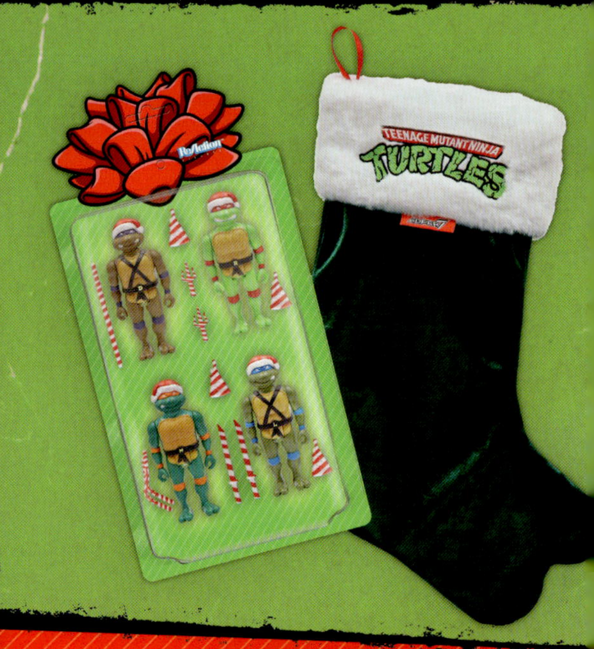
ReAction
TEENAGE MUTANT NINJA
TURTLES
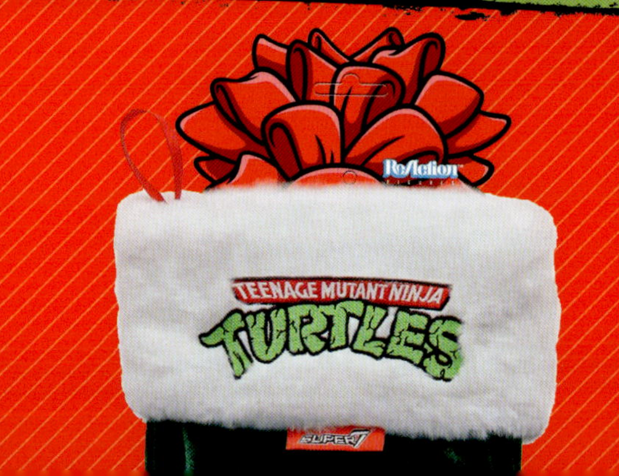
ReAction
TEENAGE MUTANT NINJA
TURTLES

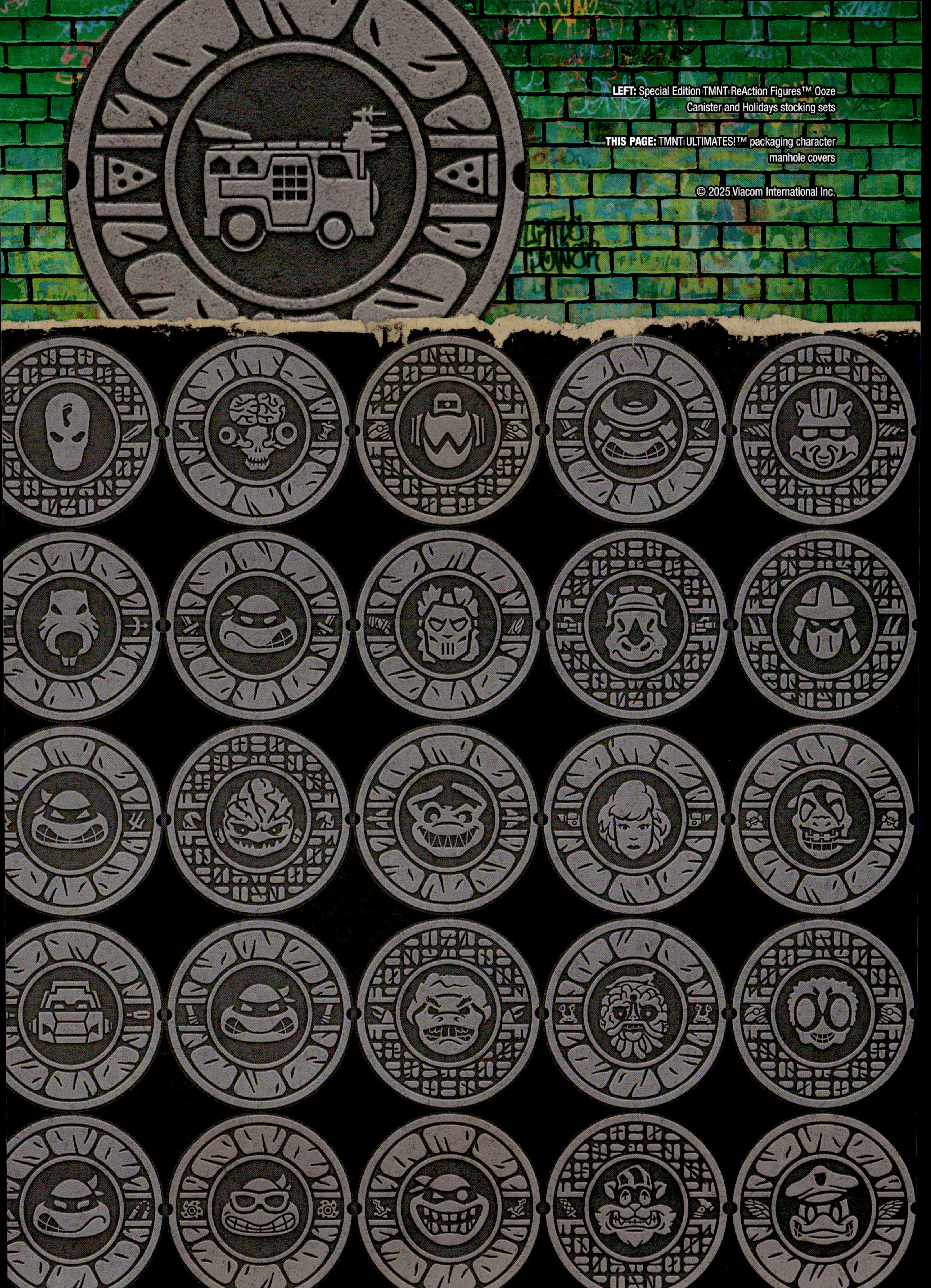

LEFT: Special Edition TMNT ReAction Figures™ Ooze Canister and Holidays stocking sets

THIS PAGE: TMNT ULTIMATES!™ packaging character manhole covers

© 2025 Viacom International Inc.

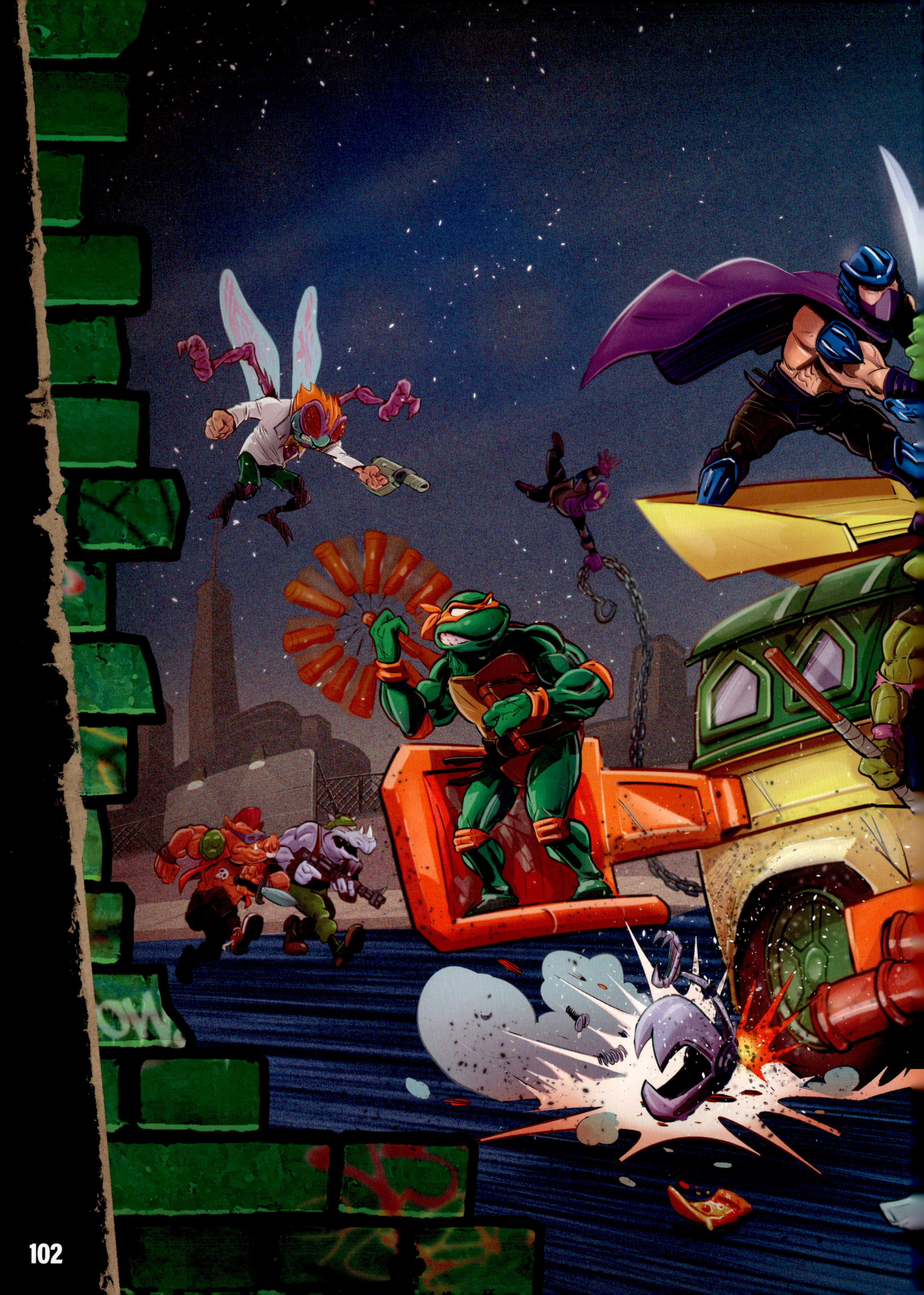

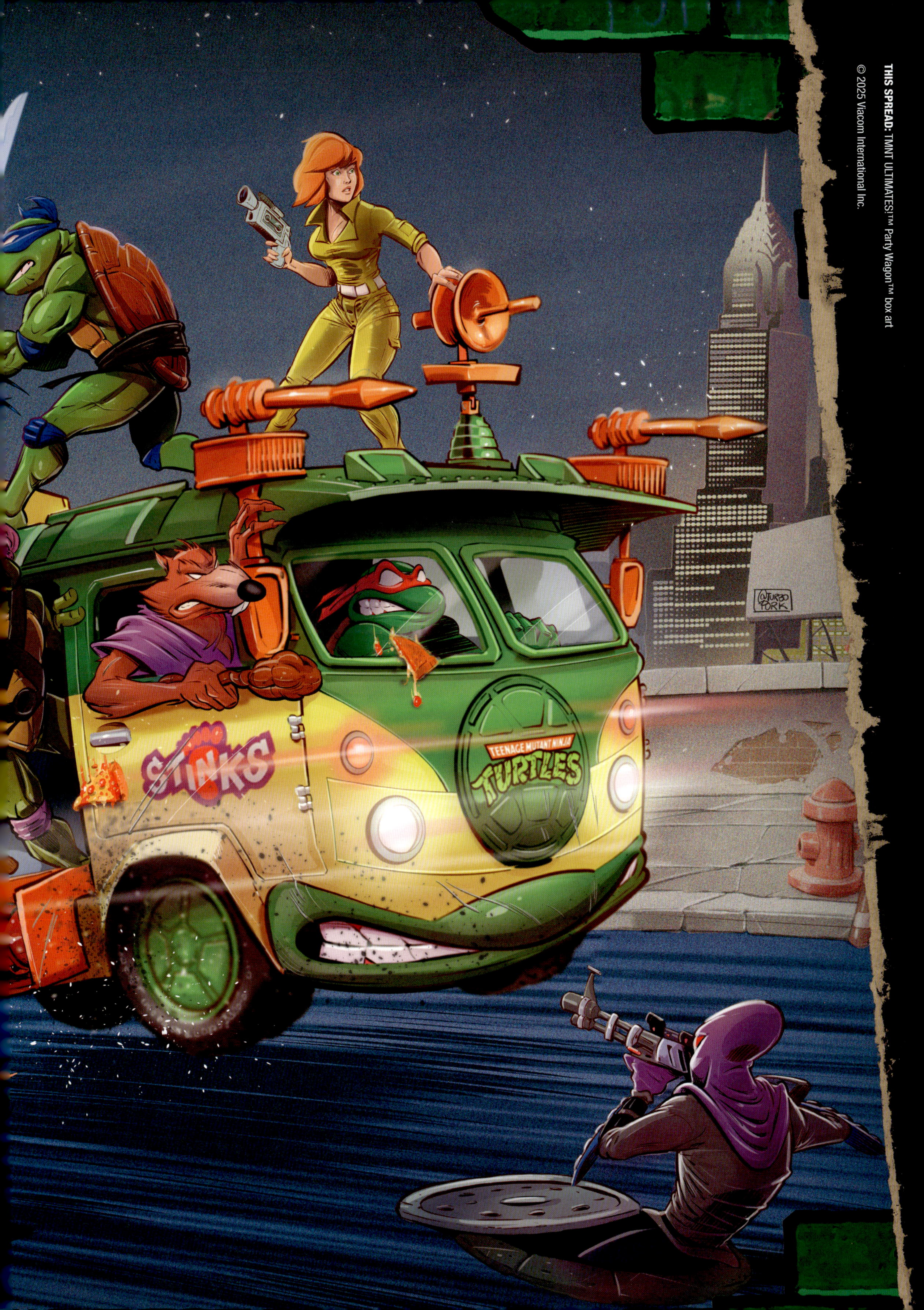

THIS SPREAD: TMNT ULTIMATES!™ Party Wagon™ box art

© 2025 Viacom International Inc.

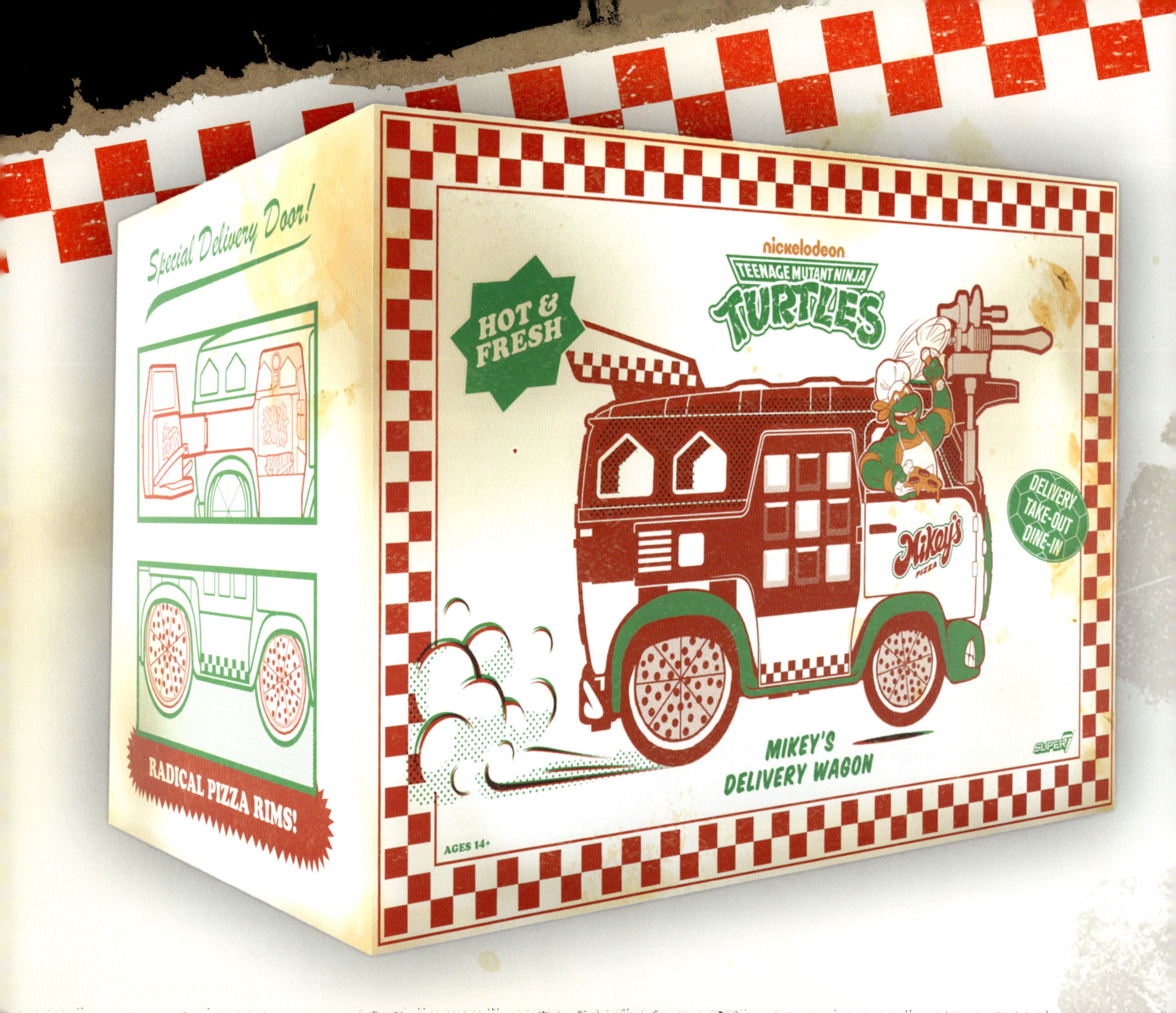

Special Delivery Door!
RADICAL PIZZA RIMS!
HOT & FRESH
nickelodeon
TEENAGE MUTANT NINJA
TURTLES
Mikey's
PIZZA
DELIVERY
TAKE-OUT
DINE-IN
MIKEY'S
DELIVERY WAGON
SUPER7
AGES 14+

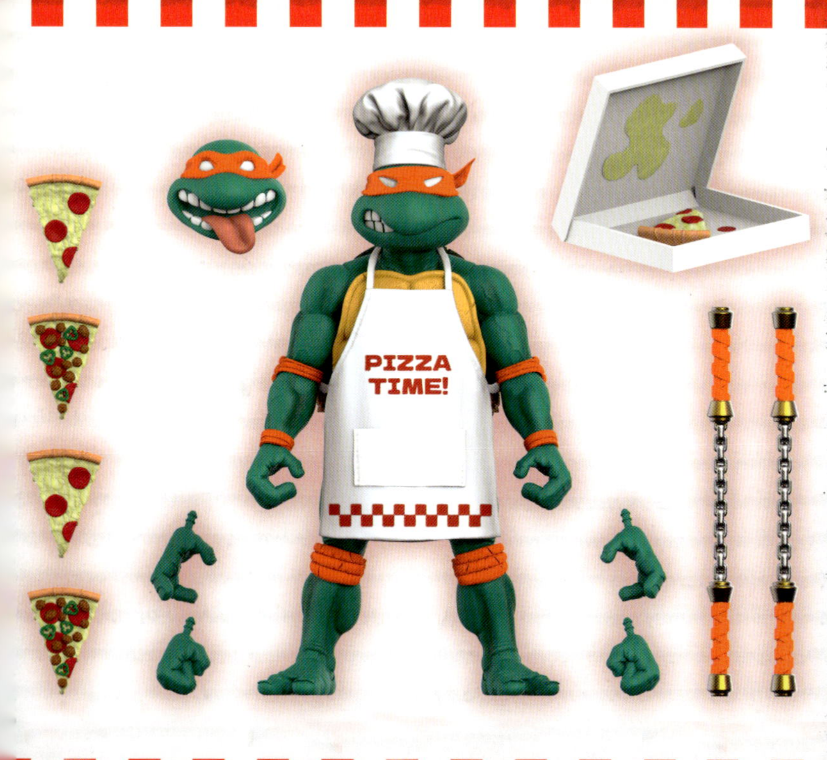
PIZZA
TIME!

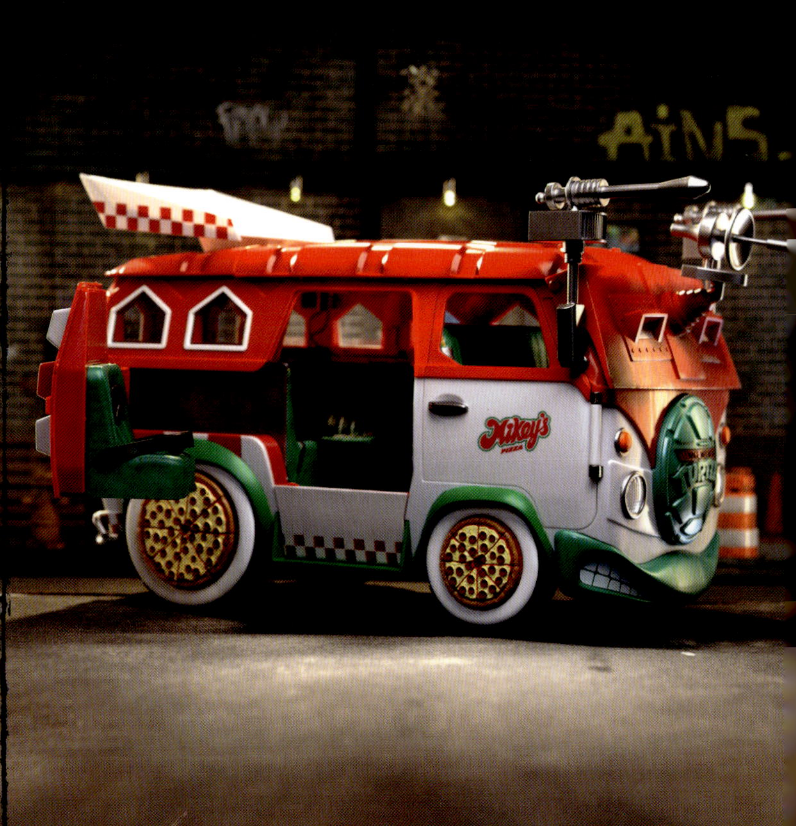
Mikey's

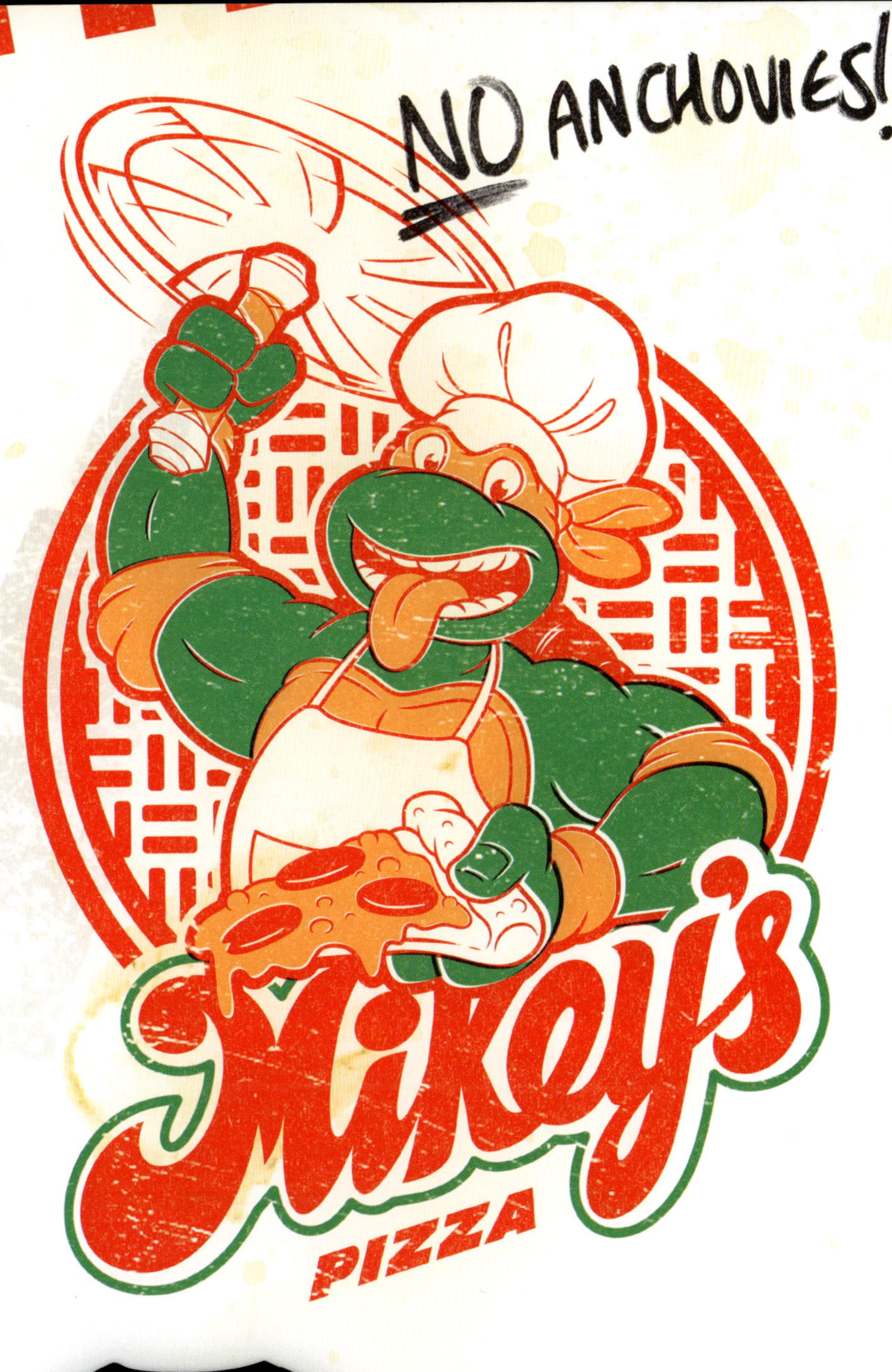

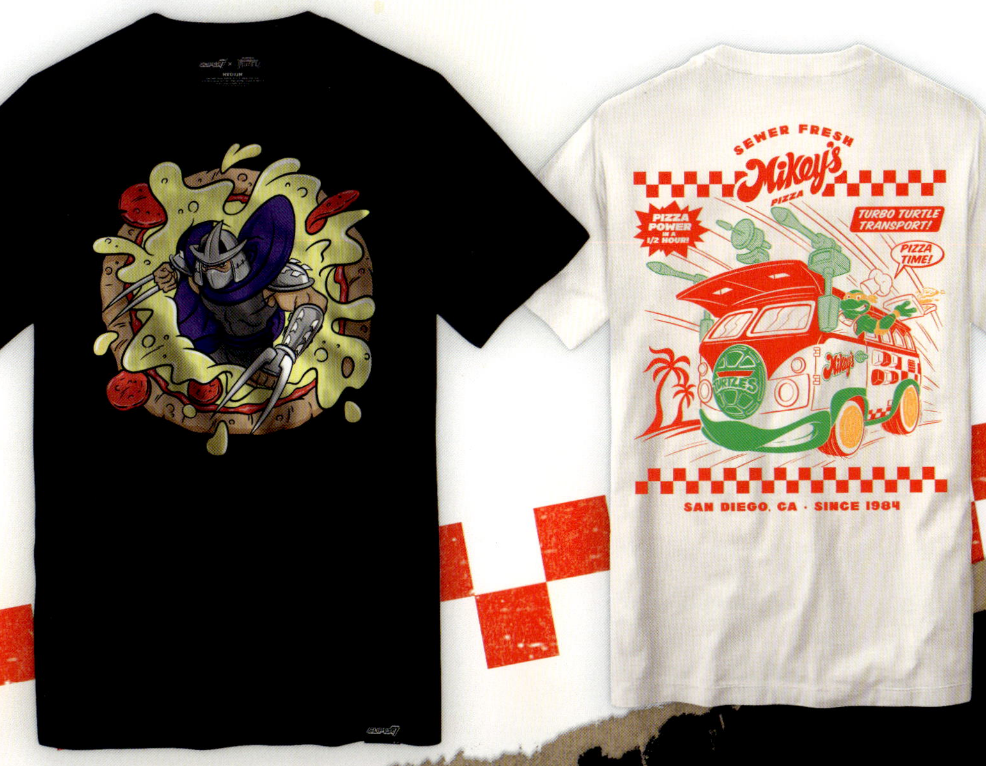

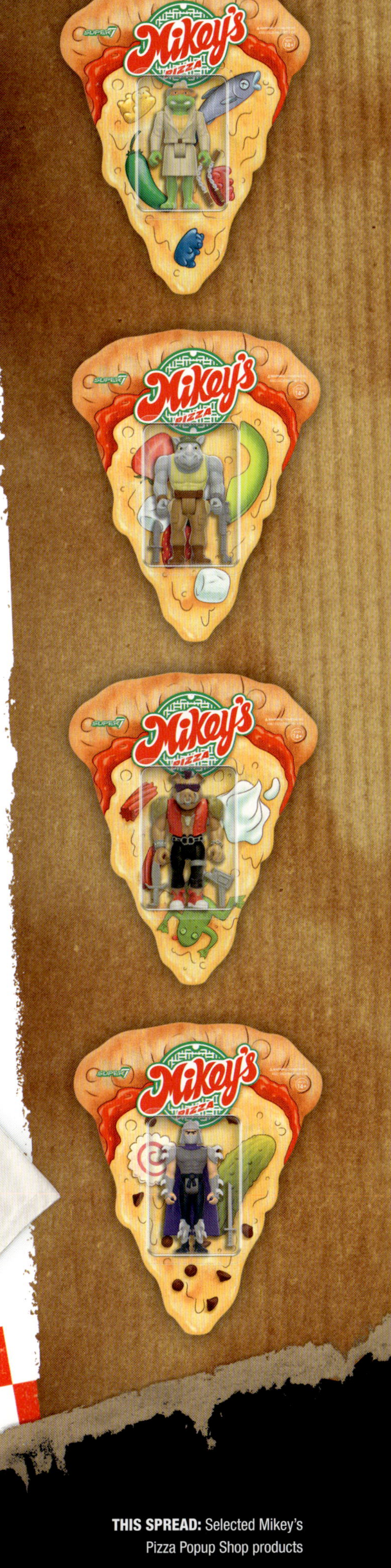

THIS SPREAD: Selected Mikey's Pizza Popup Shop products

© 2025 Viacom International Inc.

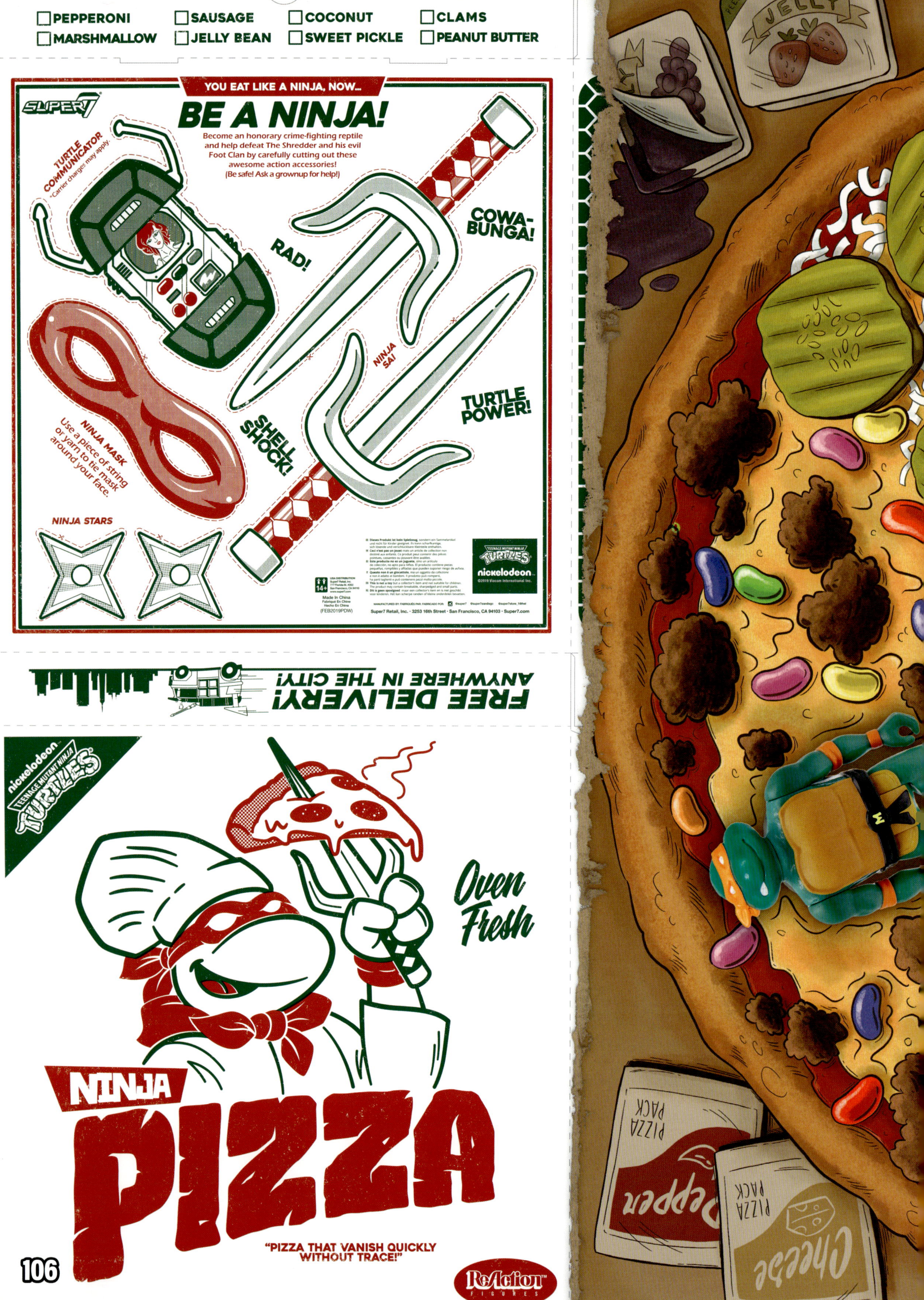
PEPPERONI
SAUSAGE
COCONUT
CLAMS
MARSHMALLOW
JELLY BEAN
SWEET PICKLE
PEANUT BUTTER
YOU EAT LIKE A NINJA, NOW...
SUPER7
BE A NINJA!
Become an honorary crime-fighting reptile and help defeat The Shredder and his evil Foot Clan by carefully cutting out these awesome action accessories!
(Be safe! Ask a grownup for help!)
TURTLE COMMUNICATOR
*Carrier charges may apply.
RAD!
COWA-BUNGA!
NINJA SAI
TURTLE POWER!
SHELL SHOCK!
NINJA MASK
Use a piece of string or yarn to tie the mask around your face.
NINJA STARS
Made In China
(FEB2019PDW)
nickelodeon
Super7 Retail, Inc. · 3253 16th Street · San Francisco, CA 94103 · Super7.com
FREE DELIVERY!
ANYWHERE IN THE CITY!
nickelodeon
TEENAGE MUTANT NINJA TURTLES
Oven Fresh
NINJA PIZZA
"PIZZA THAT VANISH QUICKLY WITHOUT TRACE!"
ReAction FIGURES
JELLY
PIZZA PACK
Pepper
PIZZA PACK
Cheese

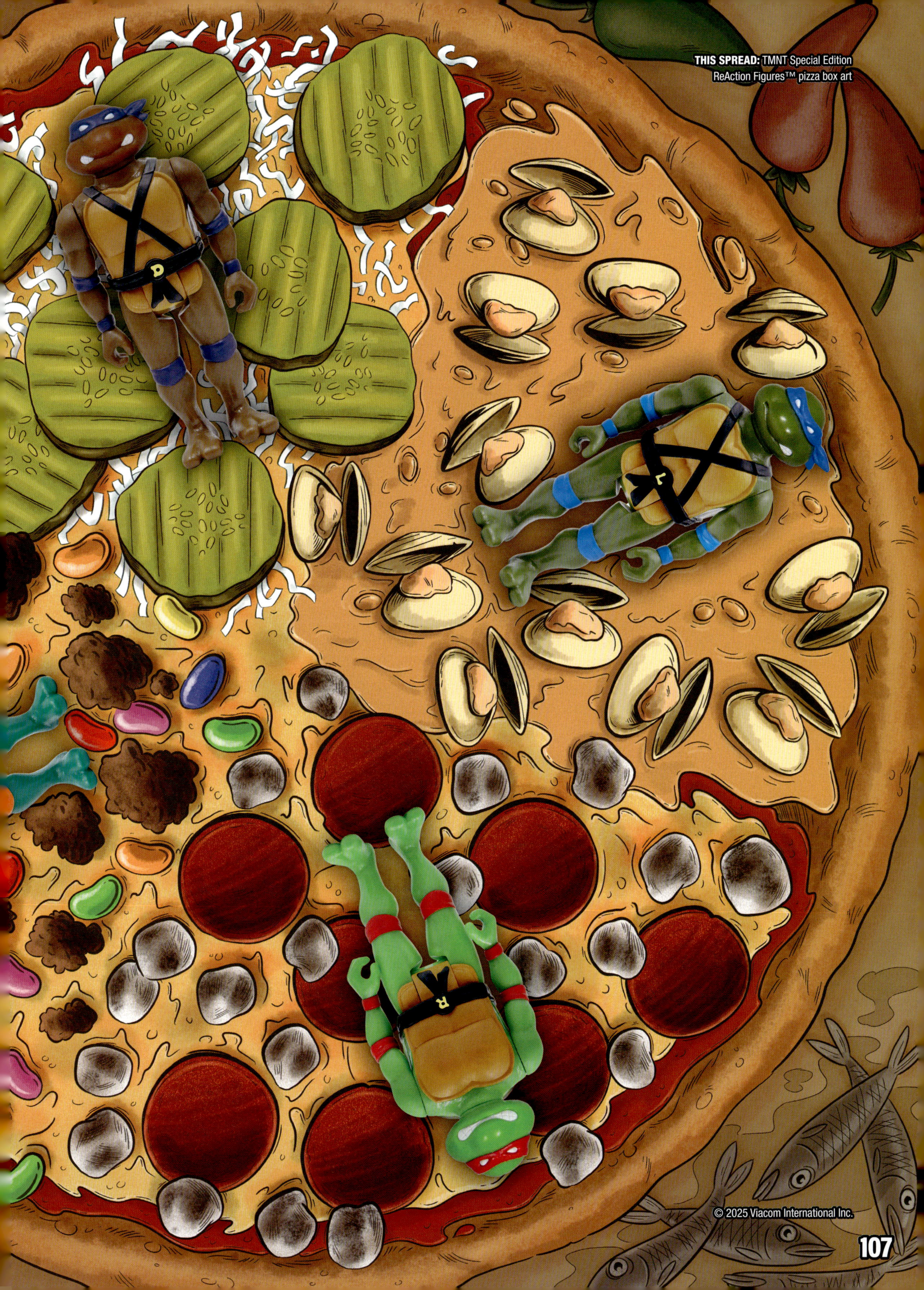

THIS SPREAD: TMNT Special Edition ReAction Figures™ pizza box art

© 2025 Viacom International Inc.

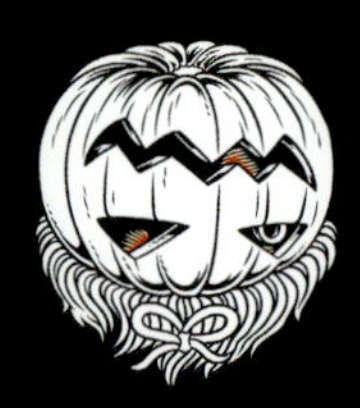
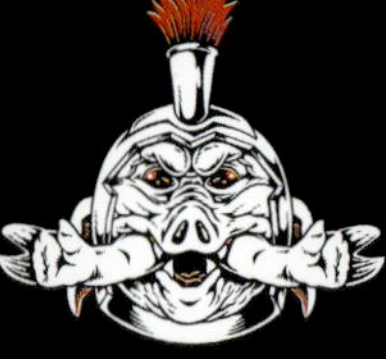
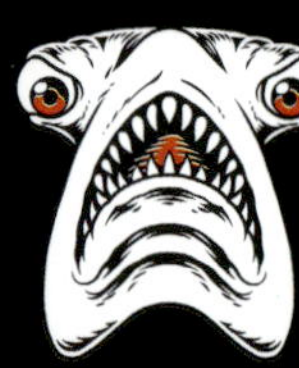
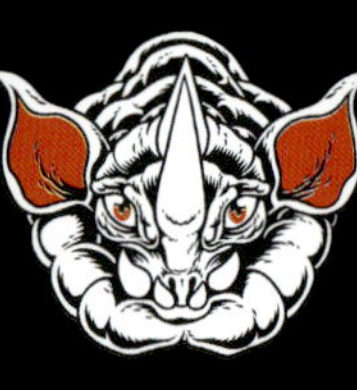
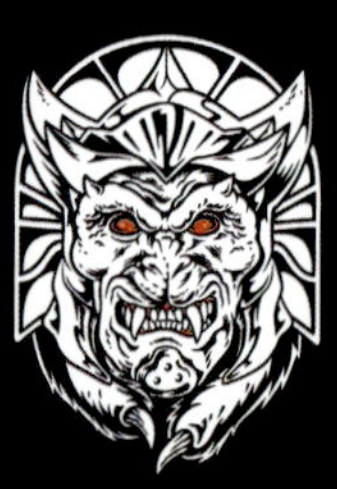
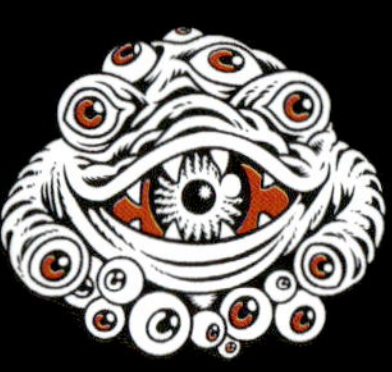
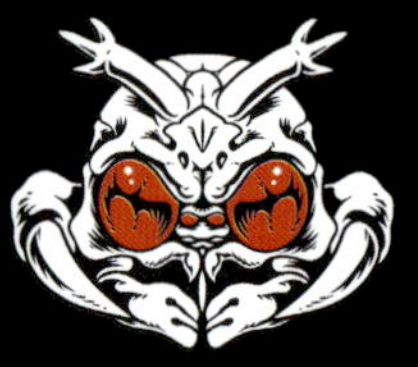
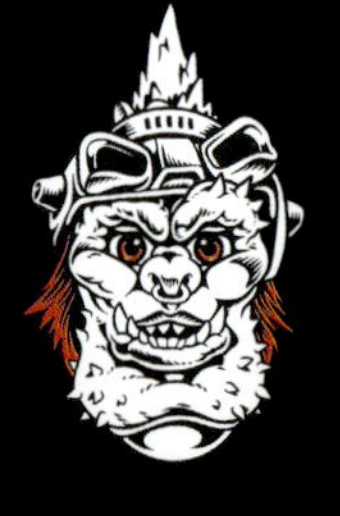

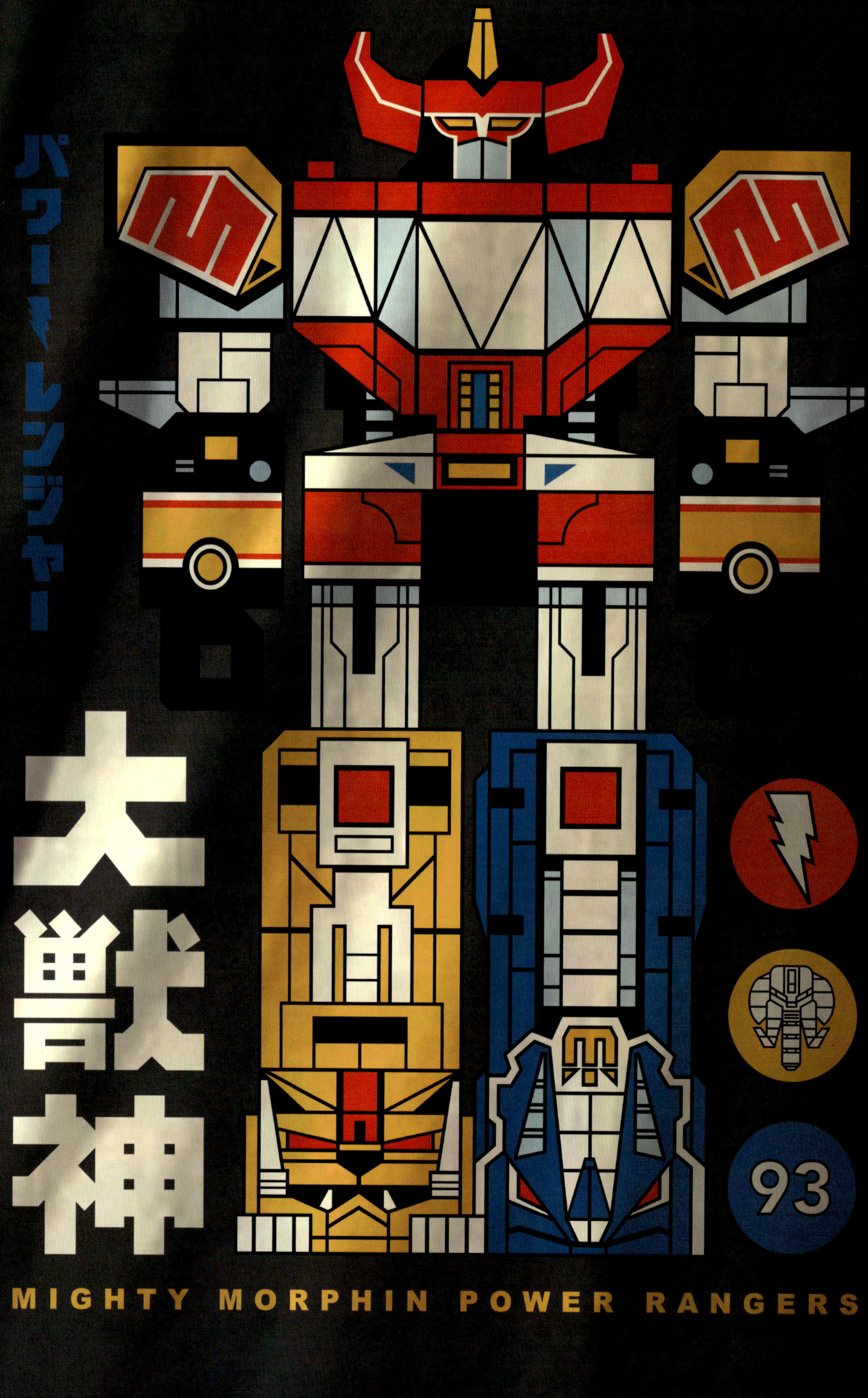

パワーレンジャー

大獣神

93

MIGHTY MORPHIN POWER RANGERS

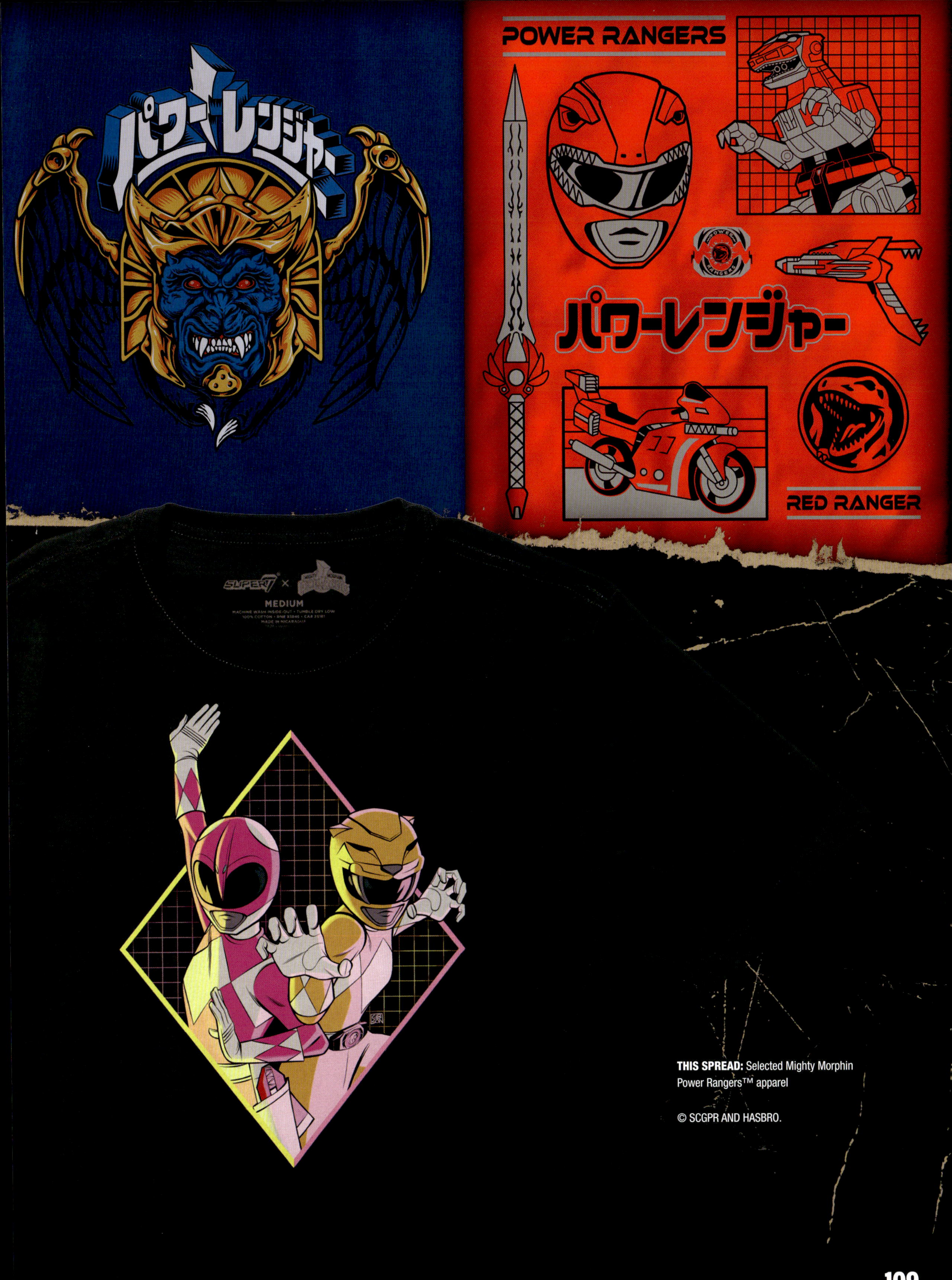

THIS SPREAD: Selected Mighty Morphin Power Rangers™ apparel

© SCGPR AND HASBRO.

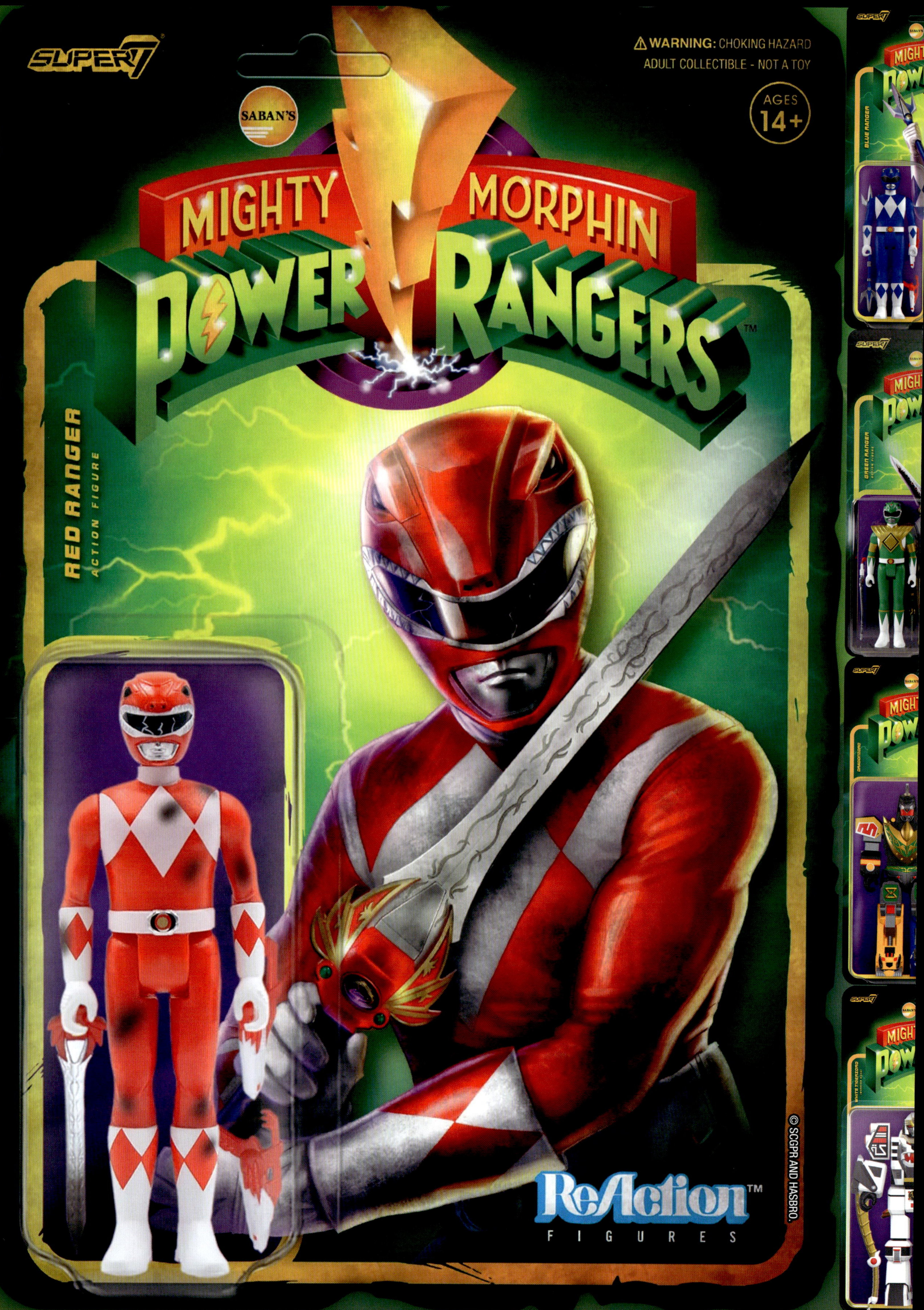

SUPER7
⚠ WARNING: CHOKING HAZARD
ADULT COLLECTIBLE - NOT A TOY
AGES 14+
SABAN'S
MIGHTY MORPHIN
POWER RANGERS™
RED RANGER
ACTION FIGURE
ReAction™
FIGURES
© SCGPR AND HASBRO.

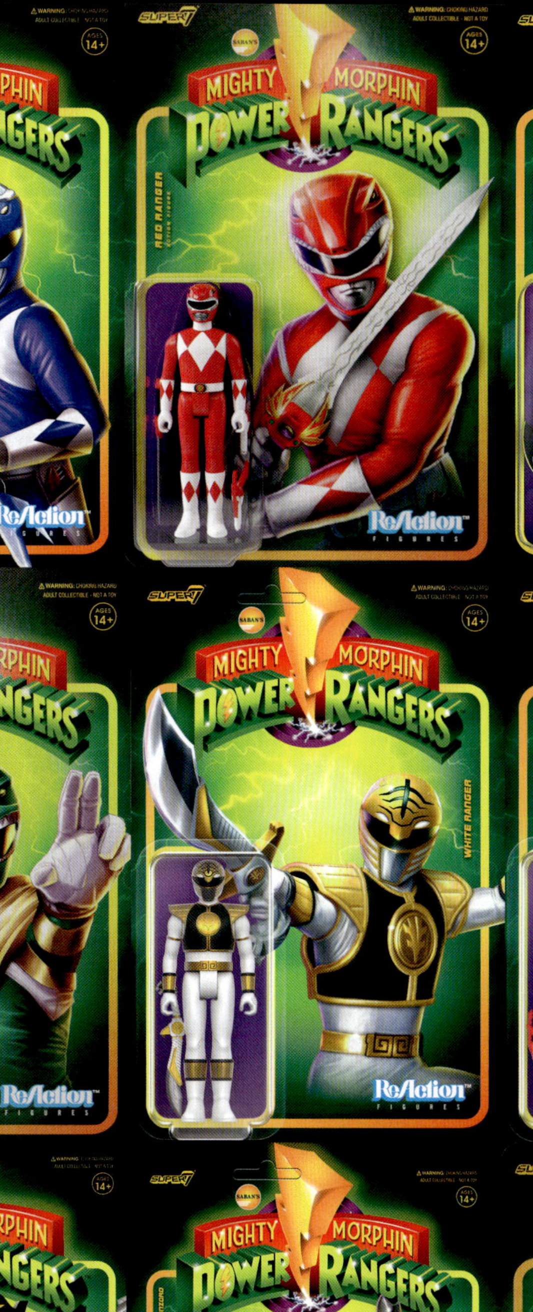
ReAction

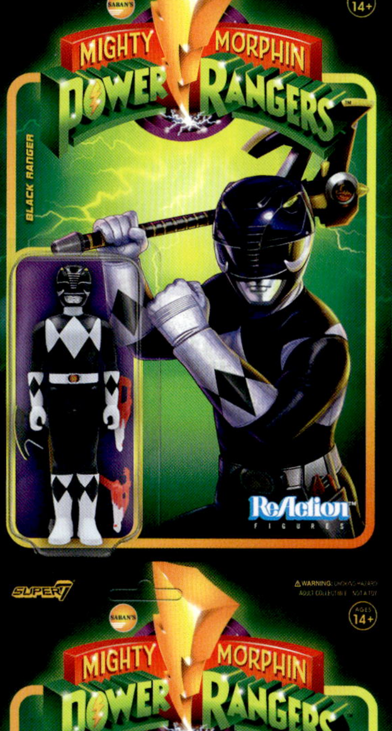
MIGHTY MORPHIN
POWER RANGERS
RED RANGER
ReAction

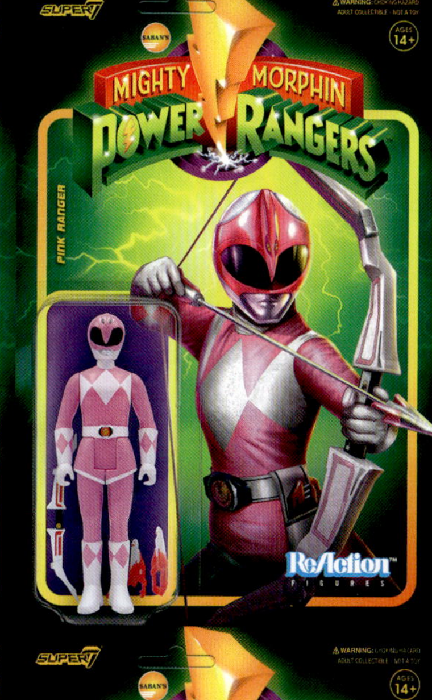
MIGHTY MORPHIN
POWER RANGERS
BLACK RANGER
ReAction

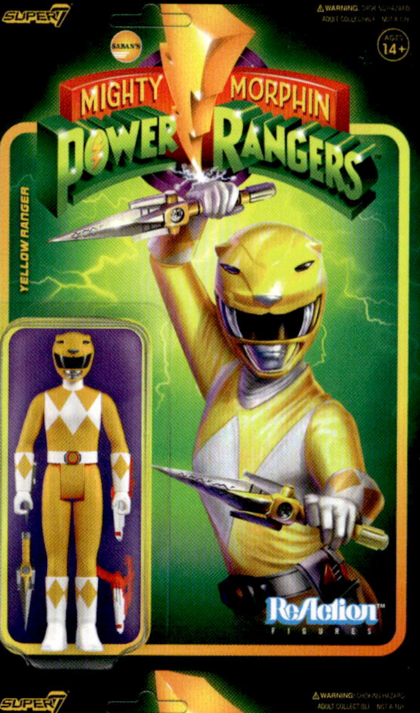
MIGHTY MORPHIN
POWER RANGERS
PINK RANGER
ReAction

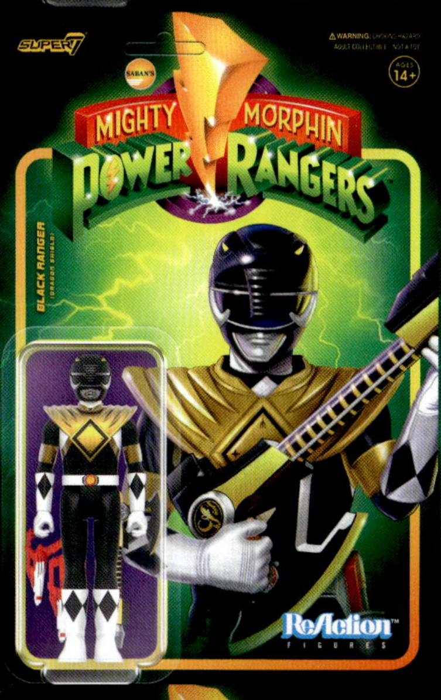
MIGHTY MORPHIN
POWER RANGERS
WHITE RANGER
ReAction

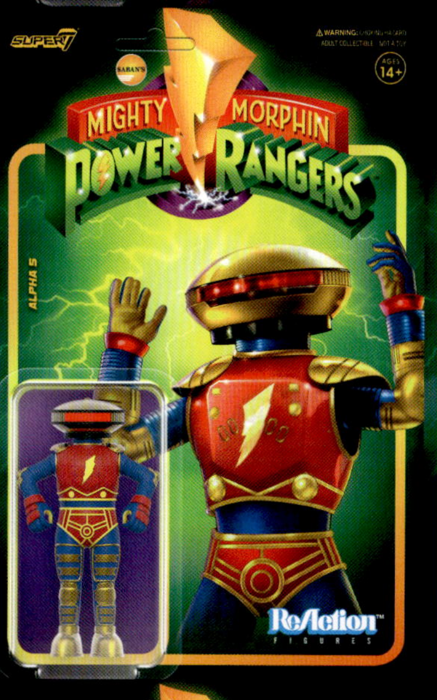
MIGHTY MORPHIN
POWER RANGERS
BLACK RANGER
ReAction

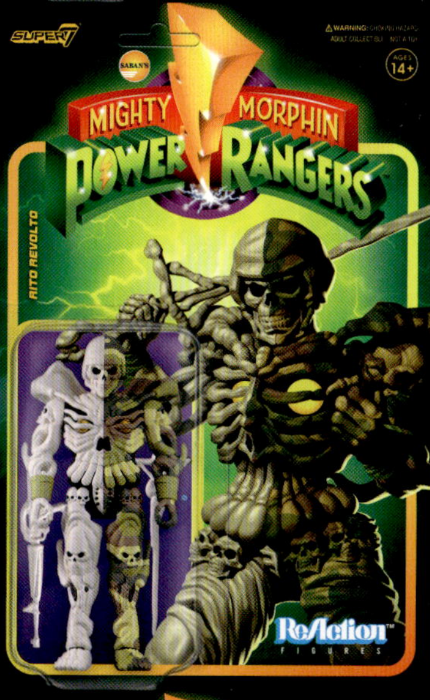
MIGHTY MORPHIN
POWER RANGERS
ALPHA 5
ReAction

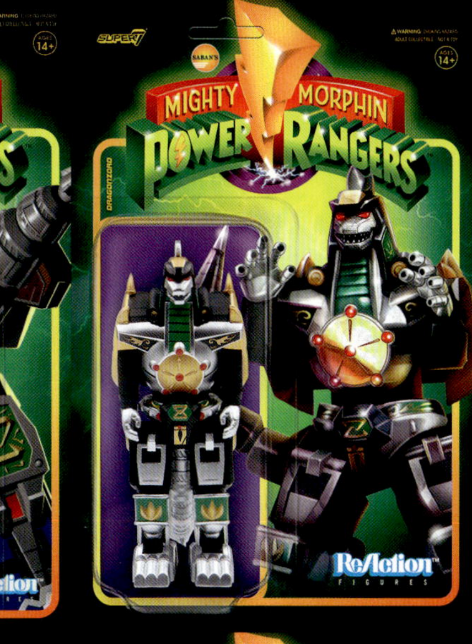
MIGHTY MORPHIN
POWER RANGERS
ReAction

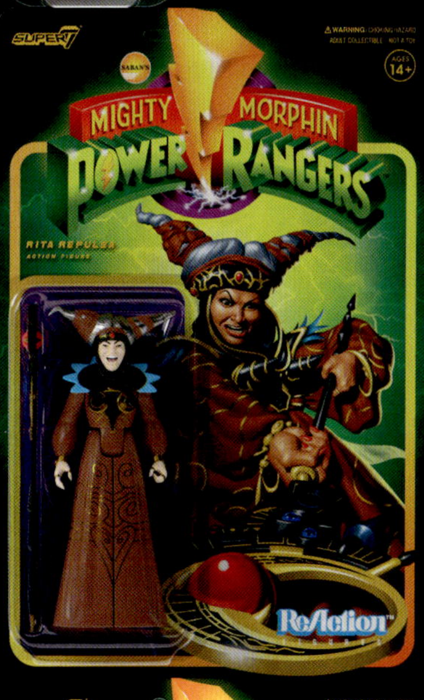
MIGHTY MORPHIN
POWER RANGERS
RITA REPULSA
ReAction

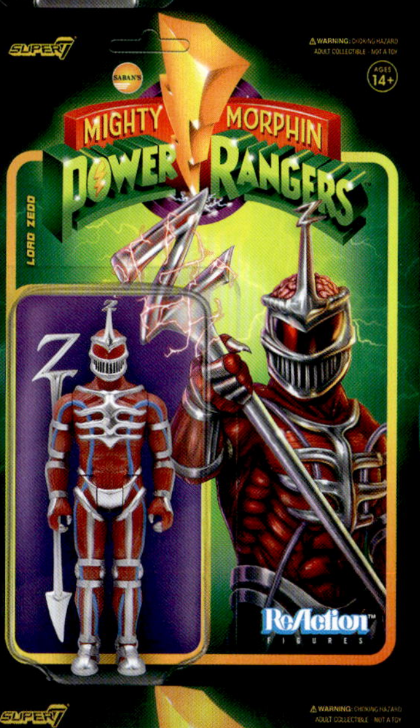
MIGHTY MORPHIN
POWER RANGERS
LORD ZEDD
ReAction

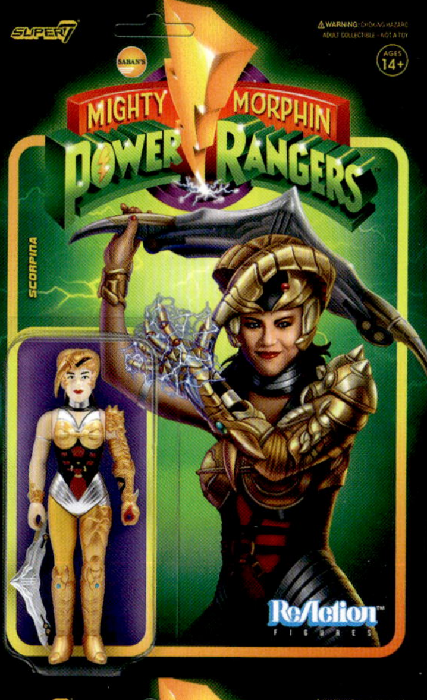
MIGHTY MORPHIN
POWER RANGERS
SCORPINA
ReAction

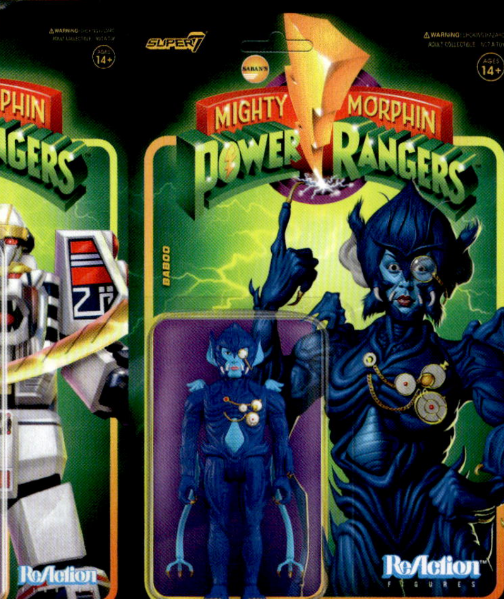
MIGHTY MORPHIN
POWER RANGERS
BABOO
ReAction

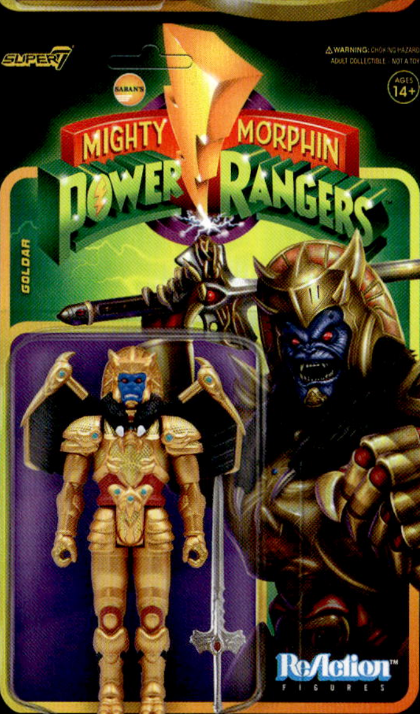
MIGHTY MORPHIN
POWER RANGERS
GOLDAR
ReAction

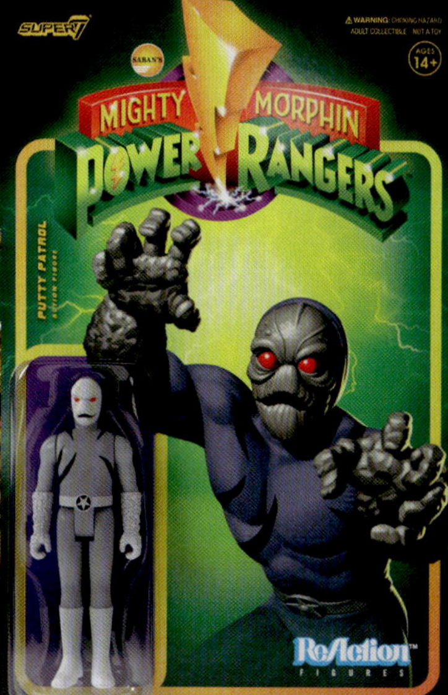
MIGHTY MORPHIN
POWER RANGERS
PUTTY PATROL
ReAction

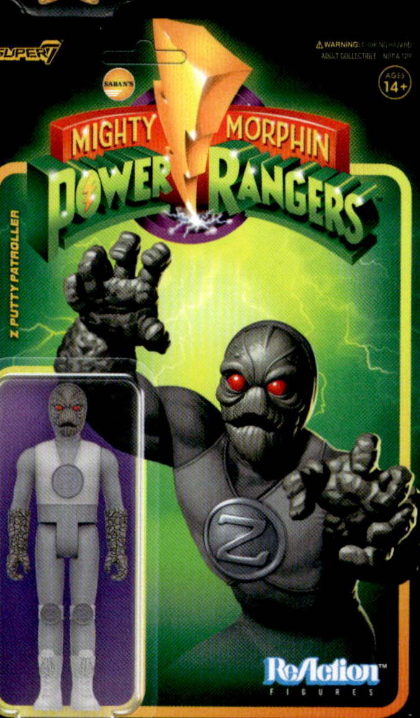
MIGHTY MORPHIN
POWER RANGERS
ReAction

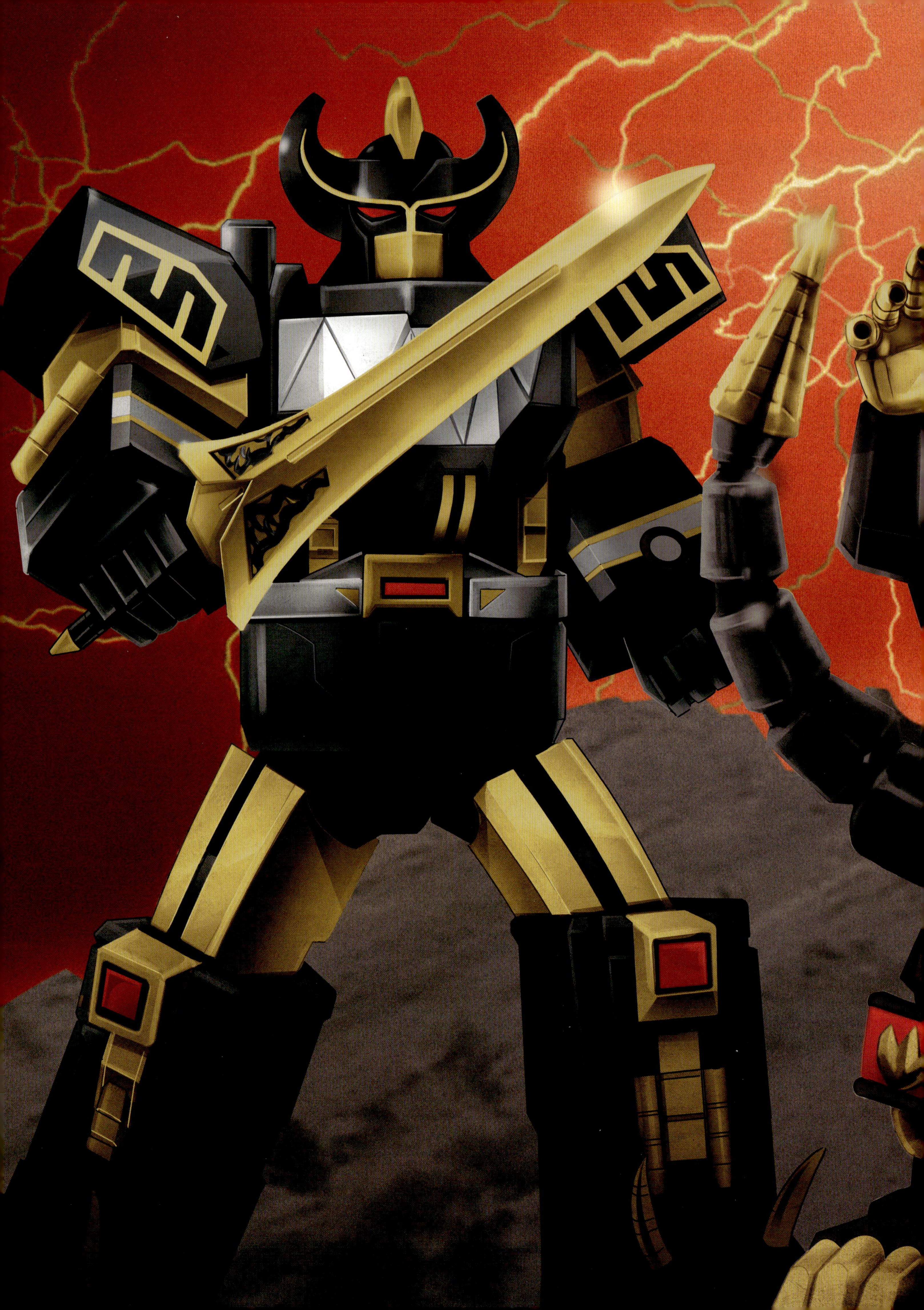

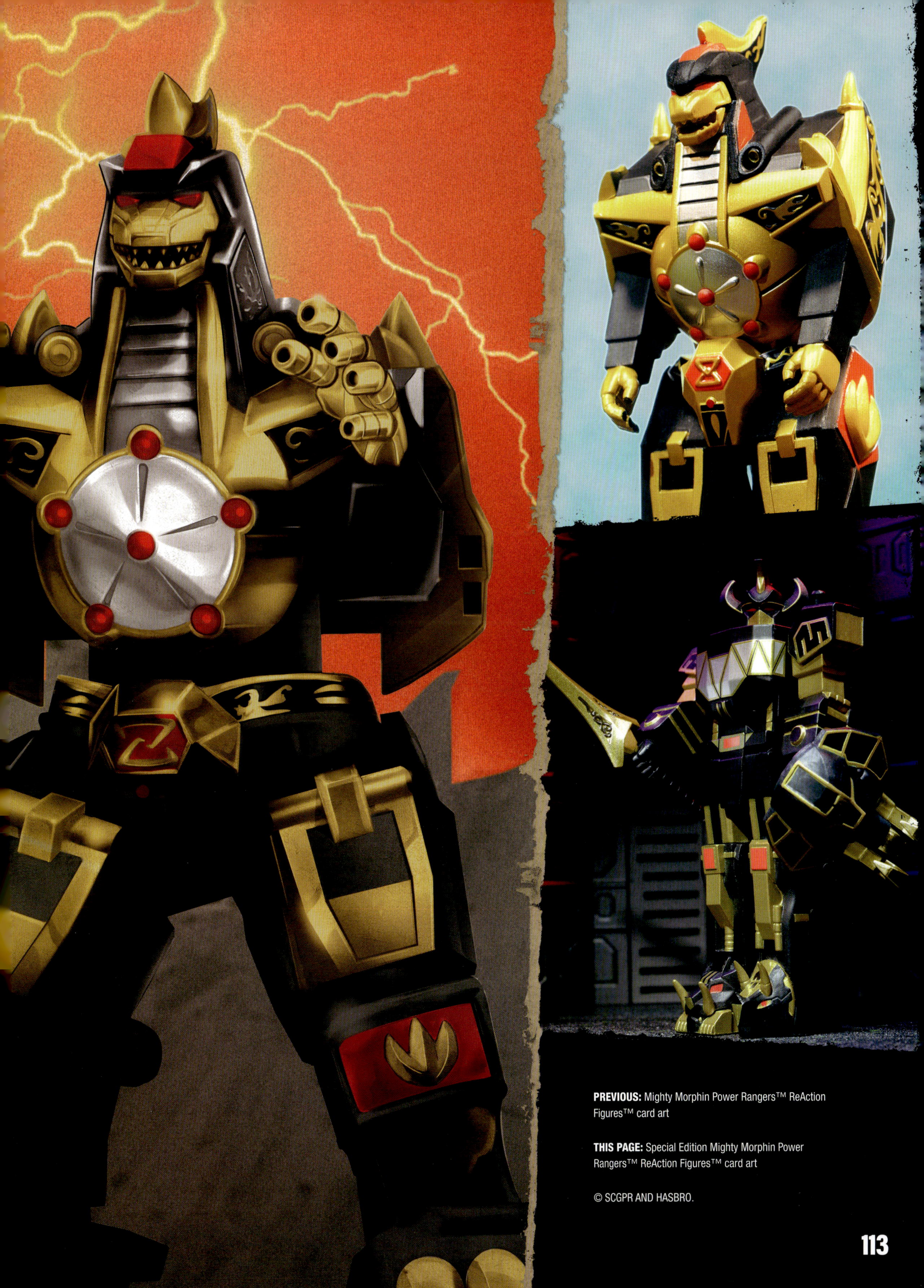

PREVIOUS: Mighty Morphin Power Rangers™ ReAction Figures™ card art

THIS PAGE: Special Edition Mighty Morphin Power Rangers™ ReAction Figures™ card art

© SCGPR AND HASBRO.

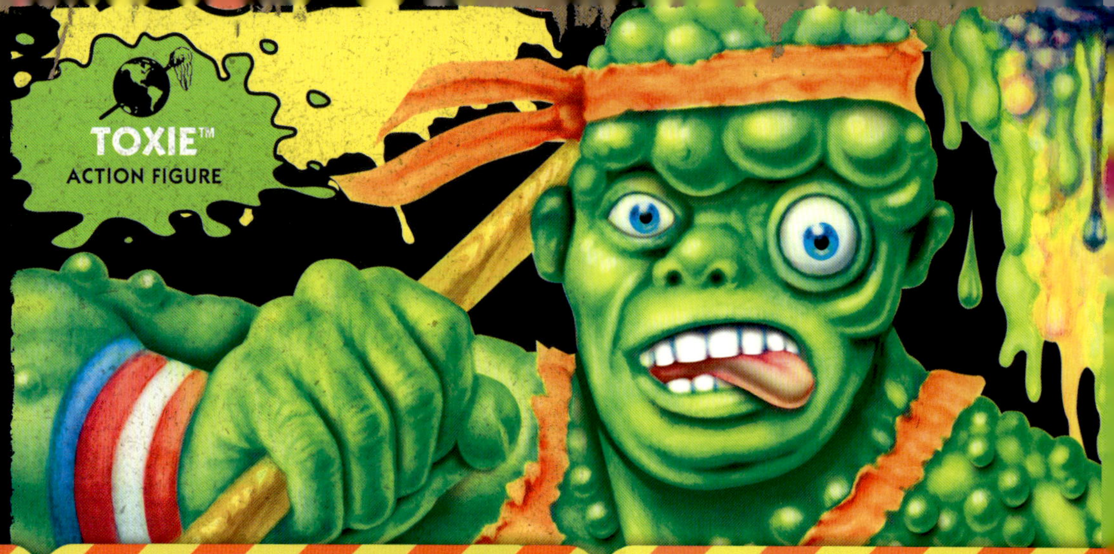

LEFT: Toxic Crusaders™ ReAction Figures™ card art

THIS PAGE: The Toxic Avenger™ ReAction Figures™ card art

© & TM Troma Entertainment Inc.

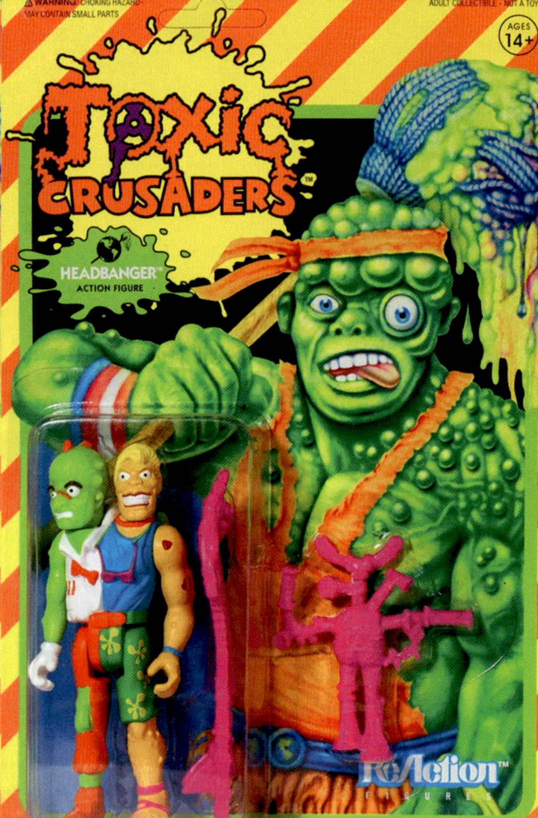

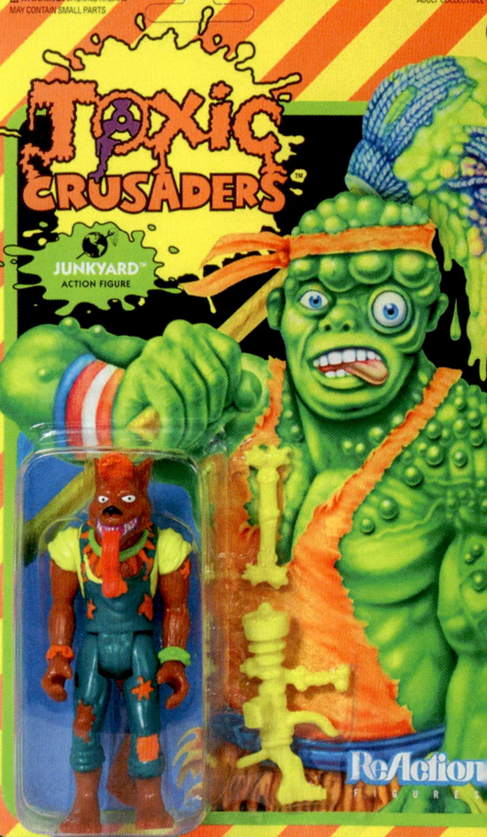

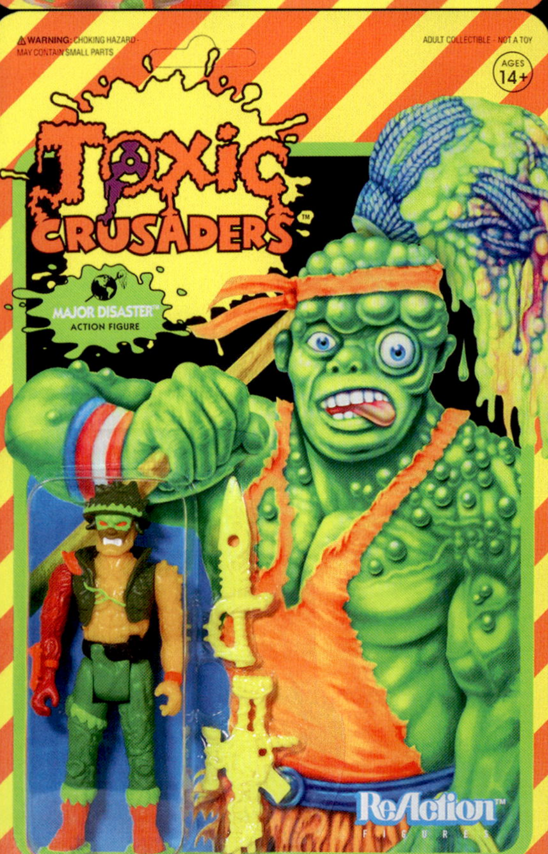

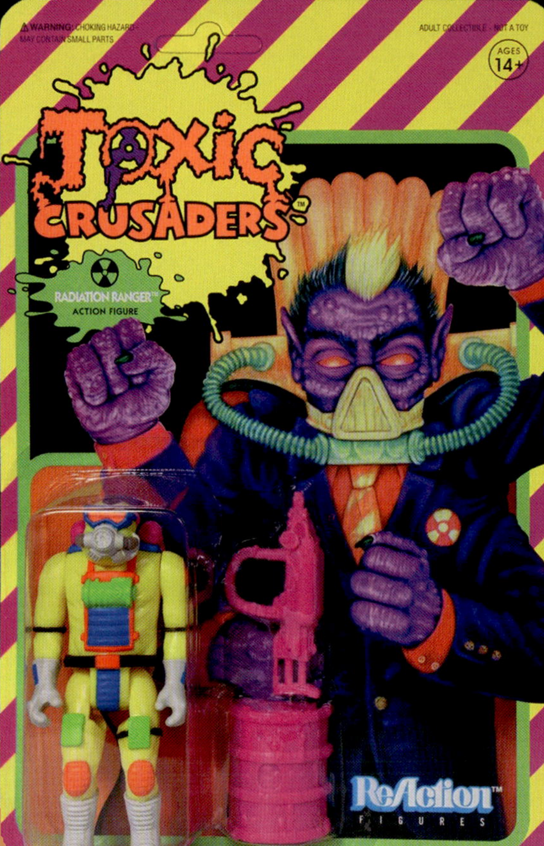

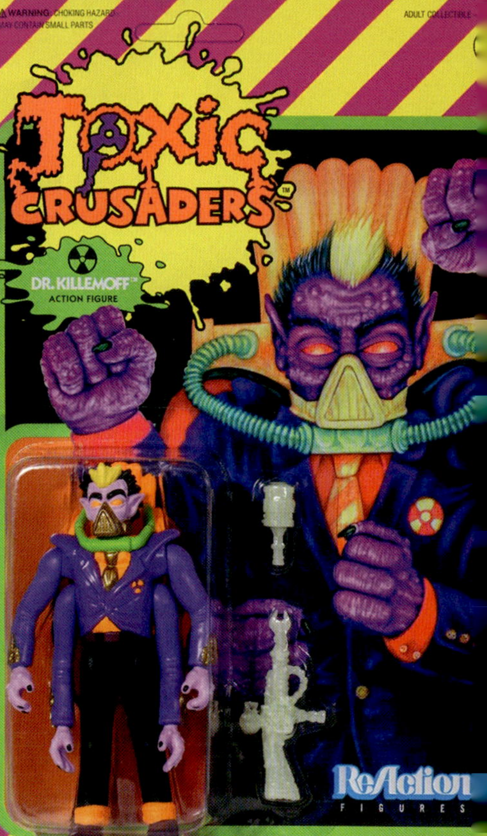

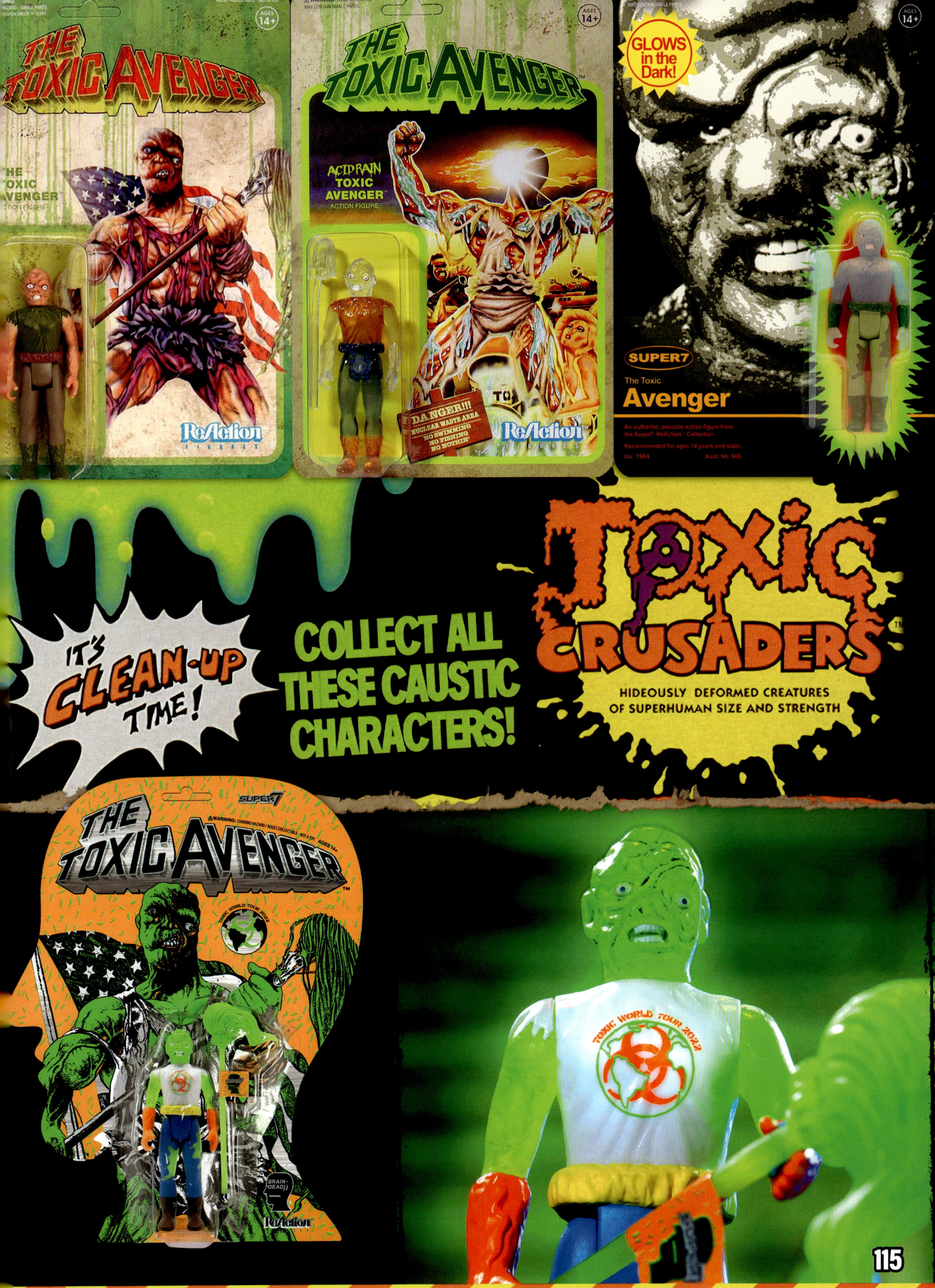
THE TOXIC AVENGER
ReAction FIGURES
THE TOXIC AVENGER
ACID RAIN TOXIC AVENGER ACTION FIGURE
DANGER!!! NUCLEAR WASTE AREA NO SWIMMING NO FISHING NO NOTHIN'
ReAction FIGURES
GLOWS in the Dark!
SUPER7
The Toxic
Avenger
IT'S CLEAN-UP TIME!
COLLECT ALL THESE CAUSTIC CHARACTERS!
TOXIC CRUSADERS
HIDEOUSLY DEFORMED CREATURES OF SUPERHUMAN SIZE AND STRENGTH
SUPER7
THE TOXIC AVENGER
TOXIC WORLD TOUR 2022
ReAction

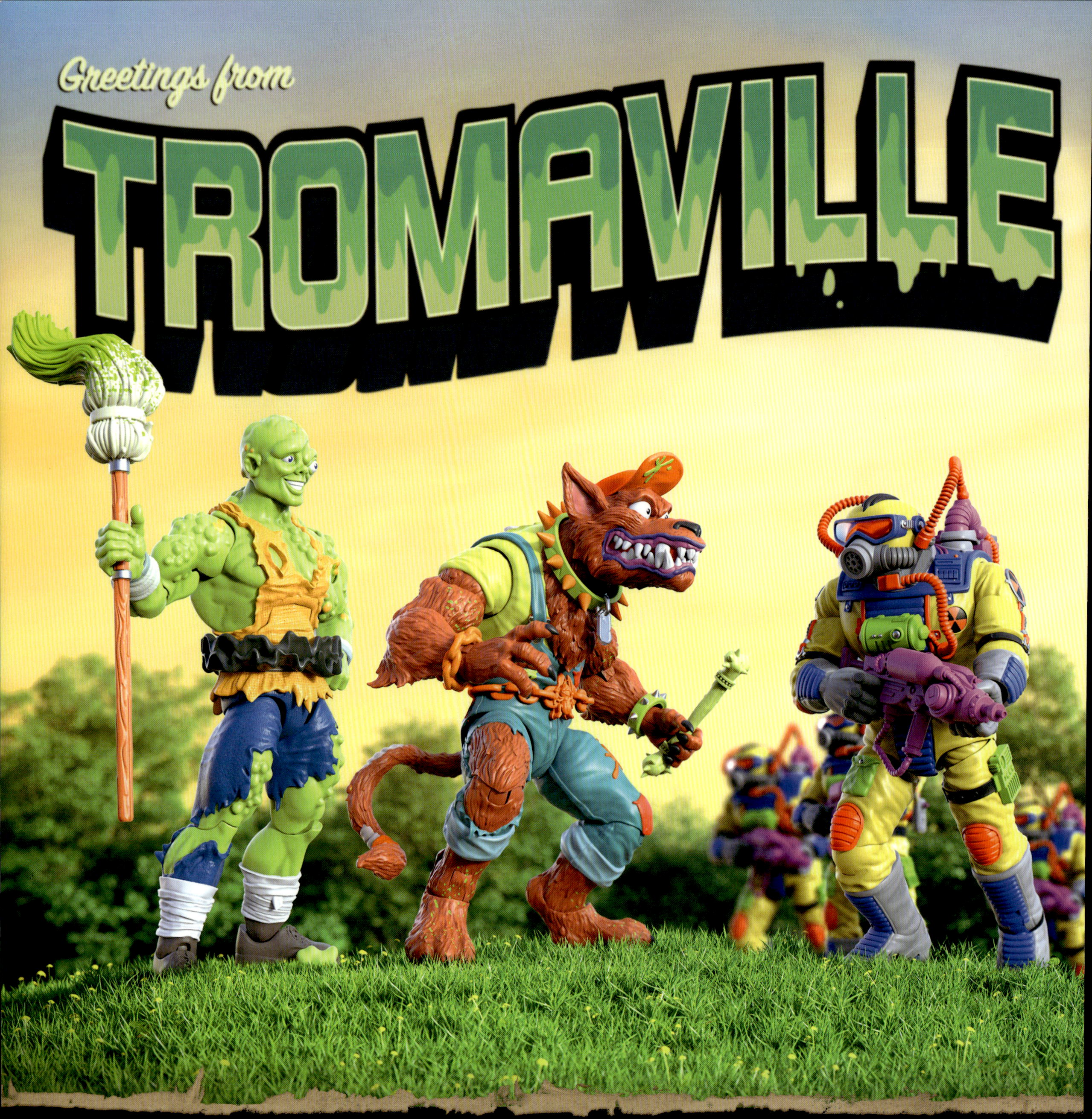

Greetings from TROMAVILLE

THIS PAGE: Toxic Crusaders™ ULTIMATES!™ box art

RIGHT: My Pet Monster™ ReAction Figures™ card art and apparel

© & TM Troma Entertainment Inc.

© 2025 Hasbro

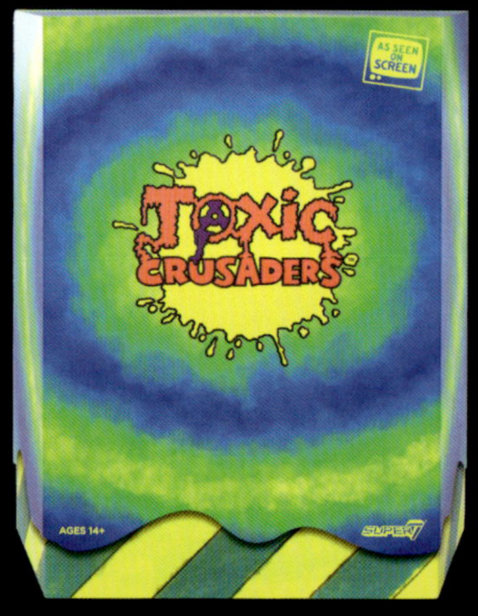

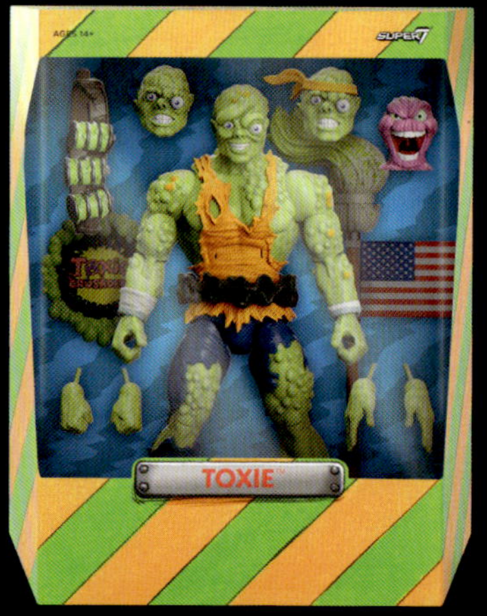

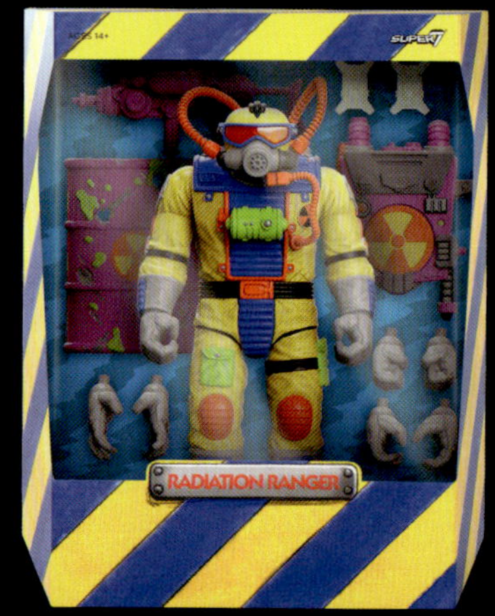

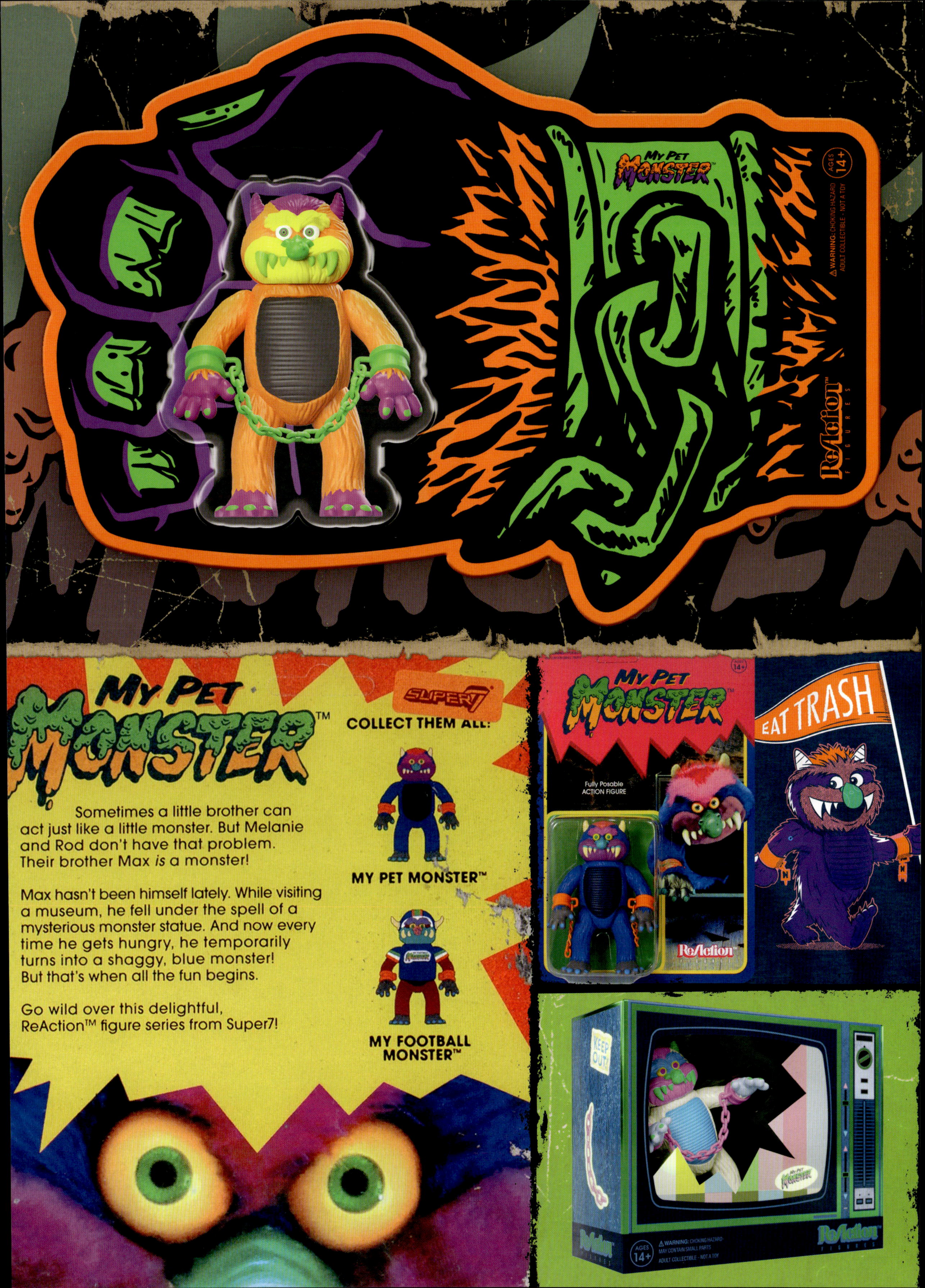

MY PET MONSTER
AGES 14+
ReAction FIGURES
MY PET MONSTER™
SUPER7
COLLECT THEM ALL!
Sometimes a little brother can act just like a little monster. But Melanie and Rod don't have that problem. Their brother Max *is* a monster!
Max hasn't been himself lately. While visiting a museum, he fell under the spell of a mysterious monster statue. And now every time he gets hungry, he temporarily turns into a shaggy, blue monster! But that's when all the fun begins.
Go wild over this delightful, ReAction™ figure series from Super7!
MY PET MONSTER™
MY FOOTBALL MONSTER™
MY PET MONSTER™
14+
Fully Posable ACTION FIGURE
ReAction
EAT TRASH
KEEP OUT!
MY PET MONSTER
ReAction
AGES 14+
WARNING: CHOKING HAZARD MAY CONTAIN SMALL PARTS
ADULT COLLECTIBLE - NOT A TOY
ReAction

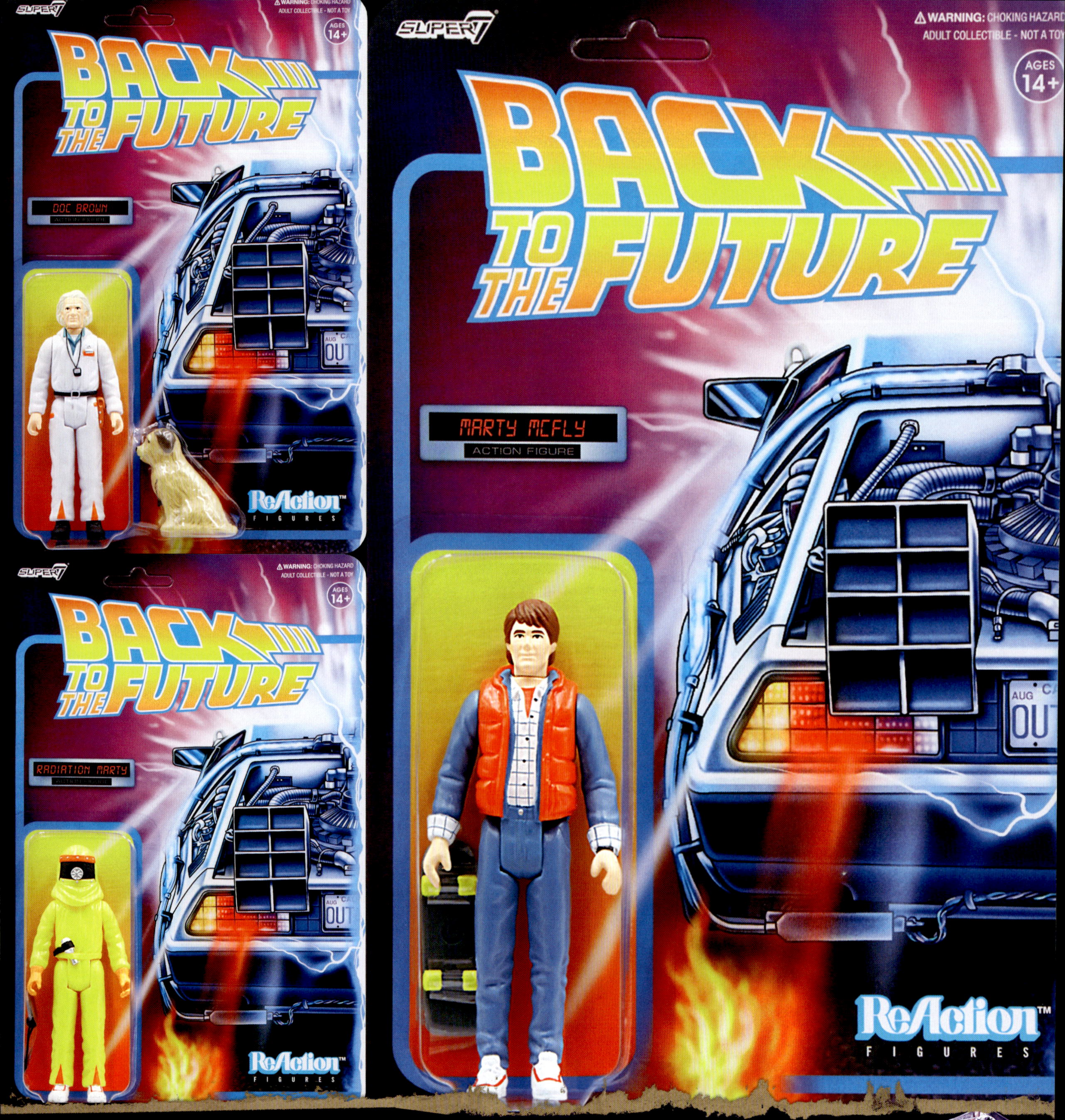

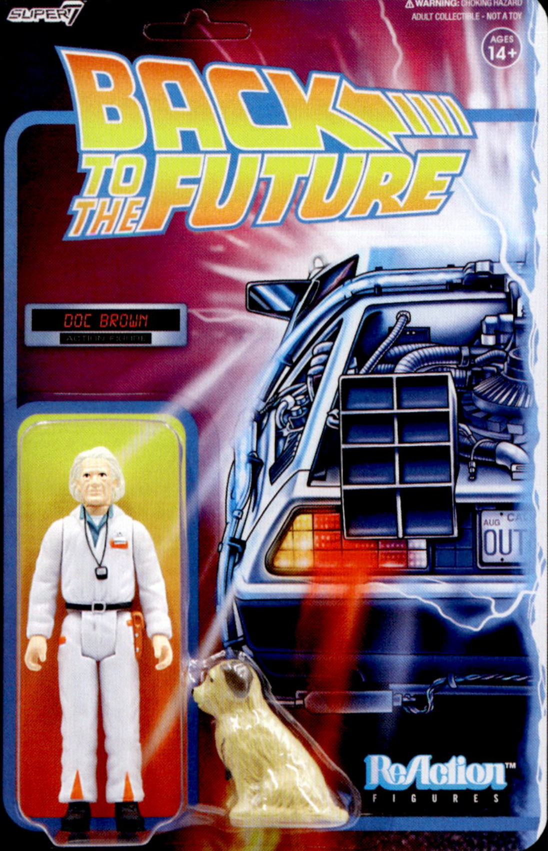

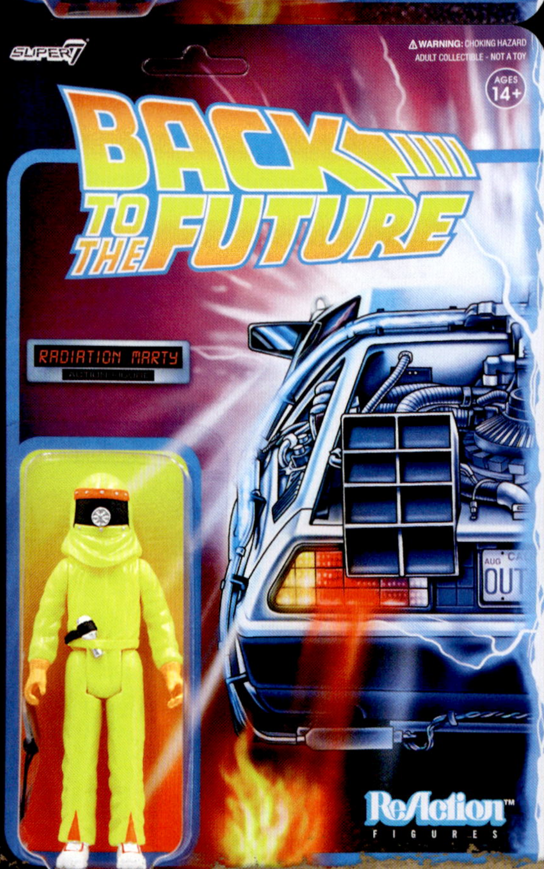

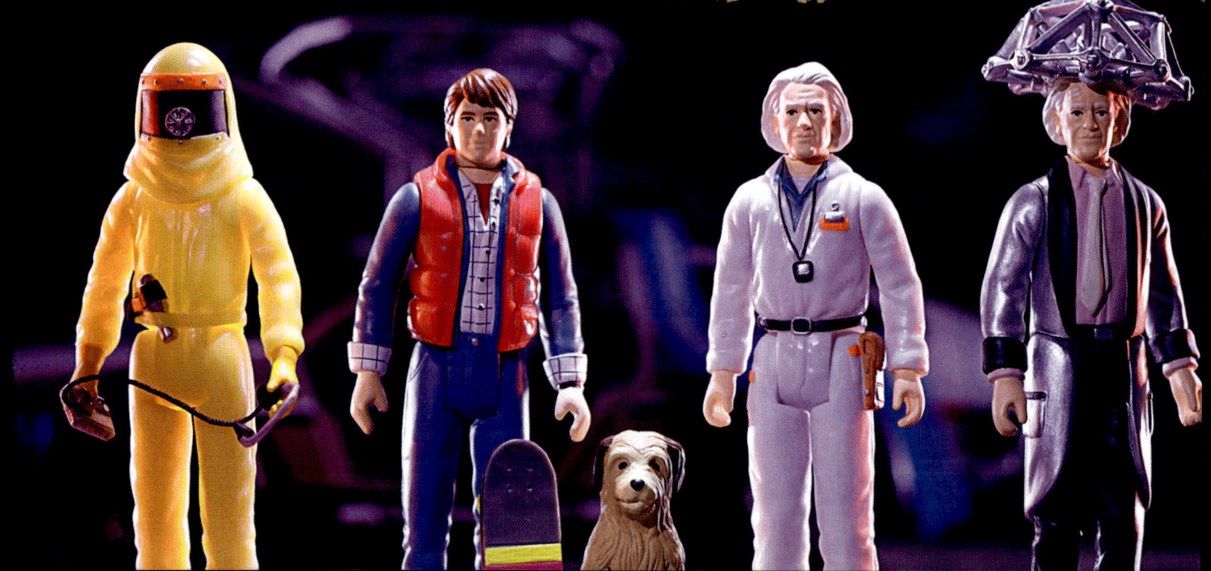

THIS SPREAD:
Back to the Future ReAction Figures™ card art

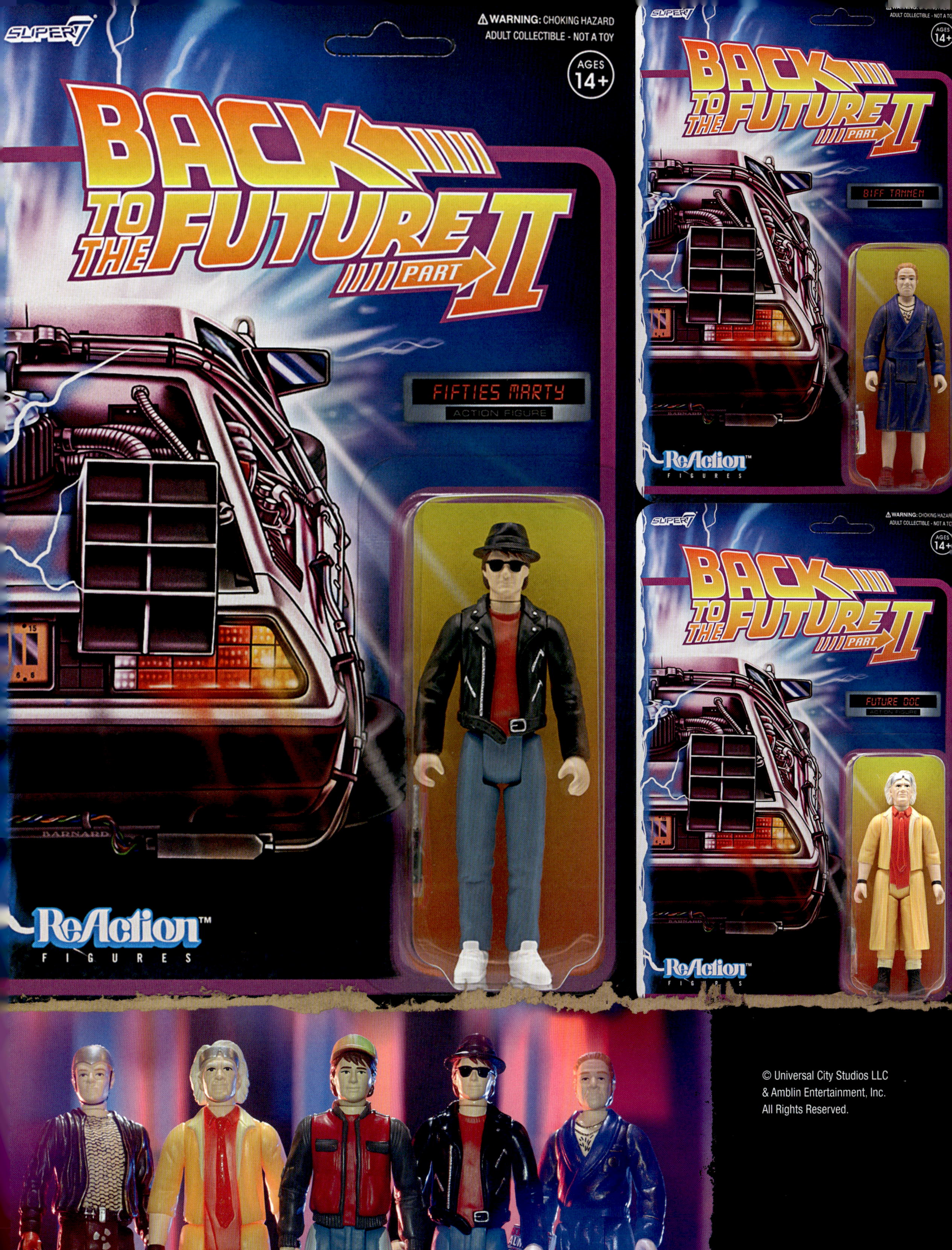

© Universal City Studios LLC
& Amblin Entertainment, Inc.
All Rights Reserved.

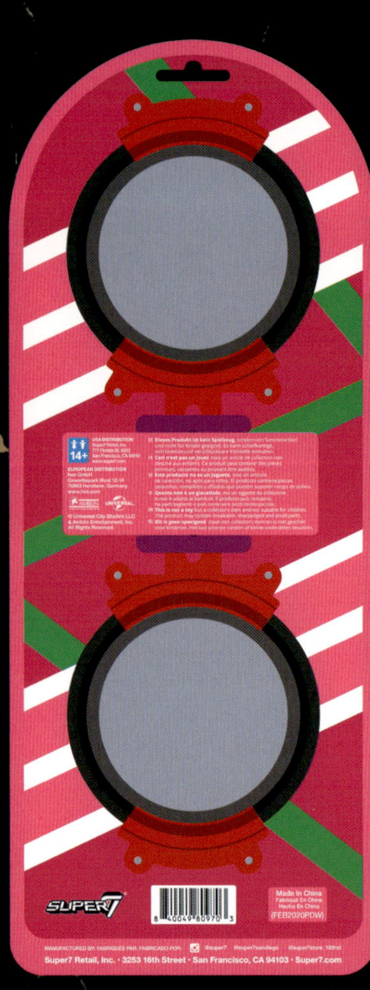

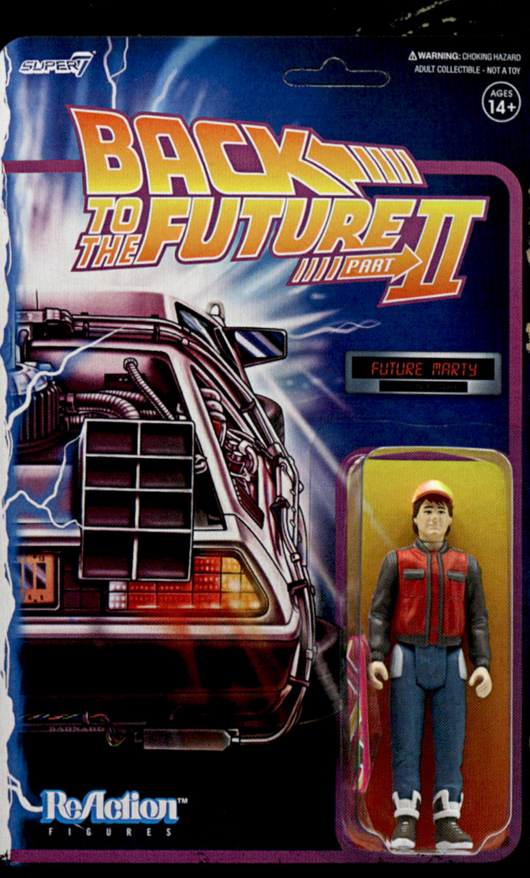

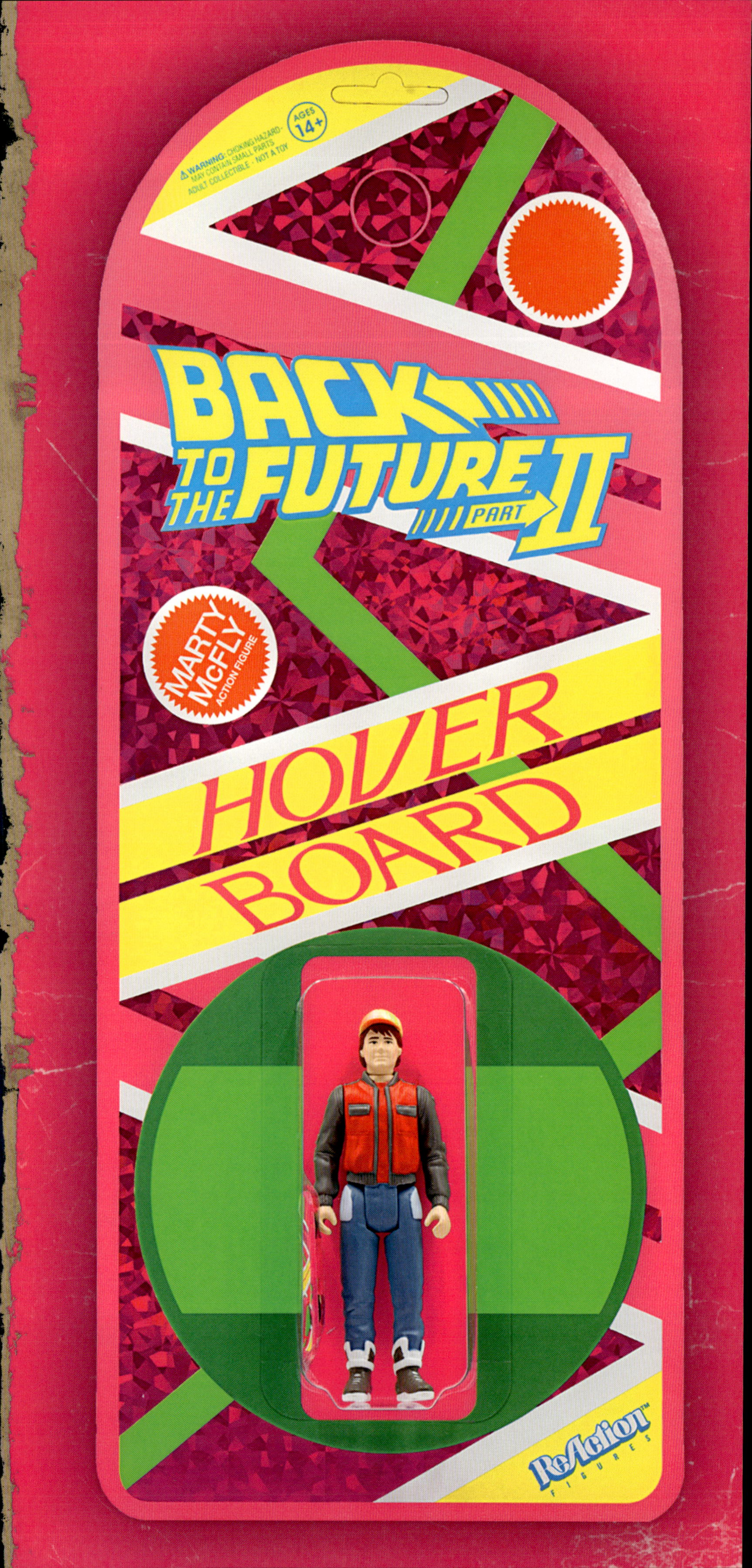

THIS SPREAD: Special Edition Back to the Future Part II ReAction Figures™ Hoverboard cards

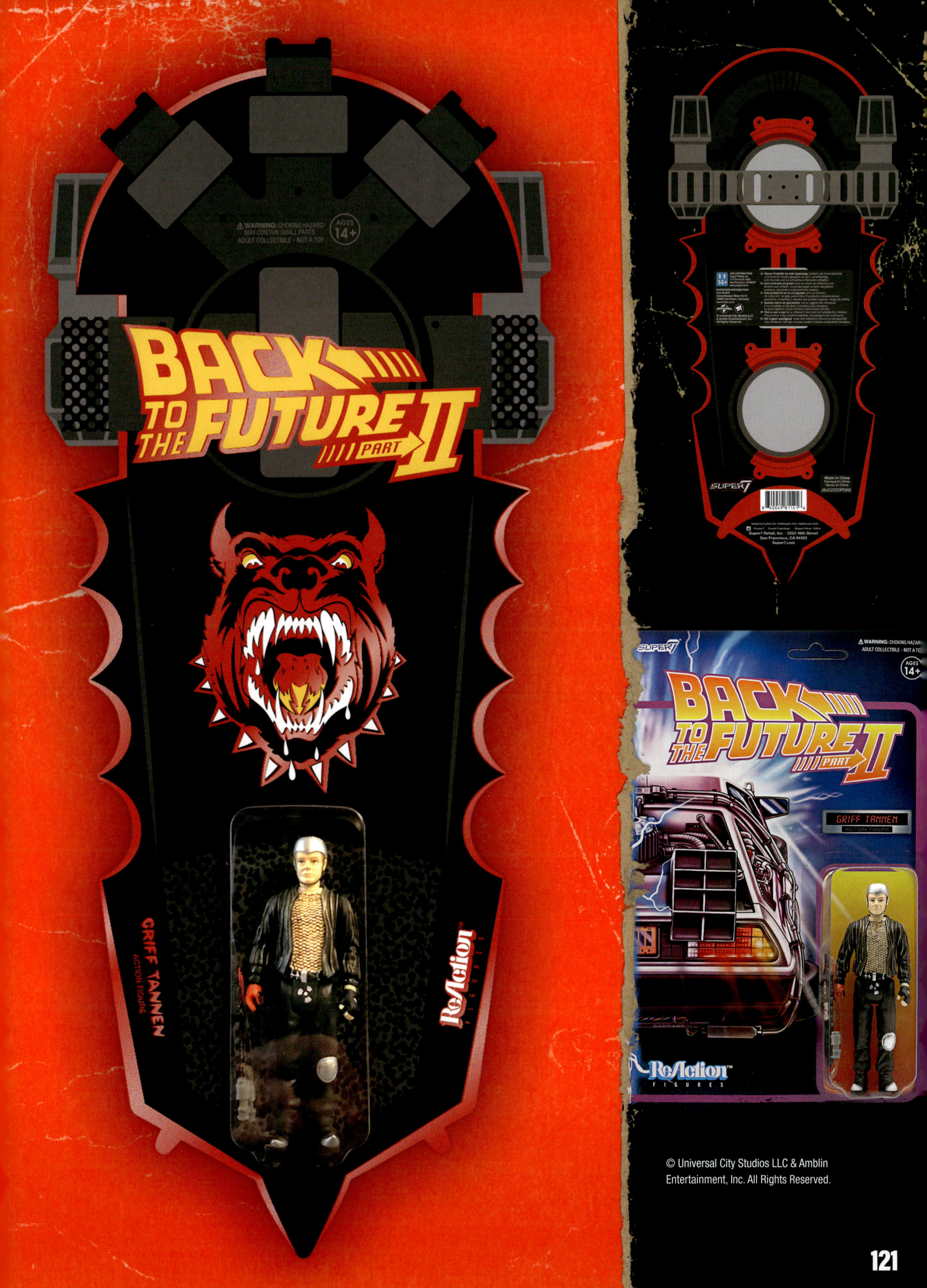

© Universal City Studios LLC & Amblin Entertainment, Inc. All Rights Reserved.

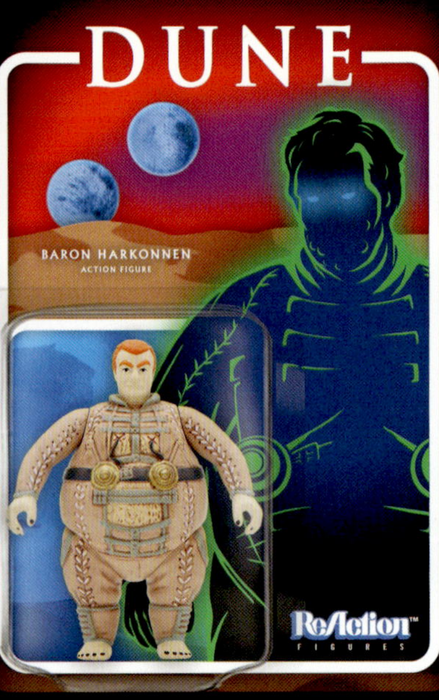

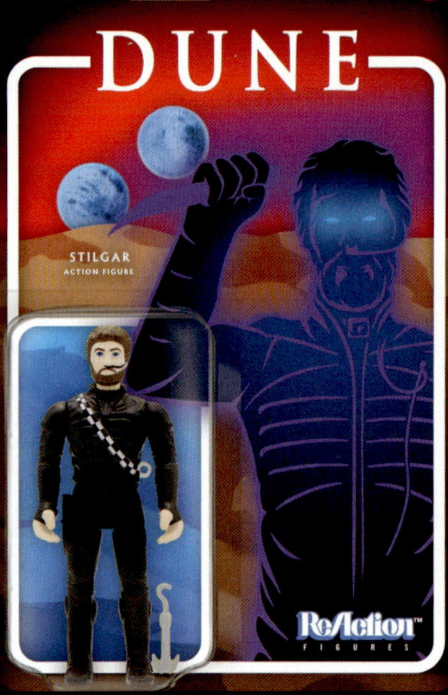

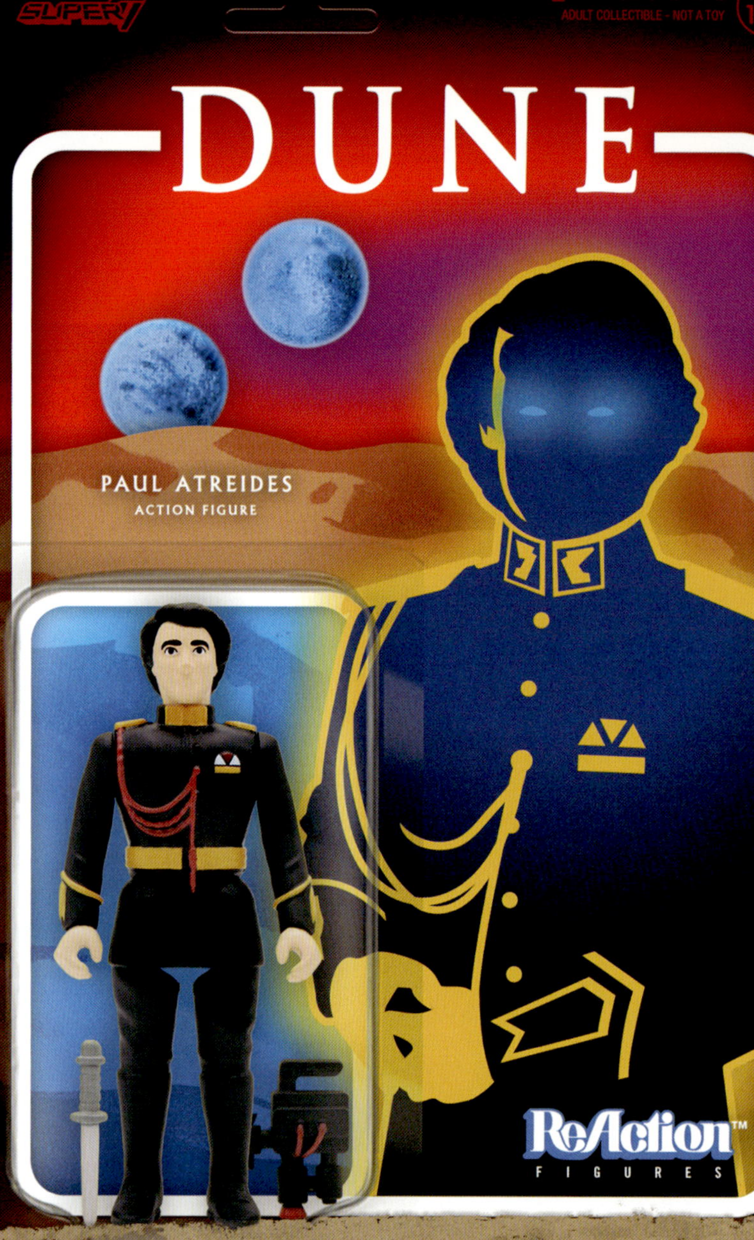

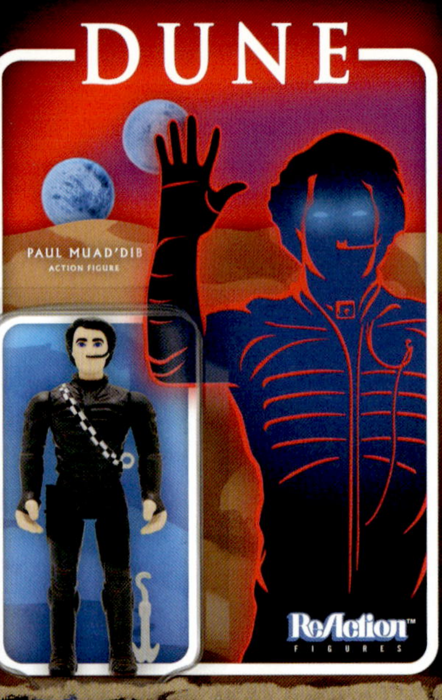

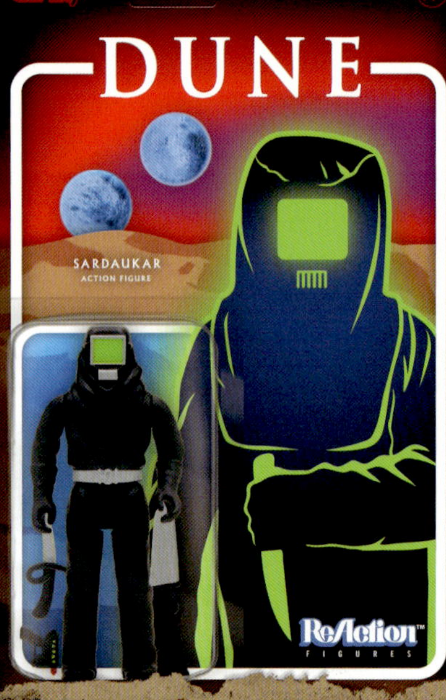

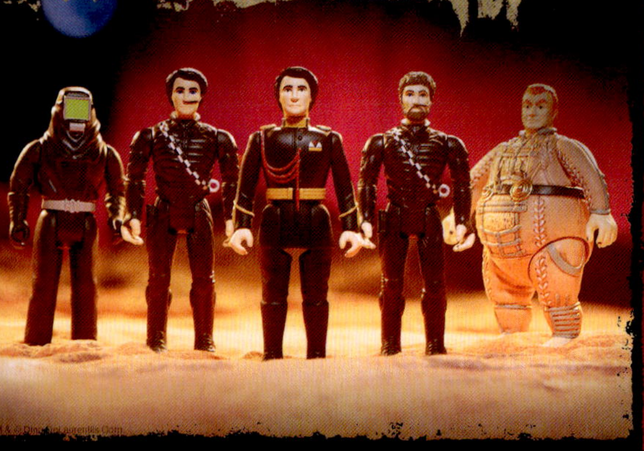

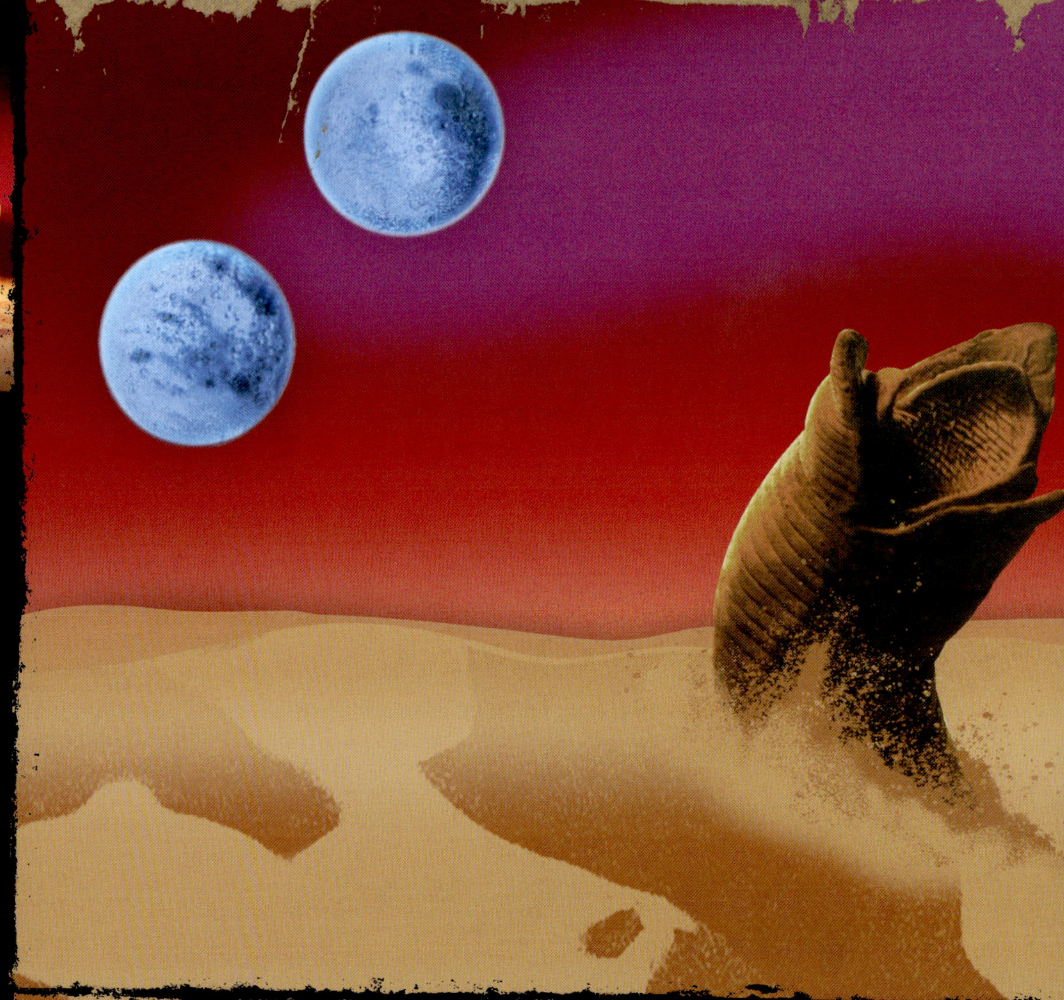

THIS PAGE: Dune ReAction Figures™ card art

RIGHT: Army of Darkness™ ReAction Figures™ card art

Dune is a TM & © of Dino De Laurentiis Corp. Licensed by Universal Studios. All Rights Reserved.

ARMY OF DARKNESS ™ & © 1993 Orion Pictures Corporation. © 2025 Metro-Goldwyn-Mayer Studios Inc. All Rights Reserved.

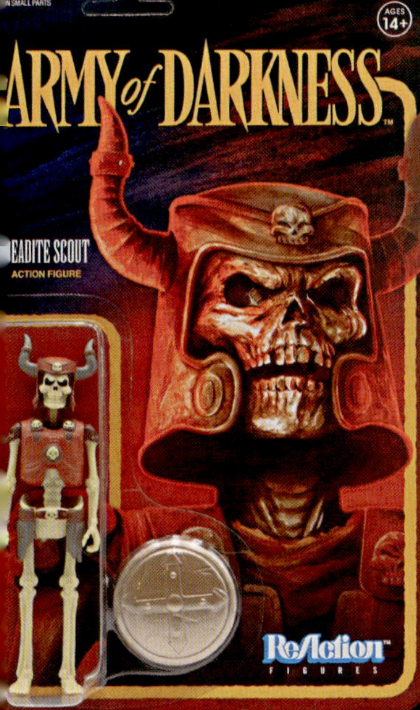

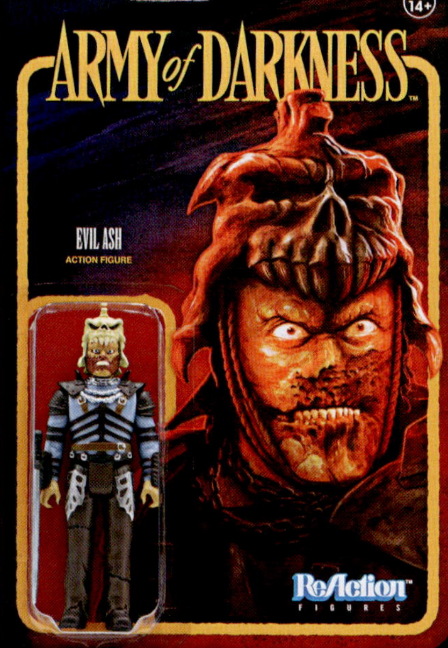

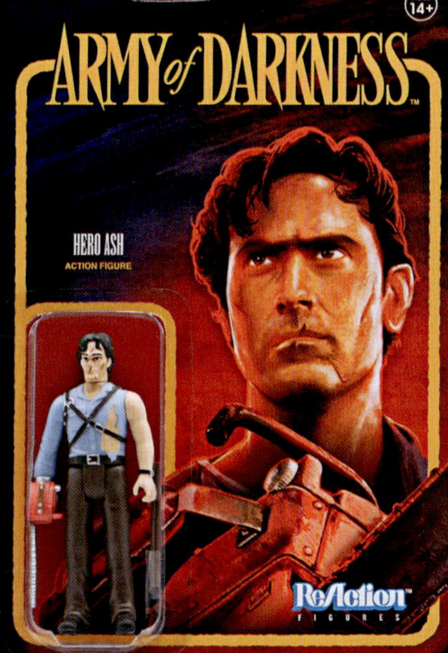

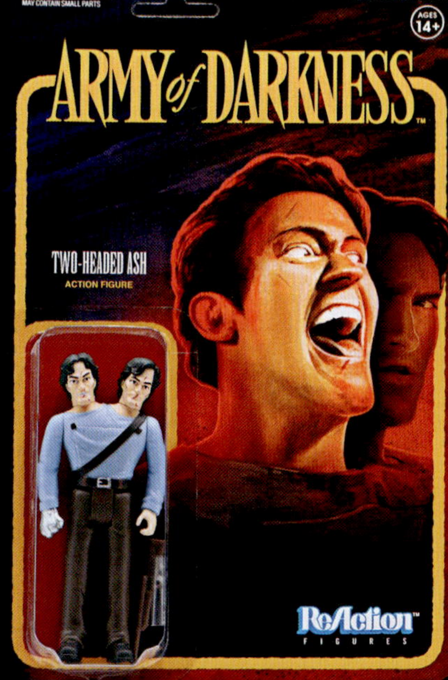

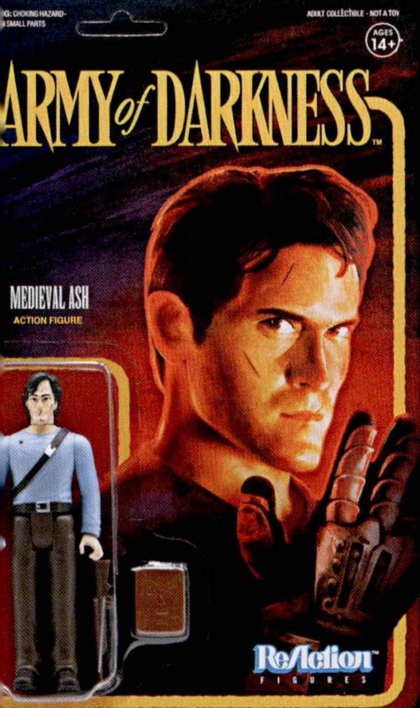

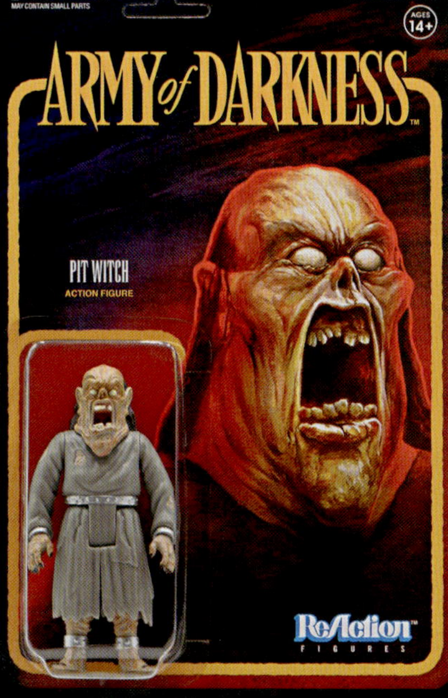

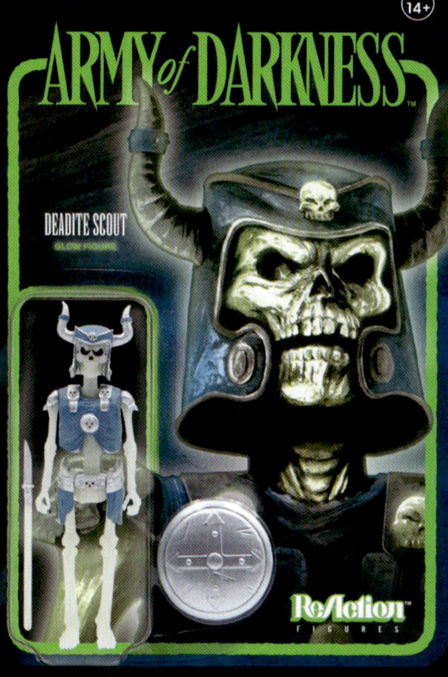

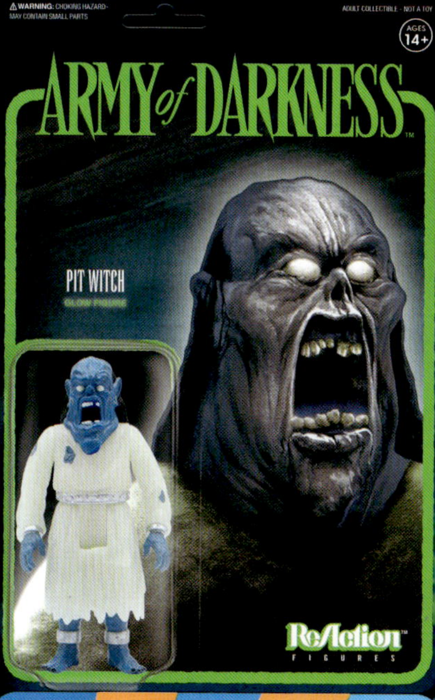

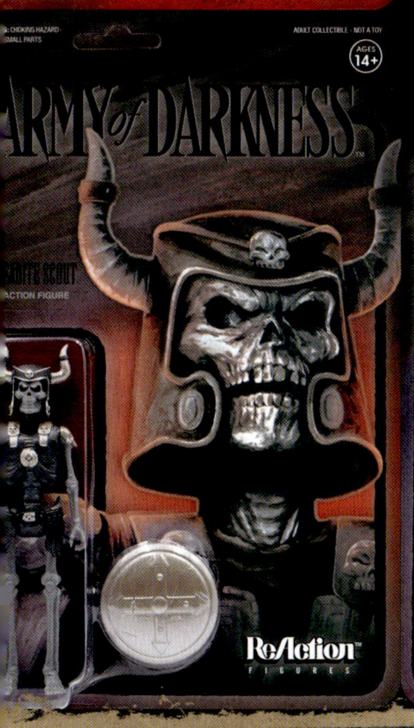

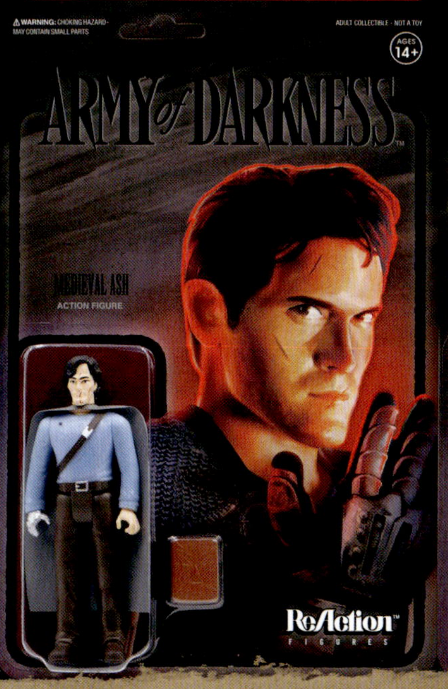

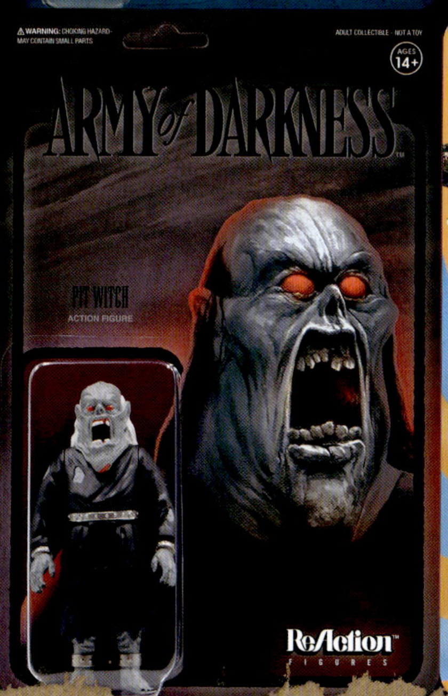

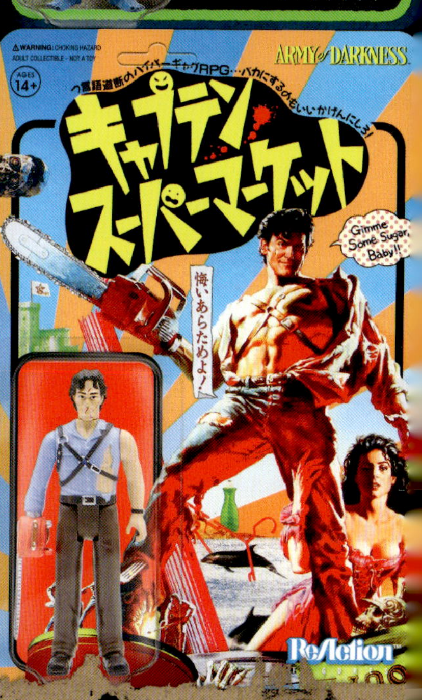

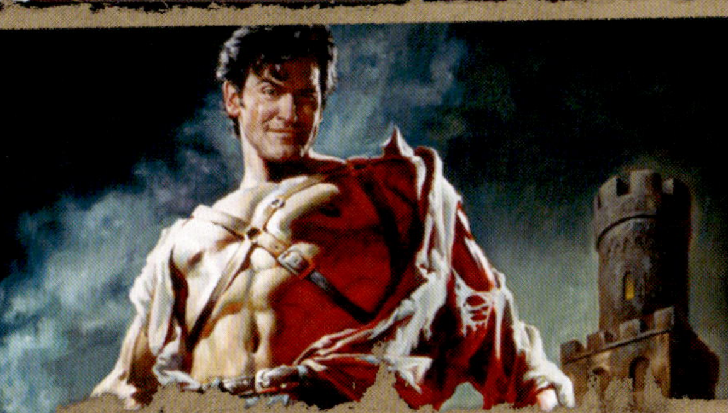

ARMY of DARKNESS™

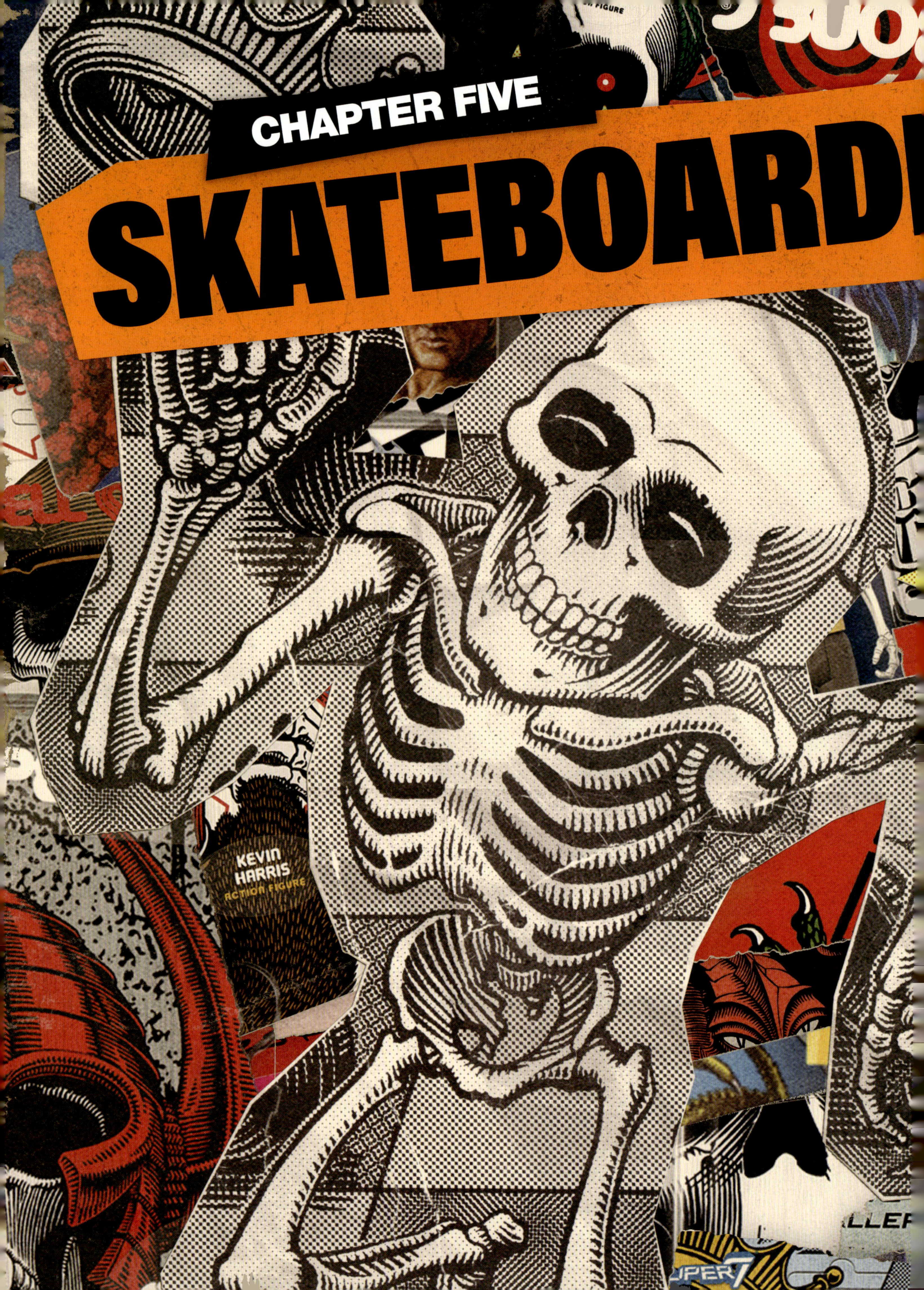
CHAPTER FIVE
SKATEBOARD
KEVIN
HARRIS
ACTION FIGURE

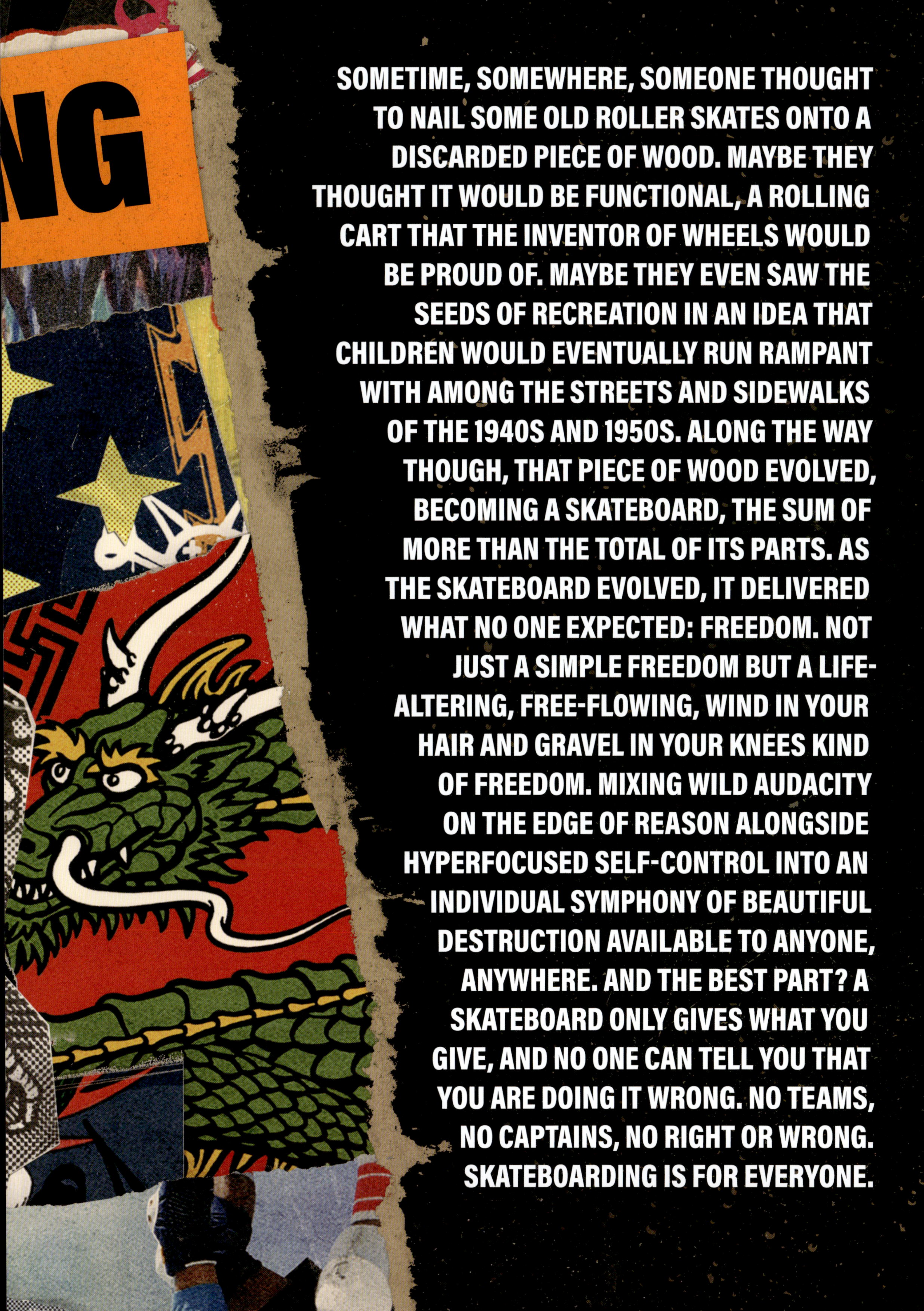

SOMETIME, SOMEWHERE, SOMEONE THOUGHT TO NAIL SOME OLD ROLLER SKATES ONTO A DISCARDED PIECE OF WOOD. MAYBE THEY THOUGHT IT WOULD BE FUNCTIONAL, A ROLLING CART THAT THE INVENTOR OF WHEELS WOULD BE PROUD OF. MAYBE THEY EVEN SAW THE SEEDS OF RECREATION IN AN IDEA THAT CHILDREN WOULD EVENTUALLY RUN RAMPANT WITH AMONG THE STREETS AND SIDEWALKS OF THE 1940S AND 1950S. ALONG THE WAY THOUGH, THAT PIECE OF WOOD EVOLVED, BECOMING A SKATEBOARD, THE SUM OF MORE THAN THE TOTAL OF ITS PARTS. AS THE SKATEBOARD EVOLVED, IT DELIVERED WHAT NO ONE EXPECTED: FREEDOM. NOT JUST A SIMPLE FREEDOM BUT A LIFE-ALTERING, FREE-FLOWING, WIND IN YOUR HAIR AND GRAVEL IN YOUR KNEES KIND OF FREEDOM. MIXING WILD AUDACITY ON THE EDGE OF REASON ALONGSIDE HYPERFOCUSED SELF-CONTROL INTO AN INDIVIDUAL SYMPHONY OF BEAUTIFUL DESTRUCTION AVAILABLE TO ANYONE, ANYWHERE. AND THE BEST PART? A SKATEBOARD ONLY GIVES WHAT YOU GIVE, AND NO ONE CAN TELL YOU THAT YOU ARE DOING IT WRONG. NO TEAMS, NO CAPTAINS, NO RIGHT OR WRONG. SKATEBOARDING IS FOR EVERYONE.

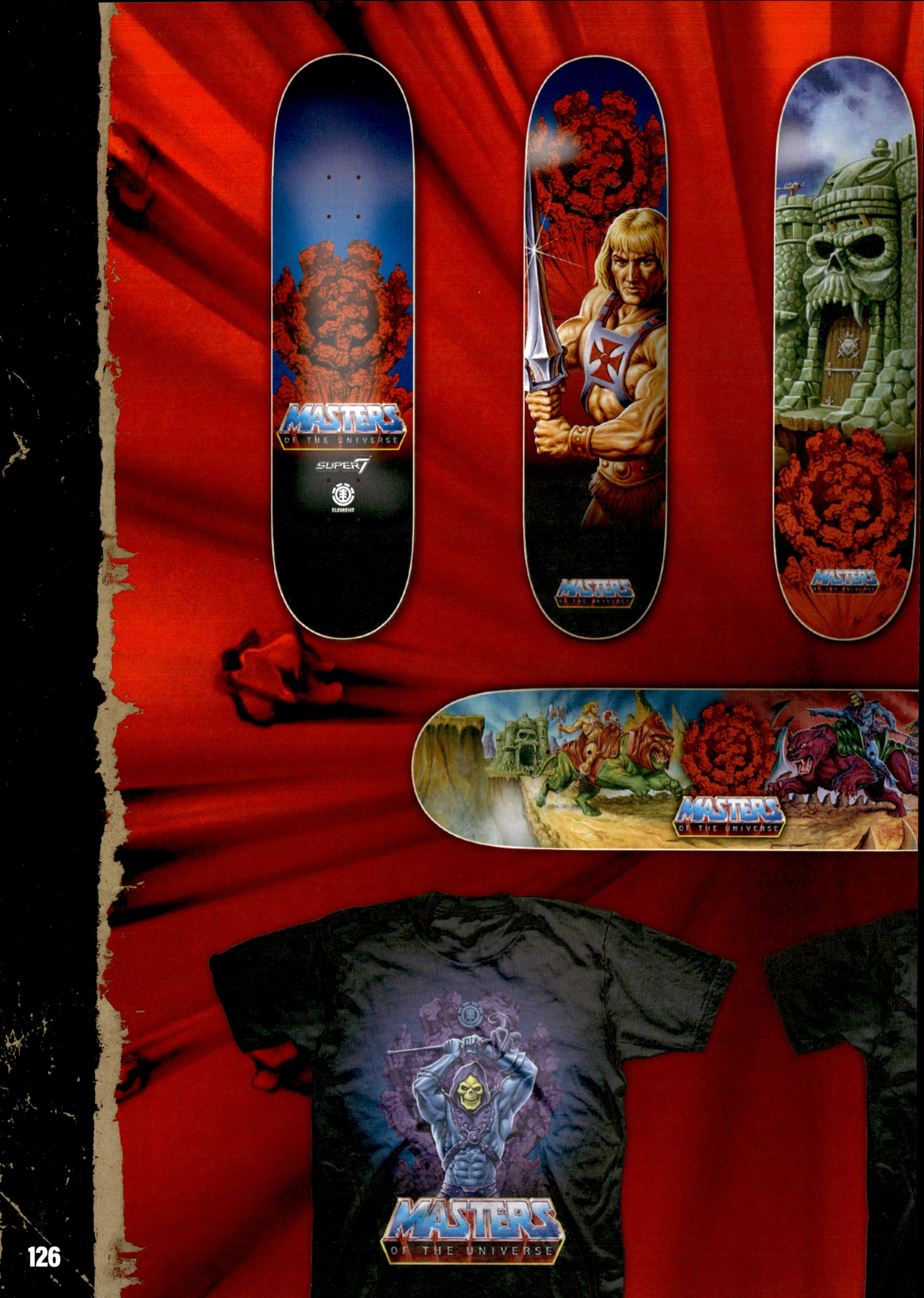
MASTERS
OF THE UNIVERSE
SUPER7
ELEMENT
MASTERS
MASTERS
MASTERS
OF THE UNIVERSE
MASTERS
OF THE UNIVERSE

THIS SPREAD: Element™ x Masters of the Universe® skateboards and apparel

© 2025 Element.
© MATTEL

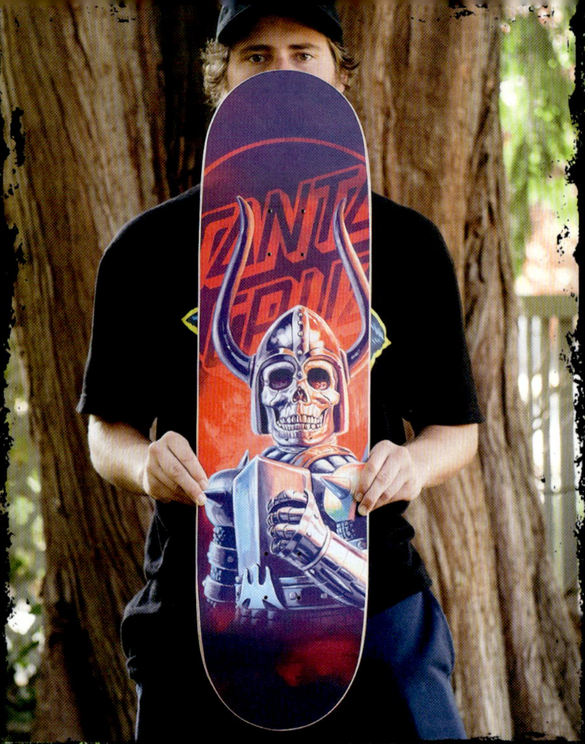

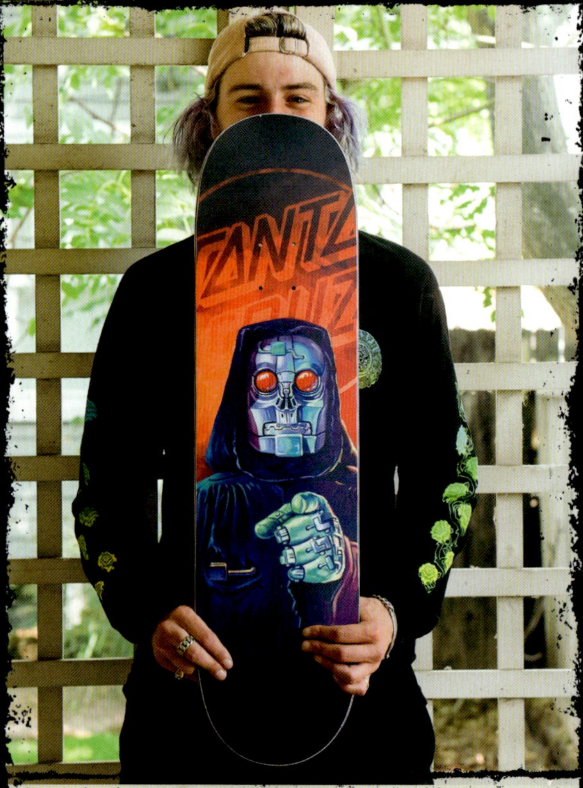

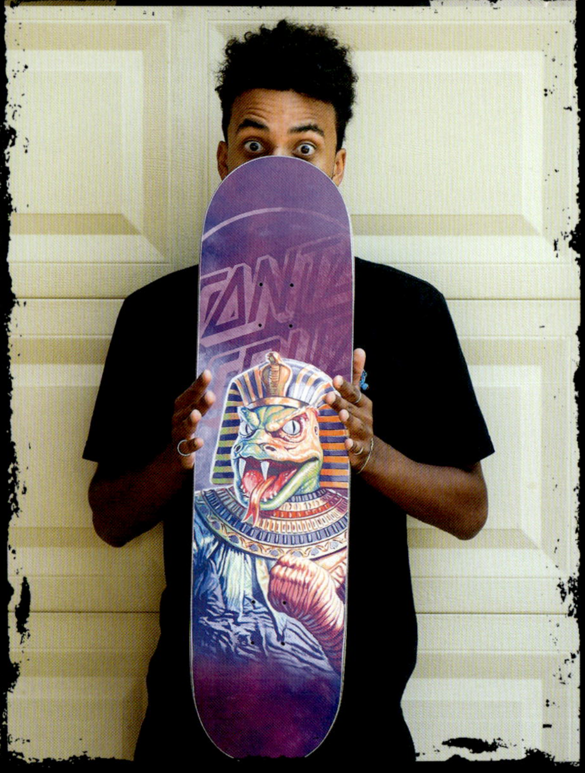

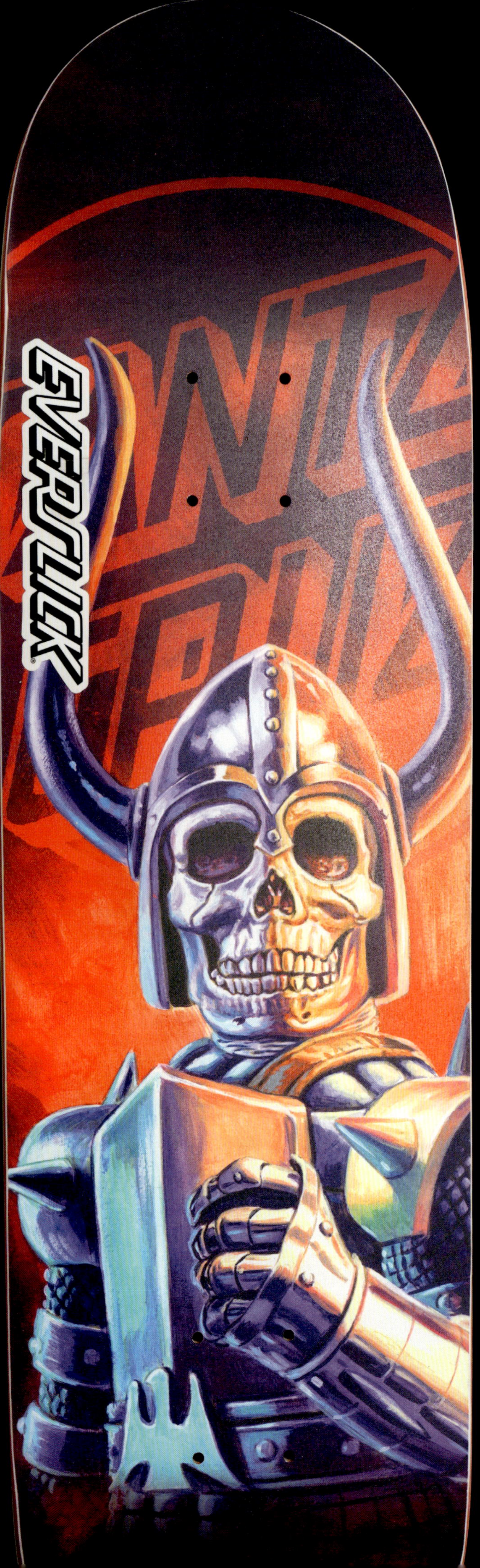

EVERSLICK

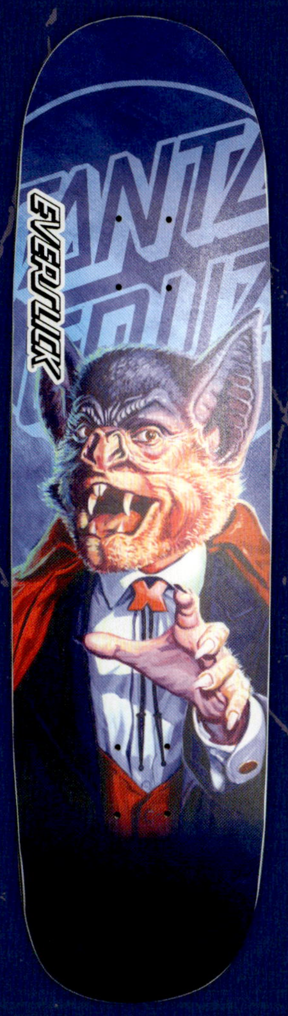

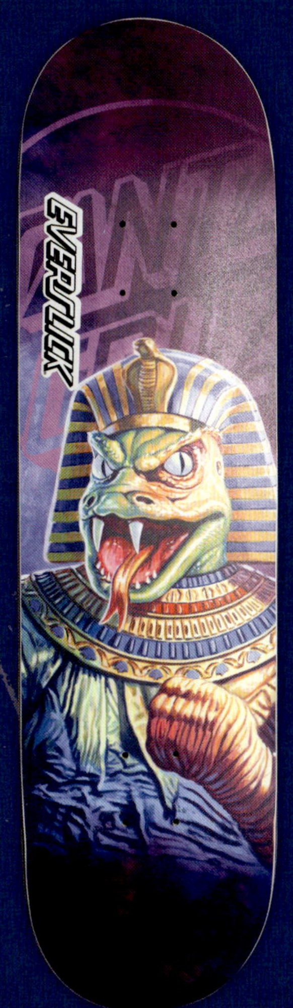

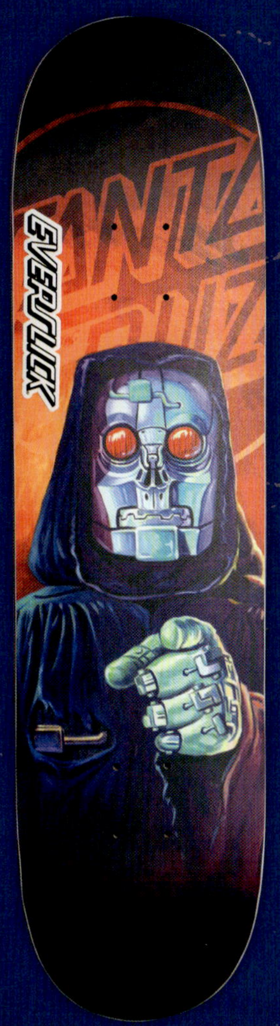

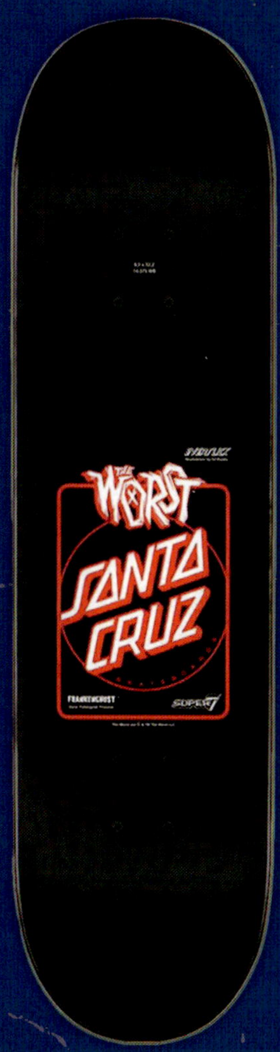

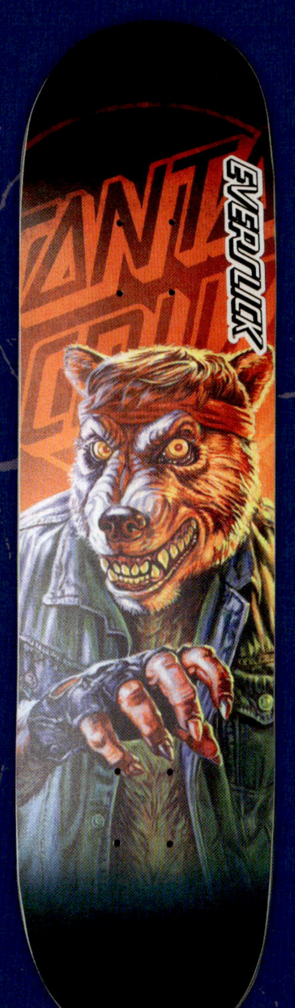

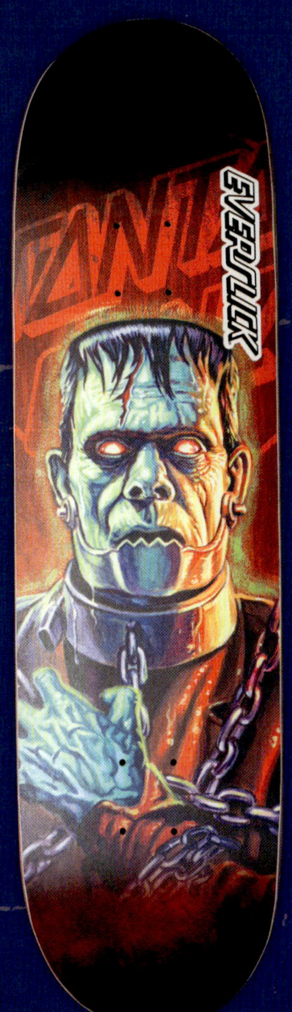

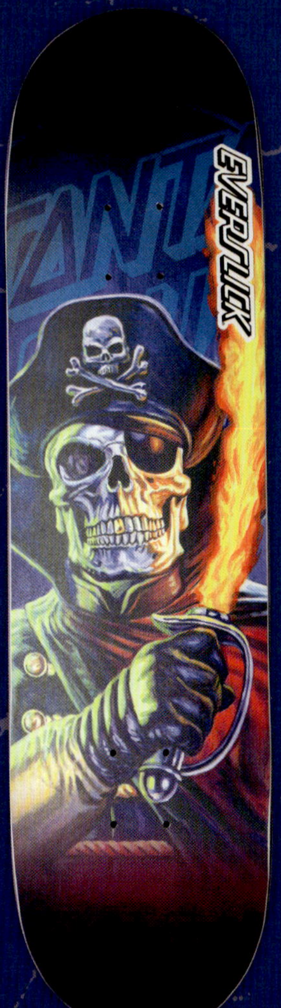

THIS SPREAD: Santa Cruz x The Worst™ skateboards

The Worst TM & © Super7 OpCo LLC

© 2025 NHS, Inc.

EXPERIMENTAL:

In the mid '80s, the Powell-Peralta R&D department began issuing team riders with prototype board shapes that were either screened or bore a sticker that branded them as "experimental" models. Although this was mainly done to ensure a rider wouldn't appear in any photos skating a blank board devoid of company logos, the concept proved to be an ingenious marketing ploy, inadvertently or otherwise, and became the premier harbinger of things to come from Powell-Peralta—not to mention the stickers themselves becoming one of the most elusive and coveted items for hardcore Bones Brigade fans. Each figure represents the "prototype" nature in which the original experimental boards were produced with single, solid color paint jobs.

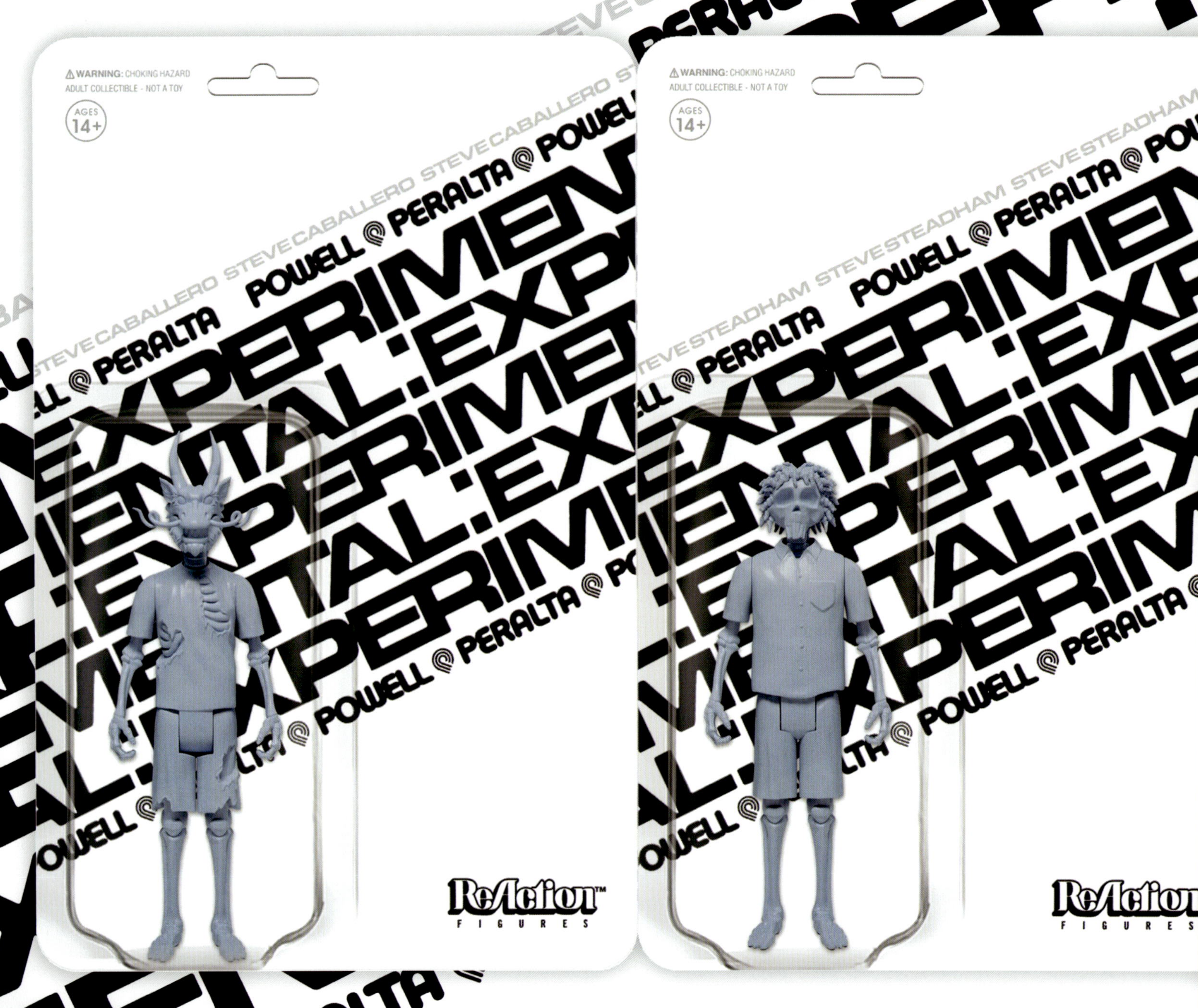

THIS SPREAD: Powell-Peralta "Experimental" ReAction Figures™ card art

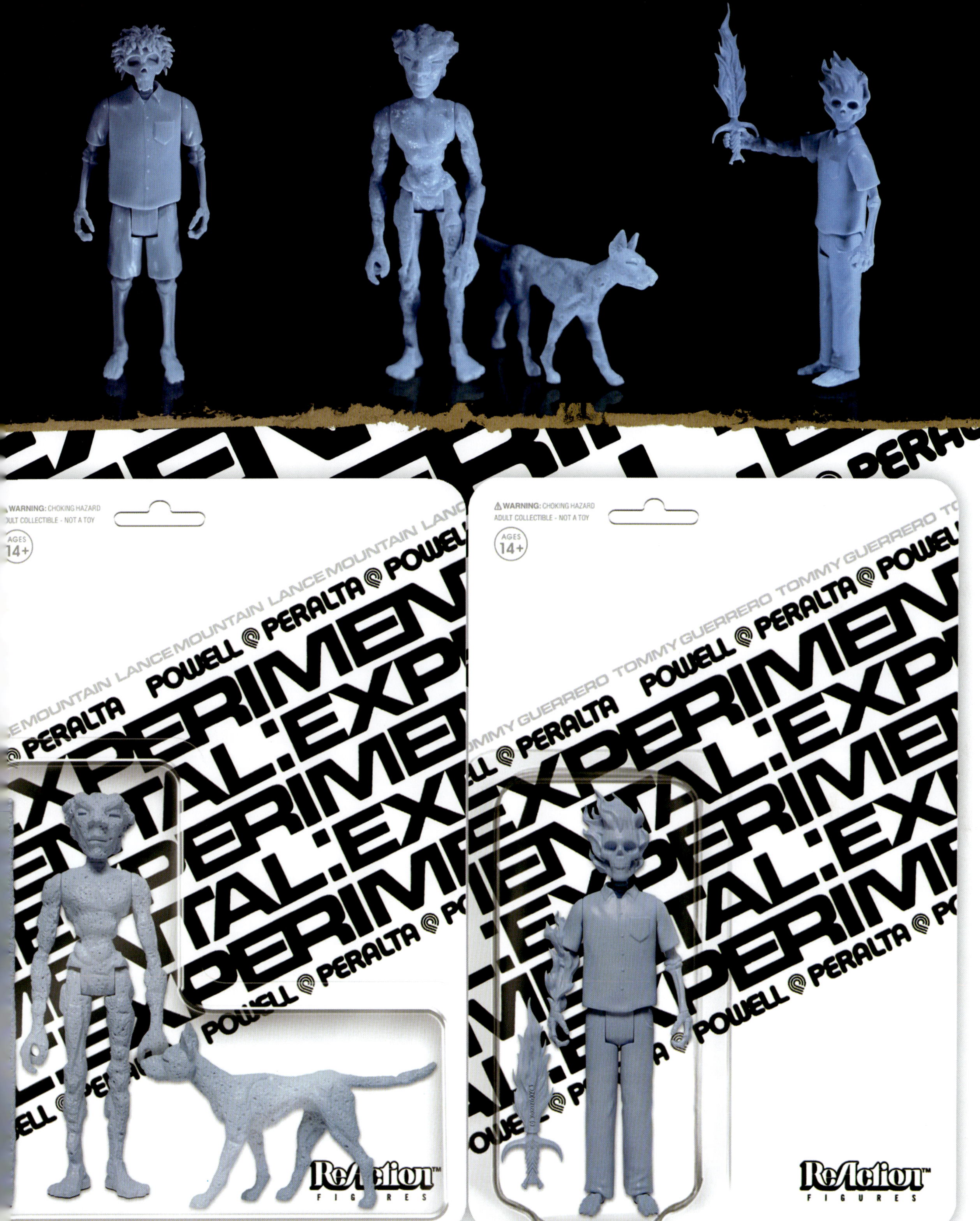

© 2025 Skate One Corp

THIS SPREAD: Selected Powell-Peralta ReAction Figures™ card art and inspiration

© 2025 Skate One Corp

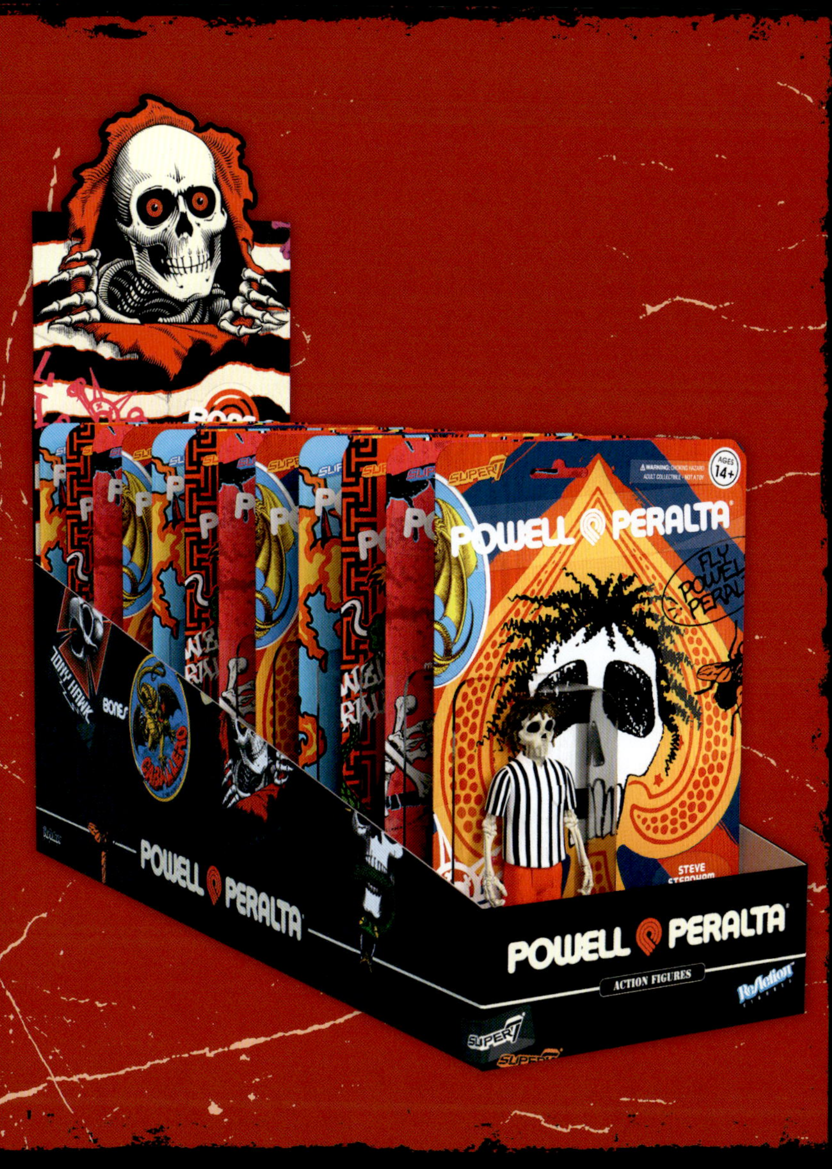

THIS SPREAD: Powell-Peralta™ ReAction Figures™ Wave 1 card art

© 2025 Skate One Corp

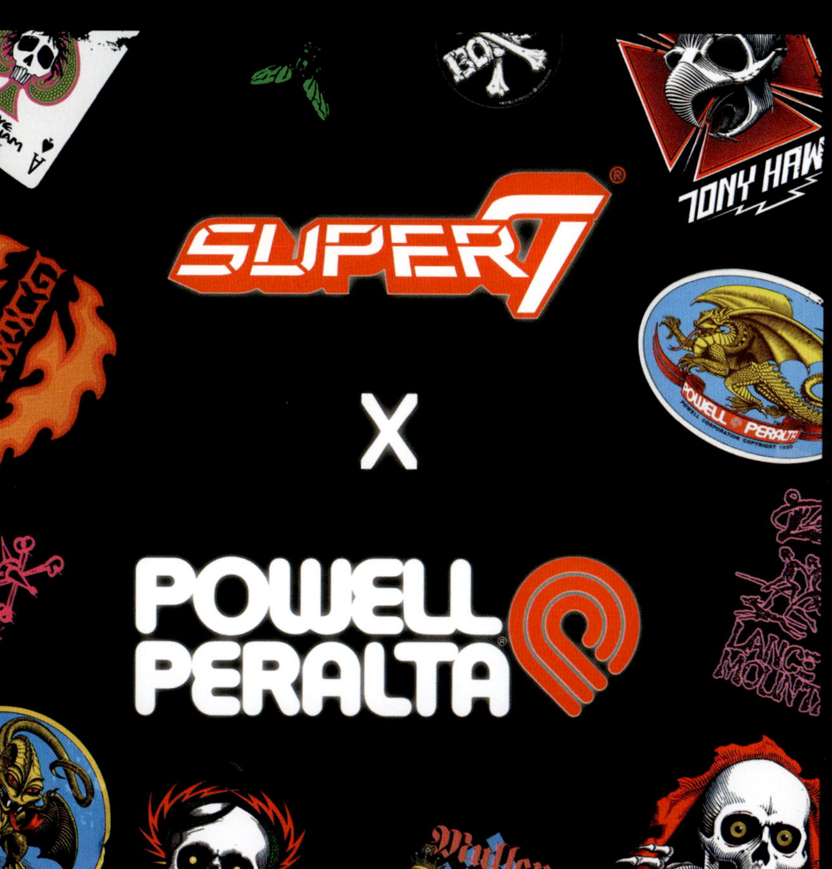

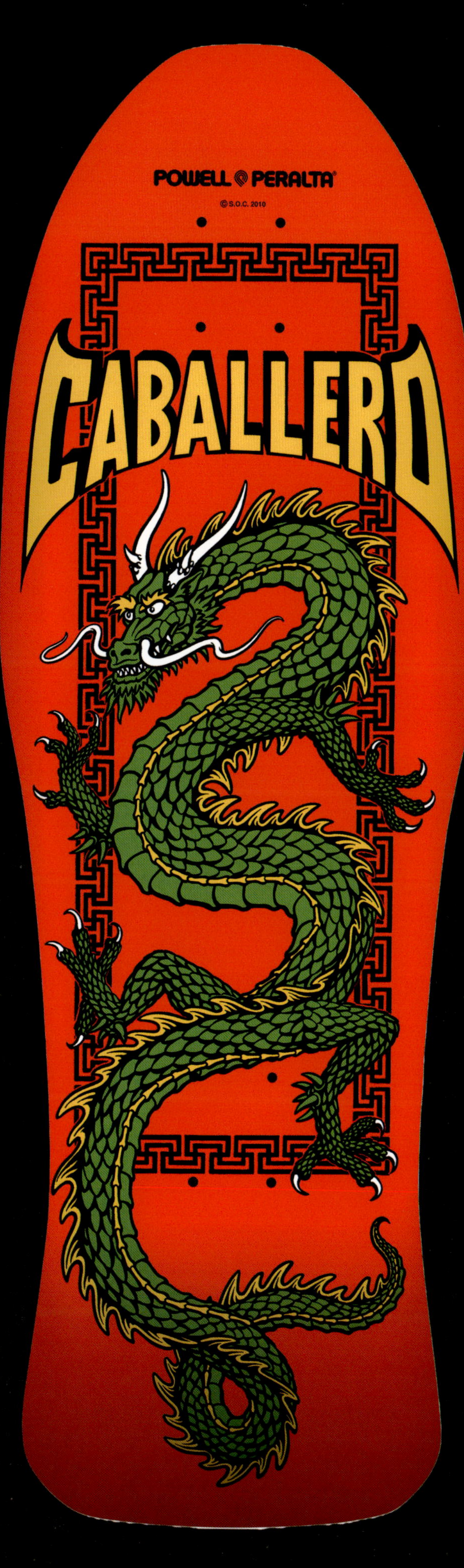

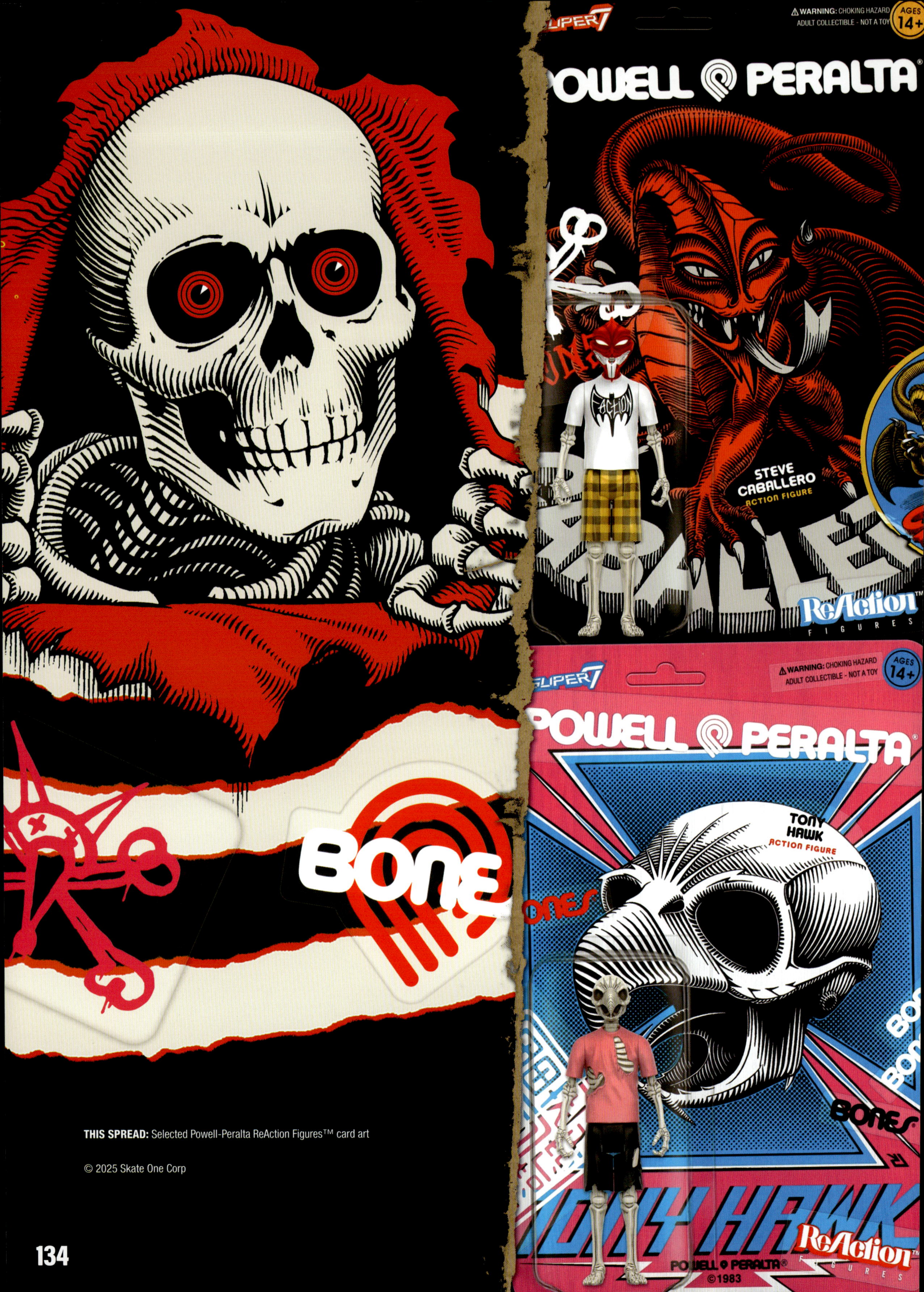

THIS SPREAD: Selected Powell-Peralta ReAction Figures™ card art

© 2025 Skate One Corp

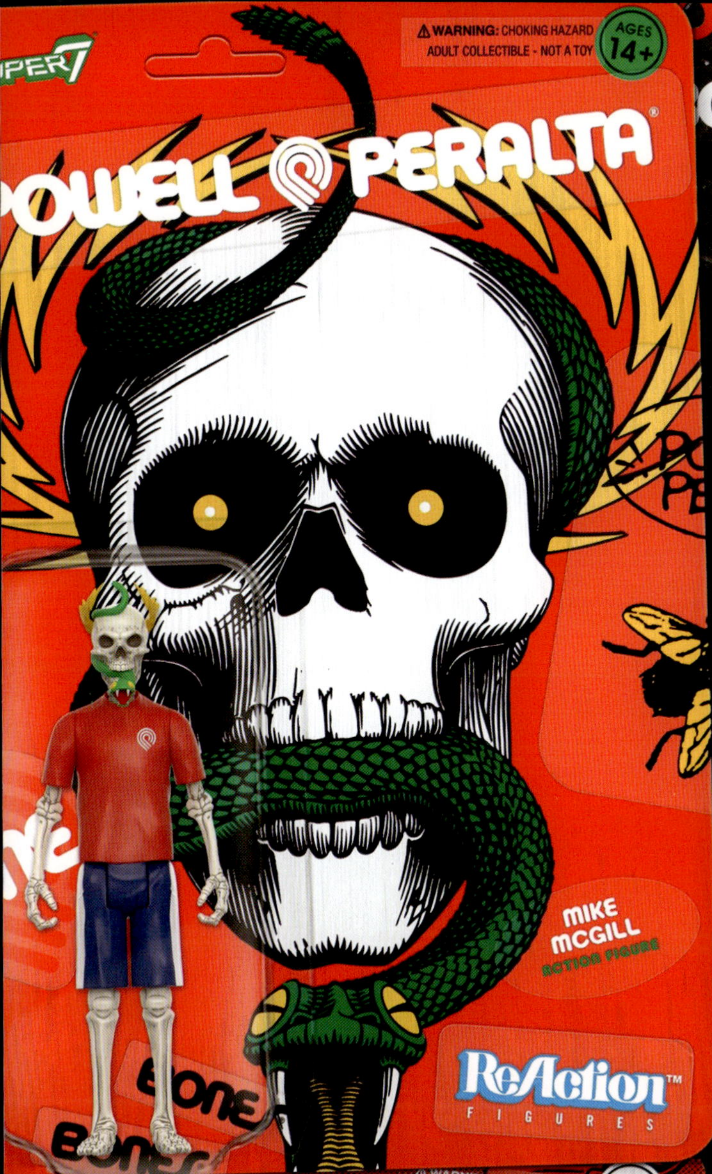

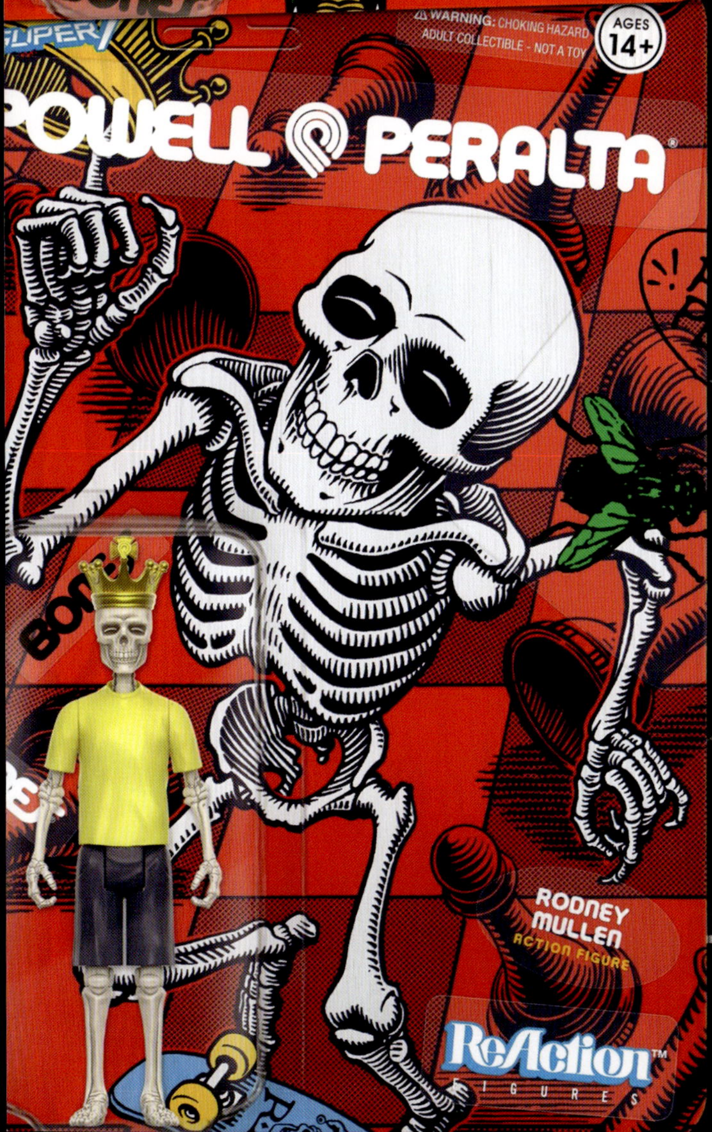

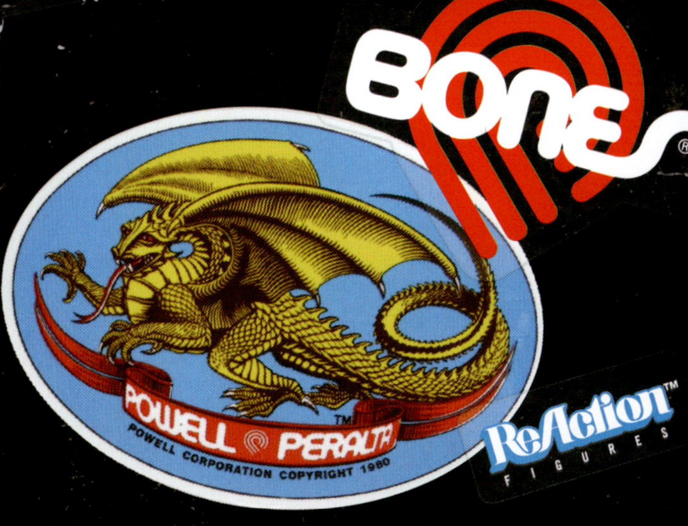

POWELL PERALTA

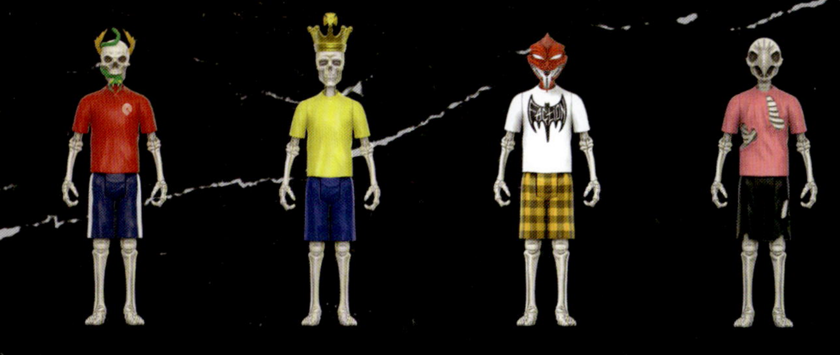

MIKE MCGILL • RODNEY MULLEN • STEVE CABALLERO • TONY HAWK

MIKE MCGILL
BONE HEAD

When it came time for Mike McGill's second pro model at Powell-Peralta, V. Courtlandt Johnson drew upon the environmental elements from McGill's home state of Florida—most notably the lightning bolts and snake—to add yet another long-lasting, classic skull to the company's line, circa 1984.

STEVE CABALLERO
DRAGON HEAD

Inspired by the fact he was born in the Year of the Dragon, Steve Caballero submitted a rough sketch of a dragon to Powell-Peralta artist V. Courtlandt Johnson, who turned the beast into an iconic emblem that stayed in continuous production from 1980 to 1986.

RODNEY MULLEN
CHESS KING

Owing to Rodney Mullen's renown as the reigning world champion freestyle skateboarder and the Bones Brigade's resident brainiac, V. Courtlandt Johnson envisioned a skeleton dramatically poised upon a chess field for the skater's second Powell-Peralta pro model, circa 1985, based on the phrase, "Only death wins in war."

TONY HAWK
SKULL & CROSS

The second and most popular of the Powell-Peralta designs for Tony Hawk, the "Skull & Cross" (what Tony fondly refers to as the "Screaming Chicken Skull") was created by V. Courtlandt Johnson, circa 1983. It went on to become the template for many of Tony's ensuing graphics throughout the years.

ReAction FIGURES

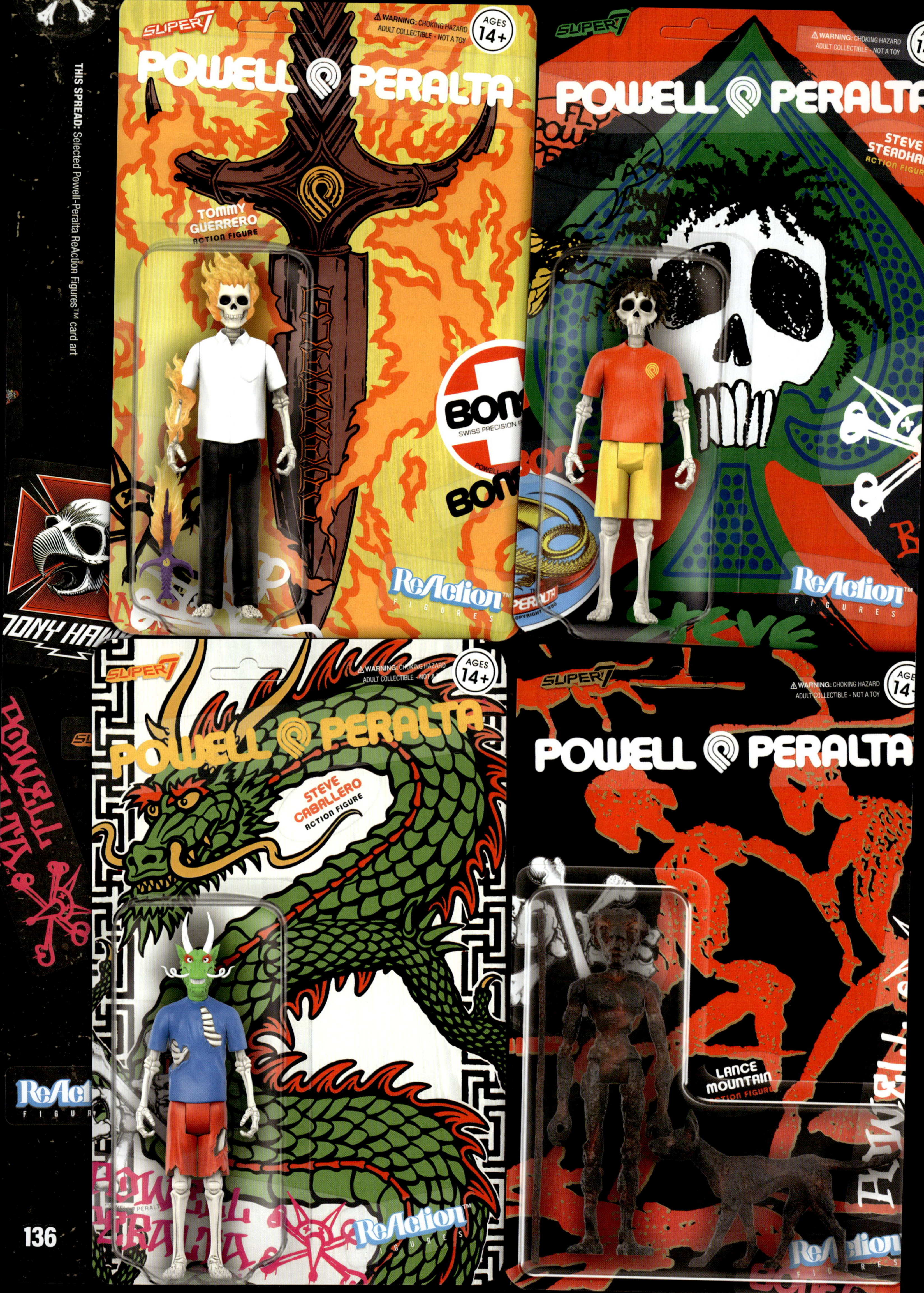

THIS SPREAD: Selected Powell-Peralta ReAction Figures™ card art

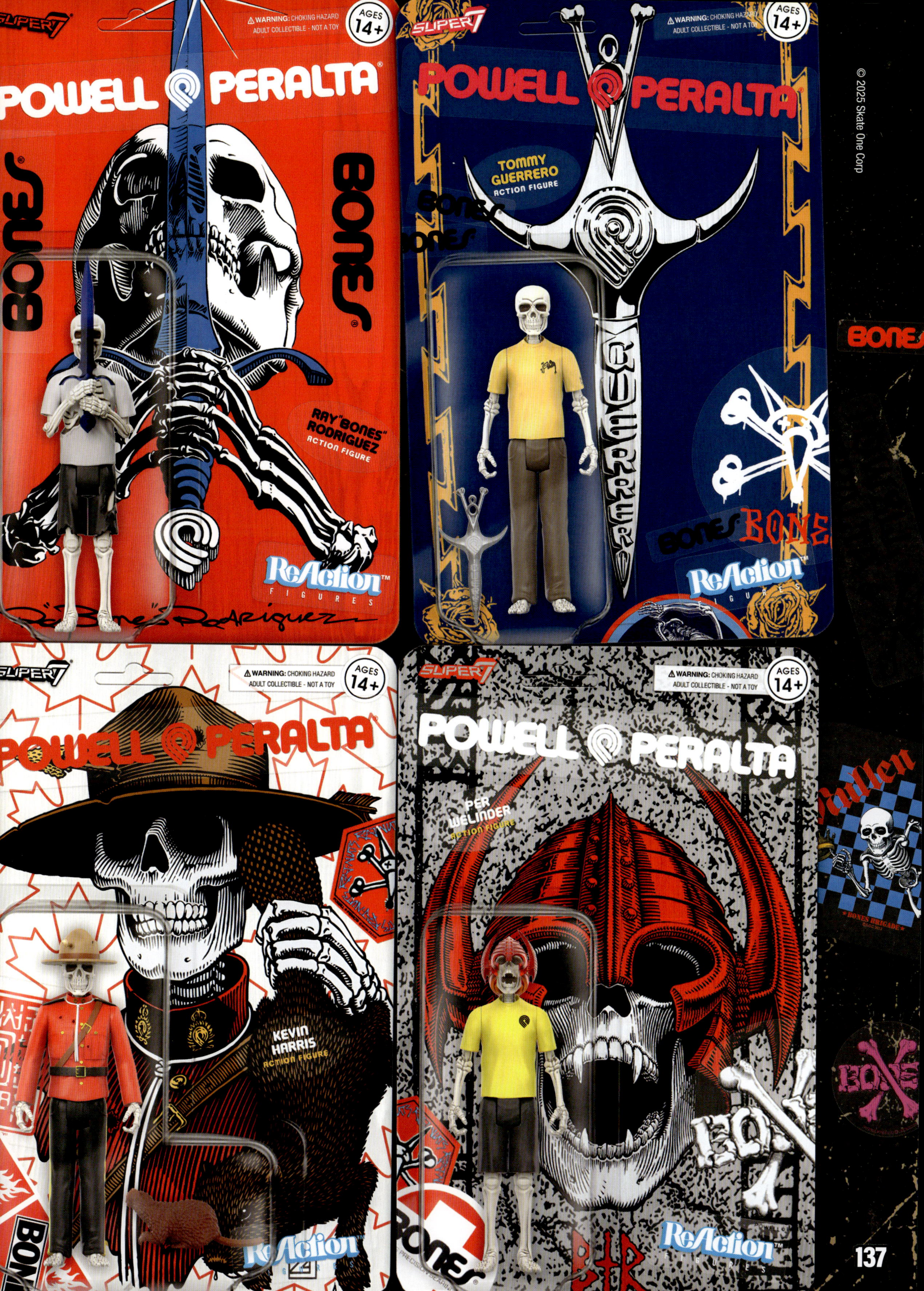

© 2025 Skate One Corp

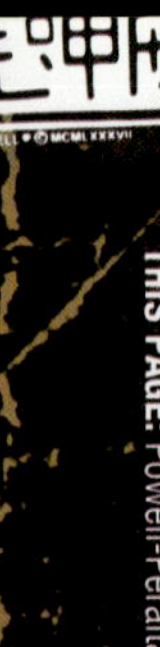

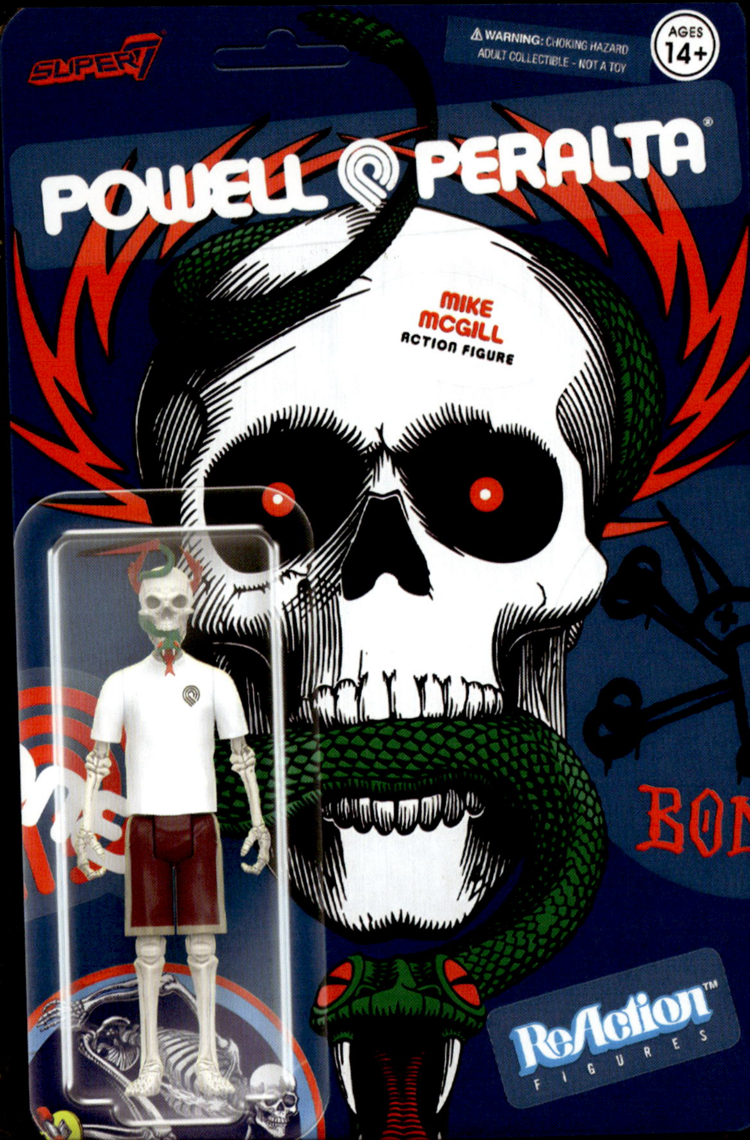

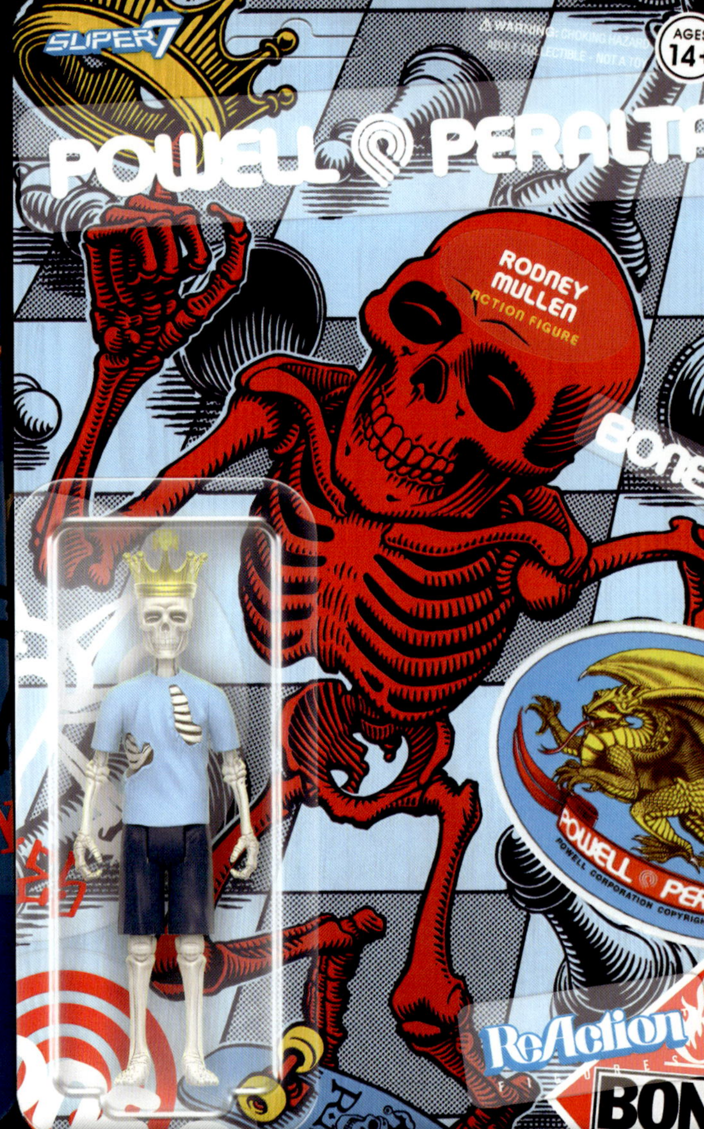

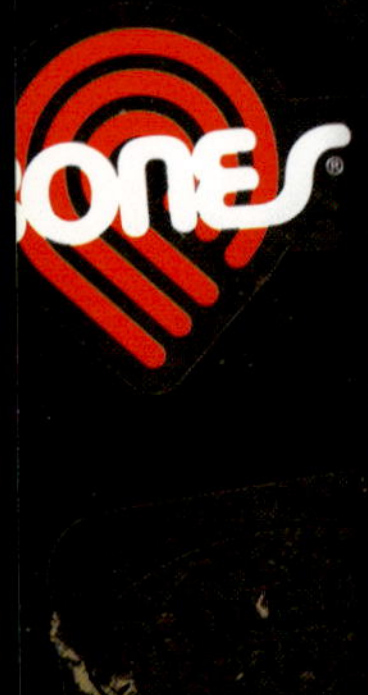

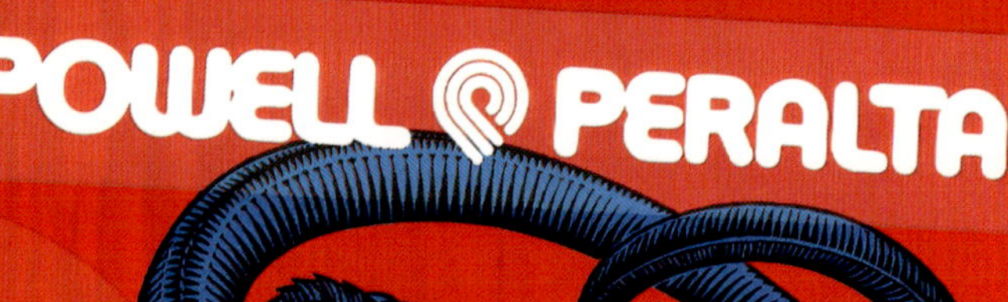

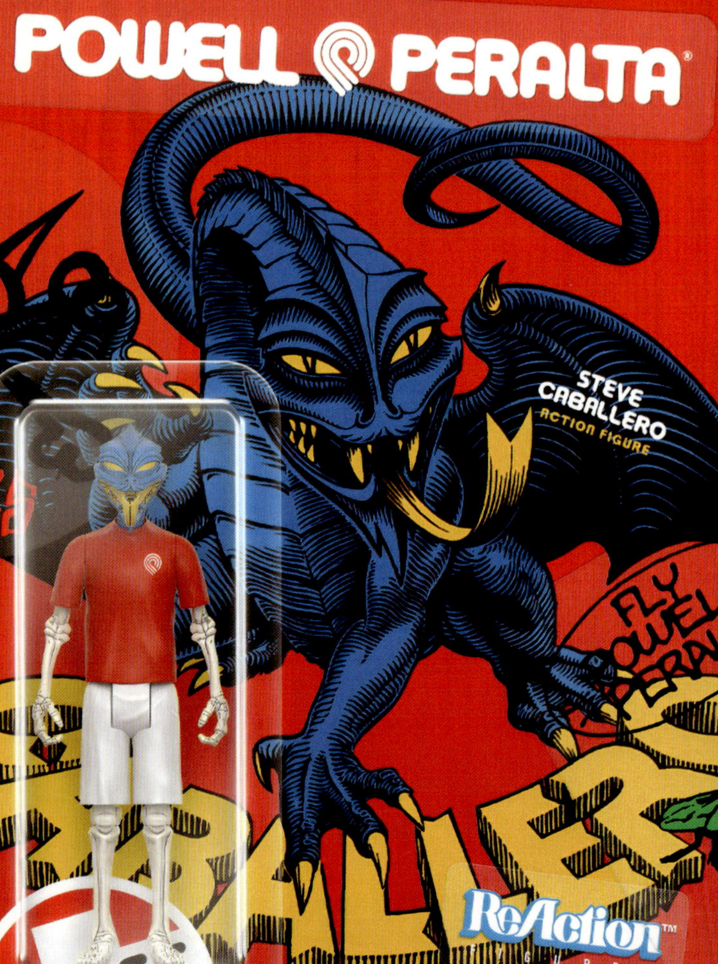

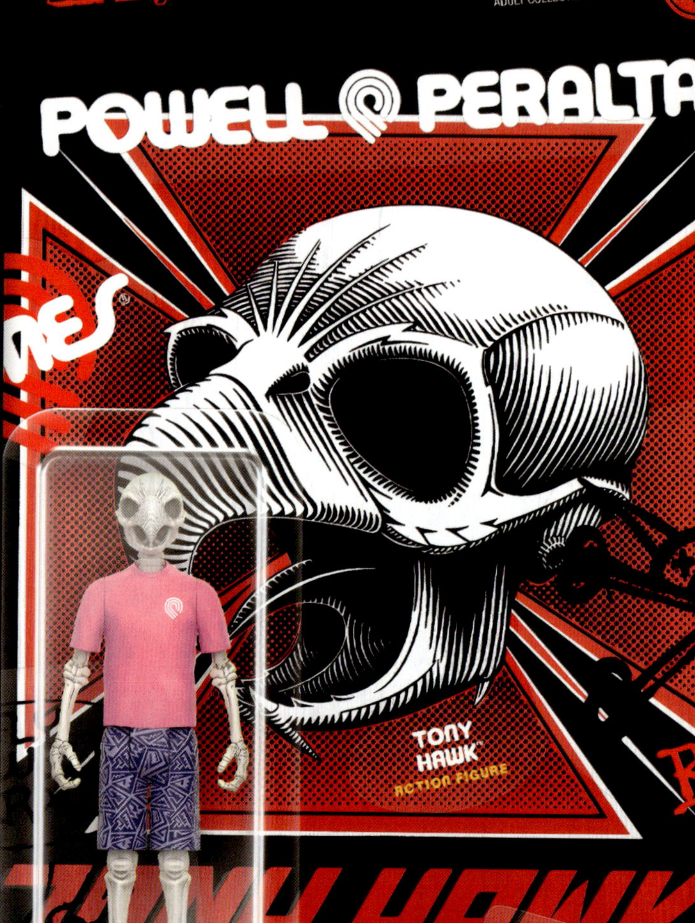

THIS PAGE: Powell-Peralta™ ReAction Figures™ Wave 5 card art

© 2025 Skate One Corp

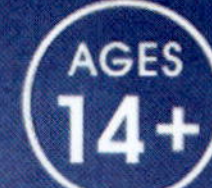

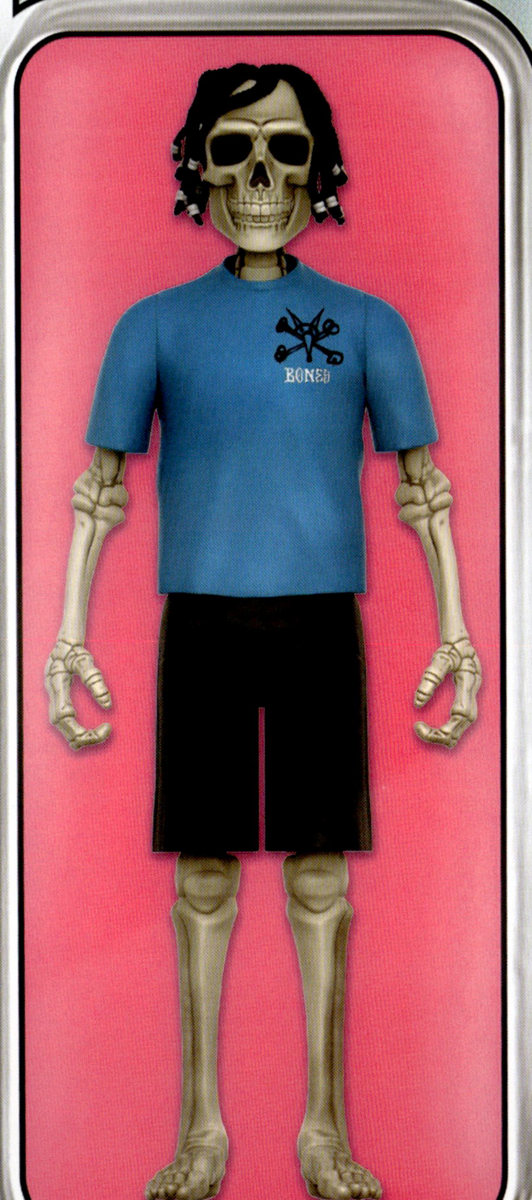

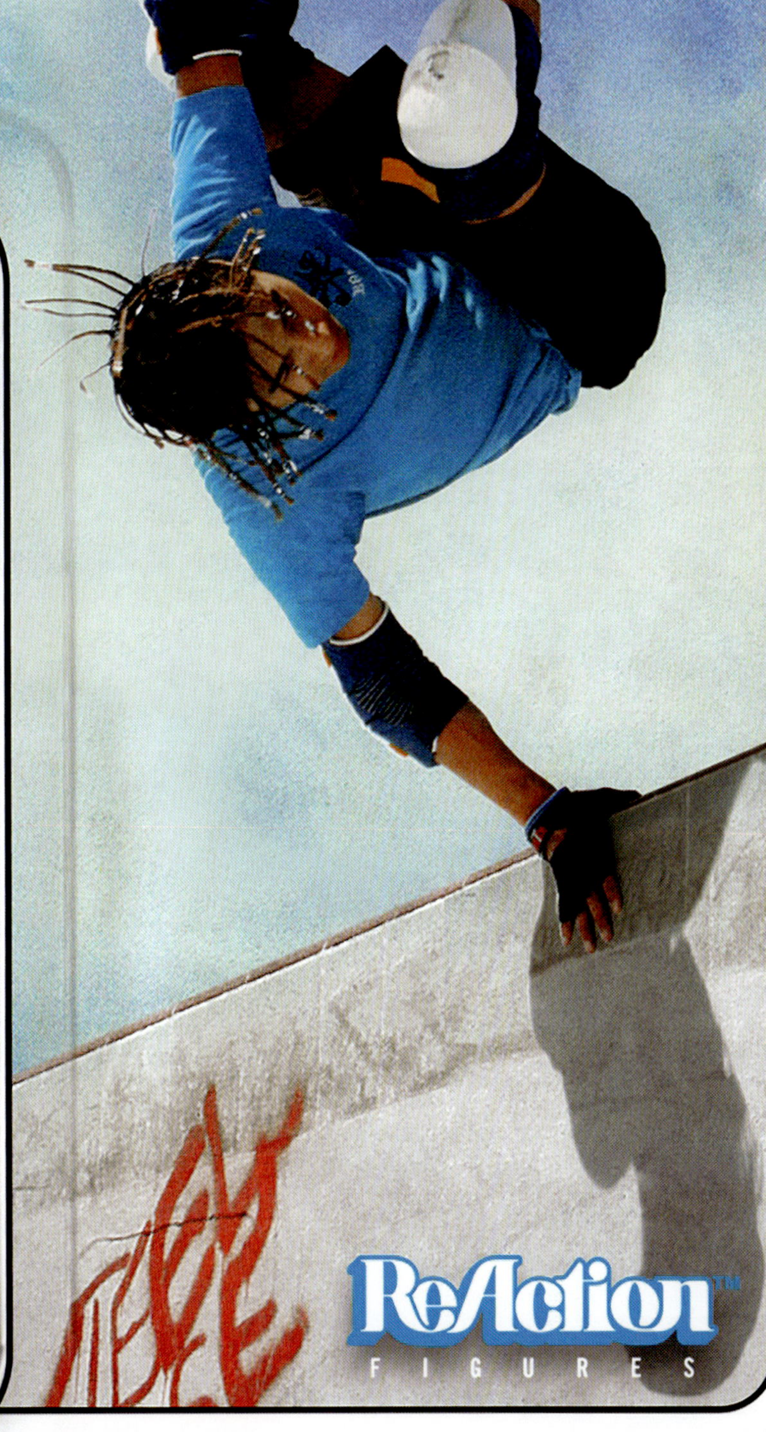

THIS PAGE: Special Edition Thrasher™ x Powell-Peralta™ ReAction Figures™ card art

Thrasher Magazine Legal © 2025 High Speed Productions all rights reserved.
© 2025 Skate One Corp

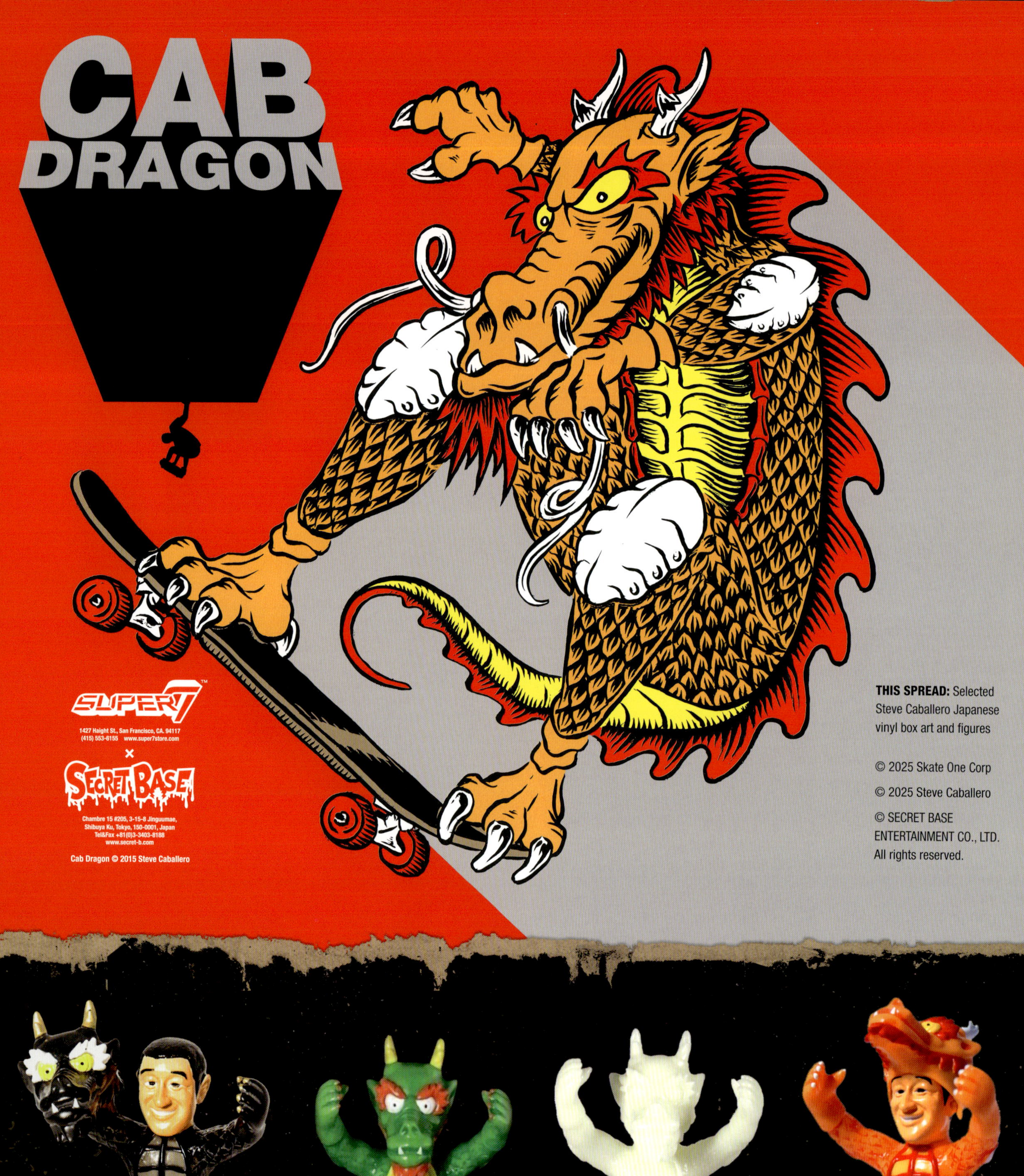

THIS SPREAD: Selected Steve Caballero Japanese vinyl box art and figures

© 2025 Skate One Corp

© 2025 Steve Caballero

© SECRET BASE ENTERTAINMENT CO., LTD. All rights reserved.

KROOKED
SKATEBOARDING

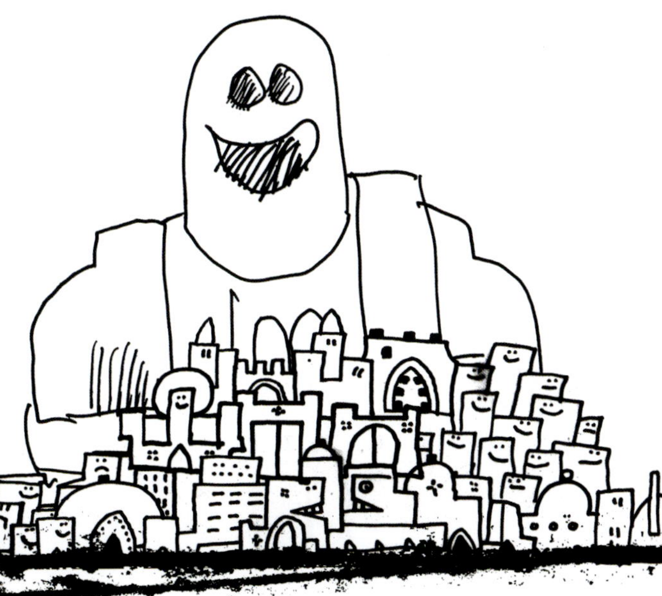

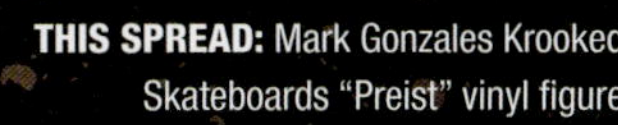

THIS SPREAD: Mark Gonzales Krooked Skateboards "Preist" vinyl figure

© 2025 S.F. Deluxe Productions, Inc.

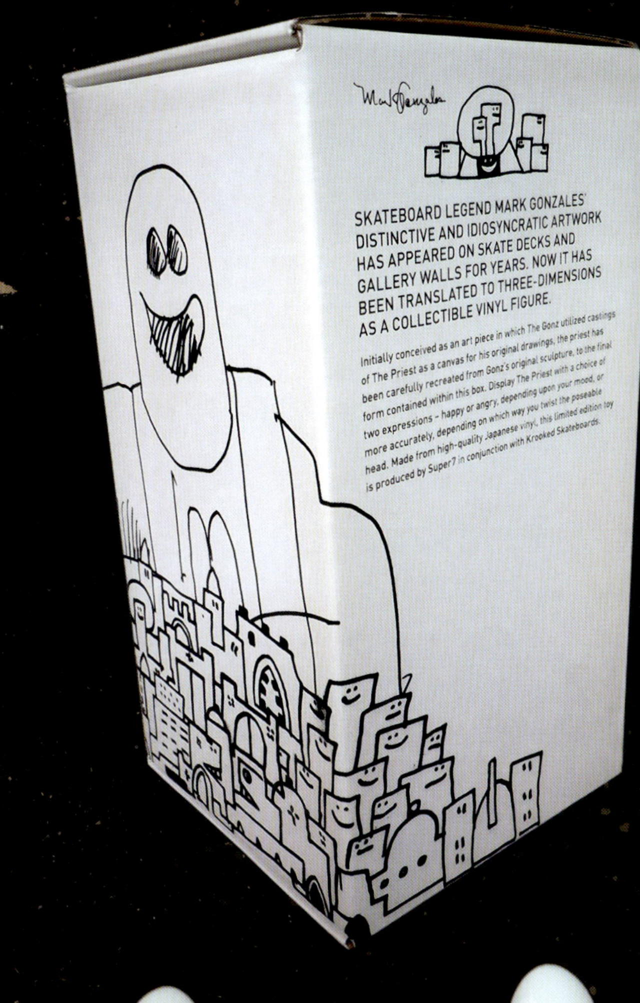

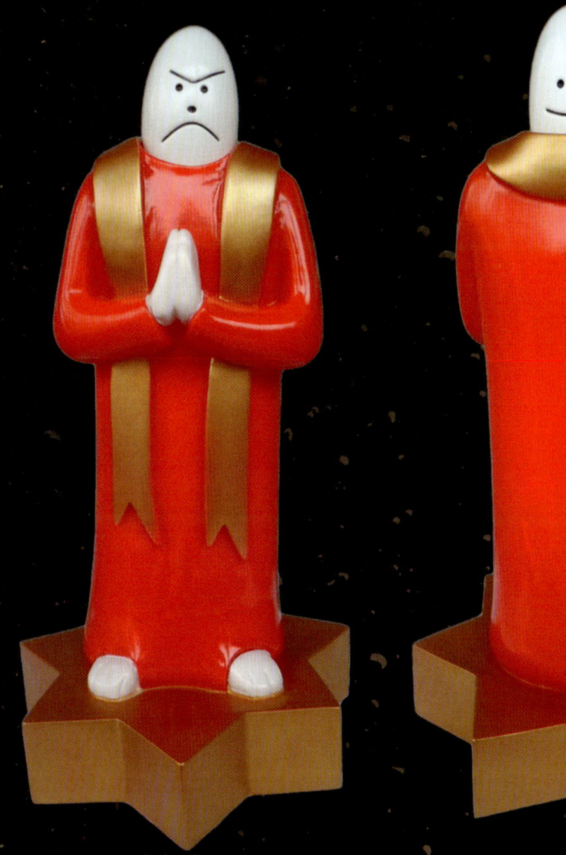

THE EXCITEMENT! THE ACTION! THE ARTWORK! ADVENTURES AND EMOTIONAL RELATIONSHIPS WRAPPED UP IN BLACK LINES AND COLOR-BLASTED EXPLOSIONS, BURSTING OFF THE PAGE AND SCREEN INTO YOUR HANDS AND HEARTS. FROM MUTANTS TO CRUSADERS, SUPERHEROES TO SIDEKICKS, ALONG WITH EVERY MANNER OF DEVIOUS VILLAIN FROM NEFARIOUS TO NONSENSICAL, IT ALL WAS A PLEASURE TO PERUSE. AS KIDS, COMICS AND CARTOONS WERE THE FIRST PLACE WE WERE TRANSPORTED TO STORIES AND CHARACTERS BEYOND THE WALLS OF OUR HOMES. AS ADULTS, WE STILL LOOK AT THESE CHARACTERS AND STORIES AND TRAVEL TO WORLDS UNKNOWN . . . WHETHER OTHER PEOPLE THINK IT IS COOL OR NOT.

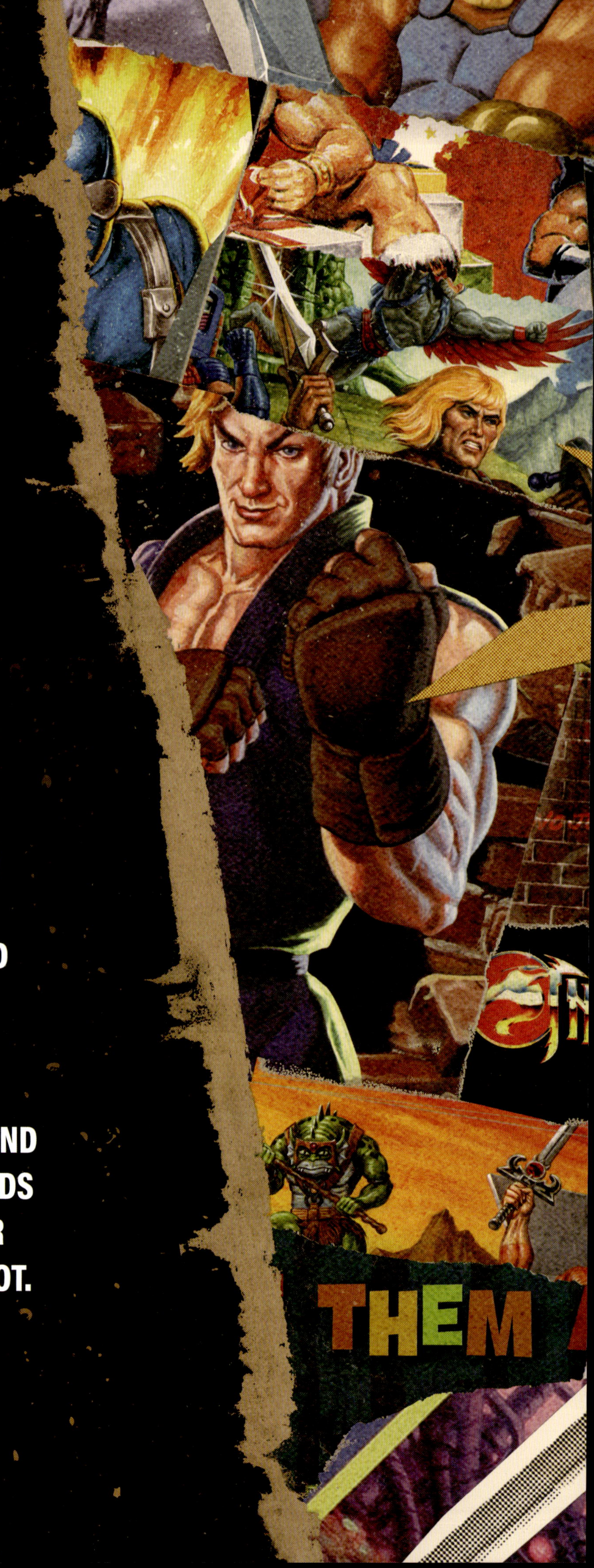

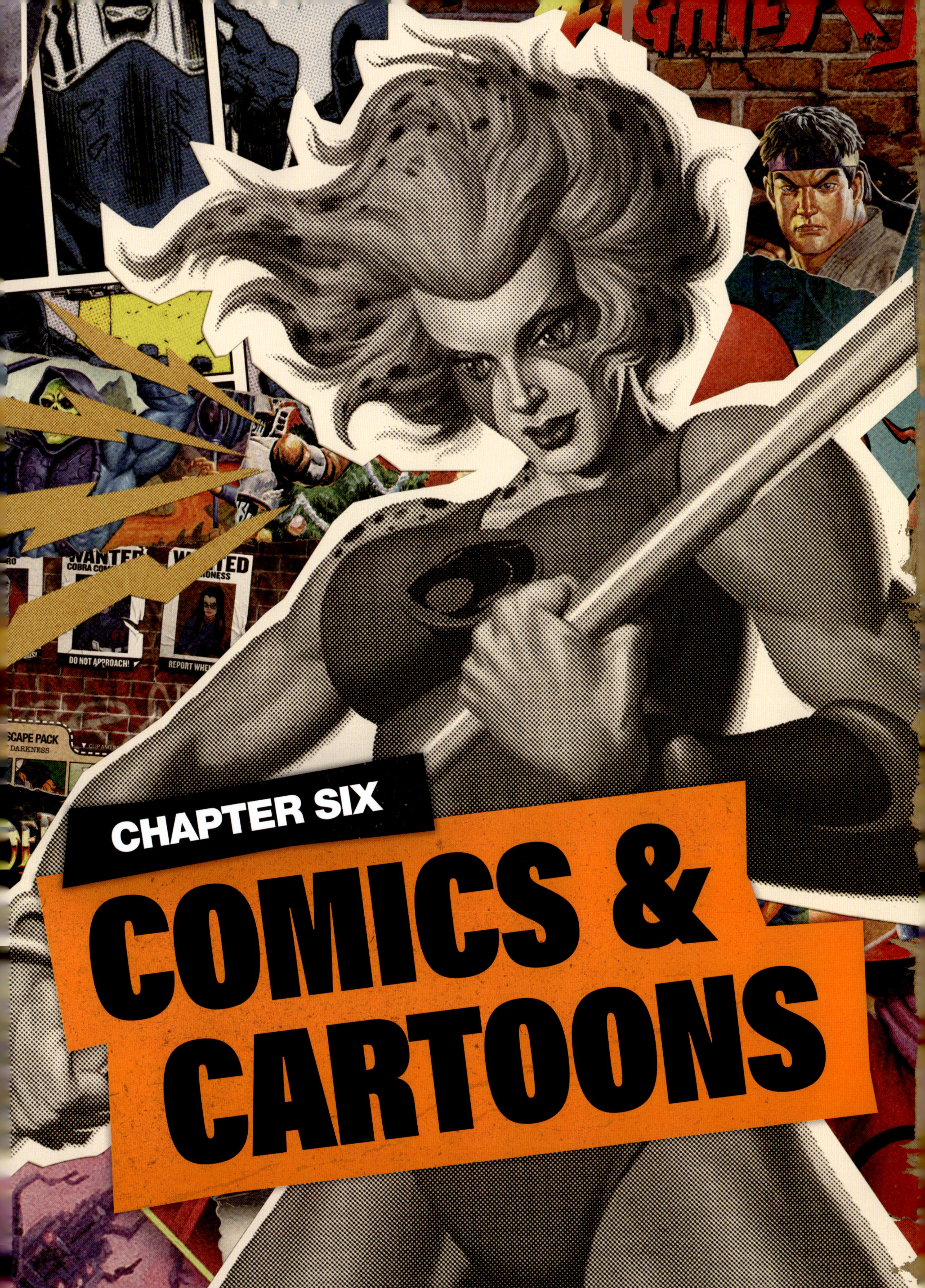

CHAPTER SIX

COMICS & CARTOONS

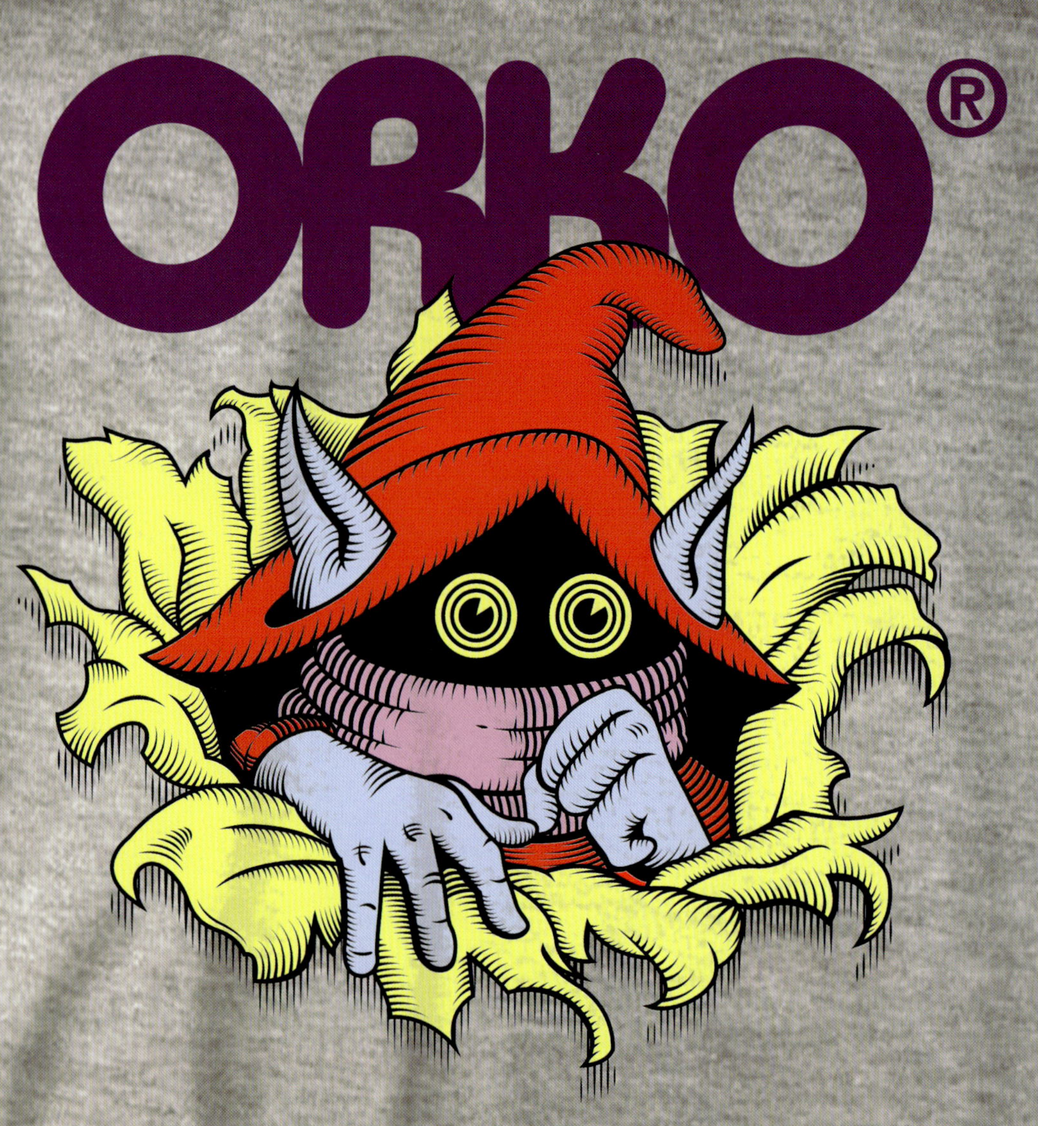

THIS SPREAD: Selected Masters of the Universe® apparel and accessories

© 2025 Mattel

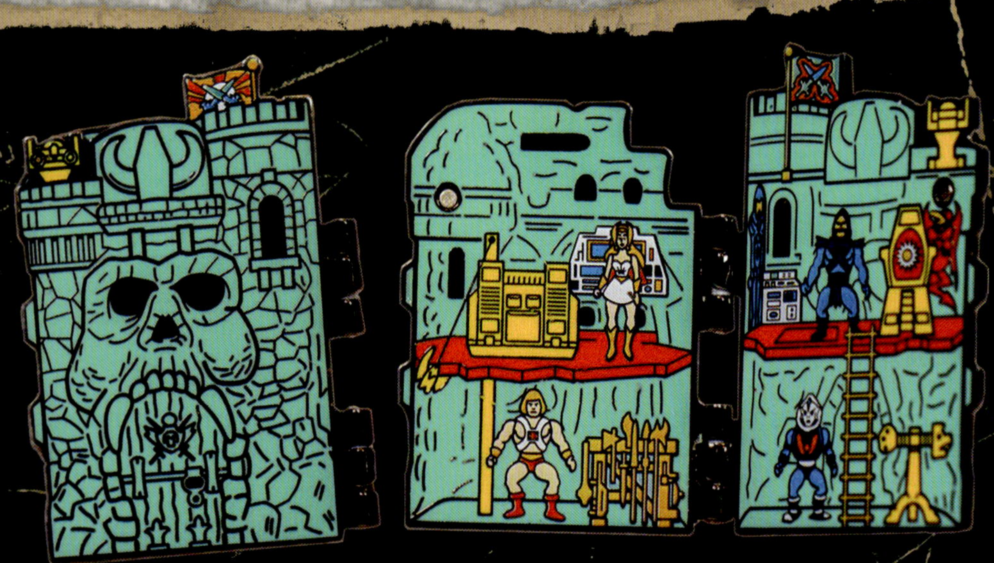

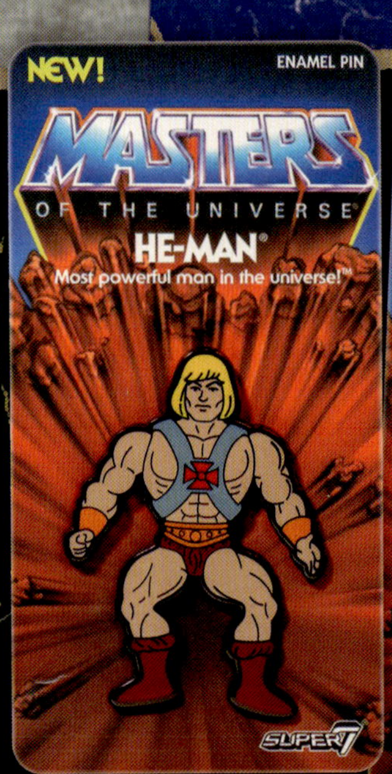

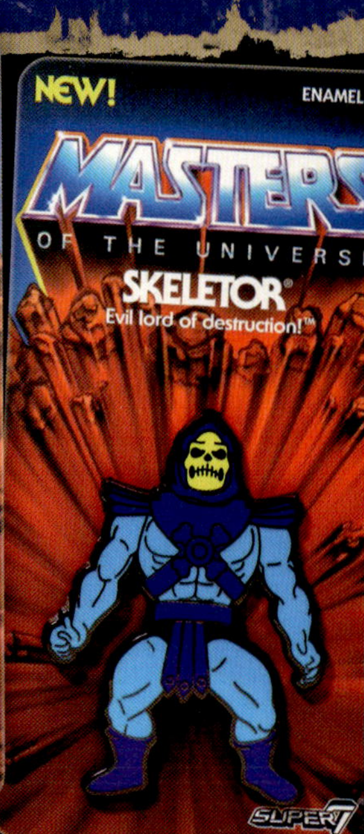

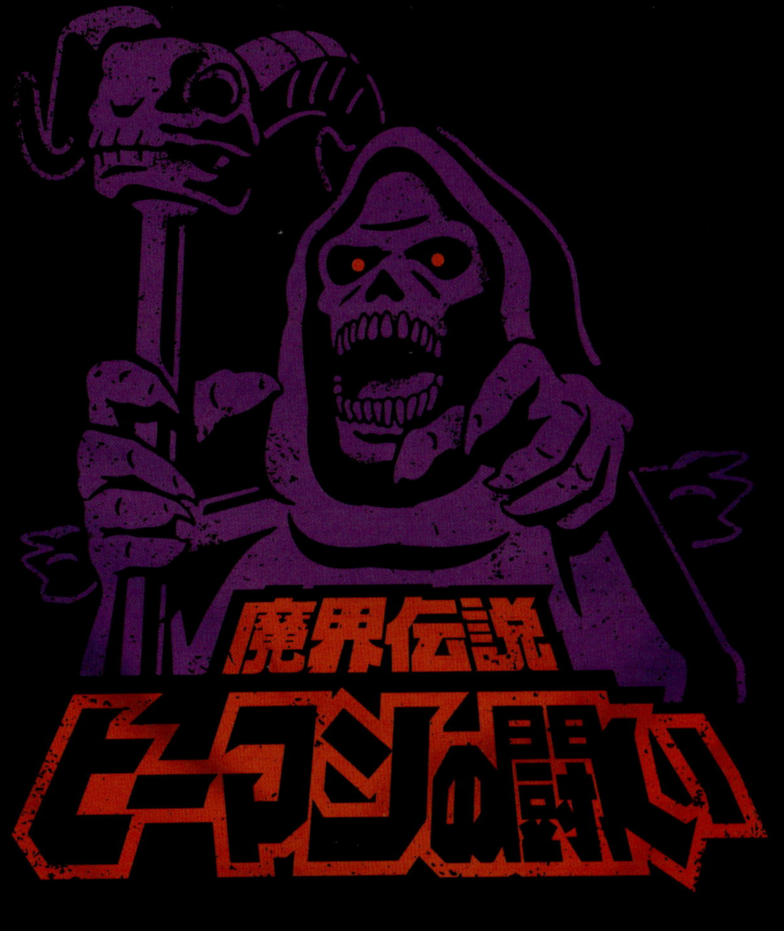
魔界伝説
ヒーマンの闘い

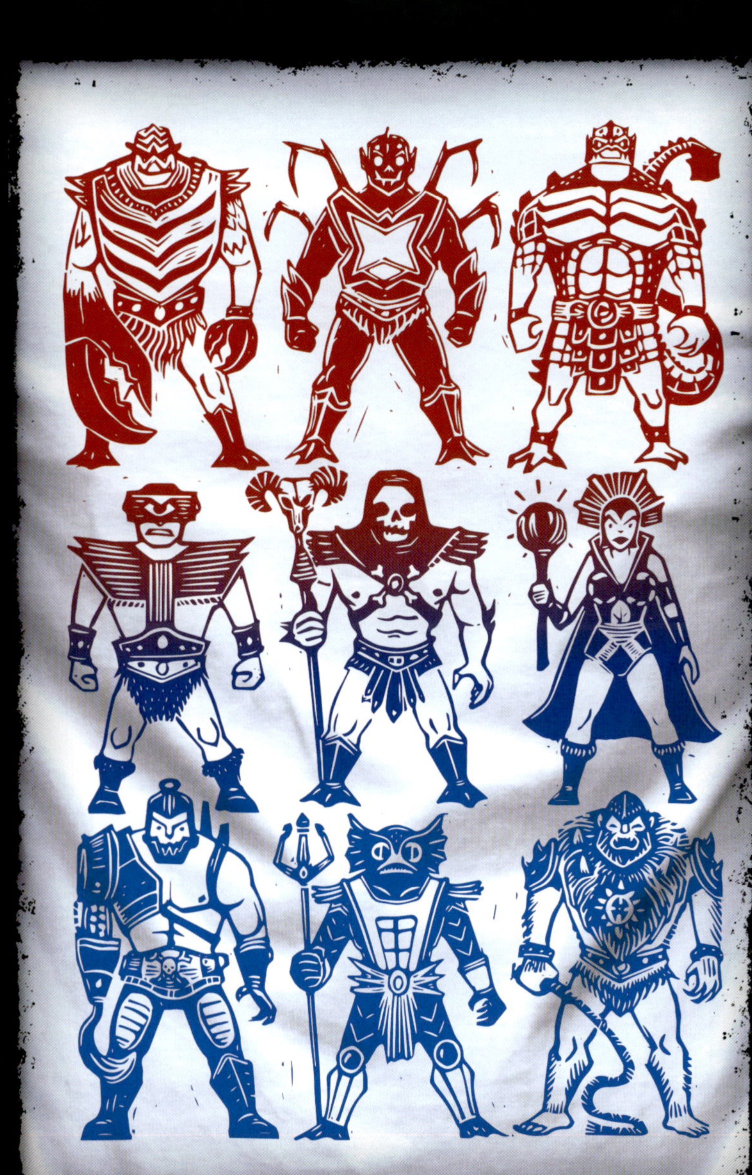

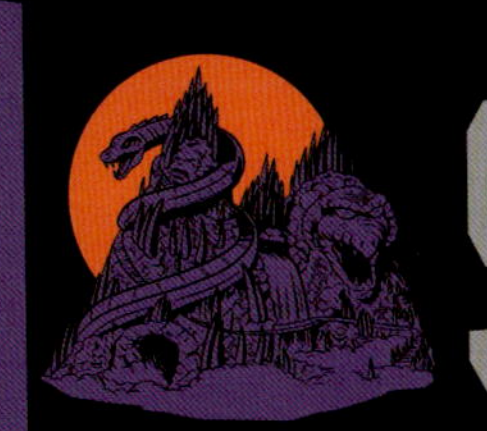
SNAKE MOUNTAIN

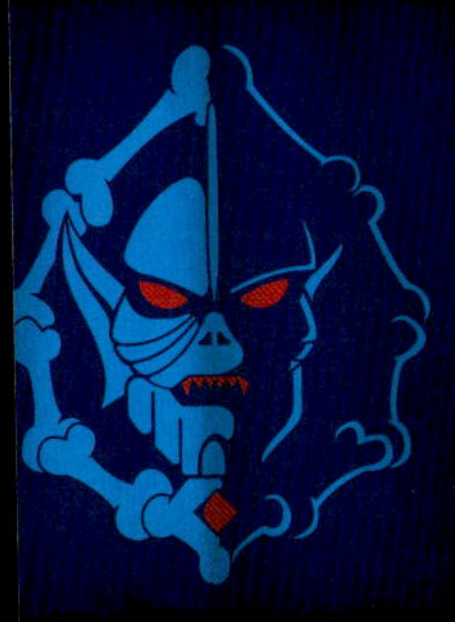

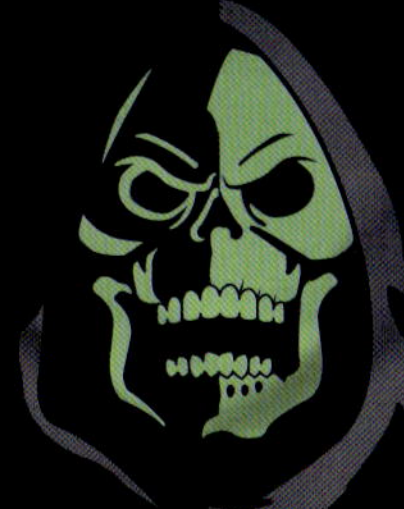

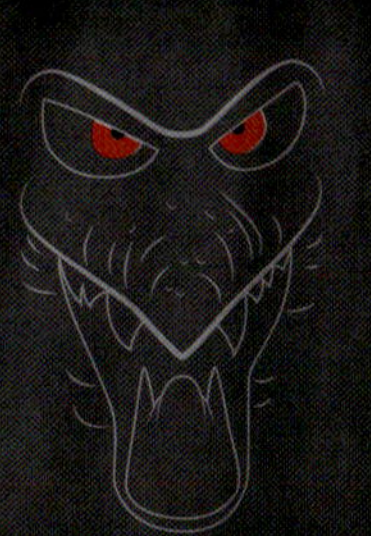

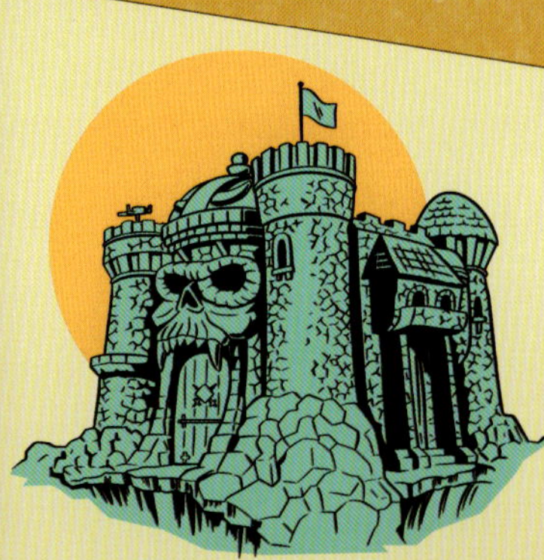
GRAYSKULL

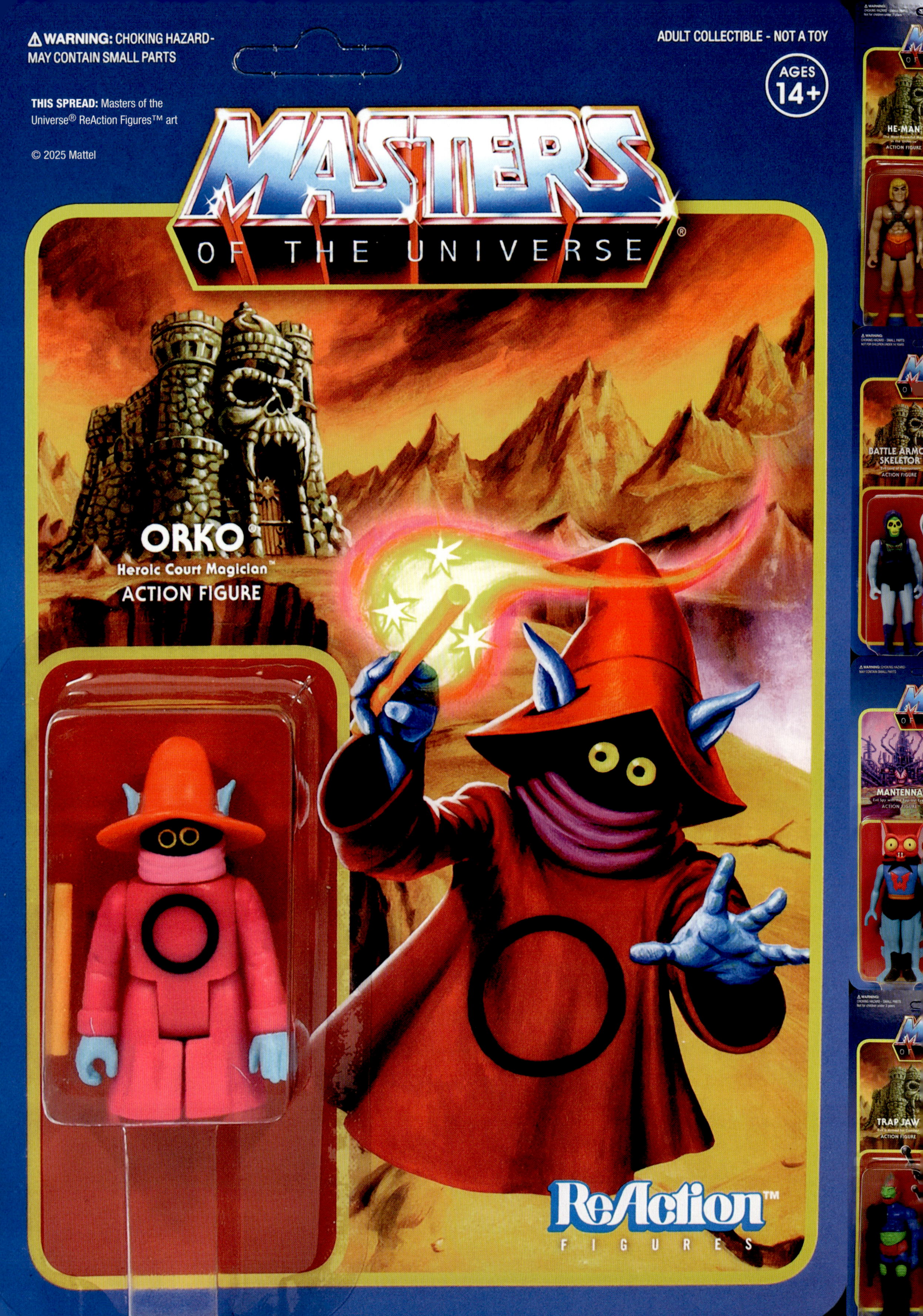

THIS SPREAD: Masters of the Universe® ReAction Figures™ art

© 2025 Mattel

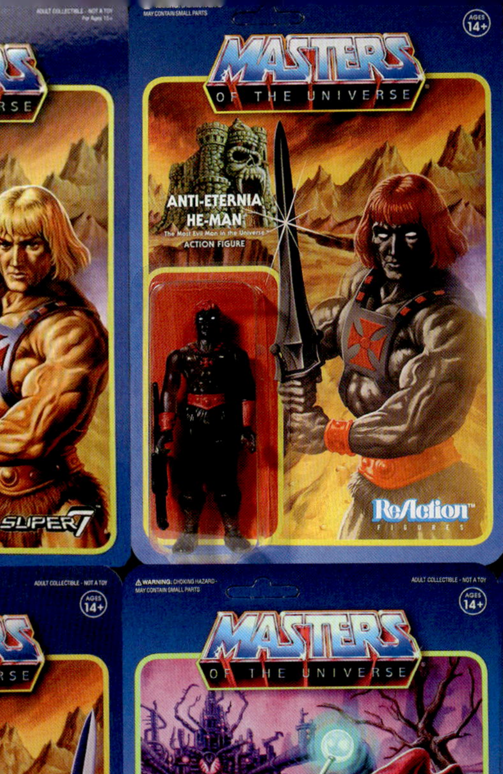
MASTERS OF THE UNIVERSE
ANTI-ETERNIA HE-MAN
ACTION FIGURE
SUPER7
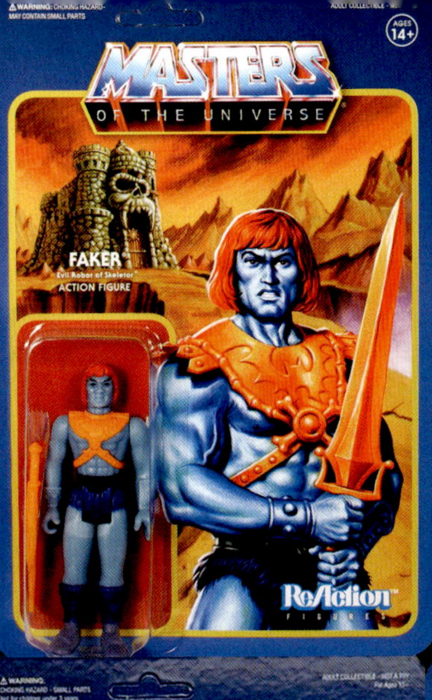
MASTERS OF THE UNIVERSE
FAKER
ACTION FIGURE
ReAction
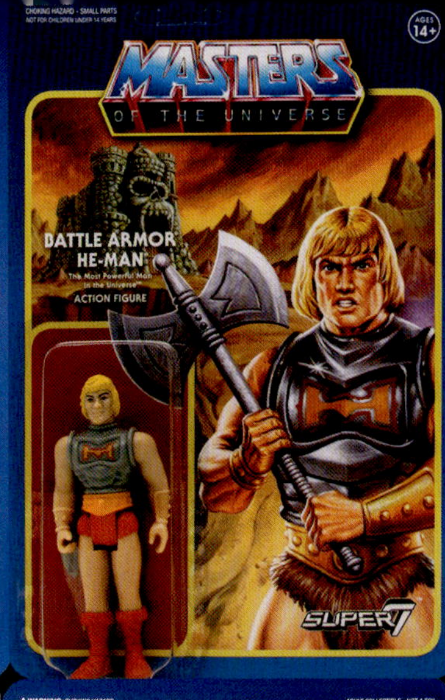
MASTERS OF THE UNIVERSE
BATTLE ARMOR HE-MAN
ACTION FIGURE
SUPER7
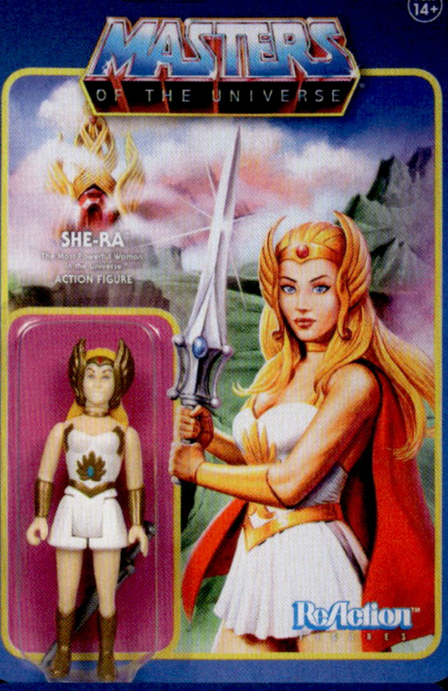
MASTERS OF THE UNIVERSE
SHE-RA
ACTION FIGURE
ReAction
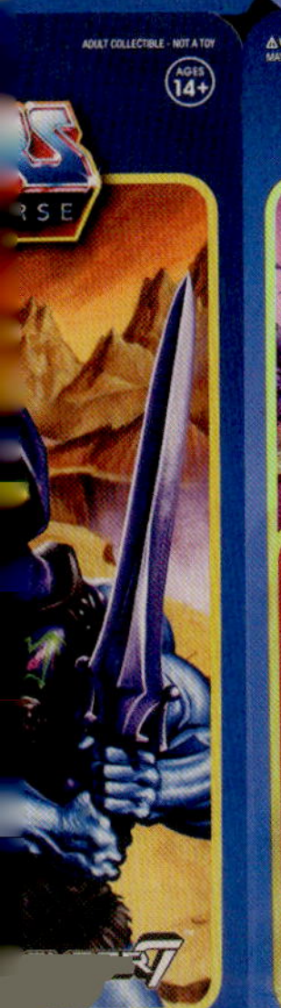
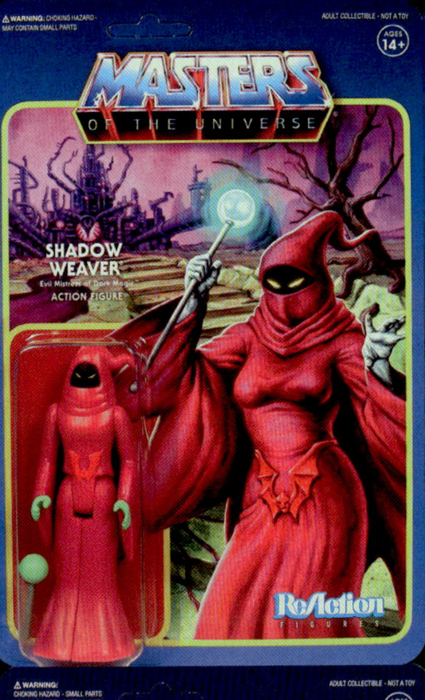
MASTERS OF THE UNIVERSE
SHADOW WEAVER
ACTION FIGURE
ReAction
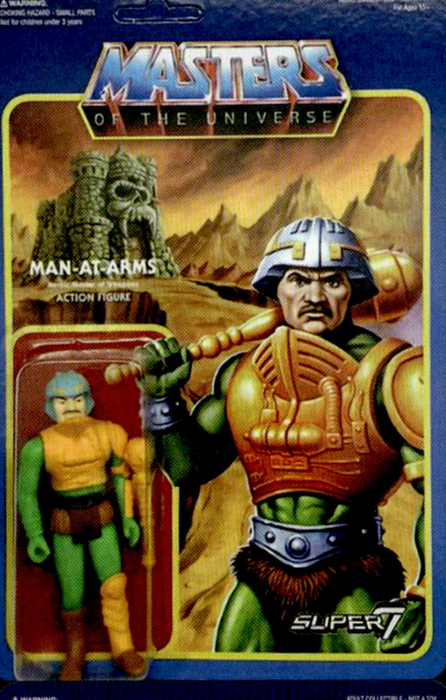
MASTERS OF THE UNIVERSE
MAN-AT-ARMS
ACTION FIGURE
SUPER7
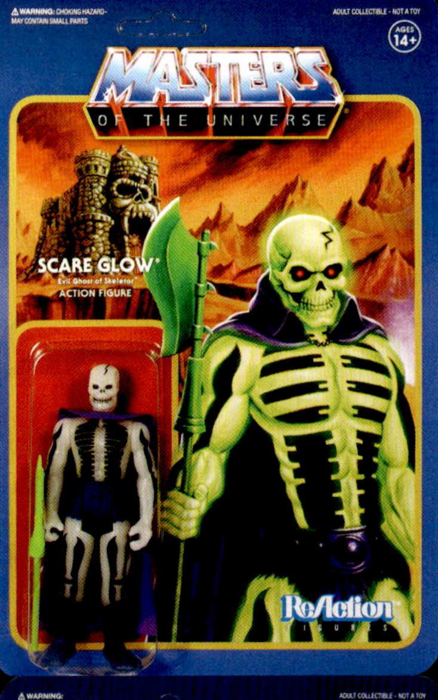
MASTERS OF THE UNIVERSE
SCARE GLOW
ACTION FIGURE
ReAction
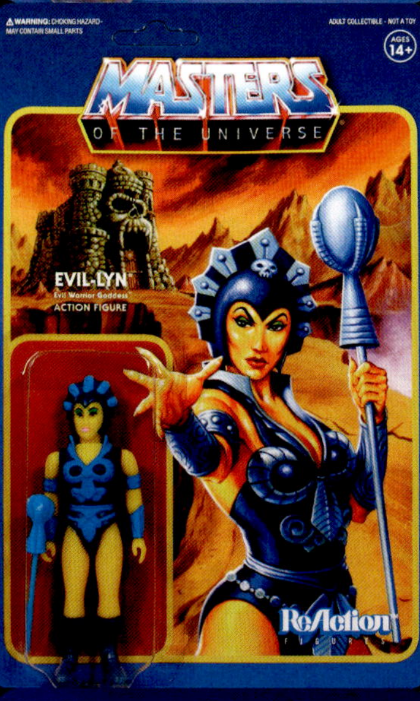
MASTERS OF THE UNIVERSE
EVIL-LYN
ACTION FIGURE
ReAction
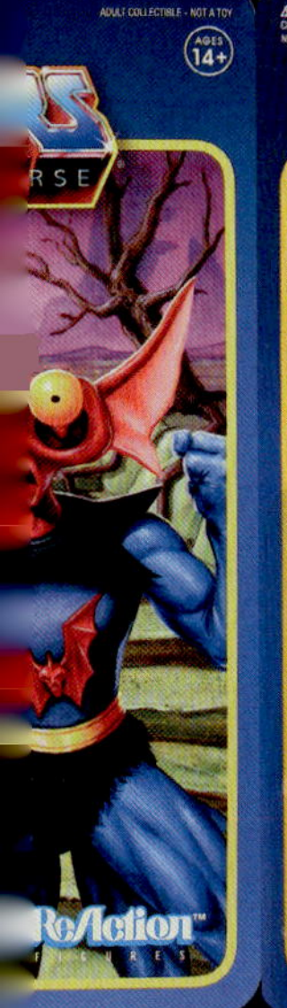
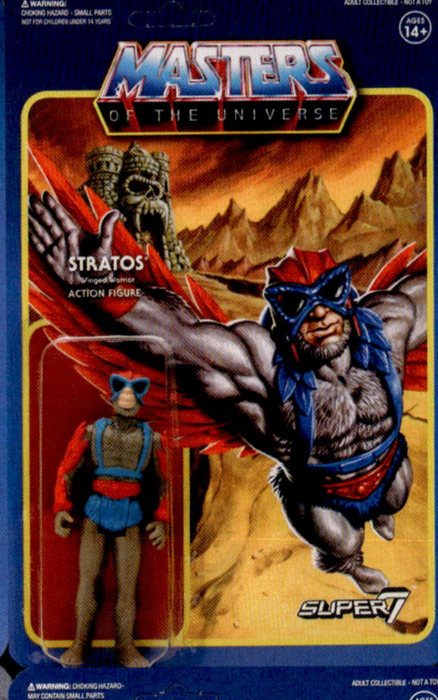
MASTERS OF THE UNIVERSE
STRATOS
ACTION FIGURE
SUPER7
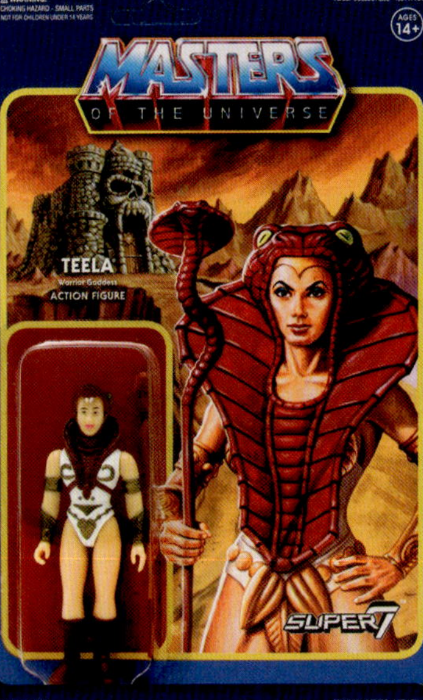
MASTERS OF THE UNIVERSE
TEELA
ACTION FIGURE
SUPER7
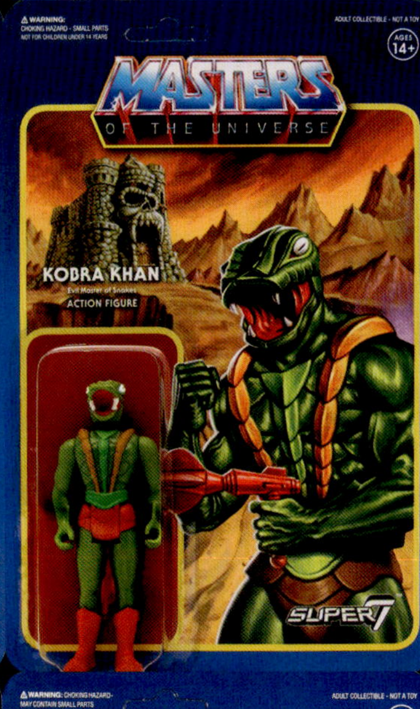
MASTERS OF THE UNIVERSE
KOBRA KHAN
ACTION FIGURE
SUPER7
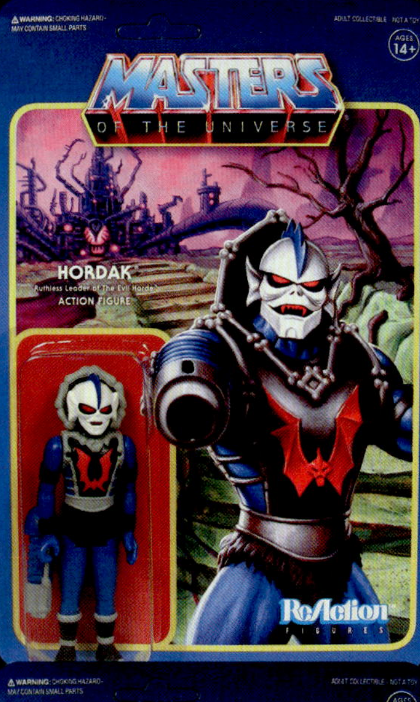
MASTERS OF THE UNIVERSE
HORDAK
ACTION FIGURE
ReAction
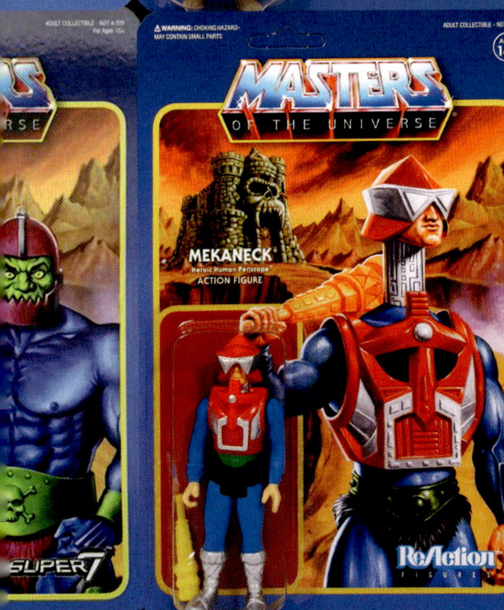
MASTERS OF THE UNIVERSE
MEKANECK
ACTION FIGURE
ReAction
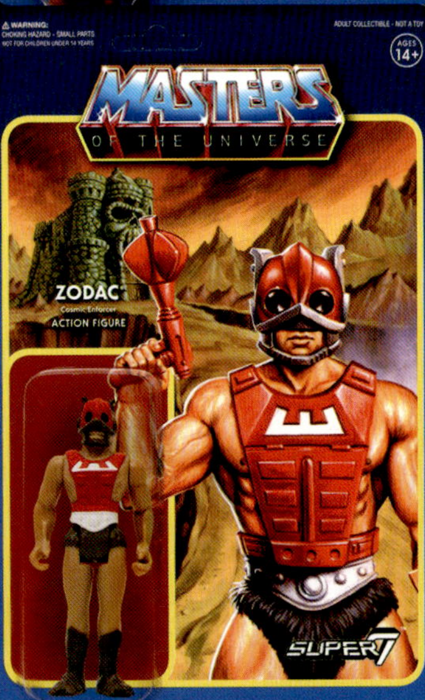
MASTERS OF THE UNIVERSE
ZODAC
ACTION FIGURE
SUPER7
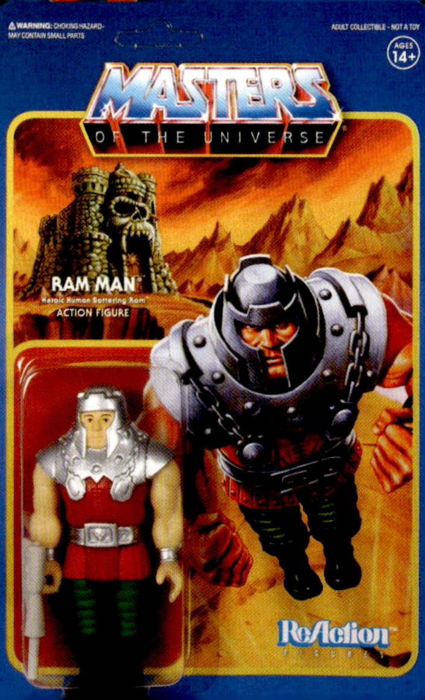
MASTERS OF THE UNIVERSE
RAM MAN
ACTION FIGURE
ReAction
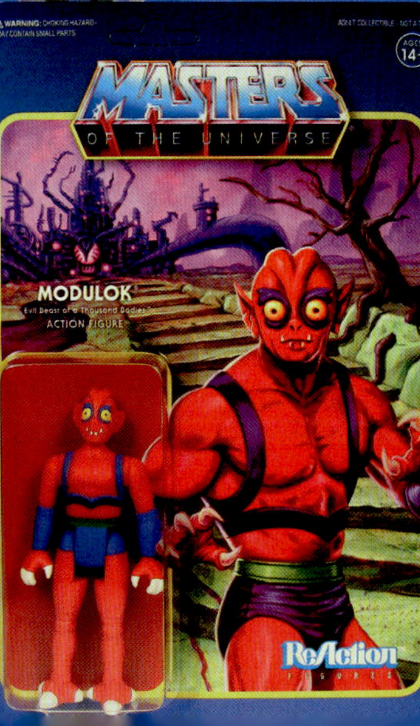
MASTERS OF THE UNIVERSE
MODULOK
ACTION FIGURE
ReAction

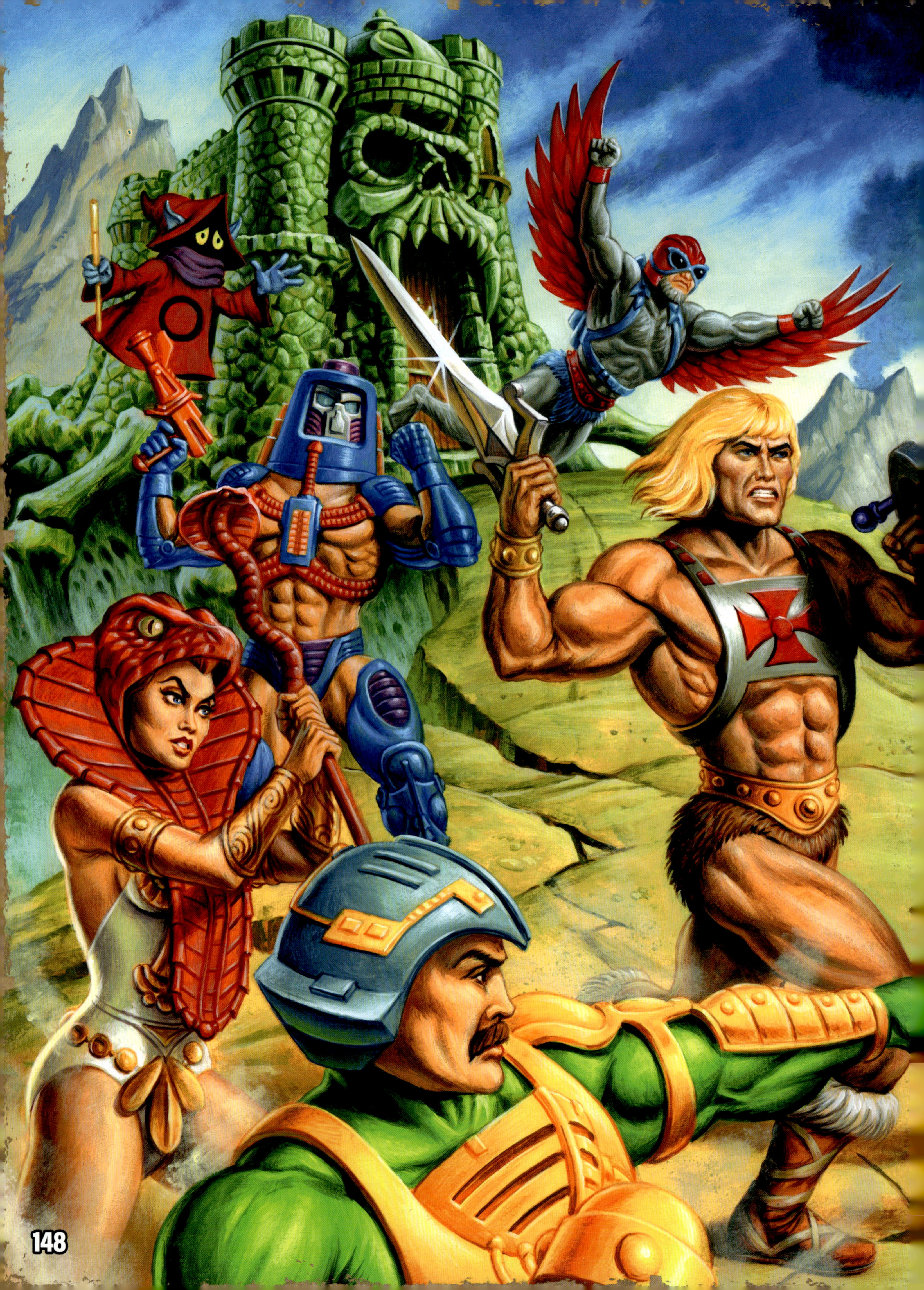

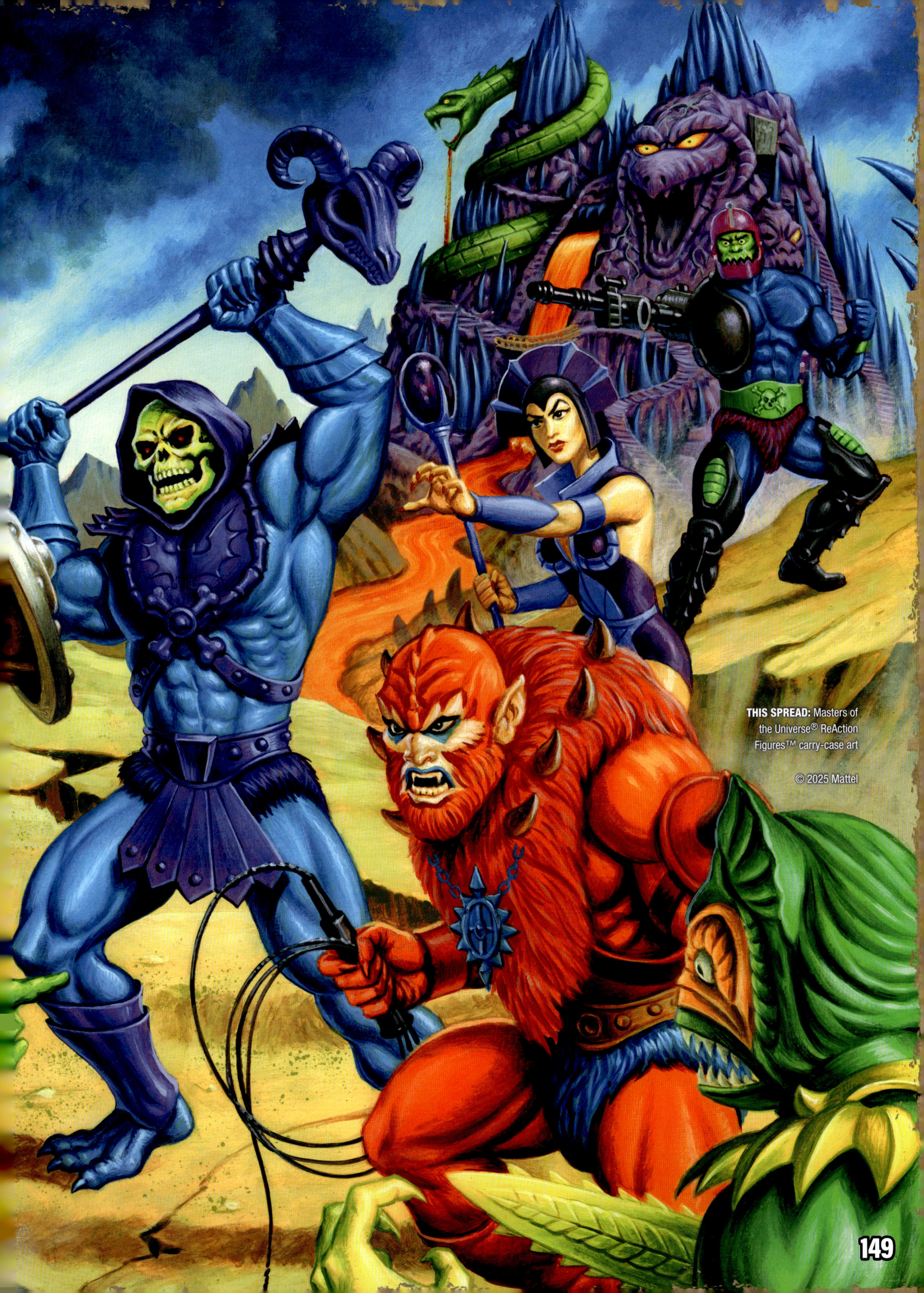

THIS SPREAD: Masters of the Universe® ReAction Figures™ carry-case art

© 2025 Mattel

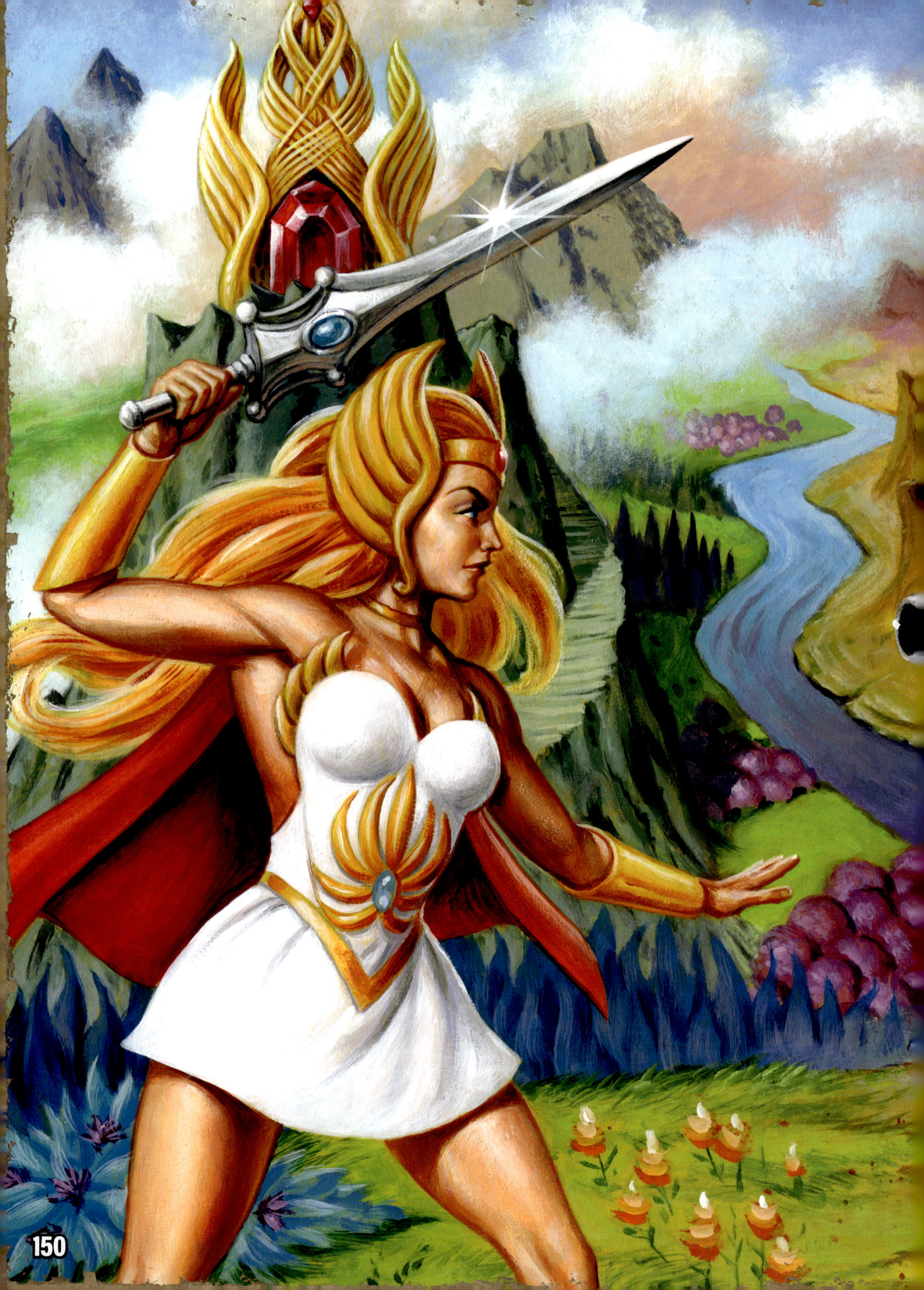

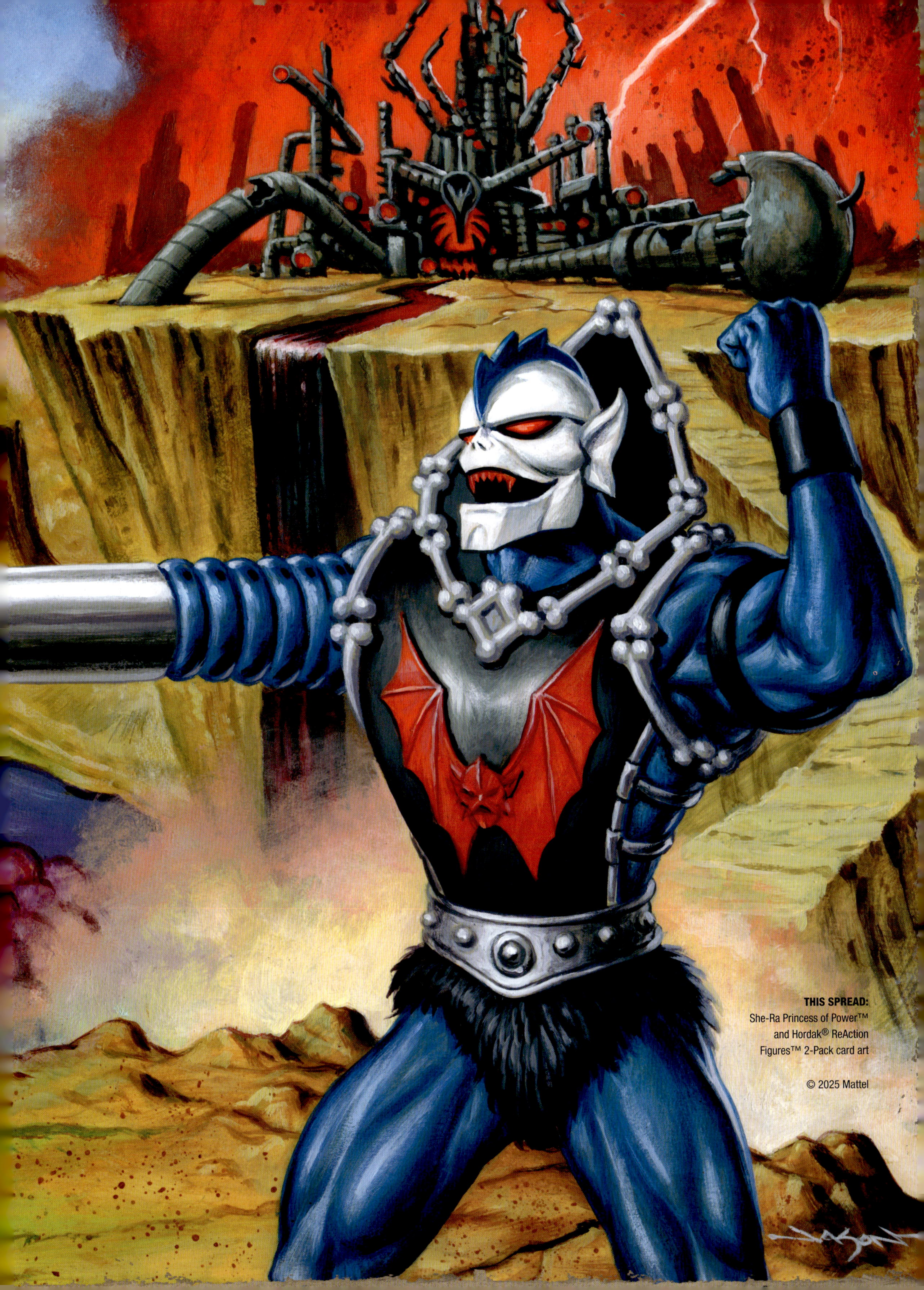

THIS SPREAD:
She-Ra Princess of Power™ and Hordak® ReAction Figures™ 2-Pack card art

© 2025 Mattel

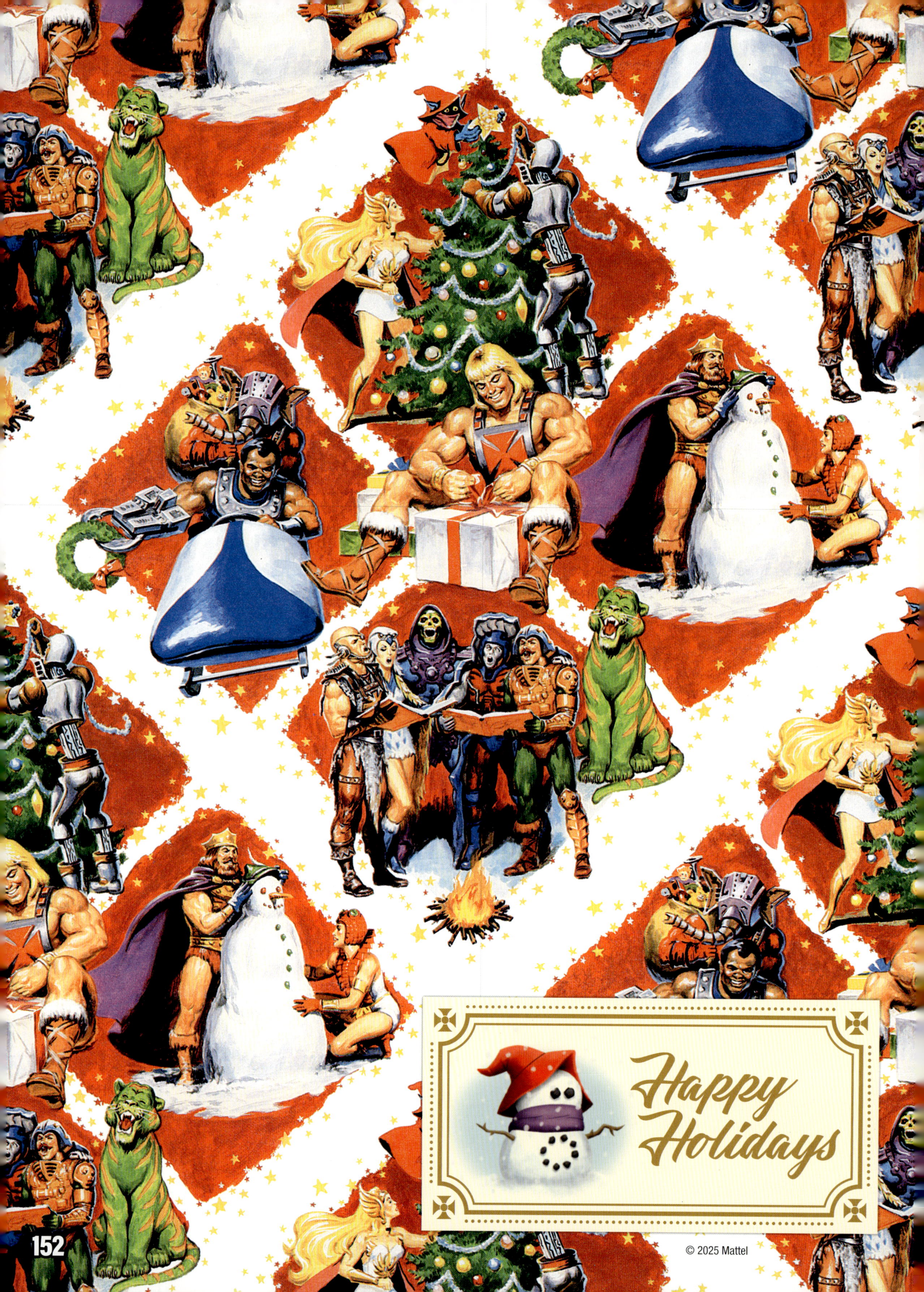

© 2025 Mattel

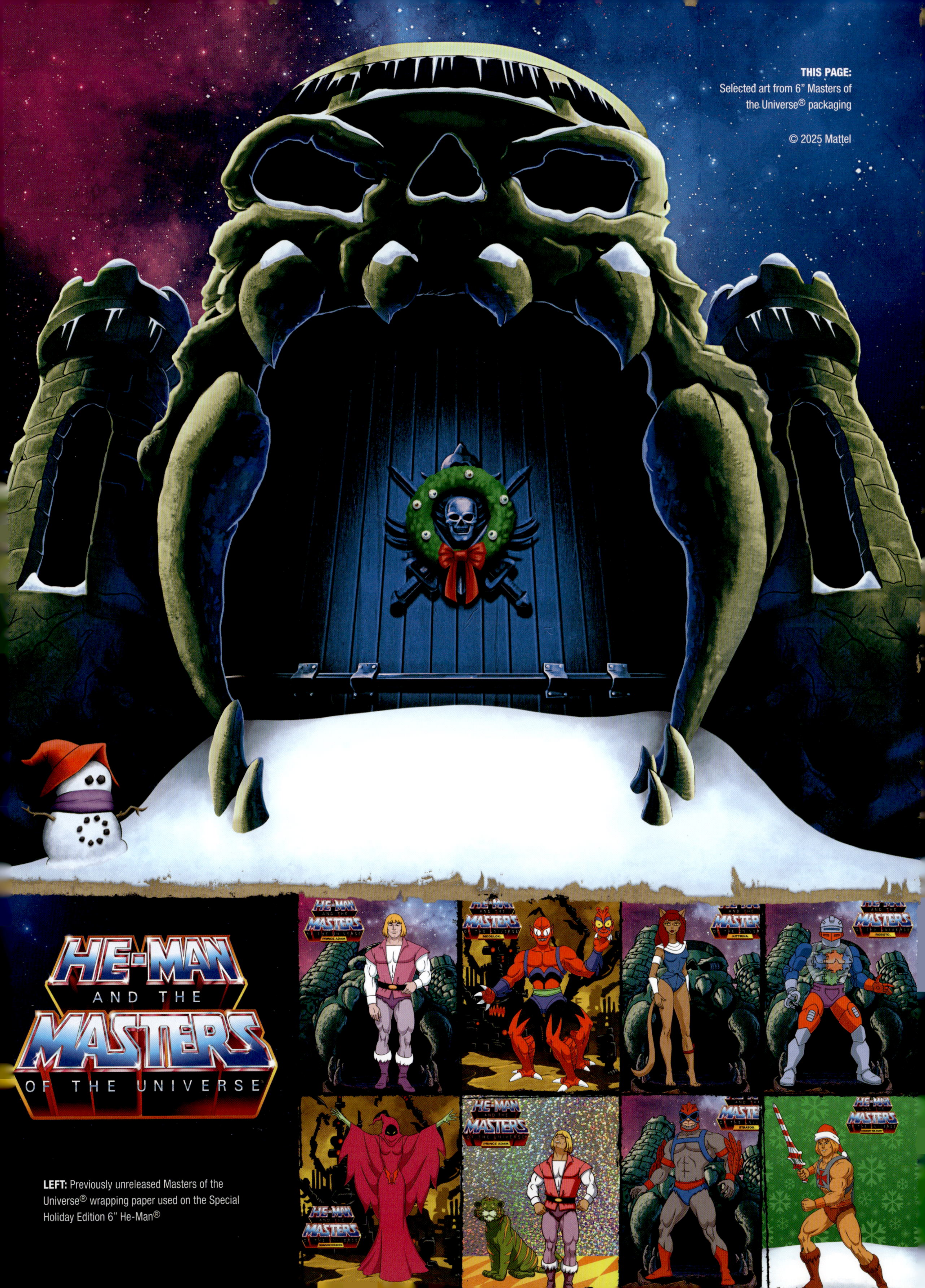

THIS PAGE: Selected art from 6" Masters of the Universe® packaging

© 2025 Mattel

LEFT: Previously unreleased Masters of the Universe® wrapping paper used on the Special Holiday Edition 6" He-Man®

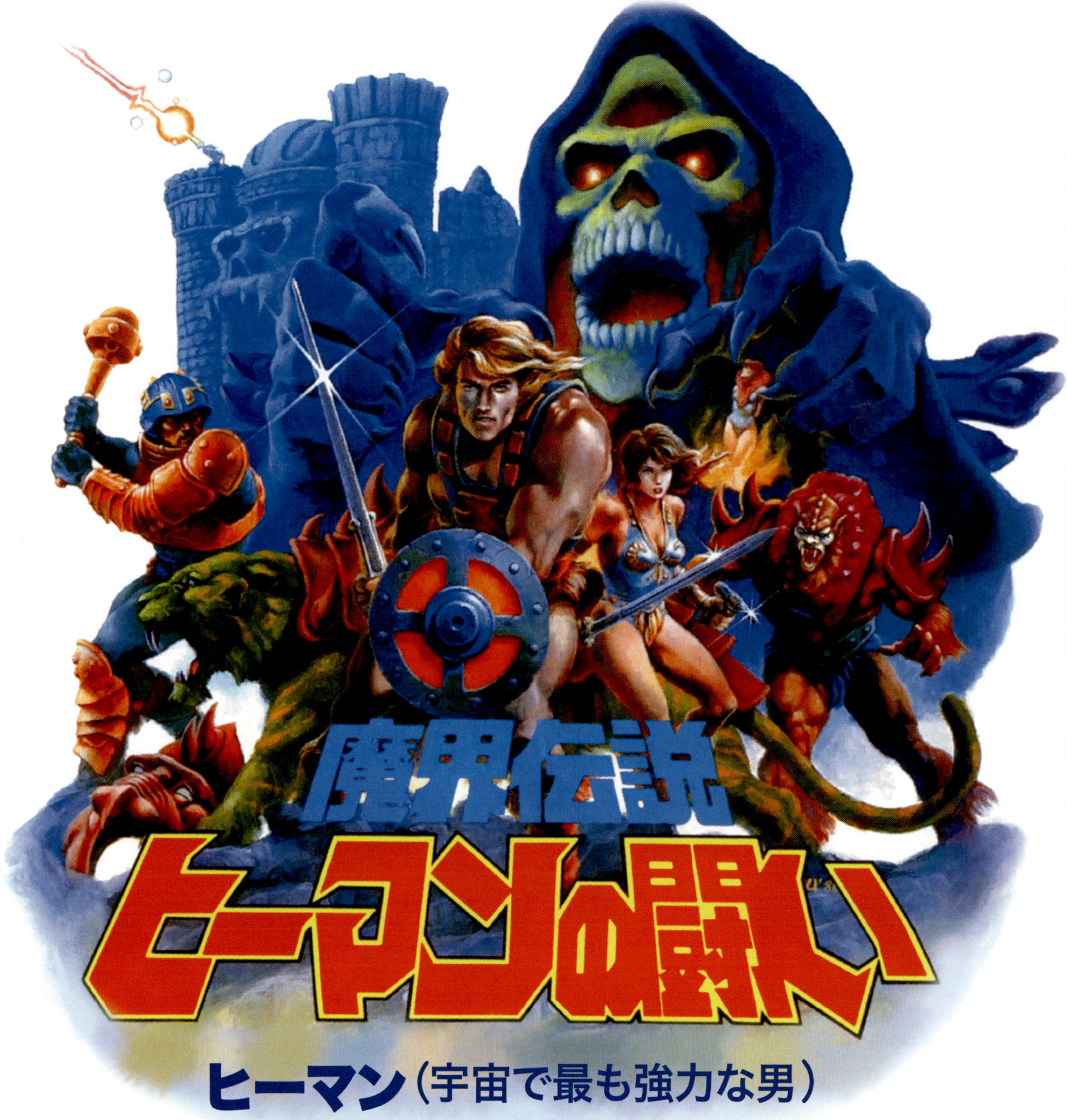

魔界伝説

ヒーマンの闘い

ヒーマン（宇宙で最も強力な男）

THIS PAGE: Japanese edition Masters of the Universe® Retro Figure box art

RIGHT: Masters of the Universe® ReAction Figures™ Blind-Box art

© 2025 Mattel

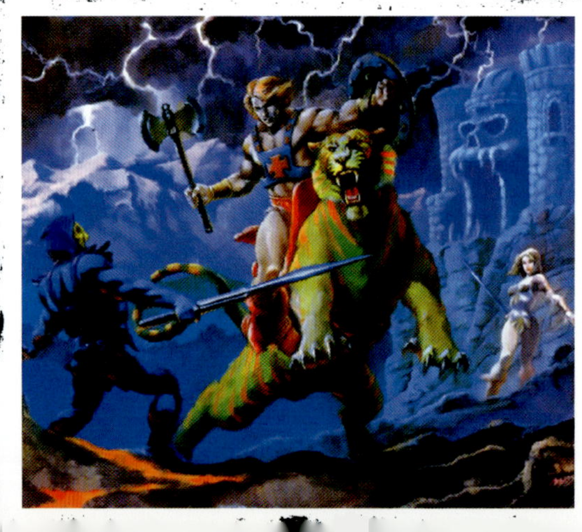

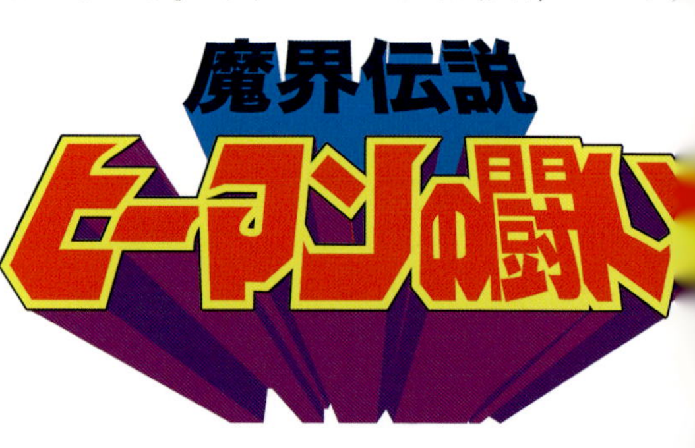

MASTERS OF THE UNIVERS

ヒーマン（宇宙で最も強力な

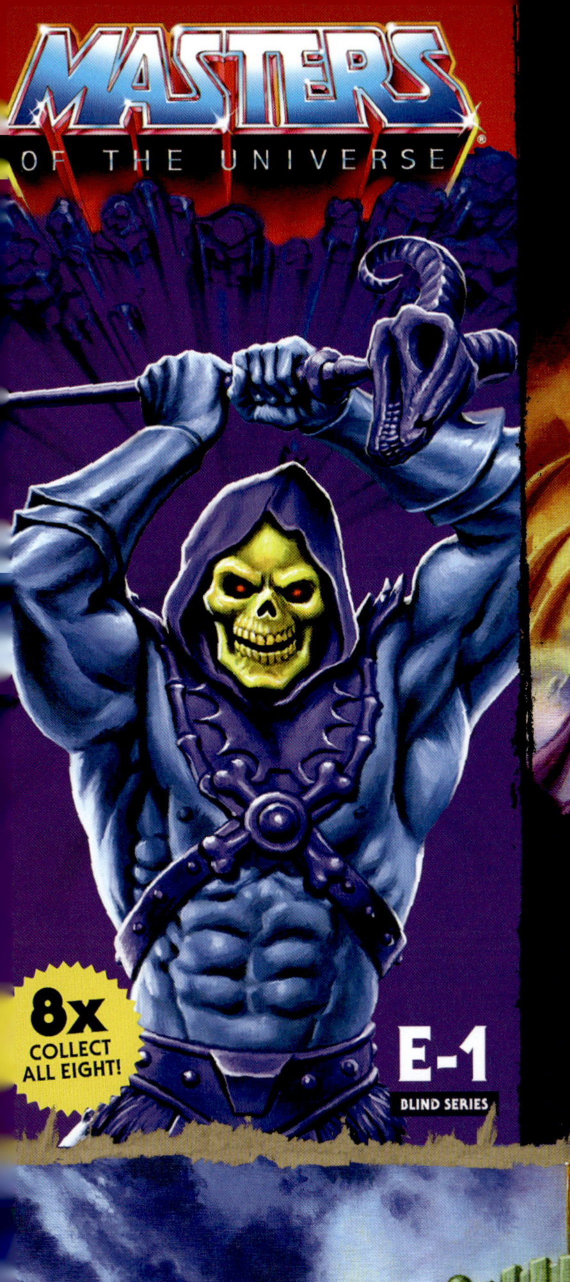

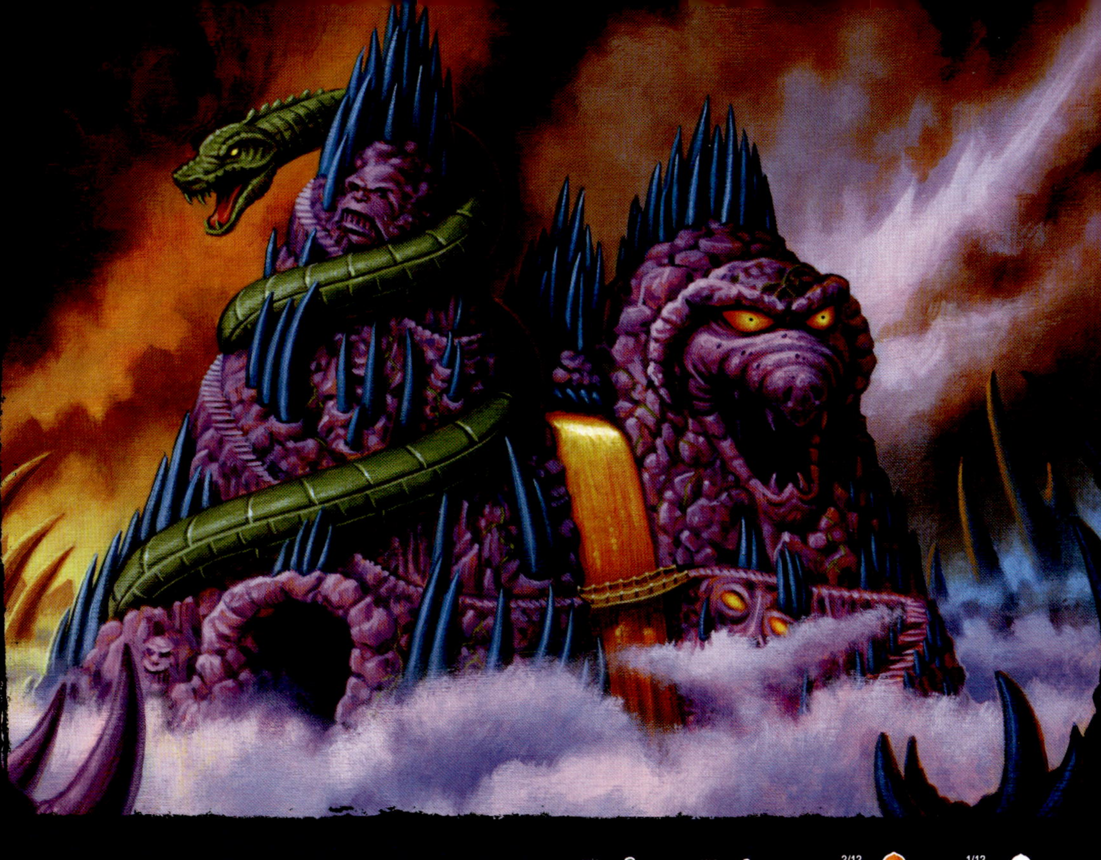

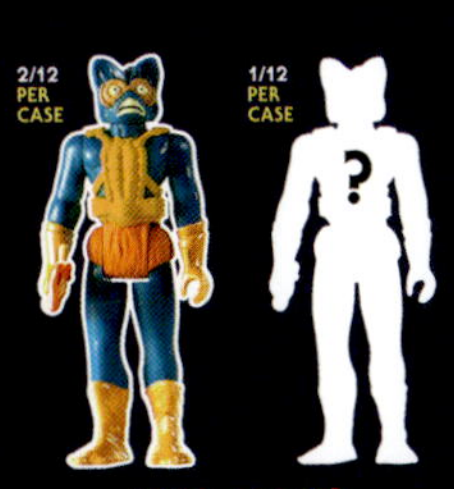

MER-MAN®
Skeletor's Ocean Warrior™

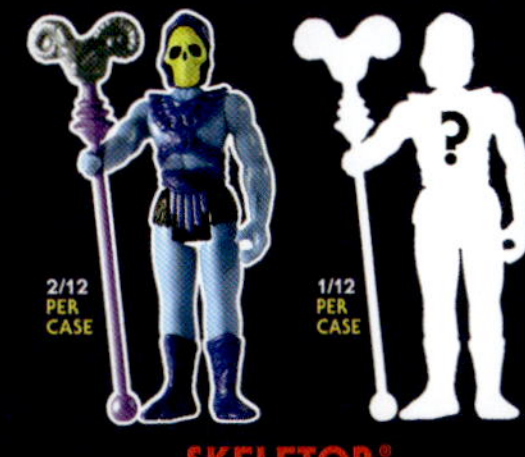

SKELETOR®
Evil Lord of Destruction™

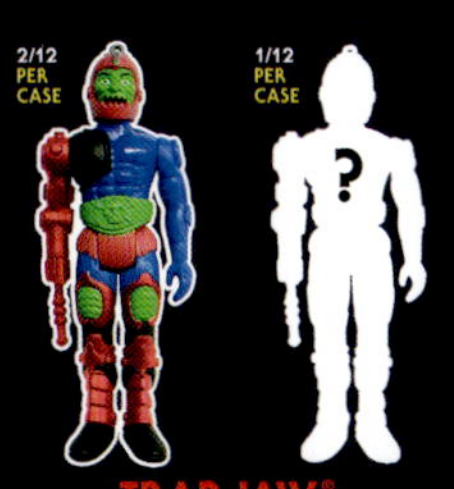

TRAP JAW®
Evil & Armed for Combat™

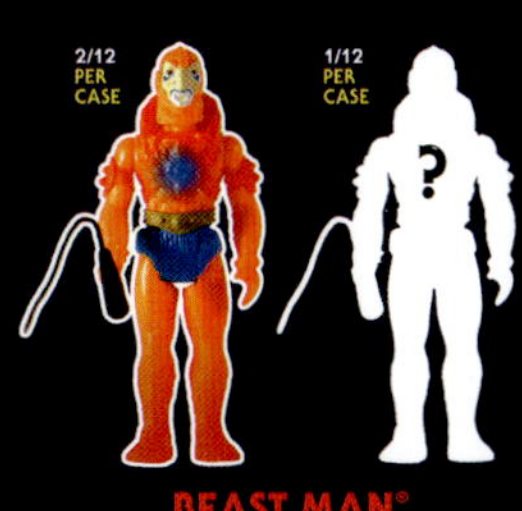

BEAST MAN®
Skeletor's Savage Henchman™

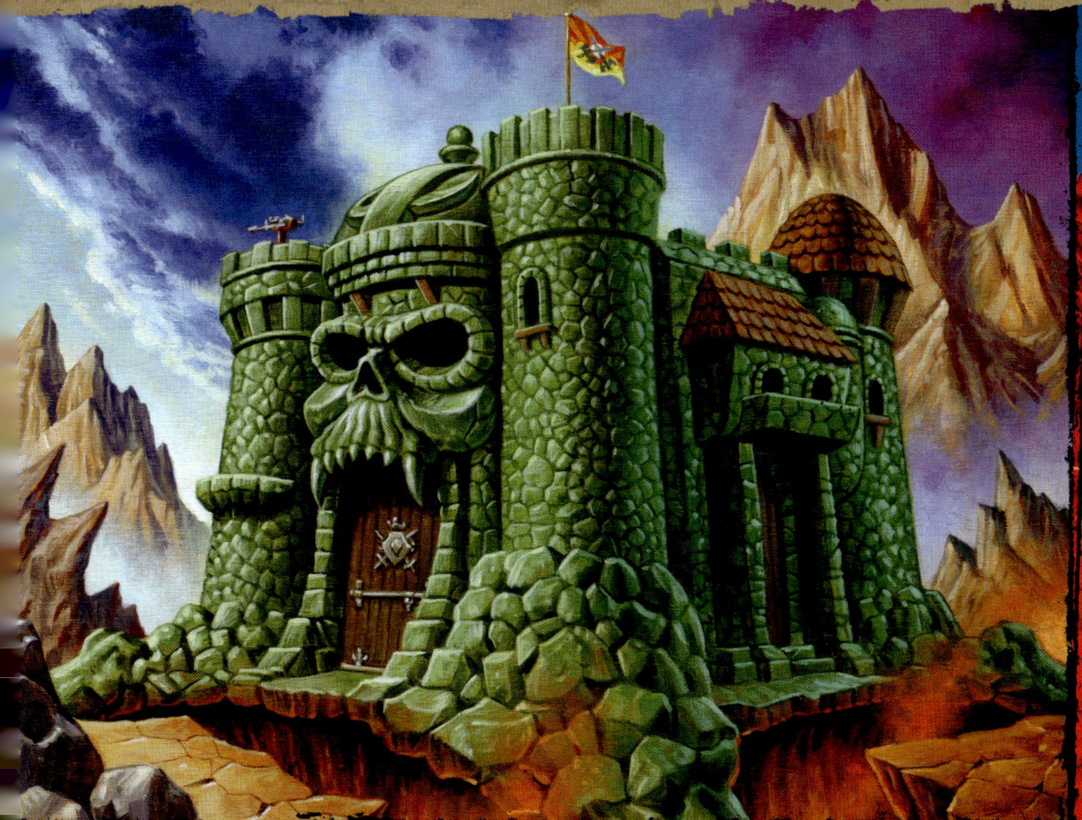

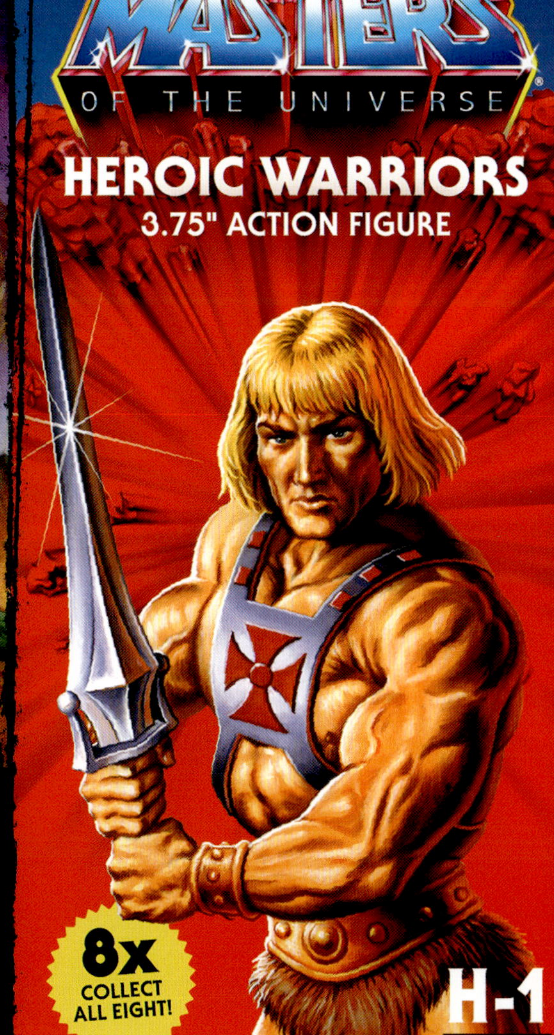

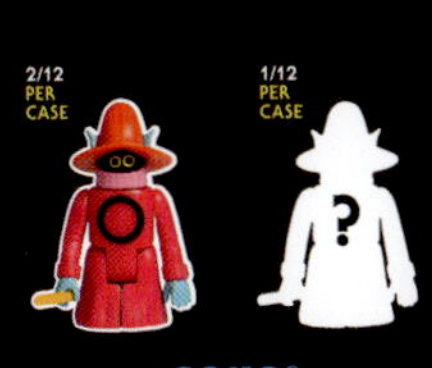

ORKO®
Heroic Court Magician™

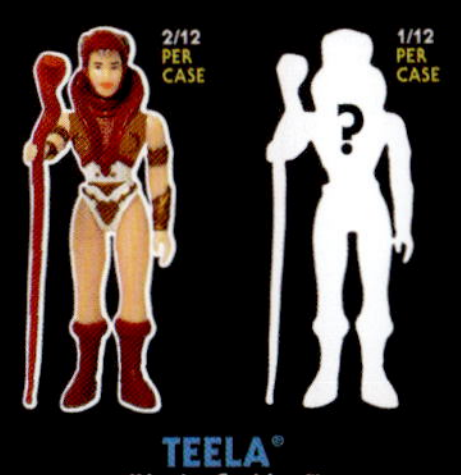

TEELA®
Warrior Goddess™

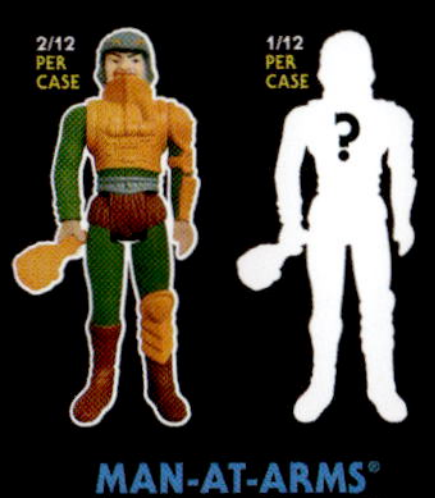

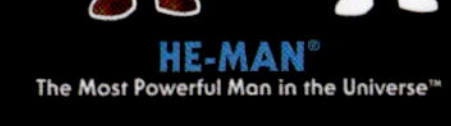

MAN-AT-ARMS®
Heroic Master of Weapons™

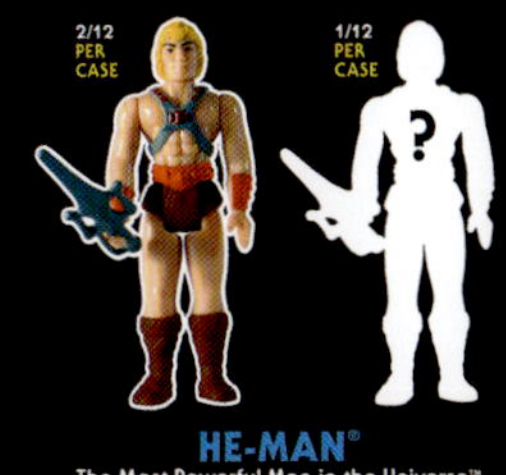

HE-MAN®
The Most Powerful Man in the Universe™

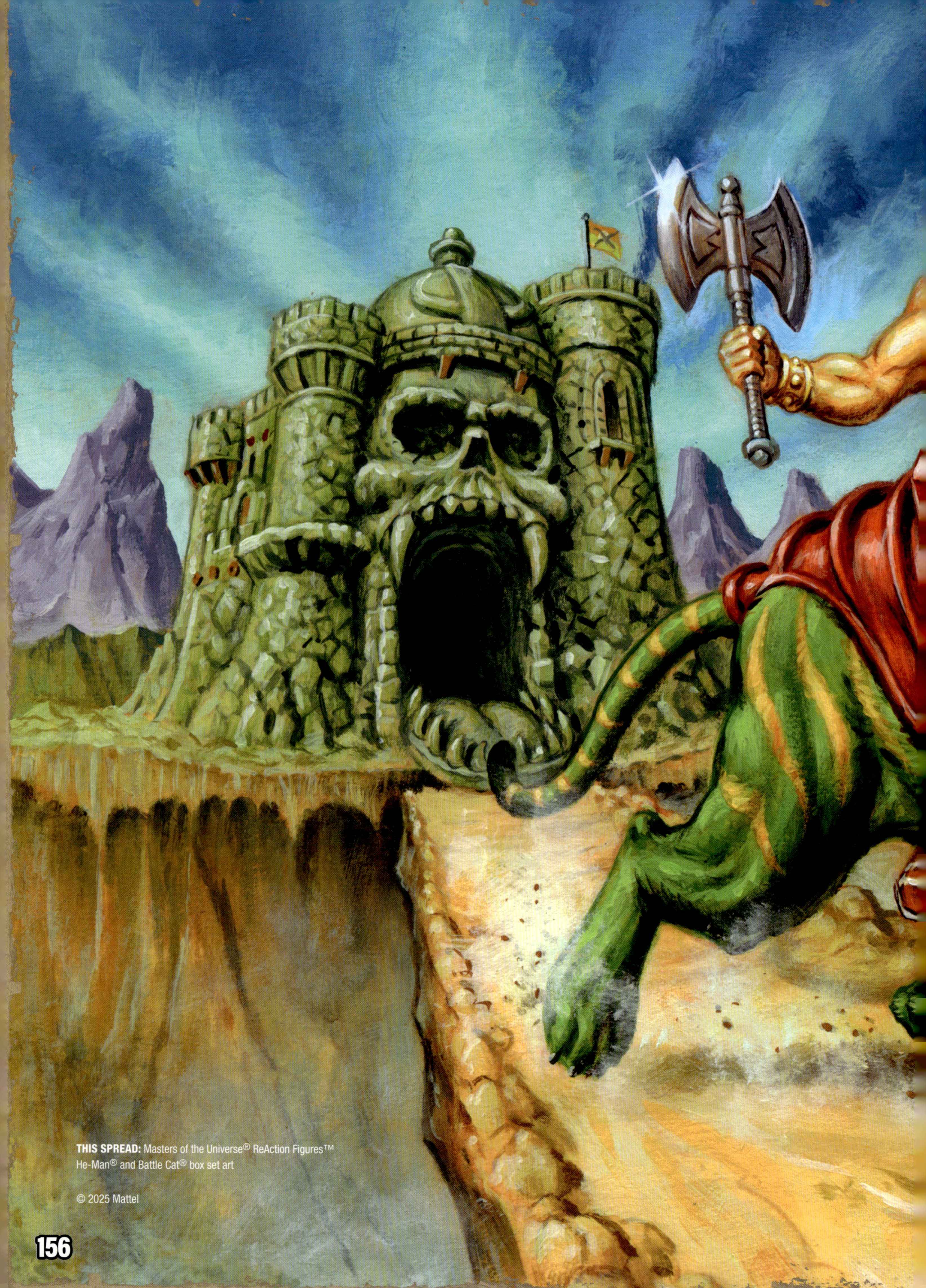

THIS SPREAD: Masters of the Universe® ReAction Figures™ He-Man® and Battle Cat® box set art

© 2025 Mattel

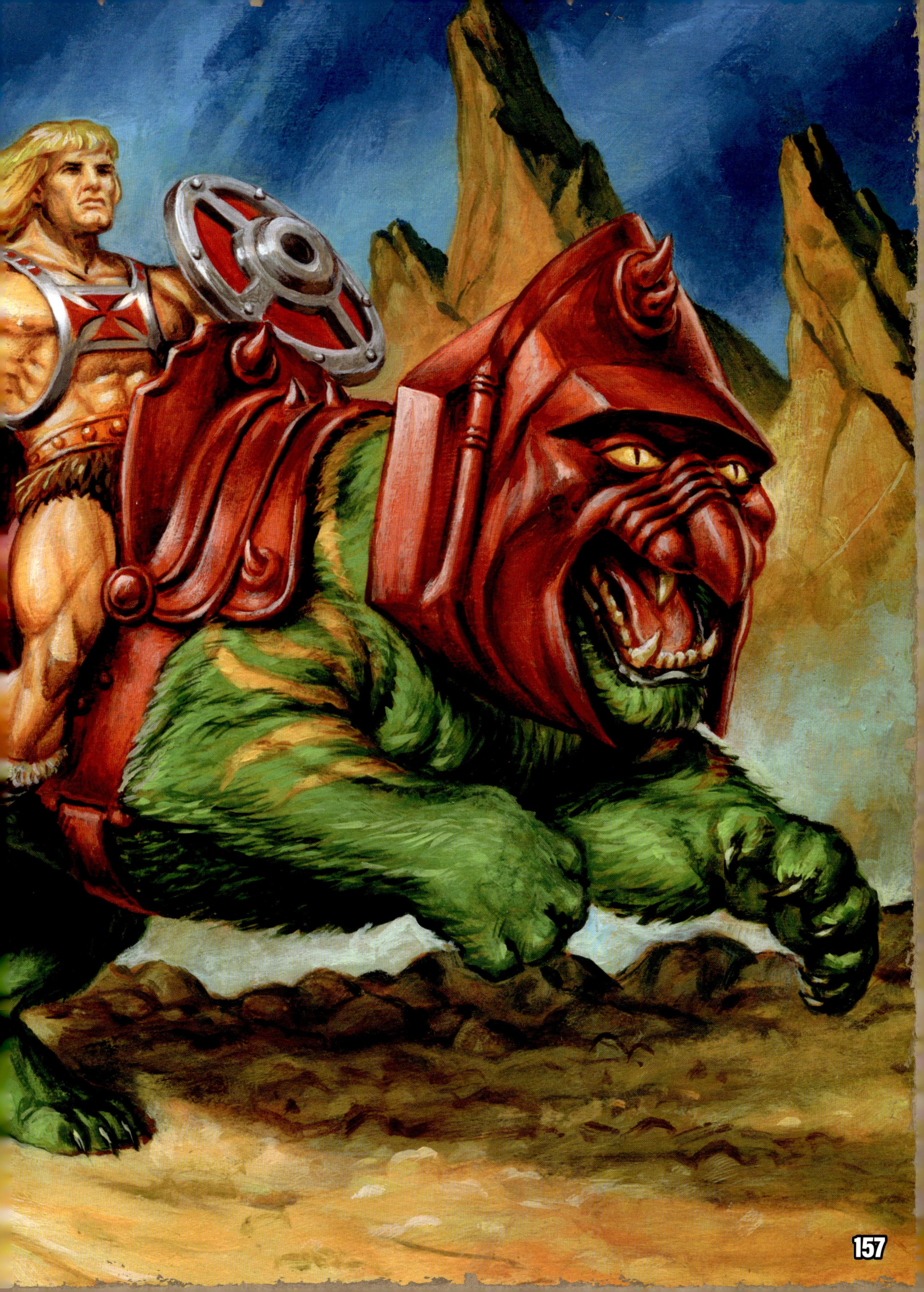

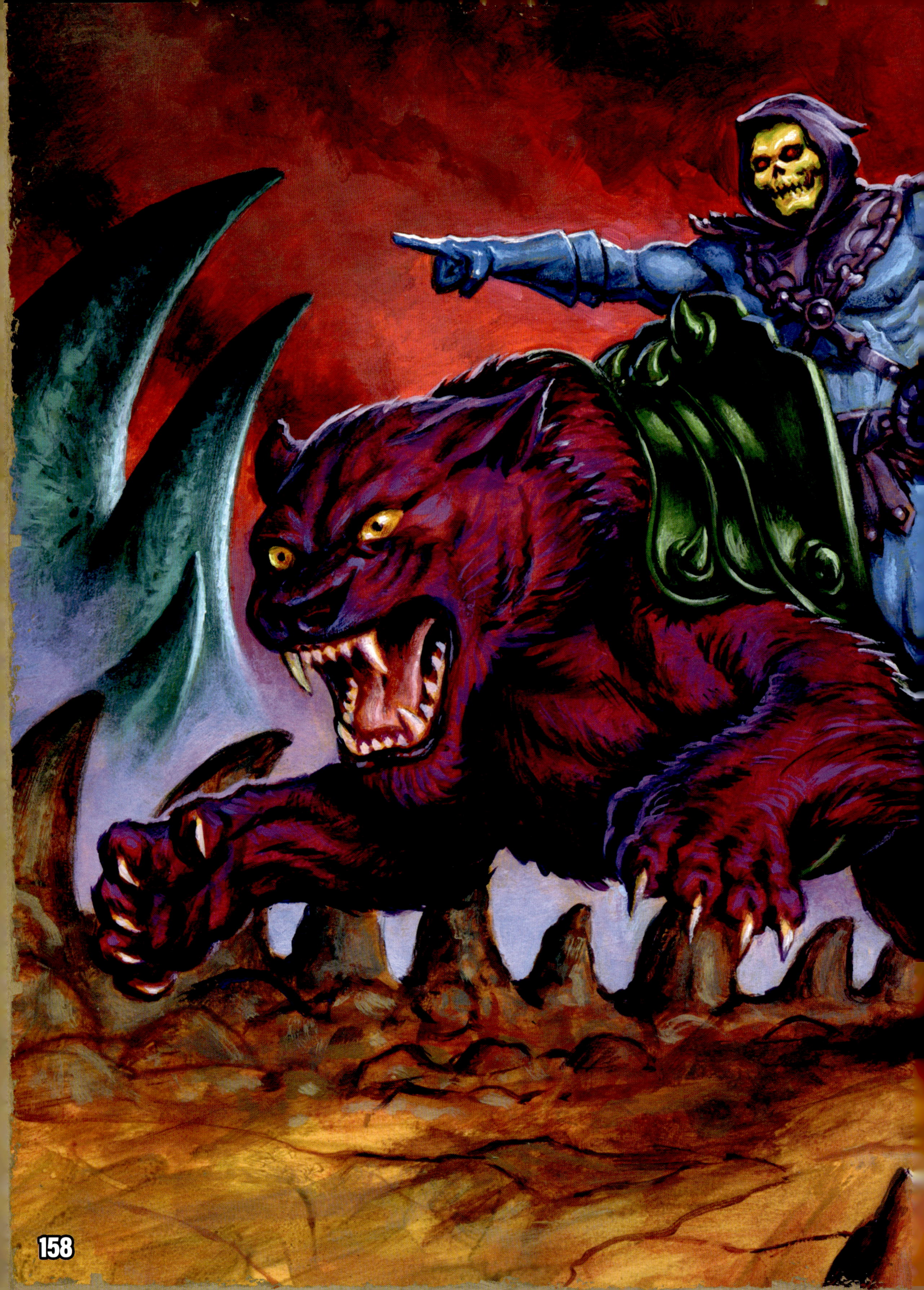

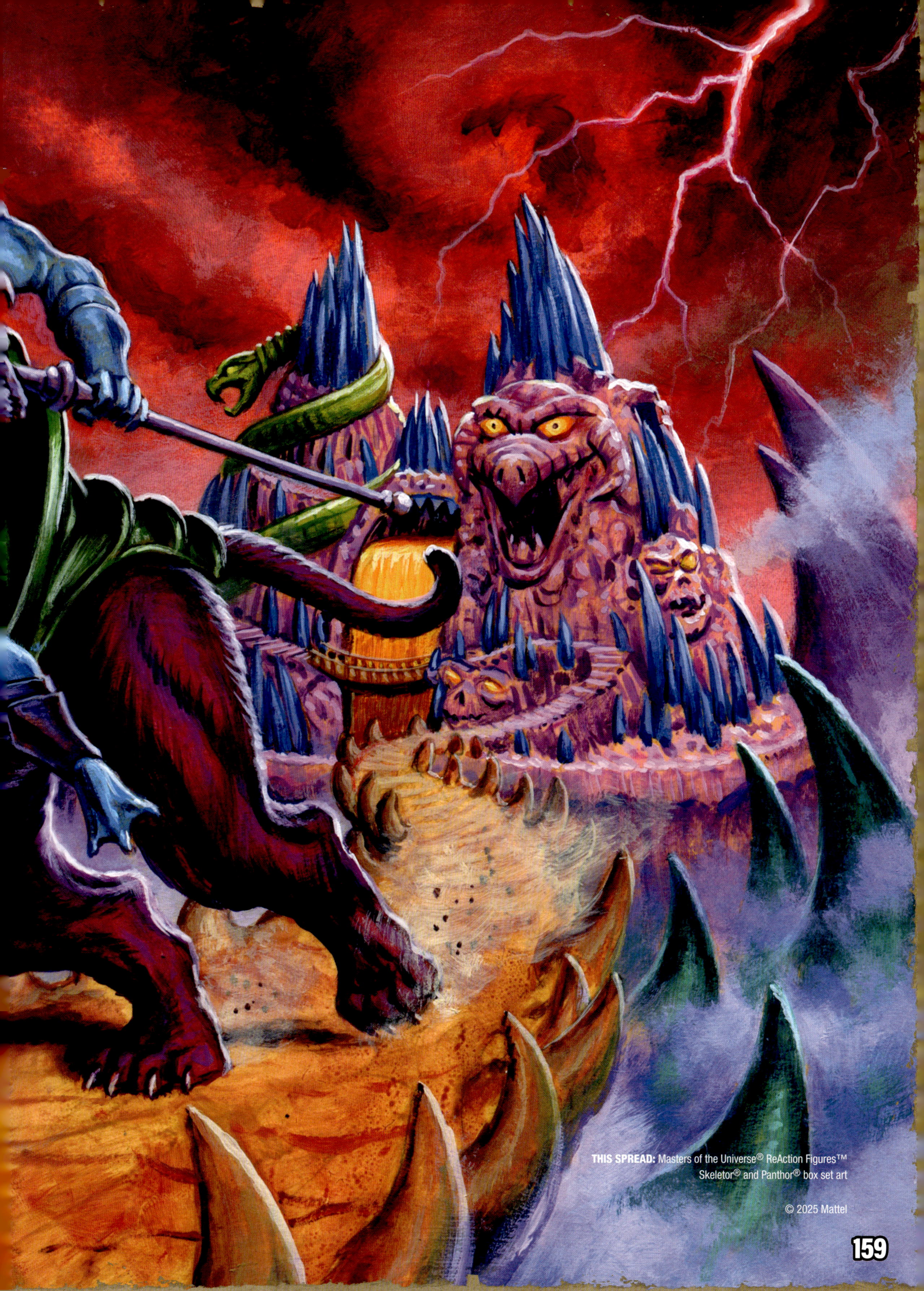

THIS SPREAD: Masters of the Universe® ReAction Figures™ Skeletor® and Panthor® box set art

© 2025 Mattel

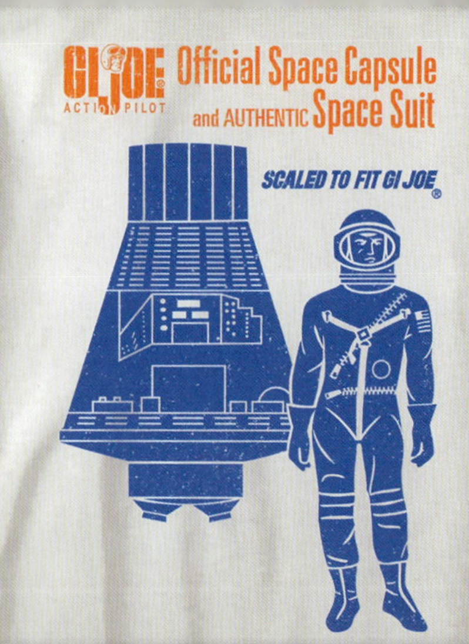

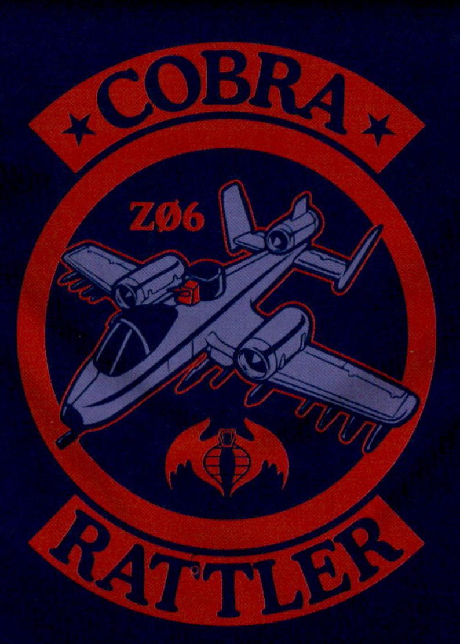

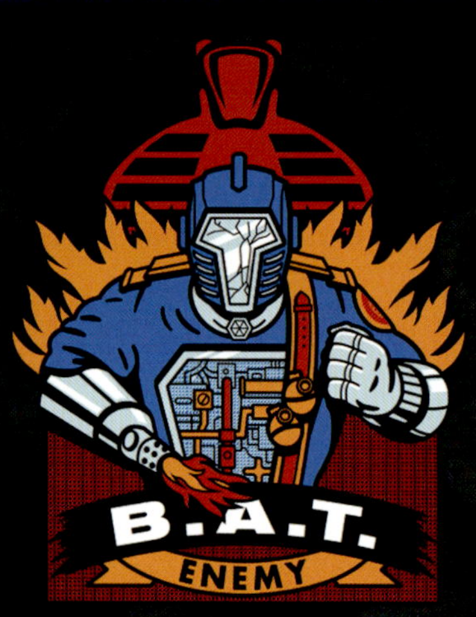

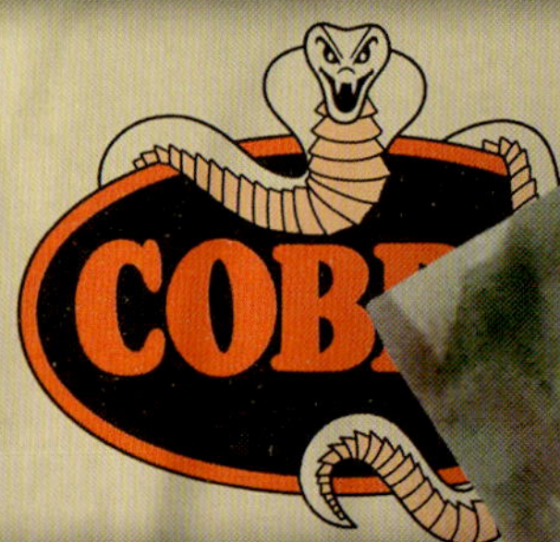

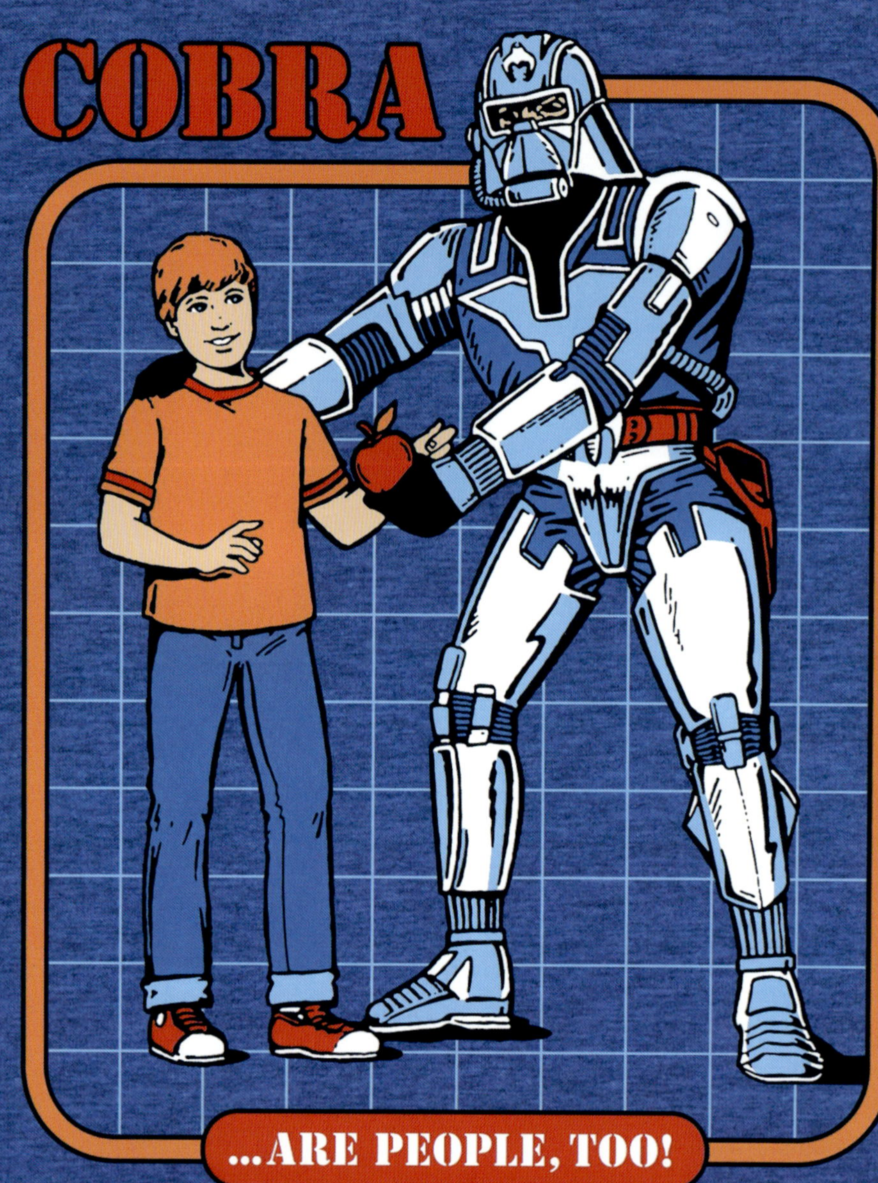

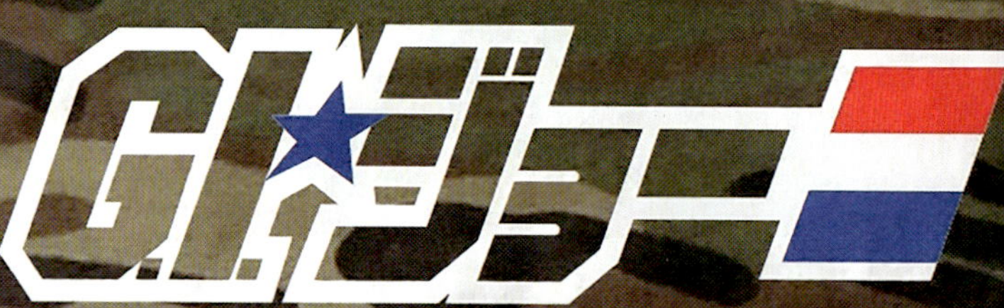

THIS PAGE: Selected G.I. Joe® apparel art

© 2025 HASBRO

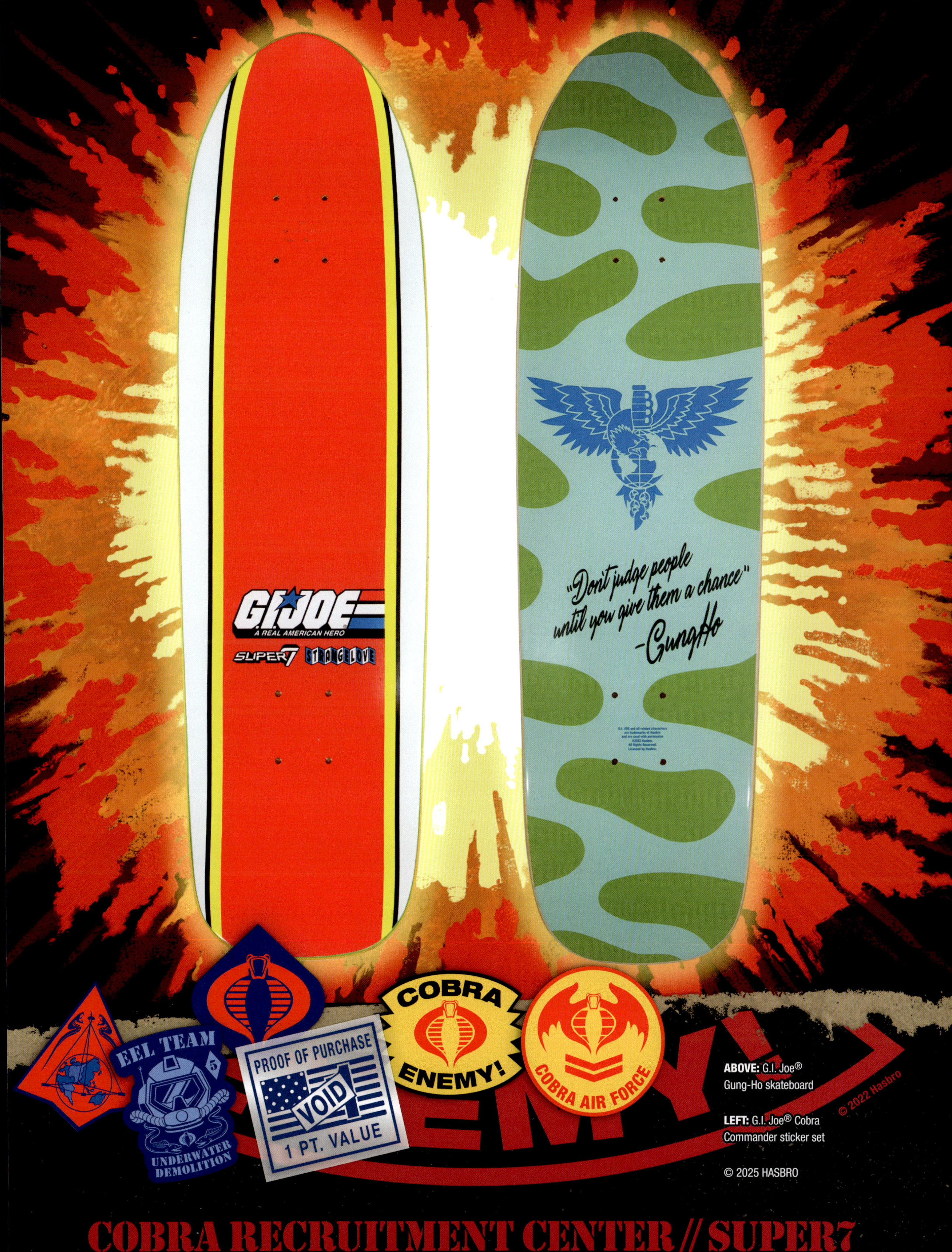

ABOVE: G.I. Joe® Gung-Ho skateboard

LEFT: G.I. Joe® Cobra Commander sticker set

© 2025 HASBRO

COBRA RECRUITMENT CENTER // SUPER7
701 8TH AVENUE, SAN DIEGO

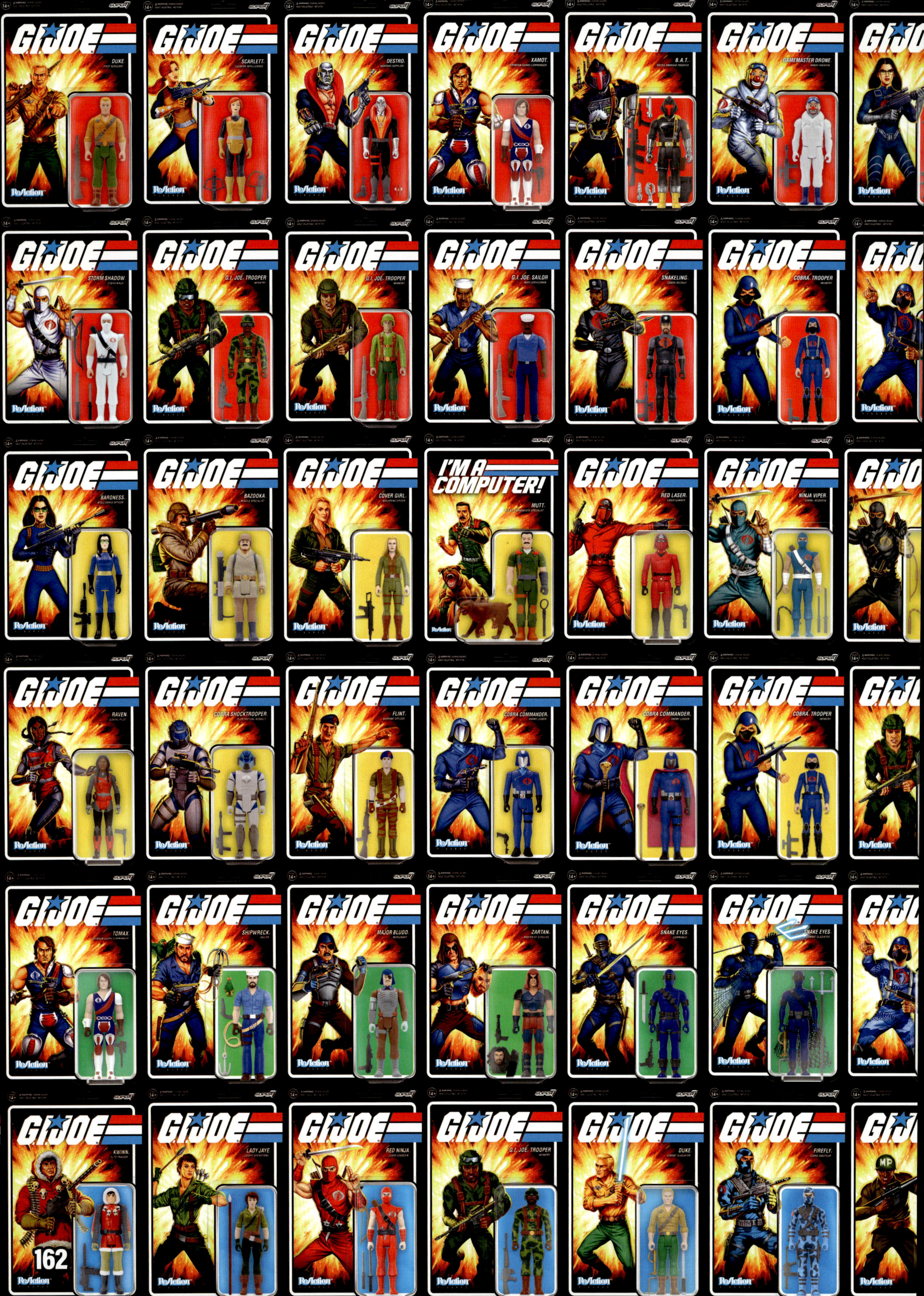
G.I.JOE
DUKE
SCARLETT
DESTRO
XAMOT
B.A.T.
GAMEMASTER DRONE
STORM SHADOW
G.I. JOE TROOPER
G.I. JOE TROOPER
G.I. JOE SAILOR
SNAKELING
COBRA TROOPER
BARONESS
BAZOOKA
COVER GIRL
I'M A COMPUTER!
MUTT
RED LASER
NINJA VIPER
RAVEN
COBRA SHOCKTROOPER
FLINT
COBRA COMMANDER
COBRA COMMANDER
COBRA TROOPER
TOMAX
SHIPWRECK
MAJOR BLUDD
ZARTAN
SNAKE EYES
SNAKE EYES
KWINN
LADY JAYE
RED NINJA
G.I. JOE TROOPER
DUKE
FIREFLY
ReAction

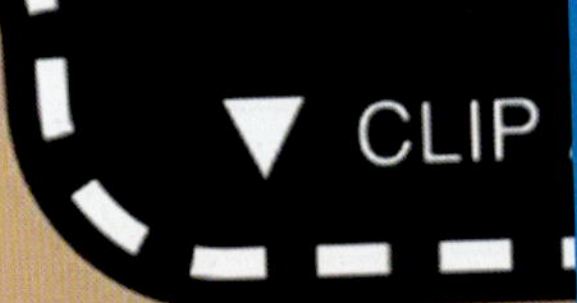

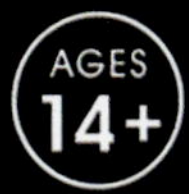

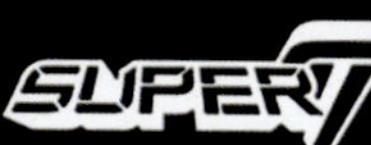

THIS SPREAD:
G.I. Joe® ReAction Figures™ card art

© 2025 HASBRO

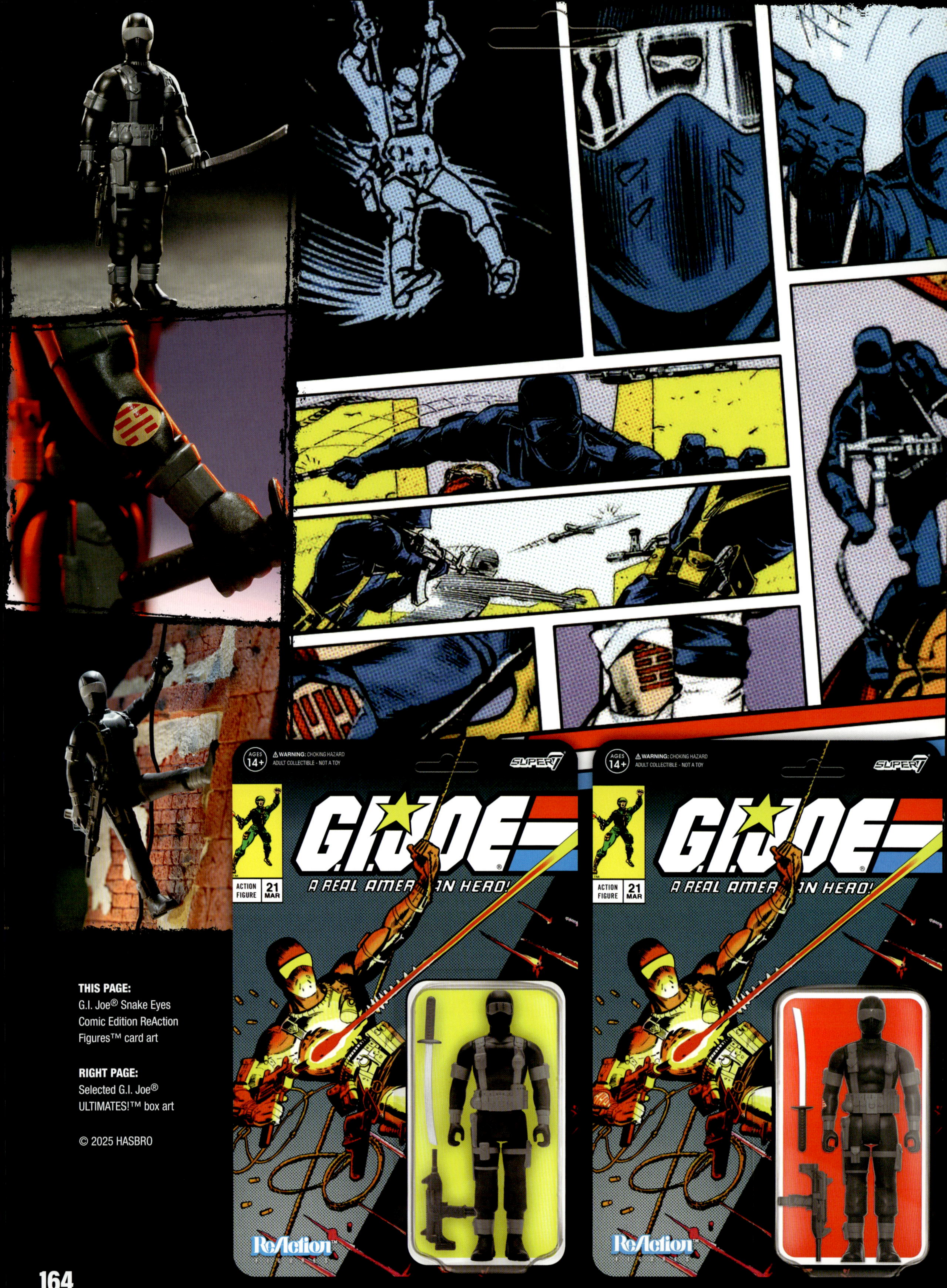

THIS PAGE:
G.I. Joe® Snake Eyes Comic Edition ReAction Figures™ card art

RIGHT PAGE:
Selected G.I. Joe® ULTIMATES!™ box art

© 2025 HASBRO

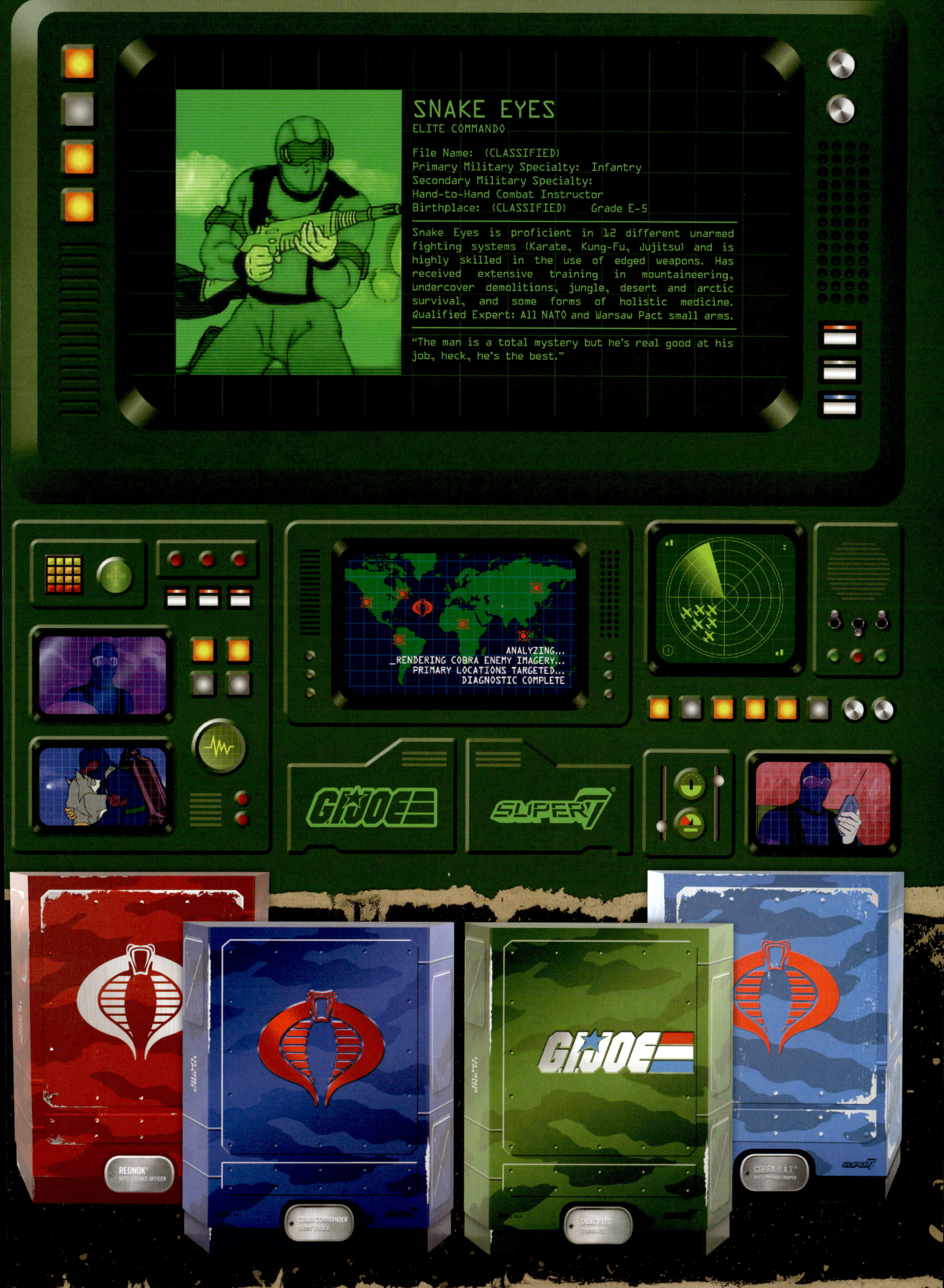
SNAKE EYES
ELITE COMMANDO
File Name: (CLASSIFIED)
Primary Military Specialty: Infantry
Secondary Military Specialty:
Hand-to-Hand Combat Instructor
Birthplace: (CLASSIFIED) Grade E-5
Snake Eyes is proficient in 12 different unarmed fighting systems (Karate, Kung-Fu, Jujitsu) and is highly skilled in the use of edged weapons. Has received extensive training in mountaineering, undercover demolitions, jungle, desert and arctic survival, and some forms of holistic medicine. Qualified Expert: All NATO and Warsaw Pact small arms.
"The man is a total mystery but he's real good at his job, heck, he's the best."
ANALYZING...
_RENDERING COBRA ENEMY IMAGERY...
PRIMARY LOCATIONS TARGETED...
DIAGNOSTIC COMPLETE
G.I. JOE
SUPER7
G.I. JOE
REDNOK
INTELLIGENCE OFFICER
COBRA COMMANDER
SNAKE EYES
COBRA B.A.T.

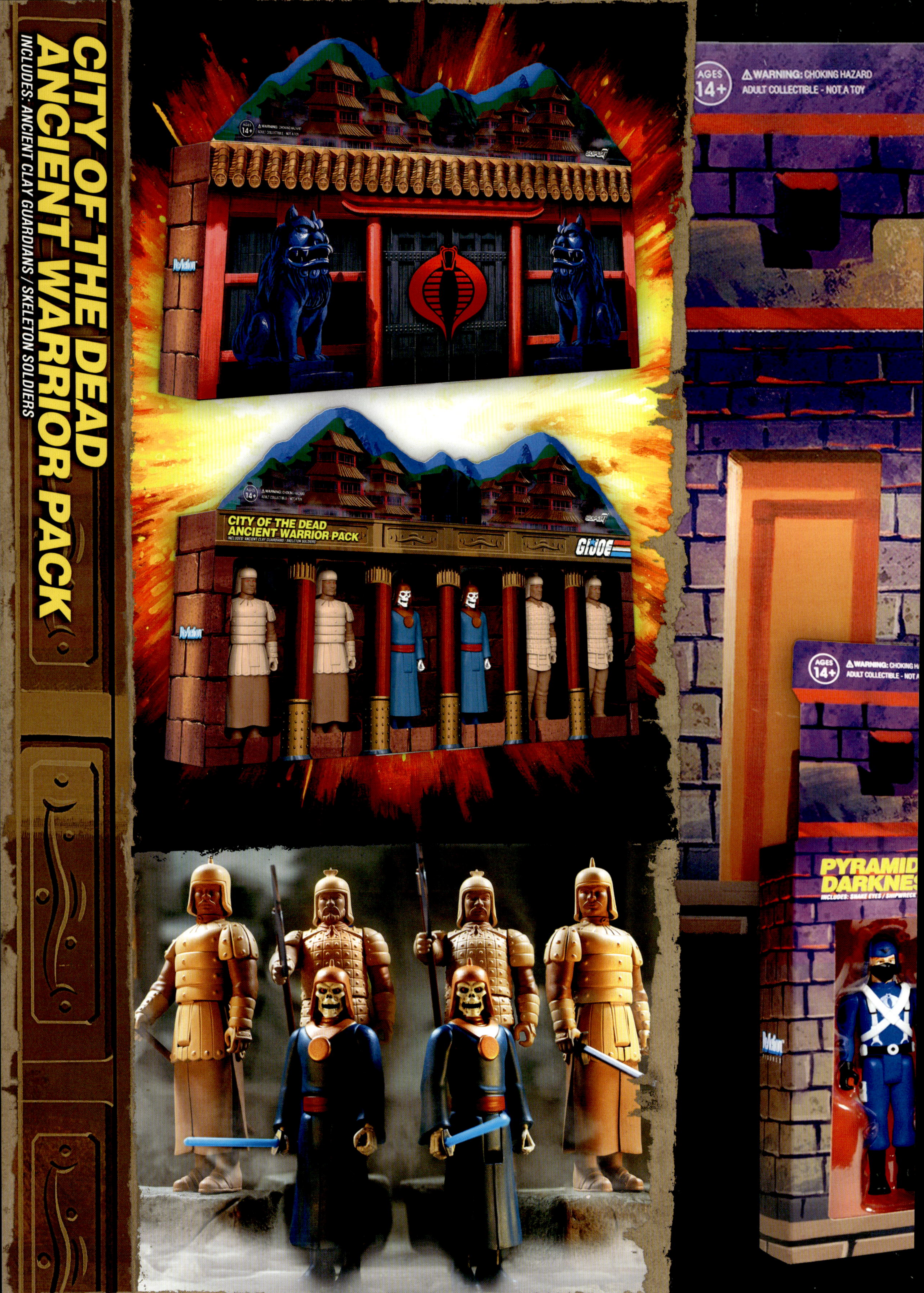
CITY OF THE DEAD
ANCIENT WARRIOR PACK
INCLUDES: ANCIENT CLAY GUARDIANS / SKELETON SOLDIERS
AGES 14+
WARNING: CHOKING HAZARD
ADULT COLLECTIBLE - NOT A TOY
CITY OF THE DEAD
ANCIENT WARRIOR PACK
GI JOE

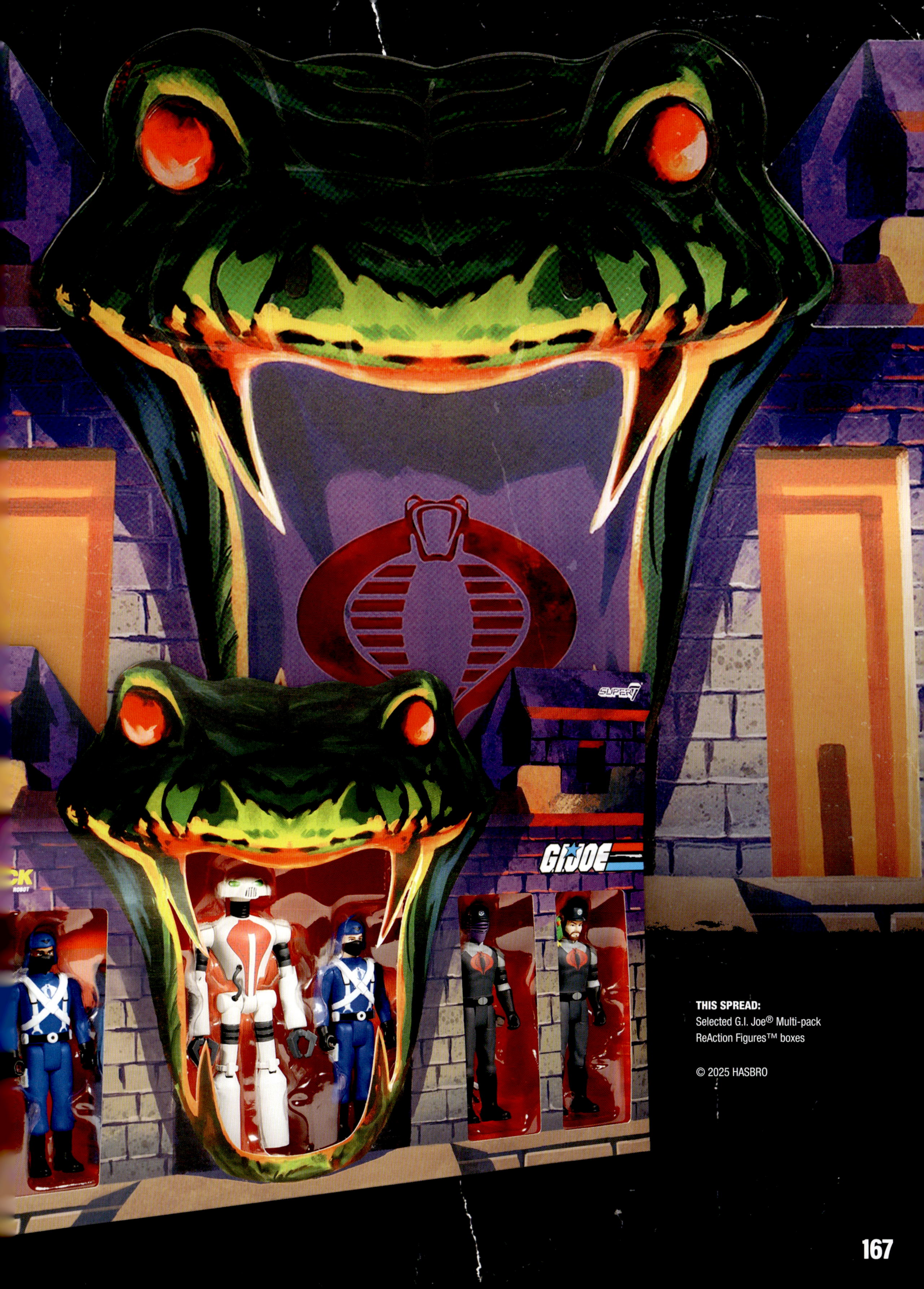

THIS SPREAD:
Selected G.I. Joe® Multi-pack ReAction Figures™ boxes

© 2025 HASBRO

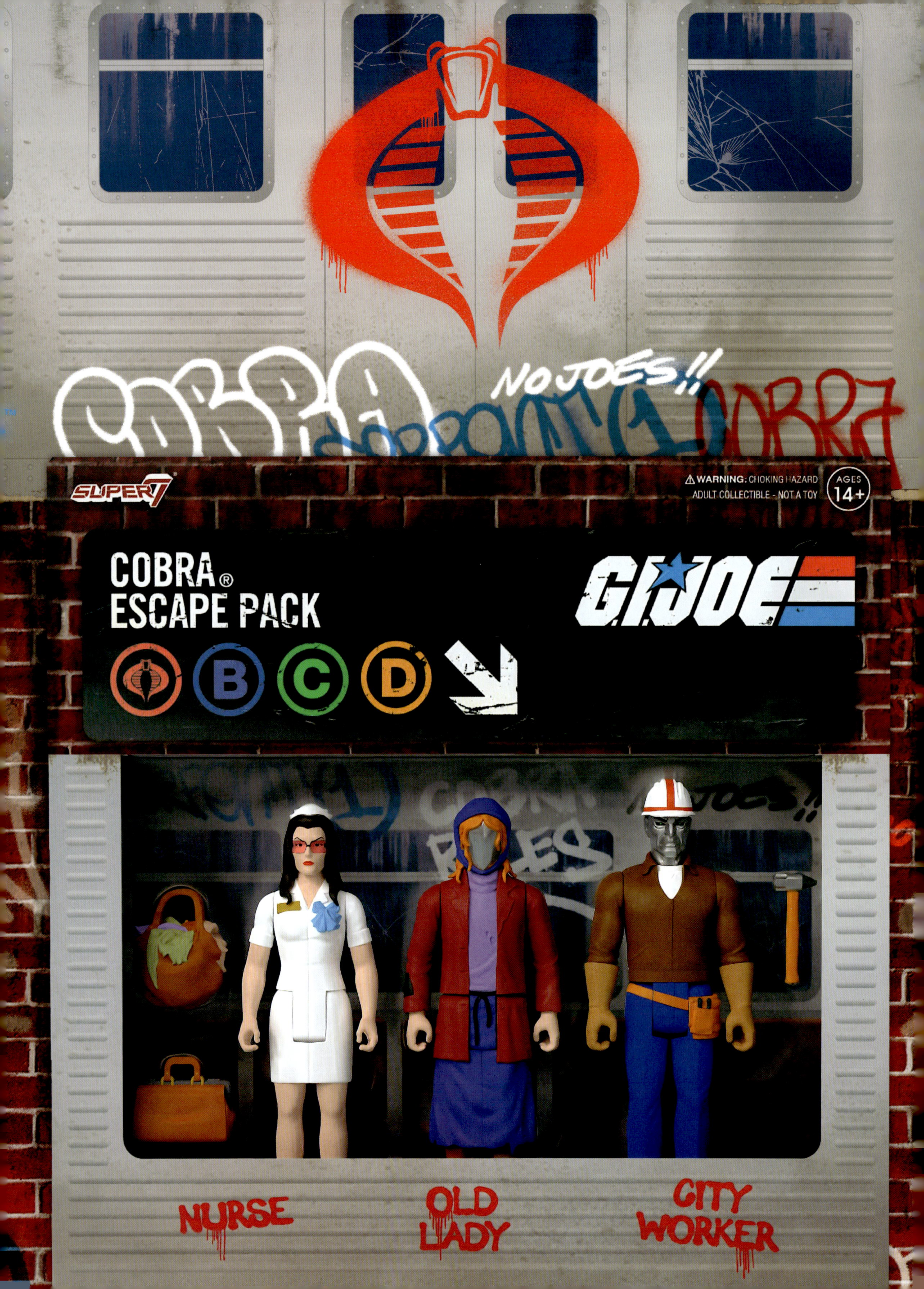

NO JOES!!

SUPER7

⚠ WARNING: CHOKING HAZARD
ADULT COLLECTIBLE - NOT A TOY

AGES 14+

COBRA®
ESCAPE PACK

B C D

G.I. JOE

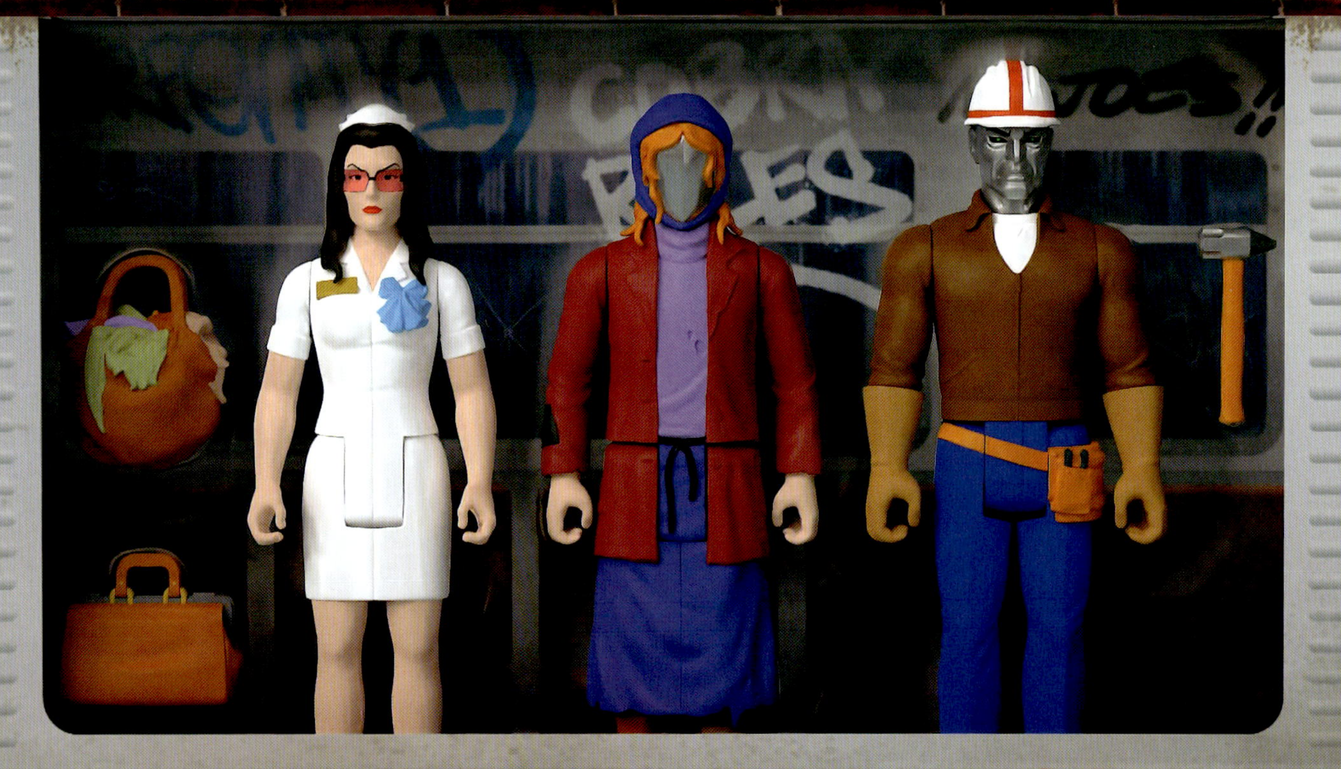

NURSE

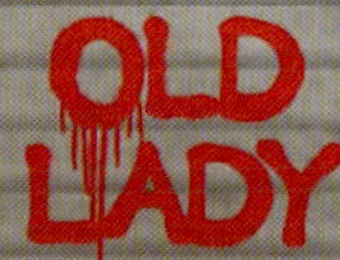

CITY
WORKER

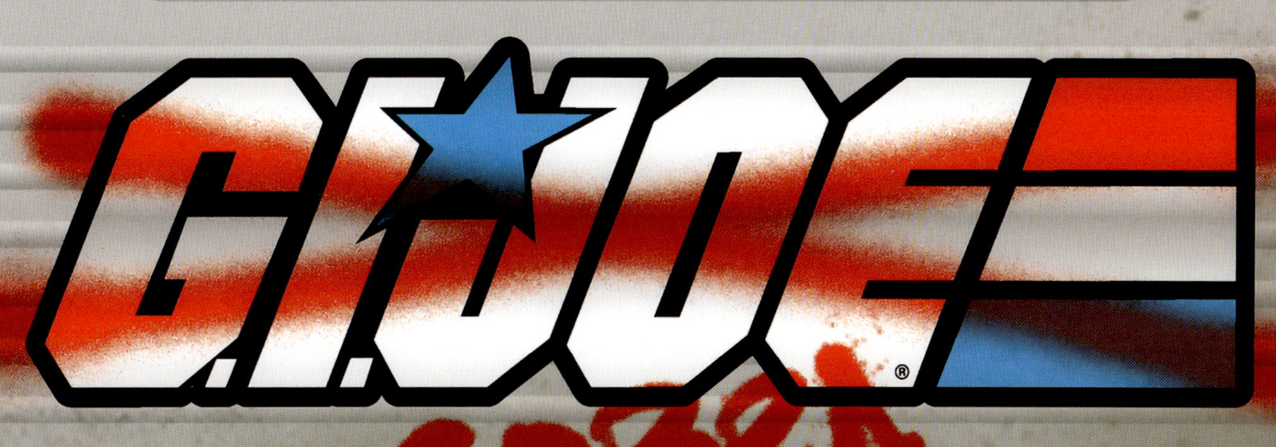

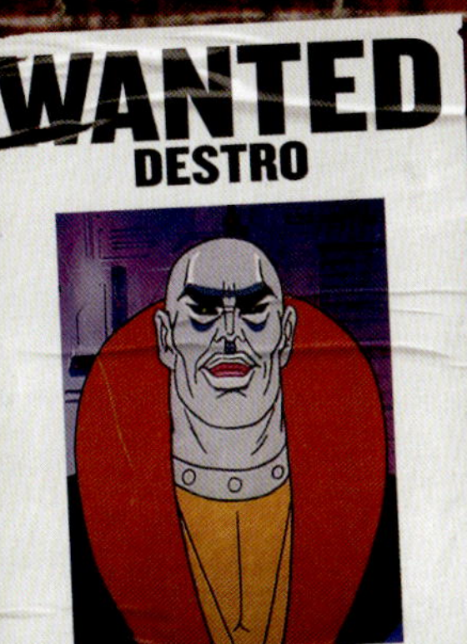

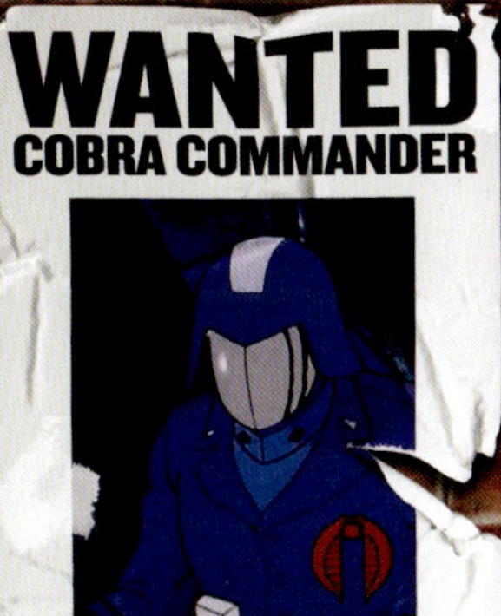

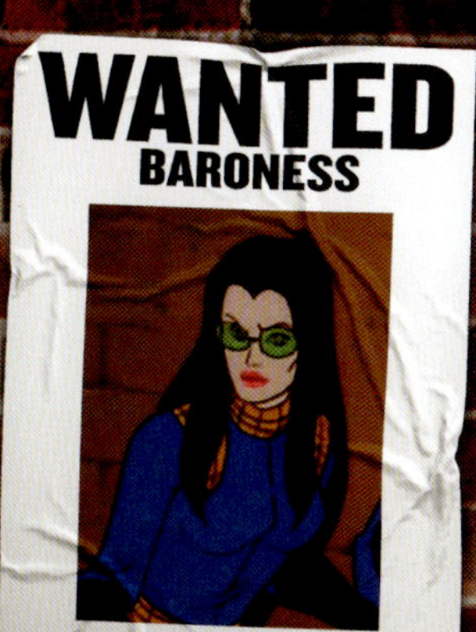

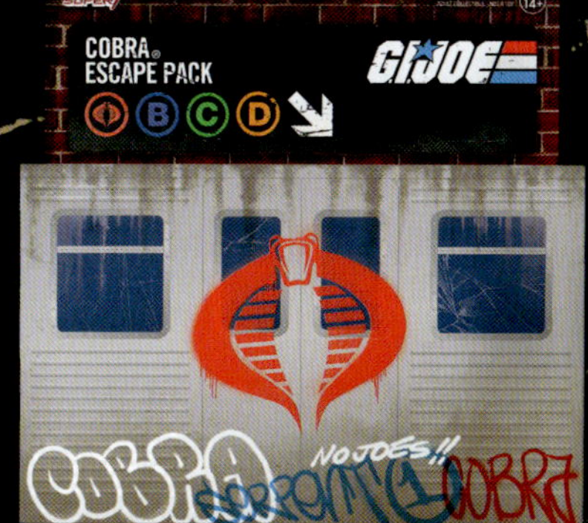

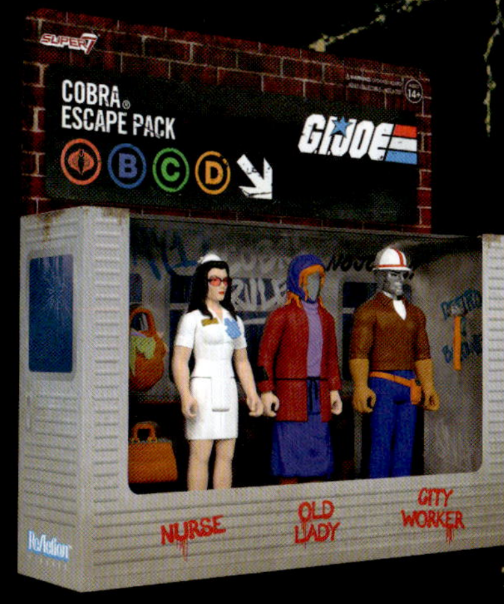

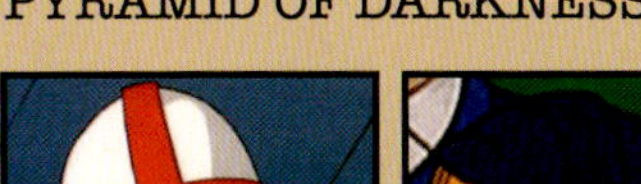

COBRA® ESCAPE PACK

PYRAMID OF DARKNESS

▼ CLIP AND SAVE FOR YOUR G.I. JOE COMMAND FILES

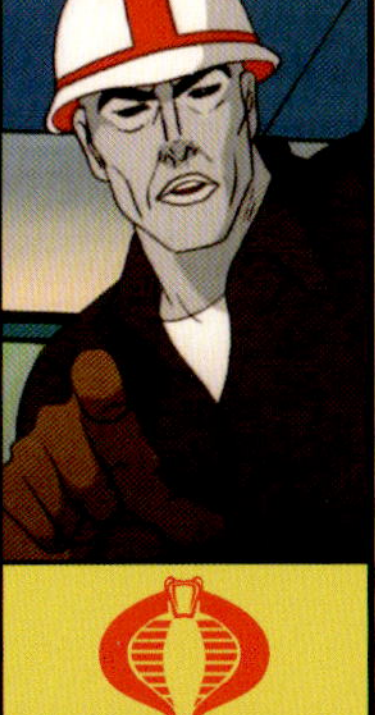

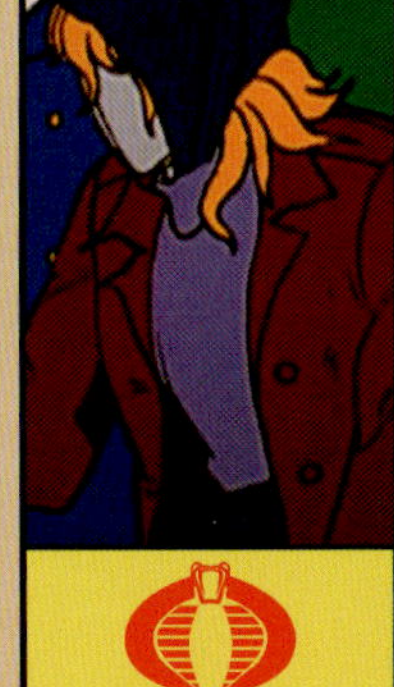

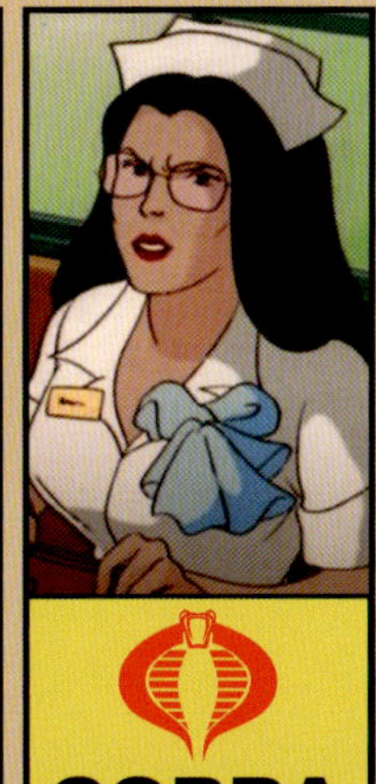

G.I. JOE sends teams to different parts of the world in order to stop COBRA from planting their Cubes of Darkness. Cobra Commander is betrayed by his own team taking control of Delta Space Station and the Pyramid of Darkness for themselves. The JOEs successfully destroy the Pyramid of Darkness, sending the COBRA leadership to escape in disguises to avoid capture.

THIS SPREAD: G.I. Joe® Cobra Escape 3-Pack ReAction Figures™ art

© 2025 HASBRO

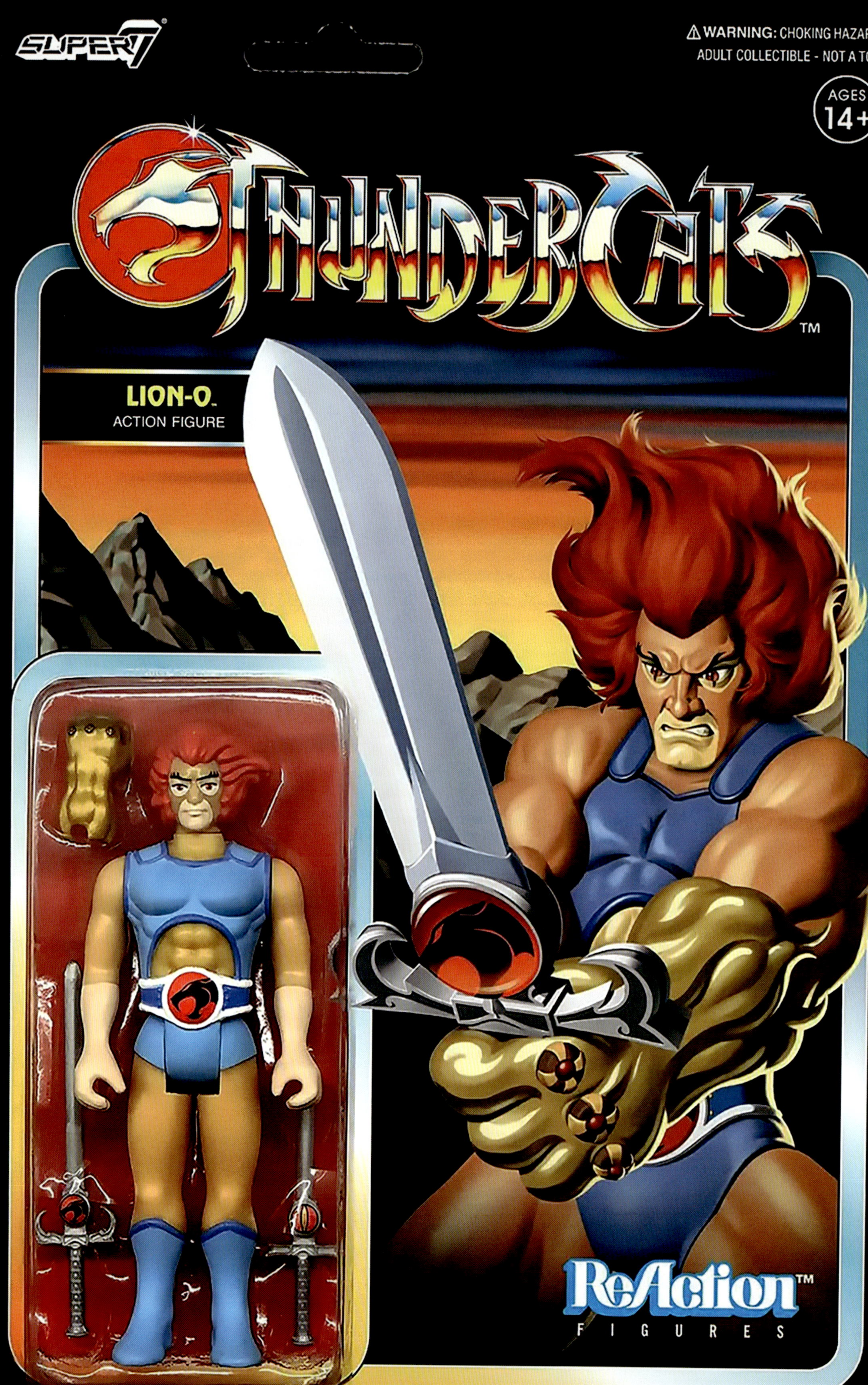
SUPER7
⚠WARNING: CHOKING HAZARD
ADULT COLLECTIBLE - NOT A TOY
AGES
14+
THUNDERCATS™
LION-O™
ACTION FIGURE
ReAction™
FIGURES
COLLECT THEM ALL! COLLECT THEM ALL! COLLECT THEM ALL! COLLECT THEM ALL! COLLECT THEM ALL!

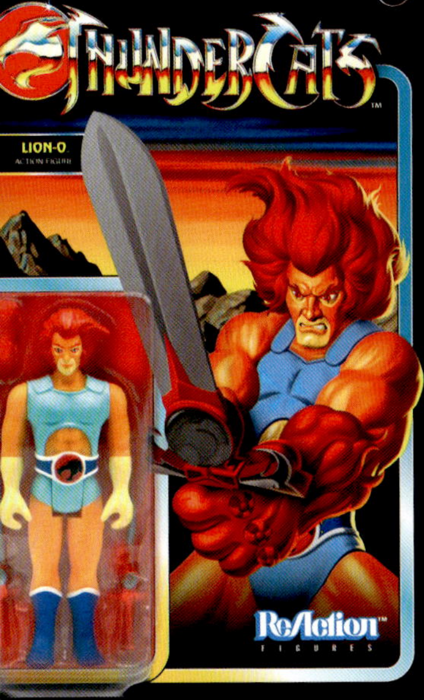

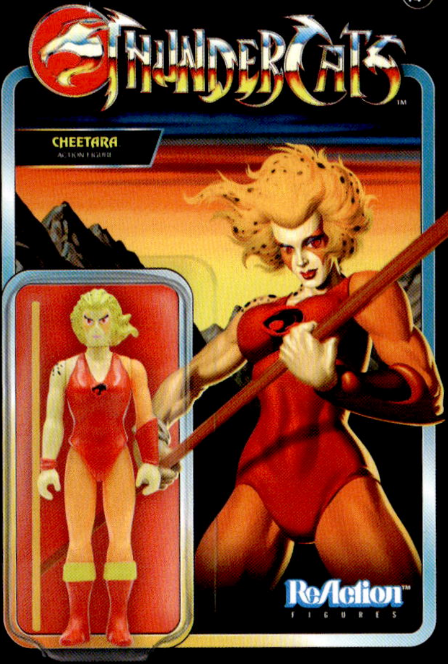

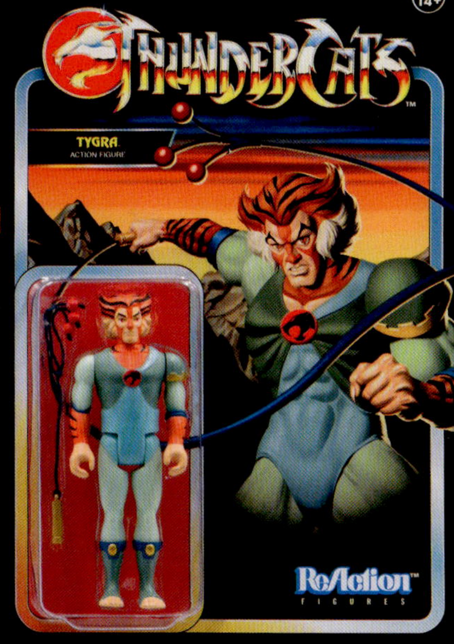

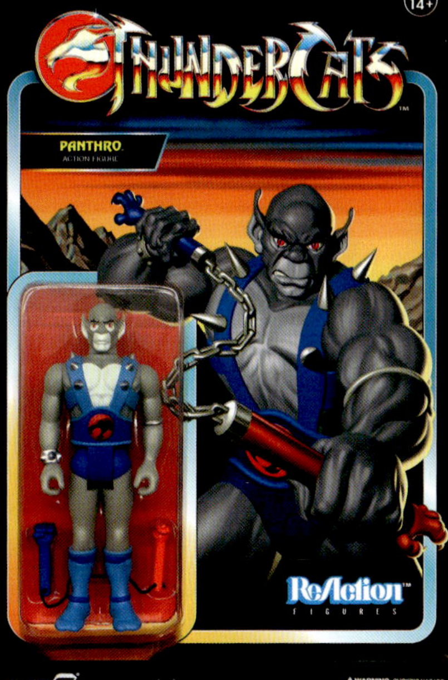

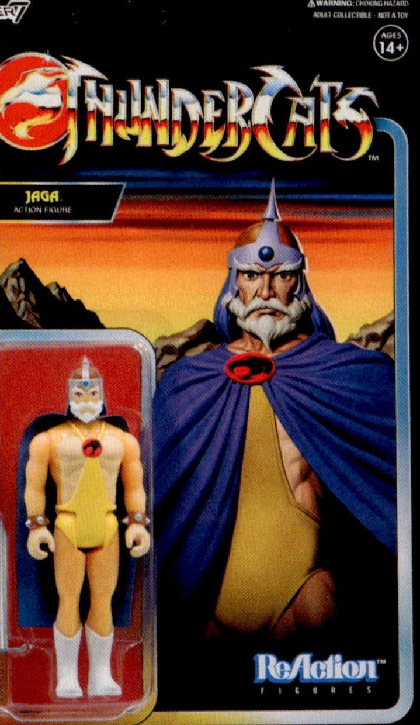

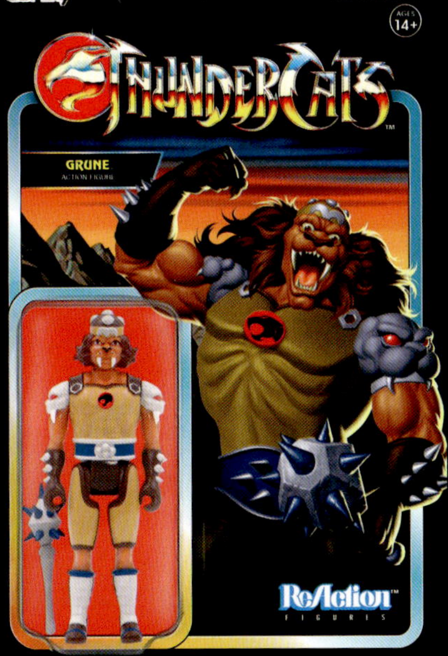

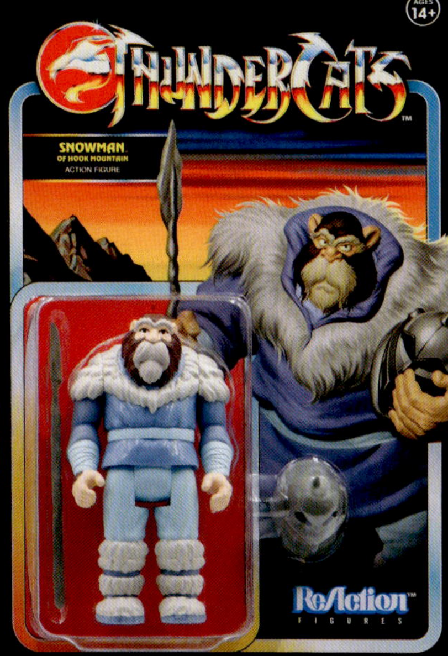

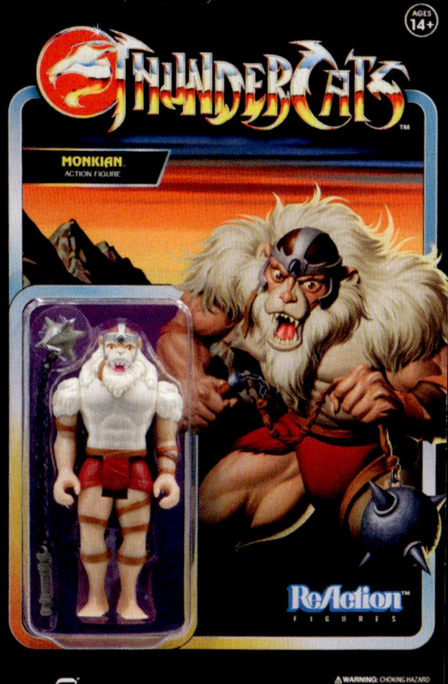

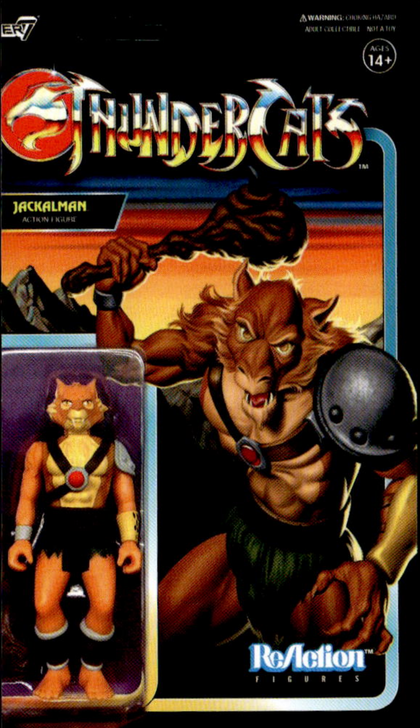

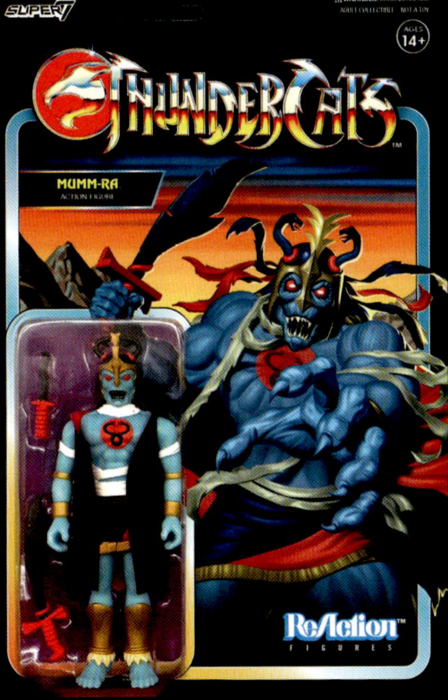

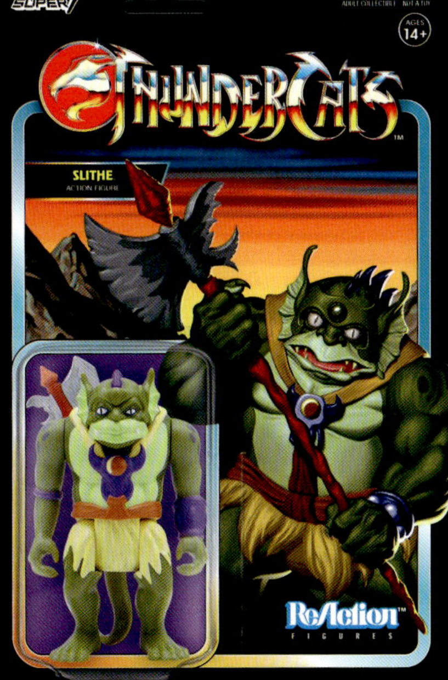

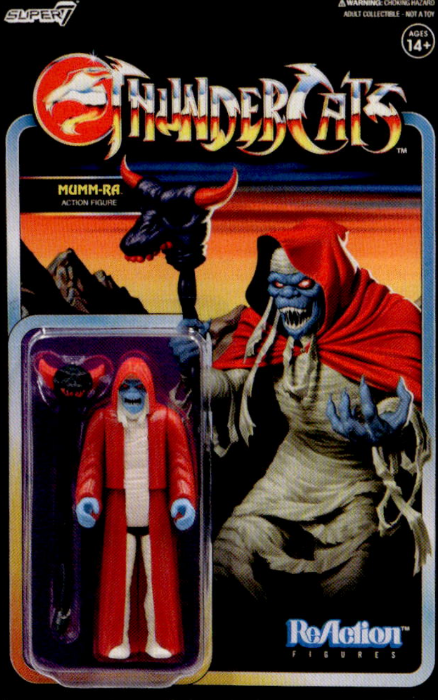

THIS SPREAD: Selected ThunderCats™ ReAction Figures™ card art

© WBEI & Wolf (s25)

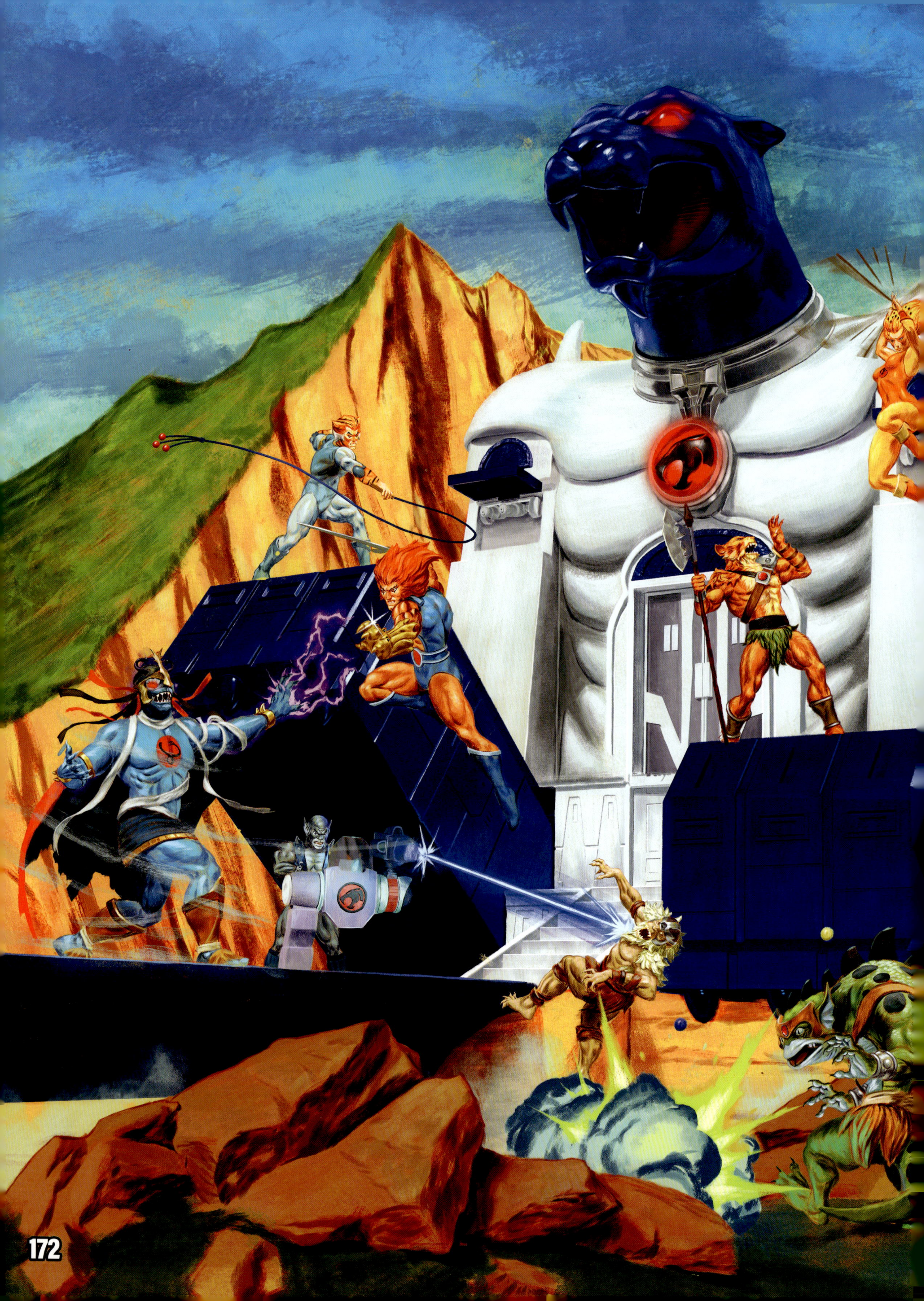

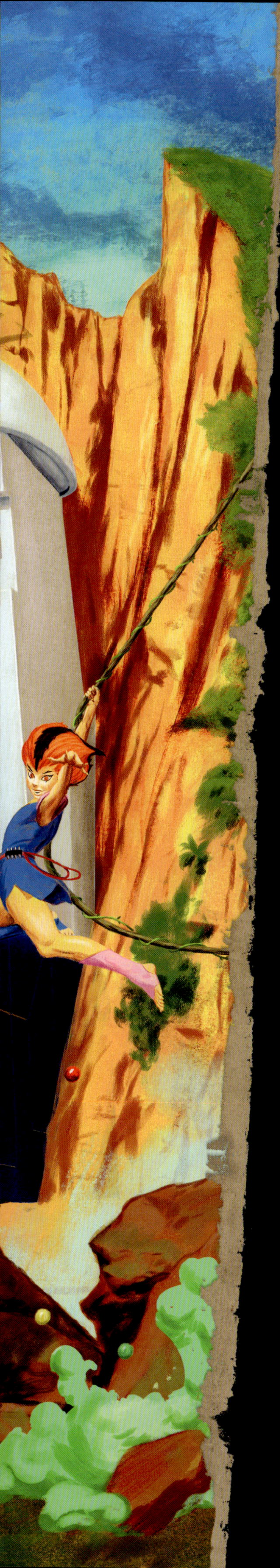

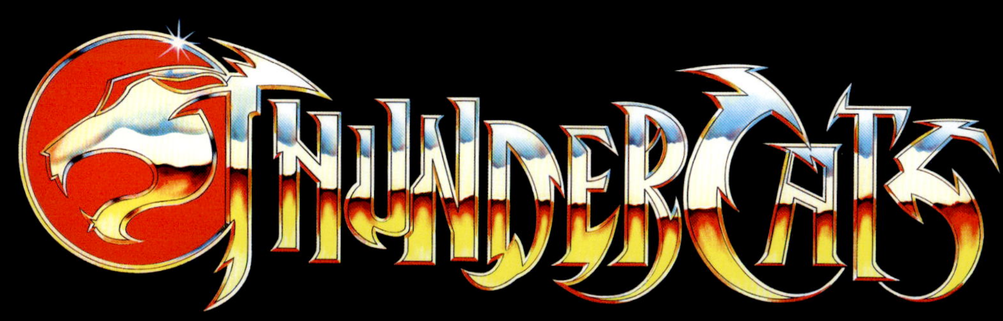

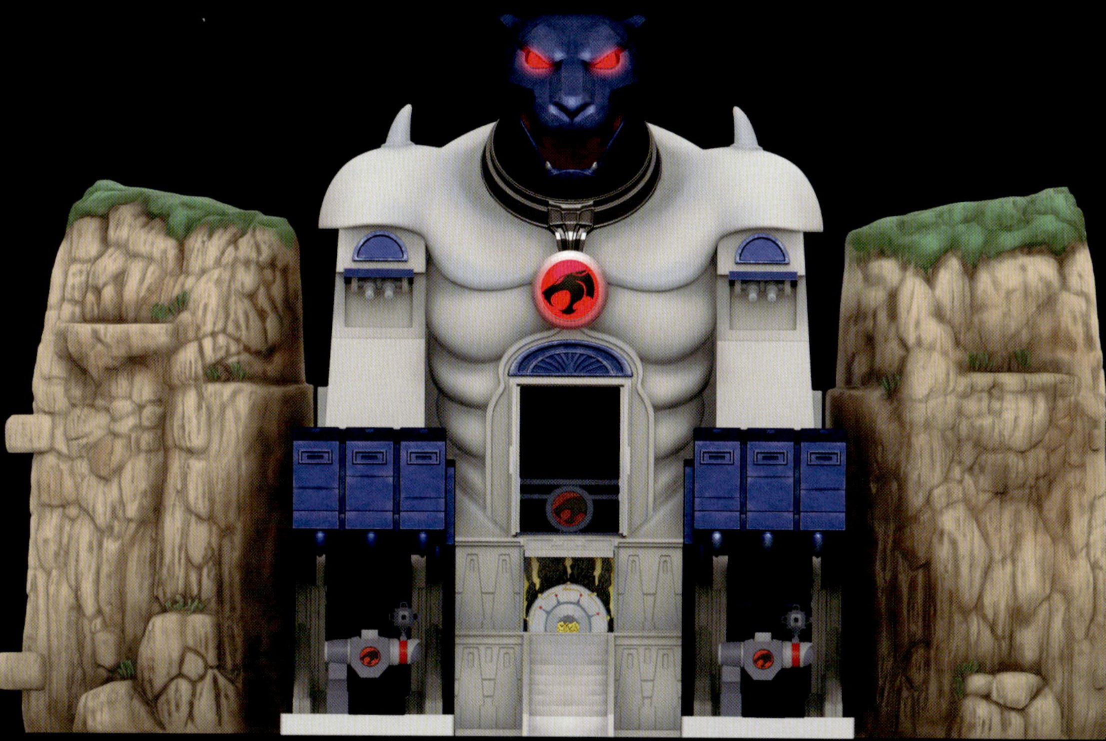

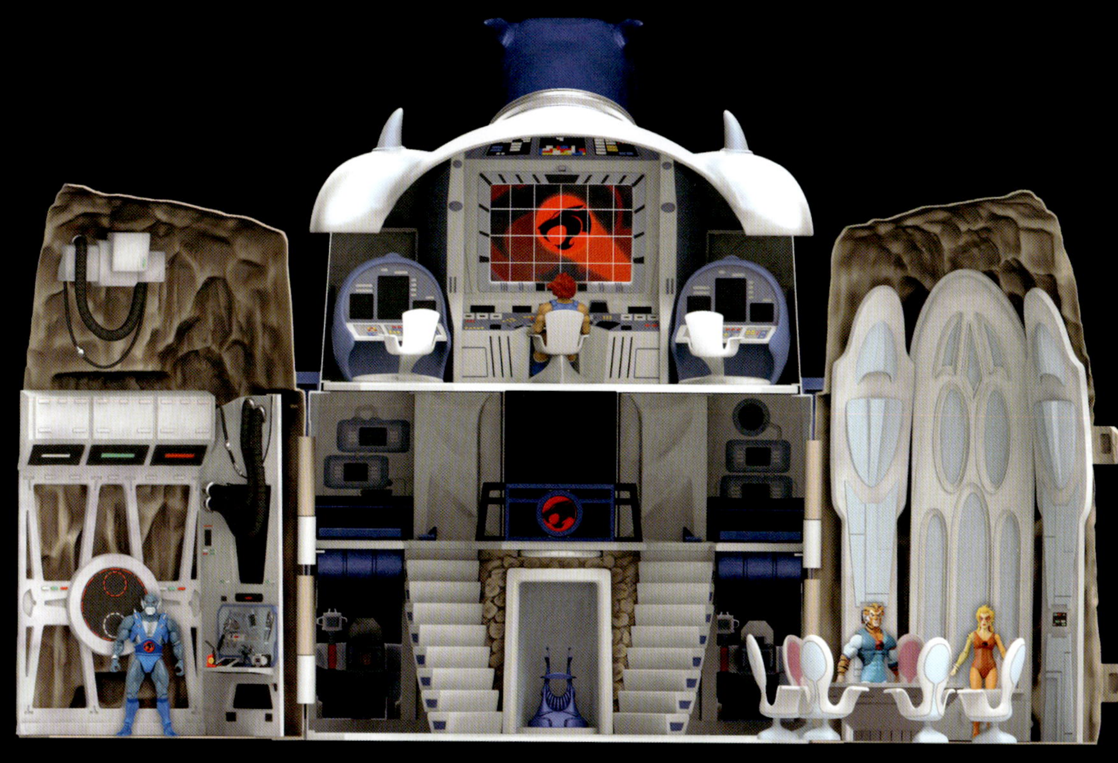

THIS SPREAD: ThunderCats™ Cats' Lair™ box art

© WBEI & Wolf (s25)

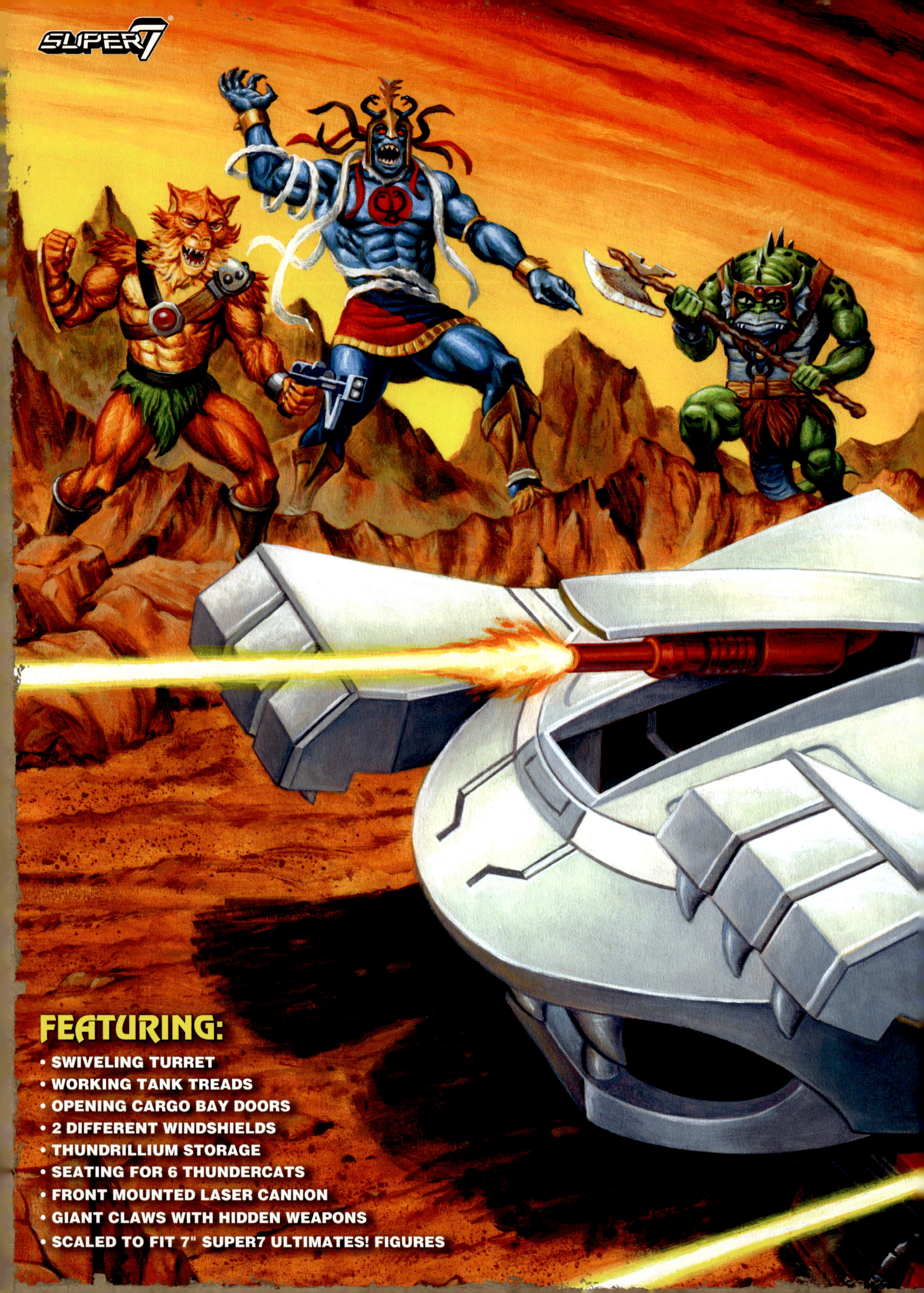
SUPER7
FEATURING:
• SWIVELING TURRET
• WORKING TANK TREADS
• OPENING CARGO BAY DOORS
• 2 DIFFERENT WINDSHIELDS
• THUNDRILLIUM STORAGE
• SEATING FOR 6 THUNDERCATS
• FRONT MOUNTED LASER CANNON
• GIANT CLAWS WITH HIDDEN WEAPONS
• SCALED TO FIT 7" SUPER7 ULTIMATES! FIGURES

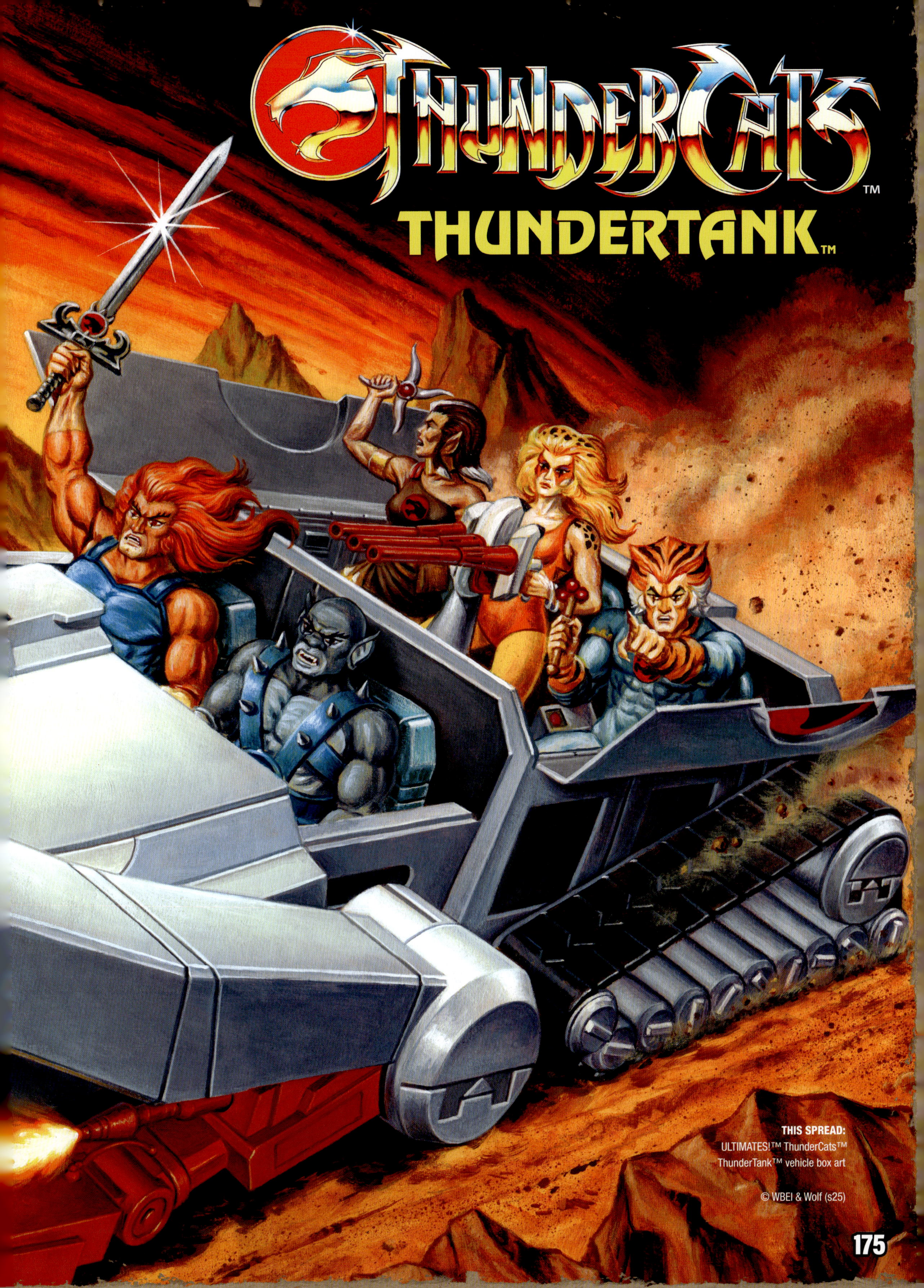

THIS SPREAD:
ULTIMATES!™ ThunderCats™ ThunderTank™ vehicle box art

© WBEI & Wolf (s25)

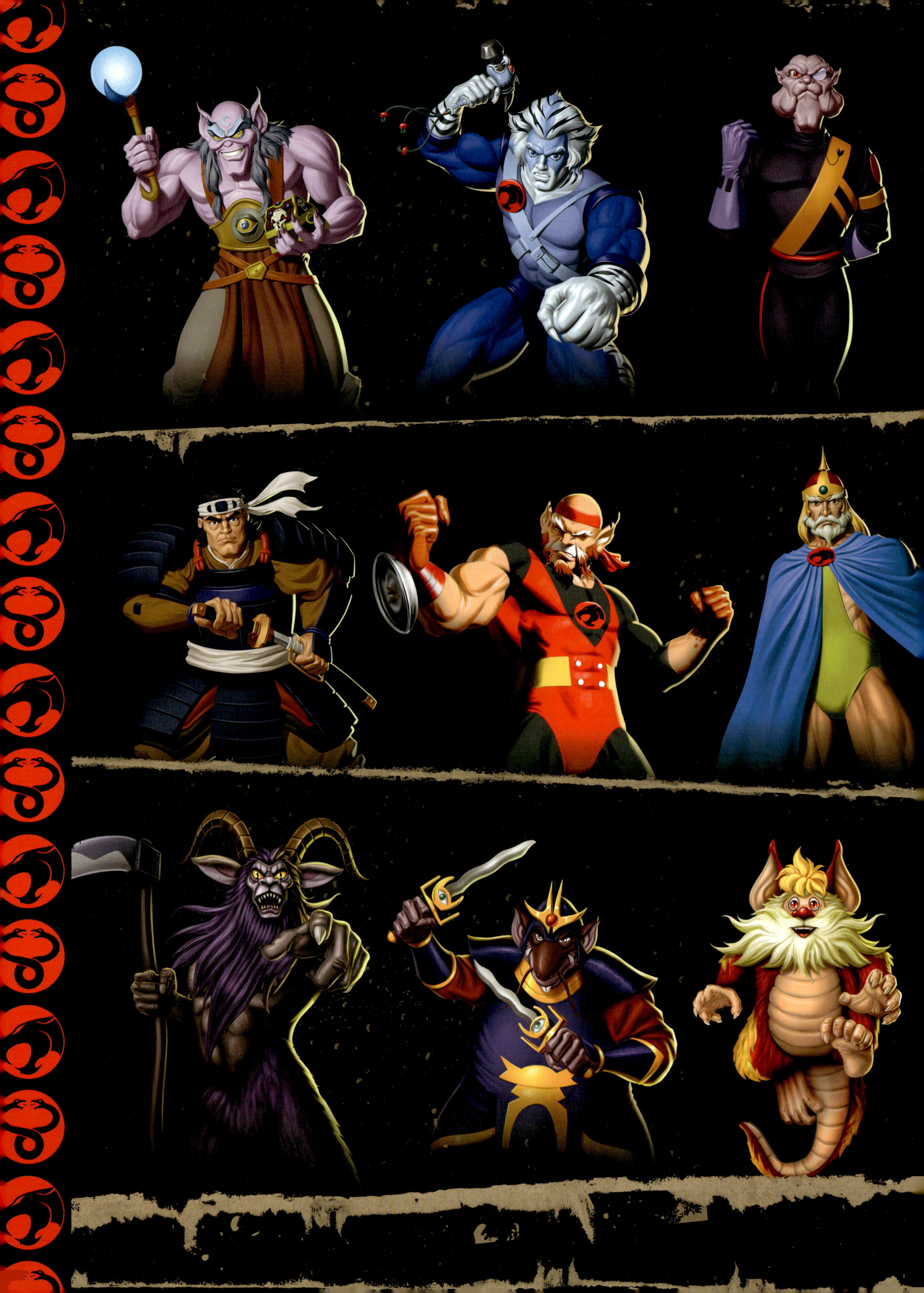

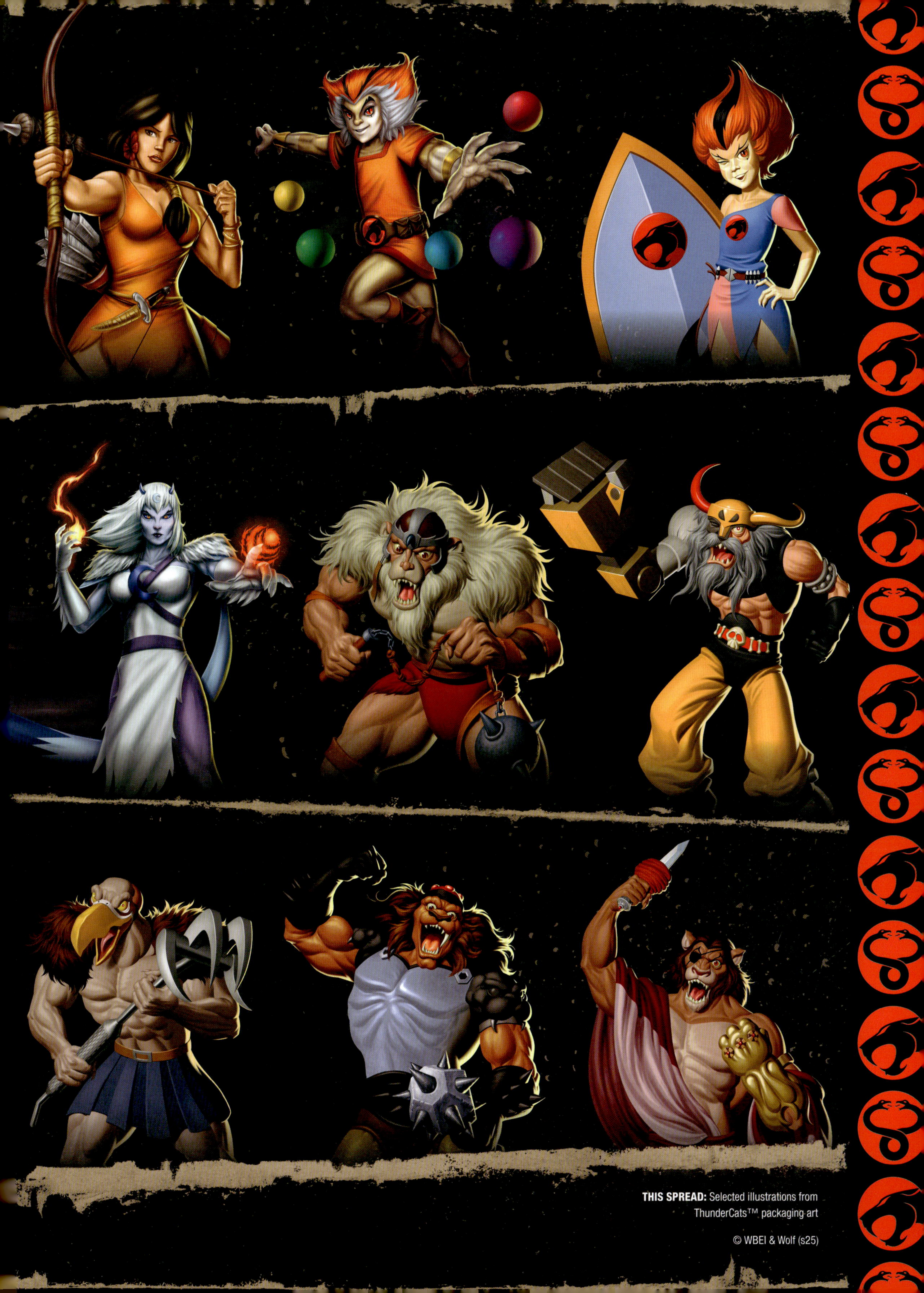

THIS SPREAD: Selected illustrations from ThunderCats™ packaging art

© WBEI & Wolf (s25)

You can COLLECT THEM ALL!

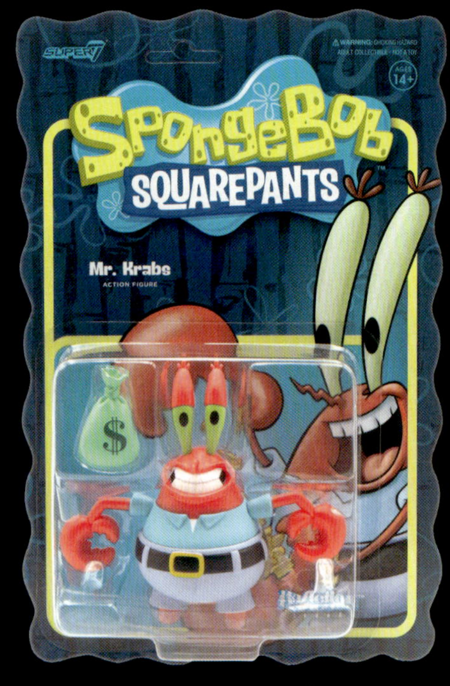

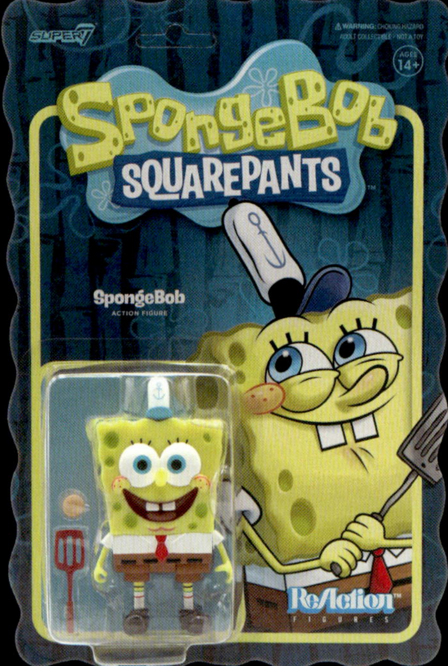

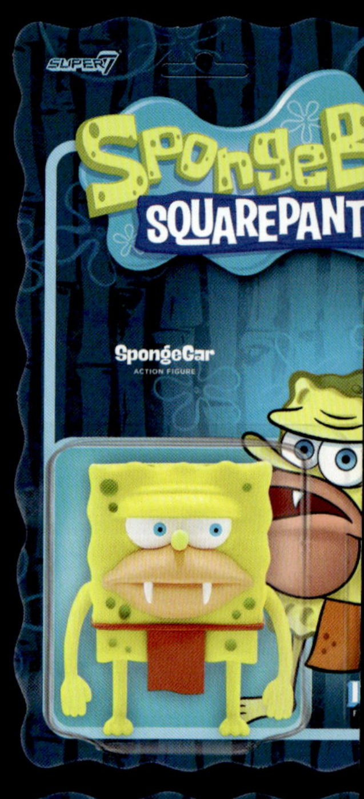

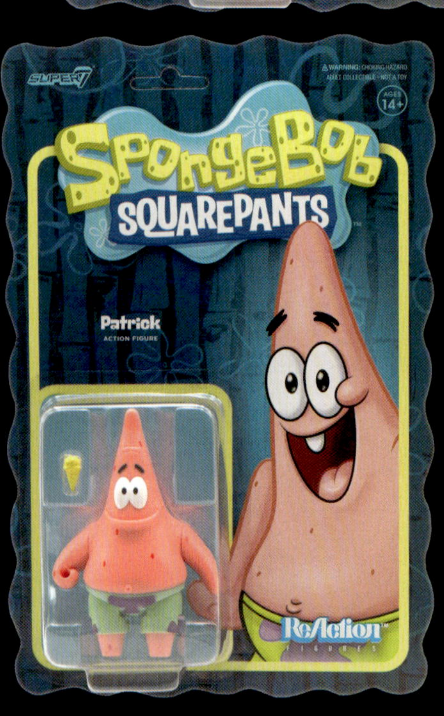

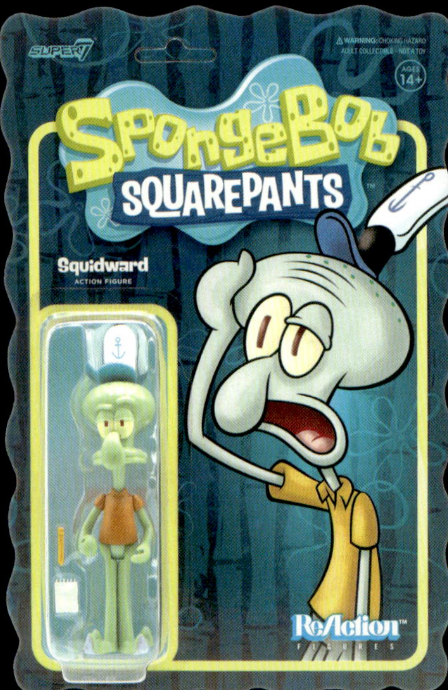

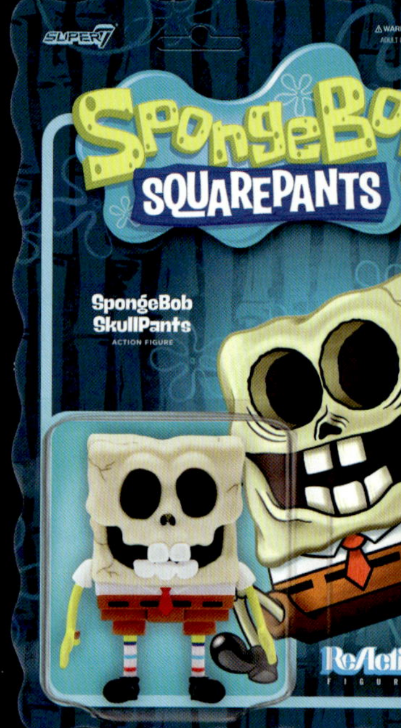

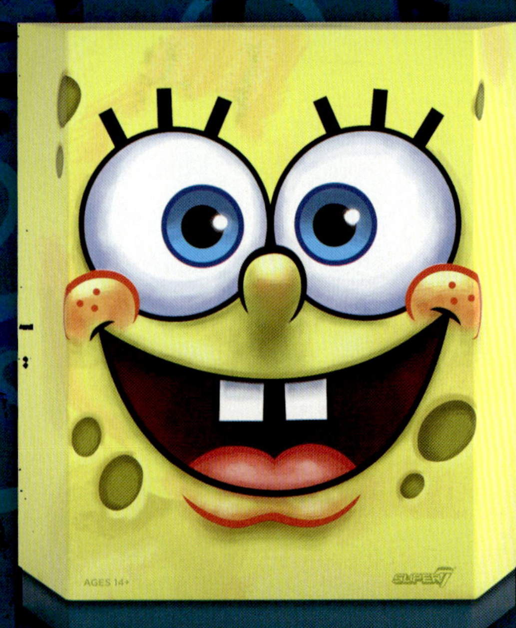

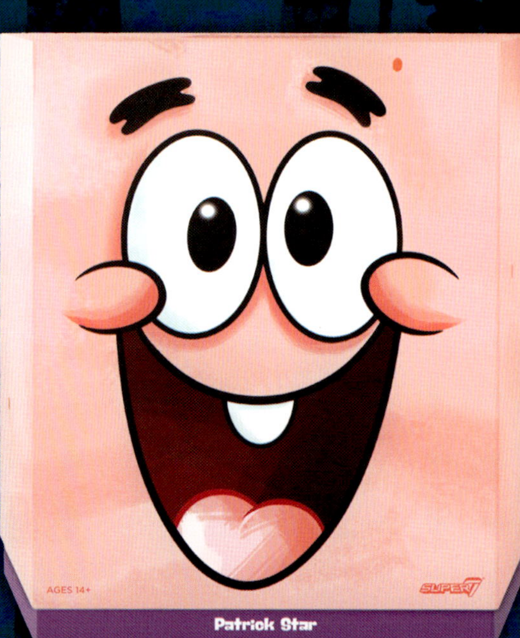

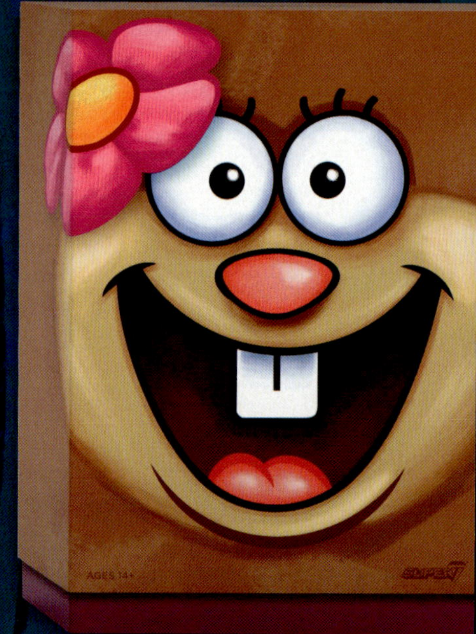

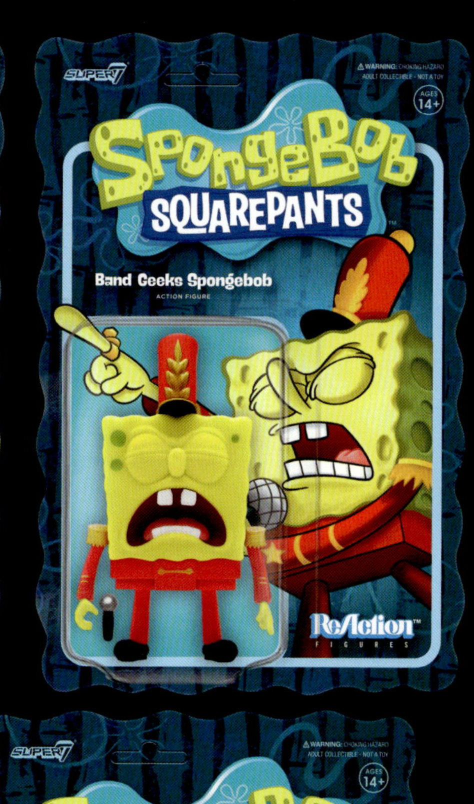

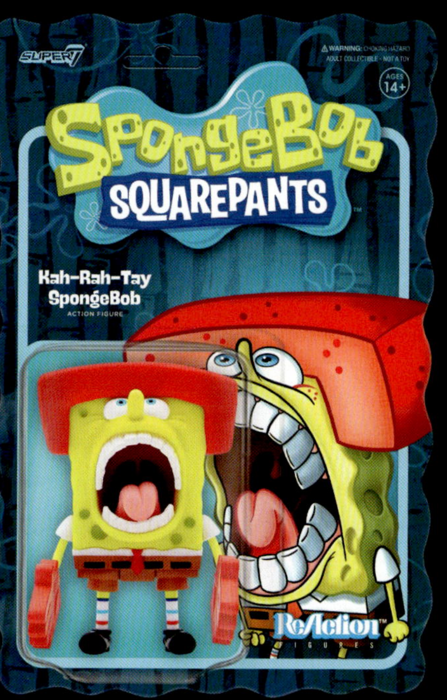

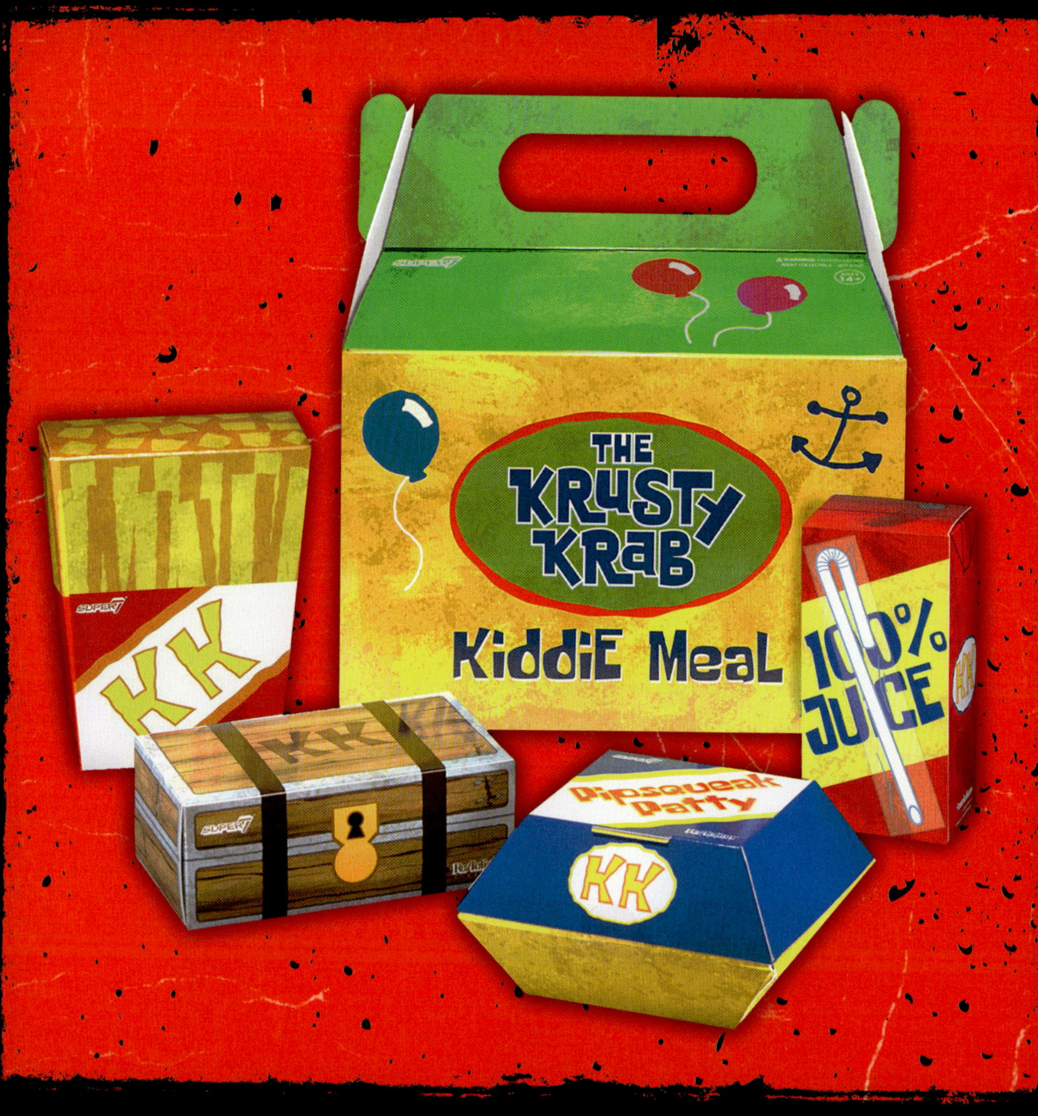

THIS SPREAD: Selected SpongeBob SquarePants™ ReAction Figures™ cards and ULTIMATES!™ boxes

© 2025 Viacom International Inc.

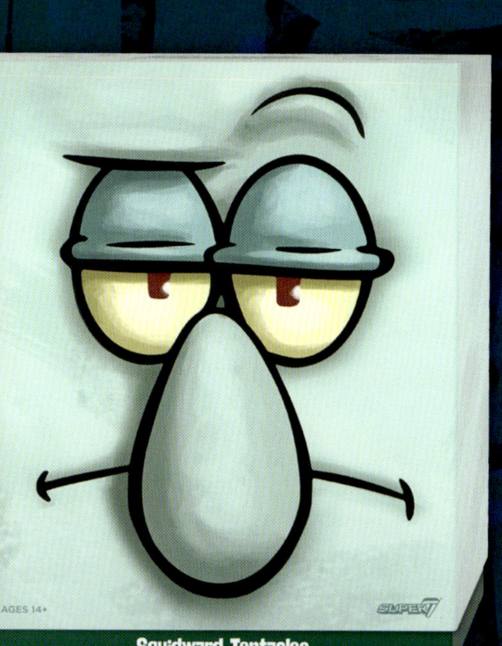

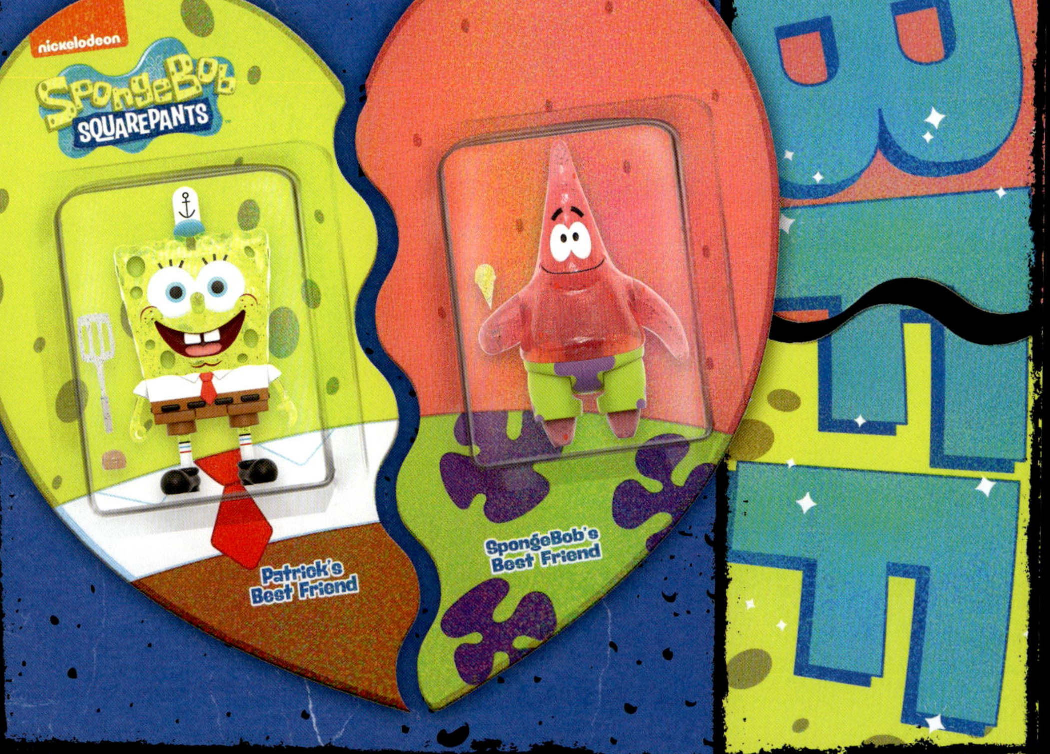

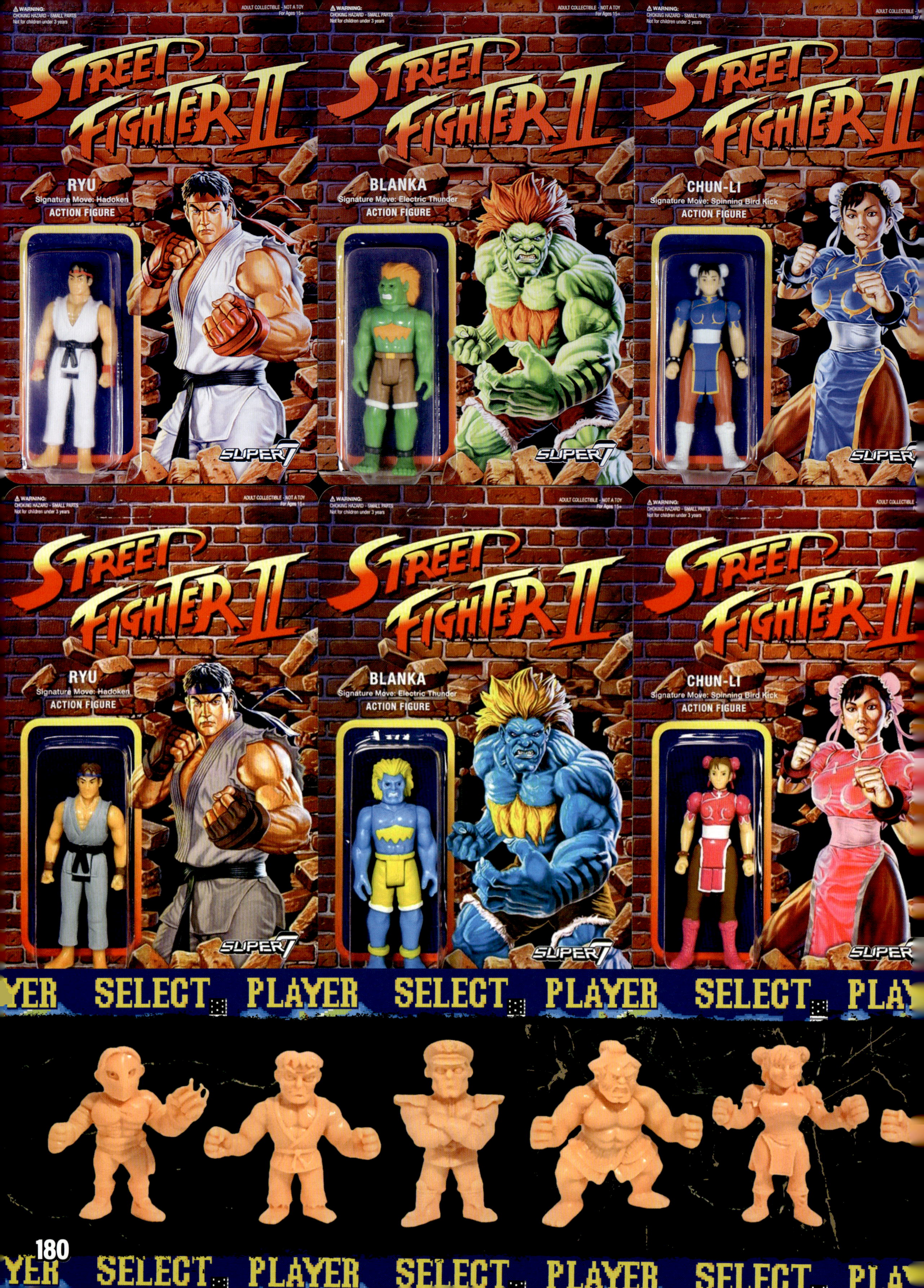
STREET FIGHTER II
RYU
Signature Move: Hadoken
ACTION FIGURE
SUPER7
STREET FIGHTER II
BLANKA
Signature Move: Electric Thunder
ACTION FIGURE
SUPER7
STREET FIGHTER II
CHUN-LI
Signature Move: Spinning Bird Kick
ACTION FIGURE
STREET FIGHTER II
RYU
Signature Move: Hadoken
ACTION FIGURE
SUPER7
STREET FIGHTER II
BLANKA
Signature Move: Electric Thunder
ACTION FIGURE
SUPER7
STREET FIGHTER II
CHUN-LI
Signature Move: Spinning Bird Kick
ACTION FIGURE
SELECT PLAYER SELECT PLAYER SELECT
SELECT PLAYER SELECT PLAYER SELECT

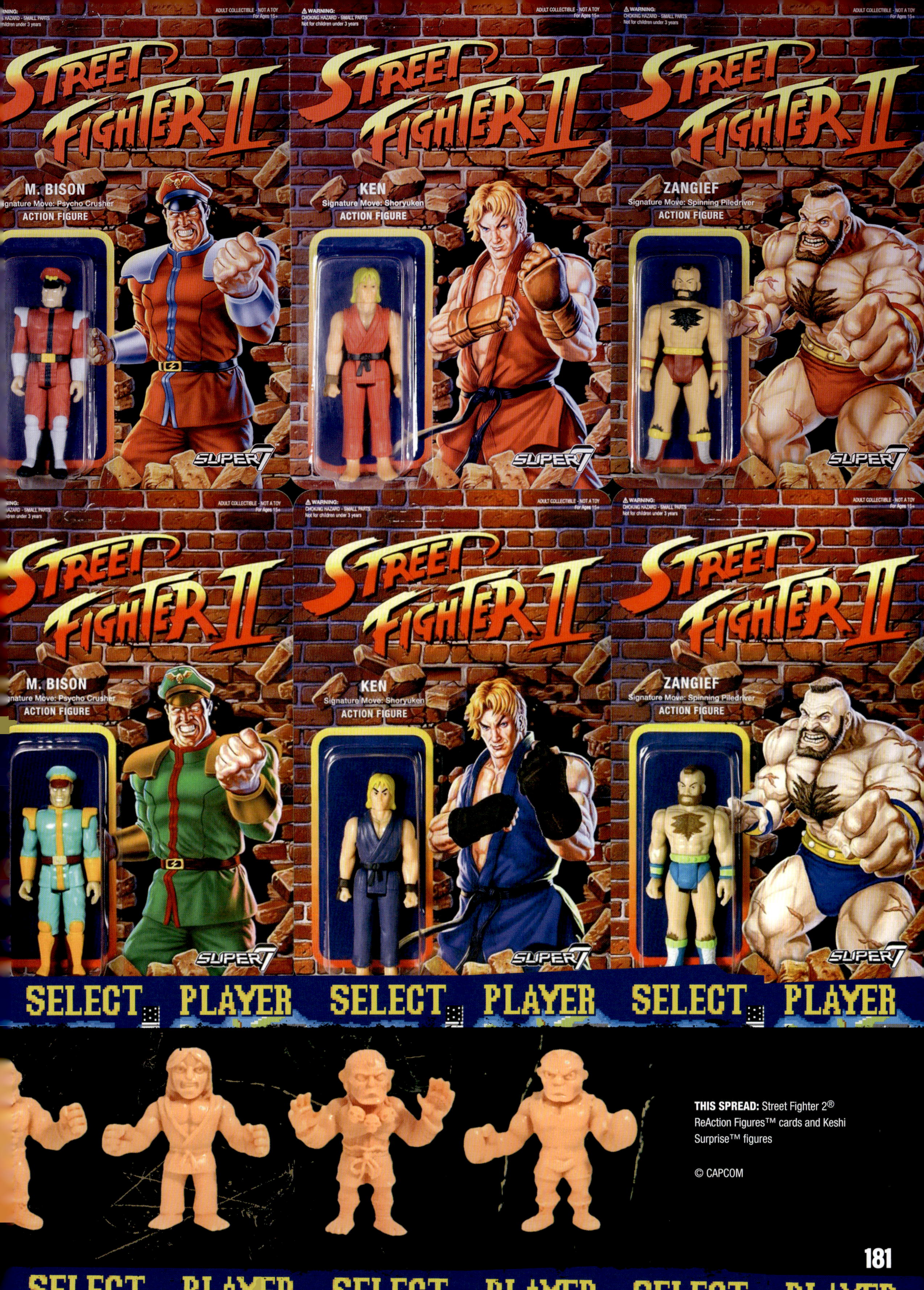

THIS SPREAD: Street Fighter 2® ReAction Figures™ cards and Keshi Surprise™ figures

© CAPCOM

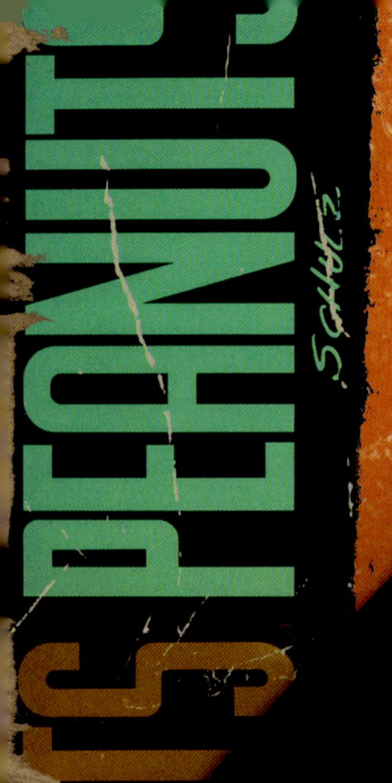
PEANUTS

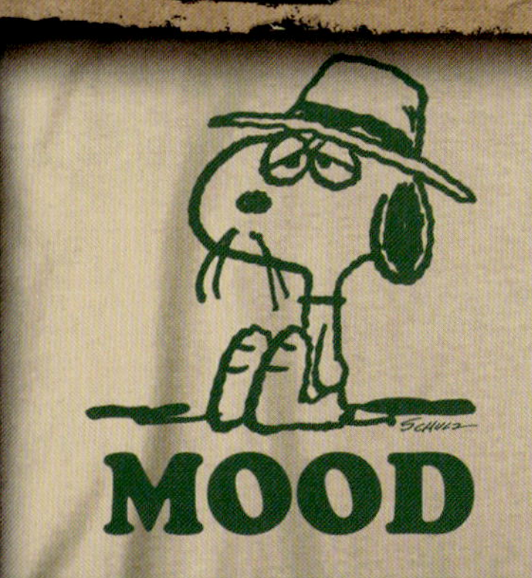
MOOD

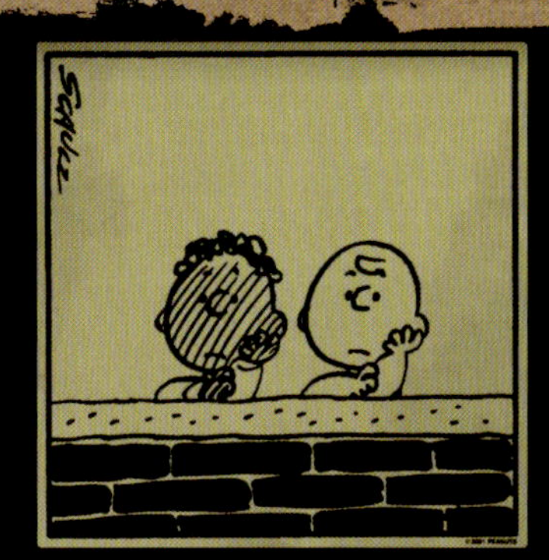

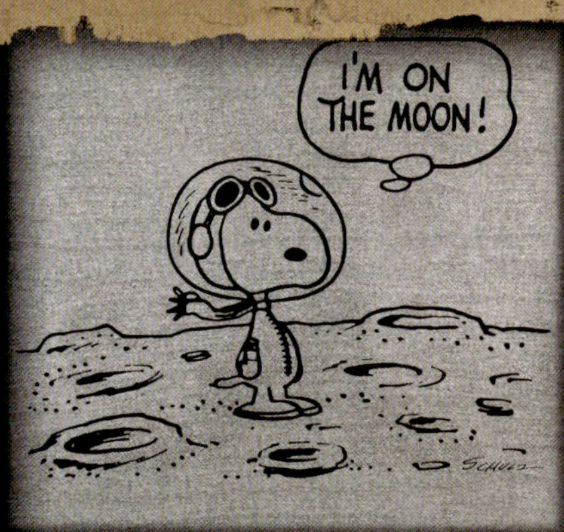
I'M ON THE MOON!

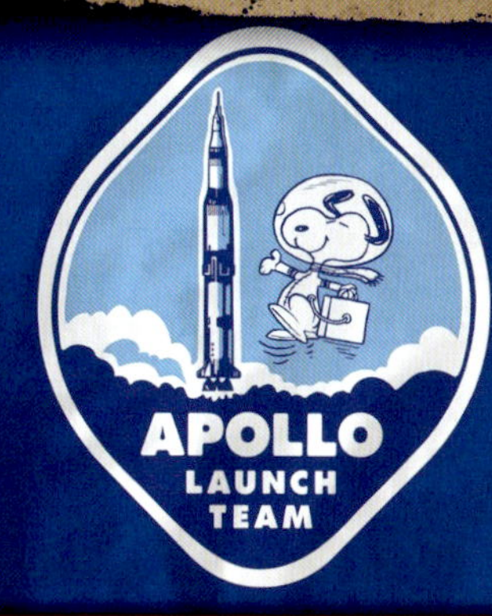
APOLLO
LAUNCH
TEAM

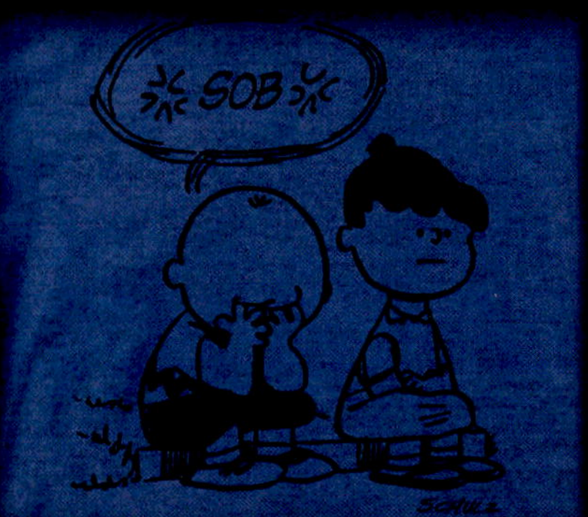
SOB

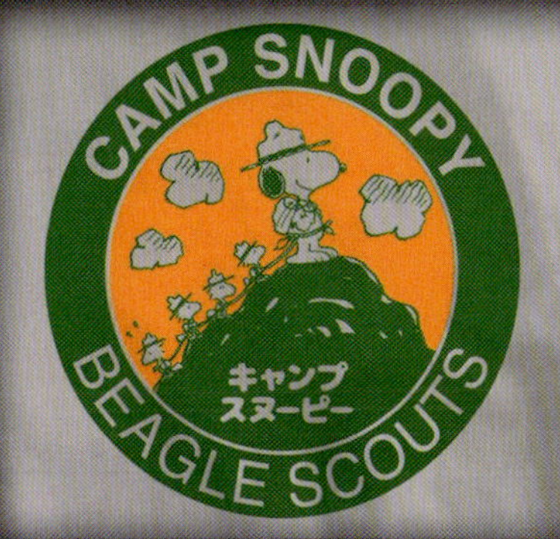
CAMP SNOOPY
キャンプ
スヌーピー
BEAGLE SCOUTS

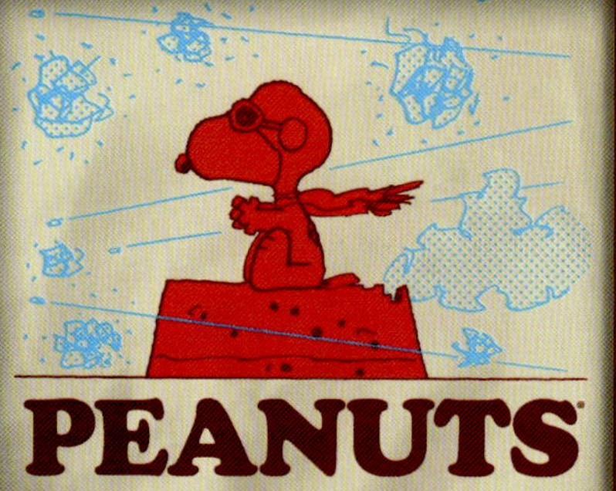
PEANUTS

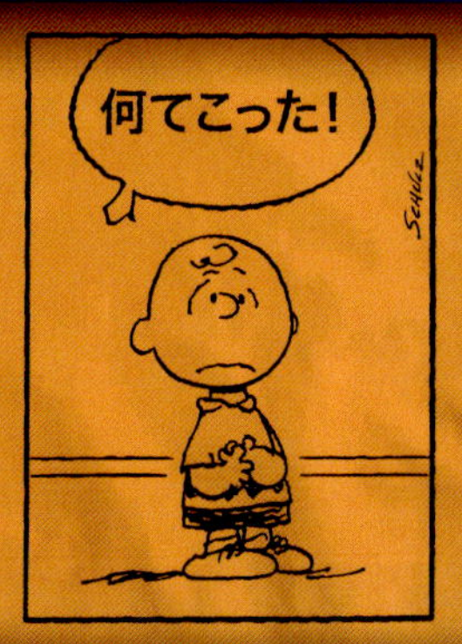
何てこった!

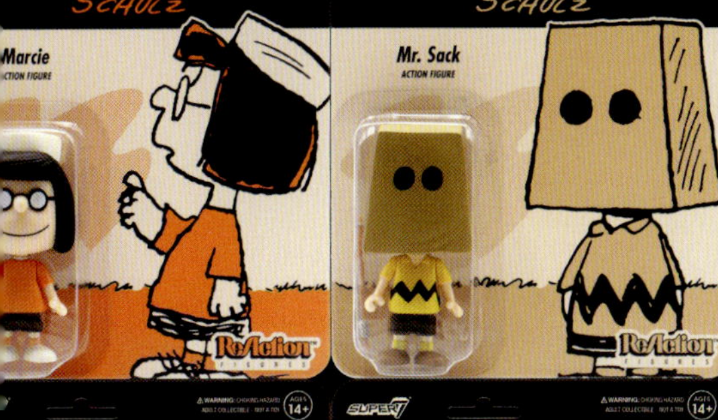

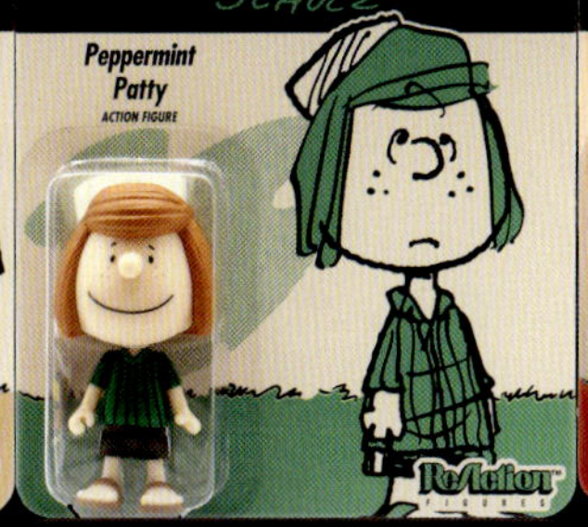

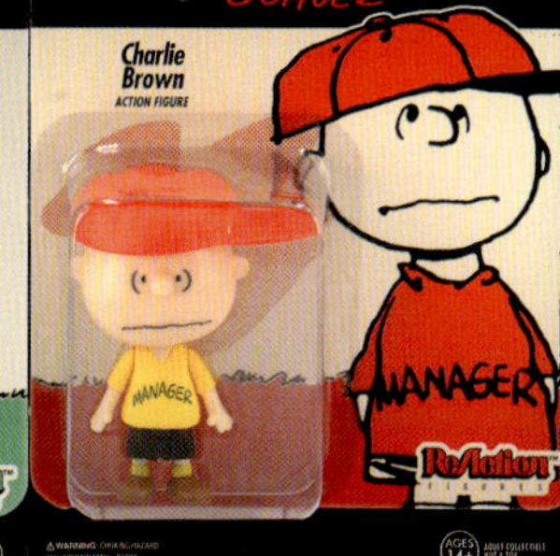

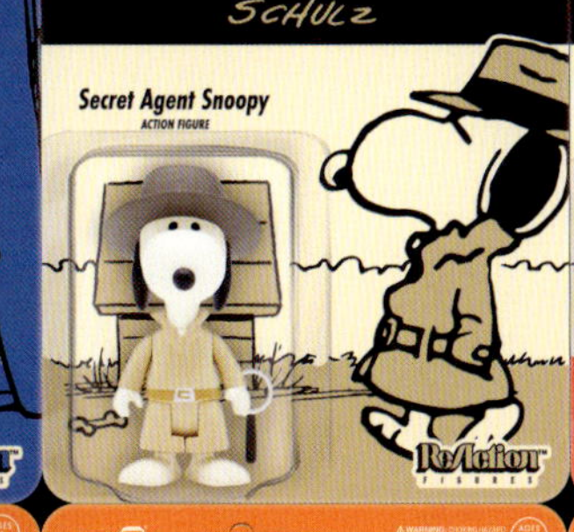

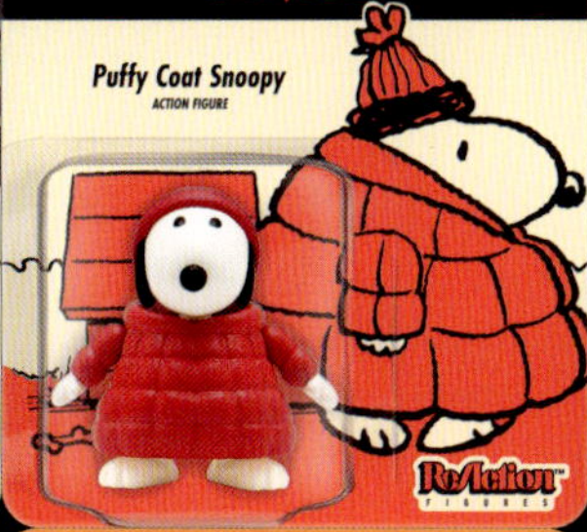

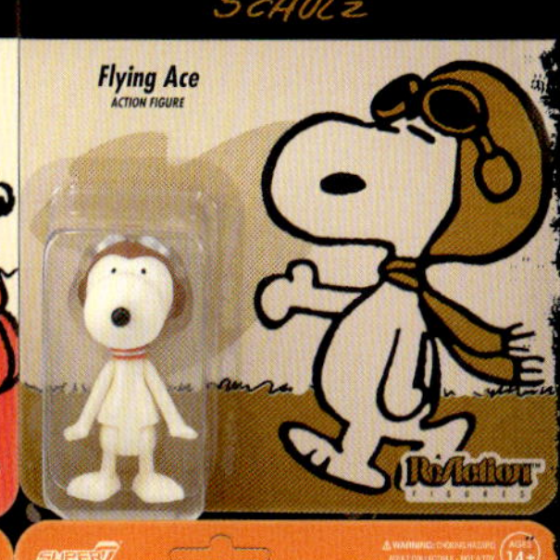

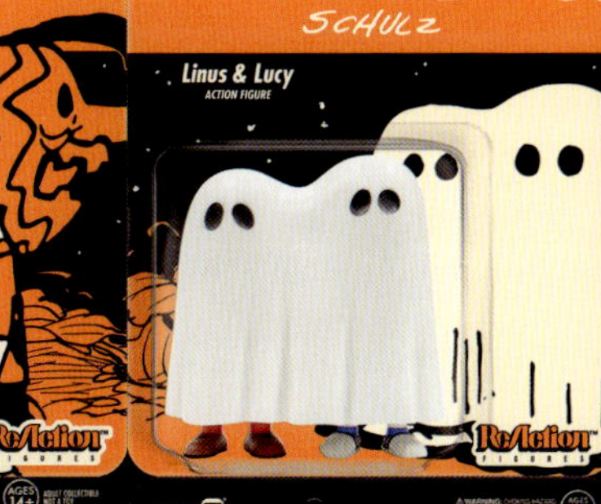

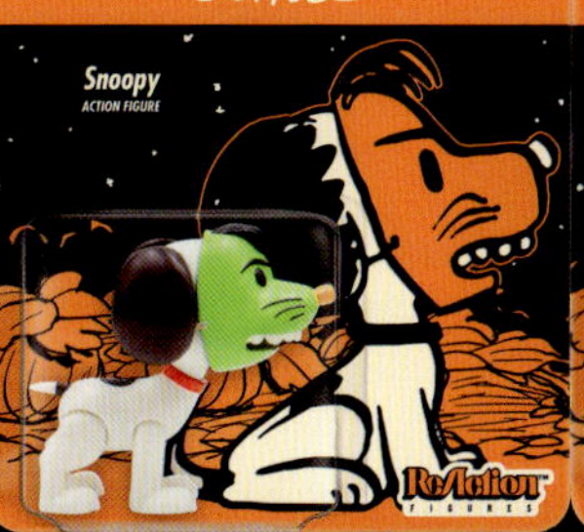

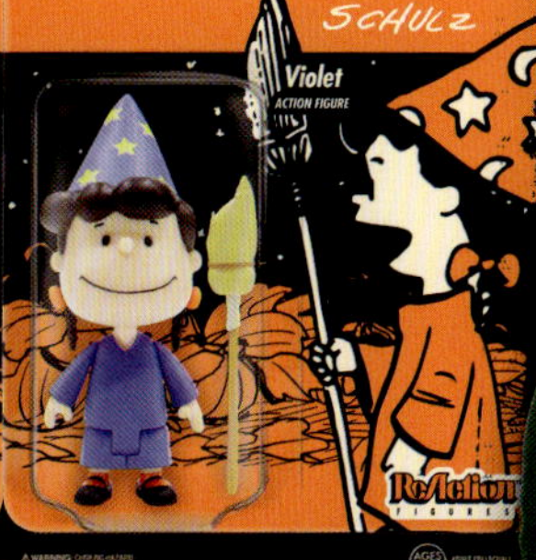

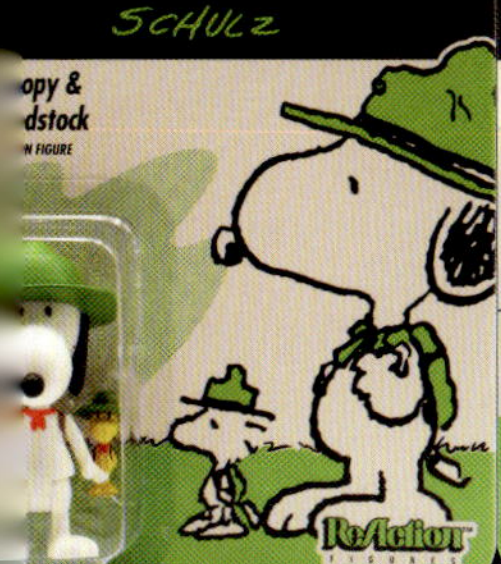
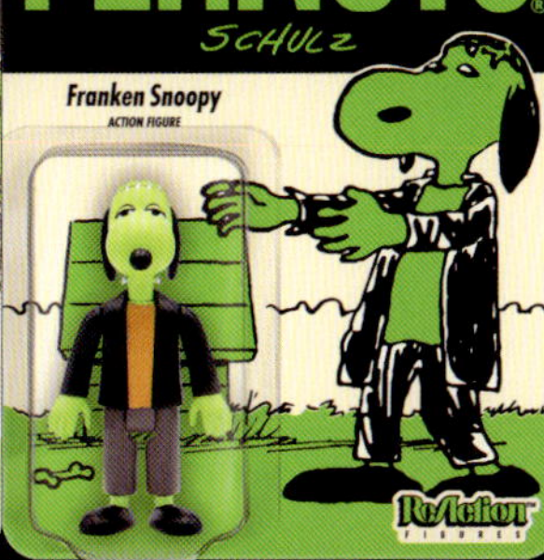

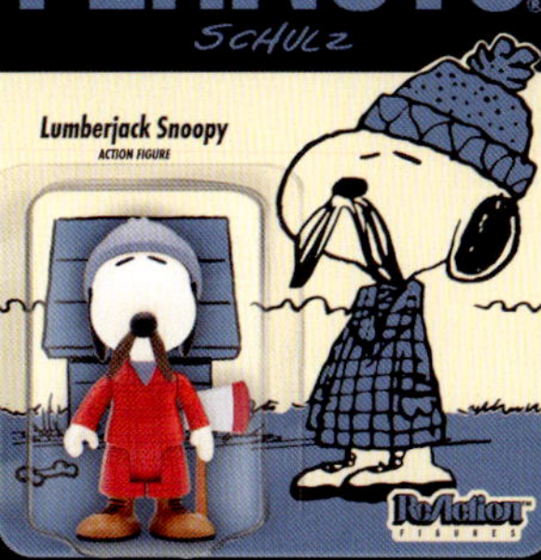

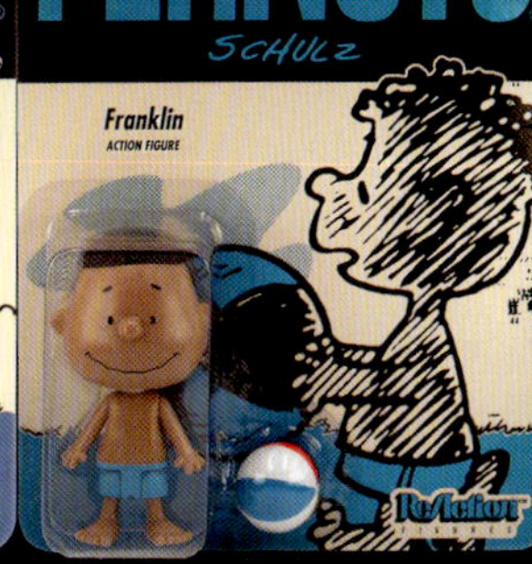

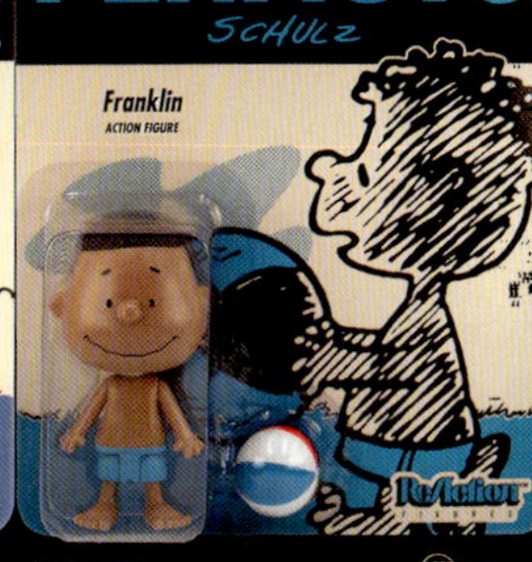
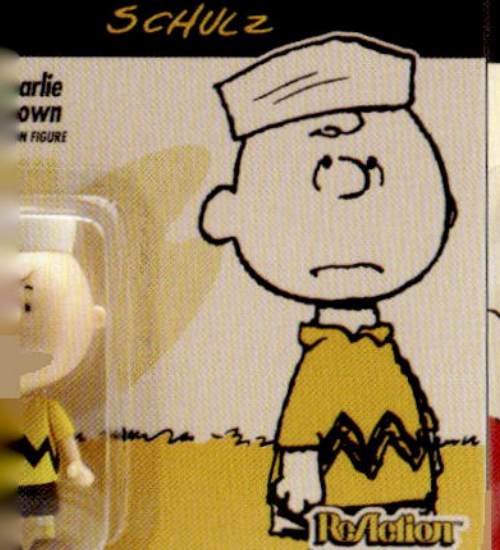
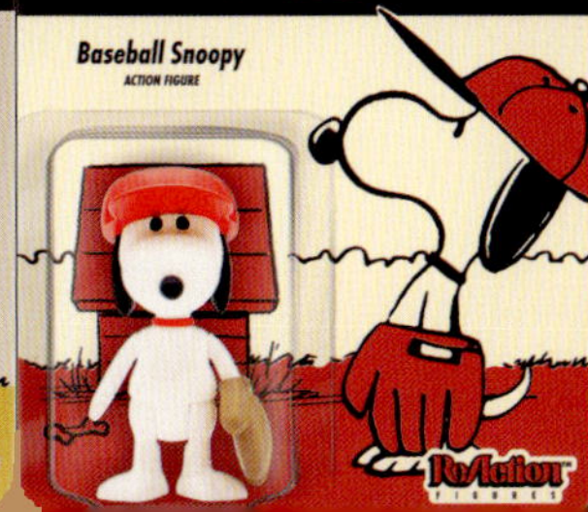

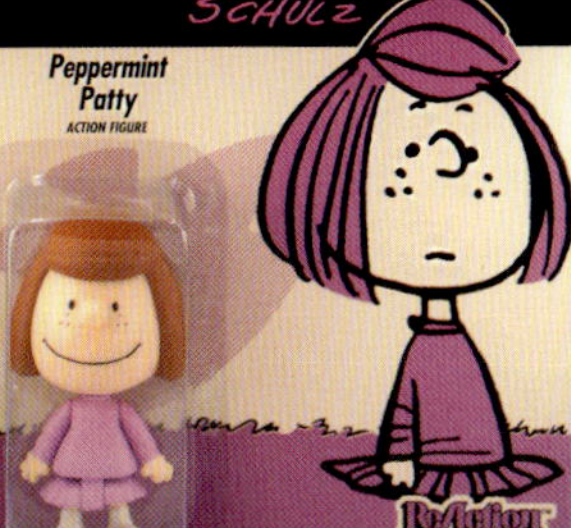

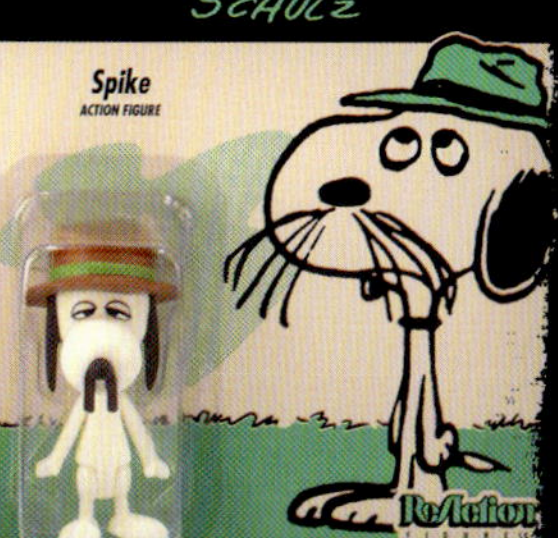

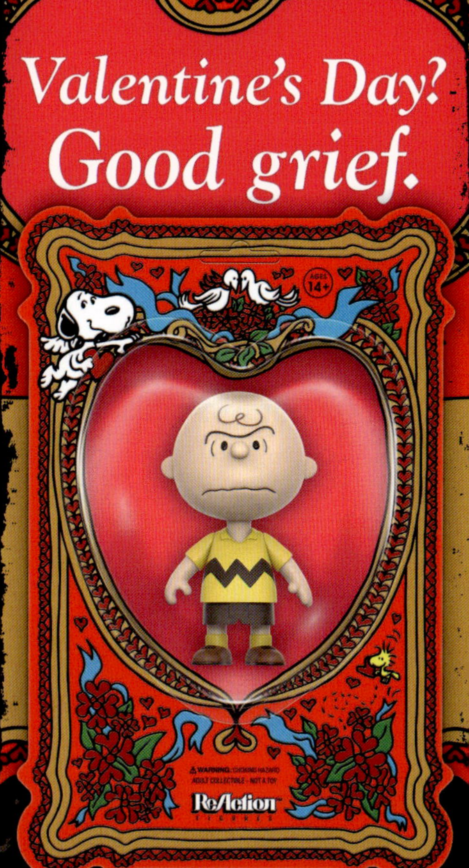

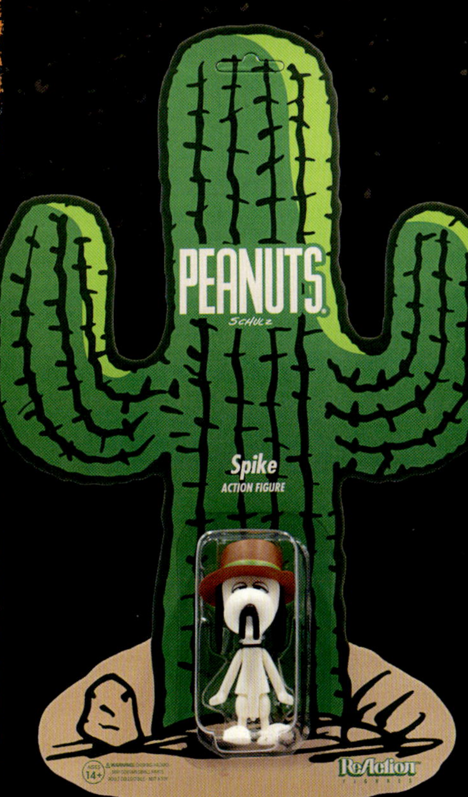

THIS SPREAD:
A selection of Peanuts® ReAction Figures™ and apparel

© 2025 Peanuts

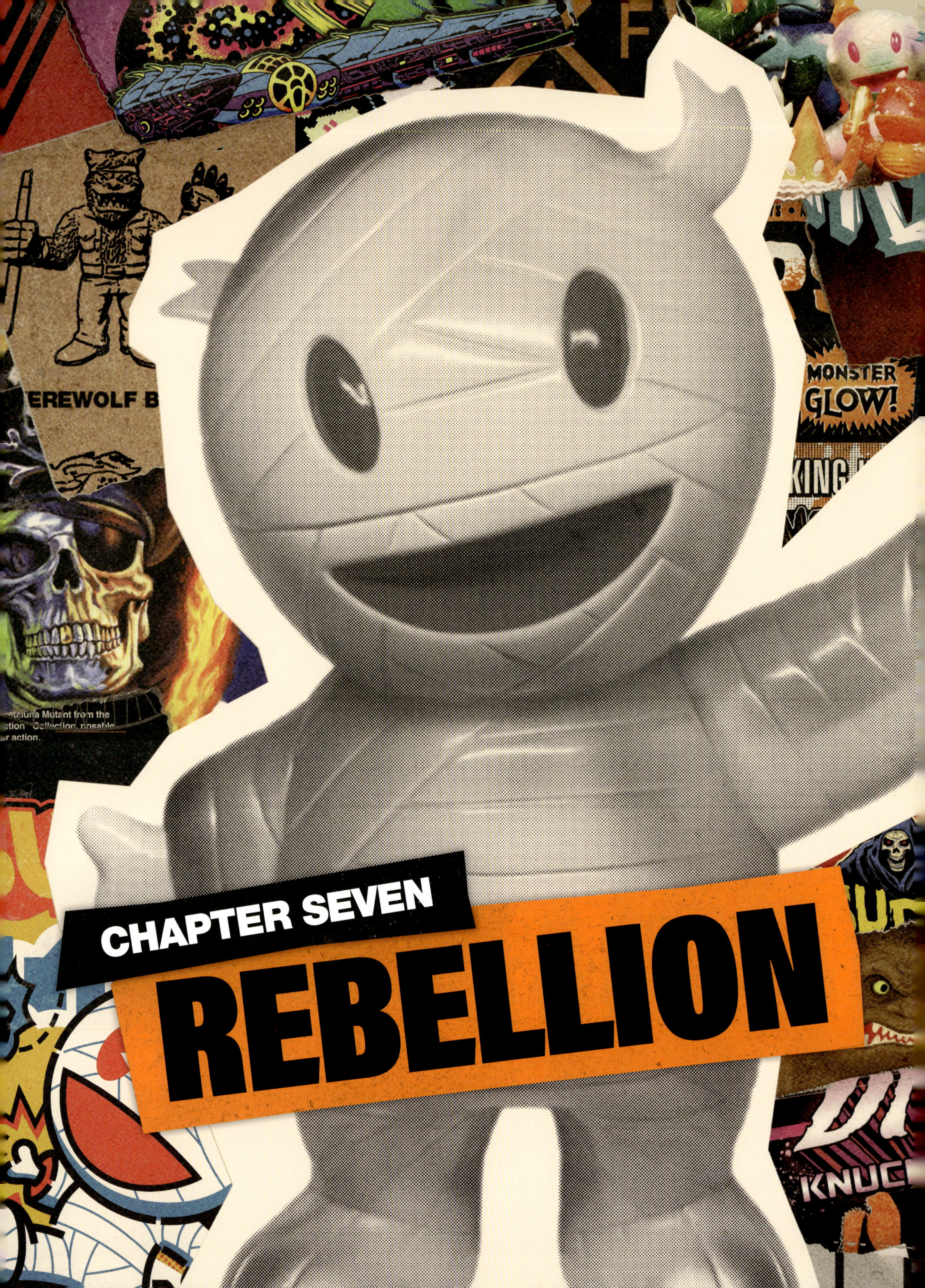

CHAPTER SEVEN
REBELLION

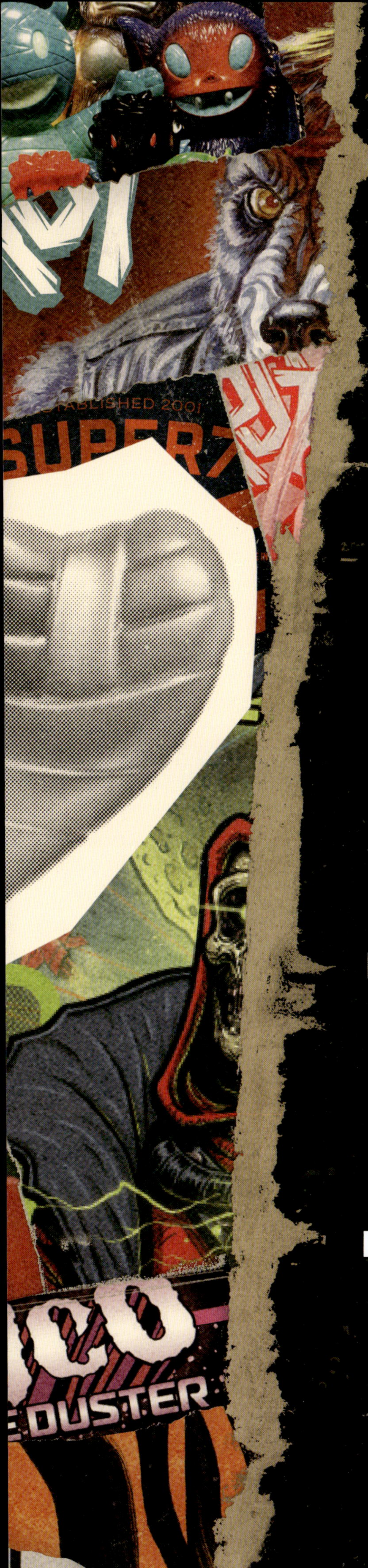

TO QUOTE THOMAS JEFFERSON, "A LITTLE REBELLION NOW AND THEN IS A GOOD THING." NOW, WE AREN'T ADVOCATING TO OVERTHROW ANY GOVERNMENTS, BUT THE FACT IS, DOING THE SAME THING AS EVERYONE ELSE ALL THE TIME HAS NEVER REALLY BEEN OUR STYLE. WHEN EVERYONE GOES RIGHT, WE TEND TO GO LEFT. YOU CAN SEE IT IN THE CHARACTERS WE CHOOSE, THE FORMATS WE MAKE, AND THE STYLES WE SCULPT IN. IT IS NOT ALWAYS FOR EVERYONE—QUITE OFTEN, IN FACT, IT IS ONLY FOR A FEW—BUT YOU CAN NEVER ACCUSE US OF PLAYING IT SAFE. THE WORST THING EVER WOULD BE TO CONSIDER WHAT WE DO AS BORING.

SPEAKING OF THE WORST, WHAT MORE COULD YOU REALLY ASK FOR? INSTEAD OF THE LATEST MOVIE, LET'S JUST MAKE AN ARMY OF BAD GUYS—WHO NEEDS GOOD GUYS ANYWAY? BUT NOT JUST BAD GUYS: THE WORST OF THE BAD GUYS. TERRIBLE BAD GUYS. HORRIFIC BAD GUYS. THE WORST OF THE WORST. BAD GUYS THAT ARE ACTUALLY TERRIBLE AT THEIR JOBS, AND HONESTLY QUITE WORTHLESS IN MOST ASPECTS—THEY JUST HAPPEN TO HAVE THE BEST OUTFITS. REBELS WITHOUT A CAUSE OR CARE, AND MOST LIKELY WITHOUT A BUDGET FOR WORLD DOMINATION EITHER. THE WORST VILLAINS EVER.

BELOW: The Worst™ apparel

RIGHT: Super7®'s own The Worst™ ReAction Figures™ card illustrations

™ & © the Worst, LLC

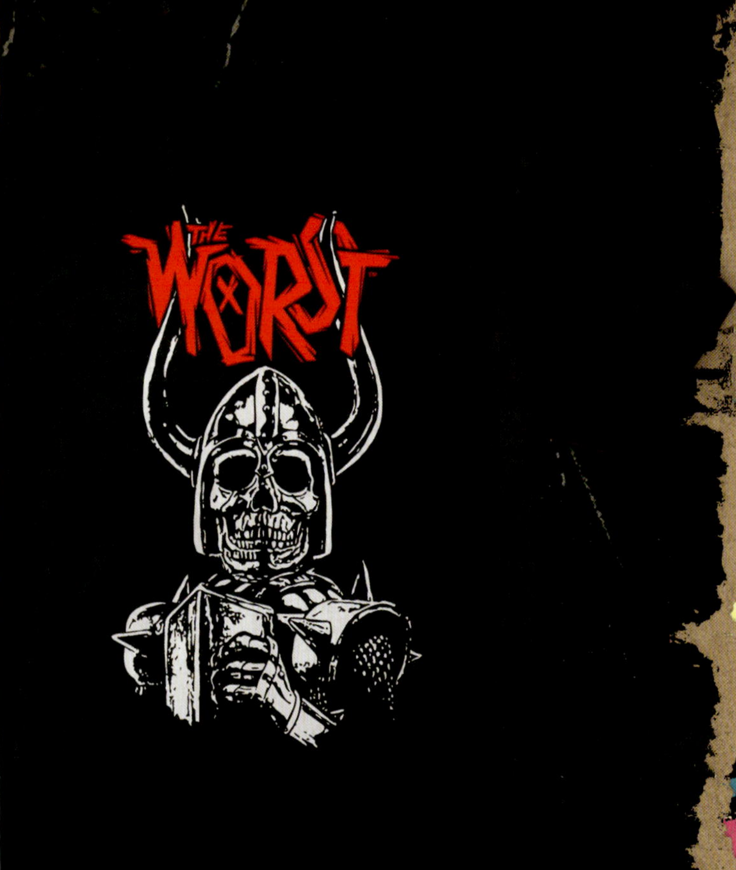

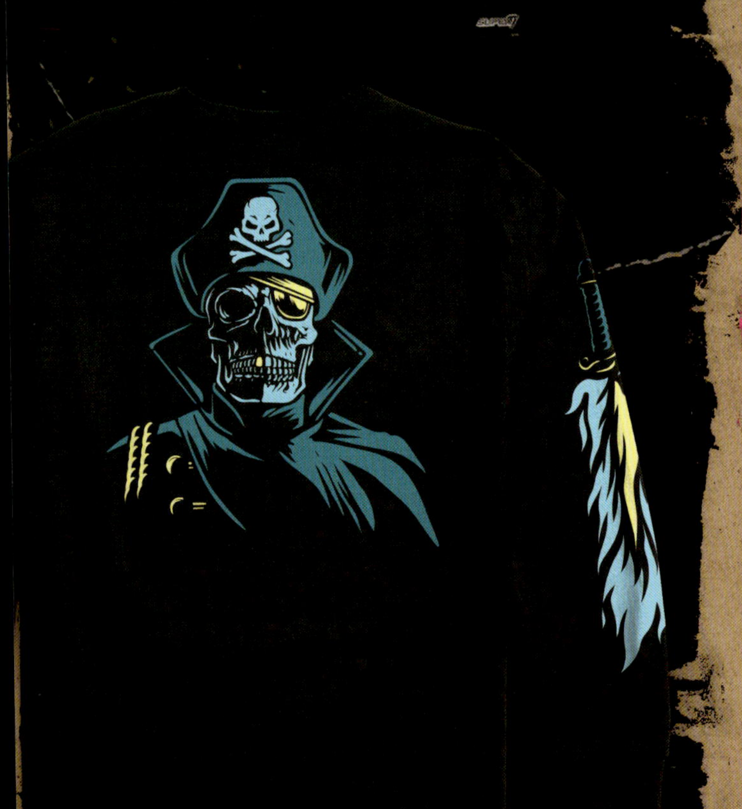

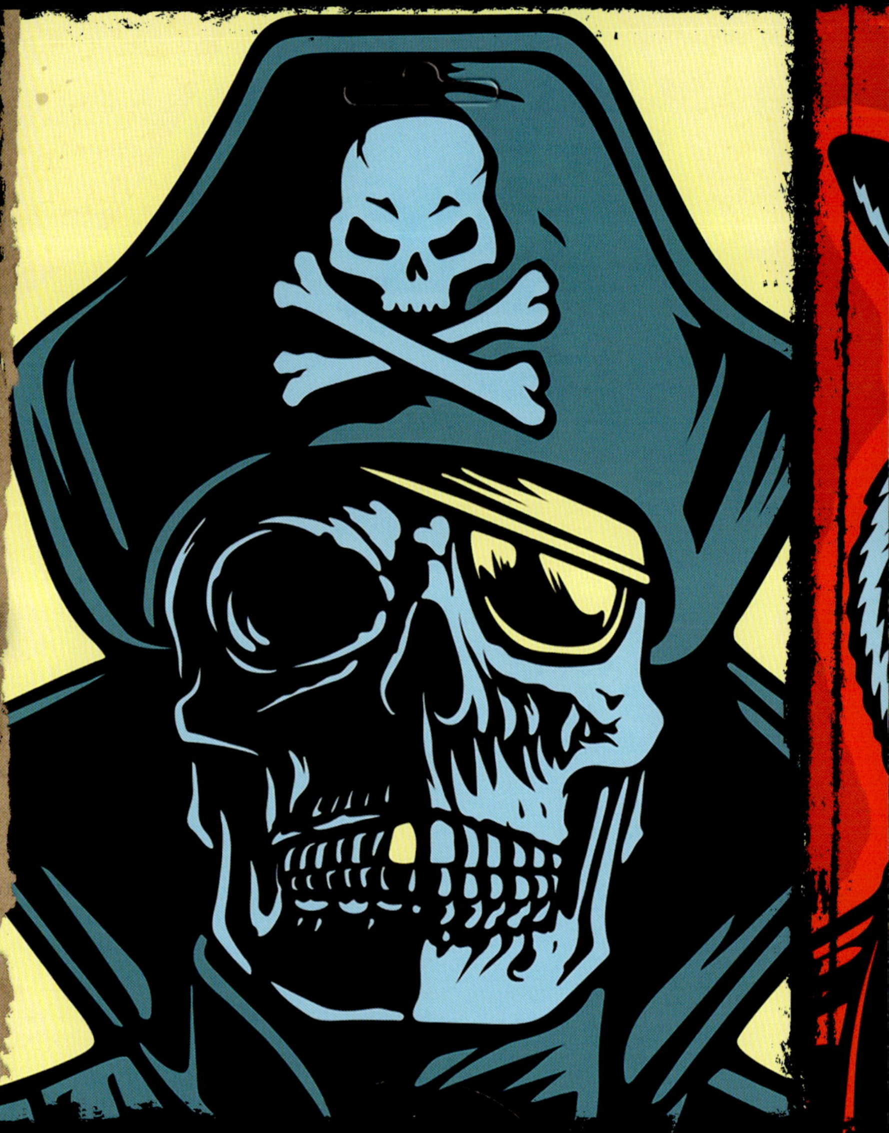

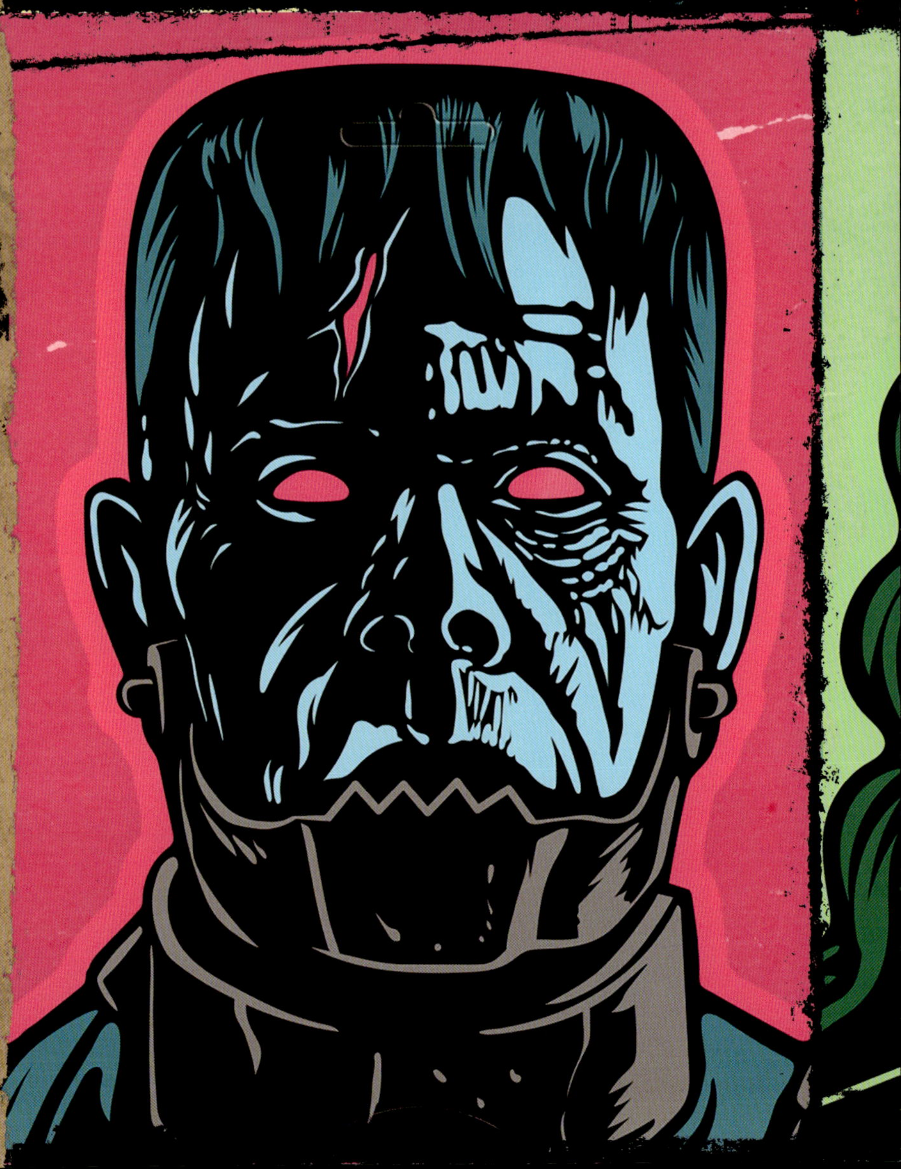

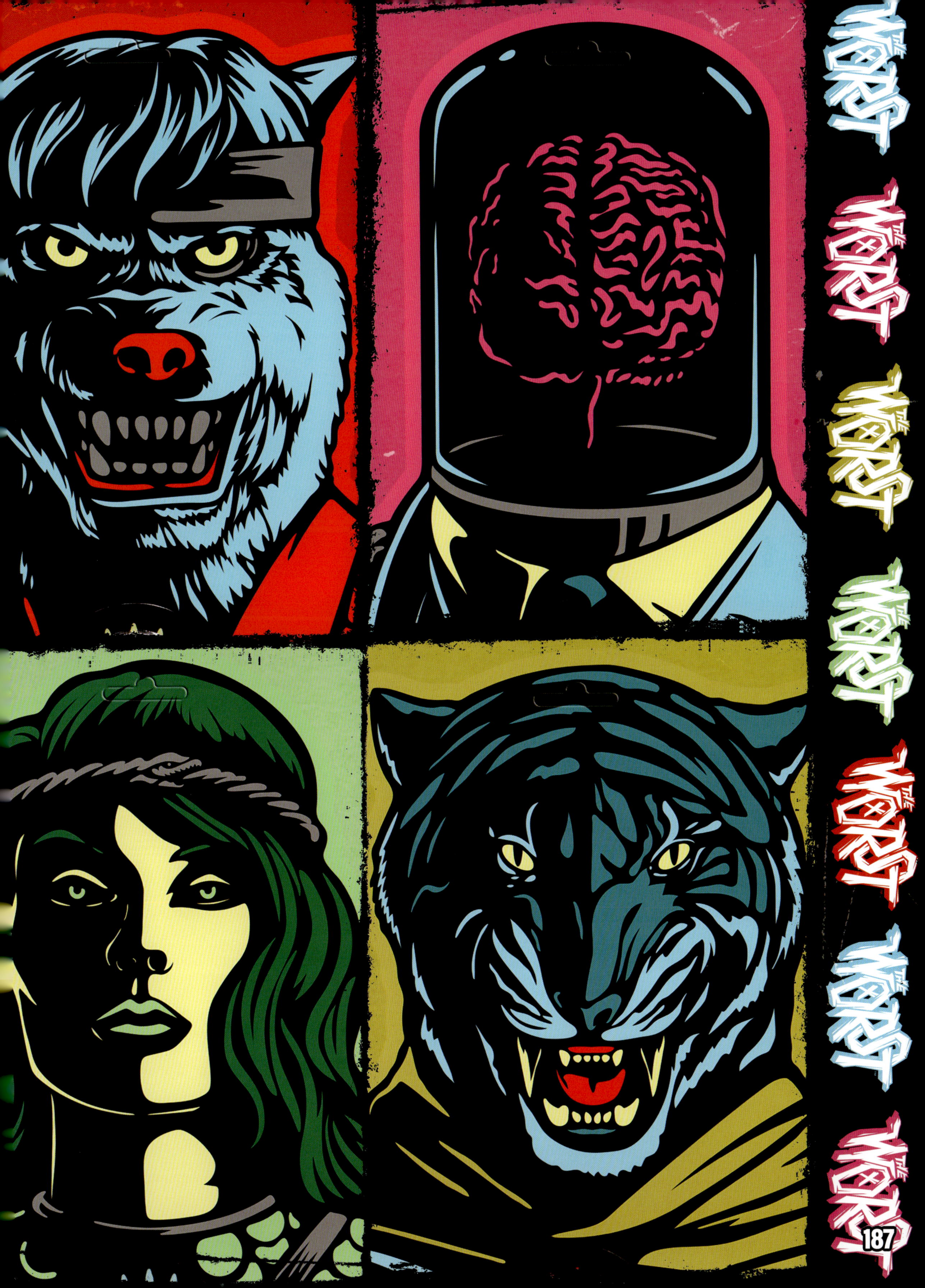
THE WORST
THE WORST
THE WORST
THE WORST
THE WORST
THE WORST
THE WORST

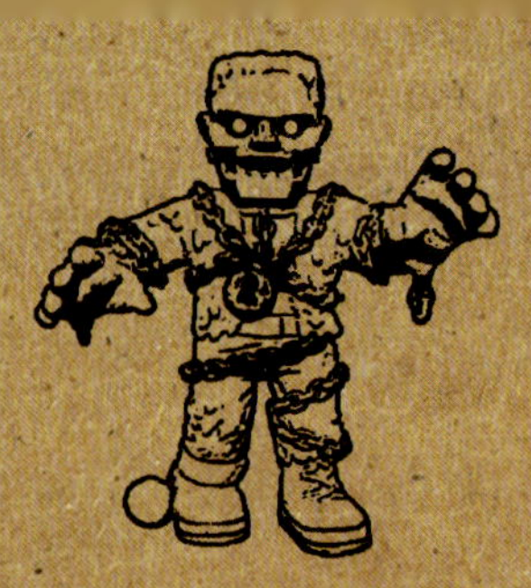
FRANKENGHOST™

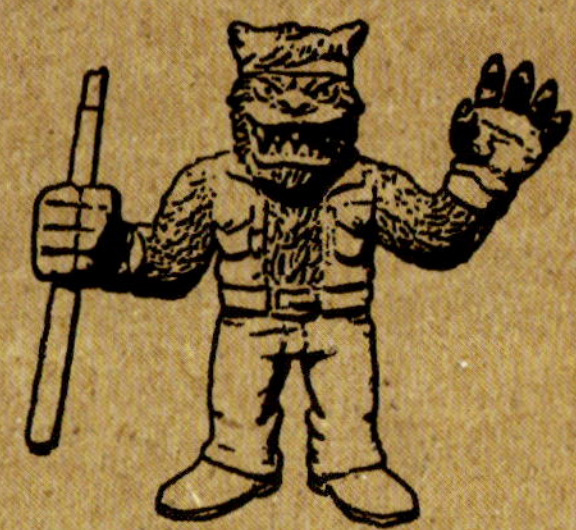
WEREWOLF BIKER™

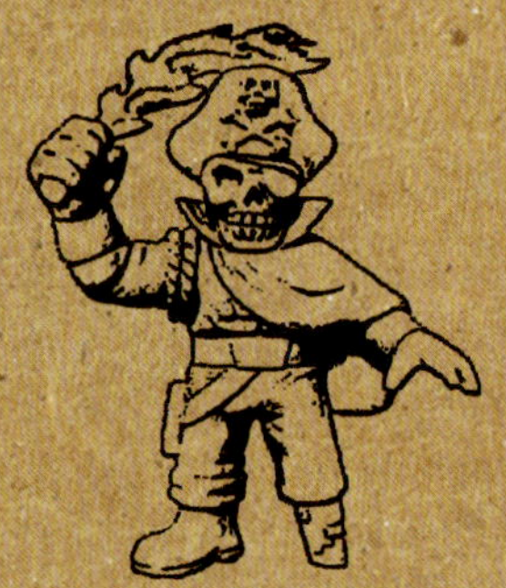
CAPTAIN DEADSTAR™

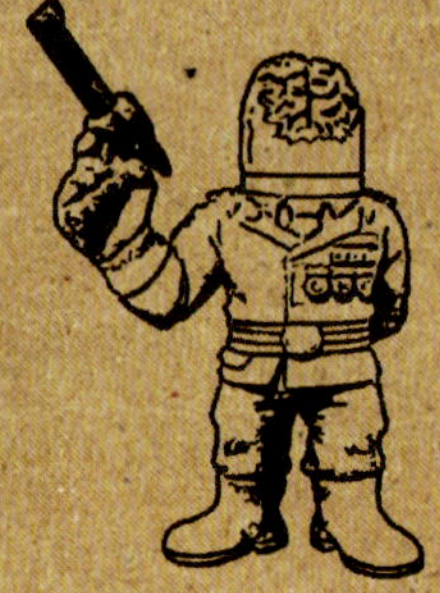
CORTEX COMMANDER™

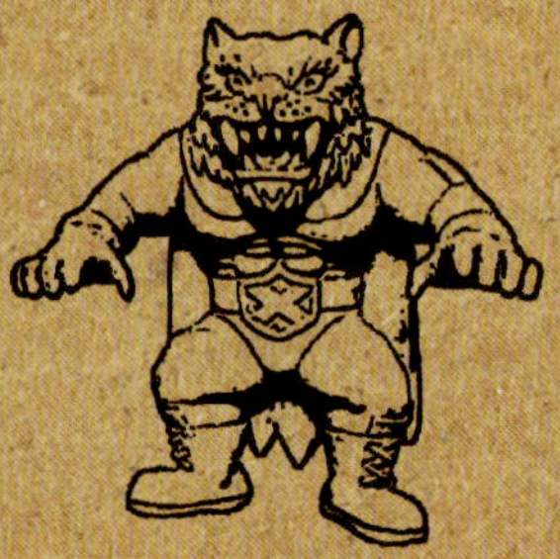
RED TIGER™

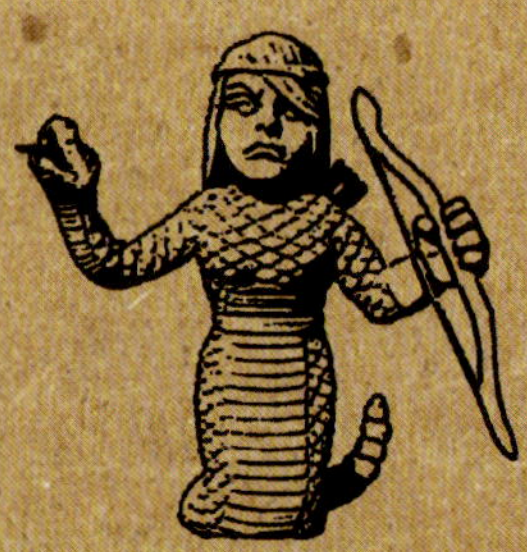
SHEDUSA™

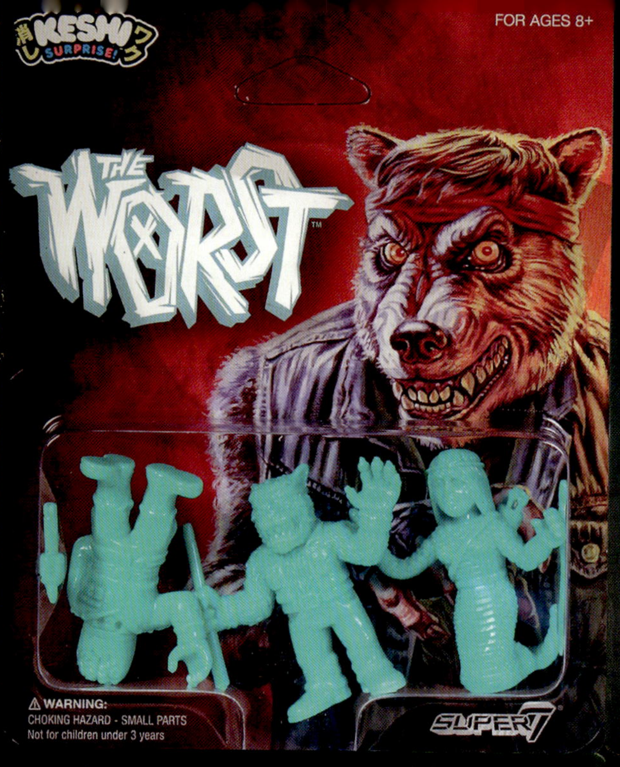

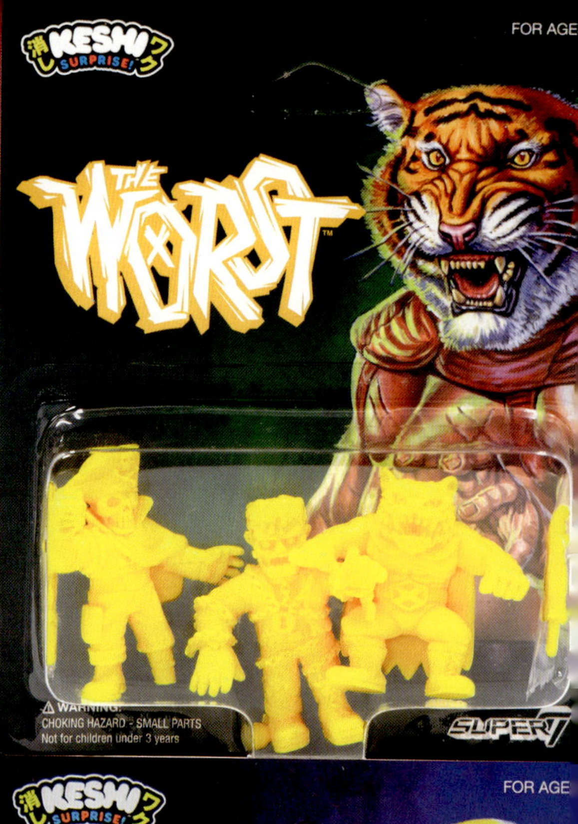

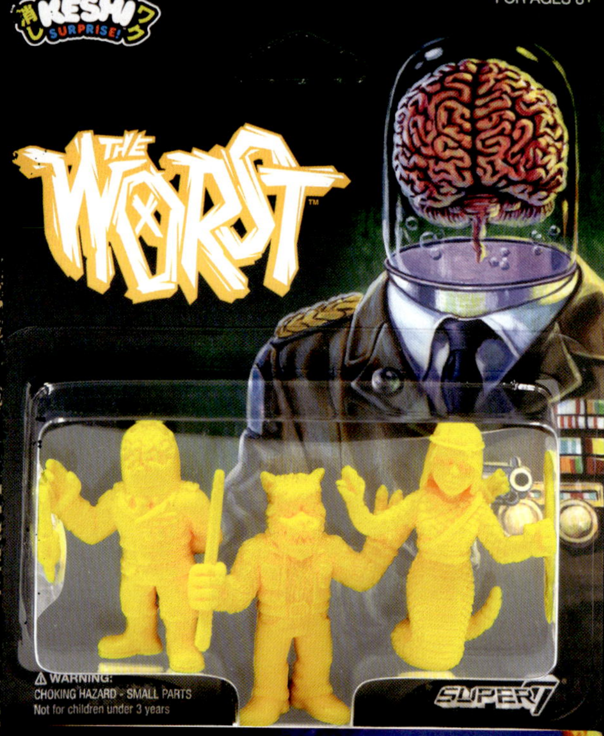

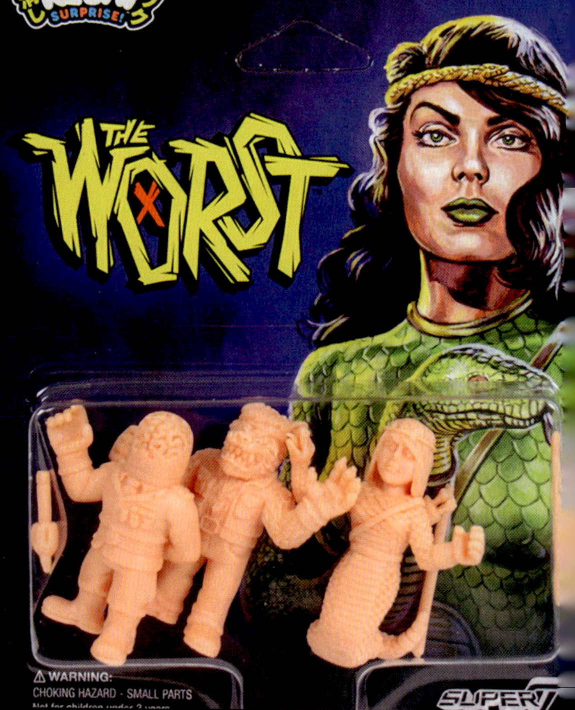

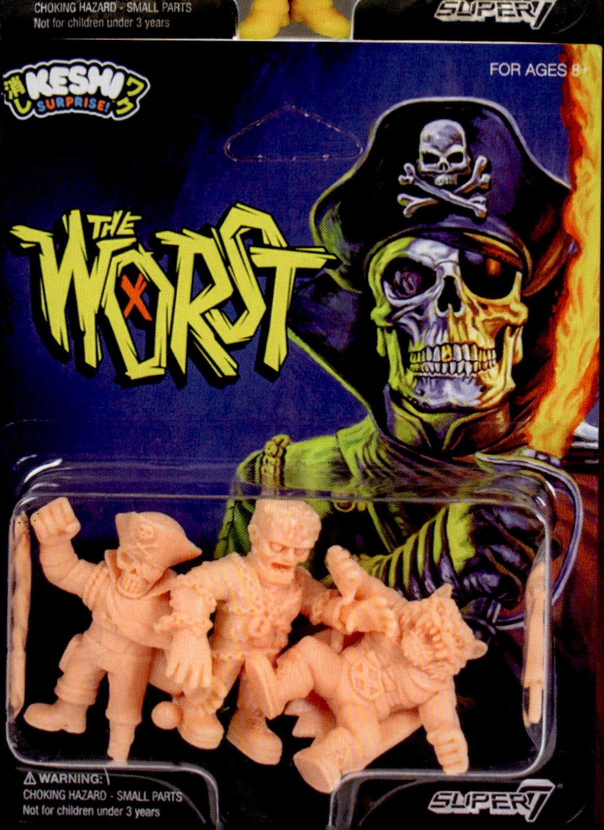

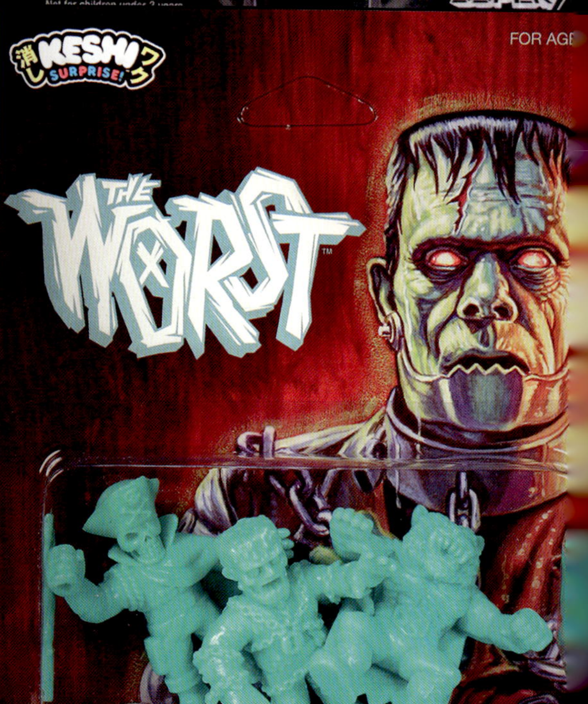

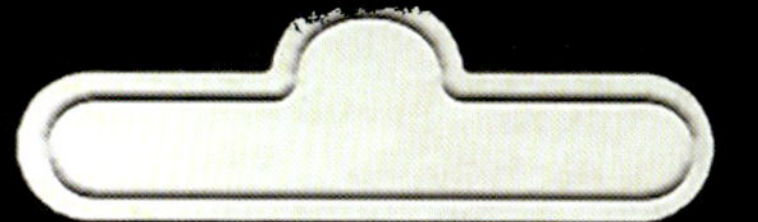

ORDER
NO. 666

THE WORST VILLAINS OF ALL TIME • COLLECT THEM ALL OR PERISH

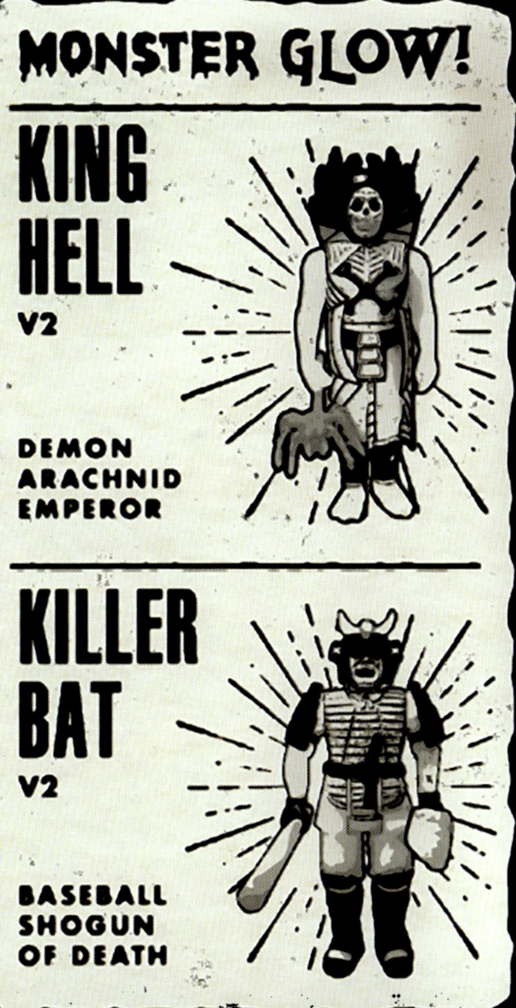

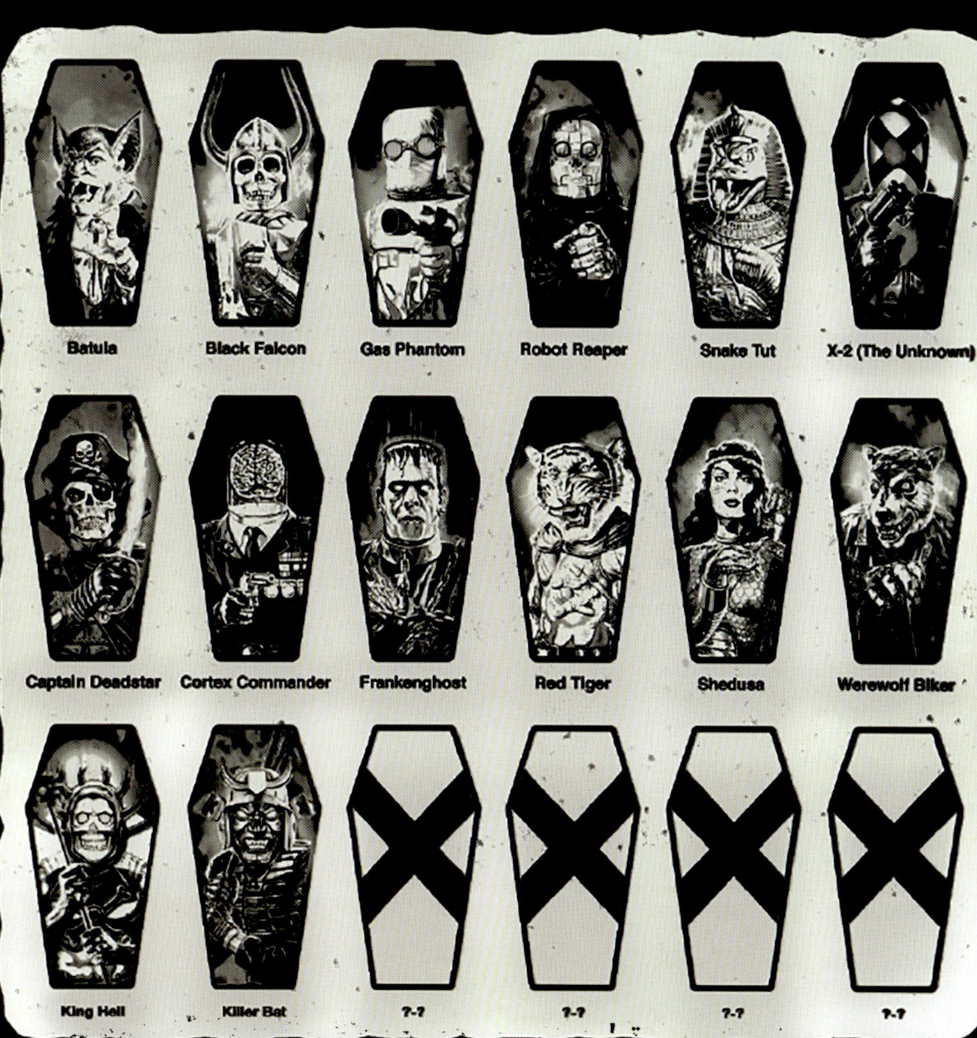

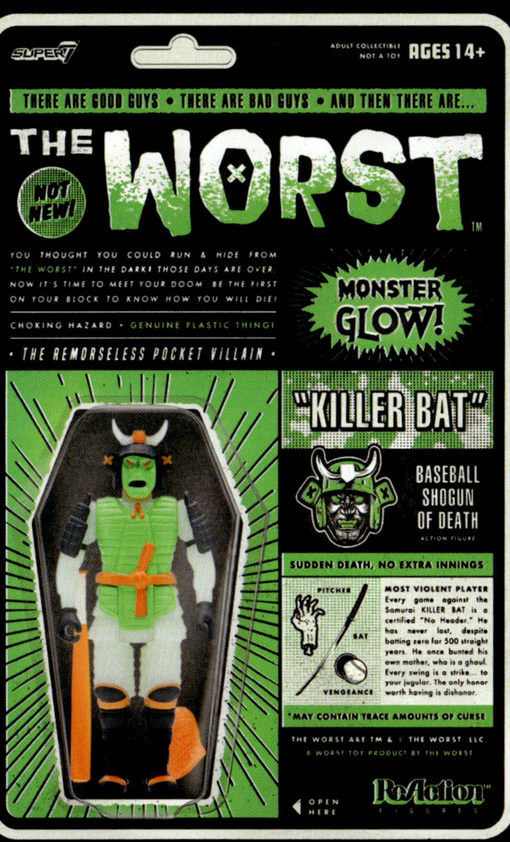

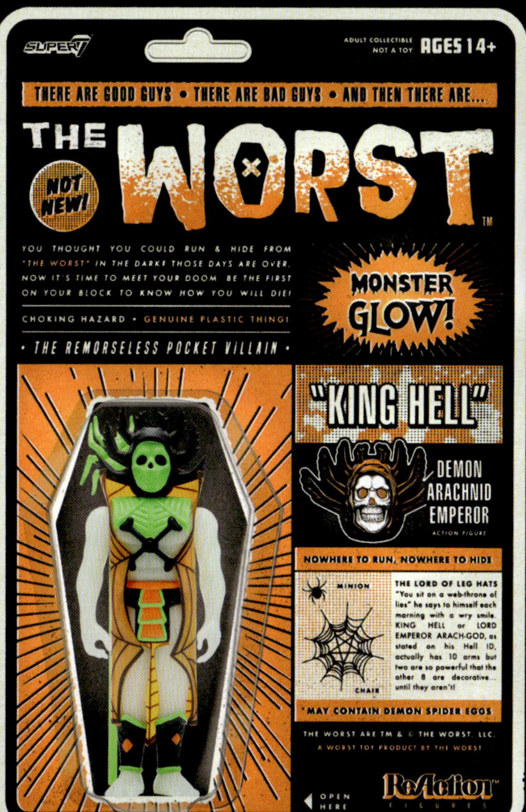

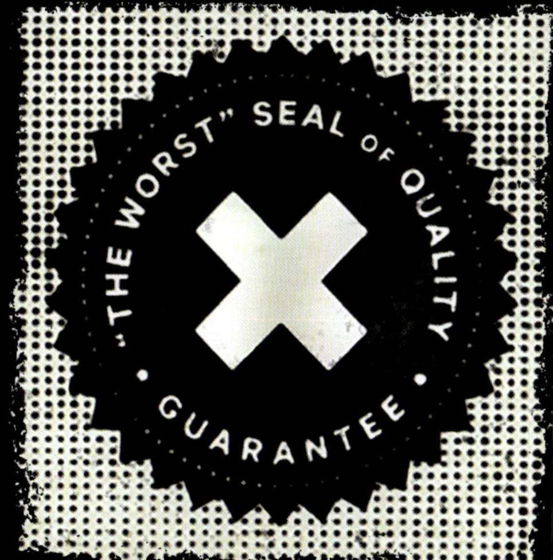

THIS SPREAD:
The Worst™ ReAction Figures™
and Keshi Surprise™

™ & © the Worst, LLC

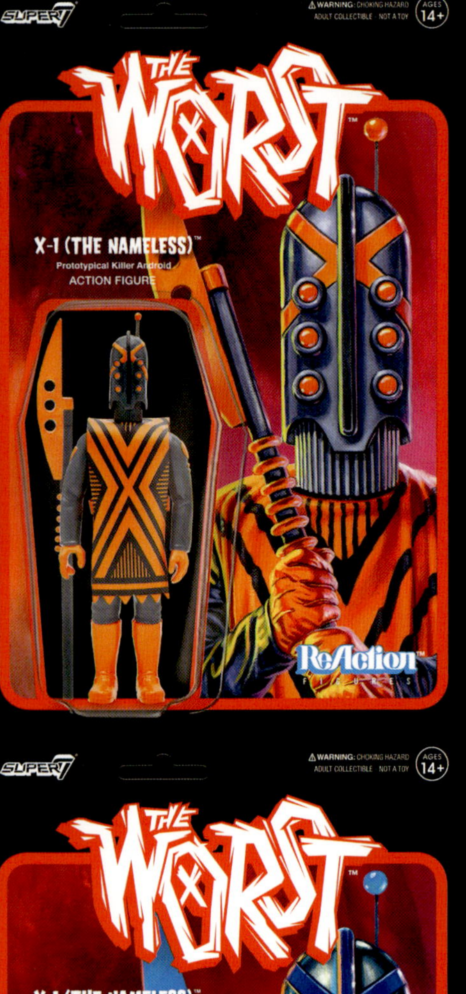
SUPER7
WARNING: CHOKING HAZARD
ADULT COLLECTIBLE · NOT A TOY
AGES 14+
THE WORST
X-1 (THE NAMELESS)
Prototypical Killer Android
ACTION FIGURE
ReAction
FIGURES

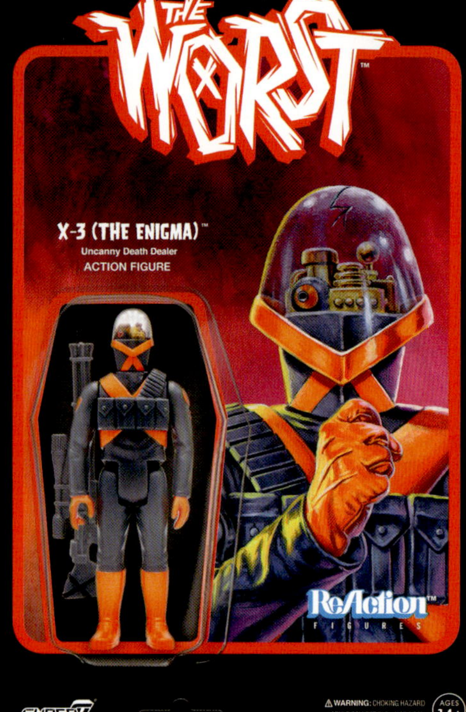
SUPER7
WARNING: CHOKING HAZARD
ADULT COLLECTIBLE · NOT A TOY
AGES 14+
THE WORST
X-3 (THE ENIGMA)
Uncanny Death Dealer
ACTION FIGURE
ReAction
FIGURES

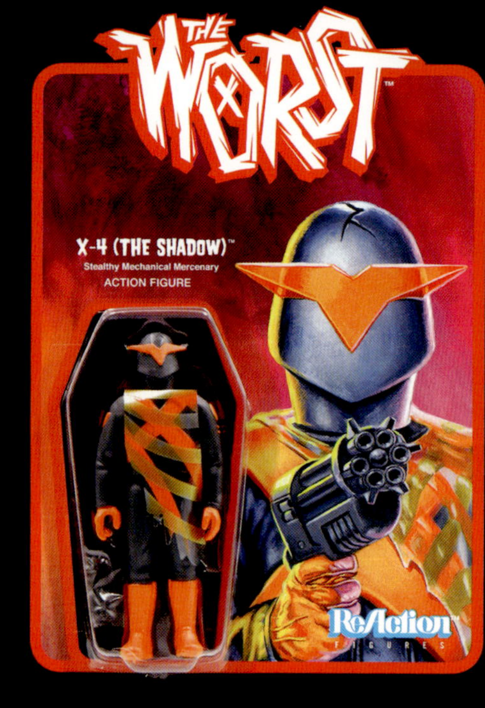
SUPER7
WARNING: CHOKING HAZARD
ADULT COLLECTIBLE · NOT A TOY
AGES 14+
THE WORST
X-4 (THE SHADOW)
Stealthy Mechanical Mercenary
ACTION FIGURE
ReAction

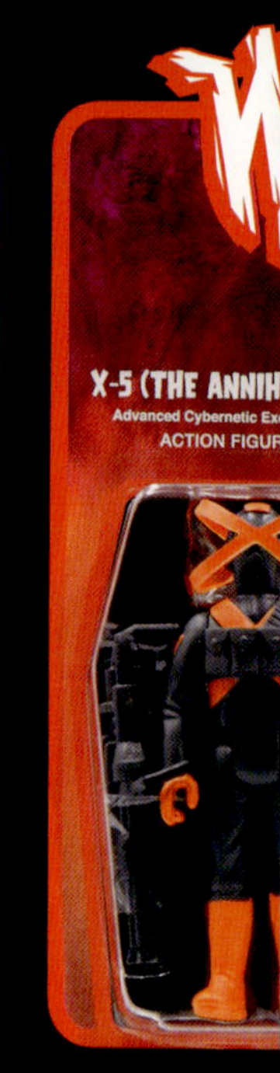
SUPER7

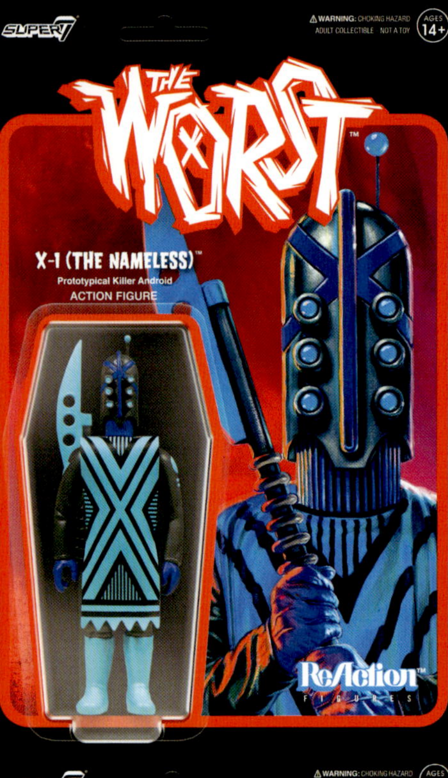
SUPER7
WARNING: CHOKING HAZARD
ADULT COLLECTIBLE · NOT A TOY
AGES 14+
THE WORST
X-1 (THE NAMELESS)
Prototypical Killer Android
ACTION FIGURE
ReAction
FIGURES

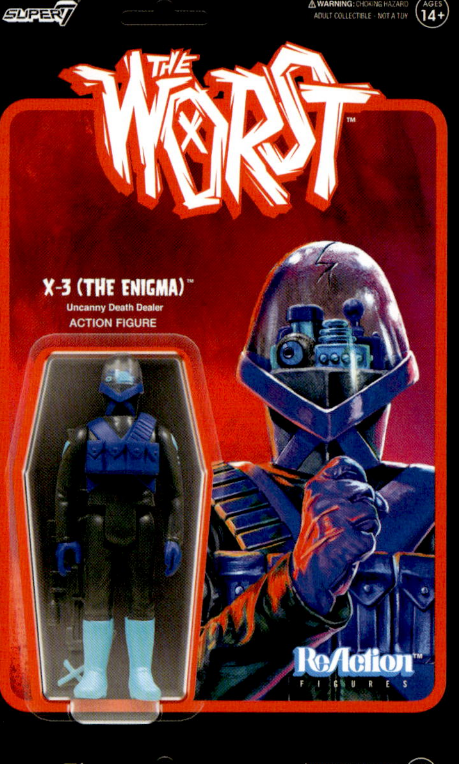
SUPER7
WARNING: CHOKING HAZARD
ADULT COLLECTIBLE · NOT A TOY
AGES 14+
THE WORST
X-3 (THE ENIGMA)
Uncanny Death Dealer
ACTION FIGURE
ReAction
FIGURES

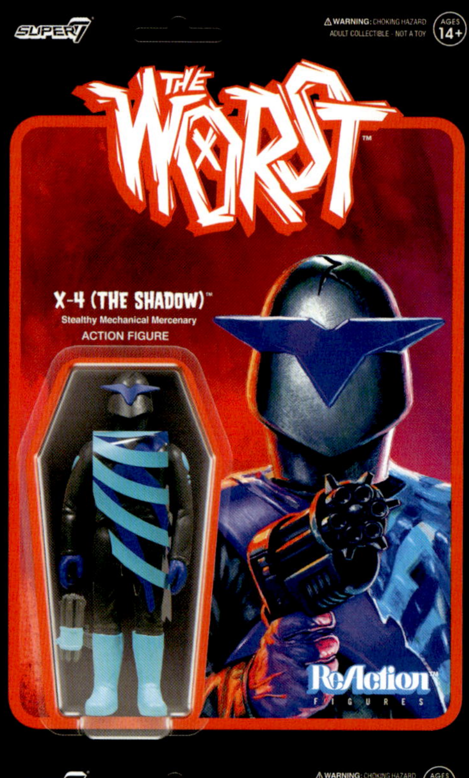
SUPER7
WARNING: CHOKING HAZARD
ADULT COLLECTIBLE · NOT A TOY
AGES 14+
THE WORST
X-4 (THE SHADOW)
Stealthy Mechanical Mercenary
ACTION FIGURE
ReAction
FIGURES

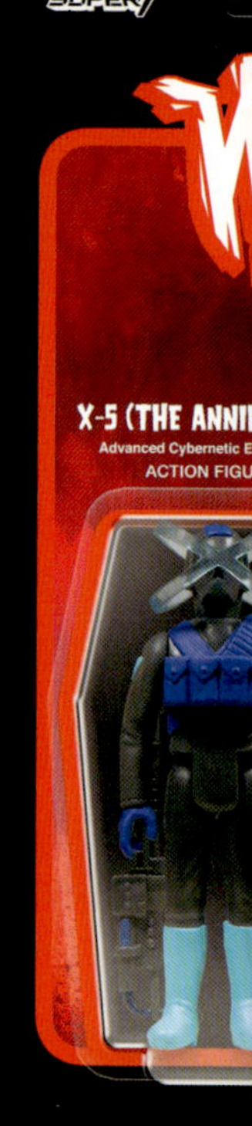

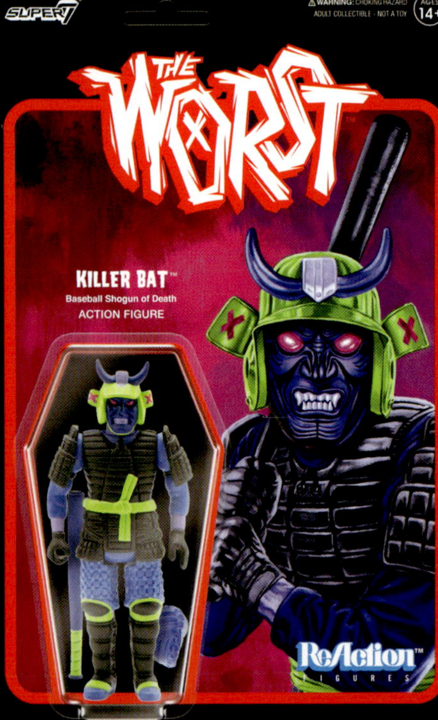
SUPER7
WARNING: CHOKING HAZARD
ADULT COLLECTIBLE · NOT A TOY
AGES 14+
THE WORST
KILLER BAT
Baseball Shogun of Death
ACTION FIGURE
ReAction
FIGURES

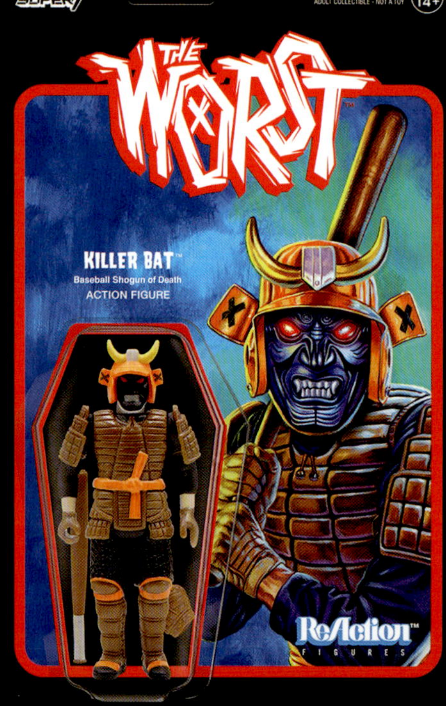
SUPER7
WARNING: CHOKING HAZARD
ADULT COLLECTIBLE · NOT A TOY
AGES 14+
THE WORST
KILLER BAT
Baseball Shogun of Death
ACTION FIGURE
ReAction
FIGURES

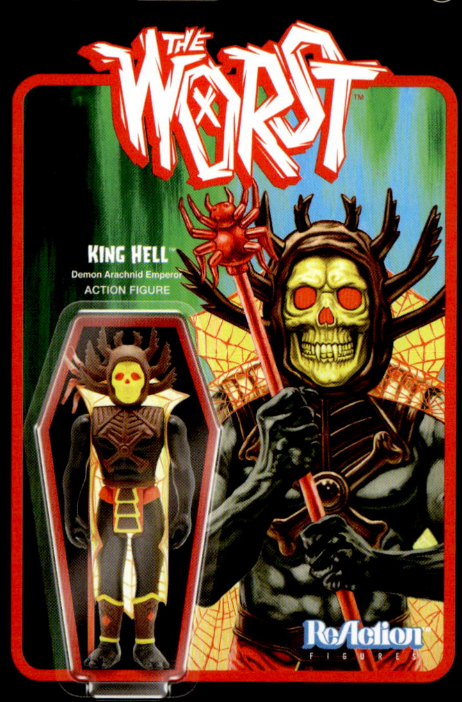
SUPER7
WARNING: CHOKING HAZARD
ADULT COLLECTIBLE · NOT A TOY
AGES 14+
THE WORST
KING HELL
Demon Arachnid Emperor
ACTION FIGURE
ReAction
FIGURES

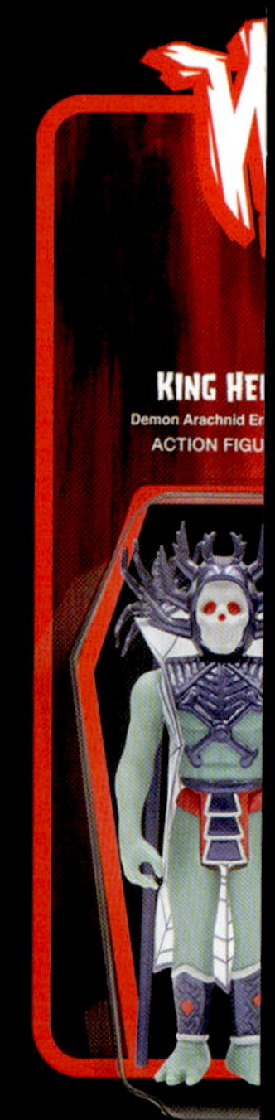
SUPER7

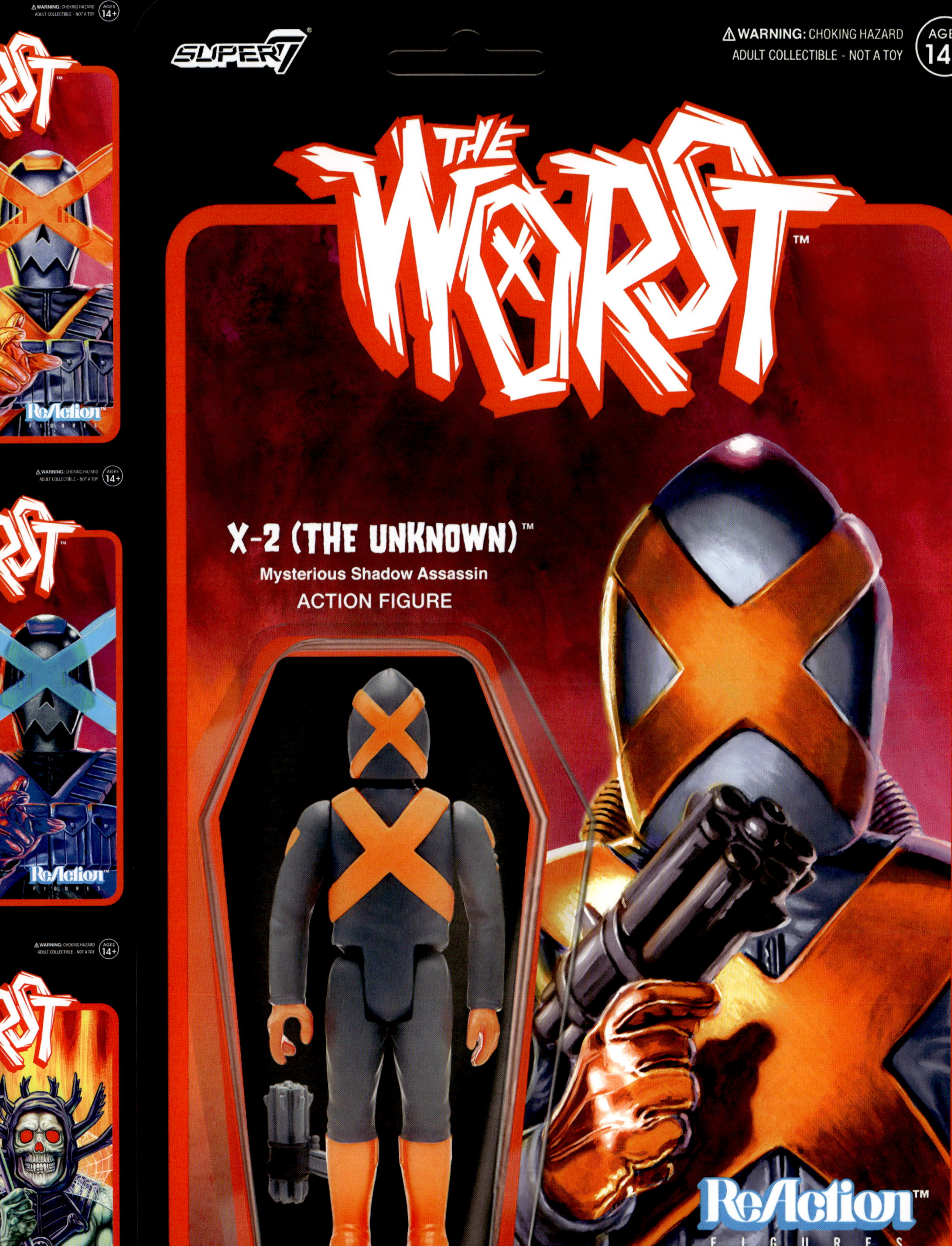
SUPER7
⚠ WARNING: CHOKING HAZARD
ADULT COLLECTIBLE - NOT A TOY
AGES 14+
THE WORST™
X-2 (THE UNKNOWN)™
Mysterious Shadow Assassin
ACTION FIGURE
ReAction™
FIGURES
™ & © the Worst, LLC

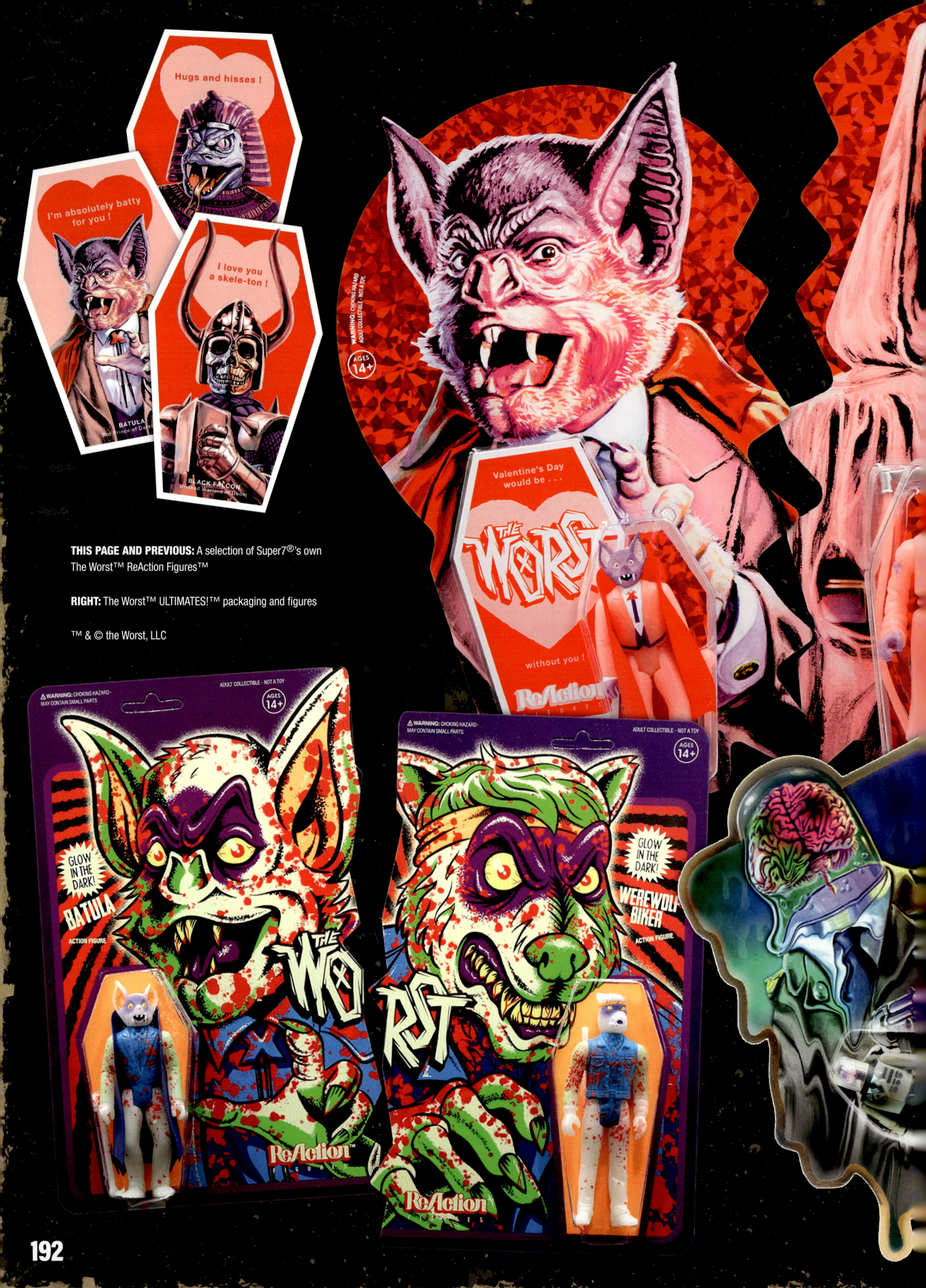

THIS PAGE AND PREVIOUS: A selection of Super7®'s own The Worst™ ReAction Figures™

RIGHT: The Worst™ ULTIMATES!™ packaging and figures

™ & © the Worst, LLC

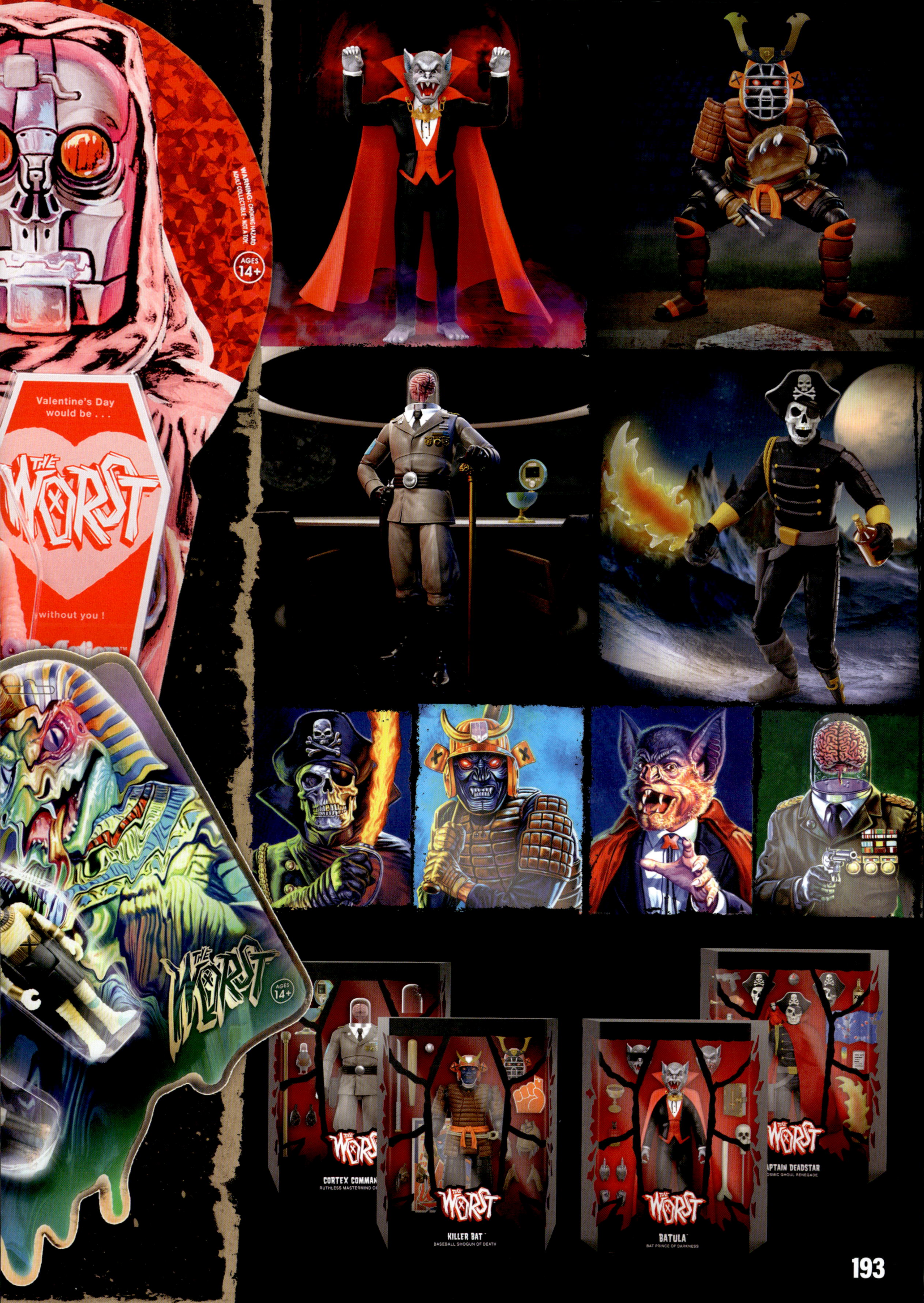

WARNING: CHOKING HAZARD
ADULT COLLECTIBLE - NOT A TOY.
AGES 14+
Valentine's Day
would be . . .
THE WORST
without you !
THE WORST
AGES 14+
THE WORST
CORTEX COMMAN
THE WORST
KILLER BAT
BASEBALL SHOGUN OF DEATH
THE WORST
BATULA
BAT PRINCE OF DARKNESS
THE WORST
APTAIN DEADSTAR

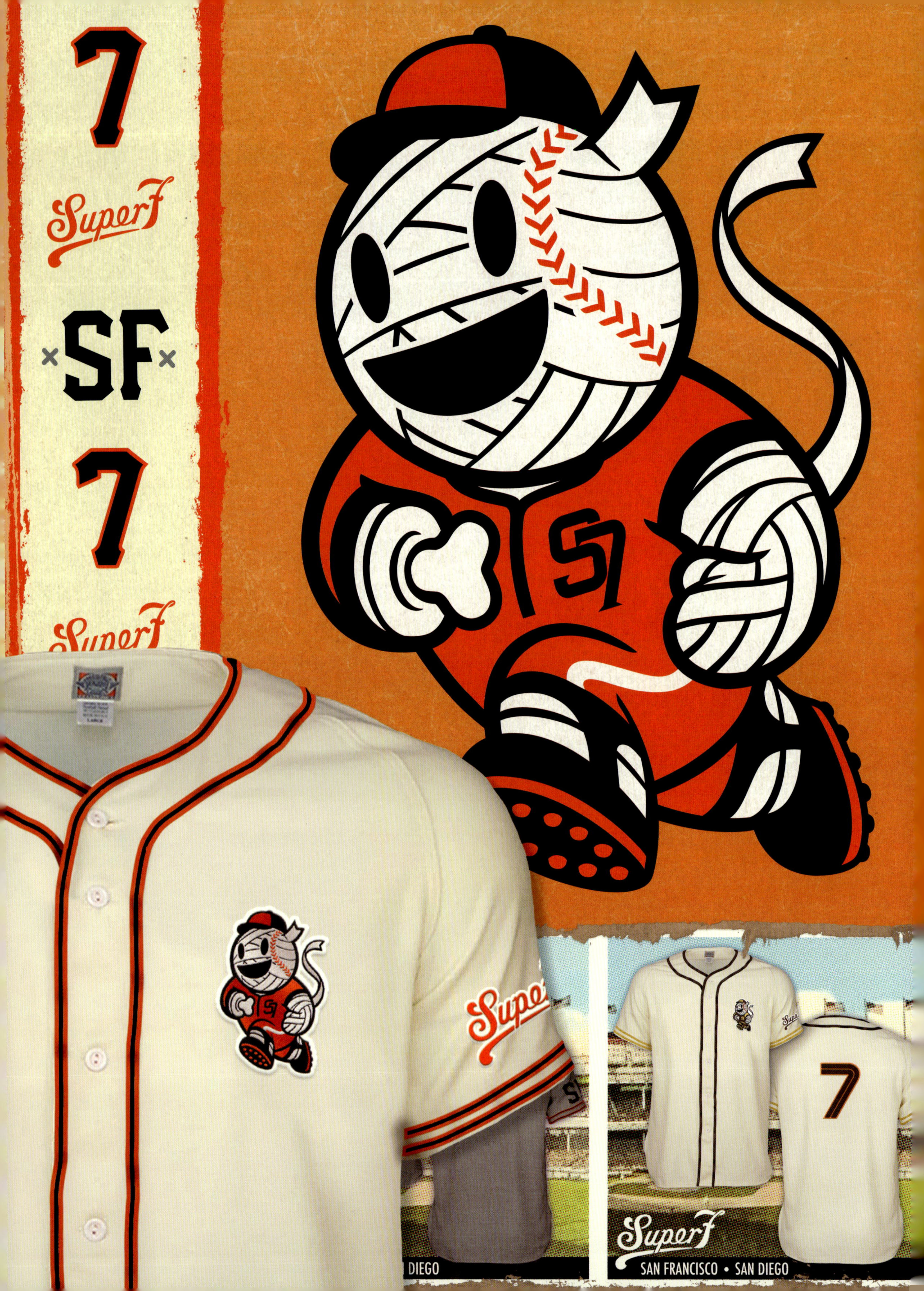

7

Superf

SF

7

Superf

DIEGO

Superf

SAN FRANCISCO • SAN DIEGO

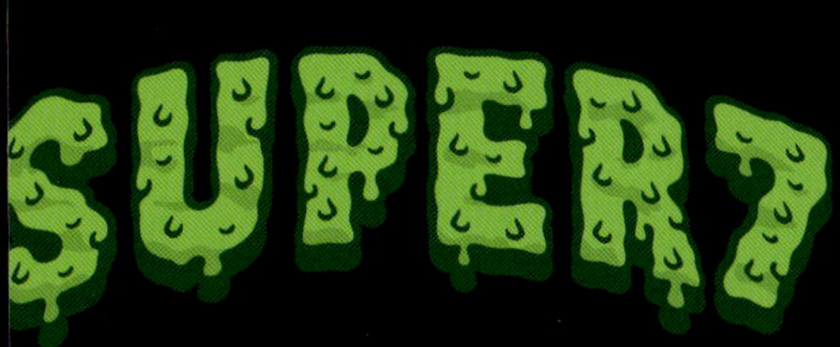

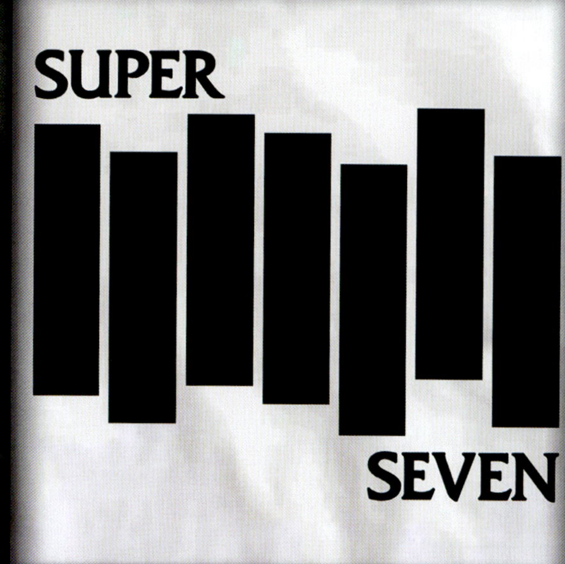

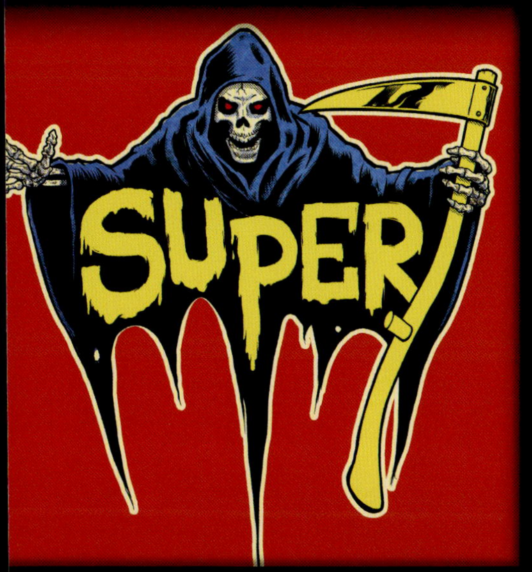

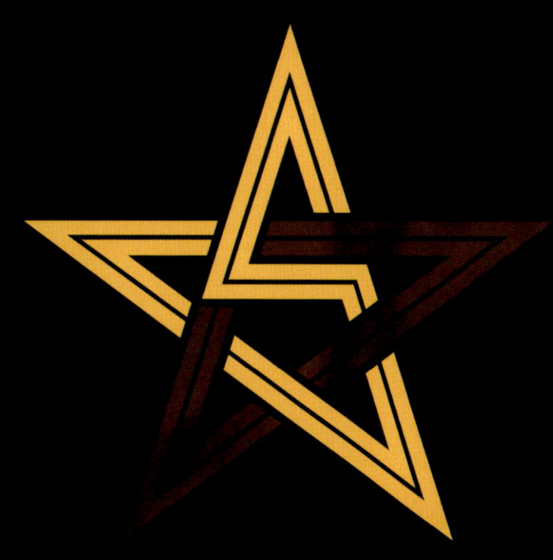

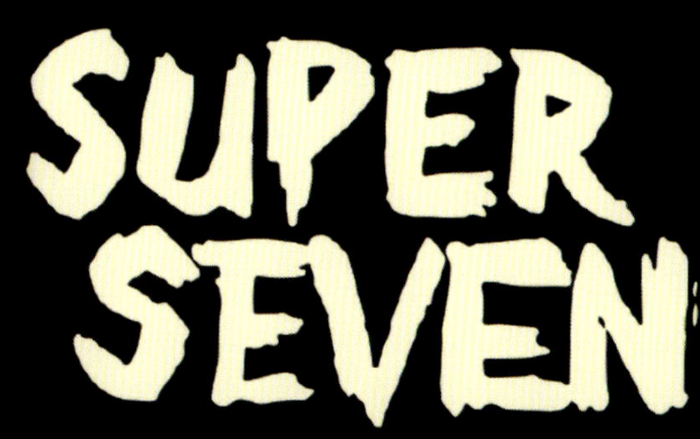

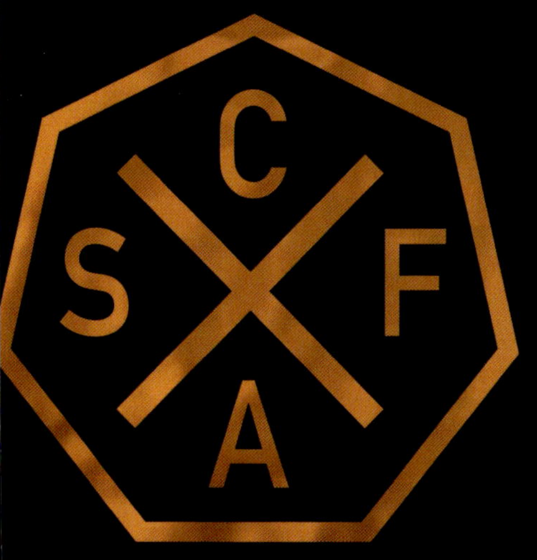

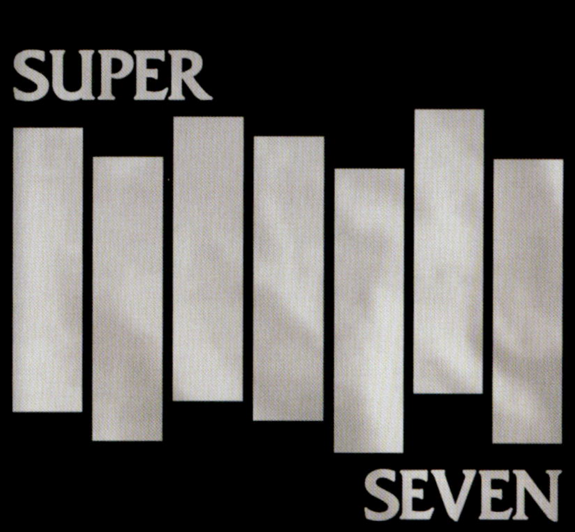

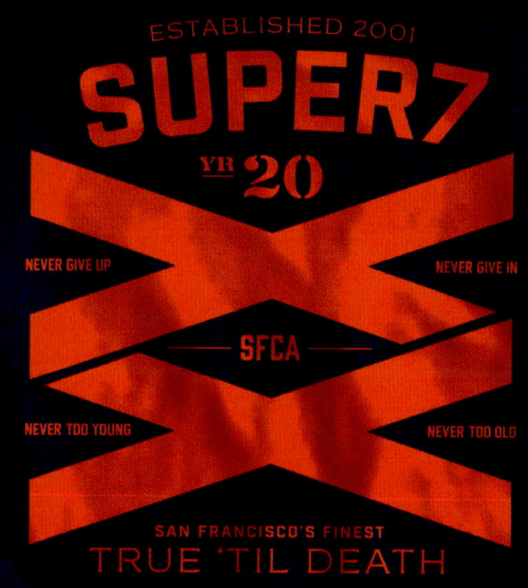

SUPER7
AGAINST
THE WORLD

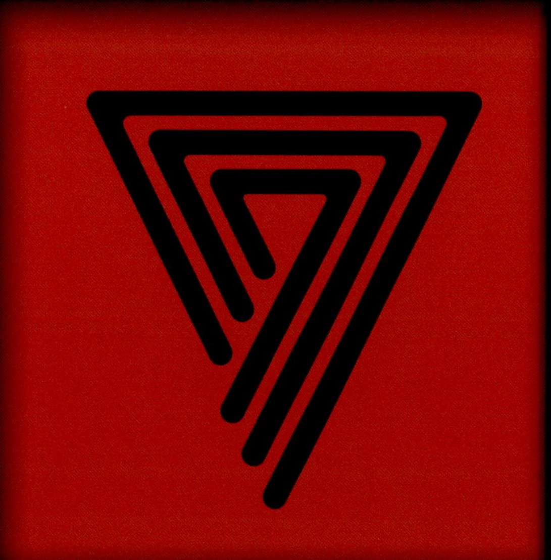

THIS SPREAD: Selected Super7® brand apparel

© 2025 Super7 OpCo, LLC

⚠ WARNING: CHOKING HAZARD - MAY CONTAIN SMALL PARTS

ADULT COLLECTIBLE - NOT A TOY

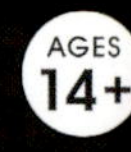

PHANTOM STARKILLER

RHAMNUSIA'S REVENGE
ACTION PLAYSET

INCLUDES ALL NEW! SPACE GLOW FIGURES

SOME ASSEMBLY REQUIRED.
ACTION FIGURES INCLUDED.

CONTENTS: Aquatic Moon Base and Cosmic Backdrop

ReAction™ FIGURES

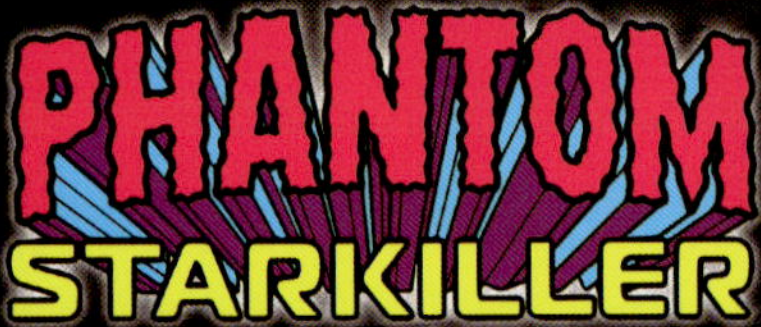

RHAMNUSIA'S REVENGE
ACTION PLAYSET

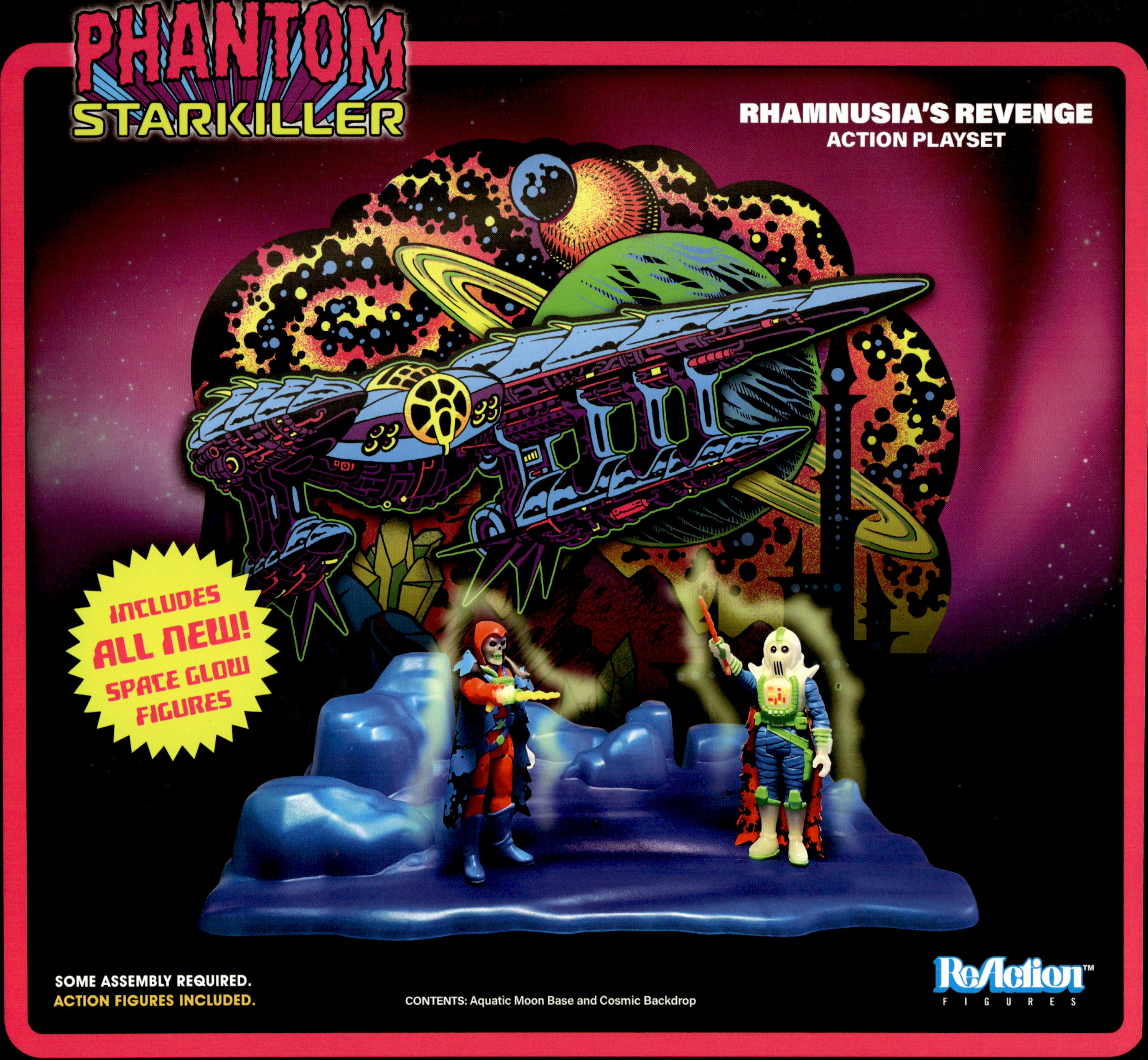

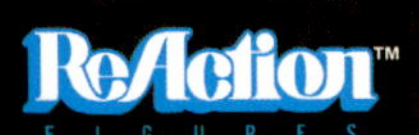

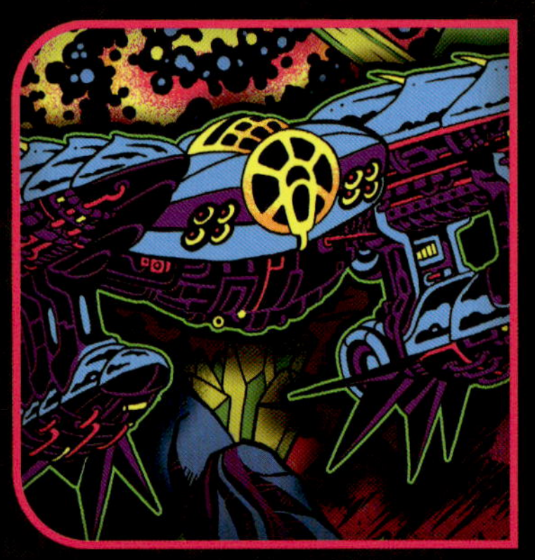

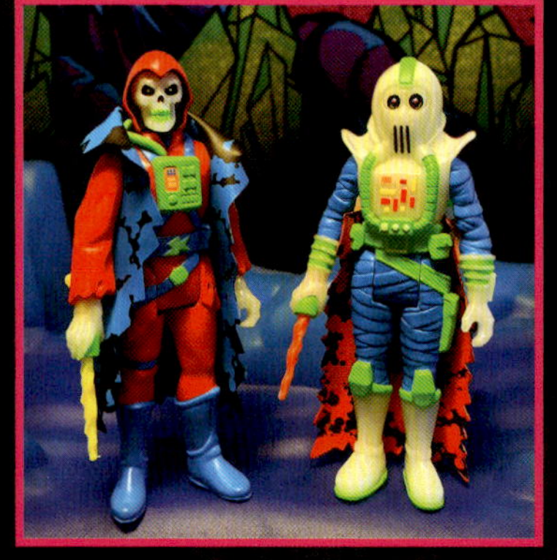

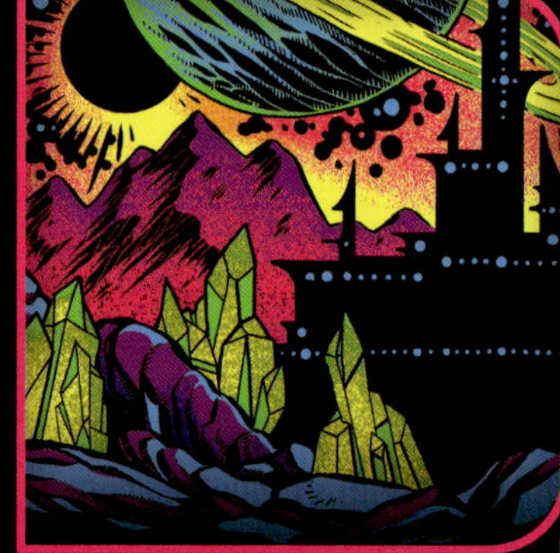

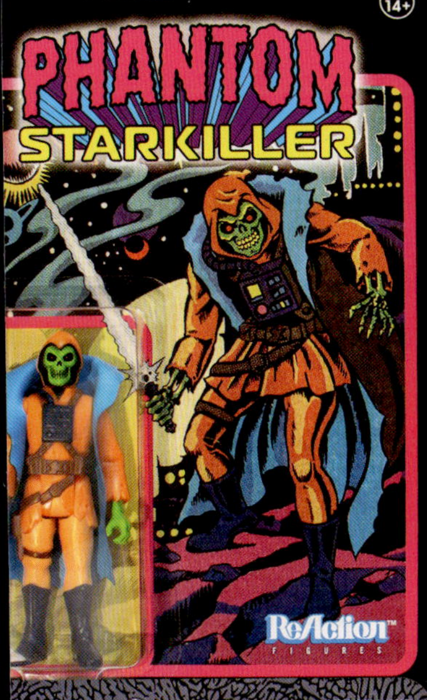

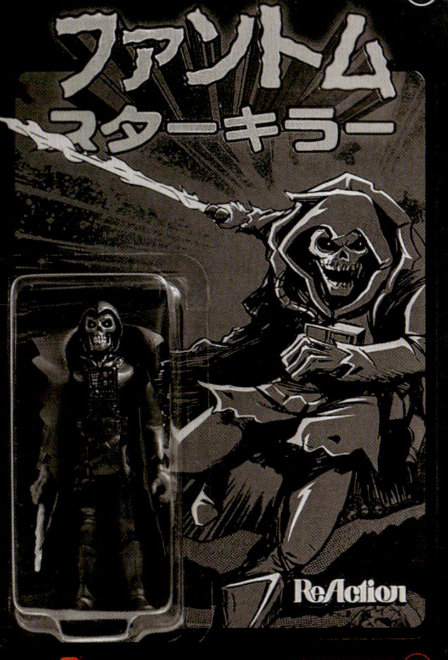

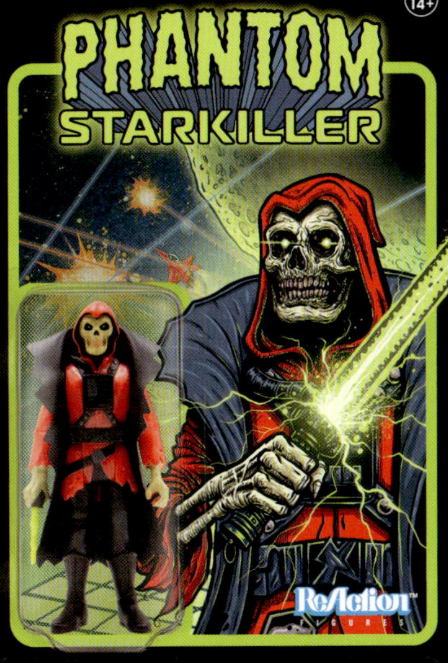

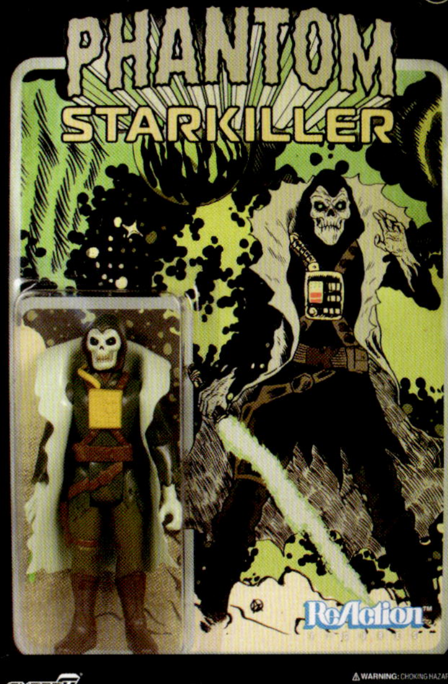

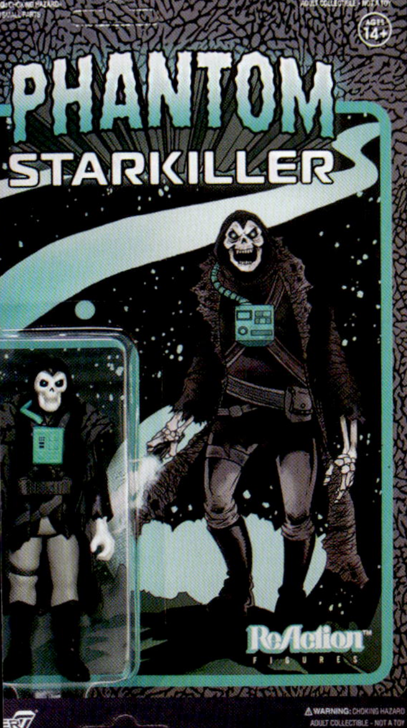

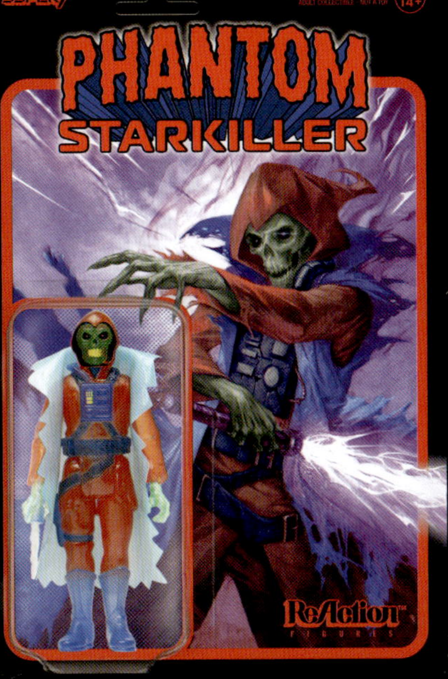

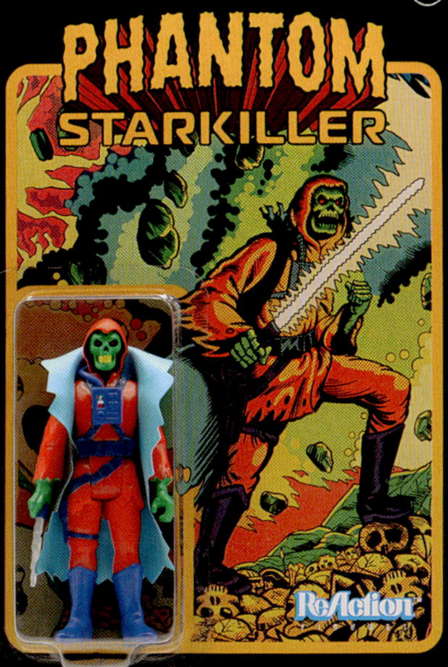

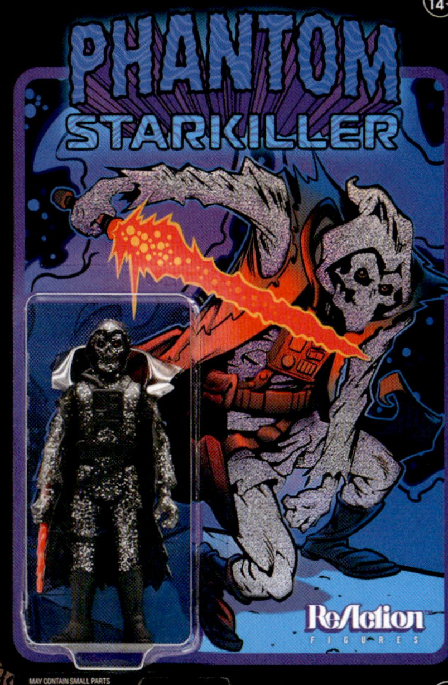

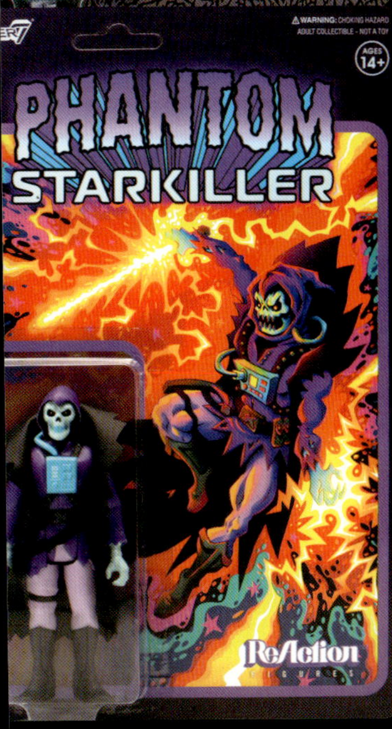

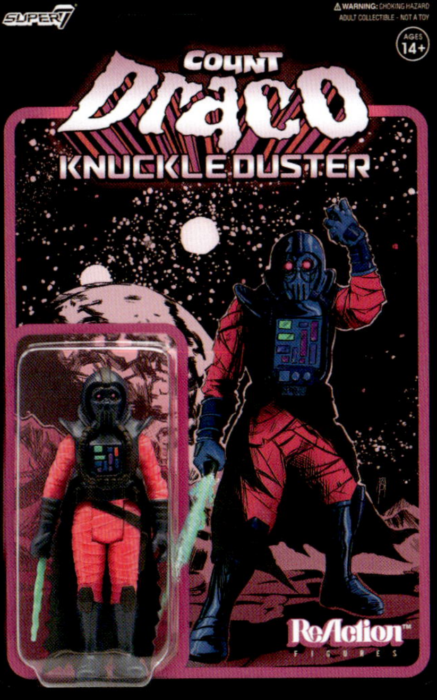

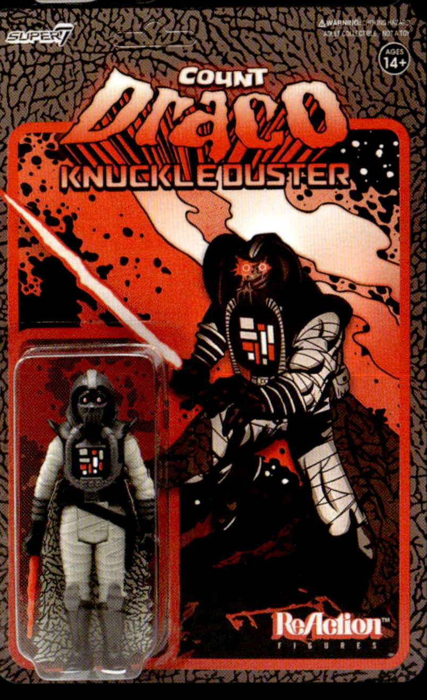

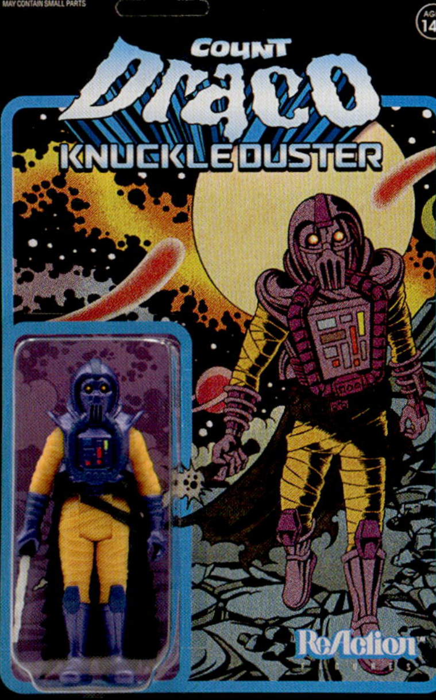

LEFT: Phantom Starkiller playset box art

ABOVE: Selected ReAction Figures™ cards from the Killer Bootlegs Universe

© Killer Bootlegs
© 2025 Super7 OpCo, LLC

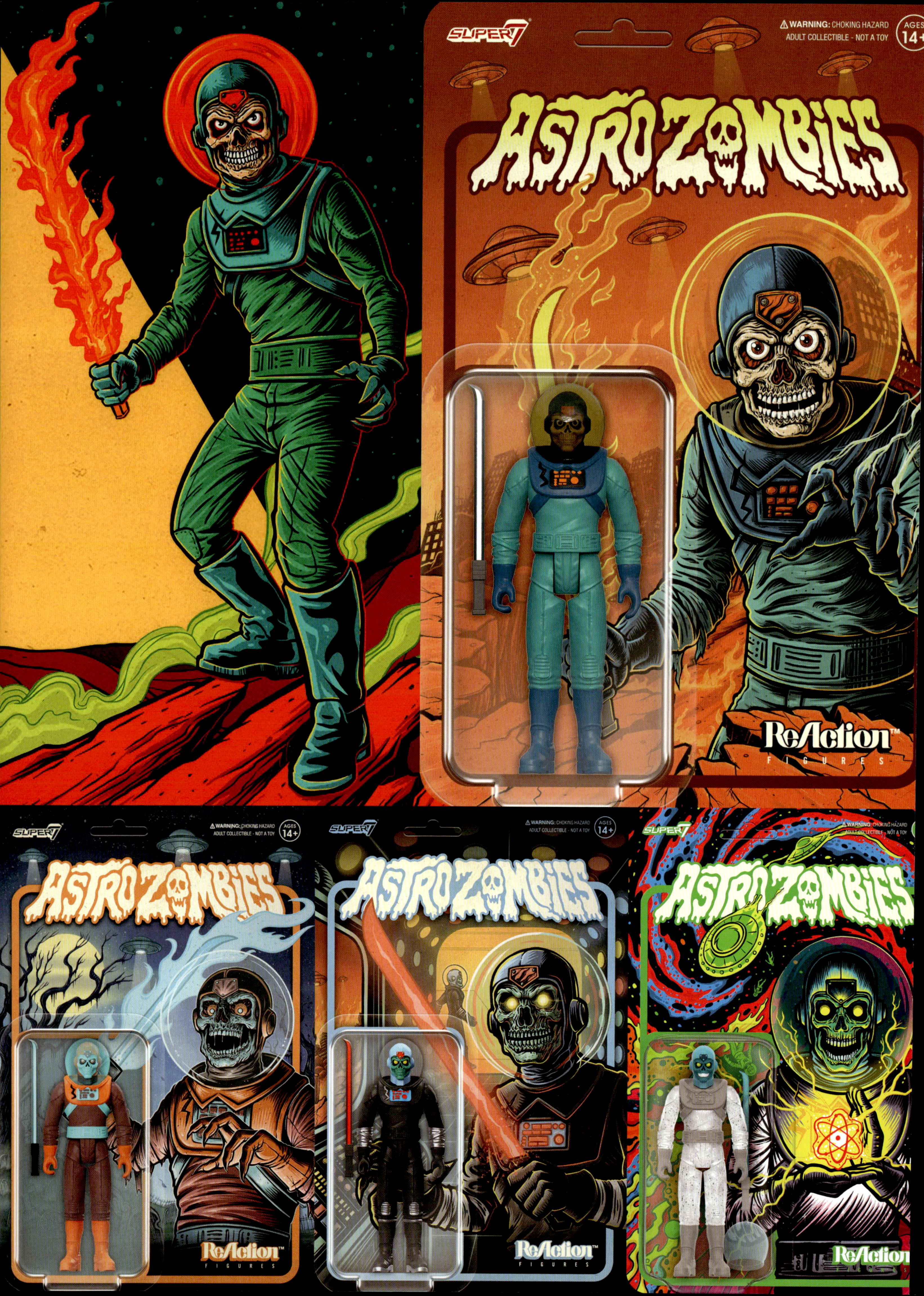

SUPER7
WARNING: CHOKING HAZARD
ADULT COLLECTIBLE - NOT A TOY
AGES 14+
ASTRO ZOMBIES
ReAction
FIGURES

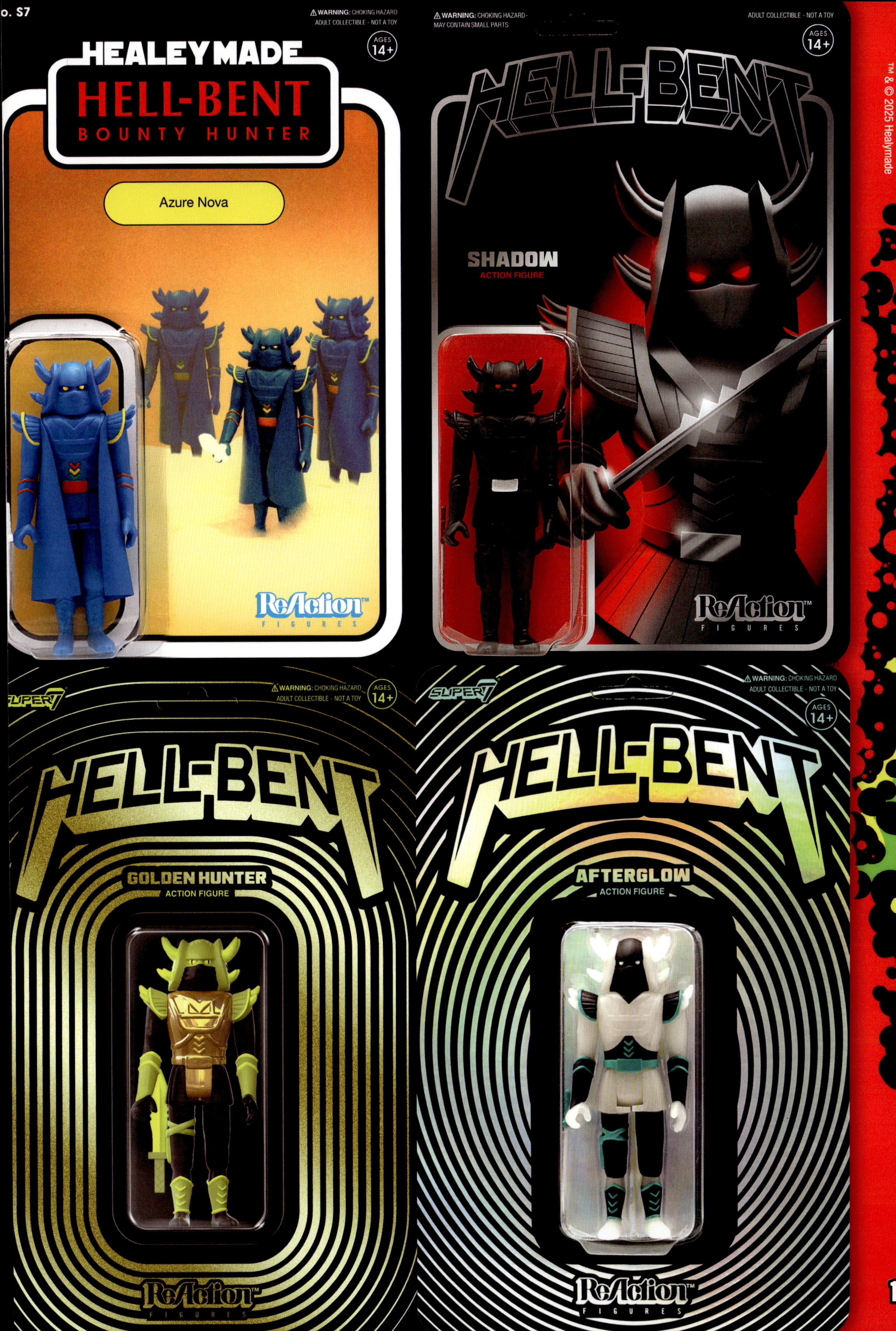

© Tim Baron
TM & © 2025 Healymade

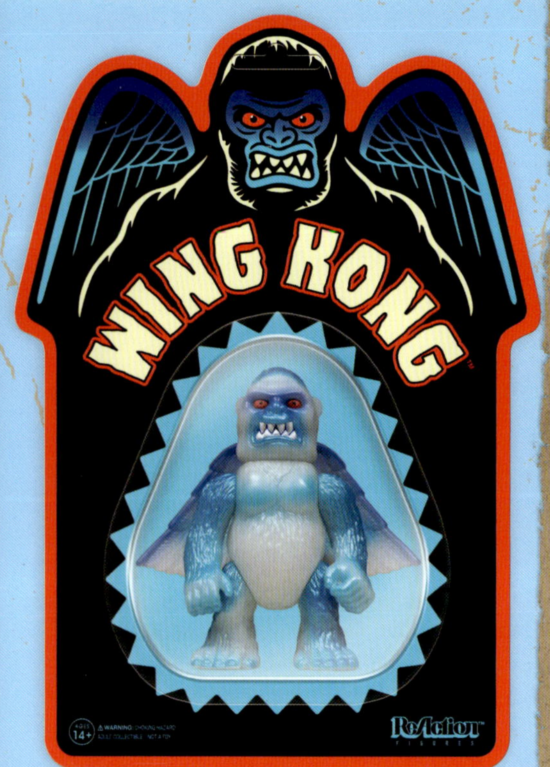

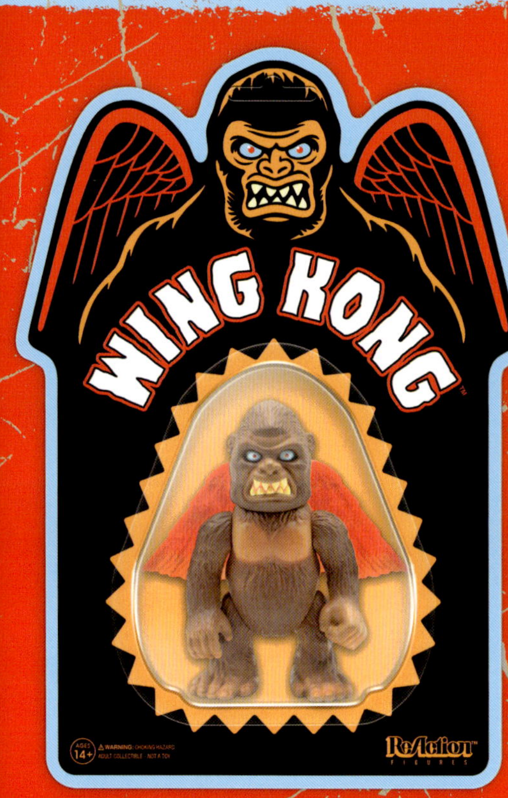

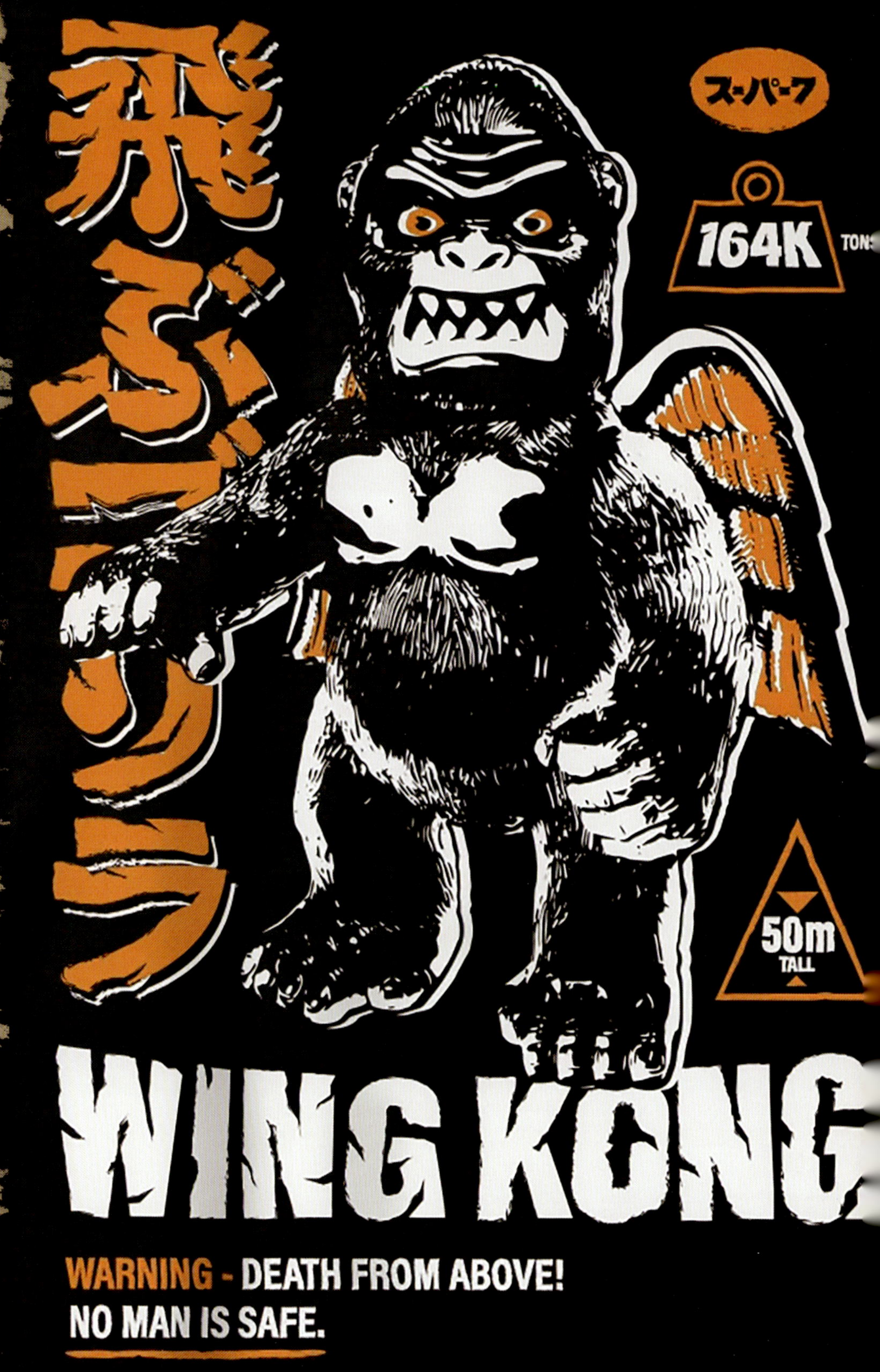

飛ぶゴリラ

スーパーフ

164K TONS

50m TALL

WING KONG

WARNING - DEATH FROM ABOVE!
NO MAN IS SAFE.

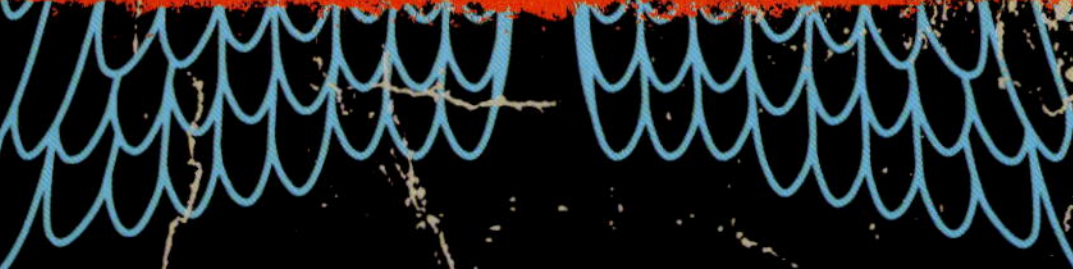

WING KONG

THE "WING KONG" IS A BIPEDAL, WINGED SIMIAN THOUGHT TO BE ONLY A MYTH. ESTIMATED 18 - 20 FEET IN HEIGHT AND WEIGHING 164,000 TONS, IT IS A TRUE WONDER HOW THIS CREATURE REMAINS ELUSIVE IN THE WILD!

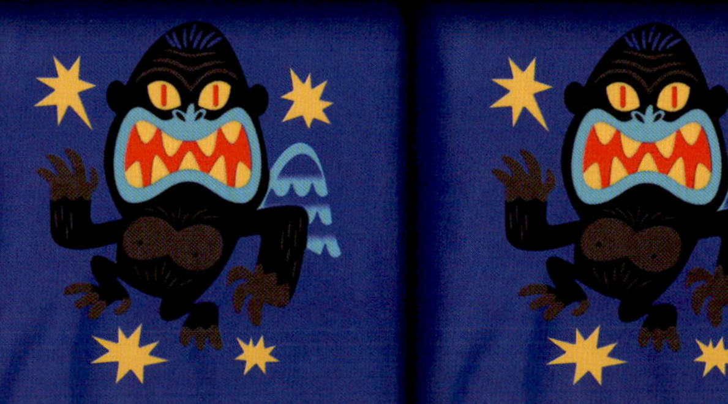

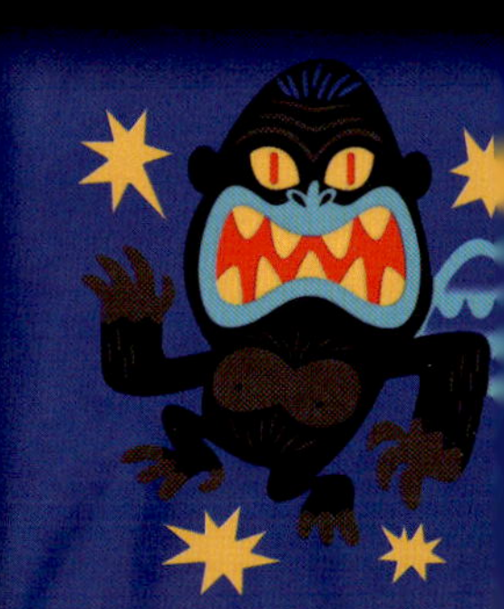

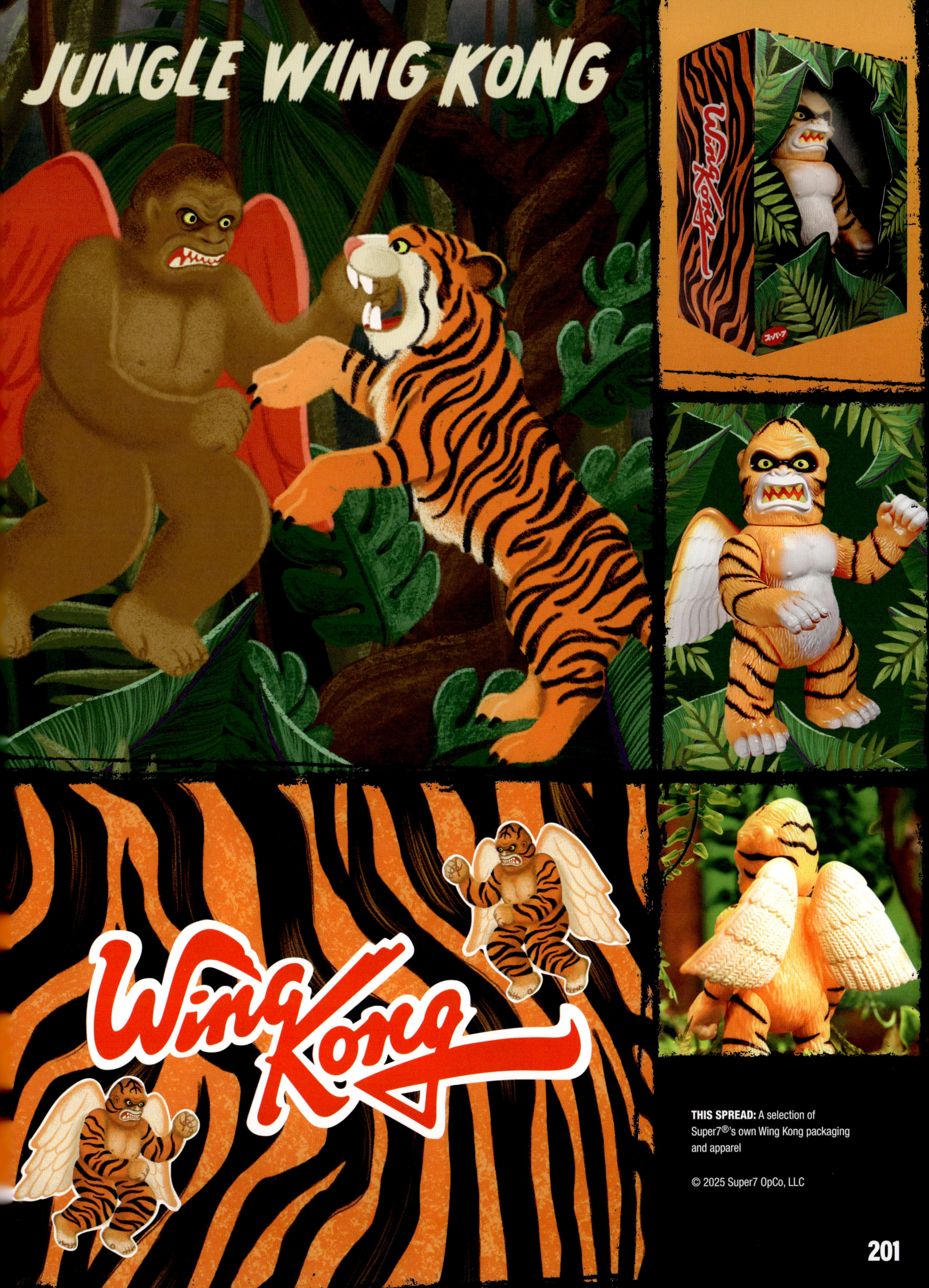

THIS SPREAD: A selection of Super7®'s own Wing Kong packaging and apparel

© 2025 Super7 OpCo, LLC

マミーボーイ

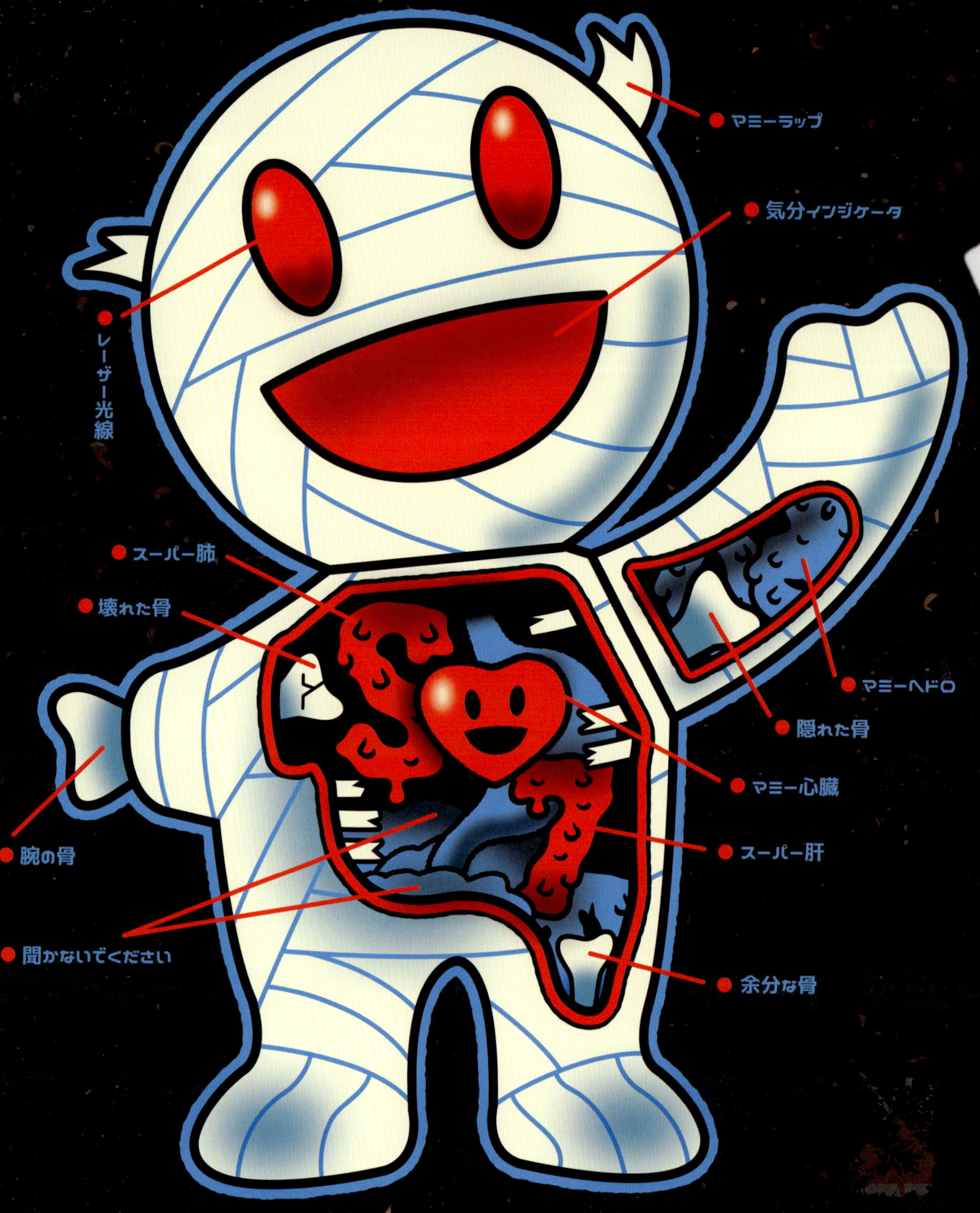

マミーラップ
気分インジケータ
レーザー光線
スーパー肺
壊れた骨
マミーヘドロ
隠れた骨
マミー心臓
腕の骨
スーパー肝
聞かないでください
余分な骨

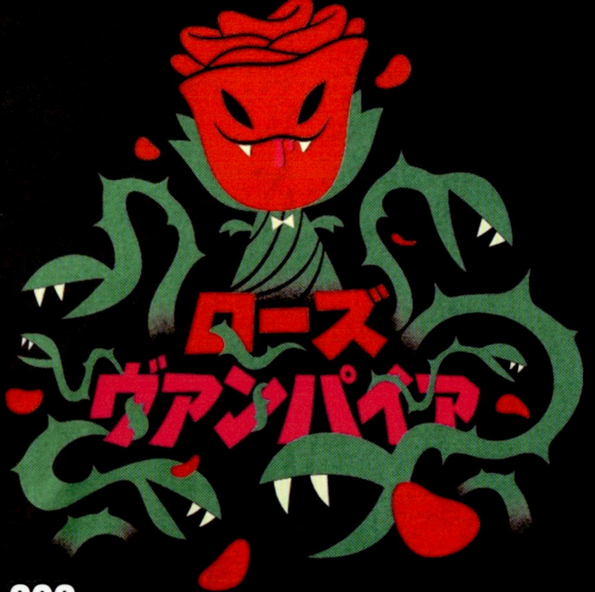

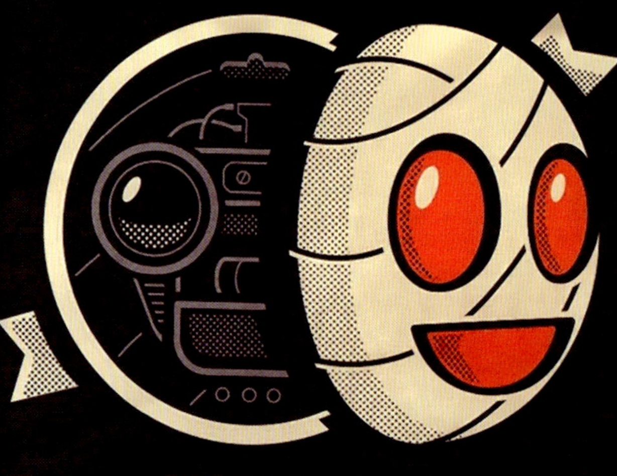
SUPER7 • スーパー7

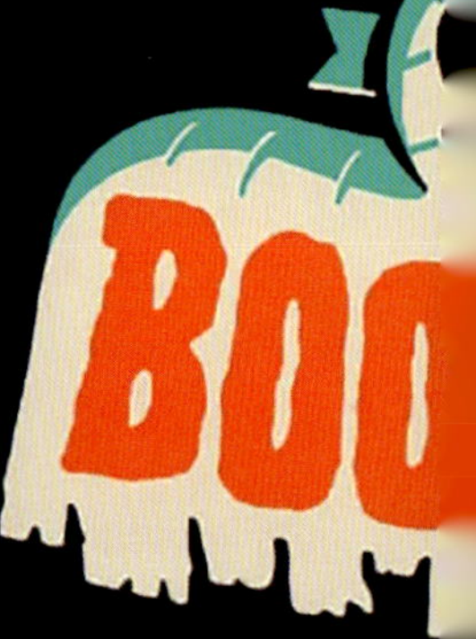

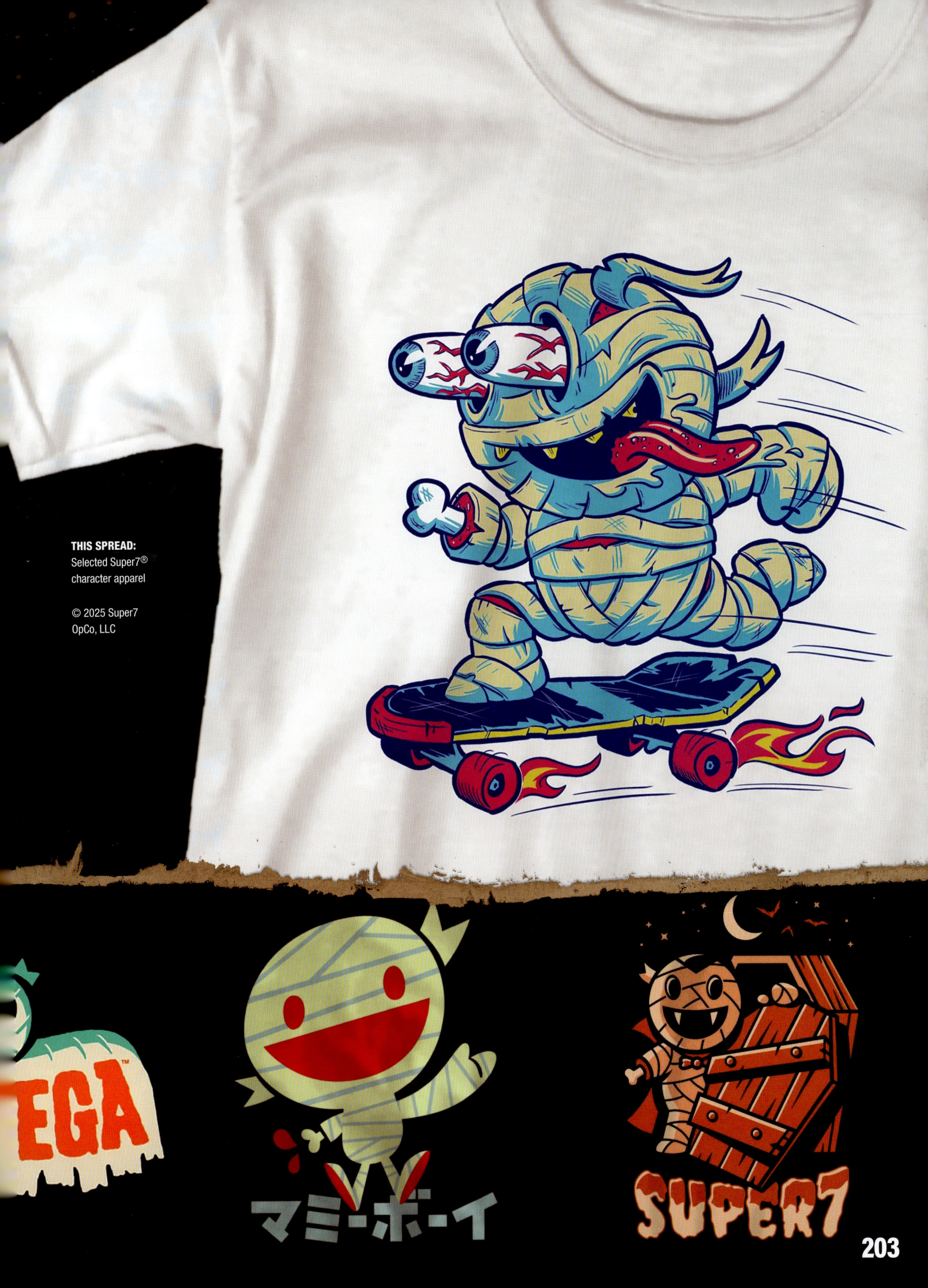

THIS SPREAD:
Selected Super7® character apparel

© 2025 Super7 OpCo, LLC

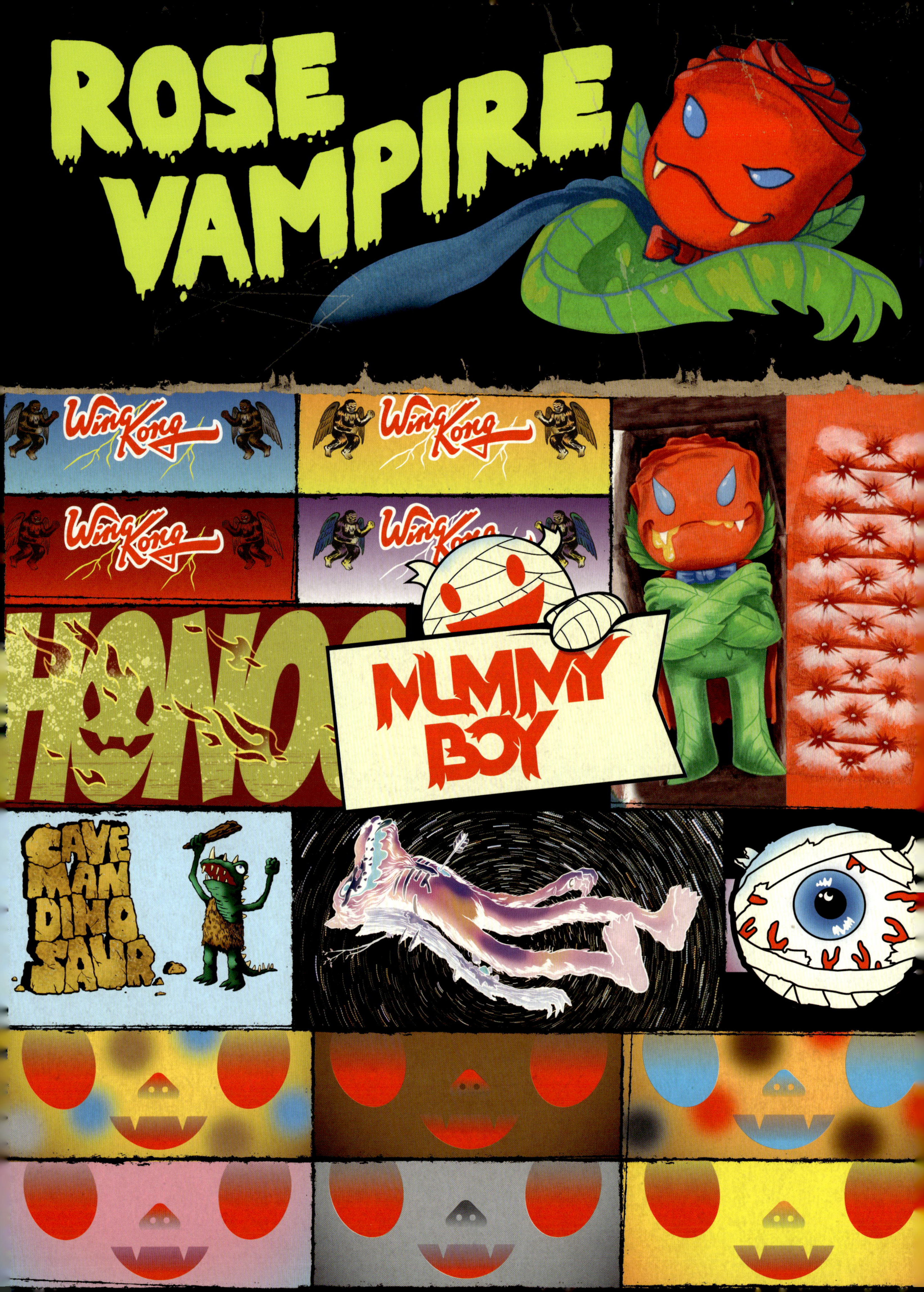
ROSE VAMPIRE
Wing Kong
Wing Kong
Wing Kong
MUMMY BOY
CAVE MAN DINO SAUR

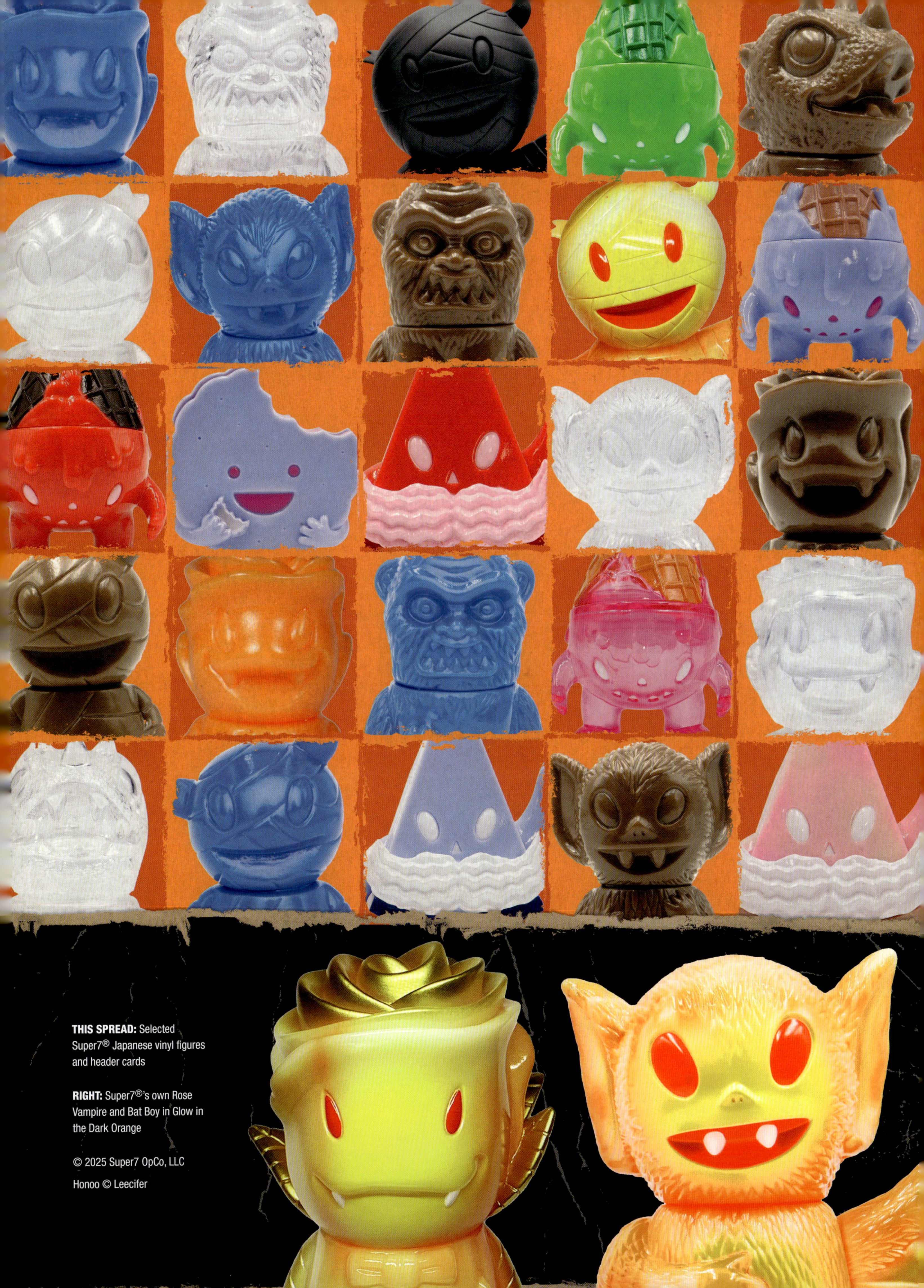

THIS SPREAD: Selected Super7® Japanese vinyl figures and header cards

RIGHT: Super7®'s own Rose Vampire and Bat Boy in Glow in the Dark Orange

© 2025 Super7 OpCo, LLC

Honoo © Leecifer

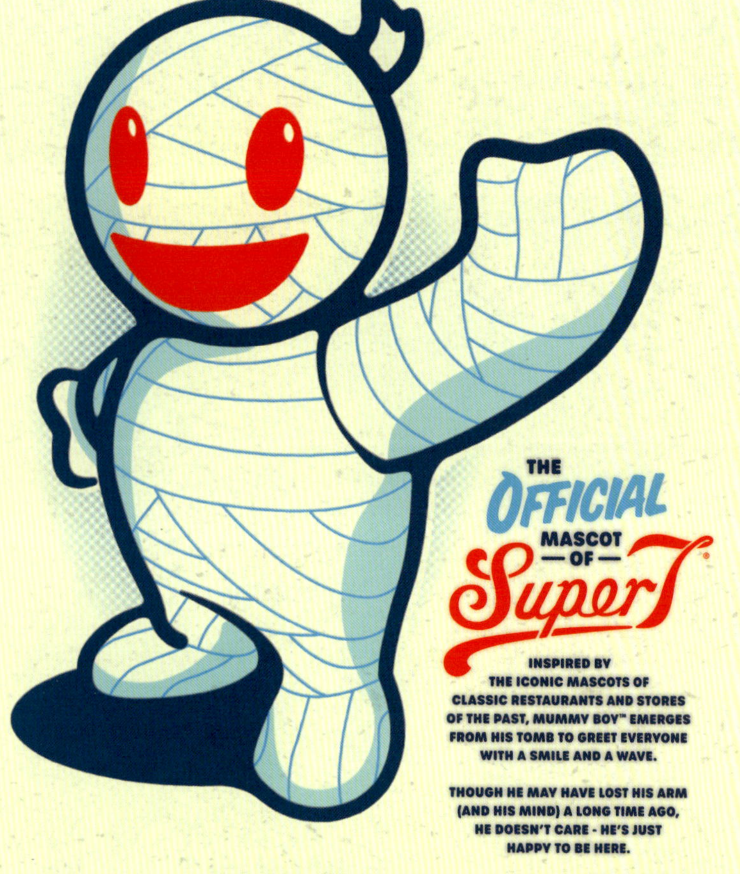
THE
OFFICIAL
MASCOT
—OF—
Super7
INSPIRED BY THE ICONIC MASCOTS OF CLASSIC RESTAURANTS AND STORES OF THE PAST, MUMMY BOY™ EMERGES FROM HIS TOMB TO GREET EVERYONE WITH A SMILE AND A WAVE.
THOUGH HE MAY HAVE LOST HIS ARM (AND HIS MIND) A LONG TIME AGO, HE DOESN'T CARE - HE'S JUST HAPPY TO BE HERE.

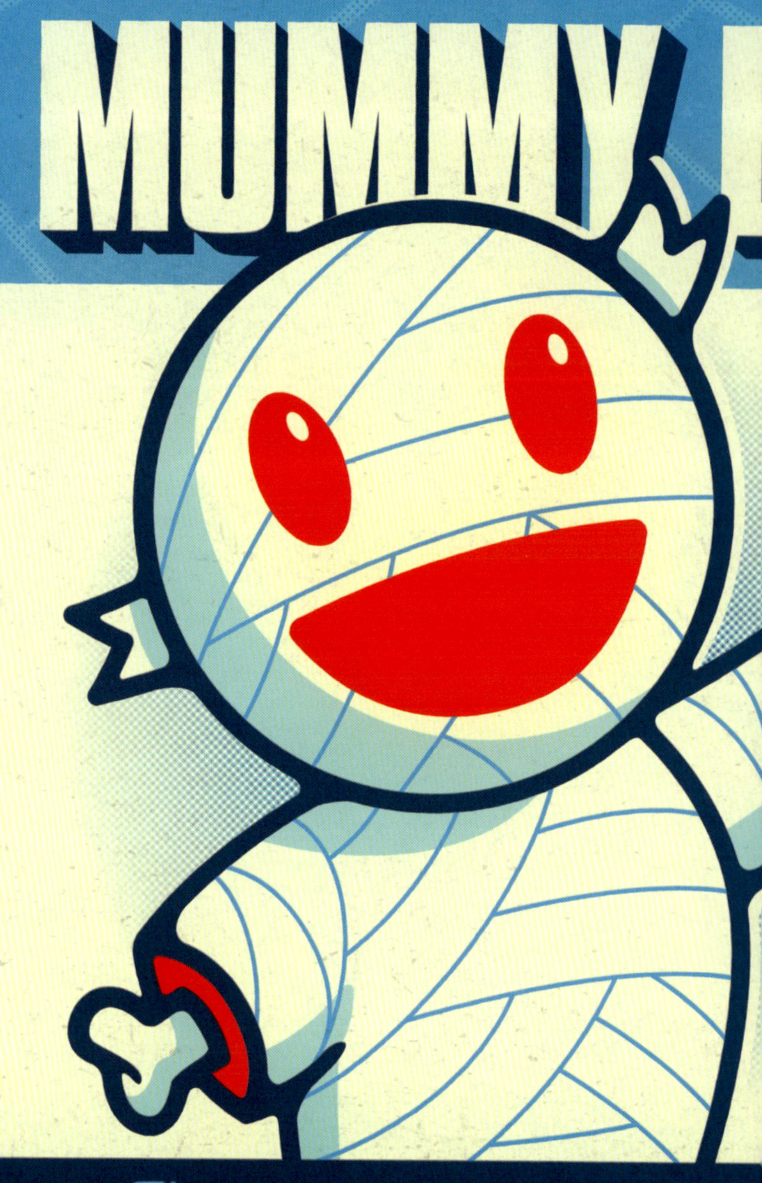
MUMMY B
SUPER7
AGES 14+

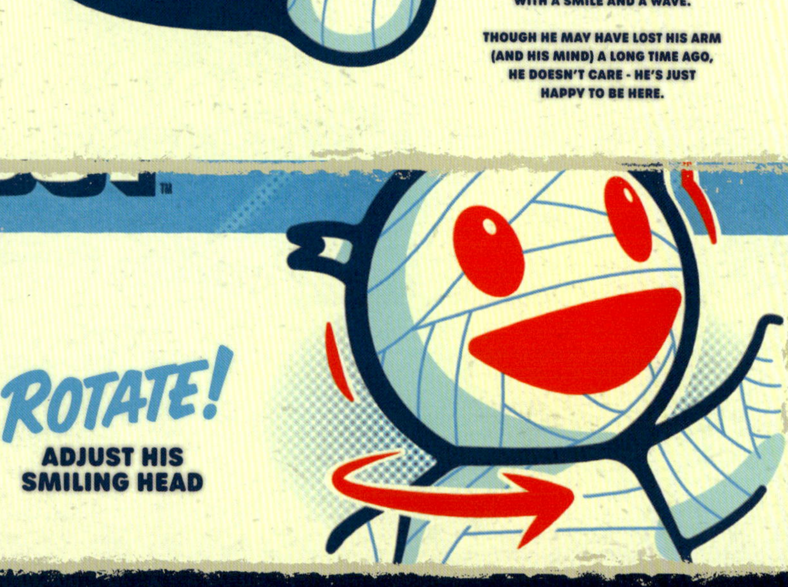
ROTATE!
ADJUST HIS SMILING HEAD

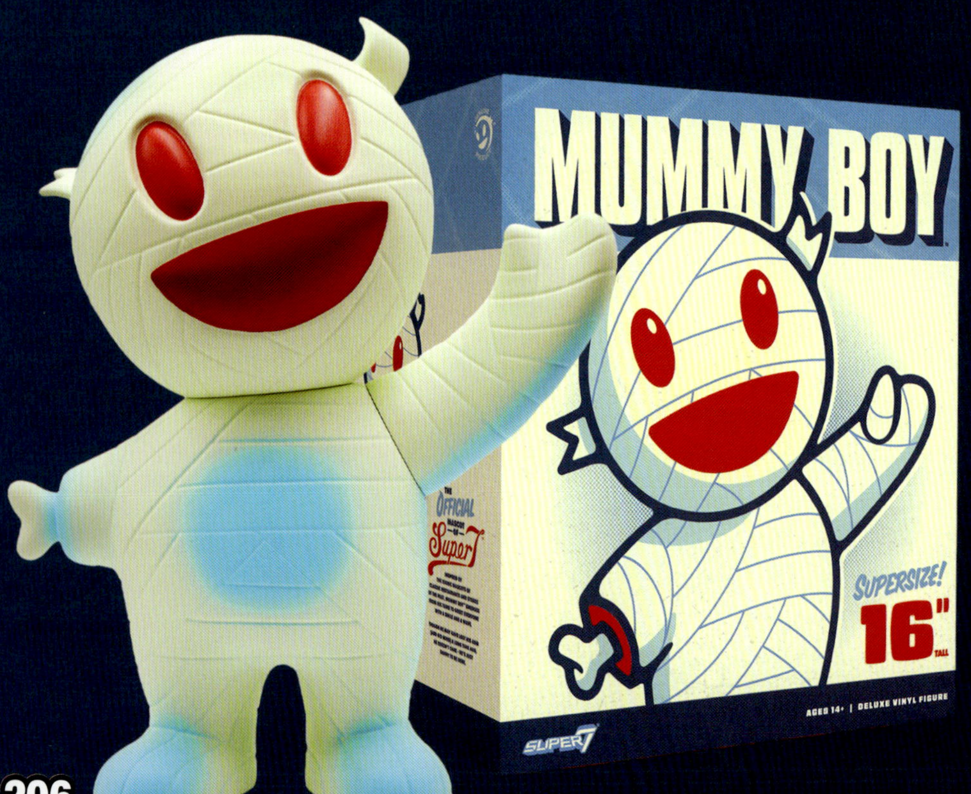
MUMMY BOY
SUPERSIZE!
16" TALL
AGES 14+ | DELUXE VINYL FIGURE
SUPER7

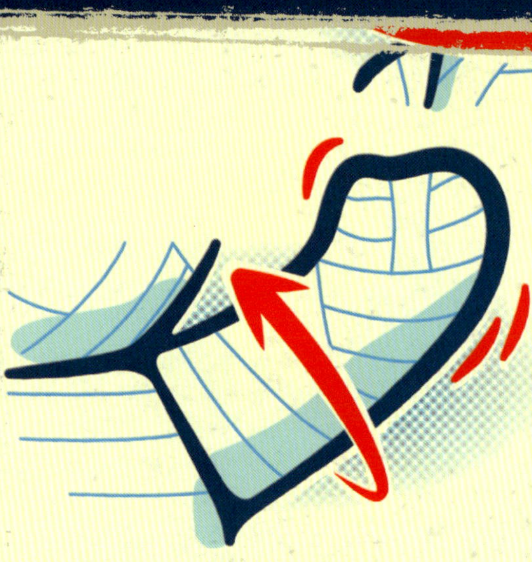

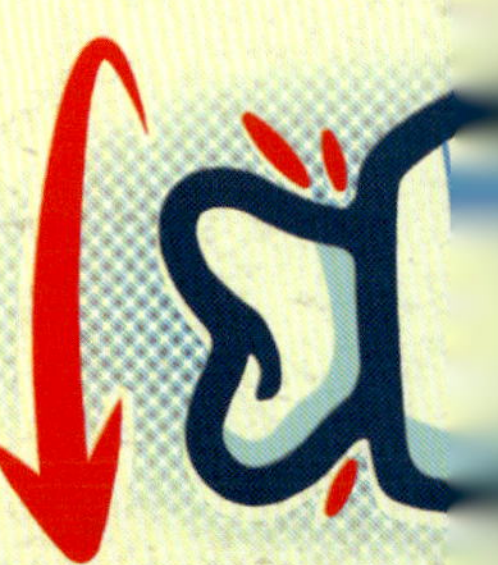
AND
WIGGLE!
TURN THE
EXPOSED HUMERUS

THIS SPREAD: Super7®'s own Mummy Boy in Glow in the Dark SuperSize format

© 2025 Super7 OpCo, LLC

AFTERWORD

"NO ONE MADE WHAT WE WANTED—SO WE MADE IT OURSELVES." FROM DAY ONE, THAT IS HOW OUR MANIFESTO HAS ENDED. THAT PHRASE HAS BEEN OUR CALL TO ACTION AND GUIDING MESSAGE SINCE WE STARTED MAKING THE VERY FIRST MAGAZINE IN 2001. BUT IT IS MORE THAN THAT. IT IS NOT SIMPLY A MESSAGE MEANT FOR SUPER7—IT IS MEANT FOR EVERYONE. THAT PHRASE IS A CALL TO ACTION TO ANYONE READING THIS BOOK TO MAKE THE WORLD EXACTLY WHAT THEY WANT TO SEE IN IT. IT IS ATTITUDE AND OPTIMISM, ACTION AND DIRECTION, INTENT AND OPPORTUNITY. IT IS EVERYTHING WE CAN DREAM, AND HOPEFULLY IT CAN BE EVERYTHING YOU CAN DREAM AS WELL. WE INVITE YOU TO USE THIS PHRASE AS DIRECTION AND MOMENTUM TO CREATE A FUTURE THAT ONLY YOU CAN SEE. AND WHEN YOU DO, WE HOPE TO MEET YOU THERE!

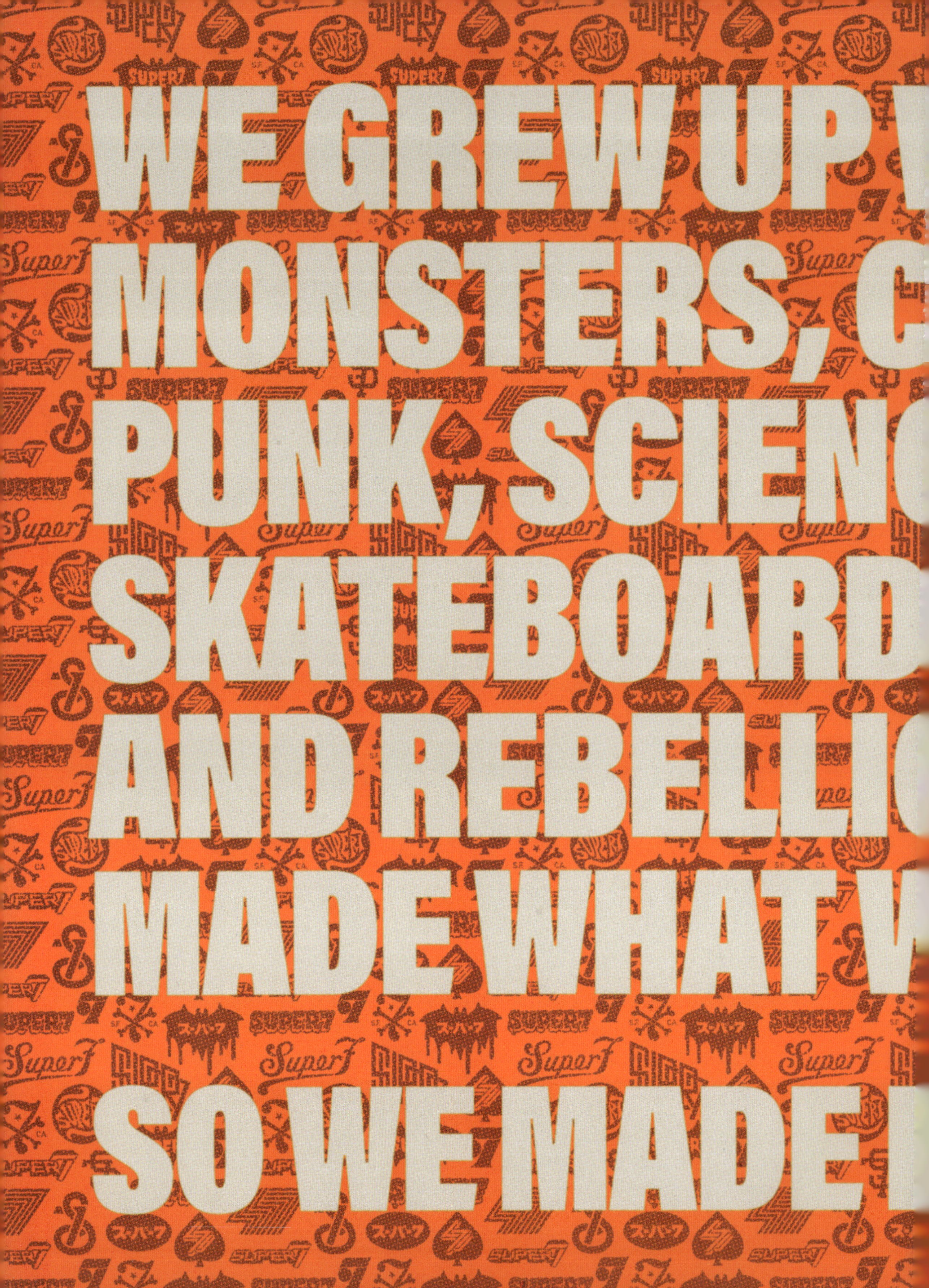
WE GREW UP
MONSTERS,
PUNK, SCIEN
SKATEBOARD
AND REBELLI
MADE WHAT
SO WE MADE